Eating & Drinking

in Great Britain & Ireland

timeout.com

Time Out Guides Limited
Universal House
251 Tottenham Court Road
London W1T 7AB
Tel + 44 (0)20 7813 3000
Fax + 44 (0)20 7813 6001
Email guides@timeout.com
www.timeout.com

Published by Time Out Guides Ltd, a wholly owned subsidiary of Time Out Group Ltd.
Time Out and the Time Out logo are trademarks of Time Out Group Ltd.

Previous edition 2003
10 9 8 7 6 5 4 3 2 1
This edition first published in Great Britain in 2004 by Ebury
Ebury is a division of The Random House Group Ltd, 20 Vauxhall Bridge Road, London SW1V 2SA
Random House Australia Pty Limited, 20 Alfred Street, Milsons Point, Sydney, New South Wales 2061, Australia
Random House New Zealand Limited, 18 Poland Road, Glenfield, Auckland 10, New Zealand
Random House South Africa (Pty) Limited, Endulini, 5A Jubilee Road, Parktown 2193, South Africa
Random House UK Limited Reg. No. 954009
Distributed in USA by Publishers Group West
1700 Fourth Street, Berkeley, California 94710
Distributed in Canada by Penguin Canada Ltd
10 Alcorn Avenue, Toronto, Ontario, Canada M4V 3B2
For further distribution details, see www.timeout.com
ISBN 1-904978-23-1
A CIP catalogue record for this book is available from the British Library
Colour reprographics by Icon, Crowne House, 56-58 Southwark Street, London SE1 1UN
Printed and bound by Cayfosa-Quebecor, Ctra. De Caldes, KM 3 08 130 Sta, Perpètua de Mogoda, Barcelona, Spain

Reviews in this guide were written by:
London taken from the *Time Out Guide to Eating & Drinking in London.* **England** Jennifer Alexander (Sussex); Patricia Ambrose (Suffolk); Ismay Atkins (Cambridgeshire, Cornwall); Roslyn Atkins (Cambridgeshire, Cornwall); Helen Barnard (Berkshire, Buckinghamshire, Oxfordshire); Sophie Blacksell (Bristol, *Bar crawl: Bristol*); Anna Britten (Somerset); Elizabeth Carter (Cambridgeshire, Essex, Kent, Suffolk); Robert Cockcroft (Yorkshire); Jonathan Cox (Gloucestershire); Peterjon Cresswell (Sussex); Simon Cropper (Herefordshire, Shropshire); Fiona Cumberpatch (Lincolnshire); Alison Davison (Birmingham, *Bar crawl: Birmingham*, Staffordshire, Worcestershire); Laura Dixon (Bristol); Lily Dunn (Cornwall); Sarah Ewbank (Yorkshire); Peter Fiennes (Kent); Will Fulford-Jones (Essex, Sussex); Janice Fuscoe (Cambridgeshire, Hampshire, Sussex); Helen Gilchrist (Cornwall); Charlie Godfrey-Fausset (Somerset); Sarah Guy (Lincolnshire, Norfolk, Sussex); Derek Hammond (Birmingham, Leicestershire, Rutland); Lindsay Harriss (Cornwall); Phil Harriss (Norfolk, Oxfordshire); Jane Howard (Dorset); Pippa Hudson (Yorkshire); Angela Jameson Potts (Bedfordshire); Ruth Jarvis (Cornwall, Leeds); Sarah Kent (Norfolk); Melanie Leyshon (Oxfordshire, Warwickshire); David Lloyd (Cheshire, Derbyshire, Lancashire, Manchester, *Bar crawl: Manchester, Bar crawl: Liverpool*); Sharon Lougher (Surrey); Julie Manniche (Cornwall); Lesley McCave (Suffolk); Norman Miller (Surrey, Sussex); Chris Moss (Liverpool & Merseyside); Tony Mudd (Hertfordshire, Northamptonshire, Suffolk); Anna Norman (Kent); Emma Perry (Cambridgeshire, Oxfordshire, Suffolk); Cath Phillips (Yorkshire); Sam Le Quesne (Jersey); Nick Rider (Warwickshire); Rosamund Sales (Shropshire); David Sandhu (Nottinghamshire, *Bar crawl: Nottingham*); Derryck Strachan (Devon, *Cream Teas*, Gloucestershire); Caroline Taverne (Suffolk); Jill Turton (Leeds, Yorkshire, *Bar crawl: Leeds*); Andrew White (Oxfordshire, Wiltshire); Arabella White (Oxfordshire, Wiltshire); Mario Wynn Jones (County Durham, Cumbria, Hampshire, Northumberland, Newcastle, Tyne & Wear, Wiltshire); **Scotland** Keith Davidson. **Wales** Philip Moss. **Ireland** Caroline Workman (Northern Ireland, *Bar crawl: Belfast*); John McKenna (Republic of Ireland). *Bar crawl: Dublin* adapted from the *Time Out Dublin Guide*.

Maps JS Graphics (john@jsgraphics.co.uk).

Photography pages 3, 11, 73, 77, 78, 85, 89, 95, 100, 105, 110, 115, 119, 123, 126, 133, 139, 201, 205, 214, 219, 222, 227, 230, 231, 235, 295, 309, 310, 312, 313, 314, 317, 321, 322, 325, 329, 333, 336, 339, 340 Paul Carter; pages 5, 28, 29, 143, 148, 152, 159, 167, 170, 175 Alys Tomlinson; pages 8, 9, 13 Sam Bailey; pages 15, 355, 359, 364 Karl Blackwell; pages 19, 28, 35, 49, 52, 57, 61, 64, 65 Tricia de Courcy Ling; pages 41, 44, 67 Thomas Skovsende; page 67 Britta Jaschinski; pages 179, 183, 191, 194, 198, 199 Heloise Bergman; pages 237, 241, 244, 249, 254, 260, 263, 343, 348 Phil Taylor; pages 265, 269, 271, 277, 283, 284, 285, 291 Ian Stuart; pages 298, 299, 302, 305 Muir Vidler. The following image was provided by the featured establishment/artist: page 363.

The Editor would like to thank Kathleen Guy, Susan Guy, Phil Harriss, David Marshall, Jane Marshall, Caroline Stacey.

Contents

About the guide

For ease of use, we've split the guide into counties (or major cities) within larger areas, such as the North West, and then by village, town or city within that county. If you know the name of an establishment, but don't know where it is, turn to the alphabetical index on page 367. For guidance on particular cuisines, look at the subject index on page 375. We've included a range of establishments – restaurants, gastropubs, cafés and tearooms – that are all notable in some way. What we haven't featured are pubs with great beer but food that only runs to cellophane-wrapped sandwiches; stuffy country house hotels with sepulchral dining rooms; over-rated local performers that rely on location alone to fill the tables; and places that are run for the convenience of the staff, rather than the customers. For more places in London, see our guides to *Eating & Drinking in London, Cheap Eats in London* and *Pubs & Bars*; we also publish the *Eating & Drinking in Edinburgh & Glasgow* guide.

The listings

- Throughout the guide we've listed phone numbers as dialled from within the country in question, but outside the village, town or city.
- The times given are those observed by the kitchen; in other words, the times within which one is fairly certain to be able to sit down and order a meal. These can change according to the time of year and the owners' whims, so it's often a good idea to call ahead. It's wise to book for popular and more fashionable restaurants, especially on Fridays and Saturdays, and it's essential if you're travelling any distance for a meal.
- Main course prices are a range, from the cheapest to the most expensive – obviously these prices can and will change over the year.
- We list the credit cards accepted by initials: AmEx (American Express), DC (Diners Club), MC (MasterCard) and V (Visa), plus JCB (Japanese credit card) in London.

Stars

The star system is to help you to identify top performers at a glance. A red star – ★ – by the name of a restaurant means that our reviewers found it to be one of the best in the area. A green star – ★ – indicates that a budget meal is possible at that establishment.

The reviews

The reviews in this guide are based solely on the experiences of Time Out restaurant reviewers. All the cafés, restaurants, bars and gastropubs listed were visited anonymously over a period of a few months, and Time Out footed the bills. No payment of any kind from restaurant owners has secured or influenced a review in this guide. While every effort has been made to ensure the accuracy of the information contained in this guide, the publishers cannot accept any responsibility for errors it may contain. Opening times, menus, chefs and other details can change at any time, and it's always advisable to phone and check before setting out.

Sponsors & advertisers

We would like to thank our sponsor, MasterCard, for their involvement in this guide. However, we would like to stress that sponsors have no influence over editorial content. The same applies to advertisers. No restaurant, café or pub has been included because its owner advertised in the guide: an advertiser may receive a bad review or no review at all.

Pig in clover

Written by Peter Watts

Nathan Outlaw's Black Pig. It sounds more like the name of a pirate and his ship than a possible template for how to take a restaurant from opening night to Michelin star in eight months, leaving nothing but impressed tourists and flattered locals in its wake. But that's what young chef Outlaw has done for the Black Pig, and that's why we decided to examine his exceptional Cornish restaurant in this, the second edition of the *Time Out Guide to Eating & Drinking in Great Britain & Ireland.* This isn't to say that the Black Pig represents the only route to gastronomic success in the UK (indeed, individuality is part of the appeal), but it's certainly one that deserves acclaim, offering further evidence that some of the country's most exciting and ambitious restaurants are to be found outside urban centres.

Outlaw served his apprenticeship at City Rhodes and Chavot in London, Lords of the Manor in Gloucestershire, Vineyard in Newbury and with Rick Stein in Padstow, just across the Camel estuary from the Black Pig. 'It was time for me to either go it alone as a head chef or do my own thing,' he says from Rock, a speck of a town on the north coast above Newquay. Outlaw teamed up with his brother-in-law Colin Morris and Morris's partner Nicki Tigwell to open the restaurant. The trio, all still in their 20s, made their youthful enthusiasm a selling point and the bank was eventually persuaded that they were worth a punt. The restaurant opened in May 2003.

'I'd known for about five years I'd wanted to come back to Cornwall,' says Outlaw, whose wife is from Padstow. 'We found the property, and it was just ideal. I mean, it's not the best location, we haven't got a sea view or anything like that, but we've got all-year trade, which in Cornwall, unless you are Rick Stein, you just don't get.'

Nicki Tigwell, Graham Walker, Nathan Outlaw, Colin Morris and Michael Hamilton.

Rock is one of the wealthiest places in the region, a summertime haunt for the rich that's described as Chelsea-on-sea. But cashing in on cut-glass accents and blue blood isn't the only reason for the Black Pig's prodigious success. Outlaw has worked hard at getting the locals on side, important anywhere but especially in Cornwall.

'If you haven't worked in Cornwall, there's no way you could open a restaurant here,' says Outlaw. 'You have to have spent some time here, purely to know the suppliers and understand the attitude of the local people. You could come here and cook the best food in the world but if they don't know who you are...

'We could easily be posh, stiff upper lip and upset all the locals, and we'd probably still survive as a restaurant, but that makes your life difficult everyday,' he continues with a Kent-border twang that makes him sound as if he could never be posh or stiff upper lip. 'I've got to live and work here, and my son's going to grow up here. A lot of chefs couldn't give a shit and stamp all over everyone, but you can't do that.'

When the summer season ends, Outlaw brings out a less expensive menu specifically designed to appeal to local tastes and pockets. He also holds an end-of-season party, to which all the locals are invited, among them the small hotel and B&B owners who put more business his way. 'At first they were all a bit suspicious: "Giving away something for nothing, what's that all about?", 'cause it hadn't happened before but it makes a lot of difference; now when I walk down the road everybody says hello.'

The social interaction doesn't end there. Outlaw recounts how 'one old boy who keeps chickens always has too many eggs so he'll bring a few in and they make fantastic ice-cream. If I see him coming I'll give him a taste, he loves it. We've got a herb garden out front and the old dears come by and take clippings off it.'

Outlaw's other contribution to the north Cornwall community can be found on the menu. He uses only local suppliers (stretching to Gloucestershire for cheese) and all are listed on the menu. 'A few years ago in Cornwall that just didn't

Feedback

We hope you enjoy this book and discover some wonderful places through using it. Please let us know if your experiences differ from ours, or if you feel we've missed somewhere that really should be included. You can do this by emailing us on eatingguide@timeout.com or by writing to us at the address given on page 2.

happen. Now it's all changing and the farmers, instead of just ploughing fields and fields of potatoes and cauliflowers, are thinking of things like globe artichokes or salad leaves. And it all goes on the menu – if there's a product that needs exploiting, we put it down. Even with fish, we'll put the name of the fisherman, the name of his boat. If they give me a better product, I cook a better product, the customer eats better and they get some of the credit. That's what we're trying to work on.'

It's an attitude that you'll find repeatedly stated at the better restaurants in this book: the use of organic produce, locally sourced and seasonally adjusted. Gradually, people, unwittingly are not, are becoming more educated about what should be eaten and when. It's a slow process in many areas: certain counties have a paucity of restaurants and almost no food culture to speak of, while others, thanks to tourism, moneyed locals, a few passionate individuals, or a happy combination of them all (Ludlow, for example) seem blessed.

However, if the ingredients are familiar at the Black Pig, the meals are not. 'What puts a twist on it is that my cooking's a lot different from anything else they've had round here,' says Outlaw. 'They might recognise the produce, they might even know the farms it comes from, but they won't have seen it cooked like this. We take familiar food and make it that little bit different. If you're paying £21 for a beef fillet, you don't want it done how you can do it or you might as well cook it yourself.'

The type of meal you almost certainly can't cook at home might include (from a 2004 summer menu): cured and grilled black bream with soused vegetables and potatoes cooked in duck fat; followed by crisp pork belly with scallops, cauliflower and red onion; with elderflower cream, apple sherbet and English toffee jelly to finish.

Outlaw believes his restaurant offers value for money, and that nobody is going to walk out feeling ripped off. 'If you have three courses for lunch here, it's cheaper then going to the pub and having bacon, egg and chips and a couple of pints.'

Bacon, egg and chips and a couple of pints don't win Michelin stars, either. Outlaw is one of the youngest British chefs to have won a star and to do so in such short time makes his achievement all the more impressive. 'I know the Michelin system and all the restaurants I've worked in have had that accolade,' he says. 'I knew I was capable of doing it, and I knew we were capable as a kitchen, but consistency comes in and I thought they'd have wanted to see that over a longer time. It was well deserved but at the same time it was a surprise.'

His long-term ambition is to rack up three stars, preferably without taking his restaurant to London ('it can be a nasty place'), although he concedes larger premises will probably be necessary. And having come so far so quickly, he's prepared to wait a little longer. 'I'd rather do it in my own time and get it right than rush to it. It takes some people 30 years and they know their craft perfectly. I mean, you can run to it and kill yourself in the process but I've got a family and it's important to see them. I already have to stop myself from being here 24 hours a day.'

See page 118 for a review of the Black Pig.

A free bottle of house wine

When you order at least two main courses at the participating restaurants listed here, you'll get a free bottle of house red or white wine.
All you have to do to take advantage of this offer is cut out one of the vouchers (below left) and take it along to a participating restaurant. Present the voucher to your waiting staff when you order your two main courses to get your complimentary bottle of house wine. If you don't want to cut into your book, take the Guide along with you to the restaurant and the waiting staff will cross the voucher off. There are three vouchers so you can use them at any three of the following great restaurants – or visit your favourite three times!

TimeOut 1 **One FREE bottle of house red or white wine**

2005 Eating & Drinking in Great Britain & Ireland

Valid any time between September 30 2004 and September 29 2005 except Christmas Day 2004 and New Year's Day 2005. See below for full terms and conditions.

TimeOut 2 **One FREE bottle of house red or white wine**

2005 Eating & Drinking in Great Britain & Ireland

Valid any time between September 30 2004 and September 29 2005 except Christmas Day 2004 and New Year's Day 2005. See below for full terms and conditions.

TimeOut 3 **One FREE bottle of house red or white wine**

2005 Eating & Drinking in Great Britain & Ireland

Valid any time between September 30 2004 and September 29 2005 except Christmas Day 2004 and New Year's Day 2005. See below for full terms and conditions.

SOUTH EAST

Chesil Rectory
1 Chesil Street, Winchester, Hampshire (01329 851555). See p82.

Grapevine
121 High Street, Odiham, Hampshire (01256 701900). See p78.

Nurse's Cottage
Station Road, Sway, Hampshire (01590 683402). See p82.

Sandgate Hotel
8-9 Wellington Terrace, The Esplanade, Sandgate, Kent (01303 220444). See p88.

Surin
30 Harbour Street, Ramsgate, Kent (01843 592001). See p88.

Westover Hall
Park Lane, Milford-on-Sea, Hampshire (01590 643044). See p78.

White Star
28 Oxford Street, Southampton (02380 821990). See p80.

SOUTH WEST

The Bay
Briton's Hill, Penzanze, Cornwall (01736 363770). See p116.

Bistro on the Beach
Solent Promenade, Southbourne, Bournemouth, Dorset (01202 431473). See p130.

Blostins
29 Waterloo Road, Shepton Mallet, Somerset (01749 343648). See p139.

Bohemia
Green Street, St Helier, Jersey (01534 880588). See p116.

Brace of Pheasants
Plush, Dorset (01300 348357). See p133.

The Smokery
Bowdens Farm, Hambridge, Langport, Somerset (01458 250875). See p138.

Casa Mexicana
29-31 Zetland Road, Redland, Bristol (0117 9243901). See p118.

The Hole in the Wall
16-17 George Street, Bath (01225 425242). See p136.

Terms and conditions

This voucher can only be used at the restaurants listed on these pages. To receive your free bottle of house wine, you must order at least two main courses from the restaurant's main menu. The voucher must then be redeemed by the waiting staff – or the Guide given to them, so that the voucher can be crossed off as used. The offer cannot be exchanged for any cash alternative and cannot be used in conjunction with any other offer. Voucher can be used anytime between September 30 2004 and September 29 2005 except Christmas Day 2004 and New Year's Day 2005. The management reserve the right to refuse admission. No photocopies will be accepted. To avoid disappointment always try to book in advance, mentioning this offer when you do so. Time Out cannot take responsibility for any change in a restaurant's proprietorship, where the restaurant may subsequently not be able to honour the offer. Promoter: Time Out Group Ltd, Universal House, 251 Tottenham Court Road, London, W1T 7AB.

Lords
43 Corn Street, Bristol (0117 926 2658). See p110.

Rajpoot
4 Argyle Street, Bath (01225 466833). See p138.

Storm Fish
16 High Street, Poole, Dorset (01202 674970). See p134.

CENTRAL

Annie Baileys
Chesham Road, Great Missenden, Buckinghamshire (01494 865625). See p153.

Bar Meze
146 London Road, Headington, Oxford (01865 761106). See p167.

Cowpers Oak
High Street, Weston Underwood, Buckinghamshire (01234 711382). See p155.

Old Plow Bistro & Restaurant
Flowers Bottom, Speen, Buckinghamshire (01494 488300). See p154.

The Park, Stoke Park Club
Park Road, Stoke Poges, Buckinghamshire (01753 717144). See p154.

The Stag
The Green, Mentmore, Buckinghamshire (01296 668423). See p154.

The Windmill
Salisbury Road, Marten, Wiltshire (01264 731372). See p176.

EAST ANGLIA

Earsham Street Cafe
11-13 Earsham Street, Bungay, Suffolk (01986 893103). See p185.

Lemon Tree
48 St Johns Street, Colchester, Essex (01206 767337). See p185.

Peking
21 Burleigh Firget, Cambridge (01223 54755). See p182.

Queens Head
The Street, Bramfield, Halesworth, Suffolk (01986 784214). See p194.

St Peter's Hall
St Peters South Elmham, Bungay, Suffolk (01986 782322). See p199.

Sun Inn
High Street, Pedmam, Essex (01206 323351). See p186.

The Volunteer
Trumpington Road, Cambridge (01223 841675). See p183.

MIDLANDS

The Elms
Stockton Road, Abberley, Worcestershire (01299 896666). See p234.

Firenze
9 Station Street, Kibworth Beauchamp, Leicestershire (0116 279 6260). See p215.

Lasan Restaurant & Bar
James Street, St Pauls Square, Birmingham (0121 212 3664). See p207.

Old Post
43 Holywell Street, Chesterfield, Derbyshire, (01246 279479). See p212.

The Restaurant at the Jews House
15 The Strait, Lincoln (01522 524851). See p218.

Sayonard Thali
49 Belgrave Road, Leicester (0116 266 5888). See p217.

Colwall Park Hotel
Walwyn Road, Colwall, Worcestershire (01684 540000). See p234.

Shagorika
16 St Mary's Road, Market Harbourgh, Leicestershire (01858 464644). See p217.

Sharmilee
71-73 Belgrave Road, Leicester (0116 261 0503). See p217.

Thai Edge
7 Oozells Square, Brindleyplace, Birmingham (0121 643 3993). See p210.

Zafroni
4th & 5th Floors, Virage Point, Walsall Road, Bridgtown, Staffordshire (01543 505023). See p228.

NORTH WEST

The Monro
92-94 Duke Street, Liverpool (0151 707 9933). See p254.

Valparaiso
4 Hardman Street, Liverpool (0151 708 6036). See p255.

NORTH EAST

Flannels
68-78 Vicar Lane, Leeds (0113 242 8732). See p271.

Tin Tin
29 East Parade, Leeds (0113 245 1245). See p275.

SCOTLAND

Ashoka
108 Elderslie Street, Glasgow (0141 221 1761). See p307.

Inverlochy Castle Hotel
Torlundy, Fort William (01397 702177). See p320.

9 Cellars Restaurant
1-3 York Place, Edinburgh (0131 557 9899). See p302.

Old Pines
Spean Bridge, Highland (01397 712324). See p322.

Otago
61 Otago Street, Glasgow, (0141 337 2282). See p312.

Suruchi
14A Nicolson Street, Edinburgh (0131 556 6583). See p305.

Suruchi Too
121 Constitution Street, Leith, Edinburgh (0131 554 3268). See p306.

IRELAND

Allo's
41 Church Street, Listowel, Co Kerry (068 22880). See p360.

Caviston's
59 Glasthule Road, Sandycove, Dun Laoghire, Co Dublin (01 280 9120). See p355.

Coxtown Manor
Laghey, Co Donegal (074 973 4575). See p354.

Cube
5 Roden Place, Dundalk Co Louth (042 932 9898). See p362.

Grapefruit Moon
Main Street, Ballycotton, Co Cork (021 464 6646). See p352.

Restaurant Nuremore
Nuremore Hotel, Carrickmacross, Co Monaghan (042 966 1438). See p362.

Slatefort House
Slatefort, Bulluan, Loughrea, Co Galway (091 870667). See p360.

Wild Geese
Main Street, Adare, Co Limerick (061 396451). See p361.

Overview

Kirkwall
Thurso
Stornoway
Inverness
Peterhead
Aberdeen
Mallaig
SCOTLAND
(p295)
NORTH
SEA
ATLANTIC
OCEAN
Oban
Perth
Dundee
Glasgow
Edinburgh
Ayr
Londonderry
NORTHERN
IRELAND
(p343)
Belfast
Stranraer
Carlisle
Newcastle
Durham
Middlesbrough

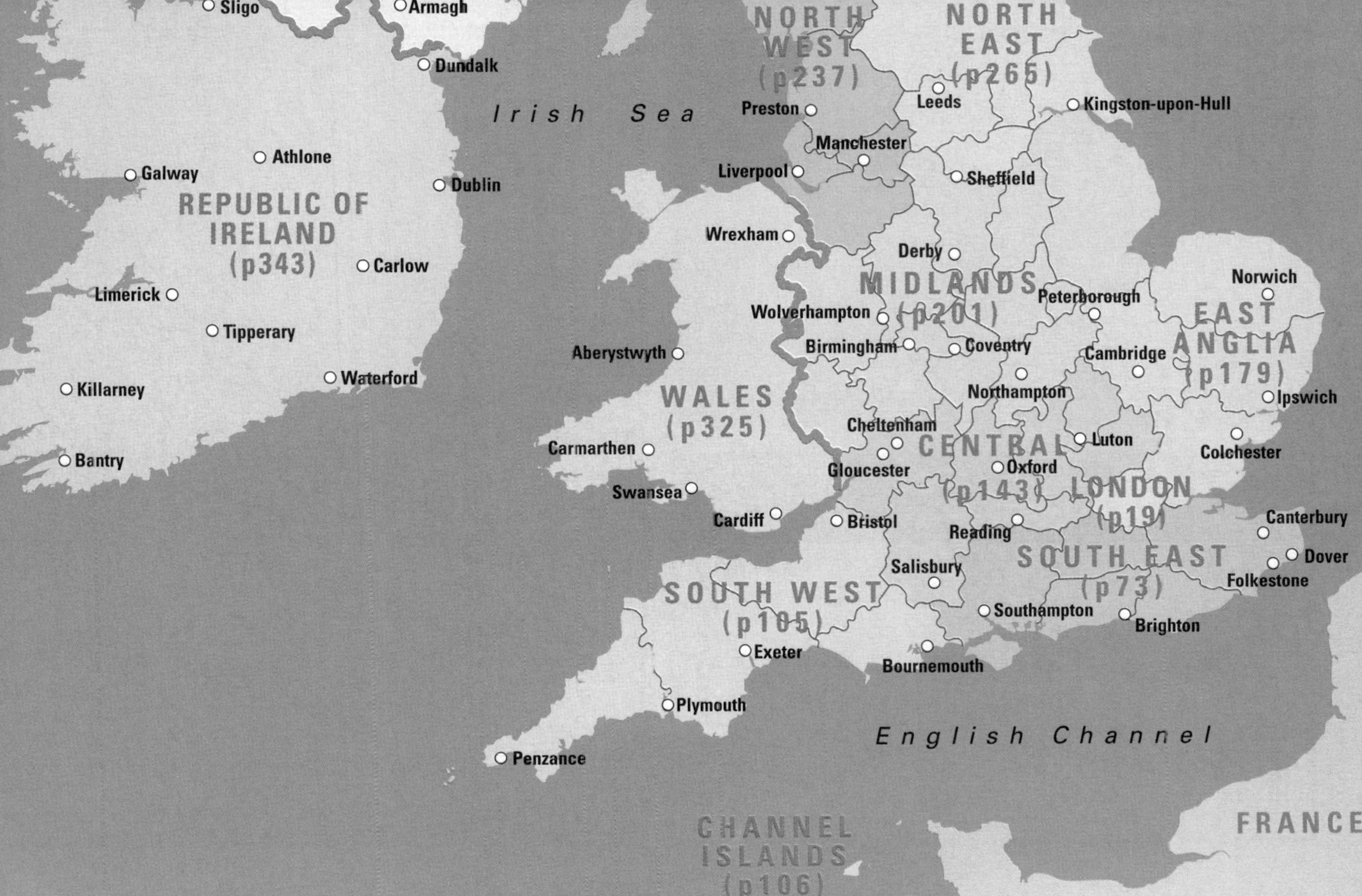
Sligo
Armagh
Dundalk
NORTH WEST (p237)
NORTH EAST (p265)
Irish Sea
Preston
Leeds
Kingston-upon-Hull
Manchester
Liverpool
Sheffield
Athlone
Galway
Dublin
REPUBLIC OF IRELAND (p343)
Carlow
Wrexham
Derby
MIDLANDS (p201)
Norwich
Limerick
Peterborough
EAST ANGLIA (p179)
Wolverhampton
Tipperary
Birmingham
Coventry
Cambridge
Aberystwyth
Waterford
Killarney
WALES (p325)
Northampton
Ipswich
Cheltenham
Luton
Colchester
CENTRAL (p143)
Carmarthen
Gloucester
Oxford
Bantry
LONDON (p19)
Swansea
Cardiff
Bristol
Reading
Canterbury
SOUTH EAST (p73)
Dover
Salisbury
Folkestone
SOUTH WEST (p105)
Southampton
Brighton
Exeter
Bournemouth
Plymouth
English Channel
Penzance
CHANNEL ISLANDS (p106)
FRANCE

London

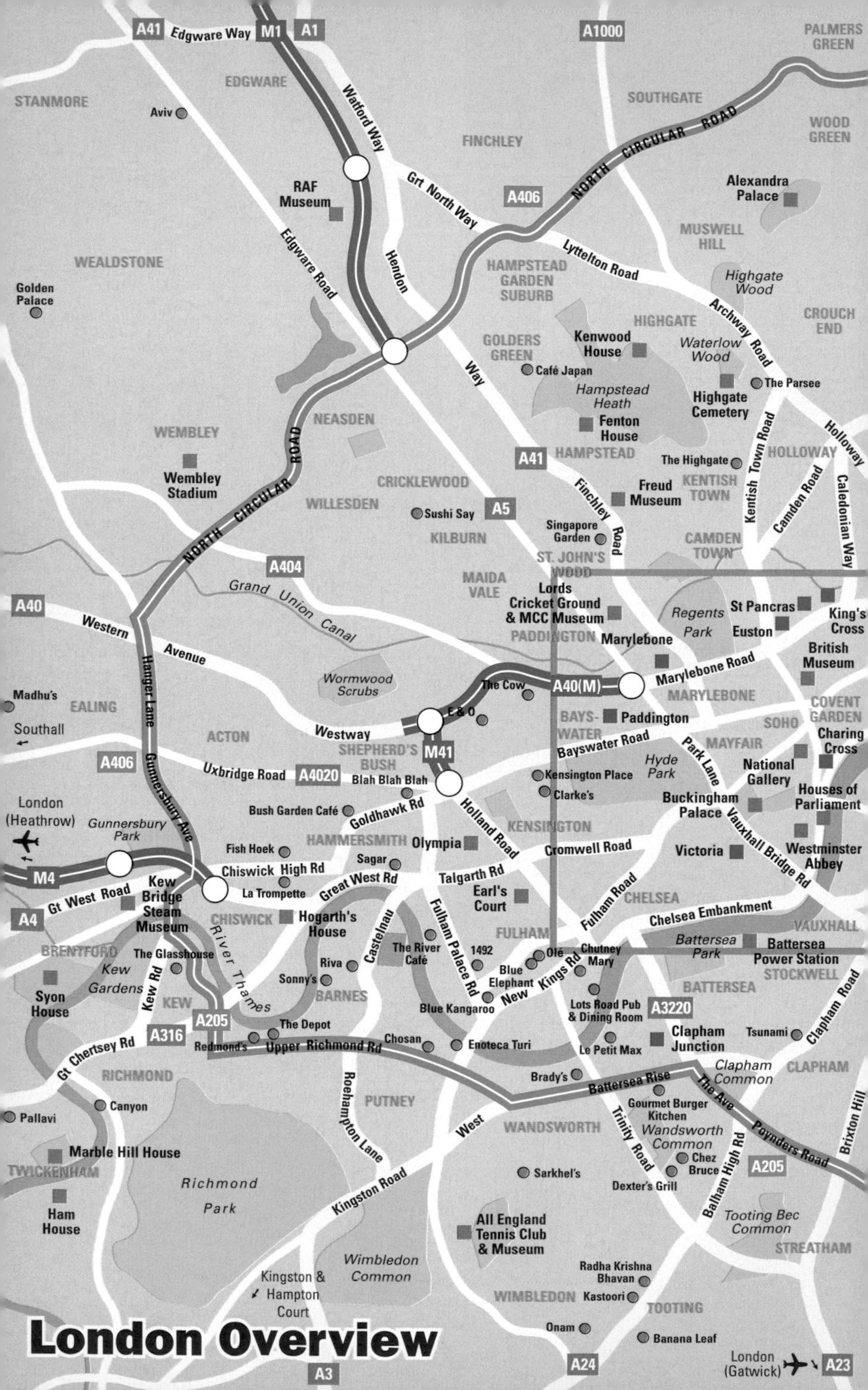

London Overview
A41
Edgware Way
M1
A1
A1000
Palmers Green
Edgware
Stanmore
Southgate
Wood Green
Watford Way
Finchley
Aviv
North Circular Road
RAF Museum
Grt North Way
A406
Alexandra Palace
Muswell Hill
Edgware Road
Hendon
Lyttelton Road
Wealdstone
Hampstead Garden Suburb
Highgate Wood
Golden Palace
Highgate
Archway Road
Crouch End
Golders Green
Kenwood House
Waterlow Wood
Way
Café Japan
The Parsee
Hampstead Heath
Highgate Cemetery
Neasden
Fenton House
Wembley
Hampstead
Holloway
A41
The Highgate
Kentish Town Road
Wembley Stadium
Cricklewood
Finchley Road
Freud Museum
Kentish Town
Camden Road
Caledonian Way
Willesden
Sushi Say
A5
Kilburn
Singapore Garden
Camden Town
St. John's Wood
A404
Maida Vale
Grand Union Canal
Lords Cricket Ground & MCC Museum
Regents Park
St Pancras
King's Cross
A40
Western Avenue
Paddington
Marylebone
Euston
British Museum
Hanger Lane
Wormwood Scrubs
The Cow
A40(M)
Marylebone Road
Marylebone
Madhu's
Ealing
E&O
Bayswater
Paddington
Covent Garden
Southall
Acton
Westway
Soho
Charing Cross
Shepherd's Bush
M41
Bayswater Road
Mayfair
A406
Gunnersbury Ave
Uxbridge Road
A4020
Hyde Park
Park Lane
National Gallery
Blah Blah Blah
Kensington Place
Clarke's
Houses of Parliament
London (Heathrow)
Buckingham Palace
Gunnersbury Park
Bush Garden Café
Goldhawk Rd
Holland Road
Kensington
Hammersmith
Olympia
Vauxhall Bridge Rd
Fish Hoek
Cromwell Road
Victoria
Westminster Abbey
Sagar
M4
Chiswick High Rd
Talgarth Rd
Kew Bridge Steam Museum
Great West Rd
Earl's Court
Gt West Road
La Trompette
Fulham Road
Chelsea
A4
Chiswick
Hogarth's House
Chelsea Embankment
Vauxhall
River Thames
Castelnau
Fulham Palace Rd
Fulham
Brentford
The River Café
1492
Olé
Chutney Mary
Battersea Park
Battersea Power Station
The Glasshouse
Kew Gardens
Riva
Blue Elephant
Stockwell
Sonny's
New Kings Rd
Syon House
Kew Rd
Kew
Barnes
Battersea
Clapham Road
Lots Road Pub & Dining Room
A3220
A205
Blue Kangaroo
A316
The Depot
Clapham Junction
Tsunami
Gt Chertsey Rd
Redmond's
Upper Richmond Rd
Chosan
Enoteca Turi
Le Petit Max
Clapham Common
Clapham
Richmond
Brady's
Battersea Rise
Roehampton Lane
The Ave
Brixton Hill
Putney
Gourmet Burger Kitchen
Canyon
Trinity Road
Pallavi
West
Wandsworth
Wandsworth Common
Poynders Road
Marble Hill House
Chez Bruce
Twickenham
Sarkhel's
Balham High Rd
A205
Kingston Road
Richmond Park
Dexter's Grill
Ham House
All England Tennis Club & Museum
Tooting Bec Common
Streatham
Kingston & Hampton Court
Wimbledon Common
Radha Krishna Bhavan
Wimbledon
Kastoori
Tooting
Onam
Banana Leaf
A3
A24
London (Gatwick)
A23

A10
EDMONTON
A112
A104
M11
London (Stansted)
NORTH CIRCULAR ROAD
Great Cambridge Road
WOODFORD
CHIGWELL
A406
Southend
Road
TOTTENHAM
William Morris Gallery
Forest Road
Epping Forest
Green Lanes
HARRINGAY
High Road
WALTHAMSTOW
A12
Eastern Ave
Cambridge Park
FINSBURY PARK
Seven Sisters Road
STAMFORD HILL
A104
LEYTONSTONE
Wanstead Park
WANSTEAD
A118
A107
Stoke Newington Road
Leytonstone
STOKE NEWINGTON
CLAPTON
LEYTON
A12
ILFORD
Iznik
Sariyer Balik
DALSTON
Mangal
A11
FOREST GATE
HACKNEY
Road
HIGHBURY
River Lea
STRATFORD
High Rd
Huong Viet
Sutton House
West Ham Park
The House
New North Rd
Kingsland Road
A102(M)
BARKING
Armadillo
Victoria Park
Stratford High St
WEST HAM
ISLINGTON
HOXTON
A13
Museum of Childhood
BOW
EAST HAM
City Road
Frizzante
MILE END
PLAISTOW
Bow Rd
SHOREDITCH
BETHNAL GREEN
Mile End Rd
A12
NEWHAM
Whitechapel Rd
Newham Way
Liverpool Street
STEPNEY
A406
BECKTON
CITY
East India Dock Road
CANNING TOWN
St Paul's Cathedral
WHITECHAPEL
Blackwall Tunnel
London City Airport
LIMEHOUSE
Tower of London
Wapping Food
Royal China
Plateau
Tower Bridge Rd
WAPPING
Canary Wharf
Dome
North Woolwich Rd
Albert Rd
THAMES MEAD
Waterloo
River Thames
Thames Barrier
Woolwich Ferry
ROTHERHITHE
ISLE OF DOGS
New Kent Rd
BERMONDSEY
A102(M)
Woolwich Road
Maryon Park
WOOLWICH
A206
Royal Naval College
Old Kent Road
Romney Road
CHARLTON
See pp22-23
DEPTFORD
Cutty Sark
National Maritime Museum
Thai Thume
Museum of Artillery
Academy Road
A205
PLUMSTEAD
CAMBERWELL
GREENWICH
Greenwich Park
A207
Camberwell New Rd
Peckham Rd
Queens Road
Royal Observatory
Shooters Hill Road
Oxleas Park
Brixton Rd
NEW CROSS
Lewisham Way
PECKHAM
NUNHEAD
BLACKHEATH
Well Hall Rd
Sea Cow
Lee High Rd
BRIXTON
LEWISHAM
East Rochester Way
A2
Dulwich Picture Gallery
Lordship Lane
Peckham Rye
Lewisham High St
Eltham Road
Brockwell Park
ELTHAM
DULWICH
Westhorne Ave
Horniman Museum
SOUTH CIRCULAR ROAD
Brownhill Road
Christ-Church Rd
Dulwich Common
London Road
Stanstead Rd
Sidcup Road
A205
FOREST HILL
CATFORD
A20
0 1 2 3 miles
0 1 2 3 4 5 km
Crystal Palace Park
Numidie
CRYSTAL PALACE
A21
BROMLEY

Central London
PRIMROSE HILL
CAMDEN
SOMERS TOWN
ST JOHN'S WOOD
MAIDA VALE
REGENT'S PARK
Queen Mary's Gardens
London Zoo
Euston
Marylebone
Paddington
FITZROVIA
MARYLEBONE
BAYSWATER
SOHO
MAYFAIR
HYDE PARK
KENSINGTON GARDENS
The Round Pond
The Long Water
The Serpentine
GREEN PARK
ST JAMES'S
ST JAMES'S PARK
BUCKINGHAM PALACE GARDENS
KENSINGTON
KNIGHTSBRIDGE
WESTMINSTER
BELGRAVIA
BROMPTON
SOUTH KENSINGTON
EARL'S COURT
CHELSEA
PIMLICO
WEST BROMPTON
FULHAM
BATTERSEA
BATTERSEA PARK
NINE ELMS
RIVER THAMES
Chelsea Physic Garden
Brompton Cemetery
Kilburn High Road
Little Venice
Grand Union Canal
Grand Union (Regent's) Canal
Marble Arch
Harrods
Science Museum
Natural History Museum
Victoria & Albert Museum
Victoria
1. Akbar/Red Fort
2. Patisserie Valerie
3. Lindsay House
4. Maison Bertaux
5. YMing
Wagamama
Mango Room
Heartstone
El Parador
Mandalay Restaurant
Green Olive
Phoenix Palace
Orrery
Sardo
Villandry
Pied à Terre
Busaba Eathai
Navarro's
Fino
La Galette
Providores
Back to Basics
Ozer
Fairuz
Golden Hind
Hakkasan
Strada
Eagle Bar Diner
Satay House
Harlem
Al Waha
Y Ming
Bodean's
Crisou
Patara Thai
Masala Zone
Yauatcha
New Mayflower
Maroush
Locanda Locatelli
Claridge's
Nipa
Momo
Chowki
Mandarin Kitchen
Le Gavroche
Kaya
Quod
Tamarind
Kiku
The Ritz
Mirabelle
The Wolseley
Nobu
Inn the Park
Mr Chow
Zuma
Nahm
Cinnamon Club
Racine
Drones
Bibendum & Bibendum Oyster Bar
Tom Aikens
Hunan
The Painted Heron

ISLINGTON
HAGGERSTON
KING'S CROSS
HOXTON
FINSBURY
BETHNAL GREEN
CLERKENWELL
SHOREDITCH
BLOOMSBURY
SPITALFIELDS
HOLBORN
THE CITY
WHITECHAPEL
ST GILES'S
COVENT GARDEN
RIVER THAMES
SOUTH BANK
BANKSIDE
WATERLOO
BOROUGH
BERMONDSEY
NEWINGTON
LAMBETH
WALWORTH
KENNINGTON/ OVAL
CAMBERWELL
PECKHAM
Viet Garden
Essex Road
Giraffe
S&M Café
Barnard Park
Shoreditch Park
Sông Quê
Viet Hoa Café
King's Cross
King's Cross Thameslink
St Pancras
Moro
Medcalf
Quality Chop House
The Eagle
Coach & Horses
Cigala
Cicada
Real Greek
Malmaison
Zetter
Sutton Arms
St John
Barbican
Flâneur Food Hall
Smith's
Club Gascon
Old Street
Cantaloupe
Eyre Brothers
Les Trois Garçons
Story Deli
Bunhill Fields
Arkansas Café
Liverpool Street
Moorgate
Aurora
Coram's Fields
British Museum
Lincoln's Inn Fields
The Gaucho Grill
The Place Below
Bank of England
Bens Marks
St Paul's Cathedral
Le Coq d'Argent
Bonds
De Gustibus
Food for Thought
The Ivy
Christopher's
The Admiralty
Paul
Rules
Hazuki
The Savoy Grill
National Gallery
Charing Cross
Nelson's Column
Fenchurch Street
Tower Hill
Cannon Street
Blackfriars
Tate Modern
Tower of London
National Theatre
Jubilee Gardens
Waterloo (East)
Hope & Anchor
Livebait
Baltic
Tas
Waterloo
Waterloo International
Fish
London Bridge
Fina Estampa
Blue Print Café
Delfina
Big Ben
Westminster Abbey
Houses of Parliament
Victoria Tower Gardens
Archbishops Park
Imperial War Museum
Newington Gardens
Tabard Gardens
The Hartley
Elephant & Castle
Burgess Park
Vauxhall
Vauxhall Park
Kennington Park
0 1/4 1/2 mile
0 500 m 1 km

Marylebone

Fairuz

3 Blandford Street, W1H 3AA (020 7486 8108-8182). Baker Street or Bond Street tube. **Meals served** noon-11.30pm Mon-Sat; noon-10.30pm Sun. **Main courses** £9.95-£18.95. **Set meze** £17.95. **Set meal** £24.95 3 courses. **Credit** AmEx, DC, MC, V.

Perhaps the most welcoming of London's Lebanese restaurants (a notoriously starchy bunch). The menu has an expansive offering of around 50 hot and cold meze. Some dishes are better than others: excellent falafel comes with a pot of tahini; chicken livers deliver a sharp little kick courtesy of a marinade of lemon and pomegranate juice, but calamares is oily. We recommend gorging on multiple meze and reordering as necessary. Of the mains farouj musakhan (£12.95) is a stand-out: a duvet of flatbread filled with chicken pieces smothered in fried onions and parsley and baked in the oven. The wine list includes Lebanese Ksara wines.

La Galette ★

56 Paddington Street, W1U 4HY (020 7935 1554/ www.lagalette.com). Baker Street tube. **Meals served** 9.30am-11pm Mon-Fri; 10am-11pm Sat, Sun. **Main courses** £5.60-£8.95. **Set lunch** (noon-5pm Mon-Fri) £6.95 2 courses. **Credit** AmEx, MC, V.

The galette is the savoury, buckwheat sibling of the crêpe – a hearty Breton staple, and the equivalent of the post-pub kebab in Paris. At this restaurant it gets very near to being glamorous, cooked with a feather-light touch and served in a setting that owes more to Scandinavia (warm lamps and pale woods) than it does to *vieille* France. There are olives, salads, pâtés and the like for starters, but skip all that for the savoury-sweet double bill. Thin, judiciously crisp and not too buttery, the galettes here are a delight: the paysanne with lardons (small bacon squares), cream and onions was miraculously unheavy, while the wild mushrooms in the forestière had a lovely, earthy meatiness. Sweet crêpes were made with a slightly flakier batter, but still worth it for the high quality toppings such as deliciously dark melted chocolate. The galette's drinking partner, cider, is extremely well represented and served in delicate ceramic bowls.

Golden Hind ★

73 Marylebone Lane, W1U 2PN (020 7486 3644). Bond Street tube. **Lunch served** noon-3pm Mon-Fri. **Dinner served** 6-10pm Mon-Sat. **Main courses** £5-£10.70. Minimum (lunch) £4, (dinner) £5. **Unlicensed. Corkage** no charge. **Credit** AmEx, JCB, MC, V.

Pride of place in this beautifully preserved art deco chippy goes to the gleaming stainless steel and Bakelite fish fryer from F Ford of Halifax. Sadly, it's no longer in use; the frying's done in the rear kitchen. The menu contains some unusual items: have deep-fried mussels in batter ever actually been ordered? Fish cakes are particularly good here, but if they are not available, scampi makes a more than adequate replacement. The main course of haddock is as fresh and flaky as you'll find anywhere. Chips the colour of proper lager are done to a turn, and even the mushy peas appear on top form. Staff are warm and personal. It's unlicensed, so bring your own booze.

Locanda Locatelli

8 Seymour Street, W1H 7JZ (020 7935 9088/ www.locandalocatelli.com). Marble Arch tube. **Lunch served** noon-3pm Mon-Sat. **Dinner served** 7-11pm Mon-Thur; 7-11.30pm Fri, Sat. **Main courses** £16-£30. **Credit** AmEx, JCB, MC, V.

It may seem that as the UK's foremost Italian chef Giorgio Locatelli can do no wrong, but someone in this outfit certainly can. Locanda Locatelli was universally praised when it opened in 2002, and tables almost impossible to secure. In such a feeding frenzy, bouts of slow service were to be expected, but by now this problem should have been sorted out. Yet once again, we spent so long waiting for our main courses we could have fallen asleep on the seductively comfy banquette. That only one of the dishes – nasello in scabeccio (steamed hake with garlic and vinegar) – was truly impressive made this all the more disappointing. Things had started well enough: a reasonably priced bottle of prosecco, a creamy soup of chickpeas with strips of grilled squid, rich oxtail ravioli, and a pleasing plate of smoked venison with celeriac. A very enjoyable restaurant that can do better.

Mandalay ★

444 Edgware Road, W2 1EG (020 7258 3696). Edgware Road tube. **Lunch served** noon-2.30pm, **dinner served** 6-10.30pm Mon-Sat. **Main courses** £3.90-£6.90. **Set lunch** £3.90 1 course, £5.90 3 courses. **Credit** AmEx, DC, JCB, MC, V.

Mandalay has been a favourite for years. OK, so the location isn't terribly salubrious, and the decor does little to evoke 'the mysterious east', but the food is a revelation. Add to that a tiny space and the care paid to guests by the two brothers who run the place and you'll see why booking is essential. Burmese cooking combines elements of Thai, Indian and southern Chinese cuisines. Coconut and tomato provide the base for curries, while stir-fries are pepped up with soy sauce. Fresh coriander, mint and lemongrass play a part, and dishes are given extra depth by the likes of shrimp paste and fish sauce; they're made tangy with tamarind, lemon and lime and lent oomph with chillies. To start, calabash fritters, cooked in chickpea flour, are served with three sauces: tamarind, chilli and soy. Mokhingar, slow-cooked fish in a coconut broth with rice noodles (a 'national dish' of Burma), has layer upon layer of flavour, while bamboo shoot curry is enlivened with tomato and red chilli, served with coconut rice.

Maroush Gardens

21 Edgware Road, W2 2JE (020 7723 0773/ www.maroush.com). Marble Arch tube. **Meals served** noon-midnight daily. **Main courses** £12-£22. **Set menu** £21-£35 (minimum 2 people). Minimum (after 10.30pm) £48 incl £7.50 cover. **Credit** AmEx, DC, MC, V.

There really is nowhere quite like Maroush. This branch of the successful London chain is housed in a handsome dark red basement that's just made for after-dark. We've never known the standard of the food to slip. Meze dishes are fresh and beautifully presented. Chickens' livers in a lemon sauce melted in the mouth. Falafel were crisp on the outside, soft on the inside and not at all greasy, served with thin tahini. A shared main course mixed grill, ample for two, consisted of a variety of well-cooked meat: lamb, liver, chicken, minced lamb. What really distinguishes this branch of Maroush, though, is its weekend entertainment. Lounge and Arabic classics from a succession of singers, plus two top-class professional belly dancers result in a lively, cosmopolitan vibe taking hold most weekends.

Orrery

55 Marylebone High Street, W1M 3AE (020 7616 8000/www.orrery.co.uk). Baker Street or Regent's Park tube. **Lunch served** noon-3pm daily. **Dinner served** 7-11pm Mon-Sat; 7-10.30pm Sun. **Main courses** £14.50-£26. **Set lunch** £23.50 3 courses. **Set dinner** (Sun) £30 3 courses incl glass of champagne. **Credit** AmEx, DC, JCB, MC, V.

This top-of-the-line Conran outlet sets out very clearly to offer luxury. The long space (on top of the Conran shop) is white, airy and sleek and the haute-cuisine cooking is refined and delicate. A tomato consommé *amuse-gueule* and frothy raspberry pre-dessert were exquisite. Of our first courses, velouté of spring garlic with parmesan, rocket and chive oil was superb, infused with multilayered flavours; crab ravioli with an étuvée of leeks and grapefruit was over-subtle, and stuffed baby artichokes with asparagus and quails' eggs surprisingly bland. Mains – Somerset lamb with roast saddle, braised shank and baby vegetables, beef fillet with lyonnaise onions, a risotto of spring vegetables, pea shoots and parmesan foam – were elaborately presented but not show-stoppers. Opulent desserts showed a return to form. The lunch menu provides a more accessibly priced way of checking out Orrery.

Phoenix Palace

3-5 Glentworth Street, NW1 5PG (020 7486 3515). Baker Street tube. **Meals served** noon-11.30pm Mon-Sat; 11am-10.30pm Sun. **Main courses** £6.50-£25. **Set meals** £14 2 courses, £24 3 courses. **Credit** AmEx, JCB, MC, V.

Without doubt, Phoenix Palace's menu is among the most exciting in Chinese London for both its dim sum list and the full menu. The latter includes such banqueting centrepieces as baked lobster and steamed Dover sole with tangerine peel, as well as seasonal specials like mixed funghi on tofu. We flitted in for lunchtime snacks: past the shiny bar area and into the capacious, windowless dining space at the rear (big round tables lend some class, though the place still resembles a hotel lounge). No dim sum menu was given to us: the first mistake in service that was confused and distant throughout. Several of the dishes are rare, if not new to London. Some are bizarre: peppered ostrich fillet on pull noodle, or mini sausage rolls containing tinned-standard frankfurters. Some were sublime: prawn and duck tientsin pasta soup exhibited a wealth of tongue-caressing textures; pork in yam croquettes melted in the mouth. The Palace has the potential to be one of the best. Its act needs tightening, though.

The Providores & Tapa Room ★

109 Marylebone High Street, W1U 4RX (020 7935 6175/www.theprovidores.co.uk). Baker Street or Bond Street tube. Providores **Lunch served** noon-2.45pm daily. **Dinner served** 6-10.45pm Mon-Sat; 6-10pm Sun. **Main courses** £15-£22. Cover (lunch Sat, Sun) £1.50. *Tapa Room* **Breakfast served** 9-11.30am Mon-Fri; 10am-3pm Sat, Sun. **Meals served** noon-10.30pm Mon-Fri; 4-10.30pm Sat; 4-10pm Sun. **Tapas** £1.50-£9. *Both* **Credit** AmEx, MC, V.

Welcome to the refined upper reaches of fusion food, courtesy of New Zealanders Peter Gordon and Anna Hansen. There are two dining areas, both small and sparely decorated. The ground-floor Tapa Room (named after a bark cloth used in ceremonies throughout the Pacific) is the more casual space; open for posh breakfast fry-ups, brunchy snacks and global tapas. Upstairs, the Providores is a serene, white room. Influences and ingredients from Asian, Middle Eastern and other cuisines appear, as do specifically Kiwi flavours (lemon myrtle, kumara, tamarillo, New Zealand venison). Some dishes read like an encyclopaedia of exotica, others are more straightforward – for example, two hunks of perfect roast halibut came with sautéed artichokes, new potatoes and puy lentils, with sweetness provided by red onions, tartness by tarragon vinaigrette. Prices upstairs match the rarefied cooking; mains hover around £20, while a starter of smoky coconut and tamarind laksa with green tea noodles was a densely flavoured affair – but cost £9.50 for a small bowlful containing one fat prawn and one small dumpling made of chicken and hijiki (seaweed). The well thought-out Kiwi wine list highlights a different New Zealand wine region every month.

Satay House

13 Sale Place, W2 1PX (020 7723 6763). Edgware Road tube/Paddington tube/rail. **Lunch served** noon-3pm, **dinner served** 6-11pm daily. **Main courses** £5-£18.50. **Set meals** £13.50, £18, £25 per person (minimum 2). **Credit** AmEx, MC, V.

Stepping into this tucked-away restaurant, with its pale pink walls and prints, is rather like entering someone's living room. A well-established eaterie, Satay House is authentically Malaysian – from its pleasantly relaxed ambience to the unmistakable smell of freshly fried blachan (shrimp paste) wafting from the kitchen. Satay and roti canai, chosen from the extensive menu, got our meal off to a promising start. The stars of the show, though, were the wonderfully flavourful ikan masak kecap (a great chunk of mackerel in a rich, soy sauce gravy) and the kangkong belacan (water spinach stir-fried with chilli and shrimp paste), both of which overshadowed the simply spiced ayam percik (chicken curry) in its turmeric-yellow gravy.

Villandry

170 Great Portland Street, W1W 5QB (020 7631 3131/www.villandry.com). Great Portland Street tube. **Open** 8am-11pm Mon-Sat; 8am-4pm Sun. **Breakfast served** 8am-noon Mon-Sat. **Brunch served** noon-3pm Sat, Sun. **Lunch served** noon-3pm Mon-Fri. **Dinner served** 6-10.30pm Mon-Sat. **Main courses** £10.50-£19.50. **Credit** AmEx, DC, MC, V.

Beyond Villandry's bar, which can get lively at night, is an airy restaurant that exudes calm, with huge picture windows, white walls and tablecloths. The setting is a perfect foil for the food, which is great but not flashy. Tip-top, carefully sourced ingredients are matched and prepared with flair (and so they should be with main courses at the £18-£20 mark). The food is Mediterranean with a twist – swordfish wrapped in speck with white bean purée, rosemary and spinach, or black olive and sun-dried tomato gnocchi with rocket and parmesan salad. There can often be a robust edge too; on the warm evening we visited there was a lack of summery options and we ended up with (very good) salt beef and carrots. Starters such as smoked black pudding, puy lentils and onion gravy or confit pork belly with shredded vegetables, noodles and ginger are in similar vein. Puddings are divine concoctions like pear, blackberry and whisky trifle and lemon curd tartlet with plum sauce. Staff are professional.

Also in the area

Carluccio's Caffé 12 Great Portland Street, W1W 8QN (020 7580 3050); **Carluccio's Caffé** St Christopher's Place, W1U 1AY (020 7935 5927); **Fairuz** 3 Blandford Street, W1H 3AA (020 7486 8108/8182); **Giraffe** 6-8 Blandford Street, W1H 3HA (020 7935 2333); **Maroush IV** 68 Edgware Road, W2 2EG (020 7224 9339); **Patisserie Valerie at Sagne** 105 Marylebone High Street, W1U 4RS (020 7935 6240); **Paul** 115 Marylebone High Street, W1U 4BS (020 7224 5615); **Royal China** 40 Baker Street, W1M 1DA (020 7487 4688); **Strada** 31 Marylebone High Street, W1M 4PY (0207 935 1004); **Wagamama** 101A Wigmore Street, W1H 9AB (7409 0111).

Mayfair & St James's

Cinnamon Club

The Old Westminster Library, Great Smith Street, SW1 (7222 2555/www.cinnamonclub.com). St James's Park or Westminster tube. **Breakfast served** 7.30-10am, **lunch served** noon-3pm Mon-Fri. **Dinner served** 6-11pm Mon-Sat. **Main courses** £11-£31. **Set lunch** £19 2 courses, £22 3 courses. **Set dinner** £60 5 courses (£95 with wine). **Credit** AmEx, DC, MC, V.

Chef Vivek Singh has put the Cinnamon Club at the forefront of Indian food in Britain. Classic dishes are cooked with due diligence, if unexpected twists (witness the flavour-suffused Hyderabadi biriani of beef, served with rich beef curry and raita), new creations are well judged (juicy tandoori swordfish was paired with a 'tomato lemon' sauce containing kaffir lime leaves), while regional rarities can be revelatory – as in a side dish of Rajasthani sangri beans: thin strips mouth-wateringly pepped up with wild berries. This, and a first course of lamb's sweetbreads (two lightly fried discs) with pungently spiced minced liver and a purple-hued version of coleslaw, were the most outstanding dishes on the daily-changing set lunch menu, though nothing was amiss. The setting (a conversion of a grand 19th-century library, with cinnamon-hued banquettes, and crisp table linen) is peculiarly apt, evoking colonial splendour. Within spitting distance of Parliament, the Club attracts the political elite.

Le Gavroche ★

43 Upper Brook Street, W1K 7QR (020 7408 0881/ www.le-gavroche.co.uk). Marble Arch tube. **Lunch served** noon-2pm Mon-Fri. **Dinner served** 7-11pm Mon-Sat. **Main courses** £27-£39. **Minimum** £60 dinner. **Set lunch** £44 3 courses incl coffee, half bottle of wine, mineral water. **Credit** AmEx, DC, JCB, MC, V.

Given the popularity of Le Gavroche, after more than 20 years at this address and a further 15 before that in Chelsea, booking a table is easy as pie and only need be done a week or so in advance. It's an expensive place, but customers are treated with consideration, which is more than can be said about many restaurants in this price bracket. Set lunches have risen from £40 to £44, although this includes everything from appetisers, water, half a bottle of wine per person, a three-course meal, coffee and petits fours. Otherwise, a typical main course will cost £35-40, while starters and desserts weigh in at another £30 each. Still, for that you'll get some of the best food in London. From the set lunch a simple combination of asparagus, truffle shavings and parmesan was packed with flavour, but a tian of crab with tomato and balsamic dressing was a bit non-committal. Fillet of poached veal, served cold with a creamy caper sauce and celeriac remoulade, was sensationally tender, beguilingly sweet and a very adult sophistication; almost equally good was a main of wild salmon trout with crackly thin ham and a meaty, thyme-infused jus. Adventurous diners may feel that the set lunch doesn't exercise their taste buds as much as the à la carte, but either event leaves you wanting to visit more often.

Gordon Ramsay at Claridges ★

55 Brook Street, W1A 2JQ (020 7499 0099/ www.gordonramsay.com). Bond Street tube. **Lunch served** noon-2.45pm Mon-Fri; noon-3pm Sat, Sun. **Dinner served** 5.45-11pm Mon-Sat; 6-11pm Sun. **Set lunch** £30 3 courses. **Set dinner** £55 3 courses, £65 6 courses. **Credit** AmEx, JCB, MC, V.

There are so many things we like about this beautiful hotel restaurant. Claridges hosts some of the best food in the capital and has the most relaxed yet glamorous atmosphere. It is also open for Sunday dinner, an absurd rarity in London. On this particular Sunday evening the calm peachy room was occupied by locals, families, courting couples and out-of-towners, not to mention a significant showing of professionals from other restaurants, educating their palates on their only night off. Foie gras mousse and crostini accompany idle browsing of menu and wine list, followed by a steaming cup of some artichoke and truffle-infused plaything. Starters begin with, possibly, a sublime smoked eel and celeriac soup garnished with mouth-poppingly soft quails' eggs, or chestnut tortellini with seared wild mushrooms and pumpkin velouté. Boiled beef is fantastically tender, three neat slabs served in its own consommé with tiny vegetables. Apple tarte tatin is a speciality but the two teaspoons of ice-cream alongside is plain mean. One of London's master chocolatiers makes the salted caramels, rounding off an unmissable experience.

Inn the Park

St James's Park, SW1A 2BJ (020 7451 9999/ www.innthepark.co.uk). Piccadilly Circus tube. **Breakfast served** 8am-11am Mon-Fri; 9-11am Sat, Sun. **Lunch served** noon-3pm Mon-Fri; noon-4pm Sat, Sun. **Dinner served** 6-10.30pm Mon-Fri; 6-10.30pm Sat, Sun. **Main courses** £8.50-£17.50. **Credit** AmEx, MC, V.

When restaurateur Oliver Peyton was given the chance to create a brand new café in St James's Park, he seized the chance. The crummy old tearoom has been demolished and replaced with a new wooden structure, with a glass front and veranda that blurs the boundary between outside and in. There's an all-day café menu – breakfast, snacks, afternoon tea – but for lunch and dinner the kitchen becomes a full-blown restaurant. Peyton already champions British produce, but good practice doesn't always follow the theory and the results here are mixed. Bury black pudding with beetroot, poached egg and watercress salad was delectable. But the mixed fish grill was nothing more than a few small, scrap-like pieces (tails, almost) for £15, and a chocolate truffle cake tasted little better than mass-produced versions – very poor value for £6.50. We liked Inn the Park, but we wanted to love it. For this to happen, the cooking needs to become much more consistent.

Kaya

42 Albemarle Street, W1X 3FE (020 7499 0622/ 0633). Green Park tube. **Lunch served** noon-3pm Mon-Sat. **Dinner served** 6-11pm daily. **Main courses** £7.50-£17. **Set lunch** £12-£15 1 course. **Credit** JCB, MC, V.

Korean restaurants don't often do 'smart'. Kaya is an honourable exception. The restaurant has had a minor facelift since last year – there's some new lighting and crockery and opera playing instead of traditional Korean music. The menu too, has had a few tweaks, although we were pleased to see that old favourites such as jellyfish and seafood in mustard sauce remain in place. For aficionados, the 'chef's specials' section is the place to look for the most interesting dishes. We were impressed with a light, flavourful broth containing meatballs, prawn, crab, beef, chicken and peppers, served in a steamboat, similar to Japanese shabu-shabu, as well as plump, deep-fried oysters and barbecued kalbi. Service is of a high standard.

Kiku

17 Half Moon Street, W1J 7BE (020 7499 4208/ www.kikurestaurant.co.uk). Green Park tube. **Lunch served** noon-2.30pm Mon-Sat. **Dinner served** 6-10.15pm Mon-Sat; 5.30-9.45pm Sun. **Main courses** £10-£28. **Set lunch** £12-£25 incl miso soup, rice & pickles. **Set dinner** £40-£60 incl miso soup, rice & pickles, dessert. **Credit** AmEx, JCB, MC, V.

A stone's throw from Nobu (*see p29*), Kiku also deals in high-end Japanese cuisine, but is a little less exciting and not much cheaper than its glamorous neighbour. The decor is highly functional but food is of a high quality. This isn't a bad place to try kaiseki, sets of which begin at £42. Selections vary, but will always include a grilled, fried, steamed, boiled and raw dish plus soup; the way the chef plays around with these basic rules is what makes a kaiseki meal so enjoyable. An edo set was excellent too.

Mirabelle ★

56 Curzon Street, W1Y 8DN (020 7499 4636/ www.whitestarline.org.uk). Green Park tube. **Lunch served** noon-2.30pm Mon-Sat; noon-3pm Sun. **Dinner served** 6-11pm daily. **Main courses** £14.50-£25. **Set lunches** (Mon-Sat) £16.50 2 courses, £19.50 3 courses; (Sun) £19.50 3 courses. **Credit** AmEx, MC, V.

With its Mayfair address, Marco Pierre White at the helm and what has to be one of the largest mirrorballs in London, Mirabelle is every inch the glamorous restaurant. The inevitable business lunches and dinners can be something of a turn-off in the glamour stakes but this isn't a starchy place, and the atmosphere is usually buoyant. The culinary events – and each dish here really is an event – commenced with lightly seared melt-in-the-mouth scallops atop a tarte tartin of sweet, caramelised endive, and an extraordinary ham omelette, with a gorgeous creamy texture. Mains continued in this perfectionist vein: a venison dish was richly flavoursome, set off by the currants on top, but it was the lobster that stole the show – beautifully seasoned, generously portioned and served with a fantastically creamy potato purée. We have come to expect impeccably suave but rarely stuffy service here, and classic French cuisine of the highest order; in short, Mirabelle is reliable splurging territory.

Momo ★

25 Heddon Street, W1B 4BH (020 7434 4040/www.momoresto.com). Oxford Circus or Piccadilly Circus tube. **Lunch served** noon-2.30pm Mon-Sat. **Dinner served** 7-11pm Mon-Sat; 7-10.30pm Sun. **Main courses** £14.50-£19.50. **Set lunch** £17 2 courses, £20 3 courses. **Credit** AmEx, DC, MC, V.

Sketch continues to hog the limelight but it is restaurateur Mourad Mazouz's earlier London venture Momo that's the real deal. It's simply gorgeous, decked out like Rick's Café Americain (of *Casablanca* fame) with wooden-screen windows, hanging brass lanterns and plenty of large tables filled every night with chattery action and a smattering of Nubians and North Africans. And if the staff, who are kitted out in custom-designed kasbah pop art T-shirts, appear to be chosen more for their looks than attentiveness to customers, well, that only adds to the glamour. The menu supplements the standard tagines and couscous of Morocco with dishes like baked cod, duck breast and sea bass. It's all very good, although not as exceptional as you might hope. Not that this seems to bother anyone. The true allure of Momo is that despite it being, what, ten years ago now since Madge opted to celebrate her birthday here, it still feels like the place to be. It's got style, it's got class, it's got attitude. It's Maroc 'n' roll, man.

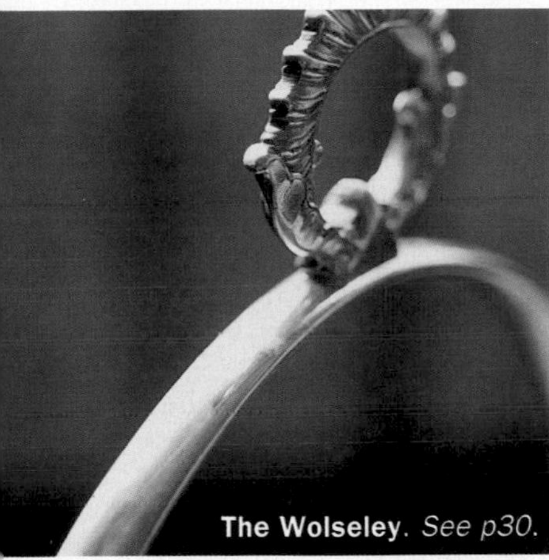

The Wolseley. *See p30.*

Nobu ★

Metropolitan Hotel, 19 Old Park Lane, W1K 1LB (7447 4747/www.noburestaurants.com). Hyde Park Corner tube. **Lunch served** noon-2.15pm Mon-Fri; 12.30-3pm Sat, Sun. **Dinner served** 6-10.15pm Mon-Thur; 6-11pm Fri, Sat; 6-9.30pm Sun. **Main courses** £5-£27.50 incl miso soup, rice & pickles. **Set lunch** £50 chef's selection, £25 bento box, £25 sushi box. **Set dinner** £70-£90 chef's selection incl green tea. **Credit** AmEx, DC, MC, V.

Bad news first: Nobu has unexpectedly unattractive features. The tables are small and packed, and the ratio of customers to square feet is emphasised by bright lighting and canteen noise levels. At these prices you may feel entitled to more seclusion than Nobu is capable of offering. Now the good news: if you're here for the food, you won't spend long worrying about your earthly surroundings. The fusion of Japanese and Peruvian traditions is no longer novel, but is still capable of inspiring surprise and delight. Tuna tataki (petals of seared sashimi in ponzu sauce) was extraordinary. So too the lobster ceviche (nuggets of marinated flesh), the sugar snap tempura (hot little life-rafts of vegetable sweetness), and the wagyu beef (priced by the 25g; you'll need 100g for two people). To follow, the sorbets burst on the tongue like the last rounds in a firework display; this is one of the few Japanese restaurants where you really should try puddings. And everything else you can get your mitts on, for that matter. Nobu continues to offer some of the best cooking and culinary invention to be had in London.

Patara

3&7 Maddox Street, W1S 2QB (020 7499 6008). Oxford Circus tube. **Lunch served** noon-3pm, **dinner served** 6.30-10.30pm daily. **Main courses** £10.95-£16.95. **Set lunch** £11.95 2 courses, £14.95 3 courses. **Credit** AmEx, DC, MC, V.

Oozing style and sophistication by the ice-bucket load, Thai restaurant Patara lets its self-assured cooking speak for itself. A tangy salad of green mango featured crisp, juicy shreds of fruit enlivened with chilli and lime. Steamed dumplings in assorted colours, from lilac to pale golden, were stuffed with prawn, chicken and pork – with some fillings working better than others. Grilled black cod with ginger and pickled yellow bean sauce was a scrumptious version of an old classic. Pineapple and tofu red curry had an intriguing mix of hot, sour, spicy and fruity flavours. More tofu featured in a delightfully piquant stir-fry with green beans, chillies and lime leaves. The soothing earthy interior, smiling staff and a buzzy crowd contribute to a highly enjoyable dining experience.

Quod

57 Haymarket, SW1Y 4QX (020 7925 1234/ www.quod.co.uk). Piccadilly Circus tube. **Breakfast served** 8am-11.30pm Mon-Fri. **Afternoon tea served** 3-4.30pm, **meals served** noon-midnight Mon-Sat. **Main courses** £8.35-£16.75. **Set meal** (4-7pm, 10pm-midnight) £10.95 2 courses, £22.95 3 courses. **Credit** AmEx, DC, JCB, MC, V.

Subtle reworking of the colours, textures and artwork in this gigantic mezzanined space has resulted in a more intimate atmosphere, though the modern portraits are still boldly unusual and the wide-screen TV is something of a distraction. The front bar area works well as a casual restaurant – a useful spot in an expensive area. The specials board offers a diversion from the standard Italian, burgers and pizza menu: duck with pak choy, mushrooms and a tasty gravy, which was executed with finesse. Pastas included good renditions of pappardelle with prawns, courgettes and cherry tomatoes, and potato gnocchi with gorgonzola and spinach sauce. Service was relaxed and pleasant.

The Ritz

150 Piccadilly, W1J 9BR (020 7493 8181/www.the ritzhotel.co.uk). Green Park tube.Bar **Open** 11.30am-11pm Mon-Sat; noon-10.30pm Sun. **Food served** noon-10pm daily. *Restaurant* **Tea served** (reserved sittings) 1.30pm, 3.30pm, 5.30pm daily. **Breakfast served** 7-10.30am Mon-Sat; 8-10.30am Sun. **Lunch served** 12.30-2.30pm daily. **Dinner served** 6-10.30pm Mon-Sat. **Main courses** £25-£56. **Set dinner** (6-7pm, 10-10.30pm) £43 3 courses; (Mon-Thur) £60 4 courses; (Fri, Sat) £70 4 courses. **Set tea** £32. **Credit** AmEx, MC, V.

It takes a brave team to renovate the revered Ritz, but the dining room is looking good. The colour scheme has subtly deepened to richer tones of garden green and cherry pink, while the over-the-top gold leaf chandeliers, framed and embellished with garlands of gilded flowers against a romantic mural, are fresh and confident. Unlike its patrons, the Ritz is not a retiring venue. A new chef is at the helm, and the archaic and unsettling old menu with its countless courses has gone. A more navigable à la carte simply displays a page of starters, a page of main courses and a separate sheet for set lunch. This gets you a light, modestly portioned meal for less than the price of most à la carte main courses. A room-temperature salad was packed to bursting with new season asparagus, artichoke, lima, french and peeled broad beans, peas, tiny carrots – 15 different veggies in all, beautifully prepared, delicious and virtuous. Beef fillet, by way of contrast, was carnivorous and satisfying. Iconic.

Tamarind ★

20 Queen Street, W1J 5PR (7629 3561/ www.tamarindrestaurant.com). Green Park tube. **Lunch served** noon-3pm Mon-Fri; noon-2.30pm Sun. **Dinner served** 6-11.30pm Mon-Sat; 6-10.30pm Sun. **Main courses** £14.50-£22. **Set lunch** £14.50 2 courses, £16.50 3 courses. **Set meal** (6-7pm) £22 2 courses. **Credit** AmEx, DC, JCB, MC, V.

Dignified and luxurious, this elegant basement Indian restaurant is synonymous with quality cooking, superlative service and a choice selection of wines. Crisp white table linen, speckled mirrors, and muted lighting are enhanced by theatrical views of skewer-wielding chefs through the glass-fronted kitchen window. Chef Alfred Prasad cooks a selection of pan-Indian dishes, but doesn't pull out the stops for new-wave choices. Saag aloo tikki – fried potato cakes stuffed with spinach and served with tamarind chutney – elevated a favourite street snack with its delicate spicing and a much appreciated velvety smooth texture. Dal makhani – black lentils simmered with garlic, ginger and chillies, enriched with cream, butter and tomatoes – was divine. Breads are light and soft. There was the occasional disappointment: tari gosht – chunks of lamb cooked in browned onion masala with mace and red chillies – lost out with an overly thick sauce, more akin to home-style cooking than the expected fine dining experience. Service is spot on.

The Wolseley ★

160 Piccadilly, W1J 9EB (020 7499 6996/www.the wolseley.com). Green Park tube. **Breakfast served** 7am-11.30pm Mon-Fri; 9am-11.30pm Sat, Sun. **Lunch served** noon-2.30pm Mon-Fri; noon-3pm Sat, Sun. **Dinner served** 5.30pm-midnight Mon-Sat; 5.30-11pm Sun. **Main courses** £8.75-£26. **Cover** £2. **Credit** AmEx, DC, JCB, MC, V.

The handsome new venture from Jeremy King and Chris Corbin, the team who made the Ivy such a success, is an egalitarian affair. The long opening hours mean that everyone can get in at short notice, even if just for breakfast, tea or a cocktail accompanied by superior bar snacks. And the sizeable, brasserie-style menu really does have something for everyone. Whether it's a simple omelette aux herbes with frites, half a dozen oysters, marinated herring with potato salad, wiener schnitzel or fillet steak au poivre – it's all there, immaculately executed and delivered with panache. The style of the place – a high-ceilinged homage to European grand cafés, created out of what was once a car showroom – is a winner too; and the details are a pleasure. And finally, the waiting staff seem pleased to see all their customers – only a chosen few receive visitations from one or other of the owners, but for the rest of us the warm service and relaxed vibe more than suffice. Prices are reasonable for the quality involved. A wonderful addition to London's dining scene.

Also in the area

Bank Westminster 45 Buckingham Gate, SW1E 6BS (020 7379 9797); **Carluccio's Caffé** Fenwick of Bond Street, W1A 3BS (020 7629 0699); **City Café** 30 John Islip Street, SW1P 4DD; **Gaucho Grill** 19 Swallow Street, W1R 4DJ (020 7734 4040); **Prezzo** 17 Hertford Street, W1J 7RS (020 7499 4690); **Strada** Panton House, 39 Panton Street, SW1Y 4EA (0207 930 8535); **Wagamama** 8 Norris Street, SW1Y 4RH (020 7321 2755).

Soho & Fitzrovia

Back to Basics

21A Foley Street, W1W 6DS (020 7436 2181/ www.backtobasics.uk.com). Goodge Street or Oxford Circus tube. **Lunch served** noon-3pm, dinner served 6-10.30pm Mon-Sat. **Main courses** £12.75-£15.95. **Credit** AmEx, DC, MC, V.

That this is a fish restaurant is clear: from the bright fish T-shirts worn by staff, through a fishy mosaic on the walls, to the innovative and colourful dishes. If you like interesting combinations and robust flavours, choosing from the menu will not be an easy task – Cornish skate with crispy bacon and mushy pea salsa? Fillet of mahi mahi, with mussels, clams, chilli and garlic? Mackerel with sun-dried tomatoes and halloumi on a bed of lentils? We went for the latter, as well as a big bowl of mussels and hot and spicy crab claws as starters. Portions are large and the food is almost always as good as it sounds. The restaurant itself is charming, small and intimate, occupying a corner site, with multicoloured globe lights and windows all around that make you feel like you are dining alfresco whatever the weather.

Bodean's

10 Poland Street, W1F 8PZ (020 7287 7575/ www.bodeansbbq.com). Oxford Circus or Piccadilly Circus tube. Deli **Open** noon-11pm Mon-Sat; noon-10.30pm Sun. *Restaurant* **Lunch served** noon-3pm, **dinner served** 6-11pm Mon-Fri. **Meals served** noon-11pm Sat; noon-10.30pm Sun. **Main courses** £6-£12. **Set meals** £15.95 (minimum 8) 2 courses, £18.95 (minimum 8) 3 courses. **Credit** AmEx, MC, V.

From the rich, sweet smell that leaks out to the street, to the pig-shaped doorknob, this place is all about roasted meat. Vegetarians beware. Everyone else: embrace your inner carnivore and plunge in for barbecue heaven. It's certainly popular – booking is necessary even midweek. Sides are good: barbecue baked beans in molasses-tinged tomato sauce, and a perfect baked potato. But what really matters is the meat – a rack of baby back ribs all but took up half the table with its juicy, marinated goodness, while a more reasonable half-slab of pork ribs is plenty big for most people. Chase it down with a Samuel Adams beer or a Lynchburg Lemonade with a kick of Jack Daniels. Now that's what we call supper.

Busaba Eathai

22 Store Street, WC1E 7DS (020 7299 7900). Goodge Street or Tottenham Court Road tube. **Meals served** noon-11pm Mon-Thur; noon-11.30pm Fri, Sat; noon-10pm Sun. **Main courses** £5.10-£9.80. **Credit** AmEx, JCB, MC, V.

This version of the popular, classy Thai canteen – from Alan Yau, the man who brought us Wagamama – does much the same as its older sister on Wardour Street, but without the queues. Big, wooden, square tables dominate the centre of the big, wooden, square room, while benches run along the sides facing out to Store Street. Tables are communal. The menu is easy to follow (spicy dishes are marked with an asterix). The choice is noodle, salad, rice, curry or wok: green vegetable curry is good, scallop and asparagus stir-fry with garlic and coconut tip is excellent and even boring old pad thai is impressively tasty in any of its three forms. There's a good vegetarian selection and a wide choice of juices, plus beer, wine and Thai whisky. Staff are friendly without ever giving you the impression you're welcome to linger.

Chowki ★

2-3 Denman Street, W1D 7HA (020 7439 1330/ www.chowki.com). **Meals served** noon-11.30pm Mon-Sat; noon-10.30pm Sun. **Main courses** £5.95-£8.95. **Set meal** £10.95 3 courses. **Credit** AmEx, DC, MC, V

Chowki is a clever concept: an unflashy diner with red leather banquettes, it showcases three Indian regional cuisines each month at unfeasibly low prices. Some dishes are good – notably moong dahl with spinach, and prawn curry; others, such as spicy mussels, merely OK. A Maharashtrian classic of rice flakes with coconut and peanuts was inexplicably replaced with layered steamed rice-flour cakes with a dried-out texture – listed under Chettinand dishes, but in fact Gujarati in origin. Cooking standards seem to vary depending on how busy the place gets, but this is a great bargain.

Eagle Bar Diner ★

3-5 Rathbone Place, W1T 1HJ (020 7637 1418/ www.eaglebardiner.com). Tottenham Court Road tube. **Open** noon-11pm Mon-Wed; noon-midnight Thur, Fri; 11am-1am Sat; 11am-6pm Sun. **Meals served** noon-11pm Mon-Wed; noon-11.30pm Thur, Fri; 11am-midnight Sat; 11am-6pm Sun. **Main courses** £4-£8.75. **Credit** MC, V.

This trendy, reliably good restaurant is an oasis off of the hellish hustle of the Oxford Street-Tottenham Court Road corner. The look here is posh American-obsessed diner – leather banquettes plonked at arty angles, tiny booths and a slick bar at the front – and the menu is pretty much the same. The grilled tuna burger is gorgeous – cooked to perfection and juicy – as is the 8oz beef burger, which we had with Danish blue cheese. Both were served with attention to detail: the rolls were fresh, the salad was crisp, the fries crisp and salty (they also do super-fatty chunky chips). Peanut butter and banana milkshake is heaven in a glass for three quid. Equally good for breakfast, brunch, lunch, dinner or drinking – there aren't enough places like this in London.

Fino

33 Charlotte Street, entrance on Rathbone Street, W1T 1RR (020 7813 010/www.finorestaurant.com). Goodge Street tube. **Lunch served** noon-2.30pm Mon-Fri. **Dinner served** 6-10.30pm Mon-Sat. **Tapas** £5-£15. **Credit** AmEx, MC, V.

It may be in a basement, but this stylish Spanish restaurant and bar is anything but gloomy. The pale wood fittings and smart lighting create a buzzy, congenial atmosphere. The small mezzanine bar is even busier. An immensely appealing menu lists tapas that run from caperberries and toasted almonds to foie gras with chilli jam. It's such a good read that greed will lead you to order too many dishes of the order of crisp fried squid rings, piping hot piquilla croqueta, moreish spicy pimentos de padron, luscious duck breast with tapenade, patatas bravas, and grilled asparagus with manchego shavings. There are classic (£17.95 per person) and gourmet (£28 per person) selections (for two or more) if you really can't make a choice. Desserts run from a shot of crème catalan foam to a chocolate brownie with pistachio ice-cream. A contemporary addition to London's Spanish dining scene.

Hakkasan ★

8 Hanway Place, W1T 1HD (7907 1888). Tottenham Court Road tube. Bar **Open** noon 12.30am Mon-Wed; noon-1.30am Thur-Sat; noon-midnight Sun. *Restaurant* **Lunch served** noon-3.15pm Mon-Fri; noon-4.30pm Sat, Sun. **Dinner served** 6-11.30pm Mon-Wed; 6pm-12.30am Thur-Sat. **Main courses** £5.90-£40; £3.50-£16 dim sum. **Credit** AmEx, MC, V.

Few London restaurants can beat the thrill of descending the green slate staircase into Hakkasan. Incense smoke and outlandish flowers greet you as you enter a subtly lit space of dark latticed screens, which evokes the old houses of pre-revolutionary China. Started by the innovative Alan Yau, Hakkasan breaks the mould by offering fine, pricey Chinese food in a place that satisfies both western and oriental tastes. The dim sum are unrivalled in London. Come at lunchtime for crisp triangular pastries stuffed with venison; translucent, emerald green dumplings filled with prawn and fragrant Chinese chive; and light-as-a-feather deep-fried snacks. Dinner is a more mixed experience. Booking a table is difficult: but the cooking can be superb. 'Tong Fong' soft-shelled crabs, deep-fried and tossed with lashings of garlic and a few curry leaves; stir-fry of asparagus, lily bulb and lotus stem with black pepper; delicious sanbei chicken. There's a fine wine list and an enticing selection of cocktails. Come here for a really special occasion.

Lindsay House ★

21 Romilly Street, W1D 5AF (020 7439 0450/ www.lindsayhouse.co.uk). Leicester Square tube. **Lunch served** noon-2.30pm Mon-Fri. **Dinner served** 6-11pm Mon-Sat. **Set meals** (6-7pm Mon-Sat) £25 3 courses. **Set dinner** £48 3 courses, £59 tasting menu, £52 vegetarian tasting menu. **Credit** AmEx, DC, MC, V.

To be buzzed into this elegant restaurant is to be given a passport to a world where cured foie gras is rolled in spiced gingerbread, where butter poached haddock comes with parsnip cream and ordinary cheeses are usurped by the likes of stinking bishop with brioche. Such ingredients are carefully sourced, often from Irish producers and often by the chef himself (Richard Corrigan is known for his hands-on approach), and once they reach the kitchen they're given a thorough and imaginative seeing-to. Creamed risotto of marinated ceps, for instance, was the seasonal highlight of a recent visit. Of the two dining rooms, the ground-floor space is more intimate, but they both share a simple aesthetic. Staff, meanwhile, strike the right balance between being pleased to see you and being happy to leave you alone; the wine list achieves a similar harmony between quality and price. One last thing: do your bit to keep gluttony on Soho's roster of deadly sins and try the £59 tasting menu. You won't regret it.

Maison Bertaux ★

28 Greek Street, W1V 5LL (020 7437 6007). Leicester Square, Piccadilly Circus or Tottenham Court Road tube. **Open** 8.30am-8pm daily. **Main courses** £1.30-£2.90. **No credit cards**.

Furnished with wonky tables and chairs that have seen better days, Maison Bertaux cocks a snook at bourgeois tastes. Friendly staff are cheerfully chatty with customers, many of whom belong to the arty/boffin brigade. No written menus either – what you get is what you see. It's quite a sight though – check out their selection of French pâtisserie, freshly baked breads and flavoursome savouries. Quiche lorraine, still warm from the oven, was encased in crumbly pastry, enriched with a creamy custard filling and flecked with bits of bacon. Top marks to the Paris Brest gateaux – we loved the nutty praline and cream filling, sandwiched between choux pastry rings. This spot gets seriously busy at tea time; better to drop in at breakfast for a buttery croissant.

Masala Zone ★

9 Marshall Street, W1F 7ER (020 7287 9966/ www.realindianfood.com). Oxford Circus tube. **Lunch served** noon-3pm Mon-Fri; 12.30-3.30pm Sun. **Dinner served** 5.30-11pm Mon-Fri; 6-10.30pm Sun. **Meals served** 12.30-11pm Sat. **Main courses** £5.50-£11. **Thalis** £6-£11.50. **Credit** MC, V.

Deserving its popularity, Masala Zone has Wagamama-fied Indian dining without compromising authenticity. The restaurant's great-value menu encompasses crisp Bombay beach snacks, meal-in-one plates, rare regional dishes (undhiyo and lentil khichdi), properly prepared curries and satisfying thalis. For dinner, a combination thali is a good way of sampling the menu, allowing a choice of any two bowls of curry from the menu as well as a starter (perhaps aloo tikki chaat: potato cake), two vegetable curries, raita, dahl, kuchumber (diced tomato and cucumber salad), popadoms and chutneys, a wholewheat chapati and rice. Lamb achari was a fine accompaniment to this, featuring a tangy, green-tinged sauce replete with freshly ground spices. Despite plentiful staff, service on our visit became a touch disjointed during the Friday-night rush. Otherwise, dining here – viewing the bustle of the open kitchen – was a pleasure.

Navarro's

67 Charlotte Street, W1T 4PH (020 7637 7713/ www.navarros.co.uk). Goodge Street tube. **Lunch served** noon-3pm Mon-Fri. **Dinner served** 6-10pm Mon-Sat. **Tapas** £1.50-£13. **Credit** AmEx, DC, MC, V.

Despite the relatively recent arrival of fresh and fancy competition round the corner in the shape of Fino (*see p33*), Navarro's continues to hold its own as one of the most enjoyable mid-range Spanish restaurants in London. The cheerful interior – dark wood and Moorish tiles – is often heaving, so you may have to book, but it's not just the atmosphere that draws a crowd. Tapas is the order of the day: fans of the simple should try perfect patatas bravas, chunky tortilla, excellent black beans and rice, good anchovies and sardines, chicken livers, or anything with prawns. For more complex tastes, there's chorizo flambéed with brandy, honey-roast lamb with mash, dried apricots and a eucalyptus honey and wine sauce, or squid stuffed with seafood. The choice is rich and the standard of ingredients, cooking and service is high. Wash it all down with good, robust Rioja. A fantastic place and, even better, no stuffed shirts (they've all gone to Fino).

New Mayflower

68-70 Shaftesbury Avenue, W1B 6LY (020 7734 9207). Piccadilly Circus tube. **Meals served** 5pm-4am daily. **Main courses** £6.50-£45. Minimum £8. **Set dinner** £12-£22 per person (minimum 2). **Credit** AmEx, MC, V.

There is a crispness to the clean, unfussy decor and the service of this popular Chinese that speaks of efficient management. Staff are knowledgeable and friendly, whether dealing with Chinese or Western customers, there is a relaxed hubbub of conversation everywhere, and the effect is comfortable enjoyment. A little bowl of complimentary sweet pickled vegetables honed our chopstick technique while waiting for the tasty starter of crispy duck and pancakes. We ordered off-menu – a fried cake of minced salted fish and pork, nicely blended with water chestnut, and on the waiter's recommendation chose as our vegetable course ung choi redolent of chillies and fermented beancurd (fu-yu). The subtleties of a mixed squid and scallop dish might have been lost in such basic company, but, thanks to freshness and well-timed cooking, they held their own. Prices are very reasonable for the quality.

Özer

5 Langham Place, W1B 3DG (020 7323 0505). Oxford Circus tube. Bar **Open** noon-11pm daily. *Restaurant* **Meals served** noon-midnight daily. **Main courses** £8.70-£15.70. **Set lunch** (noon-7pm) £9 2 courses. **Set dinner** (7-11pm) £11 2 courses. **Credit** AmEx, DC, MC, V.

One of the premier Turkish restaurants in central London. Big marinated olives and extra-smooth houmous was supplied on the table and the starters of bakla (broad beans) in yoghurt were fresh, tasty and well presented. For mains, mücver served with falafel offered complementary flavours and came with excellent basmati rice and vegetables. Tandir (shoulder of lamb) was a big portion of meat and slightly too dry and salty, although this was lessened by the kumquat and lime-quat with which it was served. The menu is varied enough to suit a wide range of tastes, with grills and stews, meat, fish and vegetarian dishes. The wine list includes French, Italian, New World and Turkish selections.

Patisserie Valerie ★

44 Old Compton Street, W1D 4TY (020 7437 3466/ www.patisserie-valerie.co.uk). Leicester Square, Piccadilly Circus or Tottenham Court Road tube. **Open** 7.30am-8.30pm Mon, Tue; 7.30am-9pm Wed-Fri; 8.30am-9pm Sat; 9.30am-7pm Sun. **Main courses** £3.75-£7.95. **Credit** (over £5) AmEx, DC, MC, V.

Indulgent cakes, marzipans and french breads provide a feast for the eyes at this landmark pastry shop and café. Decor is a throwback to the 1950s, with Formica tables, embellished with arty cartoons from the same era. It's a favourite spot for many – for a quieter setting, avoid the often cramped and gloomy ground floor and head for the lighter, more airy dining area on the first floor. The menu offers a decent choice of sandwiches and grilled snacks as well as all-day breakfasts, pastas and a variety of salads. Ciabatta bread, filled with spicy chicken, roasted peppers, melted cheese and guacamole was a resounding success, let down only by a bland salad accompaniment. A few gripes – the insipid coffee was a downer, and their signature white and dark chocolate mousse cake didn't make the grade either. Service gets harried when the place fills up.

Pied à Terre ★

34 Charlotte Street, W1T 2NH (020 7636 1178/ www.pied.a.terre.co.uk). Goodge Street or Tottenham Court Road tube. **Lunch served** 12.15-2.30pm Tue-Fri. **Dinner served** 6.15-11pm Mon-Sat. **Main courses** £27. **Set lunch** £21.50 2 courses, £26.50 3 courses. **Set dinner** £45 2 courses, £54.50 3 courses, £50-£65 8 courses. **Credit** AmEx, MC, V.

Pied à Terre goes out of its way to provide a realistically priced and relaxing gourmet experience for those canny enough to avail themselves, staff making no distinction between celebrity and everyman. This represents a mammoth achievement in the stony faced world of haute cuisine. The food is heavenly. White bean and black truffle soup was all animal attraction with crisp bacon lardons lurking in its fragrant depths. Roasted halibut was a fresh tasting, beautifully crisped dish with braised lettuce, nut butter and some gritty cockles. Desserts are stunning, light and fruity confections – poached pear came in caramel topped slices with alternating patches of liquorice ice-cream and star anise cream. If you haven't been yet, what's keeping you?

Yauatcha. *See p37.*

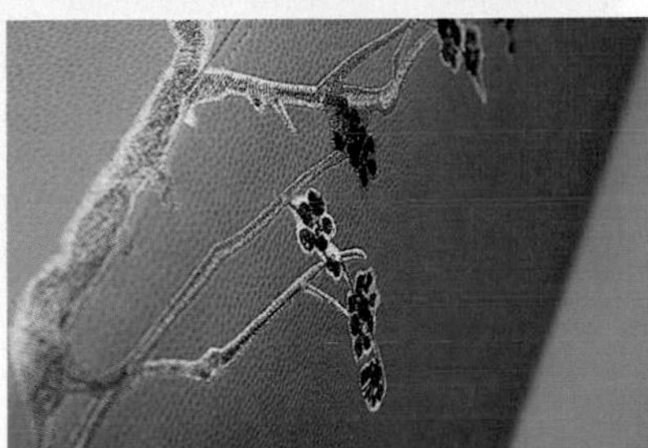

Red Fort

77 Dean Street, W1D 3SH (020 7437 2115/www.redfort.co.uk). Tottenham Court Road tube. **Lunch served** noon-2.15pm Mon-Fri. **Dinner served** 5.45-11pm Mon-Sat. **Main courses** £12.50-£20. **Set lunch** £12 2 courses. **Set meal** (5.45-7pm) £16 2 courses incl tea or coffee. **Credit** AmEx, MC, V.

Previously a *Time Out* Best Indian Restaurant award-winner, Red Fort continues to attract a clientele of deep-pocketed tourists and corporate types. Antique urns, red sandstone walls, and a sleek water feature lend a modern vibe and service never misses a beat – most of the Indian staff have been poached from five-star hotels on the subcontinent. Cooking is inspired by the regal traditions of Lucknow, characterised by complex spice mixes. Winning dishes included anaari champ – perfectly grilled lamb chops, served in a delectable meaty jus, spiked with star anise and tart pomegranate powder. Avadhi gosht biryani – chunks of spiced lamb, cooked in cardamom-scented yoghurt and braised with saffron-streaked rice – could have been lighter. The Red Fort is regaining its reputation as one of London's leading Indian restaurants.

Mint Leaf has become one of the most exciting additions to London's restaurant scene.
Serving Indian food in a beautifully designed contemporary environment, the restaurant seats 140 people offering a wonderful sense of occasion and spectacle.
Mint Leaf also features a large cocktail bar serving light snacks and drinks until 12am. A spacious and discreet private room, the Jaipur Lounge, for special events and other functions completes the restaurant seating a further 60 people.
mint leaf
Situated on Suffolk Place, just beside Trafalgar Square Mint Leaf would like you to experience their new Thali lunch menu
Open Mon-Fri 12-3 & 5:30-12AM, Sat 5:30-12AM
Mint Leaf, Suffolk Place London SW1Y 4HX
Tel: 0207 930 9020
Fax: 0207 930 6205
Email: reservation@mintleafrestaurant.com
Website: www.mintleafrestaurant.com

JIN
Korean Barbeque Restaurant
16 Bateman Street
London W1D 3AH
Tel: 020 7734 0908
Tel: 020 7734 0856

YUZU
805 FULHAM ROAD, SW6 5HE T 020 7731 0081 www.yuzu.biz
ユズ
JAPANESE | CHINESE | THAI | DIM SUM
PARSONS GREEN

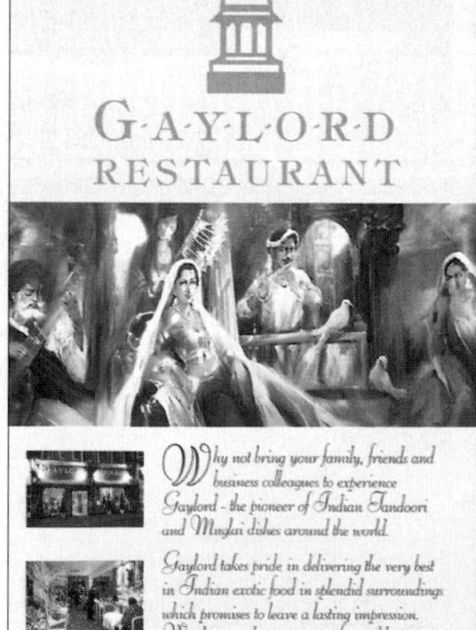
GAYLORD
RESTAURANT
Why not bring your family, friends and business colleagues to experience Gaylord - the pioneer of Indian Tandoori and Muglai dishes around the world.
Gaylord takes pride in delivering the very best in Indian exotic food in splendid surroundings which promises to leave a lasting impression. We also specialise in catering for wedding receptions.
79 - 81 Mortimer Street, London W1W 7SJ.
Tel: 0207 580 3615 / 636 0808. Fax: 0207 636 0860.

Sardo

45 Grafton Way, W1T 5DQ (020 7387 2521/ www.sardo-restaurant.com). Warren Street tube. **Lunch served** noon-3pm Mon-Fri. **Dinner served** 6-11pm Mon-Sat. **Main courses** £8.90-£18. **Credit** AmEx, DC, JCB, MC, V.

There are many popular, well-executed dishes on the menu (grilled tuna with rocket and tomatoes, say), but it's best to order from the daily specials on the blackboard, especially when fregola and shellfish are involved. Alternatively, be guided by owner Romolo Mudu, who may have just a couple of portions available of something interesting. He returns frequently to Sardinia to source new ingredients and wines and likes to try them out on a few patrons before launching them on the main menu. Our visit gleaned a tasty plate of wild boar prosciutto, and venison cooked perfectly to medium, served with blue cheese sauce. Sweet creamy polenta was an unusual but deliciously comforting finale. Sardo's fragrant breads and olives, charged at £3, are well worth the expense. Like decor and service, they may be simple, but are done extremely well and without any pretension.

Strada

9-10 Market Place, W1W 8AQ (020 7580 4644). Oxford Circus tube. **Meals served** noon-11pm Mon-Sat; noon-10.30pm Sun. **Main courses** £5.95-£13.95. **Credit** AmEx, DC, JCB, MC, V.

This modish, capital-wide chain has been expanding at a gentle rate, presumably in the hope that by keeping things on a relatively small scale, it can maintain a high level of quality. Going by our visit to this branch, spread over two handsome floors and a chunk of pavement, it seems to be working, but not quite as well as we'd hoped. A starter of polenta with a mushroom sauce was edible without being particularly memorable, and while the pizzas for which the chain is famed were well above average (we tried the ham-topped speck and the simpler bufala, both cooked in a wood-burning oven), they were also a little under-topped. This was a shame, because the ingredients are about as fresh as you'll find in any London pizzeria. Service was speedy, if a little ditzy, but the complimentary filtered water delivered immediately to every table garners the place a huge pile of brownie points.

Yauatcha

15 Broadwick Street, W1F 0DE (020 7494 8888). Oxford Circus tube. **Meals served** noon-11pm Mon-Sat; noon-10pm Sun. **Main courses** £3.50-£12. **Credit** AmEx, MC, V.

Yauatcha occupies the basement and ground floors of Richard Rogers' new Ingeni building on the corner with Berwick Street. Unlike more conventional dim sum restaurants, which are low on style and won't serve you dumplings in the evening, this one is deeply chic and open from 10am until late – so you can start the day with tea and finish with cocktails. Slithery cheung fun pasta was stuffed with spankingly fresh prawns and slices of emerald-green gai lan (Chinese broccoli), and steamed mooli cake with dried shrimp turned out to be a delicious porridgy goo. In the basement, there are cool grey tables and chairs under a dark ceiling that twinkles with star-like bulbs. Upstairs, in the exquisitely elegant tearoom, some of the most shatteringly beautiful pâtisseries in London are arrayed like works of art on a marble counter, and more than 50 different teas can be brewed to order – look out for the dark, smoky yunnanese or the magnificently sweet huang jin gui.

YMing

35-36 Greek Street, W1D 5DL (020 7734 2721/ www.yming.com). Leicester Square, Piccadilly Circus or Tottenham Court Road tube. **Meals served** noon-11.45pm Mon-Sat. **Main courses** £5-£10. **Set lunch** £10 3 courses (noon-6pm). **Set meals** £15-£20 per person (minimum 2). **Credit** AmEx, DC, JCB, MC, V.

YMing likes to be different, not sticking to the usual run of Cantonese dishes, but despite the claim of the waiter who served us, neither does it serve only Northern Chinese food. We started with steamed pork dumplings, savoury and accompanied by a simple but nicely judged sauce of tender ginger needles in vinegar. The chicken dish that followed was also simple, strips of white breast meat fried with bitter-hot red pepper slices, but our next choice, daringly made to catch the menu's adventurous spirit, was neither simple nor good, a concoction of shelled prawn balls in a thixotropic sauce studded with mango pieces, nauseatingly sweet and an insult to the prawns. The menu was surprisingly short on fresh vegetables, but 'four season beans' were agreeably authentic dry-fried dark green beans in finely chopped red chilli and black fermented soybeans. Service was friendly and efficient and the wrap-around windows of the corner site make for a comfortable, bright lunch venue.

Also in the area

Busaba Eathai 106-110 Wardour Street, W1F 0TR (020 7255 8686); **Cafe Lazeez** 21 Dean Street, W1V 5AH (020 7434 9393); **Carluccio's Caffé** 8 Market Place, W1W 8AG (020 7636 2228); **Carluccio's Caffé** St Christopher's Place, W1W 8QN (020 7935 5927); **Carluccio's Caffé** Fenwick, 63 New Bond Street, W1A 3BS (020 7629 0699); **Crazy Bear** 26-28 Whitfield Street, W1T 7DS (020 7631 0088); **De Gustibus** 53 Blandford Street, W1U 7HL (020 7486 6608); **Livebait Café Fish** 36-40 Rupert Street, W1D 6DW (020 7287 8989); **Maroush III** 62 Seymour Street, W1H 5AF (020 7724 5024); **Maroush V** 3-4 Vere Street, W1G 0DG (020 7493 5050); **Prezzo** 98 Tottenham Court Road, W1T 4TR (020 7436 5355); **Rasa Express** 5 Rathbone Street, W1T 1NX (020 7637 0222); **Rasa Samudra** 5 Charlotte Street, W1T 1RE (020 7637 0222); **Strada** 15-16 New Burlington Street, W1X 1FF (020 7287 5967); **Strada** 9-10 Market Place, W1W 8AQ (020 7580 4644); **Wagamama** 10A Lexington Street, W1R 3HS (020 7292 0990).

Covent Garden & Bloomsbury

The Admiralty

Somerset House, Strand, WC2R 1LA (020 7845 4646/www.somerset-house.org.uk). Temple tube. **Lunch served** noon-2.30pm daily. **Dinner served** 6-10.30pm Mon-Sat. **Main courses** £16.50-£22.50. **Credit** AmEx, DC, JCB, MC, V.

Gracious high-ceilinged dining rooms, hidden away in the wing of Somerset House. Prices are high, but not outrageous for French regional food that is rarely less than excellent. We relished starters of deeply satisfying crispy confit leg of lamb with nuggets of foie gras and potato champ, and hot-smoked salmon on celeriac and apple remoulade. Mains were also class acts – breast of corn-fed chicken with cabbage, bacon, onions and a buttery almond morel cream was superior comfort food, while pan-fried fillet of brill with boulangère potato and smoked bacon jus starred a sea-sweet piece of fish. Iced prune parfait with hazelnut and sultana biscotti, and dark chocolate mousse – were good if not exceptional desserts.

Christopher's

18 Wellington Street, WC2E 7DD (020 7240 4222/ www.christophersgrill.com). Covent Garden tube. *Bar* **Food served** 11.30am-11pm Mon-Sat. *Restaurant* **Brunch served** 11.30am-4pm Sat, Sun. **Lunch served** noon-3.45pm Mon-Fri. **Dinner served** 5pm-midnight Mon-Sat. **Main courses** £12-£28. **Set meals** (5-7pm, 10pm-midnight Mon-Sat) £12.95 2 courses, £16.50 3 courses. **Credit** AmEx, DC, MC, V.

One of the top London restaurants for modern American cuisine. Christopher's decor is cool and modern, with cream and chocolate tones. The menu changes seasonally: Chesapeake Bay crab salad in chilled tomato and herb bisque was a perfect summer dish, with smoky flavours and lots of fresh crab. For mains, blackened salmon was perfectly spicy, served atop fresh spring greens – very rich, and very tasty. A blackened ribeye was cooked to order and, at ten ounces, a generous size. For pudding, lemon tart with mascarpone ice-cream was so fabulous we'd come back just for that. A separate bar serves excellent cocktails.

Cigala

54 Lambs Conduit Street, WC1N 3LW (020 7405 1717/www.cigala.co.uk). Holborn or Russell Square tube. **Lunch served** noon-10.45pm Mon-Fri; 12.30-10.45pm Sat. **Main courses** £10-£17. **Tapas** £2-£8. **Set lunch** (Mon-Fri) £15 2 courses, £18 3 courses. **Set tapas** £18 5 dishes. **Credit** AmEx, DC, MC, V.

Cigala is a slick, modern Spanish restaurant decked out in white and pine, so don't come expecting a trad tapas joint. The menu, however, keeps things traditional, with Spanish classics like deep-fried padrón peppers, seafood paella and cured pork loin that are simply but effectively prepared with robust ingredients. The expertly chosen wine list is a highlight, with plenty of Spanish vintages under £30, a handful by the glass and an admirable selection of sherries. The waiting staff are usually efficient and knowledgeable, and prices are in line with the chic surroundings. Note that when busy the tapas menu may only be available in the downstairs tapas bar or on the pavement tables, and not in the restaurant.

East@West

13-15 West Street, WC2H 9NE (020 7010 8600/ www.egami.co.uk). Leicester Square tube. **Open** noon-2am Mon-Fri; 5.30pm-2am Sat. **Meals served** noon-midnight Mon-Fri; 5.30pm-midnight Sat. **Main courses** £9-£40. **Credit** AmEx, DC, MC, V.

Australian chef Christine Manfield has quickly established a fresh, funky but seriously classy dining spot here. Pass through the shiny, chic decor of the bar to the upstairs restaurant. At lunchtime, the pristine white napkin vibe is loosened by evangelical waiting staff keen to guide you through the 'tastes' of an array of small dishes on the menu. At night, discreetly dimmed lights give a more romantic air. The modern Asian menu might feature wasabi avocado cream served with asparagus tempura, or spring onion wontons floating in a rich turmeric lemongrass broth.

Food for Thought ★

31 Neal Street, WC2H 9PR (020 7836 9072). Covent Garden tube. **Breakfast served** 9.30-11.30am Mon-Sat. **Lunch served** noon-5pm daily. **Dinner served** 5-8.30pm Mon-Sat. **Main courses** £3-£6.50. Minimum (noon-3pm, 6-7.30pm) £2.50. **Unlicensed. No credit cards.**

Veggie stalwart FfT is unpretentious, reliable and great value. Diners share tables in the small narrow basement (if you're lucky, the cosy little alcoves at the back may be free) to enjoy the daily changing, globally inspired menu. Lunchtime takeaway queues can be long and dishes sometimes run out, but this is a testament to the enduring popularity of the place. There's always a soup (Thai spinach and coconut, say), a stir-fry, a quiche and chunky salads, plus specials such as aubergine and fennel timbale, layered with rice and a rich tomato sauce, and

The best Cocktail bars

Akbar
77 Dean Street, W1D 3SH (020 7437 2525).
Below Soho's Red Fort Indian restaurant, the exotic Akbar sprinkles spices and herbs from the kitchen into its cocktail collection.

American Bar
Savoy Hotel, Strand, WC2R 0EU (020 7836 4343).
The bar that brought the mixed drink to Britain, this art deco exercise in understated extravagance is a homage to the classic cocktail.

Apartment 195
195 King's Road, SW3 5ED (020 7351 5195).
This sexy/camp Chelsea bar excels at modern creations.

Baltic
See p51.
Gem of a bar attached to a gorgeous restaurant. The drinks list is adventurous, and is particularly strong on vodka.

Brixtonian Havana Club
11 Beehive Place, SW9 7QR (020 7924 9262).
This sweaty, saucy, funky bar goes a bundle on rum.

Christopher's
See p38.
Classic, beautifully made cocktails in classy surroundings.

Dusk
339 Battersea Park Road, SW11 4LS (020 7622 2112).
Sophisticated treasure with excellent drinks in a sleek, chilled environment.

Freud
198 Shaftesbury Avenue, WC2H 8JL (020 7240 9933).
Proof that cocktail bars don't have to be leather banquettes, velvet walls and mirrors, this lo-fi bunker is a satisfying dive.

Hide
125 Dawes Road, SW6 7EA (020 7385 8936).
Off the beaten track, this new Fulham venture is a good-looking venue with excellent drinks.

Hill
94 Haverstock Hill, NW3 2BD (020 7267 0033).
A design dream – Victorian dandyism meets '70s chic – with fine drinks to match.

Lonsdale
48 Lonsdale Road, W11 2DE (020 7228 1517).
This gorgeous joint has an extensive cocktail list – topped by the stunning Pear and Cinnamon Sling.

Loungelover
1 Whitby Street, E1 6JU (020 7012 1234).
Camp as cowboys, Loungelover is decked out like a Chinese junkyard and serves terrific cocktails in seductively sculpted glasses.

Match EC1
45-47 Clerkenwell Road, EC1M 5RS (020 7250 4002).
Simple but superb: try the Hackney Zombie, a nine-ingredient, Scotch-based recipe.

Monkey Chews
2 Queen's Crescent, NW5 4EP (020 7267 6406).
A hidden den of slouchy hedonism and good drinking in the Chalk Farm backstreets.

mybar
myhotel, 11-13 Bayley Street, WC1B 3HD (020 7667 6000).
Trendy hotel bar offering the likes of Nettle Martini. Low-key style at a price.

Player
8 Broadwick Street, W1F 8HN (020 7494 9125).
Sleek and seductive, this dimly lit lounge bar is one of Soho's classiest boozing joints.

Salt Whisky Bar
82 Seymour Street, W2 2JE (020 7402 1155).
The clue's in the name: this is the place for you if you like Scotch, Irish, bourbon or even Japanese whisky.

Shumi
23 St James's Street, SW1A 1HA (020 7747 9380).
Swanky bar with a short but perfect drinks list – try the Liquorice Whisky Sour and wait for the kick.

Trailer Happiness
177 Portobello Road, W11 2DY (020 7727 2700).
Trendy new bar with negligible design throwing the spotlight on killer cocktails.

topped with melted cheese. Fruit crumbles, cakes and scones are available. Produce is GM-free, and there are vegan and wheat-free options. Appealing, inviting and a little bit boho, it's no surprise that Food for Thought has remained a Covent Garden institution for three decades.

Gaucho Grill

125-126 Chancery Lane, WC2A 1PU (0207 242 7727/www.thegauchogrill.co.uk). Chancery Lane tube.
Meals served noon-11pm Mon-Fri. **Main courses** £9-£20. **Credit** AmEx, DC, JCB, MC, V.
Cowhide stools and racks of Mendozan plonk allude to the Argentine countryside, but the Gaucho Grill is a pricey, refined steakhouse (one of a small chain). But if it's far from an authentic parrilla experience, the veal sweetbreads, the fillet steak and empanadas are all tasty and the meat is evidently top-grade Argentine export-quality prime. The wine list is hefty, staff are knowledgeable and welcoming. At this outlet, there are usually more people sipping cocktails on the ground floor than dining upstairs.

Hamburger Union ★

4-6 Garrick Street, WC2E 9BH (020 7379 0412/ www.hamburgerunion.com). Covent Garden tube.
Meals served 11.30am-9.30pm Mon, Tue, Sun; 11.30am-10.30pm Wed-Sat. **Main courses** £3.95-£9.95. **Credit** MC, V.
A pleasing alternative to the fast food superpowers. Union burgers make a filling treat and, at £3.95, are pretty nicely priced for the quality. A lemony chicken sandwich and a garlicky mushroom burger were first rate. Other fillings might be steak, chorizo, or halloumi. The dining area is handsome: sleek wooden benches, a compact bar, framed artwork and – gulp – diners enjoying a glass of wine with their fries.

Hazuki

43 Chandos Place, WC2 4HS (020 7240 2530/ www.sushihazuki.co.uk). Charing Cross tube/rail.
Lunch served noon-2.30pm Mon-Fri. **Dinner served** 5.30-10.30pm Mon-Sat; 5.30-9.30pm Sun. **Main courses** £5.50-£18. **Set meals** £16-£40 3-8 courses. **Credit** AmEx, DC, JCB, MC, V.

East@West. *See p38.*

Nicely placed as a post-show destination, Hazuki has been known to find room for customers right up to the 10.30pm watershed. Service can consequently get a little frazzled, but the food is always remarkably good. The main menu is solidly Japanese, and though the specials edge towards oriental fusion, the best things are core dishes, including a spine-tinglingly good dobin mushi. To make maximum use of limited space, the restaurant is three-tiered: basement tables are fine; those at the glass-fronted entrance level are draughty; while the best are the four in the mezzanine, where vases of bamboo and dragon lilies take the edge off the spare decor.

The Ivy

1 West Street, WC2H 9NQ (020 7836 4751/ www.caprice-holdings.co.uk). Leicester Square tube. **Lunch served** noon-3pm Mon-Sat; noon-3.30pm Sun. **Dinner served** 5.30pm-midnight daily. **Main courses** £9.25-£35. **Set lunch** (Sat) £19.50 3 courses; (Sun) £22 3 courses. **Credit** AmEx, DC, JCB, MC, V.

It may be one of the most famous restaurants in the world but the Ivy has been eclipsed in terms of column inches by ex-owners Corbin and King's new restaurant, the Wolseley (*see p30*). But it's still notoriously hard to get a table; once you do, there's a menu of crowd-pleasing dishes to enjoy, at pretty reasonable prices. Potted salmon followed by shepherd's pie or roast chicken with fabulous stuffing, with sticky toffee pudding to finish, for example. Staff are well drilled, and the room is a good-looking one, decked out in wood panelling, with colourful diamond-patterned windows.

J Sheekey ★

28-32 St Martins Court, WC2N 4AL (020 7240 2565/www.caprice-holdings.co.uk). Leicester Square tube. **Lunch served** noon-3pm Mon-Sat; noon-3.30pm Sun. **Dinner served** 5.30pm-midnight Mon-Sat; 6pm-midnight Sun. **Main courses** £10.75-£29.75. **Set lunch** (Sat, Sun) £14.75 2 courses, £18.50 3 courses. **Credit** AmEx, DC, MC, V.

J Sheekey shares many wonderful things with its sister restaurant the Ivy (*see above*) – elegant and discreet design, simple but sublime food (in this case fish) – and it's always been far easier to book a table. Dressed crab, served with grated egg and parsley, was wonderfully fresh. Excellent main courses include delicately flavoured sea trout with steamed clams and samphire and slightly more robust lemon sole with soft roe shrimps and brown butter, and monkfish and tiger prawn curry. Raspberry trifle made a rich, extremely fruity end to a great meal.

Paul ★

29 Bedford Street, WC2E 9ED (020 7836 3304). Covent Garden tube. **Open** 7.30am-9pm Mon-Fri; 9am-9pm Sat, Sun. **Main courses** £3.50-£7.25. **Credit** MC, V.

This flagship café combines Parisian style with a friendly and informal atmosphere. Admire rows of picture-perfect pastries, beautiful breads and savoury tarts in the shop window, or sit in the smart, wood-panelled café at the back and watch bakers at work through the glass-fronted kitchen. Carré soleil – an open puff pastry tart, crammed with juicy tomatoes, courgettes and warm emmental was memorable for its wafer thin layers of nut-brown pastry and perfectly balanced filling. And sink a pastry fork into their dreamy patisserie selection – the chocolate éclairs and raspberry tarts are divine.

Rules

35 Maiden Lane, WC2E 7LB (020 7836 5314/ www.rules.co.uk). Covent Garden tube. **Meals served** noon-11.30pm Mon-Sat; noon-10.30pm Sun. **Main courses** £15.95-£19.95. **Credit** AmEx, DC, MC, V.

Rules dines out on its claim to be London's oldest restaurant. It certainly looks the part – you may find yourself eating under the scrutiny of a stuffed stag's head or a lordly buffer in a gilt frame – and if you're at all rich or famous, you can expect several staff members to drop by your red velvet banquette and politely enquire if everything's OK. The chances are that you'll answer in the affirmative: the cooking at Rules is nothing if not dependably good. Try stilton and walnut tart with pear and apple chutney, or the smoked haddock fish cakes – among the best we've had. Puds are classic sponges, tarts and the like.

Savoy Grill ★

The Savoy, Strand, WC2R 0EU (020 7420 2065/ www.gordonramsay.com). Covent Garden tube. **Lunch served** noon-2.45pm Mon-Fri; noon-3pm Sat, Sun. **Dinner served** 5.45-11pm Mon-Sat; 6-10.30pm Sun. **Set meal** (lunch, 5.45-6.45pm Mon-Sat) £30 3 courses. **Set dinner** £50 3 courses, (7-11pm Mon-Sat) £60 tasting menu. **Credit** AmEx, MC, V.

Where the fat cats come to ensure they don't get any slimmer, the Savoy Grill is still favoured by the old guard despite Marcus Wareing's rejuvenescence of its menu. At lunch, the work of Savile Row tailors is amply displayed, while the futures of Harley Street cardiologists are steadily secured. The dining room has lost none of its subdued glamour over the years. The sense of occasion is heightened by staff who know how to make themselves available without being present at every mouthful. Highlights were a rich starter of rillette of Scottish salmon with avocado purée, frisée salad and chives, and a brace of delicious mains (steamed fillet of sea bass with parma ham tortellini; marinated leg of rabbit with herb gnocchi). A winner.

Also in the area

Bank Aldwych 1 Kingsway, WC2B 6XF (020 7379 9797); **Livebait** 21 Wellington Street, WC2E 7DN (020 7836 7161); **Loch Fyne** 2-4 Catherine Street, WC2B 5JZ (0207240 4999); **Patisserie Valerie** 8 Russell Street, WC2 5HZ (020 7240 0064); **Prezzo** 34 New Oxford Street, WC1A 1AP (020 7436 6641); **Strada** 6 Great Queen Street, WC2B 5DH (020 7405 6293); **Wagamama** 14A Irving Street, WC2H 7AB (020 7839 2323); **Wagamama** 1 Tavistock Street, WC2E 7PG (020 7836 3330); **Wagamama** 4A Streatham Street, WC1A 1JB (020 7323 9223).

Clerkenwell & the City

Arkansas Café ★

Unit 12, Old Spitalfields Market, E1 6AA (020 7377 6999). Liverpool Street tube/rail. **Lunch served** noon-2.30pm Mon-Fri; noon-4pm Sun. **Dinner served** by arrangement. **Main courses** £5-£14.50. **Credit** MC, V.

This wonderfully eccentric restaurant hovering on the edge of Spitalfields Market is justifiably popular. Its Arkansan owner, Bubba, presides over the barbecue pit, greeting the customers with a wave of his spatula while he cooks up huge piles of tender beef brisket, pork ribs, perfect duck and juicy chicken. Customers sit on a mishmash of church pews and garden chairs, and they're happy to do so once they've tasted smoky roasted beef marinated in a tangy sweet sauce, and excellent side orders of baked beans, coleslaw, purple cabbage and cold new potatoes in a tart vinegar dressing.

Aurora ★

Great Eastern Hotel, 40 Liverpool Street, EC2M 7QN (020 7618 7000/www.aurora.restaurant.co.uk). Liverpool Street tube/rail. **Lunch served** noon-2.30pm, **dinner served** 6.45-10pm Mon-Fri. **Main courses** £15.50-£29.50. **Set lunch** £28 3 courses. **Set meal** (tasting menu) £50 6 courses, £70 6 courses with wine. **Credit** AmEx, MC, V.

Like the hotel in which it's situated, the formal, gracious Aurora is a looker; witness the stained-glass dome in the middle of the room and the decadent bar to one side. But the food is easily good enough to divert attention back towards the plate. Roast sea scallops, served with deceptively light dots of black pudding and a creamy garlic sauce, were the perfect appetite-whetter for a beautiful milk-fed veal cutlet almost overshadowed by the gnocchi, girolles and Madeira velouté that ringed it. At lunch, the place is dominated by City types giving their expense accounts a workout; in the evening, the mix is pleasingly egalitarian for such a high-end place.

Bevis Marks

Bevis Marks, EC3A 5DQ (020 7283 2220/ www.bevismarkstherestaurant.com). Aldgate tube/Liverpool Street tube/rail. **Lunch served** noon-3pm Mon-Fri. **Dinner served** 5.30-7.15pm Mon-Thur. **Main courses** £9.50-£15.90. **Credit** AmEx, MC, V.

The restaurant shares a wall with Britain's oldest synagogue, built in 1701. From the airy lattice-covered dining room you can see the old chandeliers through the synagogue windows. The setting is matched by fine-quality cutlery and tablecloths, and pleasant, unobtrusive service. The menu, which changes every few months, is inventive – what might be termed modern British/kosher. There's a nod towards Jewish tradition with chicken soup and salt beef, but far better are dishes such as confit of duck with pomegranate and walnut sauce. Book ahead and arrive early so you can see around the synagogue first.

Club Gascon ★

57 West Smithfield, EC1A 9DS (020 7796 0600). Barbican tube/Farringdon tube/rail. **Lunch served** noon-2pm Mon-Fri. **Dinner served** 7-10pm Mon-Thur; 7-10.30pm Fri, Sat. **Tapas** £6-£16.50. **Set meal** £35 5 courses. **Credit** AmEx, MC, V.

Food at Club Gascon, from conception to presentation, is challengingly imaginative, and so is the environment, lots of incongruous shapes and materials assembled into clubby, natural warmth. The 'tapas'-based menu is a little bewildering, but staff are on hand to advise. A frothed olive emulsion *amuse-gueule* preceded deep-flavoured jugged mushrooms and ham, and a Gascon pie (duck mousse with a mushroom filling) that elicited an actual frisson of pleasure. Other courses were similarly awesome, and artfully accompanied by a succession of wines by the glass. A blowout, but one you won't forget.

Coach & Horses ★

26-28 Ray Street, EC1R 3DJ (020 7278 8990). Farringdon rail/tube. **Open** 11am-11pm Mon-Fri; 5-11pm Sat; noon-3pm Sun. **Lunch served** noon-3pm Mon-Fri, Sun. **Dinner served** 7-10pm Mon; 6-10pm Tue-Sat. **Credit** MC, V.

A stylish, sophisticated gastropub that has preserved its pub identity in traditional touches such as the etched glass and wood panelling. But the real highlight is its kitchen – this is the 2004 Time Out Best Gastropub award winner. Typical starters would be a perfectly cooked globe artichoke or a gorgeously simple combination of squid, chorizo, garlic and parsley. Mains include the likes of poached organic salmon with fennel, sorrel and cucumber, or beautifully tender rabbit with judion beans, piquillo peppers and oregano. The wine list is great (and well annotated), and the service is never less than charming.

Eagle

159 Farringdon Road, EC1R 3AL (020 7837 1353). Farringdon tube/rail/19, 38, 63, 341 bus. **Open** noon-11pm Mon-Sat; noon-5pm Sun. **Lunch served** 12.30-3pm Mon-Fri; 12.30-3.30pm Sat, Sun. **Dinner served** 6.30-10.30pm Mon-Sat. **Main courses** £5-£15. **Credit** MC, V.

The original gastropub – a tiny one room, stripped and stranded affair just along the road from the

Coach & Horses. *See p43.*

Guardian offices – is constantly packed, as much with drinkers as with diners. With not a great deal in the way of starters or desserts on the blackboard menu, this is still very much a pub that serves food rather than a restaurant with a bar. Dishes are prepared in an open kitchen that segues into the bar, and are hearty: steak and shredded cabbage, sausages and lentils. The beers are from Charles Wells. A modern classic, no longer blazing a trail but still a delight.

Flâneur Food Hall

41 Farringdon Road, EC1M 3JB (020 7404 4422). Farringdon tube/rail. **Open** 9am-10pm Mon-Sat; 9am-6pm Sun. **Brunch served** 9am-4pm Sat, Sun. **Lunch served** noon-3pm Mon-Fri. **Dinner served** 6-10pm Mon-Sat. **Main courses** £9-£13.90. **Credit** AmEx, DC, JCB, MC, V.

This food hall/restaurant charms immediately with its Wonderland atmosphere and enthusiast staff. It's a handsomely converted warehouse with an element of whimsy in its improbably tall shelves and shapely wooden tables interspersed haphazardly between cabinets of sensual cheeses and toothsome deli goods. Mod Med food might include delicate yoghurt and cucumber soup, scented as much as flavoured with garlic and mint; generous, intense feta risotto; and first class salmon on potato salad. Finish with dark chocolate tart with crystalised ginger.

Malmaison

18-21 Charterhouse Square, EC1M 6AH (020 7012 3700/www.malmaison.com). Barbican tube. **Lunch served** noon-2.30pm Mon-Sat. **Brunch served** 10.30-3pm Sun. **Dinner served** 6-10.30pm daily. **Main courses** £10.95-£25.95. **Set meal** £17.95 2 courses, £21.95 3 courses. **Credit** AmEx, DC, JCB, MC, V.

Glossy stone, tall vases of orchids in a row and a fireplace of pebbles set the tone at this ultra-modern hotel, hidden behind a Victorian façade. There's just one eaterie – the Brasserie. Prices are lower than the average London hotel restaurant. Starters are soups, fancy salads and tricky little tarts. Mains might be calf's liver and bacon on a neat circle of celeriac or monkfish with jerusalem artichoke purée and roast salsify. The hotel is part of a small country-wide chain.

Medcalf ★

40 Exmouth Market, EC1R 4QE (020 7833 3533). Angel tube/Farringdon tube/rail/38 bus. **Open** 10am-11pm Mon-Fri; 7-11pm Sat; noon-10.30pm Sun. **Food served** 10am-8.45pm Mon-Thur; 10am-7.45pm Fri; noon-5pm Sun. **Main courses** £8.50-£12. **Credit** MC, V.

This former butcher's shop pitches itself perfectly for the locale: by day it's a diner, offering breakfast and lunch to local workers; from mid-afternoon to mid-evening there's a bar menu; by night it's a drinking den, with DJs playing on Friday and Saturday nights. The wines are well chosen, the beer selection great (Erdinger weissbier on draught) and the staff charming, but it's the food that's the real winner. The short menu has first-class ingredients (mainly seasonal, often organic) treated simply so their quality shines through: oysters; an excellent warm salad of artichokes, asparagus and rocket; seared Rossmore scallops with broad bean and mint purée, bacon and roasted vine tomatoes. Throw in an engaging rough and ready look, and Medcalf appeals on all counts.

Moro ★

34-36 Exmouth Market, EC1R 4QE (020 7833 8336/www.moro.co.uk). Farringdon tube/rail/19, 38 bus. Bar **Open** 12.30-11.45pm Mon-Sat (last entry 10.30pm). *Restaurant* **Lunch served** 12.30-2.30pm Mon-Fri. **Dinner served** 7-10.30pm Mon-Sat. **Main courses** £13.50-£17.50. **Credit** AmEx, DC, MC, V.

With praise from all sides, a top-selling cookbook and near-permanently busy tables, Moro has set the style for restaurants offering a fresh, imaginative, English take on Mediterranean food traditions – in this case, from Spain and North Africa. Moro's wood-fired oven and charcoal grill are made much use of: wood-roasted pork with potato, pepper and onion salad, and char-grilled lamb with leeks, yoghurt and mint. To finish, try fabulous Malaga wine and raisin ice-cream. Tapa-sized dishes are available too, at the bar. Service is as bright as the food.

The Place Below ★

St Mary-le-Bow, Cheapside, EC2V 6AU (020 7329 0789/www.theplacebelow.co.uk). St Paul's tube/Bank tube/DLR. **Breakfast served** 7.30-11am, **lunch served** 11.30am-2.30pm, **snacks served** 2.30-3.30pm Mon-Fri. **Main courses** £5.50-£7.50. **Unlicensed. Credit** MC, V.

An oasis of calm in the City, this is an ideal spot for breakfast before facing the office. Browse the morning papers with toasted oat porridge with maple syrup and cream, fruit salads or muesli; good, strong Illy coffee is a bargain 80p. If you visit at non-peak dining times, you may even have the atmospheric crypt dining room, with its impressive domed ceiling, columns and cosy alcoves, to yourself – and get £2 off main courses to boot. Soups with own-made bread are satisfying, sometimes sublime (fennel, green pea and mint deserves special mention). Other freshly made dishes include pasta with walnut pesto, roast butternut squash and parmesan shavings, leafy salads and filled ciabatta rolls. Leave space for the Valrhona chocolate brownies and fluffy muffins.

Quality Chop House

92-94 Farringdon Road, EC1R 3EA (020 7837 5093). Farringdon tube/rail. **Lunch served** noon-3pm Mon-Fri; noon-4pm Sun. **Dinner served** 6-11.30pm Mon-Sat; 7-11.30pm Sun. **Main courses** £6.95-£16.25. **Credit** AmEx, MC, V.

As its name suggests, the QCH is an updated, upgraded version of the working man's canteen. The cloth cap aesthetic remains in such details as the black and white flooring, glass panels and the wooden booths of the twin dining rooms, but the proliferation of suits at lunch leaves no doubt as to the more ambitious remit of the kitchen. An enormous salmon fish cake with spinach and sorrel sauce was a suitably impressive main; also delicious was four lamb chops with chips and grilled tomatoes. What's more, the friendly, competent waiters take the restaurant's watchwords of quality and civility (printed at the top of the menu) very seriously indeed.

St John ★

26 St John Street, EC1M 4AY (020 7251 0848/4998/www.stjohnrestaurant.com). Farringdon tube/rail. Bar **Open/food served** 11am-11pm Mon-Fri; 6-11pm Sat. **Main courses** £3-£15. *Restaurant* **Lunch served** noon-3pm Mon-Fri. **Dinner served** 6-11pm Mon-Sat. **Main courses** £13-£19. **Credit** AmEx, DC, JCB, MC, V.

Its whitewashed walls, steel kitchen counters and austere character have won St John many plaudits. A similarly praised, pared-down, daily-changing menu lists back-to-basics British cuisine such as pan-fried bacon chop with sweet prune chutney or purple sprouting broccoli salad (a starter). Puddings – a wedge of treacle tart with a lemon-and-syrup-drenched breadcrumb filling – are fabulous. The own-made bread is a must-try, too. There's an interesting wine list, available in both restaurant and bar (where filling snacks are also served). St John Bread & Wine (94-96 Commercial Street, E1 6LZ, 7247 8724) is a more casual version of the original, open throughout the day, and handy for Spitalfields and Brick Lane.

Story Deli ★

3 Dray Walk, The Old Truman Brewery, 91 Brick Lane, E1 6QL (020 7247 3137). Liverpool Street tube/rail. **Open** 8am-7pm daily. **Main courses** £2-£7.50. **Unlicensed. Credit** AmEx, MC, V.

Story Deli is an offshoot of the nearby Story fashion and interiors boutique, and it's already attracting fashionistas and celebrities. It has an arty industrial warehouse look – all exposed piping and bare brick walls. Diners are seated on heavy-duty industrial containers, and food is served in cardboard boxes and greaseproof paper. The menu lists breakfast dishes, pastas, casseroles, roasts and vibrant-coloured salads, plus cakes: juicy pear and almond with frangipane; dense, truffley chocolate underscored with orange zest. Although the cakes are fabulous, it's the pizza – made, like everything else, with organic ingredients – that's the lead character. The best we've tasted this side of Naples.

Smiths of Smithfield

67-77 Charterhouse Street, EC1M 6HJ (020 7251 7950/www.smithsofsmithfield.co.uk). Farringdon tube/rail. Café (ground floor) **Meals served** 7am-5pm Mon-Fri; 10am-5pm Sat; 9am-5pm Sun. *Bar (ground floor)* **Open** 11am-11pm Mon-Wed; 11am-12.30am Thur-Sat; noon-10.30pm Sun. **Main courses** £4-£8. *Cocktail bar* **Open** 5.30pm-midnight Mon-Thur; 5.30pm-1am Fri, Sat. **Snacks served** 5.30-11pm Mon-Sat. *Dining Room* **Lunch served** noon-2.45pm Mon-Fri. **Dinner served** 6-11pm Mon-Sat. **Main courses** £10.50-£11.50. *Top Floor* **Lunch served** noon-3pm Mon-Fri. **Brunch served** 11.30am-4pm Sun. **Dinner served** 6.30-11pm daily. **Main courses** £13-£25. **Set lunch** (Sun) £25 3 courses. **Credit** AmEx, DC, MC, V.

Smiths retains an industrial, New York warehouse feel, with exposed bricks, reclaimed wood, metal tubing and raw concrete. Of the four floors, the ground floor is the most laid-back, serving breakfast, brunch and other casual fare to a steady stream of punters. The next level up is a cocktail and champagne bar, with plush red leather booths. The second-floor Dining Room overlooks the champagne bar, and serves comfort food with a twist (mozzarella, beetroot and marinated anchovy salad followed by scallops with black pudding, mash and mustard sauce, say). The Top Floor restaurant serves excellent British food in an atmosphere of restraint (soundproofed from the noise levels on the other floors) and with great views of the Smithfield skyline.

Les Trois Garçons

1 Club Row, E1 6JX (020 7613 1924/www.lestroisgarcons.com). Liverpool Street tube/rail/8, 388 bus. **Dinner served** 7-10pm Mon-Wed; 7-10.30pm Thur-Sat. **Main courses** £12.50-£22. **Set dinner** (Mon-Wed) £20 2 courses, £24 3 courses. **Credit** AmEx, DC, JCB, MC, V.

The decor here features a grinning stuffed crocodile wearing a crown, while a similarly defunct tiger sports a tiara; antique handbags hang by threads from the ceiling; jewelled drapes sparkle in the light of Murano chandeliers. Basically, it's a little piece of restaurant theatre, and the kitchen does its best to ensure that the show goes on. Among the starring roles are starters like sautéed tiger prawns with crushed herbs, and garlic- and coconut-spiked tomato sauce. Oven-roasted chicken wrapped in Bayonne ham is beautifully tender and comes with celeriac mash and a light Dijon mustard sauce. Prices are not low, but if you choose well from the excellent wine list you can probably get away with a two-figure bill. Loungelover, the restaurant's cocktail bar just around the corner (1 Whitby Street, E1 6JU, 020 7012 1234) also has to be seen to be believed.

Zetter

86-88 Clerkenwell Road, EC1M 5RJ (020 7324 4455/www.zetter.com). Farringdon tube/rail. **Breakfast served** 7-10.30am Mon-Fri; 7-11.30am Sat, Sun. **Lunch served** noon-2.30pm Mon-Fri; noon-3.30pm Sat, Sun. **Dinner served** 6-11pm Mon-Sat; 6-10.30pm Sun. **Main courses** £10.50-£17. **Credit** AmEx, DC, JCB, MC, V.

Within days of opening, the Zetter made it into *Condé Nast Traveller*'s list of the 50 coolest new hotels in Europe. Its restaurant, headed by ex-Moro chef Megan Jones, offers modern interpretations of Italian regional cooking. Panelle (chickpea flour fritters punctuated with aniseed); olives stuffed with veal and pork and fried in breadcrumbs; baked globe artichoke stuffed with ricotta and 'wild greens' served with superb fennel-flavoured lentils; (over-salty) Roman veal chop with parma ham and sage. The brasserie-style room has big windows and something of a buzz.

Also in the area

Cafe Lazeez 88 St John Street, EC1M 4EH (020 7253 2224); **Carluccio's Caffe** 12 West Smithfield, EC1A 9JR (020 7329 5904); **Gaucho Grill** 12 Gracechurch Street, EC3V 0BL (020 7626 5180); **Livebait** 1 Watling Street, EC4M 9BP (020 7213 0540); **Livebait** 1 Plough Place, EC4A 1DE (020 7842 0510); **Living Room** 2-3 West Smithfield, EC1A 9JX (0870 442 2541); **S&M Cafe** 48 Brushfield Street, E1 6AG (020 7247 2252); **Wagamama** 109 Fleet Street, EC4A 2AB (020 7583 7889); **Wagamama** 1A Ropemaker Street, EC2V OHR (020 7588 2688); **Wagamama** 4 Great St Thomas Apostle, Off Queen Street, EC4V 2BH (0207 248 5766); **Wagamama** 22 Broad Street, EC3N 1HQ (0207 256 9992); **Wagamama** Tower Place, off Lower Thames Street, EC3R 4EB (0207 283 5897).

Chelsea, Knightsbridge, South Kensington & Victoria

Bibendum

Michelin House, 81 Fulham Road, SW3 6RD (020 7581 5817/www.bibendum.co.uk). South Kensington tube. **Lunch served** noon-2.30pm Mon-Fri; 12.30-3pm Sat, Sun. **Dinner served** 7-11.30pm Mon-Sat; 7-10.30pm Sun. **Main courses** £19-£42. **Set lunch** (Mon-Fri) £28.50 3 courses. **Credit** AmEx, DC, MC, V.

The original figurehead of the good ship Conran remains one of the organisation's more attractive venues. The spectacular dining room, on the first floor of the Michelin building – above the Bibendum Oyster Bar (a great casual dining spot, 020 7589 1480) – has a real sense of occasion, dominated by the original 1930s rich blue Michelin Man stained-glass windows. Service, if not entirely seamless, is crisply efficient and welcoming. The food doesn't shy from the rich and robust: a warm quail salad included a powerful mix of figs, fried prosciutto and a Madeira ravioli (actually, more like a pastry). For something lighter, a lettuce hearts and summer vegetable salad featured excellent ingredients, even if they were served a bit too cold. For mains, monkfish came with a luxuriant lobster sauce and chives, and grilled rabbit with stuffed artichokes was another no-holds-barred combo, almost like a rabbit mixed grill. A dessert of vodka, watermelon and mint granita and the extravagant petits fours didn't disappoint. The wine list is immense, mainly French, and pricey.

Blue Elephant

4-6 Fulham Broadway, SW6 1AA (020 7385 6595/ www.blueelephant.com). Fulham Broadway tube. **Lunch served** noon-2.30pm Mon-Fri; noon-4pm Sun. **Dinner served** 7pm-midnight Mon-Thur; 6.30pm-midnight Fri, Sat; 7-10.30pm Sun. **Main courses** £10.60-£28. **Set meals** £33-£39 3-4 courses. **Set buffet** (lunch Sun) £22 adults, £11 children. **Credit** AmEx, DC, MC, V.

You don't go to Blue Elephant for an intimate meal: from being greeted by over-eager staff upon arrival, to being led to your table through the huge, crowded space, any hope of privacy is kept at bay. The interior, filled with abundant foliage and Thai ornaments, is full-on – and a little too slick. The Thai food, however, is truly delicious and surprisingly good value. A mixed platter of starters brought succulent chicken legs, plump, well-filled spring rolls, crisp, spicy sweet corncakes and stuffed baby corn wrapped in pastry – each with a different sauce. We followed this with the khantoke platter – which included a distinctively spiced mussaman curry, beautifully flavoured aubergine and okra in chilli paste and beef stir-fried with basil. Some dishes are too mouth-scorchingly hot – but there's clearly a great deal of skill in the kitchen, the presentation is pretty, and the vegetarian menu is remarkable.

Blue Kangaroo

555 King's Road, SW6 2EB (020 7371 7622/www.thebluekangaroo.co.uk). Bus 11, 19, 22. **Meals served** 9.30am-7pm Mon-Fri; 9.30am-8.30pm Sat, Sun. **Main courses** £8-£16. **Credit** AmEx, MC, V.

It may be the most sprogcentric restaurant in London, but a family meal at the Blue Kangaroo is far from the ketchup-smeared purgatory parents might fear. For a start, food is uniformly good, prepared with enormous care and with diligently sourced ingredients. Children, if they want nuggets, get own-made, free-range ones, the salmon fish cakes are made with the wild variety and the sausages are organic. Grown-ups should try those fish cakes in a larger size, or the excellent butternut risotto, creamy wild mushroom tagliatelle or grilled chicken in ciabatta. Puddings are comforting – pecan nut pie, treacle sponge, tarte tatin. The wine list has also been assembled with some care and includes a number of affordable bottles. The restaurant sits above a whole basement of play apparatus, which diners pay about £3 to set the kids loose in. The play area can be monitored via plasma screen or the obliging staff, who are saintly.

Chutney Mary

535 King's Road, SW10 0SZ (020 7351 3113/ www.realindianfood.com). Fulham Broadway tube/ 11, 22 bus. **Lunch served** 12.30-2.30pm Sat; 12.30-3pm Sun. **Dinner served** 6.30-11pm Mon-Sat; 6.30-10.30pm Sun. **Main courses** £12.50-£24. **Set lunch** £16.50 3 courses. **Credit** AmEx, DC, JCB, MC, V.

Service can be overbearing at this iconic Chelsea favourite, complete with two contrasting dining spaces: a bright, verdant conservatory out back, and a dark cavern of an interior, entirely lit with flickering candles. Meals have always been deliciously memorable but our latest was a little disappointing. Prawns sautéed with asparagus, and asparagus stir-fried with freshly grated coconut, curry leaves and mustard seeds didn't quite hit the spot. However, a dish of three types of elaborately prepared vegetable patties was imaginatively executed and beautifully spiced. We had mixed feelings, about a platter of vegetable and lentil dishes and the bread basket – with some (such as the delicately spiced black dahl) working much better than others (cheddar-stuffed parathas). Don't miss the exquisite almond halva tarte for afters.

Drones

1 Pont Street, SW1X 9EJ (020 7235 9555/ www.whitestarline.org.uk). Knightsbridge or Sloane Square tube. **Lunch served** noon-2.30pm Mon-Fri; noon-3.30pm Sun. **Dinner served** 6-11pm Mon-Sat. **Main courses** £9.50-£22. **Set lunch** (Mon-Fri) £14.95 2 courses,£17.95 3 courses; (Sun) £19.50 3 courses. **Credit** AmEx, DC, MC, V.

To savour the full retro glamour of this Marco Pierre White venture, go in the evening, when the 1930s club-style decor comes off better. The walls are covered with photographs of showbiz legends, lighting is low and the place buzzes. During the day, grandes dames meeting their grandchildren, local ladies who lunch and suits seem to make up the clientele. The menu matches the timeless concept, with brasserie classics divided into hors d'oeuvres, salads, pastas, fish, roasts and grills, and so on. Potted shrimps or dressed crab served with melba toast, Dover sole, or grilled calf's liver with bacon and fried onions keep company with Mediterranean interlopers like gazpacho or grilled tuna with aubergines, tomato and basil, and there's a Drones burger with club sauce for the truly conservative. Prices on the mostly French wine list are steep, but a good range is offered by the glass.

Hunan ★

51 Pimlico Road, SW1W 8NE (020 7730 5712). Sloane Square tube. **Lunch served** 12.30-2.30pm, **dinner served** 6-11pm Mon-Sat. **Main courses** £8.50-£10.50. **Set meals** £31.80-£300 per person (minimum 2). **Credit** AmEx, DC, MC, V.

This is a serious Chinese, and when we booked we gave notice that we wanted the chef's recommended meal. There were 16 courses in all, not counting the 'picking dishes' up front nor the elegant red-bean pancake dessert. Many of the dishes certainly were hot-ish but none of them fiercely so. The soup was excellent, clear with minced pork and ginger and served in a bamboo tube. Chicken was minced with green chillies to be eaten wrapped in lettuce leaf and also smoked in a hot sweet sauce. The waiter said a third dish was chicken legs, but it had such small bones and was so tender that it was clearly 'field chicken' (tin gai) – Chinese for frog. There were cuttlefish balls that exploded with flavour, prawns with salt and chillies, black-cooked pork belly with preserved vegetable, spinach balls in sesame seed coating, beancurd in a star anise sauce, and more. No dish was less than good and most were excellent. Not cheap, but worth it.

Lots Road Pub & Dining Room

114 Lots Road, SW10 0RJ (020 7352 6645). Bus 11, 19, 22. **Open** 11am-11pm Mon-Sat; 11am-10.30pm Sun. **Lunch served** noon-3pm Mon-Fri. **Dinner served** 5.30-10pm Mon-Thur; 5.30-10.30pm Fri. **Meals served** noon-10.30pm Sat; noon-10pm Sun. **Main courses** £8-£13. **Credit** MC, V.

A sunny, chrome-fitted bar, beautifully finished oak floors, colourful abstract paintings and good quality food at reasonable prices add up to chic and cheerful atmosphere at this gastropub. Starters range from an avocado, halloumi, Parma ham and pear salad to a crab and broad bean omelette. While mains cover standard house burgers or sausage and mash, lamb rump with bok choy red onion and rice salad was adventurous and quality roast sirloin with seasonal veg maintain a heartily Anglo Saxon presence. Desserts are halfway twixt boarding school cuisine (bread and butter pudding) and the USA (key lime pie). Well-kept real ales and a decent wine list with a commendable range of choice by the glass are arguably this eaterie's finest feature.

Mr Chow ★

151 Knightsbridge, SW1X 7PA (020 7589 7347). Knightsbridge tube. **Lunch served** 12.30-3pm, **dinner served** 7pm-midnight daily. **Main courses** £12.50-£34. **Set lunch** £17 2 courses, £21 3 courses. **Credit** AmEx, DC, JCB, MC, V.

Fabulously expensive and glamorous in a slightly lived-in way, Mr Chow has changed little over the years. There are smoked mirrors, silver walnut-whip lampshades and good linen; a short, sexy menu and a fashionable clientele. You don't really expect such a chic restaurant to know its stuff when it comes to Chinese food, but Mr Chow does. Yes, they have sweet-and-sour pork and use more red food dye than necessary, but they also serve up some brilliantly authentic Chinese dishes. The Mr Chow noodles were a delicious rendition of a classic northern snack that is rarely found in London: lovely, springy hand-pulled pasta served with minced pork in a sweet, beany sauce. Drunken fish (slippy pieces of sole in a sweet, fragrant sauce) was superb, and the red-cooked pork knuckle sublimely tender if excessively red. The highlight of an evening here is the live noodle-making demo: a chef teasing dough into spaghetti-thin pasta in a series of crazy looping movements. Service is slick and European in style.

Nahm ★

Halkin Hotel, Halkin Street, SW1X 7DJ (020 7333 1234/www.halkin.como.biz). Hyde Park Corner tube. **Lunch served** noon-2.30pm Mon-Fri. **Dinner served** 7-11pm Mon-Sat; 7-10pm Sun. **Main courses** £19.50-£21.50. **Set lunch** £18-£26 2-4 courses. **Set dinner** £47 4 courses. **Credit** AmEx, DC, JCB, MC, V.

The old cliché 'never judge a book by its cover' is nowhere more appropriate than at this gem of a Thai restaurant inside the Halkin hotel. For despite a dull, slightly odd interior featuring muted gold surfaces and net curtains, the award-spangled David Thompson's interpretation of 'royal Thai' cuisine of ancient Bangkok is some of the best you'll find in the UK. Nahm's £47 set menu – an extraordinarily generous banquet – showcases old, forgotten Thai recipes given a modern twist with Michelin-pleasing ingredients such as white asparagus and foie gras. Dishes such as rabbit and coconut salad with lemon grass and chilli jam, red curry of 'middle white' pork, and mixed Thai vegetable salad with tamarind and palm sugar are cooked with an astonishing skill and understanding; the depth of the sweet, sour, hot and salty flavours revealing itself in degrees. Nahm is not just a great restaurant, it's a phenomenon.

Olé

Broadway Chambers, Fulham Broadway, SW6 1EP (020 7610 2010/www.olerestaurants.com). Fulham Broadway tube. Tapas bar **Open** noon-3pm, 5-11pm Mon-Sat. **Tapas** £1.55-£6. *Restaurant* **Meals served** noon-10.30pm daily. **Main courses** £6.50-£10.50. **Credit** AmEx, DC, JCB, MC, V.

The shout of 'Olé!' is all about flamboyance and skill, which makes you wonder why it was chosen as the moniker for this understated restaurant. A narrow bar brightened with mirrors leads to a small dining area with bare white walls and polished light wood furniture. The place looks cold and unfinished rather than stylishly minimalist, but fortunately the menu is more imaginative, combining simple dishes (calamares, octopus, cold meats, cheeses) with more creative ones (shredded confit of duck with Serrano ham rolls, beef with date and sun-dried tomato sauce). A moist tortilla with smoky chorizo was faultless. Juicy grilled langoustines and tender discs of pork fillet with mustard were others highlights, although the artistically arranged salad and vegetable accompaniments were oily even by Spanish standards. Two traditional staples were disappointing: patatas bravas were pale and powdery and albondigas (meatballs) were dry.

Tom Aikens. *See p50.*

Painted Heron ★

112 Cheyne Walk, SW10 0TJ (7351 5232/www.thepaintedheron.com). Bus 11, 19, 22, 319. **Lunch served** noon-2.30pm Mon-Fri. **Dinner served** 6-11pm Mon-Sat. **Main courses** £10-£12. **Set thali** £12 3 courses. **Credit** AmEx, JCB, MC, V.

You get a feeling of space at this light and airy, cream-painted, multi-roomed Indian restaurant on the edge of the Thames. Risks are taken – for example, starters of calf's liver in tandoori marinade with mango, and crab with red onion and chilli in dosa pancake; mains of wild boar jungle curry and smoked chicken in crushed pepper cashew nut sauce. This adventurous approach comes off brilliantly. Hung yoghurt and aubergine cake with red onions was loosely packed together, crispy on the outside and bursting with flavour, while tiger prawns in onion and tomato chutney sauce, served with (chopped) asparagus curry was impossible to fault. Unlikely ingredients and methods are combined with a skill that makes you wonder why everyone's not doing it.

Racine ★

239 Brompton Road, SW3 2EP (020 7584 4477). Knightsbridge or South Kensington tube/14, 74 bus. **Lunch served** noon-3pm Mon-Fri; noon-3.30pm Sat, Sun. **Dinner served** 6-10.30pm Mon-Sat; 6-10pm Sun. **Main courses** £9.50-£18.75. **Set meal** (lunch, 6-7.30pm) £15.50 2 courses, £17.50 3 courses. **Credit** AmEx, JCB, MC, V.

The essence of a Parisian brasserie transported to London. Winner of *Time Out*'s Best New Restaurant award in 2003, it continues to garner rave reviews and plays to a packed house. Draw aside the theatrical heavy drape that shields the door and step into a room lined with mirrors and deep green banquettes. Service negotiates the mêlée with impersonal efficiency. The French bourgeois food has rustic leanings, which show up in simple starters like tomatoes baked with basil and crème fraîche on toasted brioche, but the classics play a leading role. There are salty slices of Bayonne ham offset by creamy celeriac rémoulade, baked asparagus, langoustines sliced in half and grilled with lashings of garlic, butter and parsley, cod with a spicey crab butter sauce, and, of course, steak and excellent frites. Finish with a perfect petit pot au chocolat.

Tom Aikens ★

43 Elystan Street, SW3 3NT (020 7584 2003/ www.tomaikens.co.uk). South Kensington tube. **Lunch served** noon-2.30pm, **dinner served** 7-11pm Mon-Fri. **Set lunch** £29 3 courses incl coffee. **Set meal** £55 3 courses incl coffee, £70 6 courses incl coffee. **Credit** AmEx, JCB, MC, V.

This is one sleek restaurant. That's not to say it's intimidating (staff are well-drilled, formal but friendly) or overly fashionable (the decor is modern but classic). Everything is choreographed beautifully: from the arrival of the champagne trolley to the array of petits fours and madelines at the end, it's a smoothly oiled machine that paces the meal perfectly. From the excellently priced lunch menu, came a divine pea mousse with peas, pea shoots and Parma ham, and borlotti bean soup, a light foaming broth topped with summer truffle and concealing foie gras mousse and beans. Mains couldn't quite hit these transcendental heights, but roast brill with artichokes, artichoke purée and mushroom duxelle, and duck confit with roast duck breast, sliced turnips, lentil purée and fried duck egg came close.To finish, roast apple, with apple sorbet, apple beignet and wafer-thin apple slices was essence of apple in many forms. The £55 buys even more exalted haute cuisine, but given the generosity and skill of the set lunch, why upgrade?

Zuma

5 Raphael Street, SW7 1DL (020 7584 1010/ www.zumarestaurant.com). Knightsbridge tube. **Open** 5.30-11.30pm Mon-Sat; noon-2.30pm Sun. **Lunch served** noon-2pm Mon-Sat; noon-2.30pm Sun. **Dinner served** 6-11pm Mon-Sat. **Main courses** £3.50-£28.50. **Set lunch** £8.50-£14.80. **Credit** AmEx, DC, MC, V.

Has Zuma taken over from Nobu as the capital's most glamorous dining spot? Possibly, if the wait (several weeks) for a reservation is anything to go by. Not to mention the strictly enforced two-hour table-turning system. On our most recent visit, the shoals of beautiful young fashion folk who had graced the immaculately designed restaurant when it opened had been usurped by groups of businessmen. Still, the food remains compellingly good, helped by service that is well-informed and friendly (up until the two-hour deadline). Ingredients, as in our skewered scallops with green pepper and black bean sauce, are impeccable. Equally impressive were miso-marinated lamb chops, which had a powerful Sichuan pepper kick. Only one dish, a rather dry roast-duck nori roll, disappointed. To drink, Zuma has some great saké-based cocktails on its list, as well as the country's first saké sommelier.

Also in the area

Café Lazeez 93-95 Old Brompton Road, SW7 3LD (020 7581 9993); **Carluccio's Caffe** 236 Fulham Road, SW10 9NB (020 7376 5960); **Gaucho Grill** 89 Sloane Avenue, SW3 3DX (020 7584 9901); **Giraffe** 7 Kensington High Street, W8 5NP (020 7938 1221); **Loch Fyne** 676 Fulham Road, SW6 5SA (020 7610 8020); **Maroush II** 38 Beauchamp Place, SW3 1NU (020 7581 5434); **Patisserie Valerie** 27 Kensington Church Street, W8 4LL (020 7937 9574); **Patisserie Valerie** Duke of York, Sloane Square, SW3 4LY (020 7730 7094); **Patisserie Valerie** 215 Brompton Road, SW3 2EJ (020 7823 9971); **Patisserie Valerie** 17 Mortcomb Street, SW1X 8LB (020 7245 6161); **Prezzo** 35A Kensington High Street, W8 5BA (020 7937 2800); **Strada** 175 New Kings Road, SW6 4SW (020 7731 6404); **Strada** 237 Earl's Court Road, SW5 9AH (020 7835 1180); **Wagamama** 26 Kensington High Street, W8 4PF (020 7376 1717); **Wagamama** Lower Ground Floor, Harvey Nichols, 109-124 Knightsbridge, SW1X 7RJ (020 7201 8000).

Waterloo & South Bank

Anchor & Hope ★

36 The Cut, SE1 8LP (020 7928 9898). Southwark tube/Waterloo tube/rail. **Open** 5-11pm Mon; 11am-11pm Tue-Sat. **Food served** 6-10.30pm Mon; noon-2.30pm, 6-10.30pm Tue-Sat. **Credit** MC, V.

One of London's best gastropubs. The menu can stretch to such unusual combos as snail, preserved rabbit and watercress salad (delicious, by the way). The space itself is a low-key arrangement of relaxed bar area and slightly more formal dining room, elegantly partitioned by a curtain. Expect delicate starters like greens and mozzarella on toast or heartier mains such as a perfectly pink lamb neck, with green tomatoes, courgette and romerico sauce. Excellent stews and racks of meat for two or three people to share are also offered. But note – you can't book a table, and the noise levels are high.

Baltic ★

74 Blackfriars Road, SE1 8HA (020 7928 1111/ www.balticrestaurant.co.uk). Southwark tube. Bar **Open/snacks served** noon-11pm daily. *Restaurant* **Lunch served** noon-3pm Mon-Fri. **Dinner served** 6-11.15pm Mon-Sat. **Meals served** noon-10.30pm Sun. **Main courses** £9.50-£14. **Credit** AmEx, MC, V.

Baltic's spacious interior, complete with 'wall of amber' bar and amber sculptures, makes a great setting for the modern, varied menu and beautiful, efficient waiting staff. The food is a rare thing for an Eastern European restaurant: adventurous as well as authentic. There are touches of Latvian, Lithuanian, Georgian and Armenian food here, as well as Russian and Polish staples. The mixed blini plate is great: aubergine caviar, keta caviar, smoked salmon and trout, herrings, all served with fresh toppings (sour cream, onion, eggs). Roast cod served with a kasza (buckwheat) risotto was superb. The wine list is good, the cocktails even better.

Blueprint Café

Design Museum, 28 Shad Thames, SE1 2YD (020 7378 7031/www.conran.com). Tower Hill tube/Tower Gateway DLR/47, 78 bus. **Lunch served** noon-3pm daily. **Dinner served** 6-11pm Mon-Sat. **Main courses** £12.50-£22. **Credit** AmEx, DC, MC, V.

On the first floor of the Design Museum, with huge windows looking out over the river towards Tower Bridge, the Blueprint has location in spades. Given such a setting, the kitchen can't quite compete – although it does pretty well, the food as refreshingly unfussy as the descriptions on the plain-speaking menu. Asparagus, poached egg and parmesan might precede roast Middlewhite pork or tender roast loin of rabbit. Acoustics are challenging – a further reason to try to bag one of the balcony tables.

Delfina

50 Bermondsey Street, SE1 3UD (020 7357 0244/ www.delfina.org.uk). London Bridge tube/rail. **Lunch served** noon-3pm Mon-Fri. **Dinner served** 7-10pm Fri. **Main courses** £9.95-£12.95. **Credit** AmEx, MC, V.

Opened ten years ago, part gallery, part eaterie, Delfina manages both roles with aplomb. Tables are well spaced, decor is a soothing palette of white, pale green and navy, and the atmosphere is informal. An innovative monthly-changing menu might feature a huge, tender scallop in pancetta with a rich white bean aïoli, followed by well-cooked barramundi on a zingy bed of pomelo, peanut and beanshoot salad, and on to chocolate tart topped with poached pear.

Fina Estampa

150 Tooley Street, SE1 2TU (020 7403 1342). London Bridge tube/rail. Bar **Open** noon-10pm Mon-Fri; 6-10pm Sat. *Restaurant* **Meals served** noon-10.30pm Mon-Fri; 6-10.30pm Sat. **Main courses** £7.95-£14.95. **Credit** AmEx, DC, MC, V.

An oasis of Peruvian charm. The large bar area looks out to Tower Bridge, where you can enjoy a pre-dinner Pisco Sour (the national drink of Peru) on one of the inviting leather sofas. The restaurant at the back is small and intimate, with floor-length white tablecloths and Peruvian artefacts on the walls. Cebiche (white fish marinated in lemon, onions and coriander) and papa à la huancaina (potatoes with a fromage frais sauce) are typical starters. Next, there's seco of chicken with a light coriander sauce and deliciously thick stewed beans, and lomo saltado (strips of glazed beef stir-fried with chunky chips, red onions and tomatoes). There's a small but well-chosen list of Latin American wines.

fish!

Cathedral Street, SE1 9AL (020 7407 3803/ www.fishdiner.co.uk). London Bridge tube/rail. **Meals served** 11.30am-11pm Mon-Fri; noon-11pm Sat; noon-10.30pm Sun. **Main courses** £8.95-£17.95. **Credit** AmEx, MC, V.

A handsome, light-filled room, close to the action in Borough Market. The menu is pretty simple – the fish available each day is highlighted; you order it grilled or steamed, with either a salsa, herb and garlic butter or hollandaise sauce. Or there might be filling and lemony salmon fish cakes with spinach. Cod, fish and mushy peas are highly recommended. Puds are the likes of ice-cream and apple crumble.

The Hartley ★

64 Tower Bridge Road, SE1 4TR (020 7394 7023/ www.thehartley.com). Borough tube/London Bridge tube/rail. **Open** noon-11pm Mon-Sat; noon-10.30pm

The Hartley. See p51.

Sun. **Lunch served** noon-3pm Mon-Fri. **Brunch served** noon-5pm Sat; noon-6pm Sun. **Dinner served** 6-10pm Mon-Sat. **Main courses** £7.50-£11.50. **Set lunch** (Mon-Fri) £5 1 course. **Credit** AmEx, MC, V.

This gastropub is easy on the eye (claret-coloured walls, exposed brick, floorboards, fun black and white prints dotted around) but, more importantly, it has an inventive menu. A specials board touts interesting combinations (pork belly with frogs' legs, chorizo, parsley and garlic), while the menu proper offers half a dozen choices in each course. Organic meat from Ginger Pig shines through in dishes like terrine of foie gras, chicken and ham knuckle or main-course roast suckling pig with new season garlic. Wines are good and affordable. As for the staff, they are polite, knowledgeable and justifiably proud of their product.

Livebait

41-45 The Cut, SE1 8LF (020 7928 7211). Southwark tube/Waterloo tube/rail. **Meals served** noon-11pm Mon-Sat; 12.30-9pm Sun. **Main courses** £9.75-£29. **Set meals** (2.30-7pm) £14.50 2 courses, £18.50 3 courses. **Credit** AmEx, DC, JCB, MC, V.

Livebait is great for a pre- or post-theatre meal, particularly at this branch with its easy proximity to the Old and New Vic. Diners get a clean, functional interior (classic fishmonger tiling), simple unfussy menu (shellfish is a big hit here) and friendly efficient staff. Added to this, the food is often pretty good: tender squid in lovely succulent batter, for example, or generous fish cake. Note that it can get quite noisy and smoky here, somehow made more so by the tiled walls and bright white lighting.

Tas ★

33 The Cut, SE1 8LF (020 7928 2111/www.tasrestaurant.com). Southwark tube. **Meals served** noon-11.30pm Mon-Sat; noon-10.30pm Sun. **Main courses** £5.25-£8.95. **Set meal** £7.45 2 courses, £17.50 11 dishes incl coffee. **Credit** AmEx, MC, V.

Something of an SE1 mini-chain (there's also one in Farringdon), each serving excellent, keenly priced Turkish food in light, airy and accommodating spaces. A fourth SE1 branch – combining a deli, restaurant and wine bar – was scheduled to open in the arches behind Southwark station in September 2004. So far expansion hasn't harmed the cooking at this big flagship operation: bread is terrific – fresh, fragrant and filling, but go easy or you won't be able to enjoy classic starters of borek (feta and spinach in filo pastry), calamares, houmous, halloumi and garlic sausages. Mains cover grills (kofte, iskender and the rest), fish (baked swordfish) and casseroles (diced lamb, tomatoes, onions, mushrooms and peppers cooked with herbs) with rice and salad on the side. Enjoyable food at very reasonable prices.

Also in the area

De Gustibus 4 Southwark Street, SE1 1TQ (020 7407 3625); **Tas Pide** 20-22 New Globe Walk, SE1 9DR (020 7633 9777); **Tas** 72 Borough High Street, SE1 O2E (020 7403 7200).

Bayswater & Notting Hill

Boozers

Cock Tavern
27 Great Portland Street, W1W 8QE (020 7631 5002).
Tadcaster brewery Samuel Smith owns this magnificent gin tavern.

Duke's Head
8 Lower Richmond Road, SW15 1JN (020 8788 2552).
Perched on the river, this two-bar Young's pub is a suntrap in summer and a cosy comfort when it's cold.

Holly Bush
22 Holly Mount, NW3 6SG (020 7435 2892).
Off Hampstead's main drag, this cosy multi-roomed pub is a dimly lit den of isolated perfection.

Lamb
94 Lamb's Conduit Street, WC1N 3LZ (020 7405 0713).
An outstanding Grade II-listed pub serving Young's bitters to a comfortable crowd.

Market Porter
9 Stoney Street, SE1 9AA (020 7407 2495).
There's excellent beer in this market pub that opens at 6am for the local workers.

Seven Stars
53-54 Carey Street, WC2A 2JB (020 7242 8521).
Time Out's 'Best Pub 2003', this modest boozer is a charm-filled winner with excellent beer and an excellent cat.

Warrington Hotel
93 Warrington Crescent, W9 1EH (020 7286 2929).
This ornate Little Venice pub serves both Young's and Fuller's ale.

Wenlock Arms
26 Wenlock Road, N1 7TA (020 7608 3406).
A superb selection of cask ales from all over the country served from an old-fashioned wooden bar.

Al Waha

75 Westbourne Grove, W2 4UL (020 7229 0806/ www.waha-uk.com). Bayswater or Queensway tube.
Meals served noon-midnight daily. **Main courses** £9-£18. **Set lunch** £12.50 5 courses. **Set dinner** £21-£25 3 courses incl coffee. **Credit** MC, V.

Ranged over two levels, painted a mellow yellow and furnished with plenty of greenery, Al Waha gives the impression of spaciousness in quite a small area. Staff are serene but efficient, the atmosphere subdued but relaxed. This is Lebanese dining at its best: quality meze and meat dishes, white tablecloths, a huge bowl of salad vegetables to dip, but none of the frosty formality of some London Lebanese restaurants. The meze list is a long affair: highlights included delicately fragrant foul moukala (broad beans cooked in lemon and oil, served with coriander); down-home bamia bil zeit (literally, okra with oil, actually served in a tomato sauce); manakeish jibneh (warmed cheese on pitta bread, spread with a dusting of mellow dried herbs); fatayer (soft pastry filled with cheesy spinach); or creamy baba ganoush. Shish taouk was tender chicken cooked to a T, and plenty for two. A light Lebanese Kefraya rosé was a perfect accompaniment.

Clarke's

124 Kensington Church Street, W8 4BH (020 7221 9225/www.sallyclarke.com). Notting Hill Gate tube.
Brunch served 11am-2pm Sat. **Lunch served** 12.30-2pm Mon-Fri. **Dinner served** 7-10pm Tue-Sat. **Main courses** (lunch) £14-£16. **Set dinner** £32-£36 2 courses; £48 4 courses incl coffee, truffles and service. **Credit** AmEx, DC, JCB, MC, V.

Sally Clarke's delightful dining room celebrates its 20th anniversary in 2004. When she first started serving Californian-inspired dishes with an emphasis on simple, freshly sourced ingredients served with the minimum of fuss, her style was unique in London. Since then, it has been honed, developed and emulated by countless others. Thankfully, Clarke and her team have remained consistent and the many regulars would attest to her success. The furnishings are plain and the menu is famously limited to a dozen or so dishes at lunch and a set no-choice menu at dinner. Welsh lamb char-grilled with mushrooms and a glossy red wine and rosemary glaze is a typical dish. A salad of buffalo mozzarella with spiced aubergine, roast red peppers, black olives and pine nuts is made with cheese flown over from Naples. To finish, there might be some soft vanilla meringue served with pineapple ice-cream and passion fruit sauce . A lot of care has gone into the wine list, with 200 bottles from lesser-known Californian, French and Italian producers.

Cow

89 Westbourne Park Road, W2 5QH (020 7221 0021). Royal Oak or Westbourne Park tube. Bar **Open** noon-11pm Mon-Sat; noon-10.30pm Sun. **Food served** noon-4pm, 6-11pm Mon-Sat; noon-4pm, 6-10pm Sun. **Lunch served** noon-3.30pm daily. **Dinner served** 6-10.30pm Mon-Sat; 6-10pm Sun. **Main courses** £8-£13. *Dining room* **Lunch served** 12.30-3.30pm Sun. **Dinner served** 6-11pm Mon-Sat; 6-10.30pm Sun. **Main courses** £13-£18. **Credit** MC, V.

It's as though the clocks have been set back to the 1950s upstairs at the lace-curtained Cow Dining Rooms. This is a classy reinvention of the old fashioned standards of British cuisine. Building on the fishy list available in the pub, the first-floor menu opens up with a fusillade of oysters, then it's into starters such as new season's garlic soup. Orecchiette pasta with broad beans, peas and artichokes sounded plain but proved divine, and among the mains proper, skate wing was a soft, fresh sensual delight, while a tiny, whole roast chicken with sauté potatoes, tender broad beans and a fine jus was gorgeous. Excellent ales are available from the bar below; the wine list is a model of taste and fiscal discretion.

E&O

14 Blenheim Crescent, W11 1NN (020 7229 5454/ www.eando.nu). Ladbroke Grove or Notting Hill Gate tube. Bar **Open** noon-11pm Mon-Sat; noon-10.30pm Sun. **Dim sum** £3-£6.50. *Restaurant* **Lunch served** noon-3pm Mon-Sat; 1-3pm Sun. **Dinner served** 6-10.30pm Mon-Sat; 6-10pm Sun. **Main courses** £6-£21.50. **Credit** AmEx, DC, MC, V.

E&O is one hip and stylish restaurant. Cream walls, huge circular lampshades and dark wooden slatted walls create a simple, oriental feel that is reflected in the interesting pan-Asian menu. The small bar is always packed, but the food is the real highlight. Take a seat at one of the brown leather banquettes and browse the glossary at the back of the menu to help make your choice. Roasted coconut and pomegranate betel leaves, beautifully presented on a pretty plate, were extremely fresh and minty. Tender marinated spicy lamb followed, accompanied by a crunchy salad of papaya and mango. Chicken pad thai was also a tasty, if less adventurous, choice. Service is admirably efficient, and booking is essential.

Harlem

78 Westbourne Grove, W2 5RT (020 7985 0900/ www.harlemsoulfood.com). Bayswater or Notting Hill tube. **Meals served** 10.30am-midnight daily. **Credit** AmEx, DC, MC, V.

When this trendy, wood-panelled restaurant/bar opened in early 2004, reviews were mixed, but it seems to have hit its stride. The place is attractive, with lots of polished wood, plus banquette and table seating. Service, from hip young things, is cool but friendly. Despite the presence of a bar downstairs the music in the restaurant was at a good level as we chose from the menu of 'home-cooking' style southern favourites. Fried corncakes and calamares were good starters, but eclipsed by mains of an enormous hamburger, juicy and perfectly cooked with a mound of excellent fries, and a thick, 10oz sirloin, grilled precisely to order, topped with onion rings, on wilted spinach. White chocolate cheesecake with fresh berries was heavenly. A couple of Brooklyn Beers and… what else do you need?

Mandarin Kitchen

14-16 Queensway, W2 3RX (020 7727 9012). Bayswater or Queensway tube. **Meals served** noon-11.30pm daily. **Main courses** £5.90-£25. **Set meal** £10.90 per person (minimum 2). **Credit** AmEx, DC, JCB, MC, V.

The British HQ of the lobster trade, this place serves 50 to a 100 of them every night, steamed, dry-fried with spices and garlic, slathered in black bean sauce, or even as Japanese sashimi. We took ours with lashings of fragrant ginger and spring onion, on a bed of noodles: it was gorgeously fresh and juicy. Six dainty oysters steamed in their rugged shells with a scattering of salted olive leaves were excellent, and stewed pork with preserved vegetables was a fine version of a rustic Chinese classic, the meat braised to melting tenderness, its flavours sharpened by the dark mustard greens. The Mandarin is a reliable bet for spankingly fresh seafood, and a magnet for discerning East Asians.

Nipa

Royal Lancaster Hotel, Lancaster Terrace, W2 2TY (020 7262 6737/www.royallancaster.com). Lancaster Gate tube. Bar **Open** 11am-11pm Mon-Sat; 11am-10.30pm Sun. *Restaurant* **Lunch served** noon-2pm Mon-Fri. **Dinner served** 6.30-10.30pm Mon-Sat. **Main courses** £8.50-£13.50. **Set meals** £25-£28 4 courses. **Credit** AmEx, DC, MC, V.

This smart Thai inside the Royal Lancaster hotel feels like the inside of a wood-panelled jewellery box filled with a treasure trove of golden Thai knick-knacks, woven gold and maroon tablecloths and patterned carpet. The service can be hit and miss – we were kept waiting a long time before being brought the menu and drinks, then suddenly overwhelmed with over-attentive waiters. Food here has an amazing clarity of flavours. Minced prawn and chicken tartlets boasted light, flaky pastry with tasty filling, and sweetcorn cake was zinged up with fresh curry paste. Vegetable green curry revealed sparkling layers of flavours, in turn subtle and fiery, and a lively mixed seafood stir-fry was packed with perfectly cooked fresh prawns and squid. Nipa is the Thai community's choice for special occasion dining.

Also in the area

Fairuz 27 Westbourne Grove, W2 4UA (020 7243 8444); **Gourmet Burger Kitchen** 50 Westbourne Grove, W2 5FH (020 7243 4344); **Livebait** 175 Westbourne Grove, W11 2SB (020 7727 4321); **Royal China** 13 Queensway, W2 4QJ (020 7221 2535); **S&M Café** 268 Portobello Road, W10 5TY (020 8968 8898).

West

Blah Blah Blah

78 Goldhawk Road, W12 8HA (020 8746 1337). Goldhawk Road tube. **Lunch served** 12.30-2.30pm, **dinner served** 7-11pm Mon-Sat. **Main courses** £9.95. **Credit** MC, V.

This lilac-hued, romantically lit restaurant offers outstanding vegetarian fare. From an imaginative global menu, try spicy, sweet-and-savoury plantain fritters, or a sophisticated artichoke, butternut squash and dolcelatte tart for starters. Follow this with tortilla filled with interesting ingredients such as yams, sweet potatoes and beguilingly smoky pasilla chillies. Or how about stuffed, couscous-coated aubergine served with beetroot and chickpea relish? Salsas, sauces and other accessories are especially noteworthy, and desserts such as light passion fruit pavlova perk up the palate.

Bush Garden Café ★

59 Goldhawk Road, W12 8EG (020 8743 6372). Goldhawk Road tube. **Open** 8am-6pm Mon-Sat; 9am-2pm Sun. **Main courses** £4-£5. **Credit** AmEx, MC, V.

Just walking into this amiable, attractive wholefood café and grocery makes you hungry. With its shelves of organic pastas, sauces, wines and treats and chilled counter full of salads, quiches, pies and pastries, it's always time for lunch. There's plenty of space for children, especially out in the garden with its grassy knoll, playhouse and rainproof canopy. Indoors, the white tongue-and-groove walls and mismatched furniture exude a busy household air. The food is cooked with enormous flair and top ingredients: even something as simple as a carrot and coriander soup is a warming dose of colour and spice; the chicken and sweet potato broth is even more satisfying, as are the big breakfasts. Salads are excellent. You can go all healthy with smoothies and raw veg, or go down the Konditor & Cook cake route with a mug of hot chocolate.

Chosan ★

292 Upper Richmond Road, SW15 6TH (020 8788 9626). East Putney tube. **Lunch served** noon-2.30pm Sat, Sun. **Dinner served** 6.30-10.30pm Tue-Sat; 6.30-10pm Sun. **Main courses** £3.30-£19.90. **Set lunch** £7.90-£13.90 incl miso soup & rice. **Set dinner** £17.90-£19.90 7 courses; £18.90-£24.90 bento box. **Credit** MC, V.

Small and unassuming though it looks from the outside, this is one of London's best spots for authentic Japanese food. Sleek and modern it isn't, however, with its profusion of varnished wood, potted plants and framed pictures hanging on brick walls. The atmosphere is comforting, but the food is serious. If you're on your own, nab a stool at the sushi counter and watch the chef work his magic; the range of fish is great, including ark shell, surf clam and wonderfully fresh uni. Daily specials might include grilled beef heart and grilled salmon heads, but we tried fried salmon skin served with a punchy ponzu sauce, and fried aubergine topped with minced pork in a savoury sauce. Sukiyaki, warm and comforting, came to the table ready-cooked in a heavy pot brimming with beef, onion, carrot, cabbage, mushrooms and shirataki (konnyaku noodles), served with rice and a little dish of raw egg for dipping. Our neighbours' bento boxes looked pretty good too. Service is sweet, the food is nigh-on perfect and the saké list is impressive.

The Depot

Tideway Yard, 125 Mortlake High Street, SW14 8SN (020 8878 9462). Barnes, Barnes Bridge or Mortlake rail/209 bus. **Open** 10am-11pm Mon-Sat; 10am-10.30pm Sun. **Lunch served** noon-3pm Mon-Sat; noon-4pm Sun. **Dinner served** 6-11pm Mon-Sat; 6-10.30pm Sun. **Main courses** £9.95-£15.50. **Set meal** (Mon-Fri lunch, Mon-Thur, Sun dinner) £12 2 courses. **Credit** AmEx, DC, MC, V.

This riverfront establishment manages effortlessly a laid-back brasserie vibe. With gleaming woodwork and well-spaced tables, it's best visited in the day or at sunset to make the most of the sweeping views over the Barnes bend of the Thames. The menu makes the most of seasonal ingredients, and prices are fair for this upmarket neighbourhood. Gruyère and sweet onion tart, and grilled goat's cheese atop a fresh-tasting salad of chicory, radicchio and beetroot salad were excellent starters. Mains offer the likes of calf's liver and bacon, pork fillet, and salmon fish cake. Blackened tuna was nicely cooked, pink inside and crisply sweet on the outside, but sweetcorn and artichoke salsa was a dull accompaniment. Shoestring chips were ace. Puds are always a highlight: moist orange and almond cake, perhaps, or velvety vanilla panna cotta with tangy rhubarb compote. A decent wine list (with 16 options by the glass, including bubbly), good coffee and proficient service all add to the class of the operation.

Enoteca Turi

28 Putney High Street, SW15 1SQ (020 8785 4449). East Putney tube/Putney Bridge rail/ 14, 74, 270 bus. **Lunch served** noon-2.30pm Mon-Sat. **Dinner served** 6.30-11pm Mon-Thur; 6.30-11.30pm Fri, Sat. **Main courses** £14-£17. **Set lunch** £12.50 2 courses. **Credit** AmEx, DC, MC, V.

A polished outfit offering Prada style at Putney prices, Enoteca Turi is decorated in mottled tones of rich terracotta and shantung gold, with stylish comfortable wood and leather chairs. Describing the wine list as comprehensive does not do it justice: the degree of annotation and cross-referencing make it an absorbing read. Food was equally impressive: the unusual dish of calf's liver with salad came topped with paper-like ribbons of potato splashed with balsamic sauce – an excellent combination. A special of beetroot and ricotta ravioli with poppy seed and butter sauce was sweet, earthy and nutty. Roast rack of lamb was juicy, served with a gorgeous sticky jus and shredded courgette and mint salad. Desserts were beautifully presented. The crocante chocolate tart was accompanied by a lovely mandarin sorbet. Staff are pleasant and capable.

Fish Hoek

8 Elliott Road, W4 1PE (020 8742 0766). Turnham Green tube. **Lunch served** noon-2.30pm Tue-Sun. **Dinner served** 6-10.30pm daily. **Main courses** £9.75-£30. **Set lunch** £11.50 2 courses, £16.50 3 courses. **Credit** MC, V.

This lovely restaurant specialises in South African fish dishes. Named after a suburb of Cape Town, it's a small, bright space decorated with sepia-tinged photos (many family pictures of Pete Gottengs, the owner). It can get busy, especially on Friday and Saturday nights when there are two fixed sittings – at 7pm and 9.30pm. Such considerations soon fade, though, thanks to a buoyant atmosphere, helpful service, and excellent cooking. The menu offers an ocean of choice, with around 30 fish and 12 shellfish dishes, most available in half or full portions rather than as conventional starters and mains. South African species to look out for include kingfish, snoek, stumpnose and kabeljou, but there are also other exotica from the Indian Ocean and Caribbean, plus domestic offerings (herring, salmon, plaice). The shellfish comes mainly from Mozambique, and the wine list – predominantly whites – is exclusively South African. A delightful one-off.

Golden Palace ★

146-150 Station Road, Harrow, Middx HA1 2RH (020 8863 2333). Harrow-on-the-Hill tube/rail. **Meals served** noon-11.30pm Mon-Sat; 11am-10.30pm Sun. **Dim sum** noon-5pm Mon-Sat; 11am-5pm Sun. **Main courses** £5.20-£7.50. **Dim sum** £2.20-£3.20. **Set meals** £18-£24.50 per person (minimum 2). **Credit** AmEx, DC, MC, V.

For years now, Chinese from far and wide have beaten a path to Golden Palace's door. The varied daytime menu boasts skilfully prepared dim sum, the standard of which surpasses many a Chinatown establishment. The restaurant also excels at vegetarian 'mock' duck and such wheat gluten-based snacks that other establishments ignore due to the sheer amount of physical work involved in their preparation. We particularly enjoyed the charcoal vegetarian roast pork. The remaining selection of dim sum was superb: light and generously filled oven-baked roast pork pastries, perfectly cooked deep-fried doughnut cheung fun and packed-to-the-rafters scallop cheung fun. Thai-style cuttlefish cake was ravishingly moist and freshly made taro cake had exactly the right taste and texture. The two dining rooms are spacious and light. Service was prompt and attentive.

Madhu's

39 South Road, Southall, Middx, UB1 1SW (020 8574 1897/www.madhusonline.com). Southall rail. **Lunch served** 12.30-3pm Mon, Wed-Fri. **Dinner served** 6-11.30pm Mon, Wed, Thur, Sun; 6pm-midnight Fri, Sat. **Main courses** £6-£12. **Set meal** £17.50-£20 16 dishes incl tea or coffee. **Credit** AmEx, DC, MC, V.

This acclaimed restaurant, recently showered with awards and accolades, stands out in Southall. A favourite with local Punjabi and Sikh families, it also attracts a younger, hipper mix of diners. Sprawled over two floors, it sports a stylish, minimal look with wood and granite floors, large glass panels on the wall, crisp white napery and a tiny backlit bar. Palak paneer was made with fresh ingredients (not frozen spinach or supermarket cheese, as is often the case), and chhole-bhature featured chickpea curry with soft, fluffy pillows of deep-fried bread; however, the smoky aromas and pomegranate-laced spicing of both dishes was a tad too similar and lacked the customary pep of chilli. Sizzling lamb chops were juicy with succulent meat. Despite a packed restaurant, service couldn't have been sweeter.

New Asian Tandoori Centre Roxy ★

114-118 The Green, Southall, Middx, UB2 4BQ (020 8574 2597). Southall rail. **Meals served** 8am-11pm Mon-Thur; 8am-midnight Fri-Sun. **Main courses** £3-£7. **No credit cards.**

Although hardly upmarket, this spot is the number-one venue for home-style cooking favoured by Punjabi families. Wipe clean tables, functional decor, and a lengthy takeaway counter by the entrance doesn't smack of romance, but boisterous bonhomie lends a cosy appeal. No one churns out lassi as well as these guys – icy cold, sometimes flavoured with mango, or left plain, these coolers make a marvellous meal when accompanied with puffed baturas (leavened deep-fried bread, similar to puris, but softer in texture) and a bowlful of sweet-sour chickpeas. Stay with tried and tested dishes and you won't be let down – street snacks such as aloo tikki (potato cakes), papdi chaat (pastry discs topped with yoghurt and tangy chutneys) and butter chicken curry (flavoured with toasted cumin, tomatoes and cream) are always dependable. Staff remain attentive, even when the place gets really busy.

1492

404 North End Road, SW6 1LU (020 7381 3810/ www.1492restaurant.com). Fulham Broadway tube. **Brunch served** 11am-3pm Sat, Sun. **Lunch served** 12.30-3pm Mon-Fri. **Dinner served** 6-midnight daily. **Main courses** £8.50-£17. **Credit** AmEx, MC, V.

Named after the year Columbus 'discovered' America, 1492 specialises in pan-Latin American food, with dishes that span the continent, from Mexico to the Caribbean. And they're the real thing: no tacky Tex-Mex or ponchos here. Burnt sienna paintwork, exposed brickwork, dark wood and colourful paintings provide a casual setting, and the South American staff are utterly charming. Starters include two kinds of ceviche, one Mexican-style, served atop a tortilla with guacamole: tasty enough, but not as good as the tangy Peruvian version. Many dishes have a touch of sweetness, from the creamily smooth Venezuelan black bean soup to tiger prawn and banana curry to Brazilian moqueca, a fabulous Bahian stew of white fish cooked with garlic, onions, tomatoes, red pepper, chilli and coconut milk, served with vatapá, a fluffy, and distinctly weird-tasting, dried shrimp purée. There are also steak (from Argentina and Uruguay) and chicken dishes (from Puerto Rico, Guatamala and Mexico). Decent cocktails are worth a go at £5.80 each.

Pallavi ★

Unit 3, Cross Deep Court, Heath Road, Twickenham, TW1 4QJ (020 8892 2345/www.mcdosa.com). Twickenham rail. **Lunch served** noon-3pm daily **Dinner served** 6-11pm Mon-Thur, Sun; 6pm-midnight Fri, Sat. **Main courses** £4.50-7.95. **Credit** AmEx, MC, V.

Located on the first floor of a concrete-fronted shopping complex, Pallavi doesn't quite transport customers to Keralan heaven, but what it lacks in looks, it makes up for with its cooking. Culinary classics such as a tongue-tingling rasam (pepper broth), delicate green banana curry, and crisp dosas (rice and lentil pancakes) are a real treat. Spinach vada – savoury doughnuts made from roughly ground lentils, bitingly hot chillies, onion and chopped spinach made a tempting teaser to our main meal, and worked well with a dollop of fresh coconut and green chilli chutney. Vellapam – a potato stew, spiked with green chillies and curry leaves was served with pancakes, light and golden on one side and deliciously soft on the other. Service is polite, but staff are not especially quick off the mark.

Redmond's ★

170 Upper Richmond Road West, SW14 8AW (020 8878 1922/www.redmonds.org.uk). Mortlake rail then 337 bus, or 33 bus. **Lunch served** noon-2.30pm Sun. **Dinner served** 6.30-10.30pm Mon-Thur; 7-10.30pm Fri, Sat. **Set lunch** (Sun) £19 2 courses, £23 3 courses. **Set dinner** £27.50 2 courses, £31 3 courses; (6.30-7.45pm Mon-Thur) £12.50 2 courses, £15 3 courses. **Credit** JCB, MC, V.

Redmond's core clientele may be middle-class and middle-aged, but there's nothing middle-of-the-road about this operation. Courteous, attentive service; a relaxed atmosphere; tastefully subdued decor: everything speaks of the confidence that comes from doing something well for many years. The set dinner is shortish, but all of it appeals. Ingredients are high-quality and change with the seasons. Murmurs of appreciation greeted the fresh clear flavours of smoked haddock tartare with chive crème fraîche. For mains, roast cod peeled into fat, juicy flakes atop pak choy, perfect mash and lemony puy lentils: an excellent combination. Tagliatelle had a moreishly

1492.
See p56.

rich mushroom sauce. Best of all was an intense lime mousse and raspberry sorbet. Oenophiles are in for a treat too; the lengthy wine list is helpfully detailed.

Riva

169 Church Road, SW13 9HR (020 8748 0434). Barnes or Barnes Bridge rail/33, 209, 283 bus. **Lunch served** noon-2.30pm Mon-Fri, Sun. **Dinner served** 7-11pm Mon-Sat; 7-9.30pm Sun. **Main courses** £11.50-£19.50. **Credit** AmEx, MC, V.

Some experts consider Riva the best Italian restaurant in London, but we've always found it patchy. A delightful starter plate included rocket salad with intense chewy chunks of bottarga, superlative vitello tonnato sprinkled with tiny capers, and sweet culatello ham with figs – the fruit marred by being fridge-cold. Penne alla matriciana was no better than could be made at home. A special of turbot with lemon and rosemary came with lovely mash. Riva's gnocchi are usually very good but ours, served with crab and creamy tomato sauce, were too chewy. The wine list is brief and only house wines are available by the glass.

River Café ★

Thames Wharf, Rainville Road, W6 9HA (020 7386 4200/www.rivercafe.co.uk). Hammersmith tube. **Lunch served** 12.30-3pm daily. **Dinner served** 7-9.30pm Mon-Sat. **Main courses** £23-£32. **Credit** AmEx, DC, MC, V.

Pray for sunny weather so you can sit in the courtyard when you visit the River Café. On colder, days patrons are crammed into the indoor dining area with only a foot or so between tables. But it's a small price to pay for dining at this highly enjoyable Italian stalwart. The large price you'll be paying is the bill. Main courses now hit £32 for the turbot, which like many of the best dishes on the menu comes from the wood-fired oven, but there are low prices on the wide-ranging wine list. Another main – three thick pieces of lamb, with salsa verde, wood-roasted aubergines, and smashed cannellini beans – was perfection and generous too. Desserts included summer pud made with valpolicella, strawberry granita, the signature chocolate nemesis, and a simple but sumptuous caramel ice-cream. Apart from delay in coming back for our wine order – we were halfway through starters before the bottle was presented – service was prompt and charming.

Sagar ★

157 King Street, W6 9JT (020 8741 8563). Hammersmith tube/299 bus. **Lunch served** noon-2.45pm, **dinner served** 5.30-10.45pm Mon-Wed. **Meals served** noon-10.45pm Thur-Sun. **Main courses** £5-£10. **Thalis** £7.95-£11.45. **Credit** AmEx, DC, JCB, MC, V.

This south Indian vegetarian restaurant is a relatively new arrival in Hammersmith, but already bustles through popular lunchtimes and busy evenings every day of the week. The all-vegetarian cuisine of Udupi in Karnataka has some similarities to Kerala with subtle flavours allowing vegetables to impress but never overpowering taste buds. Instead, dishes like onion and chilli uphappam (like a potato pancake in texture) pack a punch but can be tempered by the mellow sauce of the mattar paneer or pav bhajee. Along with potato bondas, many different dosas and side dishes including a tangy lemon rice and a subtle garlic rice, Sagar offers great regional Indian cooking for London diners.

Sonny's

94 Church Road, SW13 0DQ (020 8748 0393). Barnes Bridge rail/209 bus. Café **Open** 10.30am-6pm Mon-Sat. **Lunch served** noon-4pm Mon-Sat. **Main courses** £3.95-£9. *Restaurant* **Lunch served** 12.30-2.30pm Mon-Sat; 12.30-3pm Sun. **Dinner served** 7.30-11pm Mon-Sat. **Main courses** £10.75-£16. **Set lunch** (Mon-Sat) £13 2 courses, £16.50 3 courses; (Sun) £21 3 courses incl coffee. **Set dinner** (Mon-Thur) £16.50 2 courses, £19.50 3 courses. **Credit** AmEx, MC, V.

This polished neighbourhood restaurant has been satisfying Barnes locals for years. It's a modern, white space (the back room is best), as suitable for dinners à deux as it is for family gatherings. The operation is run with professional ease, from the well-judged wine list to the artful modern European concoctions delivered by cordial staff. The menu makes good use of seasonal ingredients, offering (in summer) the likes of tiger prawns with leeks and apple salad, roasted monkfish with caramelised fennel and aubergine cream, or lamb with tomato fondue and polenta soufflé. Sides include crisp french beans and excellent chips. The set dinner, though limited, is good value considering most à la carte mains cost £14-plus. Desserts – such as inventive sorbets or vanilla soufflé with chocolate brownie ice-cream – are always delectable.

La Trompette

5-7 Devonshire Road, W4 2EU (020 8747 1836). Turnham Green tube. **Lunch served** noon-2.30pm Mon-Sat; 12.30-3pm Sun. **Dinner served** 6.30-10.45pm Mon-Sat; 7-10.30pm Sun. **Set lunch** £21.50 3 courses; (Sun) £25 3 courses. **Set dinner** £32.50 3 courses, £42.50 4 courses. **Credit** AmEx, JCB, MC, V.

It's a vibrant room: tan leather ceiling, bamboo textured walls and plenty of enthusiastic diners. It is quite an achievement for a local to be so attractive to so many and a mark of the expertise of its owners, who also run Chez Bruce (*see p59*) and the Glasshouse (*see p60*). Starters were substantial – monkfish and plaice came wrapped in pasta with crab broth; translucent layers of smoked pork loin came with tiny carrots and toasted orange morsels of mimolette cheese. There was a slight dip in the wow factor with the mains – chicken, slowly cooked in vin jaune with mushrooms and truffles, was tender but not as fragrant as the ingredients suggested, while a fillet of turbot with pasta-wrapped crab was good but not startling. The desserts more than compensated: strawberry salad arrived, theatrically, in a tall martini glass, topped with frothy pink mousse, while the chocolate puddings included a mini-soufflé that was exquisite.

Also in the area

Carluccio's Caffé 5-6 The Green, W5 5DA (020 8866 4458); **Carluccio's Caffé** Unit 5, Charter Quay, Kingston-upon-Thames, KT1 1HT (020 8549 5898); **Giraffe** 270 Chiswick High Road, W4 1PD (020 8995 2100); **Giraffe** 30 Hill Street, Richmond, TW9 1TW (020 8332 2646); **Gourmet Burger Kitchen** 131 Chiswick High Road, W4 2ED (020 8995 4548); **Momo** 14 Queen's Parade, W5 3HU (020 8997 0206); **Prezzo** 147-149 Kew Road, Richmond, TW9 2PN (020 8605 3679); **Prezzo** 109-113 High Street, Shepperton, TW17 9BL (01932 269006); **Strada** 26 Hill Street, Richmond, TW1 1TW (020 7590 4644); **Wagamama** 3 Hill Street, Richmond TW9 1SX (0208 948 2224); **Wagamama** 16-18 High Street, Kingston-upon-Thames, KT1 1EY (020 8546 1117).

South

Asadal

180 New Malden High Street, New Malden, Surrey, KT3 4EF (020 8942 2334/020 8949 7385). New Malden rail. **Meals served** noon-11pm Mon-Fri; noon-11pm Sat; 5-11pm Sun. **Main courses** £7-£25. **Set dinner** £15 2 courses. **Credit** MC, V.

Asadal is more formal than most of New Malden's many Korean restaurants; it's a first date kind of place. The lengthy menu is peppered with expensive ingredients such as abalone. Portions are generous. Our panch'an were huge helpings of ko sari (blanched bracken shoots) and kimch'i. Deep-fried oysters weren't as light and fine as we remember them, but Asadal's beef bulgogi is an excellent version, the meat marinated in soy, sugar, garlic and sesame and cooked by white-shirted staff at your table. Wrap it up in lettuce leaves, add some koch'ujang and enjoy. Fish dishes such as cuttlefish casserole and fried cod in beaten egg are a highlight.

Banana Leaf ★

190 Tooting High Street, SW17 0SF (020 8696 1423). Tooting Broadway tube. **Meals served** noon-11pm daily. **Main courses** £2.75-£4. **Set lunch** £4.95. **Credit** MC, V.

Banana Leaf's menu is long – possibly too long, at around 100 items – but the cooking is among the best to be found in London's Sri Lankan caffs. Prices are shockingly cheap. Crab curry costs just £3, but was the best dish of several – a bowl of long limbs and shell, but with plenty of meat and a moreish bisque-like sauce. One of the most expensive dishes (£3.50) was devilled mutton, the dry-roasted spices unusually and pleasingly mild. The South Indian and Sri Lankan breakfast dish, masala dosai, is served here on a real banana leaf, just as it often is in the roadside cafés of South Asia. The real deal.

Brady's

513 Old York Road, SW18 1TF (020 8877 9599). Wandsworth Town rail/28, 44 bus. **Dinner served** 6.30-10.30pm Mon-Sat. **Main courses** £6.35-£8.95. **No credit cards.**

Treated to a fresh coat of primrose-white paint and an extra skylight, Brady's has smartened up, but retains its amiable atmosphere. Don't miss the starters: potted shrimps, packed into chilli and lemon flavoured butter, are irresistible; dressed crab (if available) is a meaty taste-bomb; and salmon fish cakes come packed with flaky pink flesh. And there's more. Choose from the board menus and dive in. Main course portions aren't huge, but if you want three courses (recommended), restraint is essential. Plaice in batter was a flavoursome, fresh fish, complemented admirably by any of five herb-flavoured mayonnaises and chips that were chunky and golden. The wine list is brief but hits the spot. Quibbles? The mushy peas are a tad sweet, and the bench seats are hard work.

Cah Chi ★

34 Durham Road, SW20 0TW (020 8947 1081). Raynes Park rail/57, 131 bus. **Lunch served** noon-3pm, **dinner served** 5-11pm Tue-Fri. **Meals served** noon-11pm Sat; noon-10.30pm Sun. **Main courses** £4.50-£14. **Set dinner** £15 3 courses. **No credit cards.**

One of our favourite Korean restaurants. Everyone is made to feel at home, there are families and groups of friends having a good time, the owners offer helpful advice on the menu, and the food is stunning. A meal here always includes a few forms of table-top cooking, as in tteokpokki (pressed rice cakes) with vegetables and noodles, cooked with chilli sauce. The signature dish is soon dae, black pudding made with rice vermicelli, and cooked in various ways (or served as is). The panch'an deserve special praise too, for both quality and variety. Don't miss the sticky soya beans cooked in a sweet sauce, or the zippy pickled squid. Cah Chi is licensed for beer, or you can bring your own wine.

Canyon

The Towpath, Richmond Riverside, Richmond, Surrey, TW10 6UJ (020 8948 2944). Richmond tube/rail. **Brunch served** 11am-3.30pm Sat, Sun. **Lunch served** 11am-3.30pm Mon-Fri. **Dinner served** 6-10.30pm daily. **Main courses** £11-£19. **Credit** AmEx, MC, V.

This breezy riverside restaurant is always a pleasure, with its striking views of the Thames and extensive outdoor terrace – the perfect location for catching dramatic sunsets. From a short menu, cod in a herb crust with cold potato salad and shrimps was a better choice than fillet of beef (a nice thick cut that wasn't cooked as requested) with 'cottage mash' (flavoured mince atop mashed potatoes). This was an interesting accompaniment, but made the dish far too heavy; vegetables would have been better. Desserts – lemon tart and chocolate pot – were impeccable. Service was faultless.

Chez Bruce ★

2 Bellevue Road, SW17 7EG (020 8672 0114/ www.chezbruce.co.uk). Wandsworth Common rail. **Lunch served** noon-2pm Mon-Fri; 12.30-2.30pm Sat; noon-3pm Sun. **Dinner served** 6.30-10.30pm Mon-Sat, 7-10pm Sun. **Set lunch** (Mon-Fri) £23.50 3 courses; (Sat) £25 3 courses; (Sun) £29.50 3 courses. **Set dinner** £32.50 3 courses. **Credit** AmEx, DC, JCB, MC, V.

Bruce Poole's scintillating restaurant is approaching its tenth anniversary, but remains unchallenged as Wandsworth's top venue. It's formal but not stuffy. The main dining space is compact (a dozen tables downstairs, a few more in the less sought-after first floor), but breezy bow windows looking on to the Common and a preponderance of white keep it feeling fresh. Bruce changes his menu regularly, favouring robust dishes with strong French or Mediterranean influences. Starters can be vitello tonnato (exquisitely thin slices of veal, salad leaves, a tuna and anchovy dressing), foie gras and chicken liver parfait on toasted brioche, or a velvety, chilled pea soup with goat's cheese. The mains are heartier. Confit and fillet of pork with chorizo and bean salad; fillet of beef came with persillade of shin and an intense bourguignon sauce; a hunk of neatly roasted cod with olive oil mash. Despite the excellence of the puddings, you should try the cheese board (£5.50 supplement). The wine list is justly acclaimed. Service is French-flavoured but nonetheless friendly.

Cocum ★

9 Approach Road, Raynes Park, SW20 8BA (020 8540 3250/8542 3843). Raynes Park rail. **Lunch served** noon-3pm Sun. **Dinner served** 5.30-11.30pm daily. **Main courses** £3.95-£7.95. **Credit** AmEx, DC, MC, V.

One year into its operation, Indian restaurant Cocum still looks spick and span with its blond wooden flooring, lemon walls incorporating a frieze of line-drawing portraits, and Keralan artefacts (kathakali dancing mask, a model of a ceremonial river boat). Keralan cuisine encompasses a few meat dishes, but fish and vegetarian dishes provide the highlights. Start with kadal soup – crab, fish, squid and mussel, finely diced in a creamy coconut-milk stock. Then move on to the likes of nadan meen curry (meaty fish in a coconut and cocum – 'fish tamarind' – sauce), mambazha pulissery (a soupy yoghurt-based curry containing mango and green banana), and cheera parippu (dahl and spinach). Finish with a sweet, cardamom-laced treat of rice pudding. Informative waiters help the meal along.

Dexter's Grill

20 Bellevue Road, SW17 7EB (020 8767 1858). Wandsworth Common rail. **Meals served** *Summer* 11am-11pm Mon-Fri; 10am-11pm Sat; 10am-10.30pm Sun. *Winter* noon-11pm Mon-Fri; 11am-11pm Sat; 11am-10.30pm Sun. **Main courses** £7-£15. **Credit** AmEx, MC, V.

This family-friendly restaurant at the edge of Wandsworth Common is a useful spot. With exposed brick walls, large windows and warm, friendly staff, it's a very welcoming place. The menu puts an emphasis on gourmet sandwiches, hamburgers and fresh salads. Butterfly prawns were steaming hot, with a Thai sauce. For mains, we went for the build-your-own salad, creating an oriental affair with chicken satay and peanut sauce – filling and fresh. A big, juicy hamburger was even better, and came with lots of crisp chips. For puddings, your best bet is to go for one of the house speciality ice-cream dishes – large enough to satisfy three. Don't overlook the smoothies and shakes either.

French Table ★

85 Maple Road, Surbiton, Surrey, KT6 4AW (020 8399 2365/www.frenchtable.co.uk). Surbiton rail. **Lunch served** noon-2.30pm Wed-Fri, Sun. **Dinner served** 7-10.30pm Tue-Sat. **Main courses** £10.80-£15.80. **Set lunch** (Wed-Fri) £12.50 2 courses, £15.50 3 courses; (Sun) £16.50 3 courses. **Credit** MC, V.

Since the French Table opened in 2001, Sarah (front of house) and Eric (chef) Guignard have been building a solid local following. A recent meal was outstanding – evidence that the kitchen has really hit its stride. The conception and execution of dishes is reaching new highs with the likes of a refreshingly light salad of crab with julienne of vegetables, subtly flavoured with curry, and an exceptional canneloni of spinach and almonds with pan-fried frog's legs and garlic cappuccino. The spirit of carefully restrained playfulness extends to the main courses: the sweet-sharp contrasts of the caramelised pork belly with celeriac purée, green tomato chutney, tomato panisse with port reduction, and the multi-flavour/texture explosion of Barbary duck with spinach, rillette croustillant and parsnip ice-cream. Service remains exemplary. Look out for the Guignards' new venture, the Food Room (123 Queenstown Road, SW8 3RH, 020 7622 0555).

The Glasshouse ★

14 Station Parade, Kew, Surrey, TW9 3PZ (020 8940 6777). Kew Gardens tube/rail. **Lunch served** noon-2.30pm Mon-Sat; 12.30-2.45pm Sun. **Dinner served** 7-10.30pm Mon-Thur; 6.30-10.30pm Fri, Sat; 7.30-10pm Sun. **Set lunch** £17.50 3 courses; (Sun) £25 3 courses. **Set dinner** £32.50 3 courses; £45 tasting menu. **Credit** AmEx, MC, V.

Two sides of this wedge-shaped modern European-serving dining room are glass; on warm days, the windows at the sharp, street end are thrown open. The place is packed and everyone seems delighted to be here, including the effective and unfussy staff. You really couldn't ask more of the warm squab pigeon salad (topped with an egg that was flavoured with truffles before being deep fried in yolk-yellow batter – absolutely delicious), or the thick slices of home-cured bresaola. Other dishes are substantial and pretty – pink lamb with saffron sauce was very appetising and the pork fillet tasted and looked exceptionally good, accompanied by a prune and bacon roll and stacked on a fine apple tart. Afterwards came a perfect selection of cheeses, described with verve by an enthusiastic waiter, and an exceptional apricot and almond tart that was even better than expected. A treat.

Gourmet Burger Kitchen ★

44 Northcote Road, SW11 1NZ (020 7228 3309/ www.gbkinfo.co.uk). Clapham Junction rail/49, 77, 219, 345 bus. **Meals served** noon-11pm Mon-Fri; 11am-11pm Sat; 11am-10pm Sun. **Main courses** £4.95-£7.25. **Credit** MC, V.

Le Petit Max. See p62.

Standing proud and tall, Gourmet Burger Kitchen's burgers are Scooby snacks to be proud of. The meat is 100% Aberdeen Angus Scotch beef, shaped into thick patties and cooked to your liking. You'll need two hands to eat them. The toppings are pretty imaginative too. This being a Kiwi-owned mini-chain, try the Kiwiburger, topped with beetroot, egg, pineapple, cheese, salad and relish. Other toppings include smoky barbecue sauce, fresh garlic mayo, pesto and many other great ingredients. Chicken, lamb and chorizo are also available, as are falafel or aubergine and goat's cheese burgers. Oh, and don't forget the chips, which are perfect. For drinks, choose from milkshakes, soft drinks, coffee, tea, beer or wine. Service is unfailingly polite, even when queues snake out of the door.

Kastoori ★

188 Upper Tooting Road, SW17 7EJ (8767 7027). Tooting Bec or Tooting Broadway tube. **Lunch served** 12.30-2.30pm Wed-Sun. **Dinner served** 6-10.30pm daily. **Main courses** £4.75-£6.25. **Thalis** £8.50-£16.25. **Credit** MC, V.

Diners travel from far and wide to eat the Thanki family's Gujarati-based vegetarian cooking. Savour, for example, kachori: a spicy mung dahl and pea filling encased in pastry shells, served in a vibrant sour/sweet yoghurt sauce with splashes of traffic-light colours. Or sev puri: crisp, freshly-fried pooris filled with diced potato and puffed rice, topped with sev the colour of Buddhist robes. Even the oddest-sounding dishes are good, such as the paneer stuffed with a dark coconut-and-spice mix, served in a buff-coloured creamy pasanda sauce.

Lee Fook ★

76 The Broadway, Tolworth, Surbiton, Surrey, KT6 7HR (020 8399 9793). Tolworth rail/265, 281, 406, K1, K2 bus. **Lunch served** noon-2.30pm, **dinner served** 5.30-11pm daily. **Main courses** £4-£10.50. **Set dinners** £16-£20 3 courses. **Credit** MC, V.

If you were to choose London's best Chinese restaurant on the basis of food alone, Lee Fook would win it. Chef Ringo Lo puts his passion for cooking into the creation of special menus on request. Give him a few days notice and he'll rustle up a fabulous feast. Stir-fried eel was a magnificent entwining of bamboo shoot, red pepper, celery, coriander and various mushrooms, with succulent strips of eel, served with melt-in-the-mouth wisps of fried pastry. Pièce de résistance was a platter of boned quails, stuffed with minced prawn and dark wind-dried sausage, lightly fried and draped in a delicate egg white sauce: stunning. Those seriously interested in Chinese food should beat a path to the door.

Numidie

48 Westow Hill, SE19 1RX (020 8766 6166/ www.numidie.co.uk). Gypsy Hill rail. **Lunch served** noon-4pm Sun. **Dinner served** 6.30-10.30pm Tue-Sun. **Main courses** £7.25-£12.50. **Credit** MC, V.

The decor is nothing to write home about (dark and slightly shabby), but the place has an extremely laid-back, no-nonsense French air, enhanced by an eclectic mix of Arabic and Gallic music. And when it comes to the food, the chef is deadly serious. Tender garlicky baby squid stuffed with crab in a fragrant olive-oil dressing, and gently spiced, moist, grilled filleted sardines, are followed by excellent tagines served with couscous. This is Mediterranean cooking with flair. Seafood tagine has generous chunks of cod, sea bass, scallops, prawns and mussels in a light fish broth. A tagine of lamb shank, peas and artichokes is also a winner, in a tasty reduced sauce with a hint of cumin and ginger.

Onam ★

219 Tooting High Street, SW17 0SZ (020 8767 7655/www.onam.co.uk). Tooting Broadway tube. **Lunch served** 11.30am-3pm, **dinner served** 6-11pm daily. **Main courses** £1.95-£6.95. **Credit** MC, V.

Onam's menu follows the precedents set by such earlier pioneers from Kerala. There's an extensive vegetarian selection; 'home-made' specialities; chicken, lamb or seafood curries; and 'exotic Cochin specialities' – which, bizarrely, is where they have listed chicken tikka masala. Heading straight for Kerala, we found one dish that was memorably good – the meen curry, which was big chunks of kingfish cooked with the smoky, attractively sour flavour of cocum (aka fish tamarind). Less impressive was the chicken 65, the chicken chunks smeared with red food colouring. Best to stick to what the chefs know best: sambhar, masala vadai and the appams were all up to par. Onam is open for breakfast, should you fancy some idli sambhar to get the day moving.

Le Petit Max

14 Chatfield Road, SW11 3SE (020 7223 0999). Clapham Junction rail. **Lunch served** noon-2pm daily. **Dinner served** 7-10pm Mon-Sat. **Main courses** £9.50-£20. **Set lunch** £14.50 2 courses. **Set meal** £18.50 3 courses. **Credit** DC, MC, V.

Set in an unappealing riverside development, Le Petit Max has to work hard to overcome the location. Once inside, the warm welcome, cosy red furnishings and low-key comfortableness of the place take over. The menu is a heart-warming read too: jambon de Bayonne with cornichons, Norfolk asparagus with hollandaise, and – star starter – Cantabrian anchovies with butter and shallots. Mains stick to the same reassuring classic formula. There's plenty of fish – much of it Cornish – but it was the meat dishes that shone – if there's a confit belly of pork and smoked morteau sausage with mustard sauce on the menu when you visit, order it. Finish with a classic pudding such as pot au chocolat with vanilla ice-cream.

Sarkhel's

199 Replingham Road, SW18 5LY (020 8870 1483). Southfields tube. **Lunch served** noon-2.30pm Tue-Sun. **Dinner served** 6-10.30pm Tue-Thur, Sun; 6-11pm Fri, Sat. **Main courses** £6.95-£9.95. **Set lunch** £5 2 courses. **Thali** £9.95. **Credit** MC, V.

In 2003 Sarkhel's extended next door to create Calcutta Notebook, a 'branch' that uses the same kitchen. But our recent visits to both restaurants confirmed that the 'real' Sarkhel's is the jewel in the crown. Udit Sarkhel's cooking is at its best when grounded in north Indian dishes, such as a lamb biryani. That's not to say dishes from other regions aren't good too: we relished the lemon rice with cashews. A Parsi-style dish of tiger prawns cooked with pumpkin and aubergine was also just-so. While the food quality is unquestionably high and service appreciably better than any local competitors, don't expect the low prices you find in nearby Tooting.

Sea Cow ★

7 Lordship Lane, SE22 8EW (020 8693 3111). East Dulwich rail/176, 196 bus. **Meals served** noon-11pm Tue-Sat. **Main courses** £7-£10. **Credit** MC, V.

Sea Cow adopts a simple approach to the business of eating fish. At the front is the wet fish counter with its gleaming mounds of ice; next to that the fryer, where you can order takeaway portions; and beyond that some hefty wooden tables and bench seating. The menu keeps it simple too, with dishes ranging from basic cod and chips through the more exotic delights of tilapia and bluefin tuna to crab cakes with salad and lime mayo. Perfectly cooked and fresh thanks to daily deliveries from Billingsgate, fish comes unadorned save for wedges of lime and lemon. Extras include good fat chips, fresh leafy salads and minted mushy peas. Fast-working, friendly staff keep things moving nicely.

Tsunami

5-7 Voltaire Road, SW4 6DQ (020 7978 1610). Clapham North tube. **Dinner served** 6-11pm Mon-Thur; 6-11.30pm Fri. **Meals served** noon-11.30pm Sat. **Main courses** £7.95-£16.50. **Credit** MC, V.

Daylight pours from a large triangular skylight and larger windows across satiny dark-wood tables and chairs, white walls and faux-croc banquettes the colour of Vuitton bags. Chic, no doubt about it, though thankfully the punters aren't all on the pose, and there's a healthy number of families. Tuna tataki in miso sauce, albeit costly (£9.95), was wonderful, and the nasu goma satisfyingly savoury; vegetarian ju-dan was served still sizzling fiercely, and the grilled eel was well presented. But too-dry rice meant on this occasion the place failed the ultimate litmus test for any Japanese diner.

Also in the area

Bodean's 169 Clapham High Street, SW4 7SS (020 7622 4248); **Cafe Lazeez** 93-95 Old Brompton Road, SW7 3LD (020 7581 9993); **Carluccio's Caffé** Unit 1, The Brewhouse, Putney Wharf, SW15 2JQ (020 8789 4203); **Dexter's Grill** 136 Upper Richmond Road, SW15 2SP (020 8789 5696); **Dexter's Grill** 1 Battersea Rise, SW11 1HG (020 7924 4935); **Giraffe** 27 Battersea Rise, SW11 1HJ (020 7223 0933); **Gourmet Burger Kitchen** 49 Fulham Broadway, SW6 1AE (020 7381 4242); **Gourmet Burger Kitchen** 333 Putney Bridge Road, SW15 2PG (020 8789 1199); **Livebait** 2 Northside, Wandsworth Common, SW18 2SS (0207 326 8580); **Strada** 102-104 Clapham High Street, SW4 7UL (020 7627 4847); **Strada** 91 High Street, SW19 5EG (020 8946 4363); **Strada** 375 Lonsdale Road, SW13 9PY (020 8392 9216); **Strada** 11-13 Battersea Rise, SW11 1HG (020 7801 0794);

East

Armadillo

41 Broadway Market, E8 4PH (020 7249 3633/ www.armadillorestaurant.co.uk). Bethnal Green tube then 106, 253 bus/26, 48, 55 bus. **Meals served** 6.30-10.30pm daily. **Main courses** £9.50-£16.50. **Credit** AmEx, DC, JCB, MC, V.

Blond wood tables, pre-Columbian artefacts in recesses on the walls and soft Latin beats on the stereo create a laid-back and stylish atmosphere. The Sao Paulo-born chef has put together an eclectic menu, plundered from across Latin America. The mixed relish of feta, radishes, olives, yellow beetroot and an interesting apple-like vegetable called jicama made a good start. Cheese and spring onion pasteizinhos – like maize ravioli with a delicious tomato vinaigrette to set them off – followed. Maté tea-smoked quail, chorizo and sweetcorn humitas were slightly too dry. Main courses packed a punch: Argentinian fillet steak with churrasco and sautéed taro root was lovely and tender and the fried sea bass with okra ratatouille perfectly cooked.

Cantaloupe

35 Charlotte Road, EC2A 3PB (020 7613 4411/ www.cantaloupegroup.co.uk). Old Street tube/rail/ 55 bus. **Open** 11am-midnight Mon-Sat; 11am-11.30pm Sun. **Lunch served** noon-3pm Mon-Fri. **Dinner served** 6-11.30pm Mon-Fri; 7-11.30pm Sat; 7-10pm Sun. **Main courses** £9-£16. **Credit** AmEx, DC, JCB, MC, V.

You reach Cantaloupe's restaurant through the packed bar. The menu is a fashionable Spanish-North African mix that often sound very busy, but in fact are cleverly balanced, and comprise excellent, mainly organic ingredients. The Spanish plate is recommended and we were helpfully told it would do fine for three: a platter of first-rate meats (jamón ibérico, chorizo, salchichón), manchego cheese, boquerones (marinated anchovies), tortilla, olives and capers. Moqueca (king prawns, calamares, mussels and chicken braised with peppers, garlic, tomatoes, cashews and coconut milk, with moros y cristianos – rice and beans) was full of goodies, imbued with a lovely smooth flavour from the nuts and coconut. To finish, apple and vanilla crema catalan tasted great. Drinks are reasonably priced too. The dining area is brilliantly designed so you can eat in cool comfort unharassed by music from the bar (except when DJs play at weekends).

Eyre Brothers

70 Leonard Street, EC2A 4QX (020 7613 5346/ www.eyrebrothers.co.uk). Old Street tube/rail. **Lunch served** noon-3pm Mon-Fri. **Dinner served** 6.30-11pm Mon-Sat. **Main courses** £13-£25. **Credit** AmEx, DC, MC, V.

A winning combination of stylishness (inventive lighting, long dark-wood banquettes), a friendly atmosphere and highly enjoyable food. The brothers have a part-Portuguese background, and the head chef is from that country, so Portuguese-based dishes feature strongly, along with Spanish and modern eclectic recipes. Ingredients are outstanding. Roast morcilla with red onion and potato torta gave a real taste of Iberian black pudding, rich and punchy; pan-roasted asparagus came with a smooth, romesco sauce. Next, grilled king scallops with chilli, garlic and lemon was a fine platter, but was outshone by a fabulous beef rib steak served with a refined mix of tomatoes, red peppers, wild garlic and salt-baked potatoes. Desserts include great sorbets in flavours like champagne and grapefruit. The wine list is as well thought-out as the menu. Our only grumble was with the slow service.

Frizzante@City Farm ★

Hackney City Farm, 1A Goldsmith's Row, E2 8QA (020 7739 2266/www.frizzanteltd.co.uk). Liverpool Street tube then 26, 48 bus. **Meals served** 10am-4.30pm Tue-Fri; 10am-5.30pm Sat, Sun. **Main courses** £5-£7. No corkage charge. **No credit cards.**

Sensitive souls may hesitate to order the grilled chicken skewers out of respect for the Afro-feathered bantams pecking around outside Hackney City Farm's delightful Italian café. Be assured they are delicious, as is everything else so far sampled on the

The best Family refuelling

Burgers
Dexter's Grill *p60*, **Eagle Bar Diner** *p31*, **Gourmet Burger Kitchen** *p60*, **Hamburger Union** *p41*.

Cafés
Blue Kangaroo *p47*, **Bush Garden Café** *p55*, **Frizzante@City Farm** *p63*, **Giraffe** *p63*, **Paul** *p42*, **Place Below** *p45*.

Fish & Chips
Fish! *p51*, **Golden Hind** *p24*, **Sea Cow** *p62*.

Oriental
Sông Quê *p64*, **Viet Garden** *p71*, **Viet Hoa** *p65*, **Wagamama** *p71*.

Pizza
Strada *p37*.

London

chalked-up, frequently changing menu at this lovely place. Location is all of course, especially when you've brought a young family for lunch, and here there's built-in baaing, lowing, clucking and grunting entertainment. From the frantic farmhouse kitchen – queue at the hatch for your food – come all-day breakfasts (free range eggs as standard), or interesting light-lunch choices, such as pumpkin and spinach pie, salade niçoise, spaghetti with mussels, chicken skewers with golden fried potatoes and glorious gnocchi with mushroom sauce. The ultra-thin children's pizzas (for an unbelievably cheap £2.50) have a bubbling topping of mozzarella and tomato sauce. Winner of *Time Out*'s award for Best Family Restaurant 2004.

Huong-Viet ★

An Viet House, 12-14 Englefield Road, N1 4LS (020 7249 0877). Dalston Kingsland rail then 67, 149, 242 bus. **Lunch served** noon-3.30pm Mon-Fri; noon-4pm Sat. **Dinner served** 5.30-11pm Mon-Sat. **Main courses** £4.20-£6.90. **Set lunch** £6 2 courses incl soft drink. **Credit** JCB, MC, V.

Tucked away in a Vietnamese community centre, this small café has queues and closely packed tables (go in a group and get a round one) attesting to its popularity. The red-walled interior is softened by candles and flowers, the staff are friendly (although not always on the ball) and the food satisfying. A recent addition to the menu are steamed rolls – banh cuon – soft, almost flat, translucent pancakes that slide down effortlessly. Equally scrumptious are the less elegant but more imposing-looking stuffed squid – big white sacs bulging with minced pork, prawn, carrot and vermicelli, garnished with fiery red chillies and swimming in a piquant tomato sauce. The traditional phô was light and fresh-tasting, while barbecued aubergine was fragrant with sesame seeds but oil-heavy. A steamed fish would be an excellent, lighter choice.

Plateau

Canada Place, Canada Square, Canary Wharf, E14 5ER (7715 7100/www.conran.com). Canary Wharf tube/DLR. Bar & Grill **Meals served** noon-11pm Mon-Sat; noon-4pm Sun. **Main courses** £9.75-£32. *Restaurant* **Lunch served** noon-3pm Mon-Fri, Sun. **Dinner served** 6-10.30pm Mon-Sat. **Main courses** £14.50-£27. **Credit** AmEx, DC, MC, V.

The brave new world that is Canary Wharf is mirrored in the faintly futuristic interior of Sir Terence Conran's Plateau. The place is filled with light – there's a long glass wall – and there are several distinct spaces: a bar area, grill room, restaurant and wonderfully unexpected covered terrace decorated with cacti, olive trees and lavender. The grill menu lists grills and rotisserie dishes, plus crustacea; in the restaurant there's more variety. Starters of ribbons of raw tuna with avocado and a soy-based dressing, and butternut squash and mascarpone ravioli were intensely flavoured and set a very high standard. Mains – vegetable nagé with barley and puréed broccoli, and spiced monkfish a

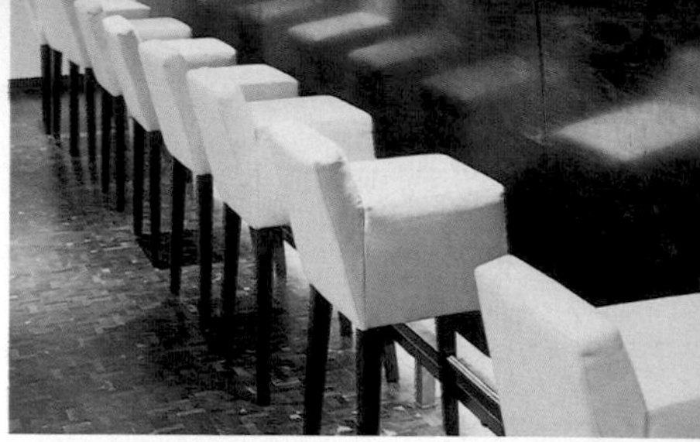

la plancha with mushroom broth – easily matched them. There are tempting desserts (chocolate fondant with fromage blanc sorbet) and a decent wine list; what's more, staff are friendly and on the ball. Finally, E14 has somewhere really special.

Royal China

30 Westferry Circus, E14 8RR (020 7719 0888). Canary Wharf tube/DLR/Westferry DLR. **Meals served** noon-11pm Mon-Thur; noon-11.30pm Fri, Sat; 11am-10pm Sun. **Dim sum** noon-5pm daily. **Main courses** dim sum £7-£40; £2.20-£4.50. **Set meal** £28-£36 per person (minimum 2). **Credit** AmEx, DC, JCB, MC, V.

Forget the Bayswater branch, with its stressful queueing and brusque staff, and go instead to this jewel in the Royal China crown. On a warm spring evening, sip cocktails outside, and watch the sun set over the glittering Thames. The menu is one of the most authentic Cantonese lists in town; a specials list offers more unusual dishes (suckling pig for £150, anyone?). Whole king prawns were deep-fried and encrusted with a delicious paste of salted duck egg yolk; slithery razor clams came stir-fried with crisp celery in a rich shrimpy sauce. Green beans tossed in a succulent relish of minced pork and dark olives were also good, but the highlight of the meal was unquestionably a garlicky hotpot of eel and bitter melon. Dim sum are excellent. Typical Royal China decor – all lacquer and gilding.

Sông Quê ★

134 Kingsland Road, E2 8DY (020 7613 3222). Old Street tube/rail/26, 48, 55, 67, 149, 242, 243 bus. **Lunch served** noon-3pm, **dinner served** 5.30-11pm Mon-Sat. **Meals served** noon-11pm Sun. **Main courses** £4.50-£9. **Set meals** £8.50-£14.50 per person (minimum 2). **Credit** AmEx, JCB, MC, V.

Plateau

Despite all the plaudits heaped upon it, Sông Quê has resisted the temptation to ratchet up the prices. Deep-fried tofu costs just £2, and even the massive, addictive pancakes served with herbs and dipping sauce are decently priced. Ignore the Chinese-y dishes and concentrate on the clean tastes exemplified by fresh rolls with pork and herbs or grilled beef rapped in betel leaf, served with dipping sauce – an absolute knock-out. Phô is a speciality, with over 20 types of the beef noodle soup listed: rare sliced steak, tendon and tripe, or mixed seafood. The functional decor's not much to write home about, the lighting is bright and the basement is very curious indeed (it's a glorified, ramshackle storage space that you have to go through to get to the loo), but Sông Quê is a must-visit Vietnamese.

Viet Hoa ★

70-72 Kingsland Road, E2 8DP (020 7729 8293). Old Street tube/rail/26, 48, 55, 67, 149, 242, 243 bus. **Lunch served** noon-3.30pm Mon-Fri; 12.30-4pm Sat, Sun. **Dinner served** 5.30-11pm Mon-Fri; 5.30-11.30pm Sat, Sun. **Main courses** £3.50-£6.90. **Credit** MC, V.

The cool and airy Viet Hoa packs in the punters by offering a multitude of exotic taste sensations with minimal fuss. Going in a group meant we were able to sample a wide range of starters, from melt-in-the-mouth deep-fried aubergine to smoky and aromatic grilled beef wrapped in betel leaves. The delicate glass noodles, coriander and tofu of the summer rolls were offset by a rich peanut sauce. Tilapia with green mango was a delight – the fish succulent beneath its hard skin, and the sweet chilli sauce conjuring up the tropics. However, we missed the usual bundles of lettuce, mint and coriander in which to wrap our spring rolls. An enjoyable bargain, but there are signs of a few corners being cut.

Wapping Food

Wapping Hydraulic Power Station, Wapping Wall, E1W 3ST (7680 2080). Wapping tube/Shadwell DLR. Bar **Open** noon-11pm Mon-Sat; noon-6pm Sun. **Main courses** £4.50-£7.50. *Restaurant* **Brunch served** 10am-12.30pm Sat, Sun. **Lunch served** noon-3pm daily. **Dinner served** 6.30-11pm Mon-Fri; 7-11pm Sat. **Main courses** £11-£19. **Credit** AmEx, DC, MC, V.

For an inner city restaurant, the setting really can't be bettered: Wapping Food is housed in what was a hydraulic pumping station, and surrounded by a gallery space. Diners are dwarfed by the dimensions, but the friendliness of the staff means there's no chance of urban alienation. The daily-changing menu is a mix of easy-going (selection of Spanish charcuterie, caper berries and olives or buffalo mozzarella, roast peppers, mixed leaves and pine nuts) and slightly more involved modern European cooking (organic leg of lamb with warm salad of artichoke, beet leaves and Agen prunes). Not everything worked on our most recent visit. A couple of dishes – seared scallops with piquillo peppers, morcilla and preserved lemon beurre blanc, and mushroom duxelle tartlet, sautéed morels and golden beetroot with baked garlic – just didn't hang together, although the individual ingredients were nice enough. Better was an assembly of smoked finnan brandade with crostini, baby capers, shallots and parsley. Still, as long as the food is at least this good (and it's frequently better), this is a must-visit destination – there's nowhere else like it in London.

Also in the area

Carluccio's Caffe Nash Court, E14 5AG (020 7719 1749); **Gaucho Grill** 29 Westferry Circus, Canary Riverside, E14 8RR (020 7987 9494); **Wagamama** Jubilee Place, Canry Wharf, E14 5NY (0207 516 9009).

North

Aviv

87-89 High Street, Edgware, Middx, HA8 7DB (020 8952 2484/www.avivrestaurant.com). Edgware tube. Lunch served noon-2.30pm Mon-Thur, Sun. **Dinner served** *Winter* 5.30-11pm Mon-Thur, Sat, Sun. *Summer* 5.30-11pm Mon-Thur, Sun. **Main courses** £9.95-£13.95. **Set lunch** (noon-2.30pm Mon-Thur) £8.95 2 courses. **Set meals** £14.95-£18.95 3 courses. **Credit** AmEx, MC, V.

In recent years both the bright airy space and the menu have expanded at Aviv. Keen to try newer offerings, we strayed from the Israeli specialities but found them disappointing (barbecued spare ribs were stewed and the roast fillet of duck was masked by an over-sweet honey sauce). Stick with starters of chopped liver, houmous and falafel. A char-grilled rib steak was faultless – rare and tender, with excellent chips. A decent glass of house red came from a wide selection of Israeli and French wines. Desserts include non-dairy tiramisu, cinnamony apple crumble and a sticky toffee pudding. Service is welcoming and careful. Aviv is great value and, if you stick to the less exotic dishes, worth the trip.

Café Japan

626 Finchley Road, NW11 7RR (8455 6854). Golders Green tube/13, 82 bus. **Lunch served** noon-2pm Sat, Sun. **Dinner served** 6-10pm Wed-Sat; 6-9.30pm Sun. **Main courses** £12-£16.50. **Set lunch** £8.20 bento box, soup. **Set dinner** £12-£17 bento box, soup. **Credit** MC, V.

Despite two changes of ownership since the mid 1990s, Café Japan continues to succeed by focusing on the raw end of the Japanese spectrum. A few years ago, chef-owner Koichi Konnai and his wife Kazuko decided to cut out the cooking (well, most of it) and concentrate on sushi and sashimi. The excellent cuts of fish are ultra-fresh and generously proportioned: stupendously in the case of the lunchtime chirashi sushi, which required a separate platter to bear its 'topping' of fatty tuna, salmon, sea urchin, salmon roe, cooked prawn, squid, octopus, marinated mackerel, bream, sea bass, clam, yellowtail and raw prawn. Keen to keep prices down, the Konnais accept cash only at lunchtime. Dinner costs a little more, but has the advantage of a specials list that offers interesting diversions.

Giraffe ★

29-31 Essex Road, N1 2SA (7359 5999/ www.giraffe.net). Angel tube/38, 56, 73, 341 bus. **Meals served** 7.30am-10.45pm Mon-Fri; 8am-10.45pm Sat; 9am-10.30pm Sun. **Main courses** £7-£10. **Set meal** (5-7pm Mon-Fri) £6.95 2 courses; (7-11pm Mon-Fri) £9.95 2 courses. **Credit** AmEx, DC, MC, V.

The Giraffe chain has struck a chord with London diners. At many branches, queueing for tables is near inevitable at weekends (when no bookings are taken), but staff work well to make the wait as painless as possible. The Giraffes cleverly maintain an appealing balance: a covering-all-bases food range and chirpily attentive service make them family-friendly, but they're not so kid-oriented that they can't also be comfortable for adults. The global-eclectic menu, plus daily specials, offers plenty to choose from: pancakes, salads, dips, burgers, plenty of veggie choices, burritos, steaks and Asian-oriented dishes like Thai chicken or miso and lime-grilled salmon, followed by crowd-pleaser puddings (cheesecakes, brownies, ice-cream combos). There's a varied drinks list too, from smoothies through teas or coffees to cocktails and decent wines.

Heartstone

106 Parkway, NW1 7AN (020 7485 7744). Camden Town tube. **Breakfast served** 8.30am-noon Tue-Fri. **Meals served** noon-9pm Tue; 8.30am-9pm Sat; 10am-4pm Sun. **Main courses** £9.50-£15. **Credit** MC, V.

This is a mellow spot, bright, calm and decorated in whites and mauves, where organic food is presented with a modern sense of style. It's as female as dark wood steak houses are male: trendy ladies lunch here, sometimes making it look like a wholefood Harvey Nichols, but the feel is relaxed rather than brittle. The menu is mainly vegetarian – with generous sandwiches as well as starters and mains – but there are always some meaty options such as house burgers. This kind of wholefood cooking is dependent on fresh ingredients, and Heartstone doesn't disappoint. Falafels were just about the best we've ever had, crisp and delicately minty, served with freshly made houmous. Drinks are invigorating fresh smoothies and hyper-imaginative juice combos, plus organic wines and beers.

The Highgate

79 Highgate Road, NW5 1TL (020 7485 8442). Tufnell Park tube/Kentish Town tube/rail. **Lunch served** 12.30-3pm Mon-Sat; 12.30-4pm Sun. **Dinner served** 6.30-10.30pm Mon-Sat; 6.30-9.30pm Sun. **Main courses** £9.50-£15. **Credit** MC, V.

Beware first impressions. Filling the ground floor of a modernish office block, the Highgate looks like a fitness centre. Closer up, the vast open-plan space with busy bar counter just inside the door and then acres of vacant tables reminded us of a Marbella hotel lobby. The cut-glass chandeliers that hang from the industrial claret-painted I-beam are a half-hearted stab at warmth and character. But forget all that and eat. The food is good. Inventive too. Chicken liver parfait came with a slithery, rubbery chutney of runner beans (sounds odd, tasted great), while another starter had a poached egg wreathed by baby leeks vinaigrette (looked great, tasted odd). Presentation peaked with a glacier of baked cod on a pebble beach of white beans and cockles, while top of the flavour charts was a crispy carapace of pork belly simmered in cider. Staff are cheerful, plus, how many London restaurants boast a view of a kneeling camel – albeit fibreglass and belonging to an oriental carpet shop across the road?

Morgan M. *See p69.*

The House

63-69 Canonbury Road, N1 2DG (020 7704 7410/ www.inthehouse.biz). Highbury & Islington tube/rail. **Open** 5-11pm Mon; noon-11pm Tue-Sat; noon-10.30pm Sun. **Meals served** 6-10.30pm Mon; noon-2.30pm, 6-10.30pm Tue-Fri; noon-2.30pm, 6.30-10.30pm Sat, Sun. **Main courses** £12.95-£45. **Credit** MC, V.

The House won *Time Out*'s Best Gastropub Award in 2003. A year later and it's doing its best to maintain high standards, largely successfully. It's got a lot going for it, not least chic decor and a lively atmosphere – a mix of groups and couples. Service doesn't always hit the spot, though. Deep-fried lemon sole in chilli ciabatta breadcrumbs was much lighter than it sounded; the fish moist on the inside but crunchy on the outside. Chips were fat, hot and salty – perfect. Corn-fed chicken vinaigrette with mashed potatoes, baby leeks and chillied hazelnuts also hit the spot, the meat juicy, the mash creamy. What's more, the wine list is interesting.

Iznik

19 Highbury Park, N5 1QJ (020 7354 5697). Highbury & Islington tube/rail/4, 19, 236 bus. **Meals served** 10am-4pm Mon-Fri. **Dinner served** 6.30pm-midnight daily. **Main courses** £7.50-£9.50. **Credit** MC, V.

Iznik has barely changed in the past few years, and there are no complaints about that. For starters mücver (grated courgette and feta cheese mixed and fried) had a beautiful texture, and came with fresh kisir. Dolma were crisp and piquant, flavoured with dill. For mains, tavuk begendi (chicken in aubergine sauce) was ideal served with good basmati rice and with a gloriously smoky flavour. Kuzu firinda (oven-cooked lamb) was mouth-wateringly tender. Mains are accompanied by a beautiful salad, with sweet pepper seeds, small sharp-tasting peppers and olives. Strongly recommended.

Mangal Oçakbası ★

10 Arcola Street, E8 2DJ (020 7275 8981/ www.mangal1.com). Dalston Kingsland rail/76, 149, 243 bus. **Meals served** noon-midnight daily. **Main courses** £6.50-£11.50. **No credit cards**.

Despite ever-growing competition in the area, the original Mangal continues to shine. People who want restaurant trappings (like menus) go to Mangal II (4 Stoke Newington Road, 020 7254 7888) round the corner. People who want a great grill come down a dark side street to Mangal. Once through the tiny entrance and past the raw kebabs there is a plain, clean, grey-tiled café. It's worth asking for dishes that aren't on display (such as stew or lahmacun). Start with houmous and cacik, big portions served on a side plate. Bread is good and plentiful, though not warmed. Pirzola (lamb chops) came with no rice, but a big fresh salad. Staff are happy to help with choices. No longer as ridiculously cheap as it once was, but still something of a bargain.

Mango Room

10 Kentish Town Road, NW1 8NH (020 7482 5065/ www.mangoroom.co.uk). Camden Town tube. **Lunch served** noon-3pm Tue-Sat. **Dinner served** 6pm-midnight Mon-Sat. **Meals served** noon-11pm Sun. **Main courses** £9.50-£12.50. **Credit** MC, V.

A visit to Camden's Mango Room is always something of a treat. Split into two rooms with natural features – raw brickwork, comfortably worn

wooden floors, skylights and large abstract pictures, it has a menu that fuses the Caribbean with international influences. Dishes like ackee and avocado or curried goat sit nicely with lamb steak, or mussels in coconut sauce. Try tender kingfish with mango sauce, rice and peas and fried plantain. Specials on our visit were all fish dishes, including grilled snapper, whole sea bass and king prawns with basmati rice. We topped off our visit with an exquisite warm sticky toffee pudding and cream, and beautifully sculpted fresh mango.

Morgan M

489 Liverpool Road, N7 8NS (020 7609 3560). Highbury & Islington tube/rail. **Lunch served** noon-2.30pm Wed-Fri, Sun. **Dinner served** 7-10pm Tue-Sat. **Set lunch** £19.50 2 courses, £23.50 3 courses. **Set dinner** £30 3 courses. **Credit** MC, V.

At the more unfashionable end of Liverpool Road, Morgan M is a new French restaurant run by chef Morgan Meunier. His previous position at the Admiralty (*see p38*) gives a fair idea of the quality that's on offer here. Dishes such as fillet of sea bass steamed with pastis, razor clams, asparagus and grilled fennel, served with saffron cream or light vanilla rice pudding with orange tuile, leave you stimulated, impressed and yet not over-full. Wine list and service are superb. Booking is essential, as the room isn't large. A word of warning – the chef always does a tour of the restaurant at the end of the evening, so be ready with your thoughts on the meal.

The Parsee

34 Highgate Hill, N19 5NL (020 7272 9091). Archway tube. **Lunch served** noon-3pm Mon-Fri. **Dinner served** 6-10.45pm Mon-Sat. **Main courses** £9.95-£12.95. **Set lunch** £4.99-£6.99 3 dishes. **Set dinner** £15-£30 3 courses. **Credit** AmEx, MC, V.

This elegant neighbourhood local serves authentic Parsee dishes in a cosy, yet contemporary setting, decked out with wooden flooring and tables, and pictures of notables from the Parsee community across walls. Cooking is influenced by mild fruity flavours of an Iranian heritage, tastefully embellished with Indian spices. Parsees love eggs so try masala no poro, a dressed-up omelette, cooked with meltingly soft sliced potatoes, toasted cumin and chillies. The real star of our vist was a sublime main course of jardaloo ma murghi (chicken curry with apricots). A classic wedding dish, this was a gorgeous marriage of rich, dried apricots and sweetly scented cinnamon, expertly combined with tender hunks of chicken and a dried red chilli masala. We especially liked the crunch of its sali topping (crisp-fried straw potatoes).

Rasa

55 Stoke Newington Church Street, N16 0AR (7249 0344/www.rasarestaurants.com). Stoke Newington rail/73, 243, 426 bus. **Lunch served** noon-3pm Sat, Sun. **Dinner served** 6-10.45pm Mon-Thur, Sun; 6-11.30pm Fri, Sat. **Main courses** £3.65-£6.85. **Set meal** £15.50 4 courses. **Credit** AmEx, DC, MC, V.

Despite gaining several siblings, the original Rasa hasn't changed: the walls are still scarily pink; the idol of blue-skinned Krishna and a spicy incense aroma still greet at the entrance, and the gentle south Indian hospitality is the same as always. Perhaps the only clues that Rasa has moved on in the world is a picture of the owner Das Sreedharan with Jamie Oliver, and a cosy new (marginally less pink) extension. All the Keralan classics are present and correct: black eye bean thoran piled with wisps of freshly grated coconut; vegetable curry redolent of cinnamon and cardamom; mango and plantain curry spiked with shredded fresh ginger, and a perfectly cooked layered paratha were the highlights on our visit. The only off-note was a tray of fried, crunchy snacks that seemed less than fresh, and slightly greasy aubergine fritters that tasted of stale cooking oil. Otherwise, we were delighted to find this iconic restaurant still in glorious form.

S&M Café ★

4-6 Essex Road, N1 8LN (020 7359 5361). Angel tube. **Breakfast served** 8am-noon Mon-Fri; 9am-noon Sat, Sun. **Meals served** noon-11pm daily. **Main courses** £5.95-£6.95. **Credit** DC, MC, V.

S for sausage and M for mash, to ward off any gross misunderstandings. This is about comfort eating; a pick 'n' mix of pick-me-up food. Select your S (from a choice including veterans like the Cumberland and gourmet fancies such as wild boar), throw in some M (we recommend the creamy, perfect traditional mash) and finish with one of three gravies. The result is served Beano-style, with sausages poking cutely out of a generous mash mountain. Alternative options include mash-accompanied pies and casseroles plus a few salads and an all-day breakfast. The original 1950s shopfront (this was once legendary Islington café Alfredo's) and interior adds to the experience. Food that invites a smile.

Sariyer Balik ★

56 Green Lanes, N16 9NH (020 7275 7681). Manor House tube then 141, 341 bus. **Meals served** 5pm-1am daily. **Main courses** £6.50-£10. **No credit cards.**

This outstanding Turkish fish restaurant is a little off the beaten track, but finding it repays the effort. The interior is tiny. It is painted black, with fishing nets suspended from the ceiling; hanging from these are a variety of stuffed fish and oddments. The starter of mussels, marinated in beer and deep-fried is full of flavour. These are served with toasted chunks from a loaf of bread rather than the more common pide, but that's not a complaint. For mains, pan-fried anchovies are a revelation. Bream was also excellent, though not our first choice – both mackerel and mullet were off. The small menu varies depending on what they can get fresh. Mains were accompanied by a large shredded salad, lightly dressed with a sour tang from a particularly tasty vinegar. A fish-shaped plate of nuts was brought as we sat digesting. Nothing was over-fancy or pretentious, and the food was perfect.

The best Gastropubs

Anchor & Hope
See p51.
Duck's heart risotto in Waterloo? No wonder this place has become SE1's most popular.

Anglesea Arms
35 Wingate Road, W6 0UR (020 8749 1291).
This busy, well-heeled Brackenbury Village stalwart is the perfect 'local'.

Approach Tavern
47 Approach Road, E2 9LY (020 8980 2321).
Decent ales and food by royal appointment – Nigella was spotted in here apparently.

Cat & Mutton
76 Broadway Market, E8 4QJ (020 7254 5599).
Handsome Hackney renovation with exposed brickwork and skilled cooking.

Coach & Horses
See p43.
Prime ales, good service and brilliant food lift the Coach way above the norm.

Cow
See p54.
Great seafood and Guinness at this classic.

Crown
233 Grove Road, E3 5SN (020 8981 9998).
Everything on the menu is organic at this good-looking eastern outpost.

Eagle
See p43.
The original? A Farringdon institution.

Earl Spencer
260-262 Merton Road, SW18 5JL (020 8870 9244).
Great grub, a lengthy drinks list and charming service.

Easton
22 Easton Street, WC1X 0DS (020 7278 7608).
From strip joint to stripped down, the Easton is now all bare boards and chalked menus.

Fox & Hounds
66 Latchmere Road, SW11 2JU (020 7924 5483).
Italian-influenced oasis of good looks and great food in an otherwise bleak patch of South London.

Hartley
See p51.
Revamped and renamed after a former jam factory nearby, the food is the star here.

Havelock Tavern
57 Masbro Road, W14 0LS (020 7603 5374).
This beautifully balanced boozer is the daddy of the Shepherd's Bush gastro scene. A flawless local.

House
See p67.
As far from a boozer as a pub can get, this is Islington's finest spot for 'pub' grub.

Junction Tavern
101 Fortress Road, NW5 1AG (020 7485 9400).
Tufnell Park trendification continues apace with this gastro overhaul towards aubergine and open-plan.

Lansdowne
90 Gloucester Avenue, NW1 8HX (020 7483 0409).
Haunt of Primrose Hill's privileged with great food and great atmosphere.

Lots Road Pub & Dining Room
See p48.
A beacon for brilliant food. Hard to get to, worth the effort.

Masons Arms
169 Battersea Park Road, SW8 4BT (020 7622 2007).
Sample the famous fish cakes at this long-running, chilled-out gastropub.

Paradise by Way of Kensal Green
19 Kilburn Lane, W10 4AE (020 8969 0098).
Mismatched furniture, Gothic looks and exotic snacks add up to a healthy portion of W10 cool.

Salusbury
50-52 Salusbury Road, NW6 6NN (020 7328 3286).
Popular Queens Park boozer with a vast wine list and ambitious food.

Wells
30 Well Walk, NW3 1BX (020 7794 3785).
Former geezers' boozer that dropped the 'Tavern' from its name and joined Hampstead's posh set.

Singapore Garden ★

83A Fairfax Road, NW6 4DY (020 7624 8233). Swiss Cottage tube. **Lunch served** noon-2.45pm daily. **Dinner served** 6-10.45pm Mon-Thur, Sun; 6-11.15pm Fri, Sat. **Main courses** £6-£15. **Minimum** £10. **Set lunch** (Mon-Fri) £7.50 2 courses. **Set meal** £20-£32.50 per person (minimum 2) 3 courses. **Credit** AmEx, DC, MC, V.

On a Friday evening this veteran high-class Swiss Cottage restaurant was positively humming with a cosmopolitan crowd. Diners ranged from affluent Chinese businessmen to large family groups. The menu is predominantly Chinese, but also offers several Singaporean classics rarely found in London. Tender chicken satay with a flavourful peanut sauce made a promising start. We continued with ho jien (a rich omelette generously studded with oysters – a Singapore hawker-stall favourite), authentically spiced Malaysian chicken curry in a fine-tasting coconut-milk gravy, and tauhu goreng (fried beancurd topped with beansprouts tossed in a salty-sweet nutty dressing), all washed down with Tiger beer and chendol. Polite, efficient service, combined with excellent cooking.

Sushi-Say

33B Walm Lane, NW2 5SH (020 8459 2971). Willesden Green tube. **Lunch served** 1-3.30pm Sat, Sun. **Dinner served** 6.30-10.30pm Tue-Fri; 6-11pm Sat; 6-10pm Sun. **Main courses** £6.10-£18.90. **Set dinner** £18.20-£28.60 incl miso soup, rice & pickles, dessert. **Credit** AmEx, JCB, MC, V.

Long and as low-ceilinged as a Nissen hut, with wasabi green walls, Sushi-Say might be an odd-looking fish, neither straight Japanese nor London fashionable, but it's also one of the most interesting Japanese restaurants in London. This is a good place for basics: a miso soup of balanced stock and quality tofu; edamame that reach the table al dente and piping hot (never trust a Japanese restaurant where they're served cold – if the edamame are prepared ahead of time, chances are other dishes will be too). Service is charming, the menu isn't overstretched and although the specials are reliable. Buri daikon (yellowtail and white radish in stock), for instance, was pure comfort food, the components simmered into sweet softness: a good example of the versatility of daikon. Also noteworthy is the single tatami seating area at the rear of the restaurant, available for bookings of four or more.

Viet Garden ★

207 Liverpool Road, N1 1LX (020 7700 6040). Angel tube. **Lunch served** noon-3.30pm Mon-Sat; noon-3.30pm Sun. **Dinner served** 5.30-11pm Mon-Thur, Sun; 5.30-11.30pm Fri, Sat. **Main courses** £4.50-£6.90. **Set lunch** (Mon-Fri) £5.50 2 courses. **Credit** AmEx, MC, V.

The cooking here doesn't match up to Sông Quê (*see p64*), these days the gold standard for London's Vietnamese food, but it's still good. Golden pancake was lacking in crispness and served with a slightly mean pile of lettuce leaves and herbs, and the onion in the pork and prawn filling was almost raw. After these disappointing starters, however, beef wrapped in betel leaves was juicy and seductive with a dark, caramelised taste; and spicy bun hue soup with snaking rice noodles and juicy prawns, served with the usual scattering of beansprouts and purple basil and a wedge of lemon, was enjoyable. The highlight was a delicious, mellow pork stew with fried hard-boiled duck eggs, served with a plate of clean, crisp beanspouts and fresh red chilli. Viet Garden is a simple place, with pale walls and basic tiled floors. Staff are delightfully friendly.

Wagamama ★

11 Jamestown Road, NW1 7BW (020 7428 0800/ www.wagamama.com). Camden Town tube. **Meals served** noon-11pm Mon-Sat; noon-10pm Sun. **Main courses** £5.60-£8.50. **Credit** AmEx, MC, V.

Everyone's a bit blasé about noodle bars but it pays to remember that Wagamama is one of the originals, and definitely the best. Gleaming, smoke-free cleanliness, perky staff and a wholesome menu make it perfect for groups, especially families. This branch is light and spacious, and as noisy as all the others, so stroppy toddlers' yells go unnoticed by fellow diners sharing the canteen tables. Children can choose between chicken katsu (breast of chicken fried in breadcrumbs) with dipping sauce, rice and shredded cucumber, or vegetarian or chicken noodle dishes for just £3.50. One of the most popular noodle dishes on the main menu is the savoury yaki soba, with its fiery ginger and garlic alongside crisp fried vegetables, chicken, and shrimps. Other meat and vegetarian ramen dishes come in an ocean of stock with ladles. The lip-smacking pickles and miso soup accompanying other dishes, such as the rice cha han (the rice is a bit dry but its prawns and chicken juicy enough) can be ordered separately for just £1.30, and the green tea is free, so healthy options are the cheapest ones. Conversely, a small coke is £1.80 – Wagamama gets its priorities right.

Also in the area

Carluccio's Caffé 305-307 Upper Street, N1 2TU (020 7359 8167); **Carluccio's Caffé** Fenwick, Brent Cross Shopping Centre, NW4 3FN (020 8203 6844); **Gaucho Grill** 64 Heath Street, NW3 1DN (020 7431 8222); **Giraffe** 46 Rosslyn Hill, NW3 1NH (020 7435 0343); **Gourmet Burger Kitchen** 331 West End Lane, NW6 1RS (020 7794 5455); **Living Room** Suncourt House, 18-26 Essex Road, N1 8LN (0870 442 2712); **Loch Fyne** 2 Park Road, N8 8TD (020 8342 7740); **Loch Fyne** 74-77 Chalk Farm Road, NW1 8AN (020 7428 5680); **Masala Zone** 80 Upper Street, N1 0NP (020 7359 3399); **Prezzo** 161 Euston Road, NW1 2BD (020 7387 5587); **Prezzo** Parkfield Street, N1 0PS (020 7359 8804); **Royal China** 68 Queen's Grove, NW8 6ER (020 7586 4280); **Strada** 105-106 Upper Street, N1 1QN (020 7226 9742); **Strada** 4 South Grove, N6 6BS (020 8347 8686); **Wagamama** N1 Centre, Parkfield, N1 OPS (020 7226 2664); **Wagamama** Brent Cross Shopping Centre, NW4 3FP (020 8202 2666).

South East

South East

NORTHAMPTON-SHIRE
BEDFORDSHIRE
GLOUCESTER-SHIRE
BUCKINGHAM-SHIRE
OXFORDSHIRE
HERT-
BERKSHIRE
WILTSHIRE
SURREY
HAMPSHIRE
WEST SUSSEX
DORSET
ISLE OF WIGHT
Bedford
Kempston
Sandy
Biggleswade
Newport Pagnell
Shipston on Stour
Banbury
Brackley
Stony Stratford
Milton Keynes
Ampthill
Buckingham
Bletchley
Hitchin
Chipping Norton
Bicester
LUTON
Dunstable
Woodstock
Harpenden
Aylesbury
Witney
Tring
Hemel Hempstead
Berkhamsted
Thame
OXFORD
St Albans
Fairford
Chesham
Amersham
Borehamwood
Abingdon
Watford
Chorleywood
Bushey
High Wycombe
Beaconsfield
Didcot
Wallingford
Wantage
Gerrards Cross
Marlow
Harrow
SWINDON
Henley-on-Thames
Uxbridge
Maidenhead
Madhu's New Asian Tandoori
Slough
Reading
Monsieur Max
Egham
Staines
Bracknell
Asada
Marlborough
Virginia Water
Wokingham
Newbury
Chertsey
The French Table & Lee Fook
Windlesham
Bagshot
Chobham
Weybridge
Esher
Tadley
Yateley
Lightwater
Kingsclere
Camberley
Woking
Frimley
Ripley
Leatherhead
Fleet
Farnborough
Basingstoke
Old Basing
Odiham
Aldershot
Ash
Guildford
Overton
Dorking
Whitchurch
Andover
Farnham
Shalford
Gomshall
North Holmwood
Elstead
Godalming
Abinger Common
Milford
Ockley
Sutton Scotney
Alton
Hindhead
Witley
Cranleigh
Stockbridge
Bordon
Grayshott
Chiddingfold
Headley
Wilton
Kings Worthy
Haslemere
New Alresford
Camelsdale
Horsham
Salisbury
Winchester
Liphook
Twyford
Henley
Billingshurst
Petersfield
Romsey
Eastleigh
Midhurst
Petworth
Pulborough
Bishop's Waltham
Henfield
Fordingbridge
SOUTHAMPTON
Chilgrove
Charlton
Amberley
Storrington
Stoney Cross
Wickham
Horndean
Steyning
Hamble
Lyndhurst
Hythe
Titchfield
Havant
Burpham
Ringwood
Portchester
Arundel
North Lancing
Fareham
Cosham
Chichester
Angmering
Beaulieu
Emsworth
Stubbington
Middleton-on-Sea
Worthing
Brockenhurst
Fawley
Gosport
PORTSMOUTH
Littlehampton
Bransgore
Lee-on-the-Solent
Aldwick
Sway
South Hayling
East End
Southsea
Bognor Regis
Cowes
East Cowes
Poole
Christchurch
Lymington
Ryde
East Wittering
Selsey
Shalfleet
Seaview
BOURNEMOUTH
Milford on Sea
Newport
Selsey Bill
St Helens
Yarmouth
Bembridge
The Needles
Freshwater
Sandown
Shanklin
Swanage
Ventnor
St Catherine's Point

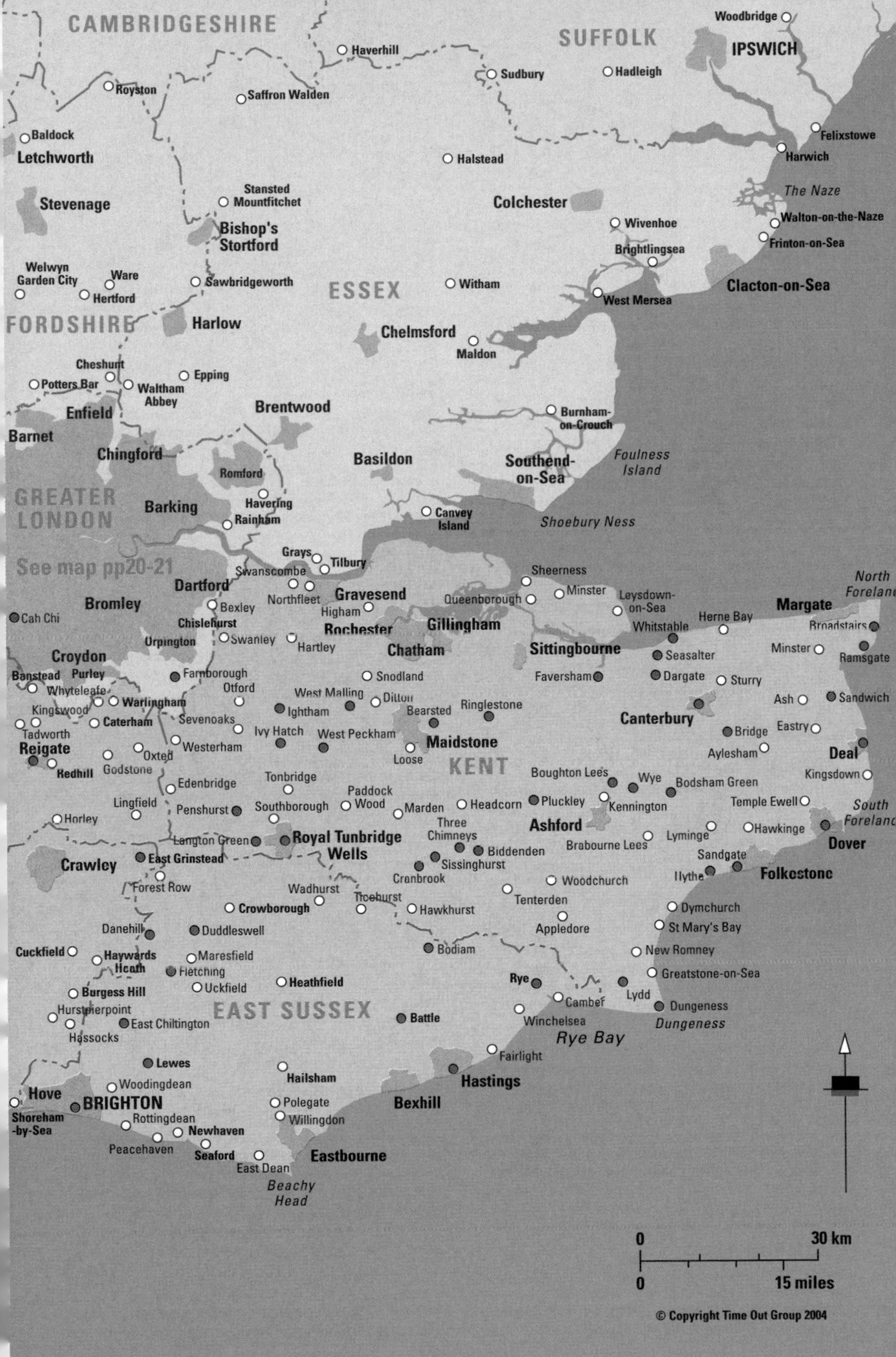

CAMBRIDGESHIRE
SUFFOLK
Woodbridge
IPSWICH
Haverhill
Sudbury
Hadleigh
Royston
Saffron Walden
Felixstowe
Baldock
Letchworth
Harwich
Halstead
The Naze
Stansted Mountfitchet
Stevenage
Colchester
Walton-on-the-Naze
Bishop's Stortford
Wivenhoe
Frinton-on-Sea
Brightlingsea
Welwyn Garden City
Ware
Hertford
Sawbridgeworth
ESSEX
Witham
Clacton-on-Sea
West Mersea
FORDSHIRE
Harlow
Chelmsford
Maldon
Cheshunt
Potters Bar
Epping
Waltham Abbey
Enfield
Brentwood
Burnham-on-Crouch
Barnet
Chingford
Basildon
Southend-on-Sea
Foulness Island
Romford
GREATER LONDON
Havering
Barking
Rainham
Canvey Island
Shoebury Ness
Grays
Tilbury
See map pp20-21
Swanscombe
Sheerness
North Foreland
Dartford
Northfleet
Gravesend
Minster
Bromley
Bexley
Queenborough
Leysdown-on-Sea
Margate
Higham
Cah Chi
Chislehurst
Rochester
Gillingham
Whitstable
Herne Bay
Broadstairs
Orpington
Swanley
Hartley
Chatham
Sittingbourne
Minster
Croydon
Seasalter
Ramsgate
Purley
Farnborough
Banstead
Snodland
Faversham
Dargate
Sturry
Whyteleafe
Otford
Kingswood
Warlingham
West Malling
Ditton
Ringlestone
Ash
Sandwich
Ightham
Bearsted
Tadworth
Caterham
Sevenoaks
Canterbury
Ivy Hatch
West Peckham
Eastry
Reigate
Westerham
Bridge
Oxted
Maidstone
Godstone
Loose
Aylesham
Deal
Redhill
KENT
Tonbridge
Boughton Lees
Kingsdown
Edenbridge
Wye
Bodsham Green
Paddock Wood
Lingfield
Southborough
Penshurst
Marden
Headcorn
Pluckley
Kennington
Temple Ewell
South Foreland
Horley
Three Chimneys
Ashford
Lyminge
Hawkinge
Langton Green
Royal Tunbridge Wells
Dover
Brabourne Lees
Biddenden
Sandgate
Crawley
East Grinstead
Sissinghurst
Folkestone
Cranbrook
Hythe
Woodchurch
Forest Row
Wadhurst
Tenterden
Ticehurst
Crowborough
Hawkhurst
Dymchurch
Appledore
St Mary's Bay
Danehill
Duddleswell
Bodiam
New Romney
Cuckfield
Haywards Heath
Maresfield
Fletching
Greatstone-on-Sea
Rye
Heathfield
Uckfield
Lydd
Burgess Hill
Camber
Dungeness
EAST SUSSEX
Hurstpierpoint
Winchelsea
Dungeness
East Chiltington
Battle
Hassocks
Rye Bay
Fairlight
Lewes
Hailsham
Hastings
Woodingdean
Hove
BRIGHTON
Polegate
Bexhill
Shoreham-by-Sea
Rottingdean
Willingdon
Newhaven
Peacehaven
Seaford
Eastbourne
East Dean
Beachy Head
0
30 km
0
15 miles
© Copyright Time Out Group 2004

Hampshire

BISHOP'S WALTHAM

Wine Bar & Bistro

6-8 High Street, Bishop's Waltham, SO32 1AA (01489 894476/www.thewinebarandbistro.co.uk). **Food served** noon-10pm Mon-Sat; noon-9.30pm Sun. **Main courses** £8.95-£16.95. **Set meals** (Sun) £8.95 1 course, £11.95 2 courses, £14.95 3 courses. **Credit** AmEx, DC, MC, V.

This converted red brick cellar is an ideal location for a wine bar. The two rooms that comprise this popular establishment are attractively decorated, nicely lit, and well supplied with air-conditioning and smoke extractors. An extensive wine list complements an imaginative menu that might, for lunch, offer Mexican crab cakes with sour cream and salsa, or toasted goat's cheese crostini with peach and rocket salad, followed by pork and leek sausages with chive mash and onion gravy, or pan-fried ribeye steak with garlic butter, hand-cut chips and rocket salad. Lighter bites such as omelettes and wraps are also available. Dinner is a more extensive version of the lunchtime carte, and identically priced.

BROCKENHURST

Simply Poussin

The Courtyard, Brookley Road, Brockenhurst, SO42 7RB (01590 623063/www.lepoussin.co.uk). **Lunch served** noon-2pm, **dinner served** 7-9pm Tue-Sat. **Main courses** £12.50-£14.50. **Set meals** (Tue-Fri, lunch Sat) £10 2 courses, £15 3 courses. **Credit** AmEx, MC, V.

Down an alleyway and hidden behind a parade of shops, Simply Poussin exudes an air of contented calm that more conventionally situated places must envy. A slate-floored conservatory leads into the restaurant itself where square beechwood tables set with shining glasses hint at treats to come. The set meals offer extremely good value since the standard of the food can be sublime and some of the dishes are taken from the à la carte menu. Pot-roast New Forest pork had been brined in beer and slow-roasted with honey and cloves, while a tomato tatin topped with fillet of red bream was based on buttery puff pastry. Passion fruit soufflé was truly memorable. A comprehensive wine list is reasonably priced.

EAST END

East End Arms

Main Road, East End, SO41 5SY (01590 626223/ www.eastendarms.co.uk). **Lunch served** noon-2pm Tue-Sun. **Dinner served** 7-9pm Tue-Sat. **Main courses** £12. **Credit** MC, V.

Booking is advisable to ensure a table at this very rural, totally unpretentious pub on the edge of the New Forest. The small garden is a popular summer retreat, while for cooler times the interior has a log fire and walls crowded with attractive framed prints. Fish is a speciality and is filleted and boneless, unless requested otherwise. Usefully, the menu is price banded, so for a fiver the choice is between baked camembert in smoked salmon; asparagus with parsley butter; pan-fried scallops; crab terrine; or warm potato and elver salad. For £12 you'll find baked cod with dill and crème fraîche; baby pork olives with sautéed rainbow chard; grilled hake with mussel sauce; and grilled salmon vinaigrette. There's a good mix of decently priced wines too.

EMSWORTH

Fat Olives

30 South Street, Emsworth, PO10 7EH (01243 377914/www.fatolives.co.uk). **Lunch served** noon-2pm, **dinner served** 7-10pm Tue-Sat. **Main courses** £11.95-£15.25. **Set lunch** £14 2 courses, £16.50 3 courses. **Credit** MC, V.

A brasserie-style restaurant created from 17th-century fishermen's cottages, and just a stone's throw from the quay. Run by husband-and-wife team Lawrence and Julia Murphy, it has a clean, simple design with plain wood tables and white walls. The food too, is uncomplicated but modern fare. Though short, the menu has plenty of variety, starters including warm potato pancake with smoked salmon and crème fraîche, Jerusalem artichoke soup, and duck confit sausage salad with honey and orange dressing. Among the mains there could be veal loin with creamed braised kohlrabi and madeira jus, or lemon sole with mussels and a cider and tarragon sauce. Lovely puds might be caramelised banana cheesecake or baked chocolate mousse with hazelnut ice-cream.

36 on the Quay ★

47 South Street, Emsworth, PO10 7EG (01243 375592/www.36onthequay.co.uk). **Lunch served** noon-2pm Tue-Fri. **Dinner served** 7-10pm Mon-Sat. **Set lunch** £17.95 2 courses, £22.95 3 courses. **Set dinner** £42 3 courses, £55 10 course tasting menu. **Credit** AmEx, DC, MC, V.

Housed in a building dating from the 17th century, 36 on the Quay stands right on the quayside overlooking Emsworth harbour. It's a true south coast gem. Chef Ramon Farthing and wife Karen moved here in 1996 and brought with them a reputation for outstanding and memorable modern

East End Arms. *See p76.*

British food. The setting is a pretty and pastel-coloured dining room with a large bay window that makes the most of the views. There's a short lunch menu of just two choices per course, as well as the carte, while for dinner there's the difficult decision of deciding between the wonderful three course carte and a sensational ten-course tasting menu that's surprisingly uncomplicated and beautifully balanced. Honey-spiced duck breast and crisp confit leg with pineapple tatin and spring onion noodles with a sherry vinegar reduction is a typical main.

LYMINGTON

Chequers Inn

Lower Woodside, Lymington, SO41 8AH (01590 673415/www.chequersinn.com). **Lunch served** noon-2.15pm Mon-Fri. **Dinner served** 6.30-9.30pm Mon-Thur; 6.30-10pm Fri. **Meals served** noon-10pm Sat; noon-9pm Sun. **Main courses** £8.25-£13.50. **Credit** MC, V.

Situated on the edge of Lymington's historic salt marshes, this picturesque 16th-century pub is a real favourite with yachtsmen. The cosy traditional interior features a mix of quarry-tiled floors and varnished floorboards, with wood-burning fires in the winter. In fine weather, however, the walled garden is great for a bite and a pint. The blackboard menu offers a choice of specials such as whole grilled plaice, a trio of fish (salmon, bass and haddock), caesar salad, and chicken and mushroom pie. Bar snacks are straightforward dishes like honey-glazed ham with double egg and chips. Try the restaurant for moules marinières and beef puddies (a sort of beef Wellington), with apple pie for afters.

MILFORD ON SEA

Westover Hall

Park Lane, Milford-on-Sea, SO41 0PT (01590 643044/www.westoverhallhotel.com). **Lunch served** noon-2pm, **dinner served** 7-8.45pm daily. **Main courses** £9.95-£16.95. **Set lunch** (Sun) £25 3 courses. **Set dinner** £35.50 3 courses. **Credit** AmEx, DC, MC, V.

The Grade II-listed Victorian mansion is a very friendly, family-run place, with a comfortable and relaxed air. Its position right on the coast means it enjoys uninterrupted views across Christchurch Bay to the Needles from both the very ornate, intimate dining room (note the fantastic ceiling), and the more informal lounge bar. Staff are warm and welcoming, and there are no restrictions on where you can eat at lunch, when anything from a sandwich upward is available. Menus are adventurous: Brixham crab mayonnaise with celery salad and gazpacho jelly, or ballotine of slow-cooked suckling pig with seared foie gras and shallot vinaigrette to begin, and oven-roasted turbot with minted peas, mashed potatoes and red wine sauce to follow. The chocolate dessert is a must.

ODIHAM

Grapevine

121 High Street, Odiham, RG29 1LA (01256 701900/www.grapevine-gourmet.com). **Lunch served** noon-2pm Mon-Fri. **Dinner served** 6-10pm Mon-Sat. **Main courses** £9.95-£15.95. **Set lunch** £9.95 2 courses. **Set dinner** (6-7pm) £14.95 3 courses incl glass of wine. **Credit** AmEx, DC, MC, V.

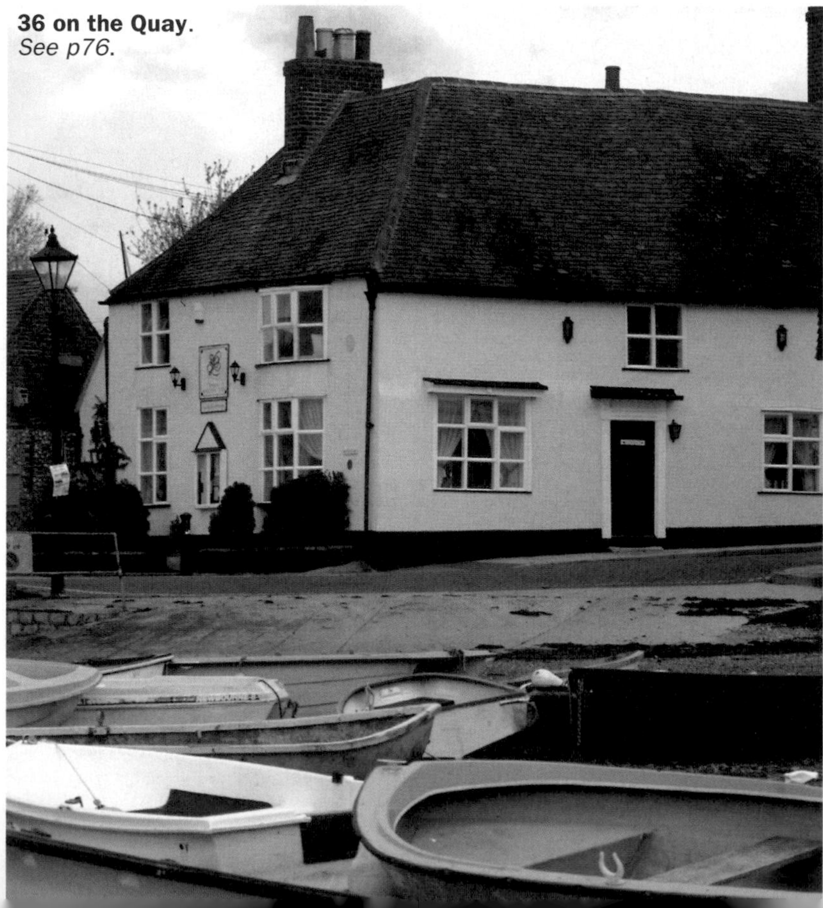

36 on the Quay. *See p76.*

Now in their tenth year, Matt and Penny Fleet run a successful bistro in a bow-windowed Georgian building and a delicatessen just down the road. The light wooden floors and print-lined colourful walls create a pleasantly cosy and intimate setting for food that's a mix of modern Italian and French cooking. There are good value fixed-price menus for lunch and early evening and some interesting vegetarian options: vegetable fritto misto with aïoli; asparagus, thyme, lemon and mascarpone risotto. A starter of caramelised onion, thyme and taleggio tart was packed with rustic flavours. To follow – succulent pot-roast leg of lamb with dauphinoise potatoes, cabbage and garlic sauce. Saffron poached pear with vanilla crème fraîche shone as a dessert.

PETERSFIELD

JSW ★

1 Heath Road, Petersfield, GU31 4JE (01730 262030). **Lunch served** noon-1.30pm, **dinner served** 7-9.30pm Tue-Sat. **Set lunch** £19.50 2 courses, £24.50 3 courses, £29.50 6 courses. **Set dinner** £29.50 2 courses, £34.50 3 courses, £39.50 6 courses. **Credit** MC, V.

Perfectly encapsulating the phrase 'small is beautiful', Jake Watkins (he of the initials JSW), has established a gastronomic haven in this picturesque market town. The dining room is minute, and while the decor may not be overly exciting, the food is truly outstanding, and is accompanied by a seriously good and extensive wine list, wonderfully strong in underappreciated, but noteworthy Alsatian vintages. The excellent value six-course tasting menu is taken from the carte, so on either menu you might enjoy such dishes as roast scallops with pea shoot salad, slow roast belly of pork and Earl Grey tea panna cotta with strawberries. This is highly sophisticated cooking, with ingredients put together with obvious care and regard to balance, resulting in dishes that are immensely enjoyable.

PORTSMOUTH

American Bar Restaurant

58 White Hart Road, Portsmouth, PO1 2JA (023 9281 1585/www.americanbar.co.uk). **Meals served** noon-10pm Mon-Thur, Sun; noon-10.30pm Fri, Sat. **Main courses** £9.25-£15.95. **Credit** AmEx, MC, V.

This converted pub has been given a bright facelift, though it retains much of its pubby character. In fine weather the patio garden and pavement tables come into their own. Inside, there's a nautically themed no-smoking dining area offering a short blackboard selection of enjoyable fish dishes, like a wonderfully sea-fresh whole plaice, and a menu that's un-American – a mix of mainly Mediterranean food including chicken liver parfait with red onion marmalade to start and confit of lamb on rosemary mash for mains. Afternoons see baguettes and tortilla wraps (all with chips) as well as Spanish omelette, moules frites and burger and chips.

Lemon Sole

123 High Street, Portsmouth, PO1 2HW (023 9281 1303/www.lemonsole.co.uk). **Lunch served** noon-2pm, **dinner served** 6-9.45pm Mon-Sat. **Main courses** £7-£22. **Set lunch** £6.95 1 courses incl coffee or tea, £9.95 2 courses, £12.95 3 courses. **Credit** AmEx, DC, MC, V.

Too few restaurants let you see the food before it's cooked and served. Here you can ogle and deliberate over precisely the variety, size, sauces and cooking method almost as soon as you arrive. The wet fish counter brims with well-presented seafood. Diners select their starters and bread from the waiter to begin, then make their way over to the fish, which is sold by weight. Sauces, vegetables and salads are ordered at the same time. John Dory was sensational, though the sauce options were a little too powerful, swamping the delicacy of the fish. There are meat and veggie options, for those so inclined. We had pleasant service here, but have had complaints concerning long waits between courses and children being made to feel unwelcome.

South East

ROMSEY

Prezzo ★

21 Palmerston Street, Romsey, SO51 8GF (01794 517353/www.prezzoplc.co.uk). **Meals served** noon-11.30pm Mon-Sat; noon-10.30pm Sun. **Main courses** £5.25-£7.95. **Credit** AmEx, DC, MC, V.

One of a chain of some 30 similar restaurants dotted around southern England. They invariably occupy buildings with some local interest – this one used to be the remarkable Mauro Bergoli's Old Manor House, before he retired. The internal decor is now more modern, and the ambience much more relaxed, though the beamed exterior remains a link with the past. The food, though retaining the Italian connection, has moved on, becoming much simpler, offering a range of pizzas, pasta, and chicken in its various guises: grilled, roasted, or baked. Food quality is on a par with the very reasonable pricing: antipasti under £4, mains under £8. As a rule, the plainer the dish, the better it tastes.

Three Tuns

58 Middlebridge Street, Romsey, SO51 8HL (01794 512639). **Lunch served** noon-2pm Mon-Sat; noon-2.30pm Sun. **Dinner served** 6.30-9pm Mon-Thur; 6.30-9.30pm Fri, Sat. **Main courses** (lunch Mon-Sat, bar menu) £5-£8; (dinner) £13-£19. **Credit** MC, V.

More of a gastropub than a boozer, though the black and white exterior reflects its 17th-century origins. Flagstone floors and dark wooden beams mean the pubby character remains, but now with a rustic-chic contemporary edge. The food is also a far cry from ploughman's. Lunch on confit of duck, foie gras and potato terrine with puy lentils, coriander and lemon vinaigrette, or delicious roast pork and apple sauce bap with chips and salad leaves. The full carte is impressively cosmopolitan with flavour-packed dishes like risotto of natural smoked cod with peas and bacon,

Isle of Wight

FRESHWATER

Red Lion

Church Place, Freshwater, PO40 9BP (01983 754925/www.redlion-wight.co.uk). **Lunch served** noon-2pm daily. **Dinner served** 6.30-9pm Mon-Sat; 7-9pm Sun. **Main courses** £8.50-£13. **Credit** MC, V.

Located in old Freshwater not far from the church and the saltings of the River Yar, the pub dates back to the 11th century, though the current building is not that ancient. The large garden at the rear is an attraction as is the varied and extensive menu. Seafood features prominently, but not exclusively. Among the starters are duck and port terrine, smoked haddock pâté, or herring roe on toast, while mains might include fish pie, Welsh rarebit-topped haddock, fish cakes, whole lemon sole, duck breast with black cherry sauce or ribeye steak with sautéed potatoes and peppercorn butter. Comfort puds such as rhubarb crumble, treacle sponge, spotted dick and apple pie make a fine finish.

SEAVIEW

Seaview Hotel

High Street, Seaview, PO34 5EX (01983 612711/ www.seaviewhotel.co.uk). **Lunch served** noon-1.30pm daily. **Dinner served** 7.15-9.30pm Mon-Sat. **Main courses** £12-£20. **Set lunch** (Sun) £16.95 3 courses. **Credit** AmEx, DC, MC, V.

A delightful, well-kept, family-run seaside hotel set back from the seafront, sporting a characterful nautical theme in its homely and inviting public areas. Whether it's bar snacks in one of the two popular bars, or a more formal meal in the smart but very relaxed main restaurant or conservatory, the style of cooking is to a uniformly high standard. Menus offer a mix of imaginative and familiar, and include local fish and seafood such as lobster, crab and sea bass. Among the meat dishes is Godshill pork three ways: roast loin, braised belly and black pudding with Isle of Wight cauliflower and apple purée. The hot crab ramekin is a speciality and is available in both bars and the restaurant. Also noteworthy is the selection of Minghella's ice-creams.

SHALFLEET

New Inn

Mill Road, Shalfleet, PO3 4NS (01983 531314/ www.thenew-inn.co.uk). **Lunch served** noon-2.30pm, **dinner served** 6-9.30pm daily. **Main courses** £6.95-£25.95. **Credit** AmEx, MC, V.

With its inglenook fireplaces, flagstone floors and original, low-beamed ceilings this 18th-century pub close to Newtown estuary is about as traditional as they come. The nautical theme of the decor is reflected in a menu that majors on tried and tested seafood dishes, with the occasional innovative touch. Local crab and prawn cocktail vies for attention with grilled sardines and moules marinières among the starters. Mains range from whole grilled local plaice to a magnificent seafood platter. There's also a smattering of old-fashioned pub favourites: cod, chips and peas; ham, egg and chips; steak and ale pie. Desserts include sticky toffee pudding, crème brûlée and tart tatin.

ST HELENS

Baywatch Beach Restaurant ★

The Duver, St Helens, PO33 1RP (01983 873259/ www.bay-watch.co.uk). **Breakfast served** 10.30am-noon, **lunch served** noon-3pm, **dinner served** 6.15-9pm daily. **Main courses** £6.90-£19. **Credit** MC, V.

On a summer's day this is the perfect place to make most of sun, sea, sand and satisfyingly filling food. Right on the beach, with tables outside for early birds, the place operates as an all-purpose café during the day and in the evening becomes an informal restaurant. The extensive daytime menus have something for everyone, from own-made local crab soup with garlic bread and pan-fried beef sirloin with lyonnaise potatoes, wild mushrooms and madeira jus. Warm chocolate fondant with caramel ice-cream and chocolate sauce is worth the short wait stated on the menu.

SOUTHAMPTON

White Star

28 Oxford Street, Southampton, SO14 3DJ (023 8082 1990/www.whitestartavern.co.uk). **Lunch served** noon-2.30pm, **dinner served** 6.30-9.30pm Mon-Sat. **Meals served** noon-9pm Sun. **Main courses** £11.50-£16.50. **Credit** AmEx, MC, V.

The ground floor of this former seafarer's hotel has been transformed into a gastropub, and now offers what is surely the city's finest food. The bright, spacious wood-floored dining area has polished wood tables and leather banquettes and a fairly extensive modern French menu. Filo-wrapped goat's cheese with rocket salad and sun-dried tomatoes, followed by fillet of beef with boulangère potatoes, fine beans, sweet and sour garlic and port jus, are typical dinner choices. The lunch menu is shorter and takes in a mix of light dishes from egg and chive baguette to spaghetti carbonara, as well as the standard three-course option.

baguette to sandwiches, burgers, pasta and pizzas. There's also a selection of simple seafood dishes: cod, haddock, scampi, shell-on prawns, whitebait and so on, but it's after 6.15pm when the quality stuff really kicks in. From a menu that's mainly seafood try a deliciously retro prawn cocktail, followed perhaps by spicy Cajun cod with baby leaf spinach and tomato salsa.

YARMOUTH

George Hotel ★

Quay Street, Yarmouth, PO41 0PE (01983 760331/www.thegeorge.co.uk). Brasserie **Breakfast served** 8-10am, **lunch served** noon-3pm, **dinner served** 7-10pm daily. **Main courses** £11.95-£29.95. **Set lunch** (Sun) £19.50 2 courses, £23.50 3 courses. *Restaurant* **Dinner served** 7-9.30pm Tue-Sat. **Set dinner** £45 5 courses incl coffee, petit fours. **Credit** MC, V.

The best hotel on the island by far has a brilliant chef and cheerful staff dishing out the food and drinks. During the day – and pray it's a sunny one – lounge in the waterside garden and take in the activity on the Solent. At other times the informal brasserie, a bright room with a sunny decor, has a modern menu featuring starters like a fresh-tasting ceviche of mackerel with crab salad and equally excellent lamb cutlets with asparagus, spinach and potato purée. Apple soufflé with calvados ice-cream is to die for. The dinner-only elegant main restaurant serves sophisticated, quite elaborate food that is worth booking a table for. There are good value house wines on a serious list of great vintages.

VENTNOR

Royal Hotel

Belgrave Road, Ventnor, PO38 1JJ (01983 852186/www.royalhotelieow.co.uk). Bar **Lunch served** noon-2pm daily. *Restaurant* **Dinner served** 7-9.15pm daily. **Set dinner** £32.50 3 courses. **Credit** AmEx, DC, MC, V.

Neat gardens front this Victorian sandstone hotel – the largest on the island. Complementing the tradition and grandeur of the Royal Hotel is a formal dining room (note that smart casual is the dress code here), where the menu consists of imaginative modern European dishes: melting pan-fried scallops on couscous with spicy chorizo and crème fraîche, very tender confit shoulder and roast best end of English lamb served with white bean and truffle purée and rosemary jus. Caramelised pineapple and rum tart with iced praline parfait makes a great dessert. Lighter lunchtime options – a speciality omelette fruits de mer, with crab, prawns, mussels and smoked haddock glazed with gruyère perhaps, or maybe pan-fried Thai fish cakes followed by garlic roasted monkfish with crushed potatoes and parsley sauce – are available in the sunny conservatory.

YARMOUTH

Sian Elin's

Quay Street, Yarmouth, PO41 0NT (01983 760054). **Meals served** 9am-2.30pm, **dinner served** 6.30-10pm daily. **Main courses** £12.50-£17.50. **Credit** MC, V.

With open decking overlooking the marina, this restaurant has a particularly great location, especially in fine weather. Spectacular sunsets are always a possibility. The carte lists a varied choice of French dishes, from roasted goat's cheese and sautéed snails with garlic butter, to crispy roast duck and boeuf en croute, but it's the fish menu that's the star attraction: locally caught prime seafood that's simply prepared and completely delicious. Fresh crab soup with crusty bread is all it should be: creamy, perfectly seasoned and packed with flavour. To follow, haddock and chive fish cakes with a decent salad and mayonnaise, then terrific sweet, rich and very moreish peach schnapps clotted cream ice-cream.

STOCKBRIDGE

Greyhound ★

31 The High Street, Stockbridge, SO20 6EY (01264 810833). **Lunch served** noon-2.30pm daily. **Dinner served** 7-10pm Mon-Sat. **Main courses** £9.50-£19.50. **Credit** MC, V.

The Greyhound comprises a rustic old pub with an inglenook, and a fine dining room where chef Darron Bunn's almost faultless cooking can be enjoyed. Tables are a little close together for conversational privacy – but who wants to talk when the food is so good? The shortish menu (six starters, six mains, six desserts) includes such delights as risotto of Dorset crab with clams, sautéed chicken livers 'on toast' with sauce béarnaise or Bunn's wonderful signature dish – a fish cake of big chunks of fish and potato, topped with a soft-poached egg and a rich but tangy beurre blanc. A main of perfectly roasted sea bass arrived on a mound of fresh al dente linguine in a smoked salmon bouillon polonnaise, while succulent fillet of beef came with seared foie gras and a rich port and lentil jus. Room must be left for desserts such as spiced pear tart tatin with cinnamon ice-cream or a selection of British cheeses with pear and saffron chutney. The wine list is extensive.

South East

Peat Spade

Longstock, Stockbridge, SO20 6DR (01264 810612). **Lunch served** noon-2pm Tue-Sun. **Dinner served** 7-9pm Tue-Thur; 7-9.30pm Fri, Sat. **Main courses** £6.75-£13.50. **No credit cards**.

This pub, with its distinctive white leaded windows, is a champion of local and organic produce. This enthusiasm is reflected in the high quality of the food on offer and in the creation of a place focused more on dining than drinking. Menus change every few weeks and among the starters there could be organic parsnip and cinnamon soup, local free-range pork and thyme pâté, and organic broccoli and stilton quiche. Main dishes range from smoked haddock kedgeree with basmati rice to fillet of wild sea bass with crab bisque, and breast of Gressingham duck with sweet chilli oil. End with tangy fresh lemon tart.

SWAY

Nurse's Cottage

Station Road, Sway, SO41 6BA (01590 683402/ www.nursescottage.co.uk). **Lunch served** 12.30-2pm Sun. **Dinner served** 6.30-8pm daily. **Set lunch** £15 2 courses, £16.50 3 courses. **Set dinner** £19.25 2 courses, £21.50 3 courses incl mineral water, coffee, chocolates. **Credit** AmEx, MC, V.

Built in 1909, and for many years the local District Nurse's house, the cottage opened as a restaurant with rooms in 1992. The charming homely quality of the setting is reflected in the unpretentious cooking served in the pristine dining room. The short dinner menu has several house specialities. A starter of mushroom millefeuille is one such: mushrooms cooked in port with shallots and cream. Among the mains there's baked chicken breast stuffed with pork, plums and ginger, while few can resist the medley of miniature desserts, a daily-changing selection of delights.

TITCHFIELD

Radcliffe

Whiteley Lane, Titchfield, Fareham, PO15 6RQ (01329 845981/www.theradcliffe.co.uk). **Lunch served** noon-2.30pm Tue-Fri; noon-4pm Sun. **Dinner served** 7-11pm Tue-Sat. **Main courses** £12.95-£20.95. **Credit** AmEx, MC, V.

Though this converted Grade II-listed farmhouse is first and foremost a glamorous members' club, its dining rooms are open to the public. The first floor restaurant features a balcony overlooking six acres of landscaped grounds. The short modern European menu lists well-prepared dishes like eggs en cocotte with chicken livers and wild mushrooms, followed by roast fillet of beef with dauphinoise potatoes, Yorkshire pudding and café au lait sauce. There's an excellent Sunday brunch (noon-4pm), and during the rest of the week light lunches can be enjoyed in the smart member lounges. The recent departure of the founders doesn't appear to have affected the cool, stylish character, and excellent staff manner.

WHITCHURCH

Red House

21 London Street, Whitchurch, RG28 7LH (01256 895558). **Lunch served** noon-2pm daily. **Dinner served** 6.30-9.30pm Mon-Sat; 7-9pm Sun. **Main courses** £9-£16. **Credit** MC, V.

This 16th-century village pub is in fact painted brilliant white, though the doors are red. The bars are traditional in character, and enormous mirrors create an illusion of space; the large garden at the rear is a popular spot. The menu is short but varied: dishes range from teriyaki duck breast with fresh cherry dressing and salmon and dill fish cakes with poached egg and chive beurre blanc to John Dory fillets on crab and saffron risotto with parmesan and pan-fried chicken breast with a truffle and roast garlic stuffing. Desserts – cranachan parfait, lemon tart are a must.

WINCHESTER

Chesil Rectory

1 Chesil Street, Winchester, SO23 0HU (01962 851555). **Lunch served** noon-1.30pm Sat. **Dinner served** 7-9.30pm Tue-Sat. **Set lunch** £35 3 courses. **Set dinner** £45 3 courses. **Credit** AmEx, DC, MC, V.

This distinctive timber-framed building is the place's oldest house, dating from some time in the 15th century. New owners and chef arrived in January 2004 and have kept the place much as it ever was, with the cosy restaurant located on two floors, the upper room being the more romantic. Everything, from bread to ice-creams to petits fours, is made on the premises. Wild rabbit and cured ham terrine with pickled girolles, followed by line-caught sea bass with asparagus and hollandaise sauce exemplify the style.

Wykeham Arms ★

75 Kingsgate Street, Winchester, SO23 9PE (01962 853834). **Lunch served** noon-2.30pm Mon-Sat; noon-1.45pm Sun. **Dinner served** 6.30-8.45pm Mon-Sat. **Main courses** £10.75-£15.50. **Credit** AmEx, MC, V.

The Wyk, as it's popularly known, is an institution. Pub, restaurant and excellent accommodation are all part of the package. The bars and maze of rooms are crammed with memorabilia and boast open log fires. The daily-changing menu is a mouth-watering collection of dishes including pork, apricot and green peppercorn terrine with apple and ginger chutney; roast rack of Hampshire Down lamb, and Bailey's panna cotta with mixed berry compote. There's an excellent choice of wines by the glass and half bottle.

Also in the area

Hotel du Vin 14 Southgate Street, Winchester, SO23 9EF (01962 841414); **Loch Fyne** Unit 2, Vulcan Buildings, Gunwharf Quays, Portsmouth, PO1 3BF (02392 778060); **Loch Fyne** 18 Jewry Street, Winchester, SO23 8RZ (01962 872930); **Prezzo** 1-2 Market Square, Alton, GU34 1HD (01420 85580); **Prezzo** 43 The Boardwalk, Port Solent, Portsmouth, PO6 4TP (023 9238 7951); **Prezzo** 25 Oxford Street, Southampton, SO14 3DJ (023 8022 6181).

Kent

South East

BEARSTED

Soufflé Restaurant on the Green

The Green, Bearsted, ME14 4DN (01622 737065). **Lunch served** noon-2pm Tue-Fri, Sun. **Dinner served** 7-9.30pm Tue-Sat. **Main courses** £16.50-£18. **Set lunch** £13.50 2 courses, £16.50 3 courses. **Set dinner** £22.50 3 courses. **Credit** AmEx, MC, V.

Gracious and genteel, Soufflé is all about civilised dining and integrity in the kitchen. The decor is so discreet that it fades into the beams, yet Nick Evenden's cooking has style to spare. A distinctive way with French-inspired Mediterranean dishes puts the emphasis on upmarket comfort food – his pan-fried Rye Bay scallops with black pudding, parsley sauce, olive oil hollandaise and creamed potatoes is a dream. For bargain Sunday lunch was a delicate terrine of salmon and langoustine with mustard dressing, and roast ribeye of beef with (the best) Yorkshire pudding. And when you end a meal with a gorgeous, oozing rich chocolate fondant and white chocolate ice-cream, life is sweet.

BIDDENDEN

West House ★

28 High Street, Biddenden, TN27 8AH (01580 291341). **Lunch served** noon-2pm Tue-Sun. **Dinner served** 7-10pm Tue-Sat. **Set lunch** (Sun) £23 2 courses, £28 3 courses. **Set dinner** £28 3 courses. **Credit** MC, V.

Passionate best describes Graham Garrett's cooking. Fizzing with flavour, it's colourful, vivid and intense. Top-class ingredients expertly pulled together in unfussy dishes redolent of the local ingredients that inform the menu. The dining room is charming, with simple polished wood tables and a wood burning stove – an antidote to designer dining. Casual it may be, but not at the expense of technique (Garrett was awarded a Michelin star less than a year after opening). After roast scallop, cauliflower panna cotta, pancetta, caper and raisin dressing; braised rabbit in Biddenden cider and mustard, carrots and fettucine; and medlar, honey and saffron brûlée, cinnamon ice-cream and almond tuile, you'll melt softly and contentedly into the night.

BODSHAM GREEN

Froggies at the Timber Batts

School Lane, Bodsham Green, TN25 5JQ (01233 750237). **Lunch served** noon-2.30pm Tue-Sun. **Dinner served** 7-9.30pm Tue-Sat. **Main courses** £12-£19. **Set lunch** (Sun) £15 2 courses, £19 3 courses. **Credit** MC, V.

Now that Joel Gross has unfurled the tricolore at this ancient English pub, it is hard to be indifferent to its Gallic charm and brilliant bistro dishes. So go ahead and order the delicate carpaccio de halibut marine or the never-off-the-menu speciality of garlicky moules farcies; then a carré d'agneau aux herbes or classic filet de boeuf grillé; you'll still be able to polish off a tarte tatin without a groan. For those with heartier appetites, Joel also caters for walkers tramping the North Downs (on glorious display outside the front door), offering ham and eggs, locally made sausages, filled baguettes and, of course, croque monsieur, alongside pints of Adnams Best or Woodforde's Wherry. Wine and cheeses are unwaveringly French (a cousin in the Loire produces the house wine), but service and setting are rural England.

BRIDGE

White Horse Inn

53 High Street, Bridge, CT4 5LA (01227 830249/ www.whitehorsebridge.co.uk). Bar **Lunch served** noon-2.30pm daily. **Dinner served** 6.30-9.30pm Tue-Sat. *Restaurant* **Lunch served** noon-2.30pm Tue-Sun. **Dinner served** 6.30-9.30pm Tue-Sat. **Main courses** £11-£19.50. **Set lunch** £10.95 2 courses, £12.95 3 courses. **Set dinner** (Tue-Thur) £19.50 3 courses, (Fri, Sat) £23.50 3 courses. **Credit** MC, V.

Two different dining experiences are provided at this village pub. The trad exterior (white paint and pretty flower boxes) is complimented inside by a rustic bar with classic pub fare. Conversely, the restaurant area is rather lacking in atmosphere, with its uninspiring mix of dark wooden furniture, chain hotel-type carpets, and ubiquitous Mark Rothko prints. Seasonally changing dishes on both menus, though, are accomplished and creative, and use locally sourced ingredients. Simple dishes might be Masterbrew battered cod or baked goat's cheese polenta. The restaurant carte features courgette and cherry tomato tart with parsley sorbet followed by ragoût of local fish and shellfish. It's all very efficiently done, but a little clinical and lacking in flavour. Service is restrained, but efficient.

BROADSTAIRS

Marchesi's

18 Albion Street, Broadstairs, CT10 1LU (01843 862481/www.marchesi.co.uk). **Lunch served** noon-2pm Tue-Sat; noon-2.30pm Sun. **Dinner served** 7-9.30pm Tue-Sat. **Main courses** £9.95-£14.25. **Set lunch** (Sun) £14.50 2 courses, £16.50 3 courses. **Credit** MC, V.

Established in 1886 as the Marchesi Brothers, this Broadstairs institution has a strong claim to being England's oldest family-owned restaurant. Now rebranded as Marchesi's with an updated decor, the new terrace and conservatory create a light-filled, space that throws the emphasis on the views of the harbour and Viking Bay. It should work, but the kitchen plays it safe with a populist menu. Wing of local skate with béarnaise sauce, and fillet steak with madeira sauce were nothing special, but prices, at least, are reasonable. There's a decent selection of wines by the large and small glass, staff are sweet natured, and the sea views are without compare.

Osteria Posillipo Pizzeria

14 Albion Street, Broadstairs, CT10 1LU (01843 601133/www.osteriaposillipo.co.uk). **Lunch served** *summer* noon-3pm daily; *winter* noon-3pm Mon, Wed-Sun. **Dinner served** *summer* 7-11pm daily; *winter* 7-11pm Mon, Wed-Sun. **Main courses** £7.95-£16.95. **Credit** MC, V.

Broadstairs wears its look of run-down seaside resort well; with milk bars, ice-cream parlours and shops selling shells, it's like stepping back in time. This classic family-friendly Italian trattoria serves up light, fresh pizzas – ranging from quattro stagioni to the seafood-laden posillipo – that can claim the title of being the best in the area. Pasta doesn't stray too far from the familiar, but pennette with aubergine, mozzarella, basil and tomato, or linguine with king prawns, clams and mussels are good. Mains might be Dover sole (not that expertly prepared on our visit) or lamb in red wine sauce with spinach. Desserts include a deliciously rich, bitter chocolate cake. The cliff-top location gives uninterrupted views of the North Sea, a feature fully exploited by the enclosed terrace-cum-veranda (just a couple of tables) and lower patio.

BOUGHTON LEES

Eastwell Manor

Eastwell Manor Hotel, Eastwell Park, Boughton Lees, TN25 4HR (01233 219955/www.eastwellmanor.co.uk). **Lunch served** noon-2pm Mon-Sat; 12.30-2.30pm Sun. **Dinner served** 7-9.30pm daily. **Set dinner** £37.50 3 courses. **Main courses** £15-£28. **Credit** AmEx, DC, MC, V.

With a huge estate as a backdrop, this sprawling, mock-Jacobean house (built 1928) can give the impression of being very la-di-da. But Eastwell Manor is a popular conference and wedding venue; sometimes the amount of corporate or conjugal activity can swamp the individual guest. The full-dress dining room is very prim and proper with dark panelling and ornate plaster work to the fore and tones are hushed. Linen is crisp and service deferential – to the detriment of atmosphere – but the good value fixed-price lunch (grilled sardines with pesto and lemon, then fricassee of maize-fed chicken with wild mushrooms, pasta and dijon mustard cream sauce) was just about worth the rigid back. The wine list assumes a very deep pocket.

CANTERBURY

Augustine's

1-2 Longport, Canterbury, CT1 1PE (01227 453063). **Lunch served** noon-1.30pm, **dinner served** 6.30-9pm Tue-Sat. **Main courses** £9.50-£15.90. **Set lunch** £10.95 2 courses, £11.95 3 courses. **Credit** AmEx, MC, V.

One of the best things about Augustine's is the amount of attention that has gone into providing diners with an unrushed and comfortable experience: there's a large amount of space between each wide, marble-topped table, and the unobtrusive but efficient service makes you feel that there's plenty of time to linger (no 'two seatings' policy here). Upon arrival, you're taken into the cosy bar to peruse the modern European menu and the carefully chosen wine list, before being escorted into the small dining room, where low lighting creates a relaxed yet formal mood. Mains of pan-fried hake with garlic and lemon or fillet of beef with sorrel and crème fraîche sauce were sophisticated, flavourful and well presented. An extremely rich banoffi-esque dessert tickled the tastebuds, but led to feelings of sickly regret. Accomplished cooking in an elegant setting makes this a good choice for a special occasion. The set lunch is also excellent value.

Goods Shed ★

Station Road West, Canterbury, CT2 8AN (01227 459153). **Lunch served** noon-2.30pm Tue-Fri; noon-3pm Sat, Sun. **Dinner served** 6-9.30pm Tue-Sat. **Main courses** £8-£16. **Credit** AmEx, MC, V.

The huge windows of this converted engine shed let in rays of light that sweep across chunky pine tables on a raised platform. A relaxed buzz from the farmers' market below adds a comforting sense of community and earthy smells of English cheese and fresh produce reassure that the food will be of the best quality. Artisan bread got the meal off to an excellent start. A main course of roast organic chicken with sorrel, Swiss chard and potatoes was good. Even better was the vegetable platter, with mushrooms, black lentils, Swiss chard, hard-boiled egg, swede, tomato relish and salad leaves. Own-made cinnamon ice-cream to finish had a perfectly creamy taste and texture. Add a well-chosen wine list, extremely friendly staff, a wood-beamed ceiling and exposed chalky brick walls, and the result is an organic whole that produces strong feelings of contentment. English food at its best.

CRANBROOK

Restaurant 23

23 Stone Street, Cranbrook, TN17 3HF (01580 714666). **Lunch served** noon-2pm Mon-Sat; 12.30-2.30pm Sun. **Dinner served** 7-9.30pm Tue-Sat. **Set lunch** (Sun) £23.95 3 courses. **Main courses** £12.50-£17.95. **Credit** MC, V.

Bravely taking over the site vacated by Soho South, this modish British restaurant has gamely retained the cluttered, old-world decor of the previous owners

– wood floors, beams strewn with dried herbs and hops – though it's all beginning to look a bit faded. But it cuts the mustard with well-heeled Weald types. No surprise then that the menu toes a familiar line of smoked chicken and fennel risotto or beef fillet with asparagus and hollandaise, with desserts such as hot chocolate fondant with sour cherries and vanilla ice-cream. Food is consistent without ever hitting the high notes, but pleasant, satisfactory cooking does not always justify such a hefty bill.

DARGATE

Dove Inn

Plum Pudding Lane, Dargate, ME13 9HB (01227 751360). **Lunch served** noon-1.30pm Tue-Sun. **Dinner served** 7-9pm Wed-Sat. **Main courses** £14.99-£16.75. **Credit** MC, V.

The Dove's strong gastronomic reputation was built on the back of its à la carte. So it was disappointing that this wasn't available on our Saturday lunchtime visit (due to a staffing problem), although the cordial service went a long way towards making up for it. The lunch menu was short but imaginative (with dishes costing half the price of the à la carte) and although the meal took a while to get going, it was worth the wait. Salt cod mash served on a tomato, bean and chorizo stew was intense and very fresh. Shepherd's pie made with local lamb was similarly satisfying, with fluffy mash and a crispy surface. Desserts were mixed: the orange and passionfruit crème brûlée was far too sweet, but the warm chocolate pudding was delicious. A light rustic interior with scrubbed pine panelling and black and white photos documenting the Victorian (Shepherd Neame) pub's history creates a calming setting.

DEAL

Dunkerley's

19 Beach Street, Deal, CT14 7AH (01304 375016/ www.dunkerleys.co.uk). **Lunch served** noon-2.30pm Tue-Sat; noon-3pm Sun. **Dinner served** 7-9.30pm Mon-Fri, Sun; 6-10pm Sat. **Main courses** £11.95-

West House. *See p83.*

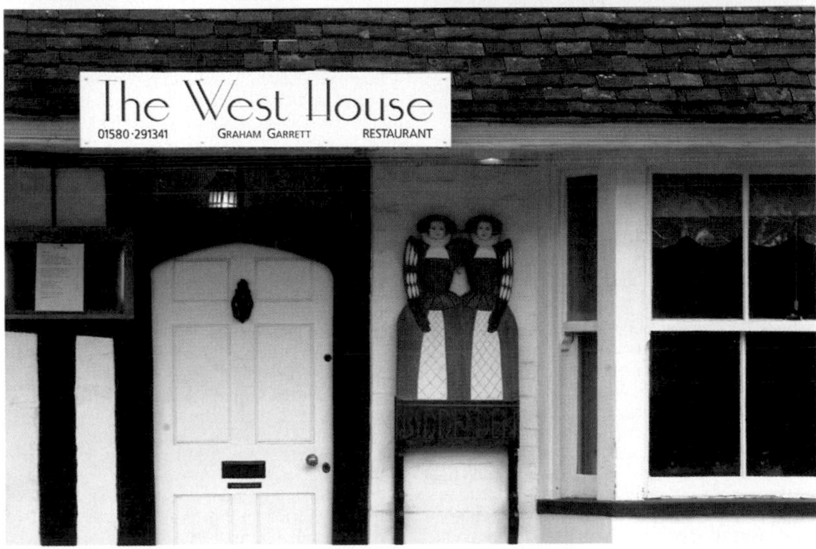

£21.95. **Set lunch** £7.50 1 course, £9.95 2 courses, £12.95 3 courses. **Set dinner** £16.95 2 courses, £20.95 3 courses. **Credit** AmEx, DC, MC, V.
Button-back caramel leather armchairs, pale wood and modern art fill the bar, but there's no escaping the hotel feel of the dining room, characterised by the busy boardroom carpet and linen tablecloths. Cooking, like the clientele, is refined but old-fashioned, offering crab bisque and whole grilled Dover sole with lemon butter and fried potatoes, alongside Sandwich Bay plaice fillet served with banana, sweet potato and spiced jus (which didn't work) and fillet of lemon sole poached with ceps in a light velouté (which did). The well-intentioned and industrious staff are a strong suit, and the likes of French onion soup and fillet of beef in a duxelle croûte mean you don't have to stick with fish, but the price tag is a little hefty for the area.

DOVER

Arlington

161 Snargate Street, Dover, CT17 9BZ (01304 209444/www.thearlington.co.uk). **Lunch served** noon-2.30pm, **dinner served** 6.30-9.30pm Tue-Sat. **Main courses** £12.95-£16.95. **Set dinner** (Tue-Thur) £20 3 courses. **Credit** MC, V.
Spadeloads of character is not a description that comes quickly to mind at this tiny restaurant. All of its former pub personality has been stripped out and the plain, no frills decor definitely needs a lift, but there's no denying the enthusiasm of the owners and the warmth of the welcome. Internationally influenced dishes are a mixed affair: a light pastry base topped with crab, mixed leaves and blue cheese fondue was a touch sickly. Far better was tossed salad of smoked salmon, quails' eggs and fresh herbs. And it is hard to go wrong with the failsafe mid-market likes of medallions of pork fillets with grain mustard mash and calvados sauce, though sirloin steak (served with parisienne potatoes and rich madeira sauce) could have been better quality.

Cullins Yard

New Cullins Yard, 11 Cambridge Road, Dover, CT17 9BY (01304 211666). **Meals served** noon-9.30pm daily. **Main courses** £9.60-£20. **Credit** MC, V.
With its waterside warehouse location, Caribbean-meets-junk-shop interior, and jazzy backbeat, Cullins Yard speaks to its customers' inner bohemian. You may have to hone your passive smoking skills (there's fine weather respite on the outside deck overlooking Wellington Dock), but you'll have no complaints about the freshness of the fish. Whether it's a generous plate of hot, buttery prawns with chilli and a good dressed salad, plump mussels cooked in wine, cream and herbs, fresh sardines with chunky chips, or baked black bream with herbs and garlic, this is simple, delicious food done exceptionally well. Venison casserole and fillet steak spread the range and customer appeal, and chocolate bread and butter pudding makes a great finish. A good wine list and lovely staff are a bonus.

Wallett's Court

Westcliffe, St Margaret's at Cliffe, Dover, CT15 6EW (01304 852424/www.wallettscourt.com). **Lunch served** noon-2pm Tue-Fri, Sun. **Dinner served** 7-9pm daily. **Set lunch** £17 2 courses, £19.50 3 courses. **Set dinner** £35 3 courses. **Credit** AmEx, DC, MC, V.
Although within easy reach of Dover, Wallett's Court is found down small roads surrounded by lush countryside. The Oakley family has lovingly converted this 17th-century farmhouse into a relaxed hotel, with the sofa-strewn lounge bar setting the tone. Beams, half-timbering and linen-draped tables define the restaurant, which produces food with a penchant for regional produce but with flavours that borrow a little from everywhere. With the sea so close, seafood is going to be as fresh as you can get, and that's the case with Rye Bay scallops caramelised with five-spice, chilli, lemongrass and coconut purée. Loin of Highland wild boar with sage mash, Bramley apples and Biddenden vintage cider sauce was a main course hit and we left feeling well-cared for, if a mite overfed.

DUNGENESS

The Pilot ★

Battery Road, Lydd, Dungeness, TN29 9NJ (01797 320314/www.thepilot.uk.com). **Lunch served** noon-2.30pm, **dinner served** 6-9pm Mon-Fri. **Meals served** *summer* noon-9pm Sat, Sun; *winter* noon-2.30pm Sat; noon-8pm Sun. **Main courses** £5.50-£8.70. **Credit** MC, V.
You can view Dungeness as the land that time forgot or its austere seascape will catch your soul. For the late film director Derek Jarman it was the latter, and his extraordinary nuclear garden is well worth the ten-minute walk from the Pilot Inn car park – across the largest expanse of shingle on earth. But make sure you're back before opening time to join the queue – this down-to-earth pub serves some of the best fish and chips in Kent. Enormous portions of battered cod, huss, skate, plaice and haddock are as fresh as can be and cooked to order, but steak and kidney pie is popular too, with a proper baked-with-the-pie pastry crust. Give the starters and puddings a miss, drink beers from Greene King and lobby the landlord to stop serving plastic sachets of sauces – it's an insult to the fish.

FARNBOROUGH

Chapter One

Farnborough Common, Locksbottom, Farnborough, BR6 8NF (01689 854848/www.chaptersrestaurant.co.uk). **Lunch served** noon-2.30pm Mon-Sat; noon-2.45 Sun. **Dinner served** 6.30-10pm Mon-Thur; 6.30-11pm Fri, Sat; 6.30-9pm Sun. **Set lunch** £16 2 courses, £19.50 3 courses. **Set dinner** £26.95 3 courses. **Credit** AmEx, MC, V.
The swish homage to pale wood, ceiling spots and glass has opened up this former roadside pub to a smart clientele. The lunchtime brasserie goes in for

posh comfort food such as fish croquette with mango salsa and curry velouté, or sweet and sour chicken, but it's the Michelin-starred restaurant that fills the car park. The good-value, fixed-price menu describes a confident, pared-down style that is strong on fresh, clear flavours as well as presentation. An underlying richness worked well in a starter of roasted quail, caramelised capers, braised turnip and honey jus, and a main course of roast black bream, ragoût of butter beans, girolles, confit garlic and red wine sauce had distinct character. But the hit of the evening was an organic lemon tart with crème fraîche sorbet and millefeuille of passion fruit. Waiting staff are efficient and discreet, but add to a rather sober atmosphere.

FAVERSHAM

Read's

Macknade's Manor, Canterbury Road, Faversham, ME13 8XE (01795 535344/www.reads.com). **Lunch served** noon-2pm, **dinner served** 7-9pm Tue-Sat. **Set lunch** £19.50 3 courses. **Set dinner** £45 5-course tasting menu. **Credit** AmEx, DC, MC, V.

The hallmark of this classic Georgian manor house is an elegant simplicity – in decor and food. David Pitchford produces seasonally tasting menus with a strong allegiance to local produce, and his food is straightforward and clearly thought through. You need just a spoonful – a pristine Rye Bay scallop with a barigoule of artichokes, crisp smoked bacon and sweet mustard dressing will do – to know that something serious is afoot. Then follow it with delicate pink fillet of Kentish lamb in a herb crust that comes with a mini shepherd's pie, shallot soubise and a tomato and tarragon sauce, and lemon tart with a red wine and elderflower sorbet, to discover how good it all is. It's perhaps even better at lunchtime, with a creative, well executed set menu that, given the quality of the cooking, is a steal at £19.50.

HYTHE

Hythe Bay Fish Restaurant & Bar ★

Marine Parade, Hythe, CT21 6AW (01303 267024). **Lunch served** 11am-3pm Tue-Sun. **Dinner served** 6-11pm Wed-Sat. **Main courses** £12.95-£17.95. **Set lunch** (Tue-Fri) £10.95 2 courses. **Credit** AmEx, MC, V.

Hythe is a sleepy seaside town untouched by candy floss and bright lights (and rated fourth in *Crap Towns: The 50 Worst Places to Live in the UK*). But even on the greyest days when south-westerly gales sweep up the Channel, this restaurant's blue-painted façade is a cheering sight – and when the sun shines the terrace comes into its own. It offers a warm welcome in a homely setting of blue-check plastic tablecloths, garish abstract art and blackboards detailing the day's catch. Generous pricing compensates for sometimes wayward execution, but hits outnumber misses. Crab, mussel and sweetcorn chowder may have owed its base to commercial fish soup, but confit of salmon with red onion and potato salad, sea bass fillets with sauté potatoes and delicate hollandaise, and garlic-roasted cod with ratatouille all came off surprisingly well.

IGHTHAM

Harrow Inn

Common Road, Ightham, TN15 9EB (01732 885912). **Lunch served** noon-2pm Tue-Sun. **Dinner served** 6-9pm Tue-Sat. **Main courses** £5.95-£7.95. **Credit** MC, V.

Narrow country lanes lead to this Kentish ragstone building that's the very picture of a modern English country hostelry. It combines informal eating with food that would not look out of place in a classier establishment and can be thought of as a gentrified pub in two parts – a front bar-brasserie and a comfortable restaurant at the back. The cooking acknowledges current trends, as well as offering tried-and-true pub dishes on the menu. So whether you are in the mood for Cumberland sausage and mash with onion gravy or pan-fried fillet of chicken with Cajun spices, you won't put the kitchen off its stroke. To drink, the choice is real ale or something from the varied wine list. The two bar rooms have real atmosphere: sunny yellow walls, open fires, fresh flowers, candles, simple wood furniture.

IVY HATCH

Plough at Ivy Hatch

High Cross Road, Ivy Hatch, TN15 0NL (01732 810268). **Lunch served** noon-2pm Mon-Sat; noon-3pm Sun. **Dinner served** 6.30-10pm Mon-Sat; 6.30-8.30pm Sun. **Main courses** £7-£16. **Credit** MC, V.

Once the village pub, the Plough has gone into overt restaurant mode over the years, building up a reputation for seafood. The interior could do with a makeover – worn carpet tiles and sagging curtains keeping out the sun in the conservatory dining room are an off note. As for food, when the criteria of simplicity and freshness are met then it really is on course. Own-potted shrimps, sweet marinated anchovies with lemon cream, and grilled haddock fillet with chips proved a hit, but steamed paupiette of sea bass filled with salmon mousse didn't deliver.

LANGTON GREEN

Hare

Langton Road, Langton Green, TN3 0JA (01892 862419/www.hare-tunbridgewells.co.uk). **Meals served** noon-9.30pm Mon-Sat; noon-9pm Sun. **Main courses** £6.95-£15.95. **Credit** MC, V.

It may be more than 100 years old, but the Hare has all the hallmarks of a modern dining pub: large windows, bare boards, well-spaced tables and blackboard menus, combining a pleasant ambience with well-executed food, friendly service and good value. And it serves food all day – a bonus when peak meal times can see the dining rooms heaving

South East

and parking impossible. Consistent delivery keeps the place afloat, the kitchen moving deftly through a repertoire of contemporary dishes with the odd classic thrown in. Warm roasted artichoke and vegetables with herb salsa and ciabatta to mop up the juices, and a crisp-skinned confit of duck with a white bean and chorizo ratatouille and red cabbage were so generous that there was no room for sticky toffee pudding with ice-cream and toffee sauce.

PENSHURST

Spotted Dog ★

Smarts Hill, Penshurst, TN11 8EP (01892 870253). **Lunch served** noon-2.30pm, **dinner served** 7-9.30pm Mon-Sat. **Meals served** noon-6pm Sun. **Main courses** £10-£17. **Credit** MC, V.

It may have all the crusty traditionalism of a typical country pub – log fires, beams, panelling and nooks and crannies – but the young team have offset it all with a healthy dose of modern thinking. The menu delivers simple enjoyment with plates of easily assembled, local ingredients, knocked out at hard-to-argue prices. Tartlet of trout on smoked salmon with beetroot oil, and rump of lamb with local asparagus and a simple bramble jelly reduction are clean and fresh. The staff know what they are doing and are in no rush to hurry along those customers who are happy to linger; maybe it's the excellent Harvey's Best that makes everybody so relaxed. Outside seating on the terrace festooned with greenery is a good option in fine weather.

PLUCKLEY

Dering Arms

Station Road, Pluckley, TN27 0RR (01233 840371/ www.deringarms.com). **Lunch served** noon-2pm, **dinner served** 7-9.30pm daily. **Main courses** £8.45-£20. **Credit** AmEx, MC, V.

This former hunting lodge may have a stark exterior, but it has got the relaxed, informal country feel exactly right inside with bare floorboards, flagstones and fresh flowers. It stands next to the railway station, two miles from the village (follow signs for Pluckley station), with a couple of high-ceilinged bars dispensing Dering Ale and blackboards advertising modern bistro staples such as moules marinière or braised rabbit with couscous and tarragon and fennel salad. A cornerstone of the cooking style is fish and more blackboards in the pretty restaurant (especially so in the evening when candles are lit) list such dishes as fillet of cod with braised red cabbage or monkfish in bacon with orange and cream sauce. Service can be slow-handed.

RAMSGATE

Surin

30 Harbour Street, Ramsgate, CT11 8HA (01843 592001/www.surinrestaurant.co.uk). **Lunch served** noon-2.30pm Tue-Sat. **Dinner served** 6-11pm Tue-Sun. **Main courses** £7-£12.95. **Set lunch** £5.95 2 courses. **Set meals** £20 3 courses incl coffee. **Credit** AmEx, DC, MC, V.

Surin's fried squid with chilli and basil leaves is hard to resist, but then so is the roast duck with tamarind sauce and the dry curry made with chicken, coconut crème and sweet basil leaves. Why is this tiny restaurant – specialising in Thai cooking (with excursions into Laos and Cambodia) – so good? Well, the produce used is fantastic – local and fresh with a strong line in seafood – and everything is cooked to order (but brace yourself for snail-paced service). Attention to detail is such that, because of problems getting deliveries of Thai beer, local micro-breweries were contacted to make Surin beer that complemented the food. The menu sports the usual suspects – spring rolls, chicken satay, chicken with cashew nuts – but here they are always what you wish you could find in every Thai restaurant – properly made and satisfying.

RINGLESTONE

Ringlestone Inn

Ringlestone Road, Ringlestone, ME17 1NX (01622 859900/www.ringlestone.com). **Lunch served** noon-2pm Mon-Sat; 12.30-2.30pm Sun. **Dinner served** 7-9.30pm daily. **Main courses** £10.50-£15.75. **Credit** AmEx, DC, MC, V.

The lost feeling that you get when searching the winding, wooded country lanes for the Ringlestone Inn is part of the charm of this remote 16th-century inn. When you finally arrive the atmosphere won't disappoint: a series of tiny rooms contribute to a dark interior that's full of worn brick and flag floors, inglenooks, dark beams and highly polished carved oak furniture. Come for the history, the acres of garden or the beer – it's taken seriously with a row of casks behind the bar dispensing Ringlestone Bitter, Marstons Pedigree, Fuller's London Pride and Adnams – but food can be hit or miss. The lunchtime buffet may be a better bet, but the evening menu delivered lacklustre mushroom and stilton tartlet, and a pie of chicken and asparagus in cowslip wine that read better than it tasted.

SANDGATE

Sandgate Hotel

8-9 Wellington Terrace, The Esplanade, Sandgate, TT20 3DY (01303 220444/www.sandgate hotel.com). **Breakfast served** 7-10am Mon-Fri; 7-11am Sat, Sun. **Lunch served** noon-3pm, **dinner served** 6-10pm daily. **Main courses** £15.50-£20. **Credit** AmEx, DC, MC, V.

A fledgling operation this may be – in its third year in 2005 – but it aims high, starting with the advantage of an elegant 19th-century house overlooking the Channel. It is an industrious kitchen, offering light meals in the bar and outside on the stepped and heated terrace. A sunny day can see the place packed, especially at weekends when food is

Harrow Inn. *See p87.*

served all day, with everyone tucking into mussels and chips; lamb, rosemary and garlic burgers; and bangers and mash. The small restaurant is a more dressed-up kind of place with an upmarket feel offering fillet of Scotch beef on a chive and celery potato cake and watercress sauce; steamed fillet of wild bass with coriander pasta; baby spinach and vanilla cappuccino sauce; and a shared caramelised banana bavarois.

SANDWICH

Quayside Bar & Brasserie

Bell Lane, The Quay, Sandwich, CT13 9EN (01304 619899/www.quaysidebar.co.uk). **Lunch served** noon-2.30pm Mon-Sat; noon-4pm Sun. **Dinner served** 6-9.30pm Mon-Sat. **Main courses** £6.95-£14.95. **Credit** MC, V.

An unprepossessing entrance up a narrow side street leads into this former grain store with its warehouse ambience. An airy setting blends pale wood tables with intense images of Miami, Bermuda and Herne Bay by Kent-based photographer Tommy Candler (all for sale), and there's a laid-back menu to match. Modern comfort food includes starters like avocado and bacon salad, moules marinière, and grilled goat's cheese with cassis; mains of steak and kidney pie, bangers and mash, and hot chicken with chorizo and sauté potato salad; with banoffi pie or pecan pie for pudding. A selection of tapas, charming service and decent wines are other bonuses. The cocktail bar is another lure.

SEASALTER

Sportsman

Faversham Road, Seasalter, CT5 4BP (01227 273370). **Lunch served** noon-1.45pm Tue-Sat; noon-2.30pm Sun. **Dinner served** 7-8.45pm Tue-Sat. **Main courses** £9.95-£17.95. **Credit** MC, V.

The classic gastropub look of polished wood floor, plain tables, chunky evening candles and contemporary art for sale, also includes terracotta potted olive and fig trees. As for food, dedication to local and seasonal raw materials produces the likes of crab, asparagus and boiled egg salad (though a single asparagus spear was ungenerous), sparkling fresh baked cod and pea sauce with puréed potatoes, and chocolate panna cotta with steamed pistachio milk. There's no doubting the quality of the materials and the skill in the kitchen, but at these prices we wanted more of a wow factor (the cod was particularly bland) and a much warmer welcome.

SISSINGHURST

Rankins

The Street, Sissinghurst, TN17 2JH (01580 713964/www.rankinsrestaurant.com). **Lunch served** 12.30-2pm Sun. **Dinner served** 7.30-9pm Wed-Sat. **Main courses** (lunch) £12.50. **Set dinner** £25.50 2 courses, £29.50 3 courses. **Credit** MC, V.

The Rankins' eponymous restaurant blends in with the rest of the weatherboarded buildings that line the road running through Sissinghurst. Nor does it look anything particularly special when you're inside inside – the homely, traditional look has remained unchanged for years. The focus, as always, is firmly on the food. Hugh Rankin is a classicist at heart – not for him any fancy modern experimentation. His cooking is an amalgamation of skill, sound technique and tried and trusted flavours. His short, seasonal menus rely on local produce such as fresh asparagus to accompany a dish of green pea mousse terrine with poached salmon, or a perfect Rye Bay scallop to go with roast cod fillet and a rich crab butter sauce, and strawberries with Gaelic coffee and muscovado cream. The wine list is reasonable, and Leonora Rankin keeps service charmingly informal and efficient.

THREE CHIMNEYS

Three Chimneys

Hareplain Road, Three Chimneys, TN27 8LW (01580 291472). **Lunch served** 11.30am-1.50pm Mon-Sat; noon-1.50pm Sun. **Dinner served** 6.30-9.30pm Mon-Sat; 7-9pm Sun. **Main courses** £10.95-£18.95. **Credit** MC, V.

It's hard not to like this country pub; you feel at home the minute you enter. Small, interlinked rooms with worn brick floors, coal fires, rough nicotine-coloured walls, distressed paint and hop-strewn beams are reassuringly rustic and speak of great age. Beers are tapped directly from the cask and suitably robust dishes fit the image – pork and leek sausages with mash, chutney and port jus – although the blackboard menu pushes some way beyond that of a typical country pub with lively mixing and matching. Prices can be high, but griddled king scallops with white wine, bacon, garlic and parmesan was well worth the hefty price tag, and starter portions can be quite generous if a white bean soup with truffle oil was anything to go by. Alas, this left little room for dessert, despite the lure of dark chocolate and praline torte with pistachio ice-cream at the next table.

TUNBRIDGE WELLS

Hotel Du Vin & Bistro ★

Crescent Road, Tunbridge Wells, PN1 2LY (01892 526 455/www.hotelduvin.com). **Lunch served** noon-1.45pm Mon-Sat; 12.30-2pm Sun. **Dinner served** 7-9.30pm daily. **Main courses** £12-£14.50. **Set lunch** (Sun) £23.50 3 courses incl coffee. **Credit** AmEx, DC, MC, V.

The hotel, part of a classy national chain, occupies a highly individualistic, grand house in the centre of town. Many non-guests dine here, but it's the hotel's resident families and courting couples that lend the restaurant its relaxed vibe. While the decor aims for an understated French country charm – a muted paint job, dark wood tables, starched linen, a smattering of Gallic antiques – the well-executed menu is more of a culinary entente cordiale. Of the regularly featured 'simple classics', pan-fried calf's liver, mash and bacon co-exists with kedgeree, cassoulet and a rich fillet steak with green peppercorn and armagnac sauce. The menu proper has a similar mix of the simple (serrano ham with celeriac to start), the familiar (fresh fillet of cod with soft olive oil mash) and the ambitious (pig's trotter stuffed with black pudding). Unobtrusive staff steer you through the mighty wine list.

Thackeray's ★

85 London Road, Tunbridge Wells, TN1 1EA (01892 511921/www.thackeraysrestaurant.co.uk). **Lunch served** noon-2.30pm Tue-Sun. **Dinner served** 6.30-10.30pm Tue-Sat. **Main courses** £17.25-£23.50. **Set lunch** £12.95 2 courses, £13.95 3 courses. **Set dinner** £55 6 course tasting menu. **Credit** AmEx, MC, V.

The pretty 17th-century Kentish house was once the home of *Vanity Fair* author William Makepeace Thackeray. Yet history is left firmly on the doorstep – inside it is as chic and savvy as chef Richard Phillips' excellent cooking. Minimalist tenets define the two ground-floor dining rooms – wear black and you'll blend in beautifully – but imagination has been allowed full reign upstairs with private dining rooms sporting red leather walls, or African tribal artifacts. With the addition of a Michelin star, all this glamour must bring expectations of high prices. While this is true of the evening menu, lunch bucks the trend with a fantastic value fixed-price menu of asparagus mousseline, poached hen's egg and truffled gnocchi, roast fillet of black bream, mussel and tomato ragoût, tian of aubergine and fish cream sauce, and almond lemon soft cake, exotic fruit salad and lemon mousse, all at an extraordinary £13.95.

WEST MALLING

Swan Brasserie

35 Swan Street, West Malling, ME19 6JU (01732 521910/www.theswanwestmalling.co.uk). **Lunch served** noon-2.30pm Mon-Sat. **Dinner served** 6-10.30pm Mon-Sat. **Meals served** noon-8.30pm Sun. **Main courses** £9-£14. **Credit** AmEx, MC, V.

The swagger and ingenuity of the decor and the liveliness of the food has the well-heeled residents of West Malling nodding with approval. From the outside the Swan resembles the pub it used to be, but inside a sophisticated bar-restaurant has been carved out with a chic, hard-edged bar; a cool, clean, polished dining area; and handsome private dining rooms that wear a glossy magazine sheen. An intelligent menu is inspired by the Mediterranean and offers simply prepared food: a light smoked red pepper, thyme and goat's cheese tart; first-class roast crusted pigeon with puy lentils and red wine sauce; rich chocolate tart with blood orange sorbet. In summer, there is no better spot than the outside patio with its Conran garden chairs and posh parasols.

WEST PECKHAM

Swan on the Green

The Green, West Peckham, ME18 5JW (01622 812271). **Lunch served** noon-2pm daily. **Dinner served** 7-9pm Tue-Sat. **Main courses** £8.95-£15.50. **Credit** AmEx, MC, V.

The Swan is effectively a rural pub with culinary aspirations. Real ales may be brewed in a microbrewery round the back (six are on offer in the bar at any time), but the main interest is in the cooking, which shows plenty of worldwide influences. The upbeat treatment of raw materials is generally well timed, portions are hearty and prices are fair. The daily-changing menu features generous portions of Thai lamb curry, lemon- and coriander-scented basmati rice and sour cream or escalope of pork coated with sage breadcrumbs and served with parsnip purée, steamed vegetables and cider jus. Relaxed, casual and simply decorated, the interior has been revamped on an open plan with lots of pale wood and soft colours – it is the sort of place you'd be more than happy to take anyone, from your mum to your best mate.

WHITSTABLE

Pearson's Crab & Oyster House

Sea Wall, Whitstable, CT5 1BT (01227 272005). **Lunch served** noon-2.30pm Mon-Sat. **Dinner served** 6.30-9pm Mon-Fri; 6-9.30pm Sat. **Meals served** noon-9pm Sun. **Main courses** £8.50-£25. **Credit** MC, V.

Old and new Whitstable stand sentinel on the beach at Horsebridge. On one side is the Whitstable Oyster Fishery Co (*see p92*) with its cool clientele and modern take on seafood; on the other there's Pearson's, a traditional seaside pub that takes care of the tastes of more conventional day trippers in its first floor restaurant. Expect chips with everything, whether it's battered fish or grilled plaice, mussels in white wine, onion, garlic and cream, or cod with parsley sauce, with the emphasis firmly on quantity rather than quality. There are oysters, of course, and whole crabs and lobsters play a big part, but at £18.95 and £24.95 respectively, are rather expensive for the dreary room, unappealing sauces and casual (sometimes offhand) service; ditto the platter of fruits de mer at £50 for two.

Tea & Times ★

36A The High Street, Whitstable, CT5 1BQ (01227 262639). **Meals served** 8.30am-5pm Mon-Fri; 9am-6pm Sat; 9am-5pm Sun. **No credit cards**.

In spite of a nonchalant attitude from some of the staff, and a distinct territorial vibe from some of the customers, this navy-fronted two-storey coffee house is still one of the best bets in town for a sandwich or an afternoon coffee and cake. The scuffed wooden interior, with deep red and cream walls, should appeal if you're into arty, organic decor, while high stools along the downstairs wooden bar are perfect if you simply want to read

South East

the paper and require regular caffeine top-ups. Newspapers and trendy magazines are on sale, as well as scattered around the upstairs room. A brie and apple sandwich with granary bread was basic but tasty enough. Chocolate cake was rightly moist and tasted home-made. There's a good selection of teas, and coffee served by the cafetière.

Wheelers Oyster Bar ★

8 High Street, Whitstable, CT5 1BQ (01227 273311/ www.whitstable-shellfish.co.uk). **Meals served** 1-7.30pm Mon, Tue, Thur-Sat; 1-7pm Sun. **Main courses** £5-£18. **Unlicensed. Corkage** no charge. **No credit cards.**

Wheelers is becoming increasingly noted, yet the staff remain refreshingly unaffected: the atmosphere inside the pink-fronted building is down-to-earth and homely, and the decor is equally unpretentious with ornamental items that are pure Victoriana (the place has existed for over 100 years). You'll need to book in advance to eat-in, though, as the tiny Oyster Parlour contains just four tables (takeaway food is available from the front bar). The seafood menu adjusts to the local seasonal catch. Starters of clam and parsley linguine in its own chowder, and roasted scallops with pancetta on a bed of puy lentils were both superb. Next, a medley of fish and shellfish in a garlic, saffron, leek and potato broth, and pan-fried sea trout with a horseradish crust and remoulade sauce maintained standards: simple presentation, sublime flavours. Bring your own booze (the place is unlicensed): the absence of a corkage fee sums this place up.

Whitstable Oyster Fishery Company

The Royal Native Oyster Stores, Whitstable, CT5 1BU (01227 276856/www.oysterfishery.co.uk). **Lunch served** noon-1.45pm Tue-Fri; noon-2.15pm Sat; noon-3.15pm Sun. **Dinner served** 7-8.45pm Tue-Fri; 6.30-9.45pm Sat; 6.30-8.15pm Sun. **Main courses** £12.50-£25. **Credit** AmEx, DC, MC, V.

The Oyster House has a classic seafood restaurant feel, but is more likely to evoke memories of Cape Cod than the traditional English seaside. Checked red and white tablecloths, cream wood panelling and fantastic sea views set the scene, and the restaurant's warehouse origins are evident from the huge windows and exposed brickwork. The blackboard menu changes regularly, but you can pretty much rely on oyster and lobster options, and a good selection of white fish, simply cooked. A plateful (enough for two) of moules marinière to start was suitably fresh, although the dish lacked the expected mopping-up juices. A main of whole roast local sea bass with garlic and rosemary was perfectly cooked. Whole Canadian lobster was also good. Desserts run the gamut from comfort (sticky toffee pudding) to posh (hazelnut and espresso chocolate tart). The adept staff can be a bit dour-faced, but the food is unlikely to disappoint. The people behind WOFC also run the restaurant at Hotel Continental (29 Beach Walk, 01227 280 280) and the East Quay Shellfish Bar (end of East Quay, Whitstable Harbour, 01227 262 003).

Williams & Brown Tapas ★

48 Harbour Street, Whitstable, CT5 1AQ (01227 273373). **Lunch served** 11.45am-2pm Mon, Wed-Fri; 11.45am-2.30pm Sat; 11.45am-2.45pm Sun. **Dinner served** 6-9.15pm Mon, Wed-Fri; 6-9.30pm Sat. **Tapas** £1.95-£9.95. **No credit cards.**

Williams & Brown bring a taste of the Med to customers at their classy deli in Harbour Street. At this new venture – on the site of the former Harbour Street Café – the food is every bit as appealing, with the menu and the cooking singing of true Spain. The simple, low-budget interior consists of white walls, a few modern prints, crowded tables and bar seating set cheek by jowl with chefs beavering in the tiny kitchen. The ingredients around which the dishes are built are prime quality and cooked to a high standard – it is all in the execution, the freshness, the flavour. Everything here is good: char-grilled sardines, twice-cooked octopus with paprika oil, squid dusted with paprika flour and deep-fried, chorizo cooked in cider. Daily specials include the likes of kidneys cooked with Marsala and cream, and spring greens and chickpea tortilla. Booking is essential at weekends.

WYE

Wife of Bath

4 Upper Bridge Street, Wye, TN25 5AF (01233 812232/www.wifeofbath.com). **Lunch served** noon-1.30pm, **dinner served** 7-9.30pm Tue-Sat. **Main courses** £17-£23. **Set lunch** £13.50 2 courses. **Set dinner** £24.50 3 courses. **Credit** AmEx, MC, V.

If you hanker after old-school English formality and sophisticated Cordon Bleu-type cooking, then this village stalwart is for you. Round tables covered with white linen tablecloths and decorated with freshly cut flowers and candlesticks create the most classic of dining room atmospheres. Mains of pan-fried fillet of salmon on a parsnip purée with oven-roasted tomatoes, and – from the à la carte – pan-fried fillet of beef on parsnip purée served with a pesto-topped field mushroom and crispy parma ham, were beautifully presented. The food is a little too rich for lunch (which is nonetheless excellent value), but we were given no reason to question the culinary skills of chef Robert Hymers. The wine list is unsurprisingly expensive but is well chosen, with plenty of half bottle options. Finally, the traditional brown bread ice-cream for dessert is a treat that is not to be missed.

Also in the area

Carluccio's Caffe Unit WVL 14, West Village, Bluewater, DA9 9SE (01322 38727); **Carluccio's Caffe** 32 Mount Pleasant Road, Tunbridge Wells, TN1 1RA (01892 614968); **Loch Fyne** 63-65 High Street, Sevenoaks, TN13 1JY (01732 467140); **Simply Italian** 52-56 High Street, Tenterdon, TN30 6AU (01580 762060); **Simply Italian** 55 High Street, Rochester, ME1 1LN (01634 408077).

Surrey

South East

ABINGER COMMON

Stephan Langton

Friday Street, Abinger Common, RH5 6JR (01306 730775). **Lunch served** 12.30-3pm Tue-Sun. **Dinner served** 7-10pm Tue-Sat. **Main courses** £10.25-£12.95. **Credit** MC, V.

Food at the Stephan Langton is a modern take on age-old British tastes: pan-fried sweetbreads came with rocket salad infused with lemon and mint; roast pork and bubble 'n' squeak was served with piccalilli and morcilla. It's all cooked impressively well and presented with care. The wine list too, is a good one: there are 20 or so reasonably priced options, each chalked up on the blackboard with many available by the glass. This place is hugely popular with walkers and cyclists at the weekend, and even mid-week both the small bar and larger dining room are busy enough to make for a convivial atmosphere.

GODALMING

La Luna

10 Wharf Street, Godalming, GU7 1NN (01483 414155/www.lalunarestaurant.co.uk). **Lunch served** noon-2pm, **dinner served** 7-10pm Tue-Sat. **Main courses** £10.50-£17.95. **Set lunch** £11.50 2 courses, £14.50 3 courses. **Credit** MC, V.

There's a strong Sicilian bent to the menu in this calm white stone-walled space flooded with light from huge windows. Fish is to the fore in each section of the menu – from antipasti such as scallops in dry martini to ravioli stuffed with swordfish. Lobster pasta came scattered with huge chunks of meat alongside punchy aubergine and red pepper. There's around 150 bottles on an impressive all-Italian wine list. Italian staff provide polished, friendly service.

OCKLEY

Bryce's

Old School House, Stane Street, Ockley, RH5 5TH (01306 627430/www.bryces.co.uk). **Lunch served** noon-2pm, **dinner served** 7-9.30pm daily. **Set meal** £22 2 courses, £27.50 3 courses. **Credit** MC, V.

Although Bryce's – a cosy, atmospheric affair – does turn out good meat and vegetarian dishes, you definitely come here for the fish. Mains start close to home (rare grilled fillet of Shetland salmon dusted with cumin and served on Arbroath smokie kedgeree) and spread to the Far East (fillets of red mullet on steamed bok choi and spring onions, sweet sesame and lime dressing) via a few sprightly offerings from the Med – and the starters pretty much follow suit. Beer-battered huss with a many-layered lattice of chips is a reminder that Bryce's still has its feet on the ground, despite its popularity with Surrey's commuter belt over the past 12 years.

REIGATE

Dining Room

59A High Street, Reigate, RH2 9AE (01737 226650). **Lunch served** noon-2pm Mon-Fri; 12.30-2.30pm Sun. **Dinner served** 7-10pm Mon-Sat. **Set lunch** (Mon-Fri) £19.50 3 courses; (Sun) £28.50 3 courses. **Set dinner** (Mon-Thur) £24.50 2 courses; (Fri, Sat) £32 2 courses. **Credit** AmEx, MC, V.

There's a slight air of smugness at TV chef Tony Tobin's latest venue – does having the salmon smoked by 'my friend Nick Nairn' really make it taste better? Such touches jar with an otherwise restrained vibe in the elegant room. Angel hair pasta with lobster, chilli, ginger and coriander, and foie gras with spiced pear chutney stood out among the half-dozen starters. A fine fillet of pork with black pudding was let down a little by over-pungent mustard mash and the meagre dribble of apple purée, but dishes like salmon, scallop and mullet with artichoke show ambition. Service can be more variable than you'd expect at these prices.

RIPLEY

Drake's

The Clock House, High Street, Ripley, GU23 6AQ (01483 224777/www.drakesrestaurant.co.uk). **Lunch served** noon-1.30pm Tue-Fri. **Dinner served** 7-9.30pm Tue-Sat. **Set lunch** £16 2 courses, £19 3 courses. **Set dinner** £30 2 courses, £36 3 courses. **Credit** MC, V.

Having earned a Michelin star at Drake's On The Pond, Stephen Drake has now taken up residence in this pretty red-brick Queen Ann house. Green and yellow pastels lift a little of the gloom in a low-ceilinged formal dining space. A starter of marinaded salmon with orange and hazelnut dressing was zinging with flavour, while wild mushrooms added a welcome rural pungency to a beautifully roasted guinea fowl. Service, led by Drake's wife Serina, is excellent. And if the sun shines, the beautiful garden beckons for pre-dinner drinks or post-dinner coffee.

Also in the area

Loch Fyne 5-6 High Street, Egham, TW20 9EA (01784 414890); **Prezzo** 2-4 High Street, Dorking, RH4 1AT (01306 644998); **Prezzo** 7 The Borough, Farnham, GU9 7NA (01252 737849); **Wagamama** 24-29 High Street, Guildford, GU1 3DY (01483 457779).

Sussex

South East

East Sussex

BATTLE

Pilgrim

1 High Street, Battle, East Sussex TN33 0AE (01424 772314/www.foodrooms.co.uk). **Lunch served** noon-3pm Mon-Sat; noon-4pm Sun. **Dinner served** 7-9.30pm Mon-Sat. **Main courses** £10.80-£18.50. **Set meal** (lunch Mon-Thur, dinner Mon-Wed) £14.75 2 courses, £19.75 3 courses. **Credit** AmEx, MC, V.

On the site of a 12th-century monastic hospital, this wonderful restaurant is housed in an impressive vaulted hall filled with period furniture, log fires, plenty of candles and efficient but friendly staff serving quality food. The weekend menu is a fine affair: scallop with a balsamic reduction was perfectly seared; lobster in a zesty lime and ginger dressing was wonderfully firm and flavoursome; good-sized fillets of brill and turbot were delivered on a fondant potato with caramelised lemon butter and fresh spinach. An à la carte main of free-range medallions of pork fillet, slow-cooked in cider and honey, was slightly overcooked and missing some contrasting crunchy crackling. A dessert of hot milk chocolate tortellini wasn't nearly chocolatey enough, and unpleasantly slippery. Chocolate tart was much better. Piquant spenwood ewe's milk and oxford blue cheeses were well matched by a glass of vintage port.

Simply Italian ★

23 High Street, Battle, East Sussex TN33 0EA (01424 772100/www.simplyitalian.co.uk). **Meals served** noon-10pm daily. **Main courses** £4.95-£8.25. **Credit** MC, V.

Exactly what it says on the… SI is a bright and airy restaurant with plenty of light wood furniture, colourful abstract paintings, fresh flowers on the tables and good Italian food. It's forte is its staff. After touring Battle Abbey, over-excited kids with newly acquired chain-mail and wooden swords are met with warm smiles and handed crayons and pictures to colour. Kids' menus are £4.95 for soft drink, pizza or spaghetti with meatballs, and dessert (three scoops of different ice-creams). Adults will make quick work of the pizzas too – ours benefited from additional (off-menu) gorgonzola and some fire-engine red chillis. Raspberry sorbet to follow provides a welcome cool-down. Bravissimo.

1066 Food

The Chapel, 55 High Street, Battle, East Sussex TN33 0EN (01424 775520). **Lunch served** noon-4pm Mon-Sat. **Main courses** £6-£10. **Credit** MC, V.

New ownership has changed little at this wholesome hideout away from the tourist bustle around the famous Abbey and battlefield. The large deli area is filled with organic and locally farmed produce (including English wines), leading to the compact dining area with its scatter of blond wood tables. Beyond, a little wooden deck terrace provides more tables beneath shady umbrellas. Daily specials chalked on the board might include smoked mackerel with rocket and mascarpone alongside more typical dishes like grilled sardines or a vegetarian tart. Meat gets more of a nod on the à la carte with minted Barnsley lamb or lipsmacking hot lemon chicken. On a hot day, though, the mixed selection 'deli starter' – heaped couscous, smoked salmon, marinated artichokes, various salads – washed down with organic ginger beer on the terrace – makes a zingy summer lunch.

BODIAM

Curlew

Junction Road, Bodiam, East Sussex TN32 5UY (01580 861394/www.thecurlewatbodiam.co.uk). **Lunch served** noon-2pm Tue-Sun. **Dinner served** 7-9.30pm Tue-Sat. **Main courses** £13.95-£18.95. **Credit** MC, V.

More of a restaurant than a pub, with most of the place given over to dining tables, the Curlew is a welcoming destination for bon viveurs. White weatherboard outside, dried hops hanging from the rafters inside, the atmosphere is country cosy, but the food is rather more sophisticated with an à la carte Mediterranean-influenced menu that changes monthly. Starters might include mussels in cream and wine, or zingy prawn, avocado and smoked salmon with mango and pepper salsa. Dishes are substantial in size and flavour: a butter-tender extra mature sirloin steak with creamy béarnaise sauce arrived with a mountain of chips, portobello mushroom, tomato, spinach and fried onions, while a vegetarian terrine comprised pan-fried pressed potato, roasted courgettes, aubergines, red and green peppers and fresh asparagus with pea foam. Desserts didn't disappoint: caramelised panna cotta with Grand Marnier and fruit was delicious. Our young waiting service was distracted, but friendly.

BRIGHTON

Blanch House

Blanch House Hotel, 17 Atlingworth Street, Brighton, East Sussex BN2 1PL (01273 645755/ www.blanchhouse.co.uk). **Lunch served** 12.30-2pm Wed-Sat. **Dinner served** 7-10pm Tue-Sat.

Set lunch £15 2 courses, £20 3 courses. **Set dinner** £25 2 courses, £30 3 courses. **Credit** AmEx, MC, V.
As simple as its *Play School* letter-b-in-a-house logo, the stark white basement interior of this hotel restaurant reflects the brevity of its menu: three-course lunches, with three selections per course, £20; three-course dinners, with four selections per course, £30. After a sumptuous appetiser of ceps and truffle oil soup, a square oriental crab salad starter sparkles with delicate touches of beet sprouts and crab mayonnaise. A main of gilt-head bream, confit tomatoes and baby artichokes with black olive oil has just the right amount of crunch and savour, and the same can be said of the sea bass with crab arrancini. Note, however, a lack of vegetarian options. Equal delicacy is applied to a dessert of lemon cake, lemon confit and raspberry sorbet, although this delicacy comes at the price of near-hour wait between main and dessert. At dinner time this might not matter; at weekday lunch, it is infuriating. Otherwise, a class act.

Café Paradiso

Hotel Seattle, Brighton Marina, Brighton, East Sussex BN2 5WA (01273 679799/www.aliashotels.com).
Lunch served noon-2.30pm Mon-Fri; 12.30-3pm Sat, Sun. **Dinner served** 7-9.30pm daily. **Main courses** £5.25-£15.95. **Credit** AmEx, MC, V.
With its vast windows facing Brighton Marina the restaurant of the stylish Hotel Seattle is a breath of fresh sea air. Providing both elegant backdrop and mooring for the boats that bring in the catch that features heavily on the menu, the marina is as integral to this slick operation as the swift staff and quirky decor. Choose from a dozen hot and cold antipasti (fresh crab with sweet pork and green mango salad, wild mushrooms on toasted brioche), some in two sizes and with vegetarian versions. Fish and seafood comprise the mains, centrepieced by a simple cold shellfish plate of oysters, langoustine and half a crab. The lunch menu is slightly less extensive than dinner, with no all-in midday specials. Children have their own mini gourmet menu, and the regular attention of friendly waitresses. Of the half-dozen imaginative desserts, peanut ice-cream with vodka and bloody orange sorbet is tangy and tasty. There are 12 wines by the glass, 80 by the bottle.

Due South

139 King's Road Arches, Brighton, East Sussex BN1 2NF (01273 821218/www.duesouth.co.uk).
Meals served noon-10pm daily. **Main courses** £10.95-£16.50. **Credit** AmEx, DC, MC, V.
The dearth of decent dining spots on Brighton's seafront has been addressed by Due South, a two-floor restaurant squeezed into a three-level space under the arches. Five prime tables face a half-moon window overlooking the sea and busy boardwalk; just below, two rows of plain mezzanine tables tremble with the traffic of staff shuttling from the sea-level kitchen down a wrought-iron staircase. Ingredients are locally and organically sourced; from the steamed, buttered Midhurst asparagus or local rabbit satay to start, to the twice-baked Stonegate sheep's cheese soufflé with rainbow chard or pedigree Sussex steak, and excellent ice-cream. The greens are from a local producer who cultivates according to phases of the moon, but the ethical dictat rarely grates given the spread of clientele from midde-aged Islingtonites to skate-rat teenagers. Five wines of each colour come by the glass. Be sure to book.

La Fourchette

105 Western Road, Brighton, East Sussex BN1 2AA (01273 722556/www.lafourchette.co.uk). **Lunch served** noon-2.30pm Mon-Sat; noon-3.30pm Sun. **Dinner served** 7-10.30pm Mon-Sat. **Set lunch** £10 2 courses, £13 3 courses; (Sun) £14 2 courses, £18 3 courses. **Set dinner** £22 2 courses, £28 3 courses. **Credit** AmEx, MC, V.
A rustic right-angle of Gallic charm and culinary authenticity between the city centre and the West Pier, La Fourchette drags in regular crowds of

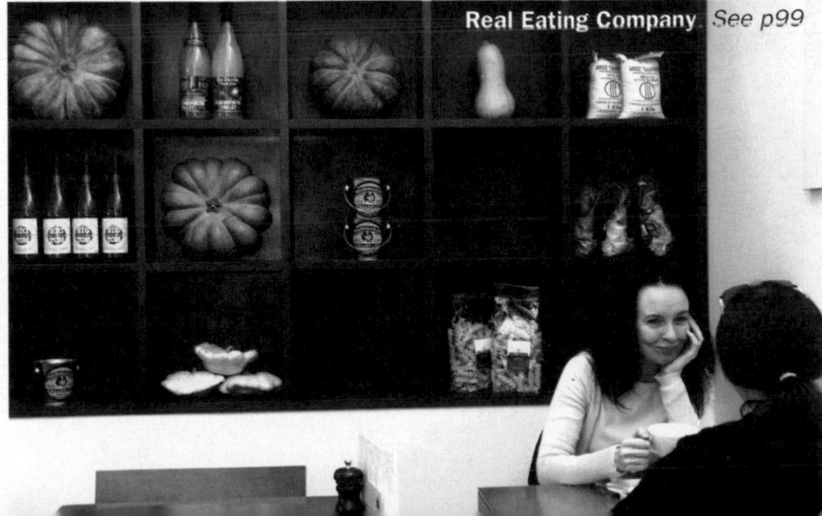
Real Eating Company *See p99*

discerning shoppers with its bargain lunchtime deals chalked up outside. This daily-changing set lunch menu is complemented by a main one of traditional French meat dishes and a fish one of the fresh variety: roast sea bream and turnip gateau, poached and butter roast brochette of monkfish and king prawns, and spinach-stuffed whiting, each as finely formed as any piscine option in town. As if in character, the service is coquettish, attentive after a fashion, charming in the right mood, annoying after your cutlery has clattered on the floor (practically an inevitability considering the tiny tables). The wines, mainly French, are well priced and the ten-strong dessert menu hides a gem or two.

Gingerman

21A Norfolk Square, Brighton, East Sussex BN1 2PD (01273 326688). **Lunch served** 12.30-1.45pm, **dinner served** 7-10pm Tue-Sat. **Set lunch** £9.95 1 course, £12.95 2 courses, £14.95 3 courses. **Set dinner** £22 2 courses, £25 3 courses. **Credit** AmEx, DC, MC, V.

Simplicity itself, Ben McKellar's Gingerman offers quality continental – mainly French – cuisine at accessible prices. The weekly changing lunch menu is an absolute winner. The main menu, available for lunch or dinner, shows style and imagination: starters include a crispy pig's trotter beignet with beetroot and tartare sauce, or warm bundles of asparagus with frisée, croutons and pancetta; mains of monkfish and sweet potato red curry with jasmine rice or braised duck leg in red wine with spätzle and spring onions. Sauces are rich and meaty but once advised, the kitchen will cater each sauce to vegetarians' wishes. Equal care is taken over the desserts, hot raspberry syrup poured into an erect soufflé. Coffee is served with delicate raspberry jam cakes, and an extensive choice of digestifs can be complemented by a seafront walk just three minutes away.

Krakatoa ★

7 Pool Valley, Brighton, East Sussex BN1 1NJ (01273 719009). **Meals served** *Mar-Dec* noon-11pm Tue-Sun. **Dinner served** *Jan, Feb* 6-11pm Tue-Sun. **Main courses** £7.50-£11.95. **Credit** AmEx, MC, V.

This modest pan-Asian café by Brighton bus station just a short stroll from the Lanes offers the authentic tastes of the Far East at prices more akin to pub lunches. Only one of the dozen main courses tops the £10 barrier, and that, a sumptuous goong samui of Thai tiger prawns and Asian salad, is worth every cent. Half the options, including the £5 starters, are vegetarian and none lack creative flair. Tum yum goong Thai soup of hot and sour prawn featured a zingy mix of flavours and two juicy prawns; Japanese salmon on fresh spinach was a confection of ginger, seaweed and peppers. Upstairs from the simple, rustic no-smoking room, cushions are scattered to cater for those who prefer a cross-legged, kneeling, nicotine-led experience, but the joy of Krakatoa is its lack of pretence. The housey soundtrack would suit any of the designer bars within a 500m radius; service is swift and without servility. Recommended.

Momma Cherri's Soul Food Shack

11 Little East Street, Brighton, East Sussex BN1 1HT (01273 774545/www.mommacherri.co.uk). **Meals served** noon-midnight Fri, Sat; noon-10pm Sun. **Dinner served** 6-11pm Mon, Tue, Thur. **Meals served** 11am-midnight Fri, Sat; 11am-9pm Sun. **Main courses** £7.50-£15.50. **Set dinner** £20 3 courses. **Credit** AmEx, MC, V.

Authentic, filling and fun, dining out at Momma Cherri's is everything that mid-range dining out should be. Run out of a modest one-level terraced house amid higgedly-piggledy buildings, Momma's is down-home and dandy. A soundtrack of soul, R&B and, on Sundays, gospel, glides out of the speakers, as smooth as the staff flitting between the narrow gaps allowed by ten tables squeezed in. Summer and special occasions (July 4th and the like) bring diners out on to the adjoining slab of pavement. And the food? Heaps of hearty goodness, grits 'n' all, typified by hulking plates of jambalaya (meat, fish or veg varieties) heavy enough to sink a paddle steamer. Other mains are categorised according to chicken, fish, pork or vegetarian staples. The three courses should come to £20 and thereafter, you shouldn't need to eat for a week. There's breakfasts and brunches too, a menu for children (celebrated rather than merely accommodated), and Dixie, Lone Star, Cave Creek and Mexican beers. Book at weekends.

Nia Café

87-88 Trafalgar Street, Brighton, East Sussex BN1 4EB (01273 671371). **Meals served** 9am-10pm Mon-Sat; 9am-6pm Sun. **Main courses** £7.50-£14. **Set dinner** (7-10pm Mon-Thur) £13.95 2 courses. **Credit** AmEx, MC, V.

By day a busy pit stop offering all-day breakfasts to market browsers, after dark the Nia dims the industrial lights hanging over its dozen wooden tables and becomes a fully fledged restaurant – without losing any of the funky chic native to the North Laines. The à la carte main menu is changed fortnightly and always features vegetarian, fish and lamb options. A Thai-infused royal dorade en papillotte, steaming as its envelope is snipped with care by a down-to-earth waitress; an accompanying side dish (£3) of mange tout in butter with a sesame seed sprinkle was big enough for three. The pork fillet rolled in parma ham on a bed of sweet potato purée with apple and ginger jus oozed succulence. Twenty well-priced wines come by the bottle, five by the large glass (£4.50). A handy short walk from the station. Book after Wednesday.

One Paston Place ★

1 Paston Place, Brighton, East Sussex BN2 1HA (01273 606933/www.onepastonplace.co.uk). **Lunch served** 12.30-1.45pm, **dinner served** 7-9.30pm Tue-Sat. **Main courses** £21-£23. **Set lunch** £16.50 2 courses, £19 3 courses. **Credit** AmEx, DC, MC, V.

Refurbished and now under the considerable expertise of Neapolitan chef and owner Francesco Furriello, Brighton's premier restaurant (arguably) has lost its upmarket French formality but gained a metropolitan buzz. The food is exquisite and presented by experienced, unstuffy staff eager to advise. The set lunch, for which many regulars happily don jacket and tie, is a delightful way to relieve yourself of £20 and step out into the trendy vibe of Kemp Town perfectly satisfied. The three main options invariably feature a fish and a lamb dish, from a lighter menu than Furriello's predecessors would have opted for, and one that is changed monthly. If you choose to go à la carte the expense will be rewarded with simple but finely tuned sauces accompanying fine cuts of fish and meat, the starters imaginative but concise: a warm salad of rabbit and goat's cheese with lemon and walnut dressing, or warm milk-poached skate with courgette and Muscat sauce, to give two examples. A somewhat formal interior of chandeliers, mirrors and a strange pastoral mural may be a hangover from the old days, but already they're warming the espresso cups and more changes might be on the way.

Real Eating Company ★

86-87 Western Road, Hove, East Sussex BN3 1JB (01273 221444/www.real-eating.co.uk). **Meals served** 9am-5pm Mon-Fri; 9am-7pm Sat; 10am-5pm Sun. **Main courses** £7.50-£15.95. **Credit** MC, V.

Opened in January 2004 as the flagship eaterie of a retail business specialising in quality foodstuffs, many sourced from local producers and/or organic, the plain and simple Real Eating Company provides all-day salads, soups and sandwiches headlined by a three-hour lunch period from noon. Seated either around the deli counter or at one of six tables in a tidy skylighted back room, diners are treated to a daily changing, seasonal choice of half-a-dozen eclectic starters – foie gras parfait, beetroot chutney and poilane toast – and eight mains – organic pork chop, quinces and curly kale, seared scallops with sautéed black pudding and new potatoes. Puddings (rhubarb and champagne sorbet), beers from microbreweries (Nyewood Gold from Ballards, £3) and hand-pressed apple and rhubarb juices from the Chegworth Valley stress the British influence. Yet to find its feet as a main lunchtime destination, but a welcome option on the otherwise bland Hove-Brighton border.

Seven Dials

1-3 Buckingham Place, Brighton, East Sussex BN1 3TD (01273 885555/www.sevendials restaurant.co.uk). **Lunch served** noon-3pm Tue-Sat; 12.30-3.30pm Sun. **Dinner served** 7-10.30pm Tue-Thur; 6.30-10.30pm Fri, Sat; 7-9.30pm Sun. **Set lunch** (Tue-Sat) £10 2 courses, £15 3 courses. **Set dinner** £20 2 courses, £25 3 courses. **Credit** AmEx, MC, V.

Award-winning chef Sam Metcalfe has given this former bank some homely touches, decking out the staircase with arty black-and-white family photos, and providing his praiseworthy restaurant with hospitable staff, who receive all of the obligatory 12% tip. Most of all, Sam has lent imaginative touches to a capable kitchen – rump of lamb on aubergine caviar with sautéed wild garlic and a tomato, olive and rosemary sauce – that is visibly active from the summer terrace bordered by a row of box trees. Traffic noise and the constant bleep of the pedestrian crossing can infiltrate quiet moments, but bonhomie overcomes all and you will soon be contentedly digesting the appetiser of tomato and basil soup while awaiting one of half-a-dozen starters. Rich, classy desserts include a rather splendid pear and walnut tart with apricot glaze. Two- and three-course deals are a snip considering the quality of fare on offer.

Terre à Terre ★

71 East Street, Brighton, East Sussex BN1 1HQ (01273 729051). **Lunch served** noon-3pm Wed-Fri. **Dinner served** 6-10.30pm Tue-Fri. **Meals served** noon-10.30pm Sat, Sun. **Main courses** £11.50-£12.50. **Credit** AmEx, DC, MC, V.

Brighton's reliably inventive flagship vegetarian restaurant enjoys a reputation that attracts hordes of weekending pan-fried weary Londoners to its simple space. Friendly, child-welcoming and with homely jars of tangy oils and preserves on sale out front, Terre à Terre spreads a fine tapestry of meat-free delights. Each of the half-dozen starter and main dishes seems to require a four-line description, which may triumphantly culminate with show-stoppers like 'dusted with caraway seed and finished with wheat berry emulsion and celeriac straw'. The result is invariably tasty, and quite often delicious, but there is a sense of tamari drenched for the sake of it. Certainly the Kibbi Our Soles of spiced soaked cane wrapped in kesthery kibbi aubergine soles, served with (for the sake of brevity) cinnamon soft onions, dry cranberry couscous and billy can escabeche, was blander than it was brilliant – although somehow you were pleased that somebody had concocted it anyway. With the addition of side salads and organic wine, prices can mount. There's a back terrace in summer.

DANEHILL

Coach & Horses

Coach & Horses Lane, Danehill, East Sussex RH17 7JF (01825 740369). **Lunch served** noon-2pm Mon-Sat; noon-2.30pm Sun. **Dinner served** 7-9pm Mon-Thur; 7-9.30pm Fri, Sat. **Main courses** £8.95-£12.95. **Credit** MC, V.

Even if its kitchen was ordinary, the Coach & Horses would be a splendid place in which to while away time with the generally jovial locals, whether round the intimate bar or the tidy beer garden. But add the dining area, as attractive a pub conversion as you're likely to find, and the ever-changing menu served there (a smaller range of food is offered in the bar), and you're left with a real gem. Gazpacho was

Duke of Cumberland Arms. *See p103.*

marginally too vinegary, but open ravioli with duck and mushrooms proved a fresh and delightful compilation. Mains, a roast rib of beef with veg and an enormous Yorkshire pud, and grilled organic veal escalope with buttered chard, were unimpeachable, as were the service, the handful of Sussex ales and Gospel Green's summery champagne-style cider.

DUDDLESWELL

Duddleswell Tea Rooms ★

Duddleswell, East Sussex TN22 3BH (01825 712126). **Open** *Feb-May, Sept-Nov* 10am-5pm Tue-Sun, bank hols; *June-Aug* 10am-5pm daily. **Lunch served** noon-2pm. **Main courses** £6-£7.50. **No credit cards**.

The sign hanging out front of the Duddleswell Tea Rooms informs passers-by that this venerable Sussex eaterie has been open since 1935. There are concessions to modernity here, sure: the list of sandwiches is supplemented by generously stuffed baguettes and the shamelessly calorific treacle tarts and Kentish apple cakes in the dessert cabinet have been joined by a creamy chocolate fudge concoction. However, in most regards (frilly decor, polite service), this is still a delightfully old-fashioned place. The lunches are substantial spreads, but the real draw is the cream teas, offering plenty of sustenance for walkers fresh from a jaunt around adjacent Ashdown Forest. In summer, take your slap-up feast out on to the immaculate, sun-soaked lawn.

EAST CHILTINGTON

Jolly Sportsman

Chapel Lane, East Chiltington, East Sussex BN7 3BA (01273 890400/www.thejollysportsman.com). **Lunch served** noon-2pm Tue-Sun. **Dinner served** 6-9pm Tue-Thur; 6-10pm Fri, Sat. **Main courses** £7.50-£16.50. **Set lunch** (Tue-Sat) £11 2 courses, £14.75 3 courses. **Credit** MC, V.

Taken over six years ago by Bruce Wass (formerly of Thackeray's; *see p91*), the Jolly Sportsman is a delight to look at, the calm and airy modernity of its roomy interior complemented by an immaculately maintained garden, complete with children's play area. But despite its excellent reputation, we found the kitchen erratic. The simple dishes were delivered well: the ingredients in a colourful crab, mango and nuoc cham salad had clearly been well sourced, as had those in a tender fillet of hake served with mushrooms and a cream-and-wine accompaniment. However, chicken and black bean broth was saltily intense, while beef bourguignon was deeply flawed, the meat lacking taste and texture and the gravy barely even extant. There's a strong selection of wine, but the real treat is the choice of obscure ales poured direct from their casks. Service was a little slow on this occasion, but full marks to the staff for acknowledging the fact and apologising by stripping our bill of its drinks and service charge. All in all, then, a mixed meal, but past experience leads us to suspect that this was an off day.

FLETCHING

Griffin Inn

Fletching, nr Uckfield, East Sussex TN22 3SS (01825 722890/www.thegriffininn.co.uk). **Lunch served** noon 2.30pm daily. **Dinner served** 7-9.30pm Mon-Sat; 7-9pm Sun. **Main courses** £9.50-£19.50. **Set lunch** (Sun) £25 3 courses. **Credit** AmEx, DC, MC, V.

The main role of the Griffin Inn, one it plays with aplomb some four centuries after opening, is as the archetypal adorable English village pub. While one bar is dark and cosy, its neighbour is airy and more modern (with sofas and a TV), and the garden to the rear offers fine views towards Sheffield Park. The kitchen is also a major draw. Staff work hard here: the menu in the restaurant – offering the likes of roast venison and harissa-fried salmon escalope – has little or no crossover with the slightly cheaper but no less appealing list scratched on a blackboard in the bar. From the latter, salad of marinated squid, lime and coriander was nicely balanced, but the houmous on the otherwise fine mixed meze platter was too dry. Pan-roasted bream arrived whole, delicately set off by a chilli, pineapple and coriander salsa. If you over indulge in the Harvey's Best or Badger Tanglefoot, there are eight rooms offering B&B accommodation, half of them in a converted coach house.

HASTINGS

Maggie's ★ ★

Above the fish market, Rock-a-Nore Road, Hastings, East Sussex TN34 3DW (01424 430205). **Meals served** *July-Sept* 5am-6pm Mon-Sat; *Oct-June* 5am-3pm Mon-Sat. **Main courses** £3.70-£5.90. **No credit cards**.

Don't be put off by the simple interior of this atmospheric café, overlooking a scattering of black timbered net huts and fish stalls by Hastings' shingle beach. Maggie's serves some of the best fish and chips in the country, huge portions of cod or rock salmon (huss), the moist white fish encased in silky smooth, whisper-thin batter. Handmade chips and perfectly cooked peas struggle to find space on the plate filled by a 'standard' portion (perhaps the 'large' helpings are intended for the hungry trawlerman who fetch up here for the 5am opening). Wine and beer are available for under £2, though most make do with mugs of strong tea, best downed on the tiny terrace, where you can sit and admire beached boats and the tangle of fishing paraphernalia in the tangy sea air.

Mermaid ★

2 Rock-a-Nore Road, Hastings, East Sussex TN34 3DW (01424 438100). **Meals served** 6.30am-3pm Mon, Tue; 6.30am-7.30pm Wed-Sun. **Main courses** £4.75-£7. **No credit cards**.

'Cod, haddock, plaice and huss, the locals call us "Fish are us".' Festooned with maritime memorabilia, the Mermaid opens early to feed the freezing, famished fisherfolk with fish so fresh it 'still has a pulse'. All freshly battered and cooked to order, and the chips aren't bad either – full, fluffy and non-greasy. The set breakfast is available throughout the day alongside familiars such as shepherd's pie, steak and kidney pie and seasoned chicken. Traditional is the word, with desserts of treacle pudding and good old spotted dick. Clientele are mixed, in age and type but include locals, yokels and DFL's (down from London's). Weather permitting, you can eat alfresco and enjoy the seaside vibe while dodging circling seagulls. At busy periods, don't wait until starvation rage is upon you – queues are common and food takes an additional half-hour. It's worth the wait.

LEWES

Circa

145 High Street, Lewes, East Sussex BN7 1XT (01273 471777/www.circacirca.com). **Lunch served** noon-2.30pm Tue-Fri; noon-2pm Sat. **Dinner served** 6-10pm Tue-Fri; 7-10pm Sat. **Main courses** £10.95-£17. **Set lunch** £11.75 2 courses. **Set dinner** £23 2 courses, £27.50 3 courses. **Credit** AmEx, DC, MC, V.

Fusion reigns at this hip restaurant and cocktail bar. Crowded tables fill the simple space where windows provide a grandstand view of the High Street bustle. The menu is as varied as the passers-by. For starters, seared salmon is paired with fried egg and fennel dahl, while wild mushrooms battle it out with tom yum toast and pickled ginger custard. Similar twists and bold pairings continue with the mains – spiced quail with mung dahl and aged pomegranate, veal with dashi and chilli pineapple and accompaniments like butternut squash vinaigrette, sour soy peas and feta bhaji. If sometimes this sort of El Bulli-influenced approach doesn't find all the notes in harmony, it's still refreshing to see such adventurous cooking, especially with such a reasonably priced lunch menu. Who needs to go to Brighton to be trendy?

RYE

Fish Café

17 Tower Street, Rye, East Sussex TN31 7AT (01797 222210/www.thefishcafe.com). **Lunch served** noon-2.30pm, **dinner served** 6-9pm daily. **Main courses** £6.50-£18. **Credit** AmEx, MC, V.

A light and airy setting for some of the best food in Rye. As you would expect from its name, the majority of the menu comprises a wide range of fish and seafood dishes, but there are also meat and vegetarian alternatives. An excellent plate of oysters, char-grilled lobster, mussels in white wine and a Thai beef salad were all satisfying dishes, but special praise goes to the delicious puddings, notably a wonderful pear tatin with blueberry ice-cream. Staff are very helpful, and can suggest appropriate wines to go with particular dishes. The café also offers a good quality children's menu (two courses and a drink for £5). Options include real cod fingers, tagliatelle, salmon fish cakes or chicken and vegetables, followed by bananas and custard, a chocolate pot or fruit fritters. The downstairs café is open for lunch only, but there is a more formal dining space upstairs offering a similar, but extended, range of dishes during the evening (when booking is essential).

Landgate Bistro

5-6 Landgate, Rye, East Sussex TN31 7LH (01797 222829/www.landgatebistro.co.uk). **Dinner served** 7-9.30pm Tue-Fri; 7-10pm Sat. **Main courses** £10-£13. **Set dinner** (Tue-Thur) £17.90 3 courses incl coffee. **Credit** MC, V.

The Landgate prides itself on its use of excellent, often local ingredients. It is very popular – with locals and visitors – so booking is a good idea. Culinary highlights include salmon and smoked cod fish cakes, English asparagus with a tangy orange hollandaise and a wonderfully garlicky squid. Noisettes of lamb was a sweet and tender dish, but another of chump of lamb with beans and bacon was dry and disappointing. Main courses come with a good selection of vegetables. Cherries with a bayleaf custard in a biscuit cup and hazelnut meringue with raspberries were much better than an indifferent crème caramel. Although we had specified on booking that our party included three young children, we got the impression that children were tolerated rather than welcomed. Children's portions of main dishes were provided, however, and service at the table was friendly.

Also in the area

Hotel du Vin & Bistro Ship Street, Brighton, East Sussex BN1 1AD (01273 718588); **Loch Fyne** 95-99 Western Road, Brighton, East Sussex BN1 2LB (01273 716160); **Quod** 160-161 North Street, Brighton, East Sussex BN1 1EZ (01273 202070); **Simply Italian** 22 High Street, Battle, East Sussex TN33 0EA (01424 772100); **Simply Italian** 10-11 The Waterfront, Sovereign Harbour Marina, Eastbourne, East Sussex BN23 5UT (01323 470911); **Simply Italian** The Strand, Rye, East Sussex TN31 7DB (01797 226024); **Simply Italian** 182 High Street, Uckfield, East Sussex TN22 1AU (01825 766555).

West Sussex

BURPHAM

George & Dragon

Burpham, West Sussex BN18 9RR (01903 883131). **Lunch served** noon-2pm daily. **Dinner served** 7-9.30pm Mon-Sat. **Main courses** £7.95-£15.95. **Credit** AmEx, MC, V.

It's a long and winding road that leads to the door of this quintessential English pub, opposite the rose-clad lych-gate of a 12th-century, flintstone church. With a menu full of modern European fare, from game terrine with celeriac remoulade, to freshly baked tartlette of crab and tiger prawn with a sweet chilli dressing, we started with pan-fried scallops and crevette in garlic butter with a lemon risotto and caper dressing and caramelised goat's cheese on crouton with chilli chutney. Both were a delight to see and savour. Main courses included slow-cooked lamb shank on a chive mash and confit of duck leg and fillet steak with Portobello mushrooms, as well as plenty of fresh fish. The only disappointment was puddings: dark chocolate and hazelnut terrine just didn't rise beyond its constituent parts. The same menu is available in the pub or a more elegant dining area, frequented by a slightly older clientele.

CHARLTON

The Fox Goes Free

Charlton, West Sussex PO18 0HU (01243 811461). **Lunch served** noon-2.30pm, **dinner served** 6.30-10pm Mon-Fri. **Meals served** noon-10pm Sat, Sun. **Main courses** £7.50-£16.50. **Credit** MC, V.

William III used to drop in at this 300-year-old country inn on breaks from hunting, though now the low, dark timbered nooks host a far more mixed crowd who pile in for a wide-ranging menu. There's an adventurousness beyond traditional pub grub – pasta comes with blue cheese and red chard, the roast birds are pigeon rather than chicken. Fish options such as bream with mushroom velouté or monkfish with wild rice and chilli jam sell out quickly. You can, of course, still comfort yourself with classic roasts, washed down with excellent beers such as the pub's own bitter or something from a short but well-chosen wine list. Lovely views across the Downs from the apple tree-filled garden are another plus.

CHILGROVE

White Horse Inn

1 High Street, Chilgrove, West Sussex PO18 9HX (01243 535219/www.whitehorsechilgrove.co.uk). **Lunch served** noon-2pm Tue-Sun. **Dinner served** 7-10pm Tue-Sat. **Main courses** £11.95-£16.95. **Credit** MC, V.

Dining at this establishment is an occasion. The energy of both proprietor and chef guarantee it. While the former plays host extraordinaire, the chef busies himself with freshly roasted nuts and salmon and cream cheese tartlets as accompaniments to aperitifs. Fresh fish is a speciality and a starter of fresh Selsey crab and avocado was exquisite. Not so poached fresh asparagus, which was rather swamped by the accompanying hazelnut and vine tomato bake with lemon and honey hollandaise. The slow-roasted half Gressingham duck on a bed of minted pea purée with rich cassis sauce was a superb mix of flavours, as was seared scallops, served with seafood risotto and bacon. After the richness of such a meal, the puddings (citrus tart and lemon soufflé on a biscuit base with Cornish ice-cream and strawberries) were tempting but beyond us – so the chef obligingly provided a plate of fresh English berries.

EAST GRINSTEAD

Gravetye Manor

Vowels Lane, nr East Grinstead, West Sussex HR19 4LJ (01342 810567/www.gravetyemanor.co.uk). **Lunch served** 12.30-1.45pm, **dinner served** 7-9.30pm daily. **Set lunch** £18 2 courses, £24 3 courses. **Set dinner** £41-£52 3 courses. **Credit** MC, V.

A very unstuffy hotel restaurant experience. The oak-panelled interior and lovely gardens set the scene; the impeccably trained staff oil the wheels. From the canapés to the coffee and Cognac in the lounge after dining, the whole experience runs like clockwork. Good-looking dishes, where possible, use vegetables from Gravetye's own kitchen garden. Dinner might centre round roast medallion of monkfish with saffron crushed potato, cockle and caper sabayon with a red wine sauce, topped by ballotine of duck confit and foie gras wrapped in Denhay ham with rocket salad and fig chutney, and tailed by a trio of cheeses. The wine cellar runs to around 400 wines and is suitably grand, in keeping with the surroundings.

HENLEY

Duke of Cumberland Arms

Henley Village, West Sussex GU27 3HQ (01428 652280). **Lunch served** noon-2.30pm daily. **Dinner served** 7-9.30pm Tue-Sat. **Main courses** £8.50-£15.95. **Credit** MC, V.

At this excellent pub, found in landscaped gardens nestling on a hillside, you can gaze out towards the Sussex Weald while sampling one of many real ales. Eager staff buzz round the cosy, quaint interior. Best known for its fresh fish and pints of prawns, the menu has become more ambitious. Cauliflower and watercress éclairs being sold out, we opted for pan-fried salmon in a dill sauce and stuffed cabbage parcels. The garden menu (bar snacks) has a choice of five caesar salads and seven ploughmans, including own-made pork and egg pie. Interesting puddings included Drambuie and oatmeal bavrois, and strawberry, elderflower and Champagne terrine. From an eclectic wine list the locally produced Nyetimber Classic Cuvée 1996 (apparently sparkling wine of the year and the Queen's favourite) exemplifies the new direction this tiny but exuberantly authentic hostelry has taken.

STORRINGTON

Sawyards

Manleys Hill, Storrington, West Sussex RH20 4BT (01903 742331). **Lunch served** noon-2pm Tue-Fri, Sun. **Dinner served** 7-9pm Tue-Sat. **Set lunch** (Tue-Fri) £19.50 2 courses, £24.50 3 courses. **Set dinner** (Tue-Sat) £29 2 courses, £34 3 courses. **Credit** MC, V.

Michelin-starred Michel Perraud's decision to retire home to France has given his former No.2 Julien Ligouri the chance to take centre stage at the former Fleur de Sel, now sporting a rustic English name despite its new owner being Scottish. The theme, however, remains: excellent French-influenced food served in chintzy English surroundings. A cucumber gazpacho amuse-bouche came delicately spiked with chilli, quickly followed by excellent starters such as scallops with cauliflower purée and red wine dressing and beautifully balanced smoked duck terrine with sweet potato, foie gras and salsify. Braised pork belly in spices showed a firm hand with robust tastes, complemented by a lighter touch for a provençal-style halibut. Vegetarian options included butternut squash tortellini with cep and hazelnut sauce. Desserts such as baked chocolate cheesecake with mascarpone ice-cream reveal a willingness to play with classics. Service from the mainly French staff is impeccable.

Also in the area

Prezzo 46 Carfax, Horsham, West Sussex BH12 1EQ (01403 230245); **Prezzo** 13 High Street, East Grinstead, West Sussex RH19 3AF (01342 300211); **Prezzo** West Street, Midhurst, West Sussex GU29 9NQ (01730 817040).

South East

South West

South West

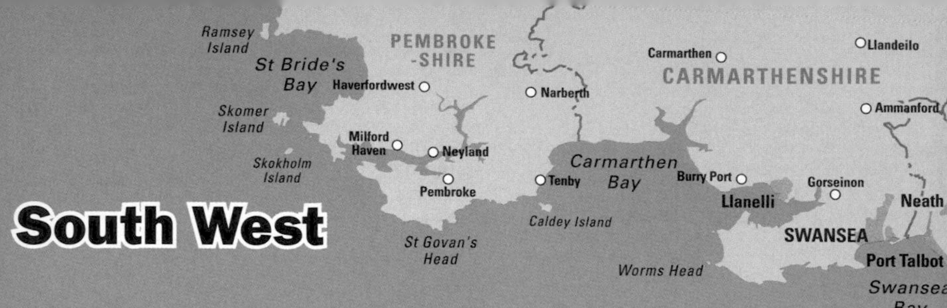

Ramsey Island
St Bride's Bay
PEMBROKE -SHIRE
Haverfordwest
Skomer Island
Milford Haven
Neyland
Skokholm Island
Pembroke
St Govan's Head
Narberth
Carmarthen
CARMARTHENSHIRE
Llandeilo
Ammanford
Carmarthen Bay
Tenby
Caldey Island
Burry Port
Llanelli
Gorseinon
Neath
SWANSEA
Port Talbot
Worms Head
Swansea Bay
Bristol Channel
Foreland Point
Lundy
Ilfracombe
Combe Martin
Lynmouth
Woolacombe
Croyde
Braunton
Northam
Barnstaple
Hartland Point
Westward Ho!
Bideford
South Molton
Hartland
Clovelly
Umberleigh
Great Torrington
Chulmleigh
Morwenstow
Merton
Chawleigh
Winkleigh
Bude Bay
Bude
Stratton
Holsworthy
Hatherleigh
DEVON
Okehampton
Boscastle
Virginstow
Portgate
Chagford
Lydford
Launceston
Lifton
Moretonhampstead
North Bovey
Port Isaac
Camelford
Widecombe in the Moor
Bolventor
North Hill
Padstow
Rock
Treburley
Tavistock
Wadebridge
Princetown
Gulworthy
CORNWALL
Gunnislake
Yelverton
Ashburton
Bodmin
Tregurrian
Bere Alston
Buckfastleigh
Newquay
St Columb Major
Liskeard
South Brent
Lostwithiel
Saltash
PLYMOUTH
Perranporth
Summercourt
St Austell
Fowey
Torpoint
Ivybridge
St Agnes
West Looe
Whitsand Bay
Pentewan
Noss Mayo
Bigbury
Goveton
Portreath
Mevagissey
Bigbury-on-Sea
Truro
Kingsbridge
St Ives
Redruth
Portloe
Bigbury Bay
Camborne
Salcombe
Hayle
Penryn
St Mawes
Penzance
Marazion
Maenporth
Falmouth
Newlyn
Helston
Constantine
Falmouth Bay
Porthleven
Mawgan
Gunwalloe
Land's End
Mount's Bay
Lizard
Lizard Point
0
40 km
0
20 miles

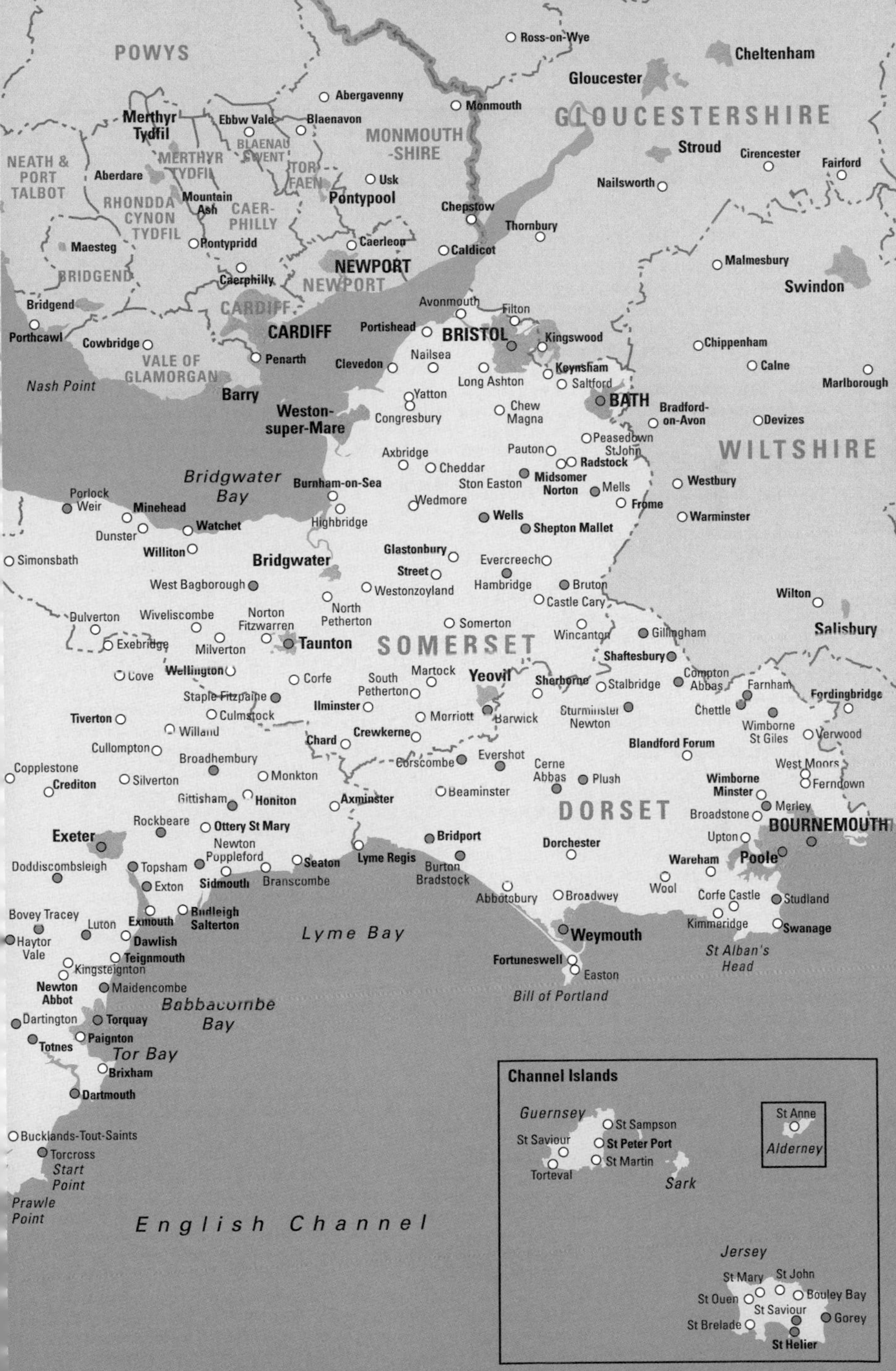

POWYS
Ross-on-Wye
Cheltenham
Gloucester
GLOUCESTERSHIRE
Abergavenny
Monmouth
Merthyr Tydfil
Ebbw Vale
Blaenavon
MONMOUTH -SHIRE
BLAENAU GWENT
MERTHYR TYDFIL
TORFAEN
NEATH & PORT TALBOT
Aberdare
Usk
Stroud
Cirencester
Fairford
Nailsworth
Pontypool
Mountain Ash
RHONDDA CYNON TYDFIL
CAERPHILLY
Chepstow
Thornbury
Maesteg
Pontypridd
Caerleon
Caldicot
Malmesbury
BRIDGEND
Caerphilly
NEWPORT
Swindon
Bridgend
Avonmouth
Filton
CARDIFF
Porthcawl
Cowbridge
CARDIFF
Portishead
BRISTOL
Kingswood
Chippenham
VALE OF GLAMORGAN
Penarth
Clevedon
Nailsea
Keynsham
Calne
Nash Point
Long Ashton
Saltford
Marlborough
Barry
Yatton
BATH
Weston-super-Mare
Congresbury
Chew Magna
Bradford-on-Avon
Devizes
Peasedown St John
WILTSHIRE
Axbridge
Pauton
Radstock
Bridgwater Bay
Cheddar
Midsomer Norton
Porlock Weir
Burnham-on-Sea
Ston Easton
Mells
Westbury
Minehead
Wedmore
Frome
Wells
Warminster
Dunster
Watchet
Highbridge
Shepton Mallet
Williton
Glastonbury
Simonsbath
Bridgwater
Evercreech
Street
West Bagborough
Hambridge
Bruton
Westonzoyland
Wilton
Castle Cary
North Petherton
Dulverton
Wiveliscombe
Norton Fitzwarren
Somerton
Salisbury
Exebridge
Milverton
Taunton
SOMERSET
Wincanton
Gillingham
Shaftesbury
Cove
Wellington
Corfe
South Petherton
Martock
Yeovil
Sherborne
Stalbridge
Compton Abbas
Farnham
Fordingbridge
Staple Fitzpaine
Ilminster
Chettle
Tiverton
Culmstock
Merriott
Barwick
Sturminster Newton
Wimborne St Giles
Willand
Crewkerne
Verwood
Cullompton
Chard
Blandford Forum
Broadhembury
Evershot
Copplestone
Corscombe
Cerne Abbas
West Moors
Crediton
Silverton
Monkton
Plush
Wimborne Minster
Ferndown
Gittisham
Honiton
Axminster
Beaminster
Merley
DORSET
Broadstone
Rockbeare
BOURNEMOUTH
Ottery St Mary
Exeter
Bridport
Upton
Newton Poppleford
Lyme Regis
Dorchester
Doddiscombsleigh
Topsham
Seaton
Poole
Wareham
Burton Bradstock
Exton
Sidmouth
Branscombe
Wool
Abbotsbury
Broadwey
Corfe Castle
Studland
Bovey Tracey
Budleigh Salterton
Exmouth
Kimmeridge
Luton
Swanage
Haytor Vale
Dawlish
Lyme Bay
Weymouth
Teignmouth
St Alban's Head
Fortuneswell
Kingsteignton
Easton
Newton Abbot
Maidencombe
Bill of Portland
Babbacombe Bay
Dartington
Torquay
Totnes
Paignton
Tor Bay
Brixham
Dartmouth
Channel Islands
Guernsey
St Sampson
St Anne
St Saviour
St Peter Port
Alderney
St Martin
Torteval
Sark
Bucklands-Tout-Saints
Torcross
Start Point
Prawle Point
English Channel
Jersey
St Mary
St John
St Ouen
Bouley Bay
St Saviour
St Brelade
Gorey
St Helier

Bristol

South West

Bell's Diner ★

1-3 York Road, BS6 5QB (0117 924 0357/www.bells diner.co.uk). **Lunch served** noon-2pm Tue-Fri. **Dinner served** 7-10pm Mon-Sat. **Main courses** £13-£19.50. **Tasting menu** £45 7 courses, Mon-Thur (max 6 people). **Credit** AmEx, DC, MC, V.

Despite stiff competition, this long-running restaurant remains at the forefront of Bristol's dining scene. The restaurant is housed in a converted grocer's shop and makes good use of the quirky space, divided into two rooms: one rustic and atmospheric, the other modern and sleek. The menu of contemporary Mediterranean-influenced British food changes daily. Among starters is a sublime dish of scallops with a rich broad bean and pea soup and a parmesan crisp; and a beetroot terrine with goat's cheese ice-cream. Roast turbot comes with smooth artichoke purée, baby artichokes and basil oil, while saddle of rabbit, black pudding and spinach is served with rabbit ravioli and tarragon foam. The wine list includes good-value regional bottles and there are surprising versions of favourite desserts for those with waistbands to spare. Highly recommended.

Casa Mexicana

29-31 Zetland Road, BS6 7AH (0117 924 3901/ www.casamexicana.co.uk). **Dinner served** 7-10pm Mon-Sat; 6-9pm Sun. **Main courses** £9.95-£10.75. **Credit** AmEx, MC, V.

The decor at this restaurant is now all tasteful beige and cream, but with Margaritas this good you'll soon be past noticing the colour scheme. The food is a cut above the usual Tex-Mex; recipes are sourced by the owners on regular trips to the Yucatan and are handled with conviction and creativity. Veggies could do a lot worse than a tostado filled with roast sweet potato, aubergines and spinach, topped with goat's cheese and garlic, while carnivores will want to get their teeth round generous enchiladas or meltingly tender pork served in a rich gravy perfumed with anco chillies and oranges. If you've survived the tequila-based cocktails, then there are Mexican beers and an Hispanic wine list to enjoy.

Clifton Sausage Bar & Restaurant

7-9 Portland Street, BS8 4JA (0117 973 1192/0117 970 6511/www.cliftonsausage.co.uk). Bar **Open** 6-11pm Mon; 11am-11pm Tue-Sat; 11am-10.30pm Sun. *Restaurant* **Lunch served** noon-2.30pm Tue-Fri; noon-3pm Sat, Sun. **Dinner served** 6.30-10pm Mon-Fri; 6.30-11pm Sat; 6.30-9pm Sun. **Main courses** £8.50-£14. **Credit** AmEx, DC, MC, V.

Understated, relaxed and welcoming, this restaurant makes bangers and mash a work of art. Eight varieties of sausage include the Clifton, a fusion of pork, cider and wholegrain mustard, and more unusual Moroccan-inspired lamb and apricot varieties. All come with creamy mash or champ and sweet onion gravy or as toad in the hole. Portions aren't massive, but with mash this rich, that's fine. Alternatives are fresh fish – try the skate wing – seafood and light vegetarian dishes. Desserts are traditional. The rustic air, intimate booths and excellent wine list make it a romantic choice or a place for special occasions.

Deason's

43 Whiteladies Road, BS8 2LS (0117 973 6230/ www.deasons.co.uk). **Lunch served** noon-2.30pm Tue-Fri. **Dinner served** 6.30-9.30pm Tue-Sat. **Main courses** £12.50-£21.50. **Set dinner** £17.50 2 courses; £21.50 3 courses. **Credit** AmEx, DC, MC, V.

Set back from the bottom of Whiteladies Road is one of Bristol's most accomplished restaurants. Faultless French service can't quite dispel the stilted atmosphere, but the unfussy interior allows the food to take centre stage. Jason Deason's travels are clearly in evidence throughout the contemporary menu of British and world fusion dishes. Careful preparation and exquisite presentation are the key notes. Mix and match from the à la carte and set menu to create a feast: a delicate glass noodle salad with scallops and duck breast, followed by a decadently rich leek and blue cheese risotto, or a supreme fillet steak on a bed of wild mushrooms. Be sure to leave room for the show-stopping assiette of desserts – white chocolate and honeycomb-filled profiterole, tiramisu and rich chocolate samosa. The French and international wine list is supported by a selection of Emilio Lustau sherries.

Entelia

34 Princess Victoria Street, BS8 4BZ (0117 946 6793). **Lunch served** noon-2.30pm, **dinner served** 6-10.30pm daily. **Main courses** £6.95-£13.95. **Credit** AmEx, MC, V.

Despite tightly packed tables, the open-plan dining room of this smart Greek restaurant is simple and stylish, with wooden floors and large picture windows. The menu features classics with a modern sensibility. Start with fish cake polpettes with a vibrant sun-dried tomato salsa or sensuous spanakopita: crisp, warm layers of filo pastry filled with feta and spinach. Follow this with fish – bass, bream, red mullet, red snapper and lemon sole are regular features – or the excellent prizzoles: a rack of red-currant-glazed lamb chops served on celeriac and thyme mash. The souvalaki are less successful, with a dryness that is unrelieved by unimaginative sides of rice and salad, but portions are generous.

Firehouse Rotisserie

The Leadworks, Anchor Square, BS1 5DB (0117 915 7323/www.firehouserotisserie.co.uk). **Meals served** noon-11pm daily. **Main courses** £10.95-£14.95. **Credit** AmEx, DC, MC, V.

Firehouse is in the perfect spot to catch hungry tourists from the @t-Bristol complex or locals from the surrounding pubs and bars. There are plenty of tables outside, and a large, airy dining room. The Californian-style menu offers rotisserie chicken, gourmet brick-fired pizzas and Southwestern specialities that are a bit of a mouthful to order but work well on the plate. Try the crayfish and rocket salad with lemon and tarragon dressing, followed by a rotisserie free-range Texas spice-rubbed half-chicken served with fries and coleslaw. Service is smiley, and the children's menu is great.

FishWorks Seafood Café

128-130 Whiteladies Road, BS8 2RS (0117 974 4433/www.fishworks.co.uk). **Lunch served** noon-2.30pm, **dinner served** 6-10pm Tue-Sat. **Main courses** £7-£20. **Credit** AmEx, DC, MC, V.

Refurbished but fortunately not reinvented, FishWorks continues to serve arguably the freshest fish and seafood in town. The catch of the day is

Bar crawl: Bristol

In the city centre, the essential stop is unmissable **Mr Wolf's** (33 St Stephens Street, 0117 927 3221) a noodle, cocktail and music bar whose inimitable laid-back vibe ensures a loyal local following. Chow down on noodles while DJs get the joint jumping. Wok-wielding Mr Wolf presides over the mayhem with unfailing good humour and enthusiasm.

If you can tear yourself away, it's a short hop to Bristol's dockside, where a converted red-brick Victorian wine warehouse shelters the much-loved **Watershed** media centre (1 Canons Road, 0117 927 5100/www.watershed.co.uk), which has an airy bar cum-café. At the weekends many of the other bars along this strip are best avoided, but **The River** (1 Canons Road, 0117 930 0498) maintains its appeal, thanks to an unfussy interior and a fab sausage and mash menu. Another good bet is the recently refurbished **E-Shed** (1 Canons Road, 0117 907 4287), a pleasantly funky hangout that's upped the style stakes with classy red leather seating and a sleek new bar.

Head east for the **Mud Dock Café** (*see p111*), the **riverstation** (*see p112*) and the **Severnshed** (The Grove, Harbourside, 0117 925 1212, www.severnshed.co.uk) a spacious former boatshed, designed by Isambard Kingdom Brunel. Its long waterside terrace is the perfect spot for summer lunch with the glorious spire of St Mary Redcliffe looking down on you from the opposite bank. Inside, a sleek mobile bar separates the formal dining room from the ultra funky drinking area.

A cluster of bars and clubs at the bottom of Park Street cater for Bristol's stylish night owls. **Nocturne** (1 Unity Street, 0117 925 7144), formerly owned by Massive Attack, is members only; easier to access is the New York-groovy **Soda Bar** (Frogmore Street, Frog Lane 0117 922 5005). The latest addition to the scene is **Three** (9 Park Street, 0117 930 4561), which has created a stir by transforming the famously dodgy Mauretania into a glammed up bar, club and restaurant empire. Head up the hill from here to the **Elbow Room** (64 Park Street, 0117 9300242) to shoot some pool or to the **Park** (38 Triangle West, 0117 940 6101), a small bar, with a classy vibe and some quality DJs entertaining the crammed-in punters.

In Clifton, the 'Strip', aka Whiteladies Road, is lined with bars and restaurants, attracting hordes of students. One of the most appealing is **Bar Humbug** (89 Whiteladies Road, 0117 904 0061/ www.barhumbug.co.uk), thanks to an outside terrace, platters of food for sharing, quality cocktails and a relaxed atmosphere. In Clifton Village, visit **Amoeba** (10 Kings Road, 0117 946 6461) a brilliant little café-bar, where all the designer furniture and original artwork is for sale, and the **Mall** (66 The Mall, 0117 974 5318) an easygoing pub with a small beer garden at the back.

For a true taste of the West Country, however, head for the **Coronation Tap** (Sion Close, Clifton Village, 0117 973 9617), a legendary cider pub, selling (among others) a cider so strong that it's only served by the half pint (ask for Exhibition). The traditional interior is usually full of rustic charm and pissed locals. Venture further afield to the **Tobacco Factory Café & Bar** (corner of Raleigh Road & North Street, Southville, 0117 902 0060) to sample its warehouse chic, restaurant-standard food and loungey beanbag atmosphere. Or head north of the centre to **one30** (*see p111*), where the cocktails are as accomplished as the tapas is tasty.

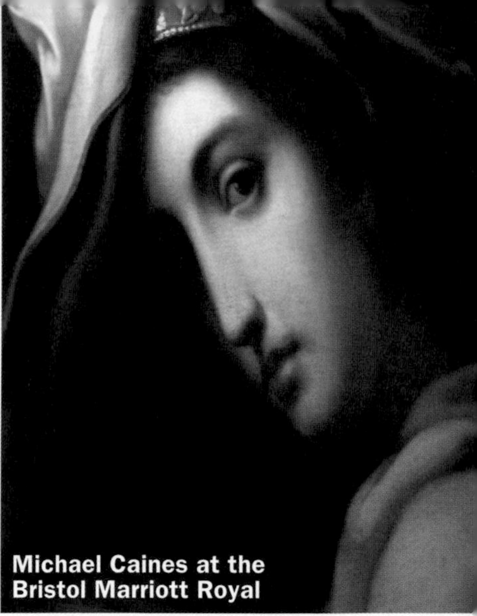

Michael Caines at the Bristol Marriott Royal

shipped in from around the British coast to ensure a specials board full of variety. Wild Icelandic halibut with hollandaise sauce was a paragon of sensitive cooking. Alongside the specials are 'classic' dishes that exemplify the kitchen's simple and respectful attitude. Try the huge vat of steamed River Fowey mussels, dripping with wine and parsley; or heaps of steamed fruits de mer served on ice. A deep blue colour scheme, a hint of nautical paraphernalia and a buzzy atmosphere provide the perfect setting. You can buy some to take home from the fishmonger's counter or learn culinary tips from the top at FishWorks' acclaimed cookery school.

Fuchsia Restaurant & Lounge Club

Nelson House, Nelson Street, BS1 2JT (0117 945 0505/www.fuchsia-bristol.com). **Lunch served** noon-3.30pm Mon, Tue, Sun; noon-3pm Wed-Sat. **Dinner served** 6.30-11pm Mon-Thur, Sun; 6-11.30pm Fri, Sat. **Main courses** £12-£18. **Set lunch** (noon-2.30pm Mon-Fri) £5.95 2 courses incl one drink. **Credit** AmEx, DC, MC, V.

Sophistication meets 1970s kitsch at this stylish oriental restaurant, where polished lacquer surfaces and Chinese fretwork are offset by neon pink lighting and flamboyant murals. There are classy cocktails to enjoy in the glam bar before moving on to contemplate the large menu that appeals to trendies as much as the Chinese community. Choices range from Szechuan king prawn and Singapore beef to stir-fried Mongolian venison or jasmine tea-smoked ribs. The lounge club upstairs has funky beats – but you have to pay to get in, even if you've racked up an impressive bill in the restaurant.

Glasnost

1 William Street, Totterdown, BS3 4TU (0117 972 0938/www.glasnostrestaurant.co.uk). **Dinner served** 7-9.30pm Tue-Thur; 6.30-9.45pm Fri, Sat. **Set dinner** £15.50 2 courses, £18.50 3 courses. **Credit** MC, V.

In an up-and-coming area, this upbeat orange restaurant is a hidden treasure. The retro menu blends Mexican, English and Mediterranean styles. Interesting starters include avocado, artichoke, orange, strawberry and baby tomato salad with a balsamic dressing, and char-grilled chicken with a mango and banana salsa. Gnocchi has a rich, creamy sauce with pesto and butterbeans and salmon is cooked in the bag with herbs and saffron vinaigrette. For dessert, try alcoholic Maltesers and Baileys cheesecake, or finish with a flavoured vodka. There's a great atmosphere, and it's good for vegetarians.

Lords

43 Corn Street, BS1 1HT (0117 926 2658/ www.lordsrestaurant.com). **Lunch served** noon-2pm Mon-Fri. **Dinner served** 6-9.30pm Mon-Sat. **Main courses** £16-£20. **Set lunch** £16.50 2 courses, £21 3 courses. **Set dinner** £33 3 courses. **Credit** AmEx, DC, MC, V.

Buried in the vaults of a former bank is one of the city's most prestigious eating venues. Interior design seems to have passed Lords by, but the staid business clientele seems untroubled by the retro surroundings and the expertly prepared Anglo-French cuisine is classy stuff. Start with an asparagus and spring pea risotto bursting with colour. Cutlets of rare English lamb are served with polenta, roast garlic and rosemary, while roast monkfish comes with sautéed spinach and shellfish sauce. An extensive wine list is dominated by high-quality French regions, and desserts include a delicious tarte tatin, dripping with smoky caramel. If food is your top priority, you're in for a treat.

Michael Caines at the Bristol Marriott Royal ★

College Green, BS1 5TA (0117 9105309/ www.michaelcaine.com). **Lunch served** noon-2.30pm Mon-Fri. **Dinner served** 7-10pm Mon-Sat. **Main**

courses £18.25-£25. **Set lunch** £17.50 2 courses, £21.50 3 courses. **Set dinner** £57.50 7-course tasting menu. **Credit** AmEx, DC, MC, V.
Michael Caines set up the Bristol outpost of his rapidly expanding culinary empire just over a year ago and brought a touch of glamour and prestige to Bristol's dining scene. Local palates are still adjusting to the brilliant cuisine now available on their doorstep. Sip a champagne cocktail on the terrace before heading to the splendid 19th-century dining room, complete with stained-glass ceiling, Greco-Roman statuary and imposing oil paintings. Such opulence might upstage less assured cooking, but here the food is the star of the show. You can opt for head chef Shane Goodway's popular weekly seven-course tasting menu, or allow the exemplary staff to guide you through the à la carte and a serious wine list. Pan-fried scallops in pancetta with aubergine truffle purée and lemon thyme jus combine depth of flavour with an exquisite lightness of touch, while a main course of ruby red fillet of beef with celeriac remoulade, roasted shallots, lardons and a rich red wine sauce was tender and oozed with intense aromas. To finish, an exquisite millefeuille of dark bitter chocolate with praline cream.

Mud Dock Café

40 The Grove, BS1 4RB (0117 934 9734/www.mud-dock.com). **Breakfast served** 7.30am-noon, **lunch served** noon-3pm, **dinner served** 6.30pm-10pm daily. **Main courses** £8.95-£14.95. **Set lunch** £5 incl one drink. **Credit** MC, V.
Mud Dock's unique formula of mountain bike shop and atmospheric bistro goes from strength to strength. The long-promised plans of bike lock-ups and showers for commuters are finally materialising and the dockside restaurant now offers a 20-minute meal deal, guaranteeing lunch is delivered on time to combat its former reputation for slack service. Highlights include venison sausages and mash, rabbit tagine with herbed couscous and plenty of fresh fish. A good range of tapas and sandwiches are perfect for lighter lunches on the small terrace. There are local Bath ales on tap, a good selection of wine, plus smoothies for the softies. By night, you can chill out to laid-back DJs, but before you get too comfortable, note the no-smoking policy throughout.

Old India

34 St Nicholas Street, BS1 1TL (0117 922 1136/www.oldindia.co.uk). **Lunch served** noon-2pm, **dinner served** 6-11.30pm Mon-Sat. **Main courses** £8-£14. **Credit** MC, V.
Housed in the former Stock Exchange and making full use of the building's grandeur, this Indian restaurant is a real eye-opener. The mahogany dining room and colonial club atmosphere provide a setting conducive to fine, modern Indian cooking. Traditional dishes are given a makeover to create delicious contemporary flavours. Start with machli purée – an aromatic fish masala chat served between wafer-thin layered purée bread, or hariyali bortha – spinach and mashed potato patties with cheese and ripe melon seeds. Main courses include moist anari lamb chops, tenderised with pomegranate juice or a spicy murga aloo – chicken and new potatoes cooked in a hot sauce. Partner these with fresh naan and a delicious stir-fried courgette side dish (louki malai).

Olive Shed

Princes Wharf, BS1 4RN (0117 929 1960/www.therealolivecompany.co.uk). **Meals served** noon-10.30pm Tue-Sat; noon-3pm Sun. **Main courses** £9.50-£13.75. **Credit** MC, V.
The ground floor of this delightful restaurant comprises the kitchen and a delicatessen, while upstairs is a dining room with picture windows and heart-warming atmosphere. The menu is dominated by vegetarian and seafood dishes made from seasonal organic ingredients. A plate of mixed tapas is an excellent way to sample the goodies – tortilla, barbecued prawns, gravadlax, anchovies and superlative olives. It's just a shame that over-chilling steals some of the flavour. Best of the main courses is arguably the sea bass sandwich: courgette and sweet potato mousse served between two delicate fillets of bass with a leek and hazelnut sauce. Olive Shed comes into its own in summer, when you can sit outside on the docks and watch the sun set.

One Stop Thali Café ★

12A York Road, BS6 5QE (0117 942 6687/www.theonestopthalicafe.co.uk). **Dinner served** 6-10pm Tue-Sat. **Set meal** thali £6.95. **No credit cards**.
Book in advance to ensure a seat at this popular eaterie. Small, eccentric and with a laid-back vibe, this is a Bristol institution. Diners share the brightly coloured space with beaded cushions and mannequins in saris, while friendly staff hand out superfluous menus to the uninitiated. Sure, you have to choose between a pakora or a bhaji as a starter; between international beer, organic wine and lassi to drink; and you will have to decide you want one chapati or two. But for your main course you'll get the thali of the day like everybody else: basmati rice, salad and four delicious vegetarian curries, served on a large, divided plate. Asian street food at its best, combining fresh ingredients, beautiful spicing and generous portions.

One30 Bar & Restaurant ★

130 Cheltenham Road, BS6 5RW (0117 944 2442/www.one30.com). **Lunch served** 11am-3pm, **dinner served** 6-10.30pm, **tapas served** 11am-10.30pm Mon-Sat. **Meals served** 11am-4pm Sun. **Main courses** £7.95-£14.50. **Credit** DC, MC, V.
Christopher Wicks of Bell's Diner (*see p108*) has created this fantastic gastrobar that's been packing in locals since late 2003. Exposed brick walls, shiny wooden floors and leather sofas create a setting that's perfect for afternoon lounging, evening drinking or informal dining on any day of the week. Hang about in the bar area for accomplished signature cocktails and a cutting-edge tapas menu that includes unmissable morcilla risotto with deep-fried sage. The restaurant offers serious bistro food,

South West

cooked with disarming flair. Start with a meltingly rich onion tart made with Mrs Kirkham's Lancashire. Main dishes might include hake with potatoes and puy lentils or braised lamb shank with mash. Portions are not over-large, but then neither are the prices and you can always fill up with a platter of Spanish cheese or a wickedly delicious praline semi-freddo. Great stuff.

Pie Minister ★

24 Stokes Croft, BS1 3PR (0117 942 9500/ www.pieminister.co.uk). **Food served** 9am-6pm Mon-Sat. **Main courses** £3-£5. **Credit** MC, V.

Who ate all the pies? Well, since the arrival of this pastry-baking, meat-marinading, potato-mashing, gravy-serving newcomer, the answer is Bristolians in their droves. All pies are made by hand, using free range meat and local seasonal veg. Combos include the humble pie (British beef, shallots, real ale and rosemary); the matador (British beef, chorizo, olives, tomatoes, sherry and butter beans) and a wonderful vegetarian version with mushrooms, asparagus, shallots, white wine and black pepper. Hungry punters can opt for a tummy filler, which includes fluffy mash and a rich veggie gravy, or round off with a sweetie pie – seasonal fruits in sugar-coated pastry. Pie Minister's success means its pies are also available in selected pubs around town.

Quartier Vert

85 Whiteladies Road, BS8 2NT (0117 973 4482/ www.quartiervert.co.uk). Bar **Open** 11am-11pm Mon-Sat; 11am-10.30pm Sun. *Restaurant* **Lunch served** noon-3pm daily. **Dinner served** 6-10.30pm Mon-Sat; *June-Sept* 6-9pm Sun. **Food served** (café menu) noon-10pm daily. **Main courses** £10.50-£19.50. **Set lunch** £14.50 2 courses, £17.50 3 courses. **Credit** MC, V.

Organic, local and seasonal are the watchwords of the Quartier Vert kitchen. Top-quality ingredients are thoughtfully prepared to create a highly effective menu of European provincial classics, ably supported by an extensive wine list. Grilled Cornish squid is served with chilli, lemon, parsley and olive oil; roast lamb shows off its vitality amid fresh greens, baby turnips, beans and a gutsy gravy. The restaurant is backed up by a café menu of tapas, lunch and supper dishes that can be enjoyed on the pavement terrace. Inside, choose the ground floor for an ebullient ambience or head up to the more sedate dining room. An organic bakery, catering service and cookery school round out this culinary empire.

riverstation ★

The Grove, BS1 4RB (0117 914 4434/www.riverstation.co.uk). **Brunch served** 10am-2.30pm Sat. **Lunch served** noon-2.30pm Mon-Fri; noon-3pm Sun. **Dinner served** 6-10.30pm Mon-Fri; 6-11pm Sat; 6-9pm Sun. **Deli menu** noon-10pm Mon-Sat; noon-9pm Sun. **Main courses** £9-£16. **Set lunch** £11.50 2 courses, £13.75 3 courses. **Set dinner** (6-7.15pm Mon-Fri) £8 incl one drink. **Credit** DC, MC, V.

One of Bristol's most stylish restaurants. The converted former HQ of the river police is an architectural fusion of stone, hardwoods and acres of glass. On the ground floor (deck one) a deli, bar and outside terrace provide the perfect pit stop for light lunches, while upstairs a second deck opens out into a 120-seater restaurant. The Modern European food is as uplifting as the surroundings. Seared Scottish scallops are given a Middle Eastern twist with lemon couscous and pistachio sauce, while Mediterranean fish soup with rouille and gruyère has all the intense flavours you could wish for. On the right night you may enjoy rack of lamb with gratin dauphinoise, cherry tomatoes and green sauce or faultless fillet of brill with baby leeks, trompettes, thyme and cream. The global wine list has been thoughtfully put together and the dessert menu sticks to favourites. A class act.

Sands

95 Queen's Road, BS8 1LW (0117 973 9734). **Lunch served** noon-2.30pm, **dinner served** 6-11pm daily. **Main courses** £7.95-£11.95. **Set lunch** £6.95 1 course, £7.95-£8.95 2 courses. **Set dinner** £14.95 2 courses, £16.50 3 courses. **Credit** AmEx, DC, MC, V.

This spacious, low-lit basement is atmospheric enough to whisk you away from the humdrum of Queen's Road while steering clear of Arabian Nights theming. In the entrance a few cushions provide a chilled-out setting in which to sample a shisha or sweet coffee, while beyond creamy plaster walls with organic alcoves are softly illuminated by lanterns. The indecisive should opt for the mezze (£16.50), or you could start with sultry, smoky baba ganoush, silky houmous, kibbeh and fatoush, served with feather-light pitta. Follow this with a mixed grill that encompasses Armenian spicy sausages, lamb koftas and lemon chicken wings. Finish with saffron, pistachio and rosewater ice-cream. Service is smiling and efficient; ambience romantic and unrushed.

Spyglass Barbecue & Grill

Welsh Back, BS1 4SB (0117 927 2800/www.spyglassbristol.co.uk). **Meals served** noon-10.30pm daily. **Main courses** £5.50-£16.95. **Credit** MC, V.

Located on a converted barge and the adjoining dockside, this seasonal restaurant has succeeded in bringing a summer holiday atmosphere to the centre of Bristol. With a canvas-covered roof and heaters, it offers alfresco dining that makes allowances for West Country weather. The food is unpretentious, tasty and great value for money. The simple but imaginative menu has no starters, just barbecue dishes and steaks, plus salads, tapas and side orders. It's all expertly cooked and presented with minimum fuss. Spyglass is buzzing throughout the week, so be prepared to queue for a table on a sunny evening.

Also in the area

Budokan 1 Whiteladies Gate, Clifton, BS8 2PH (0117 949 3030); **City Cafe** Temple Way, BS1 6BF (0117 925 1001); **Hotel du Vin** The Sugar House, Narrow Lewins Mead, BS1 2NU (0117 925 5577); **Wagamama** 63 Queens Road, BS8 1QL (0117 922 1188).

Cornwall

South West

CONSTANTINE

Trengilly Wartha

Nancenoy, nr Constantine, TR11 5RP (01326 340332/www.trengilly.co.uk). **Lunch served** noon-2.15pm, **dinner served** *bar* 6.30-9.30pm; *restaurant* 7.30-9.30pm daily. **Main courses** £6.40-£15.20. **Set dinner** £21.50 2 courses, £27 3 courses. **Credit** AmEx, DC, MC, V.

With Mike Maguire, the chairman of the Food in Cornwall Association, running the place, it's not surprising that Trengilly Wartha is a flagship for the use of local produce. Incredibly tender scallops, hand-dived just around the corner; Cornish beef steak that needs nothing more than a butter knife to eat; and the delicious Nine Maidens parfait, a frozen mousse of cream, mead and honey with prunes in Earl Grey syrup – are all superbly delivered. Add to this a 39-page wine list with over 20 by the glass, and what more could you ask? A little more ambience, perhaps? Despite Trengilly's lovely setting, the dining room feels a bit like being at grandma's. The adjoining pub has more character.

FALMOUTH

Hunkydory

46 Arwenack Street, Falmouth, TR11 3JH (01326 212997). **Dinner served** 6-10pm daily. **Main courses** £11.75-£16.95. **Credit** MC, V.

Hunkydory joined the throng of night spots in the Trago Mills end of Falmouth in 2001. The pleasing curve of its bar welcomes you, and from there you can choose either the cosy wooden-beamed front room or the brighter and less charismatic back room with its big booths. To start there's a stellar array of seafood, with crab, squid, mussels and king prawns all present, and chorizo, chillies, ginger, lime and pumpkin seeds among the supporting flavours. Hunkydory bills itself as a fish restaurant (the name refers to John Dory by way of David Bowie), but only three main courses feature fish – cod, skate and bass, and the skate was bland. However, the five-spice roast duck, moreish crème brûlée tasters and effervescent service more than compensated.

Seafarers

33 Arwenack Street, Falmouth, TR11 3JE (01326 319851). **Lunch served** noon-3pm Mon-Sat. **Dinner served** 6-10pm daily. **Main courses** £12-£19.50. **Credit** AmEx, DC, MC, V.

A recent makeover has done this previously uninspiring spot a big favour, bringing it into line with the town's other quality eating venues. Fresh local seafood is prepared with delicate but exciting flavours to enhance rather than mask that of the fish. Make sure to leave room for dessert; Scandinavian berries with meringue and white chocolate sauce is worth it. Warm terracotta walls, chunky wooden tables, candles and soft lighting, plus jazz and world music create a pleasant ambience. The chatty, arty-looking waiting staff are informal but efficient.

Seafood Bar

Lower Quay Street, Falmouth, TR11 3HM (01326 315129). **Dinner served** *July-Oct* 7-10.30pm daily; *Dec-June* 7-10.30pm Mon-Sat. Closed Nov. **Main courses** £11.95-£14.25. **Credit** DC, MC, V.

The long-established Seafood Bar remains hugely popular with locals. Its old rope fish nets and glass balls hanging from the ceiling have been removed, giving the place a crisper, candlelit bistro feel. Despite the occasional exotic sauce or fresh tomato and coriander salsa, the emphasis is on fantastic fresh local seafood cooked to simple perfection. Tiger prawns in garlic butter were just as described on the menu (messy but good), and portions are generous. Specials depend on what the fishermen bring in that day, but you won't be disappointed.

Three Mackerel

Swanpool, Falmouth, TR11 5BG (01326 311886). **Open** noon-11pm Mon-Sat; noon-10.30pm Sun. **Lunch served** noon-2.30pm, **dinner served** 6-9.30pm daily. **Terrace menu** 4-8pm, Sat, Sun. **Main courses** £10.95-£15.95. **Credit** MC, V.

The spectacular location – perched on the edge of a cliff with a lovely wooden deck overlooking clear blue waters – means people would probably come here whatever was served. The fact that the menu is an alluring mix of modern British and fusion cuisines, blending local meat and fish with Mediterranean and oriental influences to great effect, only adds to the appeal. The solid choice of European and New World wines and a buzzing, funky atmosphere don't hurt, either, so it can be difficult to get a table. Outdoor tables and window seats cannot be guaranteed, so best turn up early. There's an early-evening terrace menu at weekends.

GUNWALLOE

Halzephron Inn

Gunwalloe, TR12 7QB (01326 240406). **Lunch served** noon-2pm, **dinner served** 7-9pm daily; *July, Aug* 7-9.30pm daily. **Main courses** £8-£17. **Credit** AmEx, MC, V.

Tucked into a tiny coastal village, the Halzephron is worth searching out for its low-beamed, old-world charm and imaginative cuisine. Friendly service accompanies a menu ranging from the conservative to the downright adventurous. A starter of pan-fried pigeon breasts with poached pear, brioche croûtons and a redcurrant syrup also provided hints of Christmassy cinnamon. To follow, seared sesame-crusted ostrich fillet on stir-fried vegetables and egg noodles made perfect use of this unusual ingredient. Such tempting desserts as Roskilly's hokey pokey ice-cream and a vast raspberry pavlova with clotted cream were worthy of an encore. The varied wine list also covers much ground, from Lebanese Chateau Musar to local Cornish Camel Valley Brut.

MAENPORTH

The Cove

Maenporth Beach, Maenporth, TR11 5HN (01326 251136). **Open** *July-Sept* 10.30am-11pm Mon-Sat; noon-10.30pm Sun; *Oct-June* 10.30am-3pm, 6-11pm Mon-Fri; 10.30am-11pm Sat; noon-10.30pm Sun. **Food served** noon-9.30pm Mon-Sat. **Main courses** £10.95-£16. **Credit** MC, V.

Set well back from a beautiful view, which can only be glimpsed at a distance, this understated venue has a plain interior with a touch of flair, and friendly, informal service. A detailed list of specials adds to a varied menu; South American music complements the bistro setting. Char-grilled Falmouth Bay scallops, plus bacon, sweet baby peppers, grapes, cos lettuce and cherry tomatoes with a light mustard vinaigrette was a descriptive but satisfying starter. English venison on sweet potato mash with port wine sauce gave a full-bodied pairing of indigenous and international ingredients. The slightly limited dessert menu offers standard ice-cream, but also citrus cheesecake topped with crème fraîche, garnished with fresh berries and raspberry coulis.

MAWGAN

Trelowarren

Mawgan, TR12 6AF (01326 221224/www.trelowarren.com). **Lunch served** *Easter-Oct* noon-2.15pm daily; *Nov-Easter* noon-2.15pm Thur-Sun. **Dinner served** *Easter-June, Sept, Oct* 7-9.30pm Tue-Sat; *July, Aug* 7-9.30pm daily; *Nov-Easter* 7-9.30pm Thur-Sat. **Main courses** £12-£15. **Set lunch** (Sun) £10.50 2 courses, £12.50 3 courses. **Credit** MC, V.

In the heart of a beautiful 1,000-acre country estate, Trelowarren occupies an attractive old stableyard. Outside tables sit in the leafy courtyard between Trelowarren Pottery and the Cornwall Crafts Association Gallery. A daily blackboard lunch menu features fish caught in Helford River, and local organic farm produce prepared in simple, effective ways. Inside, the old carriage house has been converted to create a stylish rural backdrop for the more formal dinners, when a more lavish menu of modern British and Mediterranean fish, meat and game dishes is served. After a series of French chefs, a Cornish chef now heads the Yard Bistro team, but the wine list still has a strong Gallic influence.

MORWENSTOW

Rectory Tea Rooms ★

Morwenstow, EX23 9SR (01288 331251). **Lunch served** 12.30-2.30pm daily. **Food served** *April-Oct* 11am-5pm daily. **Main courses** £4.50-£6.50. **Set lunch** (Sun) £12.50 3 courses. **No credit cards.**

Idyllic is the only way to describe this old world tearoom. It's a working farmhouse purveying good honest cooking. The ploughman's is anything but standard, with each generous platter accompanied by an impressive choice of local cheeses. Baked potatoes come with a selection of fillings. On a summer's day, enjoy the garden, complete with babbling brook and bird song or take refuge in the cosy interior where high-backed settles and sepia photos set the mood. Why not finish your meal with a delicious cream tea? – scones straight from the oven, lashings of clotted cream and jam, plus teas such as Smugglers Choice or Cowslip Green. Desserts are wonderfully reminiscent of bygone days, with gems such as country fruit cake and bakewell tart.

PADSTOW

The Ebb

1A The Strand, Padstow, PL28 8BS (01841 532565). **Dinner served** *Easter-June, Oct-mid Nov* 7-9.30pm Mon, Wed-Sun; *July-Sept* 6-10pm Mon, Wed-Sun. Closed mid Nov-Easter. **Main courses** £13.50-£16.50. **Credit** MC, V.

From an unassuming back alley location, the Ebb challenges Padstow's Stein hegemony. Starting with the detail: good bread and olive oil, sparkling table settings, and just-so service in a modern room (beige, nicely lit, slightly disconcerting Schiele-esque art). Food and mood are contemporary, with an emphasis on local and organic. A short menu combines fish favourites with Asian and Mediterranean borrowings, the latter a little more successfully in our experience: while a Thai-influenced Cornish crab salad hit the spot, fish bhaji with tomato and tamarind jam, and a fish and shrimp curry went a little astray. More appreciated were the baked sea bream with sea salt, rosemary, pesto and roast tomatoes; the pine nut and herb-crusted cod with a cannellini bean salad; and, from a varied dessert list, a mint and cardamom meringue. Not revolutionary, but personal, smartly done, and popular for it.

Margot's Bistro

11 Duke Street, Padstow, PL28 8AB (01841 533441/www.margots.co.uk). **Lunch served** 12.30-2pm Wed-Sat. **Dinner served** 7-9pm Tue-Sat. **Main courses** £12. **Set meal** £21.95 2 courses, £25.95 3 courses. **Credit** AmEx, MC, V.

Margot's may not have the celebrity status of a Rick Stein, but it's almost as difficult to get a table here (we had to book a month in advance for late June). Admirably there's only one sitting per night, but the pace is slow; we were left staring at our dirty plates for a little too long. This small, quirky place has a sky- and sand-coloured interior and an intimate

Black Pig.
See p118.

atmosphere. Staff are warm and chatty. We enjoyed ample servings of good food: fluffy warm goat's cheese set off nicely by sweet roasted peppers; scallops as tender as butter, served with lardons and a rich, grainy pistachio dressing; succulent lamb with rosemary jus; and a large meaty skate wing, flavoured with garlic and anchovies on herby mash.

Ripley's

St Merryn, Padstow, PL28 8NQ (01841 520179). **Dinner served** 7-9.30pm Tue-Sat. **Set dinner** £26.50 2 courses, £31.50 3 courses. **Credit** MC, V.

Set up by a former head chef from Rick Stein's Seafood Restaurant (*see below*), Ripley's bears all the marks of a top-quality establishment. It is housed in a beautiful whitewashed cottage, with tasteful and understated decor (wooden beams, stylish furniture). From complimentary nibbles of mussels in hazelnut pesto, to the cod in a delicate mild and creamy curry sauce, and side dish of beautiful seasonal vegetables, the delivery is flawless. The small menu of local seafood and meat changes daily; vegetarians should order in advance. Desserts are innovative and light; passion fruit and nougatine parfait was outstanding. No surprise that Ripley's is usually fully booked.

The Seafood Restaurant

Riverside, Padstow, PL28 8BY (01841 532700/ www.rickstein.com). **Lunch served** noon-2.30pm, **dinner served** 7-10pm daily. **Main courses** £17.50-£39.50. **Set meal** £50 5 courses. **Credit** AmEx, MC, V.

You can't avoid the Rick Stein presence in Padstow. As well as this, his signature enterprise, he runs St Petroc's Bistro & Hotel (4 New Street, 01841 532700; quite fishy, French-Med, mains £12-£16), Rick Stein's Café (Middle Street, 01841 532700; quite fishy, global, mains £8-£14), a pâtisserie, a deli/fish and chip shop on the quay, and a seafood school. It seems a fairly benevolent hegemony, fostering a food-aware microclimate with custom to spare for other businesses. But we were surprised to have a mixed experience on this year's visit to the Seafood Restaurant. True, the seafood was unimpeachable, the stuff of pilgrimage: a vast, impeccably sourced variety, from the au naturel (a veritable menagerie of fruits de mer, £15.50 and £39.50; whole boiled crab, £17.50) to the sensitively and imaginatively prepared (soup, ceviche, curried, simply fried and grilled). Cod and chips was as good as could be imagined. Hake with sauce verte and Spanish butter beans was flat-out superb. But outside its specialism the restaurant fell down when judged against others of this (hefty) price band. We didn't appreciate being asked to take a late booking, finding the restaurant emptying out of custom and atmosphere as we arrived. Then waiters began laying tables for the next day as if the sitting were over. The conservatory decor is a little dated, and £8.50 is a lot to pay for a dessert, however fine.

PENZANCE

The Abbey ★

Abbey Street, Penzance, TR18 4AR (01736 330680/ www.theabbeyrestaurantonline.com). **Lunch served** noon-2pm Fri, Sat. **Dinner served** 7-9.30pm Tue-Sat. **Main courses** £12-£25. **Credit** DC, MC, V.

Entering the Abbey through the cavernous bright-red bar at street level, it's hard to know what to expect. Sumptuous armchairs, fake bookcases and a TV screen showing chef Ben Tunnicliffe and his team at work in the kitchen feel a little surreal, before a staircase leads you to a lovely glass, stone and wood dining room with great views. The daily-changing menu is small but exceptional, as you'd expect from a Michelin-starred restaurant; John Dory and turbot with crème fraîche, chives and Cornish asparagus was an exquisite blend. As the polite staff warn you, food is cooked to order so can take time – but not enough to make you question why this place is the talk of the town and beyond.

The Bakehouse

Old Bakehouse Lane, Chapel Street, Penzance, TR18 4AE (01736 331331/www.bakehouse-penzance.co.uk). **Lunch served** *Summer* noon-2pm Mon-Sat. **Dinner served** 6.30-10pm Mon-Sat. **Main courses** £10.50-£17. **Credit** MC, V.

Tucked at the end of a narrow alleyway in its own small courtyard, colourfully lit and fringed with lush plants, the Bakehouse lures you in like an Aladdin's cave. The name may hint at tradition, but the shiny aluminium and stylish leather upholstery within says otherwise. The bar and tables in the smoking area upstairs are popular with younger diners, while downstairs sees a mix of trendy young things and discerning diners enjoying the great food. Fresh

Jersey

GOREY

Suma's

Gorey Hill, Gorey, JE3 6ET (01534 853291/ www.longuevillemanor.com). **Lunch served** noon-2.15pm daily. **Dinner served** 6.15-9.30pm Mon-Sat; 7-9.30pm Sun. **Main courses** £12-£22. **Set lunch** £12.50 2 courses, £15 3 courses. **Set dinner** (6.15-6.45pm) £12.50 2 courses, £15 3 courses. **Credit** AmEx, DC, MC, V.

On the south-east coast, Suma's is spectacularly located in the lee of Mont Orgueil Castle, with wonderful views over Gorey Harbour. Like its sister restaurant, Longueville Manor (*see right*), it deals in quality local ingredients (the spuds are always Jersey royals, seafood is from these waters). Decor is a breezy mix of light wooden floors and white walls. Sea-fresh starters such as grilled red mullet, sardines and calamares with aïoli allow delicate, unadulterated flavours to shine, while richer combinations like oven-roasted rump of lamb niçoise with sautéed potatoes provide a robust counterpoint. Perhaps the nicest way to enjoy this restaurant is for its great Sunday brunch on the diminutive balcony.

ST HELIER

Bohemia

Green Street, St Helier, JE2 4UH (01534 880588). **Lunch served** noon-2.30pm Mon-Fri. **Brunch served** 11am-1.30pm Sat. **Dinner served** 6.30-10pm Mon-Sat. **Main courses** £17.50-£19.95. **Set lunch** £14.50 2 courses, £17.50 3 courses. **Credit** AmEx, DC, MC, V.

One year on, this newcomer is still fresh, funky and rarely less than full. A slick interior (modern art, groovy furniture, crisp tablecloths) mirrors the stylish approach of the kitchen, which specialises in hearty but elegant dishes such as braised belly pork with fondant vegetables and casserole of haricot beans. Local seafood is also well-featured (grilled Jersey scallops with boudin noir, tarragon-scented pea purée and Madeira sauce, say). Puds include a decadent lemon soufflé with milk chocolate cappuccino and pecan biscotti. The wine list is first-rate (many choices by the glass), and the service faultless. Yet at around a tenner a starter and twice that for mains, this is more a place for cigar-smoking Charlie Hungerfords than humble Jim Bergeracs.

Doran's Courtyard Bistro

Kensington Place, St Helier, JE2 3PA (01534 734866/www.revere.co.uk). **Dinner served** 6-9.45pm Mon-Sat. **Main courses** £10.95-£14.95. **Credit** AmEx, DC, MC, V.

Despite being one of St Helier's most popular restaurants, Doran's isn't complacent. Its latest addition is a Moroccan-themed section where North African trappings provide a pleasant contrast to the traditional candlelit dining room and potted greenery of the heated courtyard. The menu also reflects this change with some tasty new specials such as chicken tagine with star anise and ginger, served with couscous, or Moroccan fish soup with tomato and coriander. Otherwise, the kitchen continues with its modern eclectic repertoire to good effect; walnut-crusted cod fillet and slow-cooked lamb shank on pumpkin mash were two recent stand-outs. Puddings are equally good, and the wine list has a decent range of labels and prices. Staff could be friendlier, though.

ST SAVIOUR

Longueville Manor Hotel

Longueville Road, St Saviour, JE2 7WF (01534 725501/www.longuevillemanor.com). **Lunch served** 12.30-2pm, **dinner served** 7-9.30pm daily. **Main courses** £27-£30. **Set lunch** £12.50 2 courses, £15 3 courses. **Credit** AmEx, DC, MC, V.

The setting looks like something out of an Agatha Christie novel: a picturesque, grand, granite manor house with a fountain out front and exquisitely manicured grounds and a swimming pool around the back. The kitchen does justice to these surroundings with dishes that range from escabeche of local mackerel and sardines to oven-roasted maize-fed chicken with a cassoulet of butterbeans, artichokes and pancetta. Lunch deals are surprisingly affordable, and there's a number of excellent wines by the glass. A lighter menu ranges from steaks and pasta dishes to inventive options such as a tartlet of scrambled eggs and spinach topped with smoked salmon and chives. The service has a Jeevesian polish, whether you're having a serious supper in the oak-panelled dining room or a light lunch in the 'garden room'.

Newlyn monkfish in a nutty yellow Thai curry with spicy fried rice was superb, the monkfish less than three hours out of the water. The menu bursts with local ingredients, while the wine list swings towards the New World – with the exception of Cornwall's award-winning Camel Valley Bacchus Dry.

The Bay

Briton's Hill, Penzance, TR18 3AE (01736 366890/www.bay-penzance.co.uk). **Lunch served** noon-2pm, **dinner served** 6.15-9pm daily. **Main courses** £12.95-£18. **Credit** AmEx, MC, V.

An award-winning hotel restaurant-cum-art gallery that combines smooth interior style with panoramic views. Service is attentive but discreet, while food is imaginatively prepared by a chef who grows some of the ingredients in his own garden. There's an emphasis on local produce, but this is complemented by an enticing mixture of global influences: witness roast monkfish tail marinated in Cajun spices, vine tomato and chilli jam, with sweet potato and smoked garlic mash. Saffron bread and clotted cream pudding with mead and vanilla custard demonstrated the innovative re-creation of a classic. The mystery is, why more people aren't flocking here. Maybe its location, slightly out of town and up a steep hill doesn't help, but it's worth the climb.

Harris's ★

46 New Street, Penzance, TR18 2LZ (01736 364408). **Lunch served** noon-2pm, **dinner served** from 7pm Tue-Sat; *mid June-mid Oct* from 7pm Mon-Sat. **Main courses** £14.95-£26. **Credit** AmEx, MC, V.

Established more than 30 years ago, this family-run restaurant is worth a visit. Service is friendly but unobtrusive. Elegant decor provides a perfect backdrop to the carefully prepared, high-quality menu. A starter of grilled smoked duck breast on endive and rocket salad with walnut oil dressing burst with subtly compatible flavours, while a fresh thyme sorbet, served between starter and main course, was a delight. Main course grilled guinea fowl breast with a mushroom stuffing and lemon and basil sauce came with mouth-watering mashed potato encrusted with roasted almonds. The six-page wine list merits a mention too.

Summer House

Cornwall Terrace, Penzance, TR18 4HL (01736 363744/www.summerhouse-cornwall.com). **Dinner served** 7.30-9pm Wed-Sun. **Set dinner** £24.50 3 courses. **Credit** MC, V.

Set in a beautiful country house just off the seafront, this charming venue has received wide acclaim. Ciro and Linda Zaino have infused an English setting with Mediterranean warmth and flair, with a lovely subtropical garden set against the starched white tablecloths of the formal dining room. The regularly changing set menu uses the best seasonal local produce prepared in classic style, yet not always to maximum effect; John Dory was overpowered by its rich cream and rosemary sauce, and caramelised apple tartlet verged on the burnt. The excellent reputation of the place and high number of returning guests, however, suggests this was just a bad day.

PORTHLEVEN

Critchard's

Harbourside, Porthleven, TR13 9JA (01326 562407/ www.critchards.com). **Dinner served** 6.30-10pm Mon-Sat. **Main courses** £11-£18. **Credit** MC, V.

Situated in the heart of a picturesque fishing village, this popular, well-established seafood restaurant attracts customers from across Britain. Although the dated decor did its best to detract from the skilfully prepared menu, Critchard's worked its magic and won us over. Local seafood is effectively married to exotic, zesty flavours, seen in the starter of fresh mussels Bangkok-style, seasoned with kaffir lime leaves, lemongrass and root ginger. The Thai theme continued in an impressively piquant starter of Newlyn crab, coconut and vegetable spring roll with a sweet chilli sauce. Clever use of spices was also evident in a main course of monkfish and prawn indienne. Chocolate and prune truffle provided a suitably indulgent finale to a fine meal.

The Smokehouse

Harbourside, Porthleven, TR13 9JP (01326 563223). **Lunch served** noon-4.30pm Mon-Fri. **Dinner served** 5.30-9.30pm Mon-Wed; 5.30-10pm Thur, Fri. **Meals served** 10am-10pm Sat; 10am-9pm Sun. **Main courses** £9.50-£14.50. **Credit** MC, V.

Perched on the edge of Porthleven's fishing harbour, the Smokehouse has a head-start on many venues. It sits next to one of the area's best fish suppliers and smokeries, and its large glass frontage looks out on a picturesque scene. Service on our visit was variable, and much of the food failed to live up to expectations. Although pan-seared scallops with avocado cream, citrus fruits and tortilla offered some solace as a starter, a main of pizza was a let down. Banana brioche bread and butter pudding in some way compensated for a lacklustre meal.

PORTLOE

The Lugger

Portloe, TR2 5RD (01872 501322/www.lugger hotel.com). **Lunch served** noon-2pm, **dinner served** 7-9pm daily. **Set lunch** £15 2 courses, £20 3 courses. **Set dinner** £37.50 4 courses. **Credit** AmEx, MC, V.

On the water's edge of a beautiful fishing village, this 17th-century inn has a rich history. One landlord was hanged for smuggling in the 1890s; these days the proprietors are better behaved. The Lugger is a bastion of sophistication, frequented by wealthy weekenders. The set menu features local catches and classic meat dishes: say, pan-fried hand-dived scallops on pea purée with chardonnay, followed by Angus beef fillet wellington with Hermitage red wine jus. There's always plenty for vegetarians too. Another option is to come for lunch, when the tables on the beautiful cliff terrace come into their own.

PORTREATH

Tabb's

Tregea Terrace, Portreath, TR16 4LD (01209 842488). **Lunch served** noon-2pm Sun. **Dinner served** 7-9pm Mon, Wed-Sun. **Main courses** £11.50-£19.75. **Set lunch** £15 3 courses. **Set dinner** £19.50 3 courses. **Credit** MC, V.

Situated in Portreath, a location more attractive to surfers than gourmets, Tabb's has a reputation based upon the fine cuisine of Nigel Tabb. Bread is baked daily; ice-creams, sorbets and even chocolates

South West

are also made in house. This smoothly run operation is presided over by Melanie Tabb. Study the menu in a modern conservatory adjoining the converted granite forge restaurant. Local organic produce is used where possible and the menu includes several meat options such as roast fillet of wild rabbit.

ROCK

Black Pig ★

Rock Road, Rock, PL27 6JS (01208 862622/www.blackpigrestaurant.co.uk). **Lunch served** 12.30-2pm, **dinner served** 7-9.30pm Mon-Sat. **Main courses** £19.75-£21.50. **Set lunch** £17.50 2 courses, £22.50 3 courses. **Set dinner** £50 7-course tasting menu. **Credit** AmEx, MC, V.

Since its spring 2003 opening, the Black Pig has become Cornwall's most applauded restaurant. Despite the youthful team behind it (all under 30, led by chef Nathan Outlaw), it's an impressively mature place, every aspect carefully considered. Sited in a small strip of shops in this straggly (but monied) village, the premises include an outdoor eating area and elegant white walls. Ingredients are British and seasonal. There is an à la carte, but at dinner, the tasting menu is the best way to witness Outlaw's skills, showcasing such dishes as squab pigeon with bitter chocolate and rocket, and beef fillet with onion, beer, green beans and hazelnuts. For a smaller (but far from mean) sampling, the set lunch is top value. Dinner reservations are essential in the summer, but at other times, and at lunch particularly, it's worth phoning on the off-chance. *See p8* for more on the Black Pig.

ST IVES

Alba

Old Lifeboat House, Wharf Road, St Ives, TR26 1LF (01736 797222/www.alba-restaurant.co.uk). **Breakfast served** 10.30am-11.30am, **lunch served** noon-2.30pm, **dinner served** 6-9.30pm daily. **Main courses** £13.95-£17.50. **Set lunch** £17.50 3 courses. **Set dinner** £21 3 courses. **Credit** AmEx, MC, V.

Sitting in the corner of the harbour next to the old lifeboat, Alba has one of the best spots in town. Its front is a two-storey window offering great views across the bay. The interior is a cream and white affair, broken only by a varied selection of local art. Conversation is hushed. Food is good-looking. Tian of Cornish crab, red pepper and basil with red mullet escabeche was a delicious balance of flavours. Other starters included fillets of mackerel, pan-fried scallops, and fish and shellfish soup. The mains feature an excellent range of local fish and seafood, cockle risotto and wild sea bass being ones to watch, as well as West Country venison. Vegetables are organic, and the wine list is impressive.

Blue Fish

Norway Lane, St Ives, TR26 1LZ (01736 794204). **Lunch served** noon-3pm, **dinner served** 6-9.30pm daily. **Main courses** £7.95-£34.95. **Credit** MC, V.

Blue Fish's net-loft setting offers far-reaching views over nesting seagulls. Decor is chic and minimalist, and there's an open-air terrace. Seafood is provided by local fishmonger M Stevens & Son – one of Rick Stein's food heroes. A starter of Scottish west coast hand-dived seared scallops with asparagus tips and flaked crab hollandaise made beautiful use of fresh ingredients, while garlic-crusted cod served with sun-blushed tomato pesto, red pepper rouille and sour cream was a , full-flavoured main course. An imaginative 'digestifs and desserts' menu includes chocolate and blueberry pudding with chocolate sauce and clotted cream. Pure indulgence.

OnShore

The Wharf, St Ives, TR26 1LF (01736 796000/www.onshorestives.co.uk). **Breakfast served** 9.30-11am, **lunch served** noon-3.30pm, **dinner served** 5.30-10.30pm daily. **Main courses** £5.50-£23.50. **Set lunch** £7.95 pizza and a drink. **Credit** AmEx, MC, V.

This friendly, modern restaurant packs in the crowds. It is immaculately kitted out, from the colourful table decor to the polished steel wood-fired oven in the open kitchen. Food is 'international', though Far Eastern touches like monkfish penang curry seem superfluous in a predominantly Italian menu. For starters choose between scallops pan-fried with lemon and thyme, or gutsy Parma ham stuffed with cream cheese, pine nuts, spinach and sun-blushed tomatoes. Next, wood-roasted salmon tikka melts in the mouth, or you could opt for one of the inspired pastas and pizzas. Desserts are perfect; try the locally inspired saffron bread and butter pudding finished with a dollop of clotted cream.

Pickled Fish

3 Chapel Street, St Ives, TR26 2LR (01736 795100). **Dinner served** *Easter-Nov* 7-10pm Mon-Sat; *Nov-Easter* 7-10pm Wed-Sat. **Main courses** £12-£16. **Unlicensed. Corkage** no charge. **Credit** MC, V.

As a BYO venue, the Pickled Fish is popular with those wanting a well-prepared menu without paying the earth for wine. Ben Reeves' cooking is fresh and unfussy, with salad produce sourced from his family's own kitchen garden. Evidence of this came in a crisp side salad, with its decoration of colourful petals. Roast breast of maize-fed chicken with orange-glazed fennel bulb and chorizo sausage cream sauce demonstrated a talent for flavour combinations, while elderflower-scented baba and stem ginger ice-cream provided a further floral garnish. A quiet pleasure.

Porthgwidden Beach Restaurant ★

Porthgwidden Beach, St Ives, TR26 1PL (01736 796791). **Breakfast served** 8-10.30am, **lunch served** noon-3pm, **dinner served** 6-10pm daily. **Main courses** £5.95-£13.95. **Tapas** £3-£5. **Credit** MC, V.

The inspired Moroccan theme at this on-the-beach venue couldn't have been better chosen. The new management has gone for a decor of vibrant desert

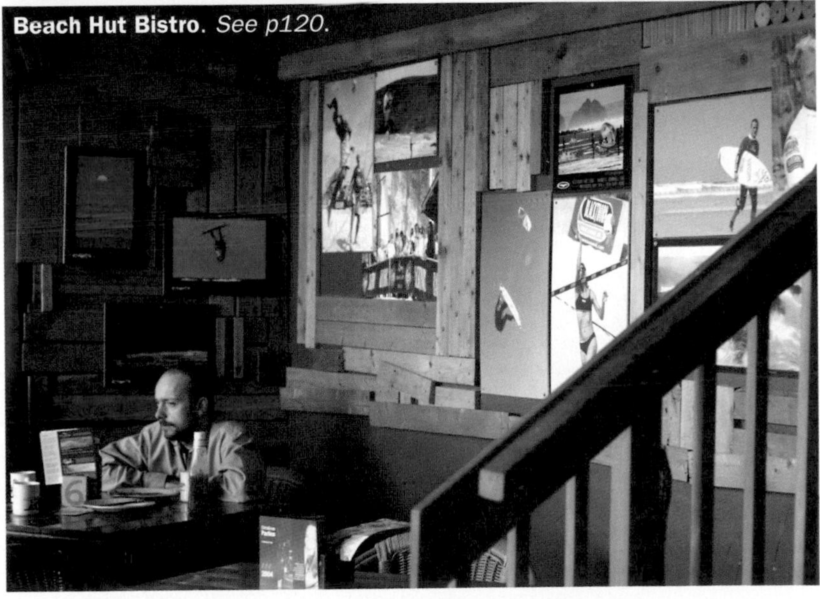

Beach Hut Bistro. *See p120.*

South West

shades that beautifully complement the striking view of white sand and aqua sea. North African touches, such as terracotta pots of cayenne, cumin and paprika on each table, all set the venue apart. Food is impressive: unpretentious and generous. Chicken andaluz was a crowd-pleaser, with crisp roast chicken and baked vegetables. The specials board included a sumptuous chocolate and coffee torte for pudding. Wonderful value, this 'new and improved' restaurant deserves great success.

Porthminster Beach Café ★

Porthminster Beach, St Ives, TR26 2EB (01736 795352/www.porthminstercafe.co.uk). **Lunch served** noon-4pm, **dinner served** 6-10pm daily. Closed Nov-Easter. **Main courses** £14.95-£17.95. **Credit** MC, V.

Overlooking Porthminster's vivid white sands, the Beach Café celebrates the best of the British seaside with its blue and white checked tablecloths, yellow plastic wine buckets and windmills on the tables. But traditional seaside nosh is cast aside in favour of a creative selection of expertly prepared Mediterranean and Asian seafood dishes: fillets of John Dory with olive crushed potatoes, wilted spinach and a delicate lemon and mint salsa verde, for instance. The wine list is equally inspired: a mix of French and Italian labels with some New World stars and plenty of by-the-glass options. By day the café bustles; evenings are more formal. Sustainable fishing methods and the use of seasonal local produce are championed here. Highly recommended.

Russets Café ★

18a Fore Street, St Ives, TR26 1AB (01736 794700/ www.russets.co.uk). **Food served** 10am-9.30pm, **dinner served** 6-9.30pm daily. **Main courses** £3.95-£7.95. **Mussels menu** £5.95. **Credit** AmEx, MC, V.

Offering superb value, Russets has a loft atmosphere complete with sloping roof and funky pictures on the walls. Local information and newspapers are kept near the sofa seating area. Food varies from snacks to full-blown meals. Crab breton with sautéed mushrooms in cream provided deliciously fresh flavours, while a cosmopolitan chicken Thai curry offered a slightly more satisfying option. A supplementary menu dedicated purely to mussels reminds you you're in Cornwall. More evidence of this came with the scone and cream dessert, served with Boddington's strawberry conserve.

Seafood Café

45 Fore Street, St Ives, TR26 1HE (01736 794004/ www.seafoodcafe.co.uk). **Lunch served** noon-3pm, **dinner served** 5.30-11pm daily. **Main courses** £7-£15.95. **Credit** MC, V.

The Seafood Café offers helpful service and great-value food. Delicious poultry and red meat options are served as well as the obligatory fish menu. Each dish is individually tailored, with customers making their choice of fish or meat from the display cabinet, then picking a sauce. Whole sea bream with hollandaise sauce and garlic-and-herb-roasted new potatoes was memorable in its generosity. But the star of the meal came from the local butcher – Curnow's award-winning sausage and mash. Sticky toffee pudding with clotted cream was also a winner.

ST MAWES

Tresanton Hotel

St Mawes, TR2 5DR (01326 270055/www.tresanton.com). **Lunch served** 12.30-2.30pm, **dinner served** 7-9.30pm daily. **Set lunch** £20 2 courses, £26 3 courses. **Set dinner** £26 2 courses, £35 3 courses. **Credit** AmEx, MC, V.

Of the growing number of exclusive, stylish Cornish hotel restaurants, the Tresanton has to be one of the best looking. This beautiful dining room has spectacular views of the Fal estuary, best enjoyed from the outdoor terrace. The fish-based menu – roast monkfish with steamed clams; grilled langoustines with fennel mayonnaise – has an air of class about it, but the results, while usually good, don't quite warrant the elevated prices. On our last visit, the place swarmed with chino-clad Londoners but few locals. Staff strike a comfortable balance between slick service and informal friendliness.

SUMMERCOURT

Viners Bar & Restaurant

Carvynick, Summercourt, TR8 5AF (01872 510544). **Lunch served** 12.30-3pm Sun. **Dinner served** 6.30-9.30pm Tue-Sat. **Main courses** £8.95-£19.95. **Set lunch** £13.90 3 courses. **Credit** MC, V.

Celebrity chef Kevin Viner's latest venture has been to take over this old boozer in a nondescript village outside Newquay and convert it into an upmarket dining venue. Surprisingly, the food remains close to the pub's roots. Huge, hearty meat-and-two-veg dishes are served, cooked to perfection. Salmon with cream and vermouth sauce, and duck with apple and calvados were delicious, but the latter was too large a portion for such rich flavours. Viner relishes tradition and customers fill the place every night.

TREGURRIAN

Beach Hut Bistro

The Beach, Watergate Bay, nr Tregurrian, TR8 4AA (01637 860877/www.watergatebay.co.uk). **Open** 10am-late, **lunch served** noon-3pm, **dinner served** 6-9pm daily. **Main courses** £11.50-£17. **Credit** MC, V.

The Beach Hut has a view to savour; watching the sun set over Watergate Bay is hard to beat. With its driftwood decor and surfer dude setting, this trendy yet unpretentious bistro has a wide-ranging clientele. Flavours are zippy – from yellow Thai vegetable curry with coconut rice, to steamed sea bass with chilli, garlic, lemongrass, coriander and ginger with new potatoes. Seared chicken breast, shallots, crispy bacon and crushed new potatoes with leeks was a perfect combination. There's chocolate fudge cake with hot chocolate sauce for afters. Service is helpful.

Devon

ASHBURTON

Agaric

30 North Street, Ashburton, TQ13 7QD (01364 654478/www.agaricrestaurant.co.uk). **Lunch served** noon-2.30pm Wed-Fri; 1st & last Sun of mth. **Dinner served** 7-9.30pm Wed-Sat. **Main courses** £14.95-£17.95. **Set lunch** £11.50-£14.50 2 courses. **Credit** MC, V.

Despite its local renown, Agaric still has the sense of being an undiscovered gem. While the front door opens straight into the dining room, the contemporary furniture and decor manage to create a warm and fuzzy feel that gets fuzzier with each glass of the excellent house wine. Chef Nick Coiley is committed to building every dish from scratch – from home-curing meat to making their own bread. They even spend their time off collecting shellfish, wild mushrooms, herbs, samphire and just about anything else that can be harvested locally. Coiley lets the ingredients do the talking in dishes such as roast pork loin with rhubarb and cranberry compote.

Moorish ★

11 West Street, Ashburton, TQ13 7DT (01364 654011). **Lunch served** noon-2.30pm Tue-Sat; 11am-2pm Sun. **Dinner served** 6-10pm Tue-Sat; 7-9.30pm Sun. **Main courses** £8.50-£14. **Credit** MC, V.

Here modern British cooking with local produce co-exists with a North African tapas menu featuring dishes like zalouk (spicy stewed aubergine) and falafel. It works – the small restaurant (which recently received a zingy makeover) is almost always busy, from the weekend brunches to evening meals where larger dishes are available. Try roasted duck with cranberry and vodka relish as a main, or organic salmon with lime crumb crust. Consistency can be a problem, especially on the tapas menu, but desserts exceed expectations, prices are reasonable and it's all delightfully moreish, if you'll pardon the pun.

BIGBURY

Burgh Island Hotel

Burgh Island, Bigbury-on-Sea, TQ7 4BG (01548 810514/www.burghislandhotel.co.uk). **Lunch served** noon-1.30pm, **dinner served** 7-8pm daily. **Set lunch** £30 3 courses. **Set dinner** £45 3 courses. **Credit** MC, V.

Agatha Christie and Nöel Coward were regular visitors during this legendary hotel's heyday and the place still resonates with art deco glamour. It serves up a mean cocktail too. The hotel recently took on chef Conor Heneghan who provides the pizzazz of Pacific rim cooking – seared baby squid with pancetta and sweet potato ravioli to start then salmon confit with green chilli and samphire curry and coconut rice as a main. Desserts are particularly good – this seems to be the only place in Devon to offer apple sorbet. It's excellent.

Oyster Shack ★

Milburn Orchard Farm, Stakes Hill, Bigbury, TQ7 4BE (01548 810876/www.oystershack.co.uk). **Lunch served** noon-2.30pm Tue-Sun. **Main courses** £6.95-£16.95. **Credit** MC, V.

The Oyster Shack goes a long way to providing what people actually want from a restaurant, as opposed to what restaurateurs think their customers

Devon teas

Avocet Café
86 Fore Street, Topsham, Exeter, EX3 0HQ, 01392 877887.
Indescribably good tarts, as well as the usual tea elements, in this modern café.

Badger's Holt
Dartmeet, Princetown, Yelverton, PL20 6SG, 01364 631213.
Gorgeous location by the river with a choice of scones or splits and generous helpings of local clotted cream. Tacky souvenirs optional.

Bovey Castle
North Bovey, TQ13 8RE, 01647 445016.
Ring ahead to reserve your table on the terrace at this grand country house hotel – the views are exceptional, as are the scones.

Corn Dolly
115A East Street, South Molton, EX36 3DB, 01769 574249.
The consummate tearoom – try the Gamekeeper's tea (with toast and pâté) or the Queen's Ransom (with crumpets). Good selection of teas.

Primrose Cottage Tea Rooms
Lustleigh, Newton Abbot, TQ13 9TJ, 01647 277365.
A delightful thatched cottage by the village green, this timeless, quintessentially English tearoom has fantastic cakes and scones.

want. As many country house hotels around the county face empty tables most weekday lunchtimes, the Oyster Shack is stuffed with punters – you must book regardless of the day. Not bad for a bring-your-own that's little more than a shack with a tarpaulin out front. Of course, the setting's part of the fun but the main draw is the ultra-fresh seafood: pan-fried sardines, potted shrimp, shell-on prawns or whatever the catch of the day might be.

BRAUNTON

Squires Fish ★

Exeter Road, Braunton, EX33 2JL (01271 815533). **Meals served** noon-9.30pm Mon-Sat. **Main courses** £4.10-£6.70. **Credit** MC, V.

In this part of the world – an area with an incredible concentration of chippies – Squires has no rival when it comes to fish and chips. Although it's been around for 25 years, it is surprisingly modern with a slick bar and friendly service. The extensive menu offers a range of other options but regulars know there's only one choice to make: fresh plaice or cod, battered, deep fried and served with glorious chips. Those not stuffed to the gills afterward might turn their attention to the ice-cream knickerbockers.

BROADHEMBURY

Drewe Arms

Broadhembury, EX14 3NF (01404 841267). **Lunch served** noon-2pm daily. **Dinner served** 7-9.30pm Mon-Sat. **Main courses** £11.50-£17. **Credit** MC, V.

The Drewe Arms balances its twin roles as local boozer and much-admired fish restaurant with great care. It's simple, pop all the drinkers in one room and give the other two areas over to diners – job done. Of course, the glue that holds it all together is the engaging personalities of the Burge family who run the joint, in particular Mrs B who presides over the dining room with warmth and humour. The fish is fresh, cooked with a minimum of fuss and with skill, despite the occasional slip up. Expect the blackboard menu to offer dishes like skate wing with black butter, langoustine, gravadlax, or whole Dover sole.

CHAGFORD

Gidleigh Park ★

Chagford, TQ13 8HH (01647 432367/www.gidleigh.com). **Lunch served** 12.30-2pm, **dinner served** 7-9pm daily. **Set lunch** (Mon-Thur) £27 2 courses, £35 3 courses; (Fri-Sun) £33 2 courses, £41 3 courses. **Set meals** £72.50 5 courses, £77.50 7-course tasting menu. **Credit** AmEx, DC, MC, V.

One of the best restaurants in the country. Chef Michael Caines seems to be able to extract about 100 times more flavour from his ingredients than most cooks, perhaps unsurprising considering the passion with which he embraces high quality local produce. Lunch Monday to Thursday provides a relatively reasonable way of indulging in his heavenly creations – terrine of foie gras, duck and guinea fowl then a embarrassingly delectable chunk of John Dory with lobster bisque, for example. A lemon tart with lemon confit sorbet was beyond belief. There's also a wine cellar of international renown. Awesome.

Mill End Hotel

Chagford, TQ13 8JN (01647 432282/www.millendhotel.com). **Lunch served** noon-2pm, **dinner served** 7-9pm daily. **Set dinner** £35 4 courses. **Credit** MC, V.

A timely makeover has invigorated the eating space at this secluded hotel with contemporary style. Now guests can enjoy chef Wayne Pearson's exciting food in an environment that does him justice. At many restaurants the *amuse-bouche* is superfluous – here an intense tomato consommé set a standard of verve and ambition that the rest of the meal maintained. Pigeon ravioli with braised chicory balanced bitter-savoury flavours with a creamy wild mushroom café crème; braised belly pork with truffle champ and foie gras was suitably unctuous and heady; while a perfect chocolate tart was unusually, but triumphantly, paired with parsnip ice-cream.

22 Mill St ★

22 Mill Street, Chagford, TQ13 8AW (01647 432244). **Lunch served** 12.30-1.45pm Wed-Sat. **Dinner served** 7.30-8.45pm Mon-Sat. **Set lunch** £21 2 courses, £24 3 courses. **Set dinner** £29.50 2 courses, £34 3 courses, £38 7 courses. **Credit** MC, V.

Chef Duncan Walker combines kitchen and front-of-house duties here. It's an idiosyncrasy that guests clearly enjoy, to say nothing of their appreciation of the food. While plaudits regularly go to Gidleigh Park (*see left*), Walker quietly produces some of the finest food in the county with considerably less recognition. Dishes like scallops with braised endive, foie gras and endive and roast squab pigeon with artichoke, chanterelle and Madeira are exquisitely conceived, but it's the puddings that really bring out the gasps of admiration – in this case a trio of raspberry (parfait, sorbet, crème brûlée) that literally had the whole restaurant cooing.

CROYDE

Hobbs

6 Hobbs Hill, Croyde, EX33 1LZ (01271 890256). **Breakfast served** *Mar-Nov* 9am-noon, **dinner served** 6.30-9.30pm daily. **Main courses** £8.95-£17.95. **Credit** MC, V.

For true surfers there's only one destination on the North Devon coast – Croyde. Thankfully, here are one or two places catering for their gastronomic needs, of which Hobbs is probably the best. Although the food isn't going to make it into any end-of-year lists, the European menu delivers robust flavours such as beef wellington, lamb tagine or whole baked sea bass. The main selling point is the atmosphere – with a buoyant crowd and the wine flowing you could make believe you were in a Mediterranean taverna – and for the morning after, the breakfasts are worth a repeat visit.

DARTMOUTH

Alf Resco ★

Lower Street, Dartmouth, TQ6 9JB (01803 835880). **Food served** 7am-2pm Wed-Sun. **Dinner served** *Summer* 6.30-9.30pm daily. **Main courses** £5-£8.50. **Set dinner** (Fri-Sun) £20.50 3 courses incl coffee. **No credit cards.**

There are few better places to eat breakfast in Devon. Alf Resco's has punters queuing up for bacon sandwiches or a monumental full English. The front courtyard is a splendid place for people-watching, while the interior has the intimacy of a bustling ship's cabin. In the summer, managers Pete and Kate launch their weekend 'rustic suppers' which could feature anything from authentic Mexican to an evening of sea shanties and seafood.

Anzac Street Bistro

2 Anzac Street, Dartmouth, TQ6 9DL (01803 835515). **Dinner served** 6.30-9.30pm Tue-Sat. **Main courses** £12-£15.95. **Credit** MC, V.

Don't turn up expecting this to be some kind of Antipodean pavement barbecue stand – it's actually a relaxed Mediterranean/British restaurant named after the road in which it's situated. The approach is straightforward – good ingredients and big flavours: crab bisque or Parma ham with celeriac remoulade to start, then lemon grass risotto with prawns or halibut and clams with white wine cream sauce. A place to enjoy a good night out.

New Angel ★

2 South Embankment, Dartmouth, TQ6 9BH (01803 839425/www.thenewangel.co.uk). **Breakfast served** 8.30-11.30am, **lunch served** noon-2.30pm Tue-Sun. **Dinner served** 6.30-10.30pm Tue-Sat. **Main courses** £14-£25. **Credit** AmEx, MC, V.

Despite its reputation and magnificent location overlooking the Dart Estuary, the Carved Angel had long been trading on past glories – that is until TV chef John Burton-Race, fresh from his French adventures, undertook a timely revamp. Resurrected as the 'New Angel', there's a vigour and energy about the place that's long been absent. Gone are the stuffiness, pretensions and wilful old-fashionedness replaced by a thoroughly urban bustle; accessible, uncomplicated food (chicken terrine with spiced pear chutney; sea bass with oyster broth) and an attention to detail. Devon needs more places like this.

Alf Resco

South West

Johnny Chick's

5 Higher Street, Dartmouth, TQ6 9RB (01803 835272). **Dinner served** 6-9.30pm daily. **Main courses** £12.95-£15.95. **Credit** MC, V.

Located in one of Dartmouth's oldest buildings, Johnny Chick's is a throbbing bistro perfectly pitched at the town's many second homers and weekend yachters. Quirkiness is the main selling point, from the open invitation to 'play on our grand piano and sing' to the friendly but frenetic service. The food – a mix of Mediterranean and British – is well priced, with a heap of modern classics on offer such as chicken liver parfait or sole with lemon butter sauce. The wine list – clearly a passion – has an interesting selection of around 50 different wines.

Little Admiral ★

27-29 Victoria Road, Dartmouth, TQ6 9RT (01803 832572/www.little-admiral.co.uk). **Food served** 6.30-9.30pm Thur-Sat. **Tapas** £2.40-£3.20. **Main courses** £11.50-£13.50. **Credit** MC, V.

A suave boutique hotel just a gull's flap away from the seafront, and also one of the town's chicest eateries. The dining room has a geometric elegance, with square wooden tables, bright art, and candlelight in the evenings. Tapas dishes are prepared with care, local seafood featuring heavily, with some interesting creations alongside old favourites – thus manchego and membrilla, and grilled chorizo can be consumed happily with a revelatory mackerel in raspberry vinaigrette.

DODDISCOMBSLEIGH

Nobody Inn

Doddiscombsleigh, EX6 7PS (01647 252394/ www.nobodyinn.co.uk). **Lunch served** noon-2pm, **dinner served** 7-10pm daily. **Main courses** £6.90-£10.50. **Credit** AmEx, MC, V.

Despite perpetuating a Victorian attitude toward children, the Nobody Inn does have its bonuses. The setting is beautiful – a historic thatched pub surrounded by an explosion of flowers, with roaring fires and low beams providing settled snugness. The food is largely traditional British – wild boar with red wine gravy, roast lamb, or pork with a creamy wine sauce – although international influences creep in (prawns with Thai dipping sauce; ostrich fillet with ox tongue sauce). However, the exhaustive wine and whiskey list is the main reason to visit.

EXETER

Café Paradiso/Bar Kino

Hotel Barcelona, Magdalen Street, Exeter EX2 4HY (01392 281000/www.aliasbarcelona.com). **Lunch served** noon-2pm daily. **Dinner served** 7-10pm Mon-Sat; 7-9pm Sun. **Main courses** £6.50-£13.95. **Credit** AmEx, DC, MC, V.

Located in a former hospital, Hotel Barcelona was a much-needed boost to cosmopolitan living in a town desperate to throw off its provincial shackles. It's something of a one-stop shop – punters head first for Café Paradiso, the hotel's restaurant, where bistro classics such as fish soup, Caesar salad and pastas rub shoulders with mains of roast rump of lamb or pan-fried duck breast. Cognoscenti head straight for the pizzas: baked in a wood oven imported from Naples, they're not only sizeable but generously topped. If that doesn't sink your battleship then it's worth a trek downstairs to the award-winning cocktail bar, Kino.

Cat in the Hat

29 Magdalen Road, St Leonards, Exeter, EX2 4TA (01392 211700/www.cathat.co.uk). **Brunch served** 10am-noon, **lunch served** noon-2.30pm, **dinner served** 7-9.30pm Tue-Sat. **Main courses** £11.50-£15.75. **Credit** AmEx, MC, V.

Although the romantically candlelit evenings at the Cat In The Hat are perhaps the best showcase for chef/co-owner Shayne Bowers' thoughtful, colourful creations – a starter of scallops with sauce vierge, then roast monkfish with rocket, red peppers and basil – this two-tiered restaurant (especially the airy upstairs conservatory) is also a great daytime hangout. A morning's shopping could be preceded by smoked salmon and scrambled eggs; lunch offerings include a tasty plate of antipasti (grilled chorizo, calamares, bruschetta), different foccacia sandwiches and hearty bowls of pasta.

EXTON

Puffing Billy

5 Station Road, Exton, EX3 0PR (01392 877888/ www.thepuffingbilly.com). **Lunch served** noon-2.30pm, **dinner served** 6-10.30pm daily. **Main courses** £9.95-£20. **Set lunch** £9.95 2 courses, £10.50 3 courses. **Credit** AmEx, MC, V.

The Puffing Billy is the kind of place that needs to be full. When it is rammed to the rafters on the Friday jazz nights, the rough edges of this upmarket pub-bistro are smoothed out by the lively atmosphere. At quieter times you start to notice the charming but slightly gawky service or the anonymity of the decor. Despite that, it's a place that attracts repeat visits. Coming from Gidleigh Park (*see p122*), chef Spencer Jones has created a menu that's largely British, with old favourites (pork with apples, steak and chips) sitting alongside more interesting offerings – foie gras mousseline with pea velouté, or halibut with curry butter.

GITTISHAM

Combe House ★

Gittisham, EX14 3AD (01404 540400/www.thishotel.com). **Lunch served** noon-2pm, **dinner served** 7-9.30pm daily. **Set lunch** £18 2 courses; (Sun) £25 3 courses. **Set dinner** £36 3 courses, £49 7-course tasting menu. **Credit** AmEx, DC, MC, V.

Leave a little extra time when travelling to Combe House – you'll want to cruise the mile-long driveway through this magnificent estate at a suitably stately pace. This Elizabethan country hotel possesses an almost unrivalled grandeur and chef Philip Leach clearly has great ambition for the kitchen. Strong ingredients underpin deceptively simple cooking with sophisticated flavours – ham hock tartlet with leek vinaigrette for example, or John Dory with roast salsify and a vanilla velouté.

GOVETON

Buckland Tout Saints Hotel

Goveton, TQ7 2DS (01548 853055/www.tout-saints.co.uk). **Lunch served** noon-1.45pm, **dinner served** 7-9pm daily. **Set lunch** £15 2 courses, £19 3 courses. **Set dinner** £37.50 3 courses incl coffee. **Credit** MC, V.

It's worth consulting a map before heading down the myriad country lanes that connect this 17th-century manor house with the outside world. Guests dine in the oak-panelled Queen Anne room, but would be advised to take coffee on the terrace overlooking the gardens. The seasonally inspired lunch menu is short and simple – asparagus, pea and mint velouté to start, followed by roast chicken breast served with veg and creamy fondant potato; expect more choice and complexity in the evenings.

GULWORTHY

Horn of Plenty

Gulworthy, PL19 8JD (01822 832528/www.thehornofplenty.co.uk). **Lunch served** noon-2pm Tue-Sun. **Dinner served** 7-9pm daily. **Set lunch** £18.50 3 courses. **Set dinner** £39.50 3 courses. **Credit** AmEx, DC, MC, V.

It may not have the reputation it once enjoyed but the Horn Of Plenty can still set Devon hearts racing, thanks largely to chef Peter Gorton's continuing residence in the kitchen. The bright conservatory extension that houses the dining room is beginning to look a little jaded, though the older parts of this attractive, ivy-clad Georgian house still seem fresh. Gorton combines subtlety with technical excellence – roast pigeon wrapped in potato on a foie gras salad with red wine and port dressing was handled with real expertise, while sea bass with white wine saffron sauce was delicate and refined.

ILFRACOMBE

11 The Quay

11 The Quay, Ilfracombe, EX34 9EQ (01271 868090/www.11thequay.com). **Tapas served** noon-10pm daily. **Dinner served** 7-10.30pm Tue-Sun. **Tapas** £2.50-£7.50. **Main courses** £15-£25. **Set dinner** £30 3 courses. **Credit** AmEx, MC, V.

At time of writing, Damien Hirst's latest venture still wasn't fully open. Overlooking the harbour, among the chippies and tourist-tat of Ilfracombe it's an incongruous burst of sophistication. The bar doesn't measure up to the hype, but is still a fine trendy boozer with upmarket 'lite bites' that are largely successful – shellfish bisque, duck confit salad, chorizo in red wine. Upstairs is a different matter – the Atlantic Room is stunning. With the right chef, this will be one of the best places to eat in the region.

IVYBRIDGE

Matisse

Plantation House Hotel, Totnes Road, Ermington, Ivybridge, PL21 9NS (01548 831100/www.plantationhousehotel.com). **Lunch served** noon-2pm Tue-Fri. **Dinner served** 7-9pm Tue-Sat. **Main courses** £17.95-£19.95. **Set dinner** £36 7-course tasting menu. **Credit** AmEx, MC, V.

A few prints and the logo aside, the artistic theme of the restaurant at this pleasant Georgian hotel seems a little tenuous. No matter – the tranquillity of the location is enough to recommend it. It's certainly worth a stroll around the gardens, perhaps even a G&T out on the terrace. The food is ambitious, although the extras (canapés, *amuse-bouche*, petits fours), added nothing to the meal except a justification for the price. The main events, though – crab bisque, followed by splendid local beef fillet with morel cream – were spot on.

KINGSBRIDGE

Pig Finca ★

The Old Bakery, The Promenade, Kingsbridge, TQ7 1JD (01548 855777/www.pigfinca.co.uk). **Meals served** 10am-4.30pm, **dinner served** 6-9pm Mon-Sat. **Main courses** £6.95-£12. **Credit** MC, V.

Apparently Pig Finca means something like pigsty in Spanish. The Iberian rather than porcine influence is in the ascendance at this buzzing café-bistro – although the informal, tapas style of dining definitely encourages troughing. The Gaudí-on-a-budget decor, attractive staff and cool music are all big factors in the popularity of the place – as is the well-priced food, which makes the most of limited ingredients. Expect uncomplicated but satisfying dishes of mashtak lamb (a north African kofte-style meal), zesty tuna with coconut and lemon, or richly spiced chorizo chicken. Regulars swear by the pizzas.

LIFTON

Arundell Arms

Lifton, PL16 0AA (01566 784666). **Lunch served** noon-2pm, **dinner served** 7.30-9.30pm daily. **Set lunch** £20 2 courses, £24.50 3 courses, incl coffee. **Set dinner** £34 2 courses, £40 3 courses, incl coffee. **Credit** AmEx, DC, MC, V.

Anne Voss-Bark has been running the Arundell Arms for over 40 years and it has gained a peerless reputation as a destination for anglers who avail themselves of the hotel's 20 miles of prime fishing water on the Tamar. It exudes old school charm with assured service, and a menu that emphasises a reliance on local produce (producers are listed) – a starter of lobster bisque and a main of duck breast with raspberry marmalade were both magnificent.

11 The Quay. *See p125.*

LUTON

Elizabethan Inn

Fore Street, Luton, TQ13 0BL (01626 775425). **Lunch served** noon-2pm, **dinner served** 7-9.30pm daily. **Main courses** £7.95-£14.50. **Credit** MC, V.

While it may not be a 'destination restaurant', locals rave about the Elizabethan Inn. You could have a creamy chicken liver parfait with just the right amount of brandy pokiness followed by a tender Catalan-style beef ragoût; sticky toffee pudding couldn't have been better. Good value too.

LYDFORD

Dartmoor Inn ★

Lydford, EX20 4AY (01822 820221). **Lunch served** noon-2.30pm Tue-Sun. **Dinner served** 6.30-9.30pm Tue-Sat. **Main courses** £12.50-£19. **Set lunch** £12.75 2 courses, £16 3 courses. **Credit** MC, V.

Owners Karen and Phillip Burgess seem amazingly pro-active in getting people to come to the Dartmoor Inn – a dining club, numerous special offers, jazz nights and art events are just some of the tactics they employ. Every element is in place to allow you to enjoy excellent food in comfortable surroundings throughout the five or so interconnecting rooms. A starter of crab mayonnaise glowed with freshness, while a sauté of chicken with new season garlic and courgettes elevated simple ingredients to lofty heights. This is probably Devon's most accomplished and consistent pub-restaurant.

LYNMOUTH

Rising Sun Hotel

Harbourside, Lynmouth, EX35 6EQ (01598 753223/ www.risingsunlynmouth.co.uk). **Lunch served** noon-2pm, **dinner served** 7-9.30pm daily. **Main courses** £17.95-£26.95. **Credit** MC, V.

You can't fault the setting of this 14th-century thatched inn, right at the water's edge of a romantically down-at-heel resort. The oak-panelled rooms are saturated with history – Shelley once stayed here, as did RD Blackmore, author of *Lorna Doone*. The food doesn't quite live up to the price tag, but an older clientele lap up the traditional take on fine dining. Local game and seafood are well represented – hare and pearl barley terrine to start, followed by venison with a blackberry sauce.

MAIDENCOMBE

English House

Teignmouth Road, Maidencombe, TQ1 4SY (01803 328760/www.english-house.co.uk). **Dinner served** 7.30-9pm Wed-Sat. **Set dinner** £21.95 2 courses, £24.95 3 courses, £27.95 4 courses. **Credit** AmEx, DC, MC, V.

Steve and Hillary Mabbutt's pleasant hotel and restaurant is a welcome addition to these parts. The crisp decor and clean finish of the dining room still have a newness to them, and it would be disingenuous to ascribe any minor delays in the service to anything other than a settling-in period. The restaurant has a modern British style that puts a strong emphasis on local ingredients and seasonality – Brixham lobster and crab salad with Netherton strawberry crisps, or a wonderfully flavoursome fillet of West Country beef.

Orestone Manor

Rockhouse Lane, Maidencombe, TQ1 4SX (01803 328098/www.orestone.co.uk). **Lunch served** noon-2pm, **dinner served** 7-9pm daily. **Main courses** £17.50-£23.50. **Set lunch** (Sun) £19.50 3 courses. **Credit** AmEx, MC, V.

Perched on a hilltop with grand views of Babbacombe Bay, Orestone Manor has a colonial feel. The restaurant has a fine reputation locally and the cooking is first class, using fresh herbs, fruit and vegetables from the garden and taking full advantage of top local seafood and meat. A fillet of beef with a foie gras crust was superbly tender, while a dessert of iced nougatine parfait with Madeira sabayon was a sweet-toothed treat. Welcoming and considerate service.

NEWTON POPPLEFORD

Dawson's

6 Greenbank, Newton Poppleford, nr Sidmouth, EX10 0EB (01395 568100/www.dawsons-restaurant.co.uk). **Lunch served** noon-1.30pm Tue-Sun. **Dinner served** 7-9pm Tue-Sat. **Set lunch** £12.50 2 courses, £15 3 courses. **Set dinner** £24.50 2 courses, £29.50 3 courses. **Credit** AmEx, MC, V.

An undistinguished frontage and unremarkable interiors aren't the attraction here, although the pervading air of calm is gently intoxicating. Glowing reports since it opened in early 2004 have brought chef Chris Dawson's fine cooking a growing reputation. Flavours are delicate: dishes like lobster with linguini and lobster cream or sea bass with artichoke, basil oil and crème fraîche are subtly delivered, working a quiet magic on the taste buds.

NOSS MAYO

Ship Inn

Noss Mayo, PL8 1EW (01752 872387/www.nossmayo.com). **Meals served** noon-9pm daily. **Main courses** £7.95-£14.75. **Credit** MC, V.

Careful where you leave your transport – car owners who park on the beach have been known to watch their vehicles float away at high tide. The kitchen serves up modern standards like Thai curry and steaks but it would seem a shame, given the location, not to partake of simple whole grilled lemon sole or a clean-tasting crab salad.

PLYMOUTH

Café JDI

Blackfriars Distillery, 60 Southside Street, Plymouth, PL1 2LQ (01752 242336/www.foodbyjdi.co.uk). *Deli* **Open** 10am-5pm daily. *Café* **Meals served** 10.30am-9pm Tue-Sun. **Main courses** £6.50-£18. **Set lunch** (1-2.15pm Sun) £15 2 courses, £18 3 courses. **Credit** AmEx, MC, V.

Part of the visitor's centre at Plymouth Gin Distillery. West Country produce is an essential component of the menu here – Dartmouth smoked salmon sandwiches, Tavistock sausages and mash, and platters of local cheeses, meat or fish are just some of the dishes on offer. The decor is funky but tasteful, with cherry leather chairs, vibrant green benches and exposed extraction pipes giving it a chic, modern feel.

Tanners ★

Prysten House, Finewell Street, Plymouth, PL1 2AE (01752 252001/www.tannersrestaurant.co.uk). **Lunch served** noon-2.15pm Tue-Fri; noon-1.30pm Sat. **Dinner served** 7-9.30pm Tue-Sat. **Set lunch** £12.50 2 courses, £15 3 courses. **Set dinner** £23 2 courses, £29 3 courses; (Fri, Sat) £33 5 courses. **Credit** AmEx, MC, V.

Set in Plymouth's oldest building, Tanners has atmosphere, the medieval feel complimented by uniformed staff, who bustle with efficiency. The food, by eponymous brothers Christopher and James, is classically influenced, imaginative but not intimidating, creativity being confined to deft touches (mussels with rosemary and citrus; sole with pancetta and lemon nut butter) and wonderful desserts. Exceptionally good value prices and an accessible wine list are also part of the attraction, but it's consistency that makes repeat visits inevitable.

PORTGATE

Harris Arms

Portgate, EX20 4PZ (01566 783331/www.theharrisarms.co.uk). **Lunch served** noon-3pm Mon, Wed-Sun. **Dinner served** 6.30-9.30pm Mon, Wed-Sat; 7-9.30pm Sun. **Main courses** £7.95-£13.95. **Credit** MC, V.

Andy and Rowena Whiteman previously ran vineyards in New Zealand and France before taking on this rural pub with stunning views over the moor. Wine is clearly a major priority with an interesting list that the hosts are more than happy to talk you through. Generous portions and full flavours characterise the cooking – a plate of hot-smoked salmon with tapenade crostini and aïoli was a thoroughly satisfying starter followed by a hearty dish of confit duck legs with grilled vegetables and mash. Definitely a place to watch.

ROCKBEARE

Jack in the Green

Rockbeare, EX5 2EE (01404 822240/www.jackinthegreen.uk.com). **Lunch served** 11.30am-2pm Mon-Fri; 11.30am-2.30pm Sat. **Dinner served** 6-9.30pm Mon-Fri; 6-10pm Sat. **Meals served** noon-9pm Sun. **Main courses** £3.75-£12.50. **Set meals** £19.75 2 courses, £24.75 3 courses. **Credit** MC, V.

The Jack in the Green doesn't seem to know whether it is a pub or a restaurant. The decoration – tearoom meets Harvester – sits well with a real ale and tankard clientele in the bar. But the good bar snacks menu (chicken kebabs, wild mushroom ravioli) and the excellent food from a bewildering number of menus (risotto with truffle oil to start, followed by lip-smacking fillets of red mullet with parsley oil and garlic chips) suggest that it aspires to – and reaches – high-end dining status. The identity crisis doesn't seem to have impacted on its popularity though.

SALCOMBE

Catch 55 Bistro

55 Fore Street, Salcombe, TQ8 8JE (01548 842646). **Dinner served** *Mar-Oct* 6.30-10pm Mon-Sat. *July, Aug* 6.30-10pm daily. **Main courses** £7.25-£12.50. **Credit** MC, V.

A vibey hangout for Salcombe's deck-shoed denizens, Catch 55 is certainly lively. Of course, many come to the bistro as a destination in itself, not just to take on ballast. The owners make a virtue of a limited set of ingredients – mussels, scallops and tuna are each available in four different preparations with numerous burger and pasta combinations in support. Service can be brusque, even surly, but the overall lack of pretension is refreshing and it's mercifully easy on the pocket.

Winking Prawn

Main Road, North Sands, Salcombe, TQ8 8JW (01548 842326). **Meals served** 10.30am-4.30pm, **dinner served** 7-9.30pm daily. **Main courses** £9.75-£14.95. **Set meal** (Summer) £14.95 steak & king prawn barbecue. **Credit** MC, V.

The beach hut style of the Winking Prawn can seem almost Californian, with young staff, informal interiors and a large deck outside. But the Union flag fluttering in the breeze, salmon pink sunbathers and the clatter of teacups in liver-spotted hands is uniquely British. Open in the day for teas, coffees and ice-cream, in the evenings the menu leans toward seafood – whole cracked crab with aïoli or big plates of shell-on prawns are good choices.

TOPSHAM

Galley

41 Fore Street, Topsham, EX3 0HU (01392 876078/www.galleyrestaurant.co.uk). **Lunch served** noon-1.30pm, **dinner served** 7-9.30pm Tue-Sat. **Main courses** £16-£23. **Credit** AmEx, DC, MC, V.

The Galley really is an extraordinary place, as unfathomable, in some ways, as the spiel on their numerous brochures and menus around the place. The nautical/aquatic theme is so utterly over-the-top – there are even fish in the toilet cistern. The food is an onslaught of flavours. Some of it is very good – Caribbean-style mussels or smoked salmon with blinis, for example; other dishes contain such a collision of flavours as to leave the diner speechless.

La Petite Maison ★

35 Fore Street, Topsham, EX3 0HR (01392 873660/www.lapetitemaison.co.uk). **Lunch served** 12.30-2pm, **dinner served** 7-10pm Tue-Sat. **Set lunch** £16.95 2 courses, £19.95 3 courses. **Set dinner** £22.95 2 courses, £27.95 3 courses. **Credit** MC, V.

La Petite Maison is so refreshing – chef Douglas Petell's technical ability is unquestionable, but he keeps dishes simple and uncluttered. Thus a tomato and goat's cheese tart had delightfully short pastry and a fantastic, melt-in-the-mouth filling; while a straightforward crème brûlée was everything you would want. The menu may not be challenging but this restaurant continues to deliver accessible, well-conceived dishes with remarkable consistency.

TORCROSS

Start Bay Inn

Torcross, TQ7 2TQ (01548 580553/www.startbayinn.co.uk). **Lunch served** 11.30am-2pm Mon-Sat; noon-2.15pm Sun. **Dinner served** 6-10pm daily. **Main courses** £4.90-£15. **Credit** MC, V.

Inside the Start Bay Inn is the kind of old world pub you wouldn't give a second thought to if you hadn't just seen the view along Slapton Sands, a long stony beach bordered by Slapton Ley freshwater nature reserve. Whether it's a sun-kissed lunch or a warming bite after a blustery walk by the sea, there can be few better locations to enjoy fish and chips. There are specials available, monkfish or sea bass, but stick with battered cod, haddock, plaice or mackerel with chips – you won't be disappointed.

TORQUAY

Blue Walnut ★

14 Walnut Road, Torquay, TQ2 6HS (01803 605995/www.thebluewalnut.co.uk). **Meals served** *Summer* 10.30am-2.30pm daily. *Winter* 11am-2pm daily. **Dinner served** *Summer* 6-8.30pm Mon-Sat. **Main courses** £4.95-£10.95. **Credit** MC, V.

This café is a beacon of individuality. There are few better cappuccinos in Torbay; they also do great all-day breakfasts and at night produce dishes like salmon with hollandaise or lamb and mint pudding – all under £5. There's jazz in the evenings too, but what really sets them apart is the 15-seater original nickelodeon cinema in the back room showing classic films such as *Battleship Potemkin* or *The Jazz Singer* – there's even piano accompaniment for some of the silent flicks. A genuine one-off.

The Elephant

3 & 4 Beacon Terrace, Torquay, TQ1 2BH (01803 200044). **Meals served** 11am-10pm Mon-Sat; 11am-4pm Sun. **Main courses** £9.75-£21.50. **Credit** AmEx, DC, MC, V.

The Elephant is a relative newcomer – lunches are still pretty quiet, although evenings are rapidly becoming populated with diners eager to try out this new venture from the owners of Orestone Manor (*see p127*). The menu leans toward contemporary brasserie fare such as tatin of smoked baby fennel followed by lamb with braised oxtail raviolo.

No.7 Fish Bistro

7 Beacon Terrace, Inner Harbour, Torquay, TQ1 2BH (01803 295055/www.no7-fish.com). **Lunch served** 12.15-1.45pm Wed-Sat. **Dinner served** *Winter* 7-9.45pm Tue-Sat. *Summer* 7-9.45pm daily. **Main courses** £11-£20. **Credit** AmEx, MC, V.

You could be in almost any decade when you step through No.7's door on to the black and white tiled floor. The classic ways of serving seafood – lobster plainly boiled or with thermidor sauce, moules marinière, hot and cold shellfish platters, or a warming seafood broth – will also never fade from popularity. Best of all are the whole fish plainly grilled and served with veg or salad – ask to see what's on offer and they'll show you a fresh, gleaming tray of plaice, sole or sea bass.

TOTNES

Effings

50 Fore Street, Totnes, TQ9 5RP (01803 863435). **Meals served** 9.30am-5pm Mon-Sat. **Lunch served** noon-2.15pm Mon-Sat. **Main courses** £8.95-£19.95. **Credit** MC, V.

Effings is a restaurant as well as a rather fine delicatessen. At the back of the shop, away from the counter with its bewildering aromas of cheese, coffee and cured meats is a little cluster of tables, available throughout the day (book for lunch) and serving superbly prepared victuals. A plate of pata negra, the king of hams, was served with manchego cheese, quince jelly and potent mostarda di voghera; duck salad with foie gras was a decadent treat.

Rumour Wine Bar

30 High Street, Totnes, TQ9 5RY (01803 864682/ www.eiaddio.com). **Lunch served** noon-3pm Mon-Sat. **Dinner served** 6-10pm daily. **Main courses** £9.50-£14.95. **Credit** AmEx, MC, V.

Rumour has something for everyone – a vibey bar with a well-priced wine list; a daytime hangout for late breakfasts and king-size cappuccinos, and a restaurant with two eating options. The pizza menu is the stuff of local legend – substantial, generously topped and affordable. The blackboard menu promises fancier offerings but nothing to break the bank – a grilled lemon chicken with slow-roast tomatoes and asparagus and rocket pesto, for example. Quality bistro food and a great atmosphere.

Willow

87 High Street, Totnes, T29 5PB (01803 862605). **Meals served** 10am-5pm Mon-Thur, Sat; 9am-5pm Fri. **Dinner served** 7-9.30pm Wed, Fri, Sat; Thur during school hols. **Main courses** £5.90-£7.50. **No credit cards.**

Given the proliferation of alternative types in the area, it's surprising how few vegetarian restaurants there are in Totnes. Willow makes up for it in spades – it's a hub for food-related issues and is particularly active in highlighting concerns over GM crops. Yet the cheerful decor, helpful staff and back room with a pile of toys for kids are anything but po-faced. The self-service counter offers salads, wheat-free quiches and caffeine-free alternatives to tea and coffee (as well as full-strength, fair trade versions of the latter). Curry nights on Wednesday and the music sessions on Friday are always busy, so it's worth booking.

Wills

2-3 The Plains, Totnes, TQ9 5DR (0800 056 3006/ www.eiaddio.com). **Lunch served** noon-2.30pm daily. **Dinner served** 7-9.30pm Tue-Sat. **Main courses** *Café* £6.95-£14.95. *Restaurant* £14.95-£22. **Credit** AmEx, MC, V.

Until recently Wills was known as the posher sister to Rumour (*see left*). Changes in the menu have brought the two much closer in style. Upstairs in this Georgian townhouse, the formal restaurant offers a modern British-style menu with plenty of interesting choice – mussel mousse with scallop carpaccio, or roast pheasant with stuffed wing and leg. The bistro-like downstairs is more informal, great for lunches such as fried halloumi with rocket or duck breast with port sauce. If you squint you could conceivably imagine you were in Vienna or Paris.

UMBERLEIGH

Northcote Manor

Burrington, Umberleigh, EX37 9LZ (01769 560501/ www.northcote-manor.com). **Lunch served** noon-2pm, **dinner served** 7-9pm daily. **Set lunch** £18.50 2 courses, £25.50 3 courses. **Set dinner** £35-£40 3 courses. **Credit** AmEx, MC, V.

This country house hotel has medieval origins but has been brought up to date with great subtlety – if you disregard the murals on the walls that add a splash of colour to the demure dining room. The food is built on French classical foundations and is most successful when it stays close to its roots – a duckling breast was pink and succulent and well sauced with Madeira gravy, whereas a starter of chicken and foie gras sausage was a misguided experiment. Vegetarians get a menu to themselves.

VIRGINSTOW

Percy's

Coombeshead Estate, Virginstow, EX21 5EA (01409 211236/www.percys.co.uk). **Lunch served** noon-2pm, **dinner served** 7-9pm daily. **Set lunch** £20 2 courses. **Set dinner** £37.50 3 courses. **Credit** MC, V.

Don't let Percy's farmhouse exterior fool you – the subtle downlighting and modern decor of the interior and progressive attitude to food are distinctly contemporary. Tina Bricknell-Webb's cooking makes the most of fantastic organic produce – the peppery salad leaves (picked that day) with sautéed squid and scallops eclipsed the seafood with their sheer freshness. There's a tendency to over-flavour – a thyme and orange sauce overpowered its attendant duck – but the commitment to local produce and engaging service redress the balance.

South West

WINKLEIGH

Pophams

Castle Street, Winkleigh, EX19 8HQ (01837 83767). **Lunch served** 11.30am-2.30pm Thur, Fri. **Set lunch** £32 3 courses. **No credit cards**.

Pophams is a masterpiece in understatement – a tiny restaurant offering a tiny choice in a tiny village miles from anywhere. Not only that, it has the briefest of opening hours, so you have to book. Owners Melvyn Popham and Dennis Hawkes prepare everything from scratch; enjoy such dishes as crab tart with crème fraîche, and chicken breast stuffed with smoked ham and a basil and Noilly Prat sauce.

WOOLACOMBE

Westbeach

Beach Road, Woolacombe (01271 870634/www.westbeachbar.co.uk). **Lunch served** *Feb-Dec* noon-2.30pm daily. **Dinner served** 6-10pm daily. **Main courses** £12.50-£30. **Set lunch** £15 3 courses. **Credit** MC, V.

Contemporary art and cool music ensure that this bar/restaurant is permanently busy. The menu combines Pacific Rim and Mediterranean offerings. Seafood is prominent and local lobster is a speciality; warm salad of scallops and red mullet followed by roast monkfish wrapped in Parma ham was great.

Also in the area

Brazz 10-12 Palace Gate, Exeter, EX1 1JA (01392 252525); **Carved Angel** 21A Cathedral Yard, Exeter, EX1 1HB (01392 210303); **Michael Caines at the Royal Clarence Hotel** Cathedral Yard, Exeter, EX1 1HD (01392 310031).

Dorset

BOURNEMOUTH

Bistro on the Beach

Solent Promenade, Southbourne, Bournemouth, BH6 4BE (01202 431473/www.bistroonthebeach.com). **Dinner served** *June-Sept* 6.30-10pm Tue-Sat. *Oct-May* 9am-4pm, 6.30-10pm Wed-Sat; 9am-4pm Sun. **Meals served** *June-Sept* 9am-4.30pm Mon, Sun. **Main courses** £10.50-£18.95. **Set dinner** £16.50 2 courses, £18.95 3 courses. **Credit** AmEx, MC, V.

A café by day, a restaurant by night, this place is popular. It's a prime spot: joggers and walkers battle with the wind on the promenade outside and the sea crashes on to the sand only metres away. In addition to fish and meat dishes, the à la carte and fixed priced menu have some interesting vegetarian choices – three cheese risotto with roasted cherry tomato oil, or camembert and walnut omelette with tapenade. Pudding lovers can indulge themselves with the chef's sweet platter. The staff are sometimes stretched to the limit, but they keep smiling despite the pressures.

Chef Hong Kong

150-152 Old Christchurch Road, Bournemouth, BH1 1NL (01202 316996). **Lunch served** noon-3.30pm, **dinner served** 6-11.30pm Mon-Sat. **Meals served** noon-11.30pm Sun. **Main courses** £5.25-£12. **Set lunch** £5.95 2 courses. **Set dinner** £15.50-£23 3 courses. **Credit** AmEx, MC, V.

Chinese families and couples were already filling this small, bright restaurant at midday in the middle of the week. Glasses sparkle in the bar area while the pale primrose walls and wooden floors give the place a modern feel. Two-course lunches offer a wide choice, while a large selection of dim sum provides some more unusual fare. As well as cheung fun, congee and steamed buns, there are rice and noodle dishes. If you need help in making your selection, the efficient waiting staff are pleased to explain.

Coriander

22 Richmond Hill, Bournemouth, BH2 6EJ (01202 552202/www.coriander-restaurant.co.uk). **Meals served** noon-10.30pm Mon-Thur, Sun; noon-11pm

Fri, Sat. **Main courses** £6.50-£11. **Set lunch** (noon-5pm) £8.50 2 courses, £11 3 courses. **Set dinner** £10.25-£11.95 2 courses. **Credit** AmEx, MC, V.
By 8pm, the two floors of this place were already packed with people having a good night out. The Mexican beers and pitchers of tequila had something to do with it, and on a Saturday night the atmosphere was pure carnival. Service is fast and friendly, and the food a mix of Mexican dishes – a selection of salsas accompanies everything and you are asked for your heat preference. A sampler starter to share offers a choice of dips with tortillas – such as chorizo and beans, chilli con carne, and jalapeno and beans – while cheese-covered enchiladas, burritos, chimichangas and quesadillas with a choice of fillings follow, together with puddings such as hot cinnamon banana wrap and fresh pineapple and tequila. A bucket of six mixed Mexican beers at £13.50, cocktails from £3.50 and Mexican Cabernet Malbec house red at £9.50 a litre all clearly meet with unreserved approval. A really fun place.

Salad Centre ★

667 Christchurch Road, Boscombe, Bournemouth, BH7 6AA (01202 393673/www.thesalad centre.co.uk). **Meals served** 10am-5pm Mon-Sat. **Main courses** £2.75-£4.95. **Credit** MC, V.
This light, bright veggie café has a modern vibe that sets it apart from the surrounding drab pedestrian precinct. As well as a choice of soups and interesting breads, there is a selection of salads – 'choose what you like, as much as you like' – or hot dishes such as broccoli and mushroom lasagne, lentil moussaka or jacket potatoes. An afternoon tea tray includes a scone, a pot of jam, butter, cream and a choice of cake, and there are half portions for children wherever possible. A steady flow of regulars lingers to chat or read newspapers. There is a commitment to additive-free food; prices are extremely reasonable too. A very welcome, unpretentious experience.

BRIDPORT

Riverside

West Bay, Bridport, DT6 4EZ (01308 422011/ www.dorset-seafood-restaurant.co.uk). **Lunch served** *Feb-Dec* noon-2.30pm Tue-Sun. **Dinner served** *Feb-Dec* 6.30-8.30pm Tue-Thur; 6.30-9pm Fri, Sat. **Main courses** £12-£22.50. **Credit** MC, V.
This light, buzzy waterside restaurant is frequently packed and, as a result, disappointed punters who have failed to book can be seen loitering outside cursing their lack of foresight. The restaurant, celebrating its 40th year under the same ownership, has a relaxed and informal atmosphere with staff who are friendly and efficient, despite sometimes being hard-pressed. The menu centres on fish and shellfish, although there are other options. The crab and razor clam chowder is particularly delicious and the daily selection of freshly landed fish arrives glistening. There is a good choice of puddings and ice-creams, and most meals are available in small portions at a 20% reduction for children.

BURTON BRADSTOCK

Anchor Inn

Burton Bradstock, DT6 4QF (01308 897228). **Lunch served** noon-2pm daily. **Dinner served** 6-9pm Mon-Sat; 6.45-9pm Sun. **Main courses** £12.95-£28. **Credit** MC, V.
Nautical knick-knacks, Christmassy decor and daunting portions confirm that no one at this popular dining pub, famed for its seafood, subscribes to the 'less is more' school. The chef likes to cook with cream – a vast seafood pancake and the smoked haddock fish cakes arrived swimming in a cream sauce, and even the tasty 'chunky fish soup' was cream-based. You could also find yourself facing chips and rice on the same plate, so this is the place to visit if you are up for a blow-out. Prices are not cheap, with soup at £6.95, or £55 for a shared seafood platter, but there's plenty of choice (including meat dishes).

South West

CERNE ABBAS

Royal Oak

23 Long Street, Cerne Abbas, DT2 7JG (01300 341797). **Lunch served** noon-2pm daily. **Dinner served** 7-9.30pm Mon-Sat; 7-9pm Sun. **Main courses** £7.75-£18. **Credit** MC, V.
The 15th-century Royal Oak, a freehouse, is most people's idea of a perfect pub. It sits in a pretty village in the heart of Dorset and has a small outside terrace for sunny days. Inside, oak beams, antique bits and the well-worn flagstone floor are straight from central casting, while the cheerfully served pub food clearly pleases a great many people. Diners eat at individual tables in the cosy bars, one of which is reserved for non-smokers. Daily specials are chalked up on the board, and dishes like dressed crab, new potatoes and salad could be on offer, while steak and Blue Vinney pie is a firm favourite. Among the range of beers, Butcombe is available.

CHETTLE

Castleman Hotel & Restaurant

Chettle, DT11 8DB (01258 830096/www.castleman hotel.co.uk). **Lunch served** noon-2pm Sun. **Dinner served** 7-9.30pm daily. **Main courses** £8.50-£15.50. **Set lunch** £18 3 courses incl coffee. **Credit** MC, V.
The ancient hamlet of Chettle has grown up around this beautiful Queen Anne house. The restaurant is now so popular that you have to book well in advance for weekends, and staff are sometimes stretched to the limit. Although not expensive, the Castleman gives the impression of grandeur – drinks are served in a blood-red bar or in the library – and the formal but comfortable dining room overlooks the lawns. The menu changes according to the season – in the summer, starters could be monkfish and crab gratin or asparagus, brie and sorrel tartlet, while mains are accompanied by a platter of fresh vegetables. The Spanish wines are recommended.

COMPTON ABBAS

Milestones Tearooms ★

Lower Blandford Road, Compton Abbas, nr Shaftesbury, SP7 0NL (01747 812197). **Food served** 10.30am-5.30pm daily. **Main courses** £6.95-£7.50. **Credit** MC, V.

This 17th-century tearoom is an ideal place for a pit stop if you're travelling along the busy A350. In the summer you can sit out on a patio overlooking the surrounding hills, while there are two snug tearooms and a conservatory for inclement weather. There are dishes such as smoked haddock pie with a selection of vegetables (a daily special), but far better are the freshly cooked light snacks, the selection of own-made cakes or the set teas – as well as various cream teas, you can have the farmhouse tea with boiled eggs, brown bread and butter and a slice of cake. Tea is served with a strainer, with not a tea bag in sight, and service is friendly if a little slow.

CORSCOMBE

Fox Inn

Corscombe, DT2 0NS (01935 891330). **Lunch served** noon-2pm daily. **Dinner served** 7-9pm Mon-Thur, Sun; 7-9.30pm Fri, Sat. **Main courses** £8.25-£17.95. **Credit** MC, V.

This rose and hollyhock-covered pub sits opposite a little green with benches. Walkers and cyclists must think they've died and gone to heaven if they come upon it unexpectedly, for as well as a comprehensive wine list and Butcombe and Exmoor beer, its food is far better than most pub offerings. The two dimly lit, characterful dining rooms are joined by a slate-topped bar with an open log fire, and there is also a light and spacious conservatory. It is essential to book for chef George Marsh's fish soup, brimful with mussels and prawns, but his local rabbit braised in cider, vanilla cream terrine and other mouthwatering dishes are popular too. The friendly service can sometimes be overstretched.

EVERSHOT

Acorn Inn

28 Fore Street, Evershot DT2 0JW (01935 83228/ www.acorn-inn.co.uk). **Lunch served** noon-2pm daily. **Dinner served** 7-9pm Mon-Thur, Sun; 7-9.30pm Fri, Sat. **Main courses** £11.25-£16.95. **Credit** MC, V.

The 16th-century Acorn Inn is situated in a pretty and unspoilt village. It features as the 'Sow-and-Acorn' in Thomas Hardy's *Tess*, and it is not difficult to imagine Hardy himself sitting in the snug bar. The two dining rooms both have handsome stone fireplaces, wooden floors and immaculate white napiery, and you get the feeling that as a guest your comfort is paramount; service is friendly and efficient. The mostly modern British food, which features fresh local produce, deserves its reputation for being several cuts above the average – strips of beef served with a sweet chilli sauce and fish cakes on a buttery lemon sauce were delicious. As well as the à la carte, bar snacks and bar meals are available during the week, but roasts are the only main course on offer in the dining rooms on Sundays.

FARNHAM

Museum Inn

Farnham, nr Blandford Forum, DT11 8DE (01725 516261/www.museuminn.co.uk). Pub **Lunch served** noon-2pm, **dinner served** 7-9.30pm daily. *Restaurant* **Lunch served** noon-3pm Sun. **Dinner served** 7-9.30pm Fri, Sat. **Main courses** £9-£20. **Credit** MC, V.

Situated in a remote, time warp hamlet, the Museum Inn draws punters from far and wide. The attractively modernised bar is frequently packed, while the restaurant tends to be more sedate. Attentive young Antipodeans serve in the bar and the restaurant, and the food is prettily presented with some interesting touches. Potted smoked trout and bruschetta of pickled mackerel could be among the starters, while Longhorn rump steak, chips and watercress salad, Gloucester Old Spot belly pork, or wild mushroom Caesar salad might be among the mains. Puddings tend towards the classics, and vintage port is available by the glass to accompany British and French cheeses. There is a comprehensive wine list with an emphasis on France, and some half bottles are available.

GILLINGHAM

Stock Hill Country House Hotel

Stock Hill, Gillingham, SP8 5NR (01747 823626/ www.stockhillhouse.co.uk). **Lunch served** 12.30-1.30pm Tue-Fri, Sun. **Dinner served** 7.30-8.45pm daily. **Set lunch** £25 3 courses. **Set dinner** £35.50 3 courses. **Credit** MC, V.

As a member of Relais & Châteaux, Stock Hill House takes itself very seriously indeed. Vast gilt mirrors, formal sofas and bizarre statuary fill the reception areas, while deferential young German waitresses whisper pleasantries as they take your coat. The food is a treat, well executed and restrained, although there can be aberrations such as turbot with braised oxtail, or rice pudding with grapefruit. It is in the finishing touches that the chef's skill really becomes apparent – a dab of celery remoulade was pure heaven, while a hot beetroot salad tasted earthy and sweet. Canapés, a complimentary appetiser, own-made bread and petits fours are included in the three-course dinner, and everything is served with old-fashioned formality. Wines, even house wines, are not cheap.

MERLEY

Les Bouviers ★

Oakley Hill, Merley, BH21 1RJ (01202 889555/ www.lesbouviers.co.uk). **Lunch served** noon-2pm Tue-Fri, Sun. **Dinner served** 7-10pm Tue-Sat. **Tea served** *May-Sept* 3.30-5.30pm Tue-Fri. **Main**

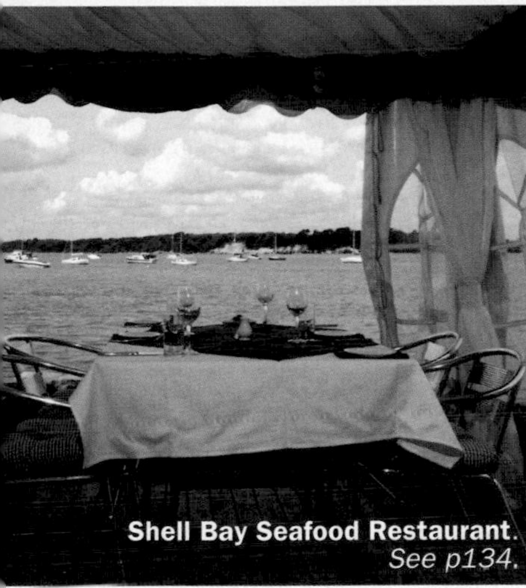

Shell Bay Seafood Restaurant. See p134.

courses £22-£27.50. **Set lunch** £12.95 2 courses, £15.95 3 courses incl coffee. **Set dinner** £26.95 4 courses incl coffee. **Set meal** £31 2 courses, £37 3 courses. **Credit** AmEx, DC, MC, V.

The minute you walk into Les Bouviers, you know from the good smells and warm greeting that the place has to be taken seriously. The experienced, perfectionist chef delivers a modern take on classical French cuisine. His beautifully presented food is intense and original and, given that all sorts of extras are included in the price, represents extremely good value. Assiette of duck or steamed wild brill appear among the à la carte choices while themed menus such as the 'Spanish Dinner' or the 'Harvest of the Sea', offer four set courses. Between June and September, Les Bouviers opens for morning coffee and afternoon tea. An impressive wine list, excellent service and memorable food make this an outstanding restaurant.

PLUSH

Brace of Pheasants ★

Plush, nr Dorchester, DT2 7RQ (01300 348357). **Lunch served** noon-2.30pm, **dinner served** 7-9.30pm Tue-Sun. **Main courses** £9.95-£16.95. **Credit** MC, V.

This country pub is the sort of place you want to keep to yourself. It serves wonderful food, interesting wines (five whites and four reds by the glass) and there is a genuinely warm welcome. The main bar has a log fire and small individual tables, while the adjoining dining room is more spacious. Starters could include crab ramekin, goose liver parfait or potted shrimps with paprika mayonnaise, while pan-roasted goose breast with blackberry sauce, Thai tuna and prawn fish cakes or beer-battered fish and chips with tartare sauce feature among the mains. For pudding, there could be mulled wine jelly with maple and pecan ice-cream, raspberry crème brûlée or Christmas pudding with calvados butter. Study the map before you set off and only approach it from the B1343 unless you have done advanced orienteering, as it is completely off the beaten track.

POOLE

Mansion House ★

The Mansion House Hotel, Thames Street, Poole, BH15 1JN (01202 685666/www.themansionhouse.co.uk). **Lunch served** noon-2pm Mon-Fri, Sun. **Dinner served** 7-9.30pm Mon-Sat. **Set lunch** £17 2 courses, £19.25 3 courses. **Set dinner** £21.95 2 courses, £27.45 3 courses. **Credit** AmEx, DC, MC, V.

Once owned by a wealthy Poole family, this elegant award-winning Georgian hotel-restaurant is a treat whatever your yardstick. The food is excellent and while the surroundings are opulent, the atmosphere manages to be relaxed and unselfconscious, due in part to attentive staff. The set dinner includes a catch of the day and is good value. Starters could feature lamb and black pudding sausages or smoked haddock rarebit, while fillet of beef with stilton mash or halibut with asparagus risotto might follow. Beautifully presented puddings and wicked petits fours served with coffee make a fitting end to a memorable meal. There are some reasonably priced wines on the exceptional wine list.

Storm Fish

16 High Street, Poole, BH15 1BP (01202 674970/ www.stormfish.co.uk). **Dinner served** 6.30-10pm daily. **Main courses** £12-£21. **Credit** MC, V.

Bare brick walls, wooden tables and stripped floorboards create a loft-like effect in this popular restaurant. The menu is almost all fish, and meals are accompanied by vegetables subtly flavoured with fresh herbs. The food is cooked so that nothing distracts from the freshness and quality of the ingredients – a starter of mixed, locally smoked fish with capers and wasabi was sweet and succulent, while a main of Brixham sole was plump and flavoursome. Local grey mullet or roast wild halibut might also be on offer, and there is a delicious-looking fruits de mer platter. Diners who could manage a pudding were chorusing their appreciation for chocolate and Bailey's truffle mousse cake with raspberry semi-freddo.

SHAFTESBURY

La Fleur de Lys

25 Bleke Street, Shaftesbury, SP7 8AW (01747 853717/www.lafleurdelys.co.uk). **Lunch served** 12.30-2.30pm Wed-Sun. **Dinner served** 7-10pm Mon-Sat. **Main courses** £16.50-£20. **Set dinner** £21.50 2 courses, £26.50 3 courses. **Credit** AmEx, MC, V.

La Fleur de Lys has recently moved to spacious, accessible accommodation. Due to the grievous misuse of capital letters, Parts Of The Menu Read Like An Exhortation, but don't let that put you off if you like complicated, rich cooking. The set menu offers the likes of asparagus tart; tenderloin of pork with apples, shallots and cranberries in a rich port sauce; or fillets of red mullet served on a light saffron sauce, while the à la carte is more comprehensive. Puddings are extremely tempting and may be accompanied by chocolate shavings or sauces made from butterscotch, praline or white chocolate.

STUDLAND

Shell Bay Seafood Restaurant

Ferry Road, Studland, BH19 3BA (01929 450363). **Lunch served** *Apr-Sept* noon-3pm daily. *Oct-Mar* 12.30-3pm Fri, Sat; 12.30-4pm Sun. **Dinner served** *Apr-Sept* 6-9pm daily. *Oct-Mar* 7-9pm Fri, Sat. **Main courses** £13-£30. **Set meal** £15 2 courses. **Credit** AmEx, MC, V.

On a sunny day, this is a good place to bring children after spending time on Studland Beach. Sailing boats and ferries pass by and you can sit outside overlooking the water, or in the Bistro, a large plastic tent with loud pop music. As well as a children's menu, the Bistro serves light, simple meals such as beer-battered cod and chips, while the light, bright restaurant offers a range of fish and shellfish dishes such as a platter of oysters, monkfish with pernod and dill or line-caught swordfish loin. The atmosphere is relaxed, despite the sometimes unenthusiastic service. Note that a refurbishment is planned, so do phone to check that the restaurant is open before setting off.

STURMINSTER NEWTON

Plumber Manor

Sturminster Newton, DT10 2AF (01258 472507/ www.plumbermanor.com). **Lunch served** 1-2pm Sun. **Dinner served** 7.30-9pm daily. **Set lunch** £21 3 courses. **Set dinner** £22 2 courses, £26 3 courses. **Credit** AmEx, DC, MC, V.

Plumber Manor, a lovely old house set in its own grounds, is much favoured by the local gentry. With its dingy lighting and '60s furniture, the bar could be an Agatha Christie stage set, while one of the dining rooms has a flickering gas log fire set in a massive marble surround. The food is unashamedly '70s, dependable and unsurprising, and portions are generous – avocado, melon and prawns with Marie Rose sauce or chicken liver pâté might be among the starters, while lemon sole with grapes or guinea fowl with black cherries and cinnamon could follow. There is even a sweet trolley, groaning with about 12 old-fashioned puddings; diners clearly enjoy giving in to temptation. A very retro experience.

WEYMOUTH

Fish 'n' Fritz ★

9 Market Street, Weymouth, DT4 8DD (01305 766386). **Lunch served** noon-2pm Mon-Fri. **Dinner served** 5-9pm Tue-Fri. **Meals served** noon-10pm Sat. **Main courses** £5.10-£5.70. **Credit** MC, V.

More promising from the outside than the inside, this café adjoining a fish and chip bar – doesn't live up to its eye-catching and freshly painted exterior. Ceramic floor tiles and scraping chairs create a noisy background while the bare tables and hard bentwood chairs seem unnecessarily austere. That said, the fish and chips are freshly cooked and the batter is unusually light. As well as a range of options such as salad instead of chips (more chips can be requested at no extra cost), pies and various vegetarian dishes, there is a choice of exotic-looking desserts. Young serving staff try hard to please and the place is run on slick and professional lines but you can expect to queue in the middle of the day.

Perry's
4 Trinity Road, Weymouth, DT4 8TJ (01305 785799/www.perrysrestaurant.co.uk). **Lunch served** noon-2pm Tue-Fri, Sun. **Dinner served** *May-Aug* 7-9.30pm Tue-Fri, Sun; 7-10pm Sat. *Sept-Apr* 7-9.30pm Tue-Fri; 7-10pm Sat. **Main courses** £10.95-£25. **Credit** AmEx, MC, V.
This small Georgian restaurant overlooks the water in Weymouth's pretty harbour area. Clever use of mirrors makes the main dining room seem larger than it is, and the buttermilk walls and soft lighting create a mellow effect. Fish features strongly but there is also a range of other dishes. The uncomplicated cooking style emphasises the quality of the ingredients – a moist terrine of duck and ham tasted sweetly rich, while turbot with mussels, leeks and new potatoes oozed freshness. As well as various desserts such as hot chocolate pudding with vanilla ice-cream, there's a generous cheese plate.

Yako Japanese Noodle Bar ★
97 St Mary Street, Weymouth, DT4 8NY (01305 780888). **Meals served** 11am-10.30pm daily. **Main courses** £3.50-£5.50. **Set lunch** £4.80 3 dishes. **Set dinner** £8.30 7 dishes. **Credit** MC, V.
You don't expect a Japanese noodle bar in the shopping area of an English seaside town, but Yako is clearly very popular. This ramen shop has low circular tables, Japanese staff and a menu of noodles served in soups with various toppings, and rice dishes, cooked to order. For £5.50, a huge bowl arrived full of noodles and vegetables with four tempura prawns on the side. Daily set lunch specials and set dinners might feature pan-fried seafood in sweet soy sauce or pork in teriyaki sauce.

WIMBORNE ST GILES

Wimborne St Giles Village Hall ★
Wimborne St Giles, BH21 5ND (01725 517255). **Tea served** *Easter-Oct* 3-5pm Sun. **No credit cards.**
Every Sunday afternoon between March and October, volunteers take over the village hall to serve teas in aid of charity. People take their mums, sporty types turn up on their bicycles, and if the weather is kind, you can sun yourself in the garden while enjoying a plateful of old-fashioned sandwiches. Everything is home-made and a round of sandwiches only costs £1. In the hall itself, tables are set with tablecloths and fresh flowers, while children's art work and village announcements decorate the walls. It is from another era and all the better for that.

Also in the area

FishWorks Seafood Café 10 Church Street, Christchurch, BH23 1BW (01202 487000); **Prezzo** 3 Bridge Street, Christchurch, BH23 1DY (01202 496100).

South West

Somerset

BARWICK

Little Barwick House
Barwick, BA22 9TD (01935 423902/www.littlebarwickhouse.co.uk). **Lunch served** noon-2pm Wed-Sat; noon-1.30pm Sun. **Dinner served** 7-9.30pm Tue-Sat. **Main courses** (lunch) £15.75-£18.50. **Set lunch** (Wed-Sat) £15.95 2 courses, £17.95 3 courses; (Sun) £19.50 3 courses. **Set dinner** (Tue-Thur) £28.95 2 courses, (Tue-Sat) £32.95 3 courses. **Credit** AmEx, MC, V.
The steps leading up to the entrance of this Georgian house, the huge cedar tree outside and the pleasing proportions of the rooms create an elegant setting, but Little Barwick House is not overly stuffy. The atmosphere is sufficiently relaxed to suit couples as well as more lively families. The three-course dinner includes nibbles and own-made bread – the food is rich, but flavours are clear and intense. Pan-fried foie gras or gateau of crab could appear among the starters, main courses might be roast squab pigeon or pan-fried veal sweetbreads – both melt in the mouth. Puddings include hot pear tart with black pepper ice-cream or iced lemon parfait with thyme sauce. There is a comprehensive wine list.

BATH

Café Retro ★
18 York Street, Bath, BA1 1NG (01225 339347). **Meals served** 9am-5pm Mon-Sat; 10am-5pm Sun. **Dinner served** 6-10pm Thur-Sat. **Main courses** £6-£11. **Set dinner** £12.95 2 courses, £15.95 3 courses. **Credit** AmEx, MC, V.
In all honesty, we include this jolly hangout as much for the location (central), imagination (vivid) and atmosphere (groovy) as for the food. Yes, its clientele of native bohos, students, smoochers, slackers and the odd knackered tourist do wax lyrical over the generously stacked club sandwiches, juicy burgers, steaks, shakes, numerous veggie delights and above-par evening tapas, but some of the pastries and smoothies are pre-packaged, and the tomato ketchup has that tell-tale eked-out vinegary quality. This is

a place to come for a snack and a chat, not a serious, chin-scratching gourmet chow. However, the well-worn, wooden shabby-chic interior (venture upstairs for more personal space) with its aged schoolroom chairs, window boxes, world music and continental café vibe brings back fans again and again.

Demuths

2 North Parade Passage, off Abbey Green, Bath, BA1 1NX (01225 446059/www.demuths.co.uk). **Breakfast served** 10-11.30am, **lunch served** noon-3.30pm, **dinner served** 6-9.30pm daily. **Main courses** £10-£13. **Credit** AmEx, MC, V.

There may be only one way to peel a carrot, but Demuths's menu blasts preconceptions about veggie food clean out of the cabbage water, finding new roles for every pulse, fruit, nut and vegetable imaginable. Be it vegetable and tofu satay wraps; fruity, colourful Gujarati curry; or ciabatta pizza fingers for kids – all arrive with side salads bristling with seeds, gratings, herbs and spices. Scrumptious smoothies, juices and lassis too. If any criticism may be levelled at an establishment working so hard for the non-carnivore it is that, occasionally, the push to prove vegetables can be fun results in aggressively strong mixes. The interior is tasty too – orange, purple, yellow and pink walls hung with giant artworks. Service is efficient, if a little detached.

Hole in the Wall

16 George Street, Bath, BA1 2EN (01225 425242/www.theholeinthewall.co.uk). **Lunch served** noon-2.30pm Mon-Sat; 11am-4pm Sun. **Dinner served** 6-10.30pm Mon-Sat; 6-9.30pm Sun. **Main courses** £13.50. **Set lunch/pre-theatre** (6-7pm) £9.95 2 courses, £14.95 3 courses. **Set dinner** £18.50 2 courses, £23.50 3 courses. **Credit** AmEx, MC, V.

Thriving and phenomenally popular since the 1960s, this Bath institution broke many hearts when it went into liquidation at the end of 2003. However, in early 2004, was rescued by new owners including chef Gerry Dowd. All praise to him, then, that one mini-refurb later the Hole's vital statistics remain intact, even enhanced: familiar yet five-star quality European staples; a jovial atmosphere; affectionate service; and a cosy flagstones-and-fireplace basement dining area. From mouthwatering starters like eggs benedict to mains such as noisette of pork with apple and stilton tatin, and desserts like raspberry crème brûlée, all are perfectly executed with aplomb, delicacy and a determination to give you something to remember. Perfect for family get-togethers – there's even a children's menu.

Hop Pole

7 Albion Buildings, Upper Bristol Road, Bath, BA1 3AR (01225 446327). **Lunch served** noon-2pm Tue-Sat; noon-3pm Sun. **Dinner served** 7-10pm Tue-Sat. **Main courses** £7.95-£15.95. **Set lunch** (Tue-Sat) £12.95 3 courses. **Credit** MC, V.

Rightly the object of both local and national press worship, Barry Wallace and Elaine Dennehy's much loved real ale boozer boasts a fantastic long and narrow, wooden-beamed restaurant in what used to be the skittle alley. Well worth the short walk out of town, it slaps egg on the face of certain fancy town centre eateries. Hearty, fresh and full-on fare assembled with a gourmet's gusto – roast pigeon, Cumberland sausages, confit leg of barbary duck or guinea fowl, followed by unashamedly comforting puddings. The portions are whopping – even the goat's cheese salad would keep a farm labourer going all day. 'Well-behaved children welcome' too (there's an adventure playground opposite for afterwards), and booking is essential at weekends.

Java ★

39 Gay Street, Bath, BA1 2NT (01225 427919/www.javarestaurant.co.uk). **Lunch served** noon-2pm Mon-Sat. **Dinner served** 6-10.30pm daily. **Main courses** £6-£8. **Set lunch** £6 1 course, £8 2 courses, £12-£14 menu (min 2 people). **Set dinner** £16-£25 menus. **Credit** AmEx, MC, V.

Turn a blind eye to the tatty woodchip decor and be deaf to the incongruous faux-jazz muzak, all of which scream 'Koa San Road backpackers' noodle bar' – this is one of the brightest new stars in Bath's culinary universe, offering a splendid alternative to those with heritage fatigue. Java serves spicy, colourful and unforgettably delicious Indonesian and Far Eastern fare, from a starter platter-for-two including satay chicken, thai fish cakes, pork dumplings and ribs, through to mains like lamb in sambal sauce or thai green curry. Symbols denote whether these are 'warm', 'fiery' or 'tingling'. Presentation and service are faultless and, although standards slip on the pudding front, this place is unlikely to disappoint. Decent house wines too.

Moody Goose

7A Kingsmead Square, Bath, BA1 2BA (01225 466688/www.moody-goose.com). **Lunch served** noon-1.30pm, **dinner served** 6-9.30pm Mon-Sat. **Main courses** £18-£19.50. **Set lunch** £17.50 3 courses. **Set dinner** £25 3 courses. **Credit** AmEx, DC, MC, V.

Quiet, refined and slightly self-conscious, The Moody Goose has for the last eight years enjoyed a reputation as one of Bath's finest purveyors of locally sourced, modern British cuisine. For the last three years, it has also boasted a Michelin star. Local-born chef-owner Stephen Shore hails from a country hotel background; the Goose itself is a hefty pottery beast that gazes across the three luxurious dining rooms, each seating about eight. Sample petits fours and aperitifs in the comfortable foyer before sitting down to chestnut mushroom and tarragon soup, followed by pan-fried calf's liver with roasted avocado and pink grapefruit, finishing with passion fruit tart with mango sorbet and fritters. Vegetarian options must be arranged in advance.

Moon & Sixpence

6a Broad Street, Bath, BA1 5LJ (01225 460962/www.moonandsixpence.co.uk). **Lunch served** noon-2.15pm Mon-Sat; noon-2.45pm Sun. **Dinner served**

5.30-10pm Mon-Thur; 5.30-10.45pm Fri, Sat; 6.30-10pm Sun. **Main courses** £10-£15.50. **Set lunch** (Mon-Fri) £7.95 2 courses; (Sun) £10.50 1 course, £13.50 2 courses, £16.50 3 courses. **Set dinners** £20.75-£24.75 3 courses. **Credit** AmEx, MC, V.

An excellent restaurant guaranteed to elicit nostalgic noises from anyone who's ever stepped into its pretty cobbled courtyard and sampled the blend of international flavours whipped together in the kitchen by chef Kevin King. Dishes such as duck with aubergine, red onion and sultana with a cinnamon and red wine sauce, or lighter plates such as pan-fried salmon fillet with potato and butternut squash purée are best taken in the bright, airy downstairs conservatory area or, on sunny days, outside (avoid upstairs if possible). The service is almost overwhelmingly amiable (they don't just bid you a good day, but a good week) and the two-course set lunch at £7.95 is such an absolute steal you'll feel you're somehow ripping them off. Not to be missed.

No.5 Restaurant

5 Argyle Street, Bath, BA2 4BA (01225 444499). **Lunch served** noon-2.30pm daily. **Dinner served** 6.30-10pm Mon-Thur, Sun; 6.30-10.30pm Fri; 6.30-11pm Sat. **Main courses** £12.50-£17. **Credit** AmEx, MC, V.

A romantic Parisian nook in the heart of Bath, all candlelight and the aroma of gently sizzling garlic. French, Roux-trained owner Michel Lemoine carefully oversees everything at this wonderful Pulteney Bridge stalwart, combining classic French cuisine with unexpected twists – like roast duck with sweet and sour sauce. Steak au poivre is flawless, the chips to kill for, and special mention must go to the fresh fish dishes. Paper tablecloths and cheerfully informal staff remove any hint of dining elitism and, with the deep orange walls and shadowy ambiance, create an atmosphere so inviting you'll need dragging away. If planning a cosy dîner-à-deux, specify when booking that you'd like the tiny, tucked away window table. Monday and Tuesday are bring-your-own-wine nights.

Olive Tree

Queensberry Hotel, Russell Street, Bath, BA1 2QF (01225 447928/www.thequeensberry.co.uk). **Lunch served** noon-2pm Tue-Sat; 12.30-2.30pm Sun. **Dinner served** 7-10pm daily. **Main courses** £12.50-£18.95. **Set lunch** (Tue-Sat) £13.50 2 courses, £15.50 3 courses; (Sun) £15.50 2courses, £18.50 3 courses. **Set dinner** (Mon-Fri, Sun) £26 3 courses. **Credit** AmEx, MC, V.

It's out with the old, genteel and traditional stylings and in with new oak floors, nu-soul music and industrial-looking cruets at the upmarket Olive Tree, located in the basement of a Georgian townhouse hotel. Those who find this dramatic makeover a travesty should know that the crucial element remains: chef Jason Horn, who becomes more imaginative as the years pass. Fresh ingredients combine in a fish-rich menu to create dazzling twists on British classics. 'Fish and chips', for example, combines tender scallops with pea purée and cocktail stick-sized fries – as witty as it is delicious. Perfection on a plate, at a price.

Pasta Galore ★

31 Barton Street, Bath, BA1 1HG (01225 463861/www.pastagalore.co.uk). **Lunch served** noon-2.30pm daily. **Dinner served** 6-10.30pm Mon-Wed, Sun; 6-11pm Thur-Sat. **Main courses** £5.90-£10.50. **Set lunch** £6 2 courses. **Credit** MC, V.

Ignore the depressing 1960s façade and daft name, this is Bath's best Italian by miles – a cheap, cheerful and charming taverna evocative of holidays in the Med, decked in red, white and green, with little packets of breadsticks and candles on the table, and run with a rod of iron by sisters Celia and Jessica. The food's the real deal too – chunky, rustic servings of own-made pasta, pizza and other Italian dishes, notable among which are pork, coriander and ginger meatballs in a red pepper, tomato, lemongrass and fresh basil sauce. For pudding try the 'hot naughty lumps' (black cherries in grappa with vanilla ice-cream and hot chocolate sauce). Popular with actors from the nearby Theatre Royal.

Pimpernel's ★

Royal Crescent Hotel, 16 Royal Crescent, Bath, BA1 2LS (01225 823333/www.royalcrescent.co.uk). **Lunch served** 12.30pm-2pm daily. **Dinner served** 7-10pm daily **Set lunches** £18 2 courses, £25 3 courses. **Set dinner** £38 2 courses £49 3 courses. **Credit** AmEx, DC, MC, V.

The finest restaurant interior in town, with soft banquettes, velvet cushions, hand-painted wall-coverings, elegant French windows… you may not have swooped down by helicopter like the many famous guests, but the full aristocratic experience can be yours for a few hours at this hotel's garden restaurant. Chef Steven Blake specialises in seasonal, classic and Mediterranean fare: in the summer try steamed, minted lamb pudding on a root vegetable purée outside on the terrace by manicured lawns or, in the winter, perch by the log fire to consume roe venison, dauphinoise, baby spinach, wild mushrooms and crisp celeriac. The 'assiette of desserts' is a tempting platter of individual puddings for two. Booking is essential at weekends, but weekday lunchtimes can be surprisingly under-populated – a good time to take up the superb two-course chef's choice lunch offer.

Pinch of Salt

11 Margarets Buildings, off Brock Street, Bath, BA1 2LP (01225 421251/www.pinchofsalt.biz). **Lunch served** noon-2.30pm Mon-Fri. **Dinner served** 7-10pm Mon-Thur; 6.30-10pm Fri, Sat. **Main courses** £15. **Set lunch** £9 2 courses. **Credit** MC, V.

Trendy new(ish) kid in town with lots of cool friends, 'the Pinch' is skippered by charismatic husband and wife team Suzy and Christophe Lacroix (maître d' and chef respectively), who have shipped in steel-topped tables, steel menu clipboards, boxes of weird and wonderfully shaped china and several giant paintings of rock stars to provide a buzzy haven for young foodies with linen-o-phobia. That's not to imply liberties have been taken with the menu – dishes such as wild sea bass with orange scented couscous and provençal-style broth, or Scottish beef fillet with bubble and squeak and roquefort cream would impress the fustiest old colonel (although he might have trouble with the outside loos).

The Priory ★

Weston Road, Bath, BA1 2XT (01225 331922/ www.thebathpriory.co.uk). **Lunch served** noon-1.30pm daily. **Dinner served** 7-9.30pm Mon-Sat; 7-9pm Sun. **Main courses** £26. **Set lunch** (Mon-Sat) £20 2 courses, £25 3 courses; (Sun) £30 3 courses. **Set dinner** £49.50 3 courses. **Credit** AmEx, DC, MC, V.

A Michelin-starred restaurant that succeeds in being neither fussy, pompous nor extortionate (the three-course dinner with coffee and petits fours at just shy of £50 really is worth it), the Bath Priory Hotel restaurant is the country house dining room of your dreams. The uncomplicated French and Mediterranean cooking uses vegetables and herbs from the hotel's own garden; every ingredient is exploited to the full and does its job perfectly. A typical menu might involve a surprise hors d'oeuvre of parsnip soup before ravioli of crab and ginger in langoustine sauce, followed by double-cooked shoulder of rosette of lamb with chive mash and thyme sauce, then crispy plum tart with crème fraîche and black pepper sorbet. Take someone you love.

Rajpoot

4 Argyle Street, Bath, BA2 4BA (01225 466833/ www.rajpoot.com). **Lunch served** noon-2.30pm daily. **Dinner served** 6-11pm Mon-Thur, Sun; 6-11.30pm Fri, Sat. **Main courses** £8-£15. **Set dinner** £18-£25 4 courses. **Credit** AmEx, DC, MC, V.

In India, suppertime is a ceremonial event. And so it is in the atmospheric, subterranean, candlelit cavern that is Rajpoot, Bath's finest (by a nose) Indian restaurant and purveyor of Tandoori, Mughlai and Bengali dishes fit for a maharajah. In short, it's far too good to thoughtlessly tumble into for a post-pub balti. Alongside freshly cooked standards like chicken tikka and onion bhaji you'll find traditional dishes such as rupchanda (a rare fish from the Bay of Bengal), rezala, fish rangamati, chicken shorisha and shahi murg mussalam, all of which demonstrate a genuine wish to introduce invigorating exotic flavours to tired Brit palates (owner Ahmed Chowdhury is director of the British-Bangladesh Chamber of Commerce). Gracious waiters are always on hand to explain the menu.

BECKINGTON

Woolpack

Warminster Road, Beckington, BA11 6SP (01373 831244/www.woolpackhotel.com). **Lunch served** noon-2.30pm daily. **Dinner served** 6.30-9.30pm Mon-Sat; 6.30-9pm Sun. **Main courses** £10.45-£16.95. **Credit** AmEx, MC, V.

The splendidly restored former coaching inn stands on a corner right at the heart of the village. An original fireplace creates a focal point for the bar, which also has 're-created' window shutters instead of curtains and re-laid traditional flagstone flooring. Of the several dining areas, the Garden Room is the most popular, leading out into a south-facing walled courtyard with high creeper-clad walls, where alfresco options are available in fine weather. The no-smoking Oak Room provides additional seating for food that's both uncomplicated and enjoyable. The all-embracing choice runs from warm chicken and bacon salad, wild mushroom and chive risotto, to cod and chips in rich beer batter with freshly-made tartare sauce, steak and ale pie, and shank of English lamb with rosemary gravy.

BRUTON

Claire de Lune

2-4 High Street, Bruton, BA10 0AA (01749 813395/www.clairedelune.co.uk). **Lunch served** noon-2pm Thur, Fri, Sun. **Dinner served** 7-9pm Tue-Sat. **Set lunch** £12.95 2 courses, £15.95 3 courses. **Set dinner** £18.95 2 courses, £21.95 3 courses, £24.95 4 courses. **Credit** MC, V.

This cheerful family-run 'restaurant with rooms' has a strong local following. Done up in shades of mustard and dark red, the restaurant has that comfortable air of small town respectability, without pompous airs or graces. The seasonally changing and very ample menu shows marginally more flair, ranging freely across the world for inspiration. Starters might be a generous panache of smoked fish, or parfait of foie gras d'oie with green tomato chutney and malt bread toast. Mains such as roast rack of West Country lamb and Cajun breast of chicken are also unlikely to disappoint, accompanied by some reliable wines and followed with an impressive array of sticky puds.

Truffles ★

95 High Street, Bruton, BA10 0AR (01749 812255/ www.trufflesbruton.co.uk). **Lunch served** noon-2pm Thur-Sun. **Dinner served** from 7pm Tue-Sat. **Set lunch** (Thur-Sat) £10 2 courses, £15 3 courses; (Sun) £15.95 3 courses. **Set dinner** £26.95 3 courses. **Credit** MC, V.

At the bottom end of the High Street, Truffles still tops the list locally for culinary finesse. It's a tiny, rose-clad little place, with pansies in the windowboxes, head room best described as cosy, starched linen tablecloths and a superb monthly changing menu that keeps locals and anyone else in the know coming back for more. (Booking is essential.) Dishes are immaculately presented: duo of smoked salmon and smoked haddock mousse with a cucumber and dill salad and saffron sauce was as refreshing as it sounded; crispy pastry cases filled with red onion marmalade, goat's cheese, and a tomato and tarragon salsa were as light on the eye as the palate. Slices of pork fillet served on caramelised apple and thyme with a calvados sauce lifted an old favourite to new heights. Fillet of red mullet pan-fried on a bed of creamed spinach and fennel with lemongrass sauce could not be faulted, a triumph of well-balanced flavours.

HAMBRIDGE

The Smokery ★

Bowdens Farm, Hambridge, TA10 0BP (01458 250875/www.smokedeel.co.uk). **Open** 10am-4pm Mon-Sat. **Lunch served** noon-2pm Mon-Sat. **Main course** £7. **Credit** AmEx, MC, V.

Light lunches and own-made cakes are available in the attractive, unpretentious slate-tiled café adjoining Brown & Forrest's successful smokery. Service is friendly and there are usually several choices for lunch, all at reasonable prices. Starters could include parma ham with baby figs or eel on rye, followed by smoked lamb or hot-smoked salmon steak served with granary bread or new potatoes, garlicky or plain, and a salad. Golden syrup bread and butter pudding is a favourite, served with a choice of low-fat yoghurt, pouring or clotted cream. The café has a small shop so that you can buy a range of vacuum-packed smoked goods, and they also do mail order. It is advisable to book for lunch.

MELLS

Talbot

Mells, BA11 3PN (01373 812254/www.talbotinn.com). **Lunch served** noon-2pm, **dinner served** 7-9pm daily. **Main courses** £11-£15. **Set lunch** (Sun) £11.95 2 courses. **Credit** MC, V.

The Talbot is a jolly old coaching inn, the sociable heart of a honeystone village, that has developed quite a reputation for the quality of its fish dishes. Fresh from Brixham, the likes of lemon sole might come simply grilled with fresh herbs, or a whole sea bass be baked with spring onions, ginger and garlic. Fresh scallops, grilled with coriander, are also a speciality. Less expensive options include standard pub grub, ploughman's, omelettes or ham and eggs. There's a large sunny garden with a pétanque pitch beneath old stone walls round the back, and the churchyard next door is worth a look for the grave of Siegfried Sassoon and an unusual equine sculpture by Sir Alfred Munnings in a side chapel.

PORLOCK WEIR

Andrews on the Weir ★

Porlock Weir, TA24 8PB (01643 863300/ www.andrewsontheweir.co.uk). **Lunch served** noon-2.30pm Wed-Sun. **Dinner served** 6.30-9.30pm Tue-Sat. **Set lunch** (Wed-Sat) £12.50 2 courses, £15.50 3 courses; (Sun) £20.50 3 courses. **Set dinner** £28 2 courses, £35 3 courses. **Credit** MC, V.

One of the most accomplished restaurants on the romantic Exmoor coast, Andrews on the Weir occupies a demure old guesthouse overlooking the little harbour at Porlock Weir. This is the crisp but faintly unlikely setting for some seriously ambitious cuisine, locally sourced and using only the freshest ingredients, favoured by couples of a certain age and families out for a special occasion. Of the six starters, tartare of scallops with lime and vermouth, mizuna salad and caviar cream proved as exotic and sensational as promised. Pan-fried langoustines with cep mushrooms, pancetta, rocket and truffle dressing were also deliciously well balanced. Mains were only marginally less successful: a delightful fillet of Porlock Bay sea bass with basil tortellini, and a succulent roast loin of Exmoor milk-fed spring lamb, with a surprising but intrusive ravioli of haggis. Very fancy puds and an exemplary selection of fine British cheeses rounded off a superb meal that was served up with quiet and charming efficiency by the excellent staff.

Mos. *See p141.*

SHEPTON MALLET

Blostin's

29-33 Waterloo Road, Shepton Mallet, BA4 5HH (01749 343648/www.blostins.co.uk). **Dinner served** 7-9pm Tue-Sat. **Main courses** £14.95-£16.75. **Set dinner** £15.95 2 courses, £17.95 3 courses. **Credit** MC, V.

A long-standing local restaurant with a loyal following. Right on the road, but quiet, clean and bright inside, it serves up largely traditional dinner combinations: seasonal mains might be loin of venison with braised red cabbage and game sauce, or escalope of veal with mushrooms and marsala, along with marginally more adventurous vegetarian options and starters (portobello mushrooms stuffed with garlic and mozzarella, sun-dried tomatoes and olives, Cornish crab pastry cases with cucumber salad and sauce grelette). Capably handled, the menu is backed up by a serious wine list. For the price, you might reasonably expect a slightly more sophisticated ambience and more imagination in the kitchen, but the place has a steady, seemingly unchanging charm all of its own.

Mulberry at Charlton House ★

Charlton Road, Shepton Mallet, BA4 4PR (01749 342008/www.charltonhouse.com). **Lunch served** 12.30-2pm, **dinner served** 7.30-9.30pm daily. **Set lunch** £14.50 2 courses, £18.50 3 courses. **Set dinner** £35 2 courses, £49.50 3 courses. **Credit** AmEx, DC, MC, V.

The Mulberry has been one of the most expensive and sophisticated operations in the area for some time. Owned by Roger and Monty Saul, founders of the Mulberry fashion label, it takes centre stage in a 17th-century manor house hotel, a comfortable showcase for their Mulberry products. Well-kept back lawns slope down from a young apple orchard to the conservatory dining room. Here the largely French menu, service and decor elevate the enjoyment of fresh seasonal produce into an elegant and theatrical treat, lunch or dinner. Carnivores and piscivores are particularly well catered for: delicious starters included the likes of poached salmon with fennel, artichoke and olive salad, and a smoked haddock and potato cake with pea purée, asparagus and red wine vinaigrette. Seared tuna with char-grilled courgette and fennel, blackened aubergine and tapenade were perfect, while the breast of duck with parsnip purée and duck confit with fig chutney with port and star anise reduction was superbly sharp and succulent. With a legendary wine list and desserts that are both sweet and rich, this restaurant all but guarantees a meal that's memorable for all the right reasons, if at a price.

STAPLE FITZPAINE

The Greyhound

Staple Fitzpaine, TA3 5SP (01823 480227). **Lunch served** noon-2pm Mon-Fri; noon-2.30pm Sat, Sun. **Dinner served** 7-9.30pm daily. **Main courses** £8.95-£16.95. **Credit** DC, MC, V.

A proper stone pub, the Greyhound is a cheerful and welcoming place. The scrum at the bar at weekends testifies to the quality of its selection of well-kept real ales, but people also travel here for some decidedly above average pub grub. Locally sourced ingredients are a speciality, including beef, venison, and lamb, as well as fish fresh shipped over from Brixham in Devon. The straightforward recipes (from king prawns or venison and cranberry terrine, to lasagne or cod supreme stuffed with baby spinach) on the extensive menu (you can choose from about 14 main courses) may not be the most imaginative you'll find in Somerset, but they're handled competently enough and can be enjoyed amid much convivial chatter.

STON EASTON

Ston Easton Park

Ston Easton, BA3 4DF (01761 241631/www.stoneaston.co.uk). **Lunch served** noon-2.30pm, **dinner served** 7-9.30pm daily. **Set lunch** (Mon-Sat) £12.50 2 courses, £17.50 3 courses; (Sun) £22.50 3 courses. **Main courses** £19-£22. **Set dinner** £34.50-£39.50 3 courses. **Credit** AmEx, DC, MC, V.

Formerly the seat of the Rees-Mogg family, Ston Easton Park is now a delightful Palladian country house hotel in the capable hands of the burgeoning Von Essen group, which also includes such high-falutin' haunts as the Royal Crescent (*see p137* under Pimpernel's) in Bath. The atmosphere is easy-going, enhanced by the resident springer and cocker spaniels, Sorrel and Sweep. They're likely to be found in the back gardens enjoying the Repton water cascades and parkland, overlooked by a dining room that's surprisingly small. The kitchen has garnered quite a reputation in the area and produces a reliable locally sourced menu (with herbs and vegetables from its own garden) that majors on French cuisine with significant nods east and west. Chicken and wild mushroom boudin proved an imaginative take on the legendary Louisiana sausage, while honey and sesame glazed duck breast with stir-fry vegetables was a delicate and delicious treat.

TAUNTON

Brazz

Castle Hotel, Castle Green, Taunton, TA1 1NF (01823 252000/www.brazz.co.uk). **Lunch served** noon-3pm daily. **Dinner served** 6-10.30pm Mon-Thur, Sun; 6-11pm Fri, Sat. **Main courses** £7.95-£15.95. **Credit** AmEx, DC, MC, V.

Attached to the Castle Hotel, but deliberately very different in atmosphere, this contemporary brasserie and bar stays busy day and night. The designer lighting, wall-mounted fish tank and easy listening sounds are possibly not the main draw. That's probably the child-friendly attitude and the straightforward, decent value meals that are quickly and efficiently presented by an eager-to-please waiting staff. The menu changes weekly, but expect to find hearty staples like mushroom tagliatelle or fish pie at reasonable prices, as well as slightly more ambitious dishes such as pan-fried fillet of sea bream with sauté potatoes and chorizo (£11.95). The bar at Brazz does have a buzz, and it's backed by considerable competence in the kitchen.

Castle Hotel ★

Castle Green, Taunton, TA1 1NF (01823 272671/www.the-castle-hotel.com). **Lunch served** 12.30-2.15pm, **dinner served** 7-10pm daily. **Main courses**

(Fri, Sat dinner) £18-£22.50. **Set menu** (lunch; dinner Mon-Thur, Sun) £12.50 1 course, £18.50 2 courses, £22.50 3 courses. **Credit** AmEx, DC, MC, V.
Still probably the smartest eaterie in Taunton, the dining room at the Castle Hotel is roomy and unpretentious, but also capable of inspiring a sense of occasion. Beautifully proportioned, with tall windows and well-spaced tables, it has proved itself a popular setting for some much better-than-average modern British cuisine, locally sourced and prepared with confidence by head chef Richard Guest. The set lunch for £18.50 offered particularly good value: two courses plus bread, a glass of wine and coffee (complete with the most delectable handmade petits fours). Very fresh chilled seafood pasta salad and a rich baked organic egg, with parmesan and white truffle butter was followed by battered plaice with pea purée, straw potatoes and a sherry vinegar reduction (superior fish and chips) and a wholesome honey roast pork belly with onion purée and buttered greens. The seasonal menu caters well for vegetarians.

Mos ★

The Crescent, Taunton, TA1 4DN (01823 326793). **Food served** 8.30am-4pm Mon-Sat. **Dinner served** 7-10pm Fri, Sat. **Main courses** £4-£7. **Set dinner** £15.50 2 courses, £20 3 courses, £23.50 4 courses, £26.50 5 courses. **Credit** MC, V.
What was once Sally Edwards' imaginative little organic café has changed its name and ownership, but otherwise remains much as it was. It still has an enthusiastic, open-to-view, family-run kitchen with the added attraction that it now offers a very select dinner menu as well. It's a cheerful place, well designed and no-smoking, which during the day provides very good coffee and healthy light lunches based on local produce. The small but carefully formed menu changes daily. A sample dinner could include a parfait of chicken's livers with pear chutney and toast, or grilled smoked salmon with orange butter, then roasted vine tomato soup, followed by either a confit duck leg, crispy duck salad, puy lentils and soy sauce, or roast fillet of salmon with asparagus and hollandaise sauce.

WELLS

Boxer's

1 St Thomas Street, Wells, BA5 2UU (01749 672317/www.fountaininn.co.uk). **Lunch served** noon-2pm daily. **Dinner served** 7-9.30pm Mon-Sat. **Main courses** £8-£13.50. **Set lunch** £7.50 2 courses, £9.95 3 courses. **Credit** AmEx, DC, MC, V.
The front first-floor room of the old Fountain Inn, just east of the cathedral, has been home to Boxer's for a couple of decades. Woody and light, and with a congenial atmosphere that prevails even at the busiest times, when diners tuck into the wide range of hearty and defiantly unfashionable options on the menu, backed up by some excellent Spanish wines. For lunch, expect the likes of chilled melon rose with a raspberry and portwine coulis, or deep-fried brie for starters, followed by cod and chips or speciality sausages and mash. The supper menu is slightly more adventurous. Sample starters might include pan-fried squid strips with a lentil salad or marinated chicken brochettes, with roast monkfish wrapped in parma ham to follow. The recipes may not be that contemporary or cool, but they're professionally prepared and served in a cheerful and easygoing atmosphere.

Ritchers

5 Sadler Street, Wells, BA5 2RR (01749 679085/ www.ritchers.co.uk). **Lunch served** noon-2pm, **dinner served** 7-9pm Mon-Sat. **Set lunch** £7.50 1 course, £10.50 2 courses, £13.50 3 courses. **Set dinner** £19.50 2 courses, £23 3 courses. **Credit** MC, V.
Tucked away behind its jolly bistro bar, Ritcher's may be furnished like a blast from the past, but the kitchen sustains an enviable reputation in the town. The place is popular with the lunching ladies of Wells and in the evening develops quite a sense of occasion, with a menu to match the atmosphere. It features high quality ingredients given a French or Mediterranean twist. Starters might include an avocado terrine, white crab salad with sauce andalouse or chicken liver pâté and blackberry marmalade on toasted brioche. They could be followed by a char-grilled sea bass, with roast veg and smoked tomato jus or a pan-fried chicken breast filled with a sun-dried tomato mousse.

South West

WEST BAGBOROUGH

Rising Sun Inn

West Bagborough, TA4 3ES (01823 432575/ www.theriser.co.uk). **Lunch served** noon-2pm, **dinner served** 7-9.30pm Tue-Sun. **Main courses** £9.95-£16.95. **Credit** MC, V.
After a disastrous fire some years back, the thatched 16th-century Rising Sun was completely renovated in oak and slate. The unusual interior, decorated with intriguing artworks and with an extra cosy dining area round the back, as well as the pub's charming location on a rising flank of the Quantocks, has kept punters coming back for more from some distance around. The menu changes regularly, but on our most recent visit was not quite as surefooted as we remembered. Starters of field mushrooms with melted goat's cheese arrived lukewarm but benefited considerably from more time in the oven. The own-cured gravadlax and red pepper marmalade was more successful, followed by a fine ribeye steak on slow roasted tomatoes with a wild mushroom ragoût. Steamed salmon fillet with sesame stir-fried veg and tarragon sauce was a welcome return to form.

Also in the area

Firehouse Rotisserie 2 John Street, Bath, BA1 2JL (01225 482070); **FishWorks Seafood Café** 6 Green Street, Bath, BA1 2JY (01225 448707); **Loch Fyne** 24 Milsom Street, Bath, BA1 1DG (01225 750120).

Central

Central
Ludlow
Bewdley
Kidderminster
Stourport-on-Severn
Bromsgrove
Redditch
Droitwich
COVENTRY
Rugby
Kenilworth
Royal Leamington Spa
Warwick
WARWICKSHIRE
Leominster
Worcester
WORCESTERSHIRE
Stratford-upon-Avon
HEREFORDSHIRE
Great Malvern
Evesham
Hereford
Ledbury
Chipping Campden
Paxford
Shipston on Stour
Banbury
Adderbury
Bloxham
King's Sutton
Buckland
Hook Norton
Deddington
Tewkesbury
Corse Lawn
Moreton-in-Marsh
Bishop's Cleeve
Winchcombe
Guiting Power
Stow-on-the-Wold
Daylesford
Oddington
Chipping Norton
Steeple Aston
Ross-on-Wye
Newent
Clifford's Mesne
Upper Slaughter
Cheltenham
Charlton Kings
Churchdown
Mitcheldean
Gloucester
Shurdington
Bourton-on-the-Water
Shipton-under-Wychwood
Charlbury
Wootton
Woodstock
Long Hanborough
Kidlington
Brockworth
Cowley
Monmouth
Cinderford
Arlingham
Burford
Witney
Eynsham
GLOUCESTERSHIRE
MONMOUTHSHIRE
Bibury
Coln St Aldwyns
Carterton
Ducklington
Wytham
Bream
Stonehouse
Stroud
Frampton Mansell
Sapperton
Barnsley
Stanton Harcourt
Sharpness
Chalford
Bampton
Boars Hill
Cirencester
Fairford
Nailsworth
Minchinhampton
Poulton
Lechlade
Clanfield
OXFORD
Dursley
Ewen
Buckland
Abingdon
Cricklade
Faringdon
Chepstow
Thornbury
Wotton-under-Edge
Tetbury
Crudwell
Highworth
Drayton
Caldicot
Stanton Fitzwarren
Watchfield
Ardlington
Purton
Shrivenham
Wantage
Easton Grey
Malmesbury
Swindon
Frampton Cotterell
Yate
Chipping Sodbury
Wootton Bassett
Wroughton
West Ilsley
Winterbourne
Lambourn
Castle Combe
Chiseldon
Ford
Kingswood
Chippenham
BRISTOL
Colerne
Ramsbury
Marlborough
Calne
Marsh Benham
Keynsham
Lacock
Hungerford
Whitley
Little Bedwyn
Kintbury
BATH
Melksham
Inkpen
Newbury
Rowde
Holt
Devizes
Bradford-on-Avon
Great Hinton
Pewsey
Marten
Trowbridge
Midsomer Norton
Radstock
WILTSHIRE
Westbury
Ludgershall
Frome
North Tidworth
Corsley
Warminster
Larkhill
Andover
Wells
Shepton Mallet
Amesbury
Glastonbury
HAMP
SOMERSET
Mere
Hindon
Teffont Evais
Wilton
Salisbury
Winchester
Fonthill Gifford
0
30 km
0
15 miles
Donhead St Andrew
Shaftesbury
Romsey
Eastleigh
Yeovil
Sherborne
Fordingbridge
SOUTHAMPTON
DORSET

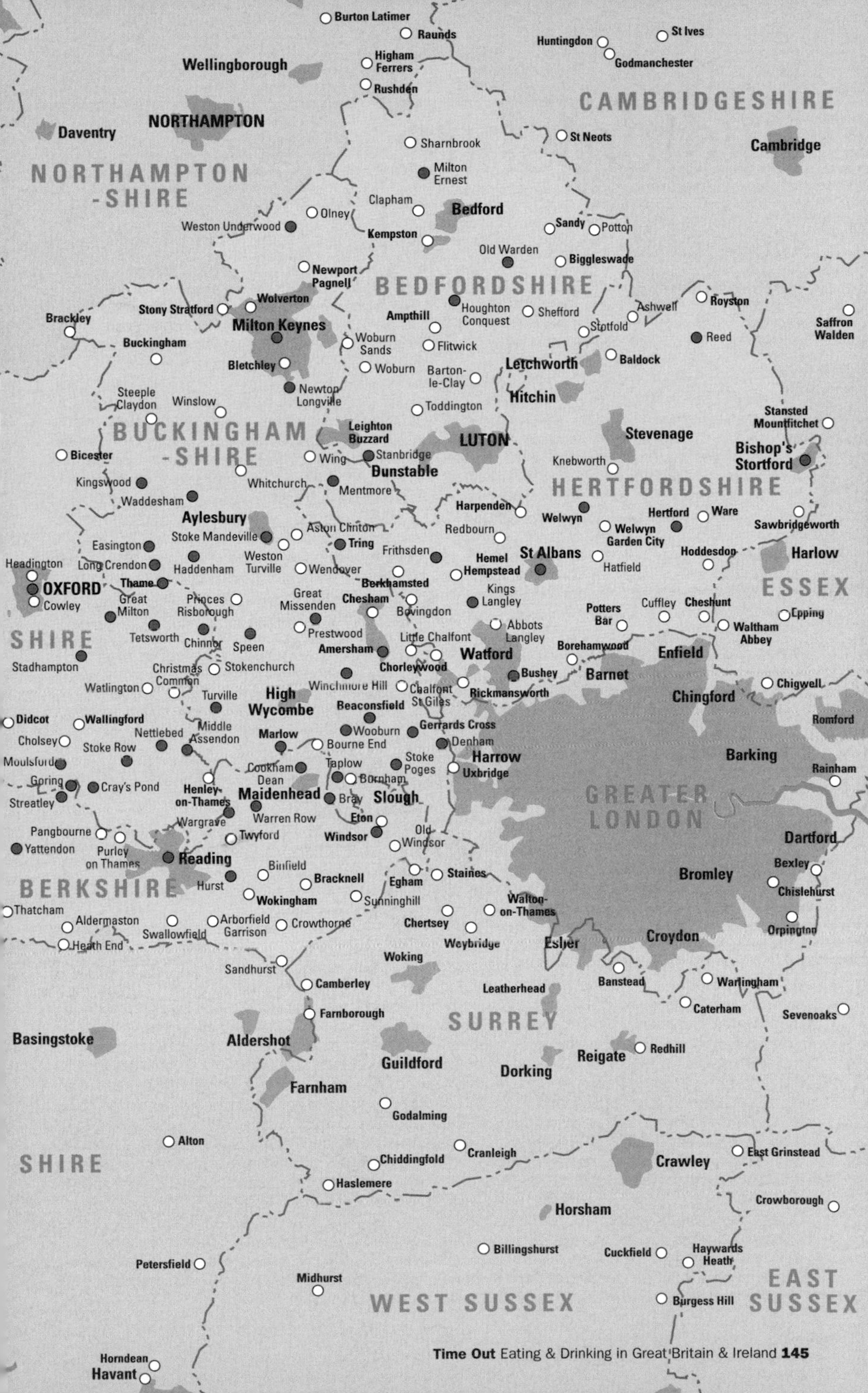
Burton Latimer
Raunds
St Ives
Huntingdon
Godmanchester
Higham Ferrers
Wellingborough
Rushden
CAMBRIDGESHIRE
NORTHAMPTON
Daventry
St Neots
Sharnbrook
Cambridge
NORTHAMPTON-SHIRE
Milton Ernest
Clapham
Bedford
Olney
Weston Underwood
Sandy
Potton
Kempston
Old Warden
Biggleswade
Newport Pagnell
BEDFORDSHIRE
Wolverton
Royston
Ashwell
Houghton Conquest
Shefford
Saffron Walden
Stony Stratford
Ampthill
Brackley
Milton Keynes
Stotfold
Reed
Woburn Sands
Flitwick
Buckingham
Baldock
Bletchley
Woburn
Barton-le-Clay
Letchworth
Newton Longville
Hitchin
Steeple Claydon
Winslow
Toddington
Stansted Mountfitchet
BUCKINGHAM-SHIRE
Leighton Buzzard
LUTON
Stevenage
Bishop's Stortford
Bicester
Wing
Stanbridge
Dunstable
Knebworth
Kingswood
Whitchurch
Mentmore
HERTFORDSHIRE
Waddesham
Harpenden
Hertford
Ware
Aylesbury
Welwyn
Sawbridgeworth
Aston Clinton
Redbourn
Welwyn Garden City
Stoke Mandeville
Tring
Easington
Frithsden
Hemel Hempstead
St Albans
Hoddesdon
Harlow
Headington
Long Crendon
Haddenham
Weston Turville
Wendover
Hatfield
OXFORD
Thame
Berkhamsted
Kings Langley
ESSEX
Cowley
Great Milton
Princes Risborough
Great Missenden
Chesham
Bovingdon
Potters Bar
Cuffley
Cheshunt
Epping
Abbots Langley
Waltham Abbey
SHIRE
Tetsworth
Chinnor
Speen
Prestwood
Little Chalfont
Borehamwood
Enfield
Amersham
Watford
Stadhampton
Christmas Common
Stokenchurch
Chorleywood
Bushey
Barnet
Chigwell
Watlington
Turville
High Wycombe
Winchmore Hill
Chalfont St Giles
Rickmansworth
Chingford
Didcot
Wallingford
Beaconsfield
Romford
Nettlebed
Middle Assendon
Marlow
Wooburn
Gerrards Cross
Cholsey
Stoke Row
Bourne End
Denham
Harrow
Barking
Moulsford
Cookham Dean
Taplow
Stoke Poges
Uxbridge
Rainham
Goring
Cray's Pond
Burnham
Henley-on-Thames
Maidenhead
Bray
Slough
GREATER LONDON
Streatley
Warren Row
Eton
Wargrave
Pangbourne
Twyford
Windsor
Old Windsor
Dartford
Yattendon
Purley on Thames
Reading
Binfield
Staines
Bexley
Bracknell
Egham
Bromley
BERKSHIRE
Hurst
Chislehurst
Wokingham
Sunninghill
Walton-on-Thames
Thatcham
Aldermaston
Arborfield Garrison
Crowthorne
Chertsey
Orpington
Swallowfield
Weybridge
Esher
Croydon
Heath End
Woking
Sandhurst
Banstead
Warlingham
Camberley
Leatherhead
Caterham
Sevenoaks
Farnborough
SURREY
Basingstoke
Aldershot
Reigate
Redhill
Guildford
Dorking
Farnham
Godalming
Alton
Cranleigh
Crawley
East Grinstead
SHIRE
Chiddingfold
Haslemere
Horsham
Crowborough
Billingshurst
Cuckfield
Haywards Heath
Petersfield
Midhurst
EAST SUSSEX
WEST SUSSEX
Burgess Hill
Horndean
Havant

Bedfordshire

Central

HOUGHTON CONQUEST

Knife & Cleaver

Houghton Conquest, MK45 3LA (01234 740387/ www.knifeandcleaver.com). **Lunch served** noon-2.30pm Mon-Fri, Sun. **Dinner served** 7-9.30pm Mon-Sat. **Set lunch** £12.95 2 courses, £14.95 3 courses. **Set dinner** £22 3 courses. **Main courses** £10.95-£16.50. **Credit** AmEx, DC, MC, V.

A bit of a mishmash this place – with a bar, small dining room and large, unexciting conservatory restaurant, you get the feeling that you could be gatecrashing a wedding reception. On our visit there was little atmosphere to speak of and the few suits were all strictly business enjoying the restaurant's forte of fresh fish. Opt for Loch Fyne rock oysters (£15 per dozen) or a half lobster with a choice of serving suggestions, such as Thai-style linguine, pesto and sun-dried tomato cream sauce. Once you wander away from fish, however, interest dissipates. Following a deliciously sweet starter of marinated herring fillets with lobster and dill dressing, we were presented with a chicken and bacon suet pudding which was more suet than meat. Dessert was an improvement: apple and calvados custard brioche with strawberry sauce was delicious. Some strong points, but decor and menu could do with an overhaul.

MILTON ERNEST

Strawberry Tree

3 Radwell Road, Milton Ernest, MK44 1RY (01234 823633). **Lunch served** noon-2pm Wed-Fri. **Dinner served** 7-8.30pm Wed-Sat. **Main courses** (lunch) £15-£20. **Set dinner** £41.50 3 courses. **Credit** MC, V.

The Strawberry Tree is housed within three white thatched cottages. Proprietor Wendy Bona does the meeting, greeting and waiting while her sons Jason and Andrew offer a pared-down menu of four starters, four mains and four desserts. Simplicity but with precise attention to detail, from the source (all traditionally reared meat, free-range chicken, local game, organic eggs, veg and herbs) to the sauce. A starter of grilled mackerel with beetroot cubes, pine nuts, capers, parsley and horseradish cream was a wake-up call for the tastebuds; the follow-up of roast monkfish was cooked to moist, flaky perfection; the warm bitter chocolate fondant with double cream sorbet was worth the 15-minute wait. With so much attention to detail, it's easy to see why a request for something vegetarian might be construed as an insult – as was the impression left when we made the requisite 'prior warning'. Thus our only bone of contention: a telephone manner that was brusque to the point of rudeness.

OLD WARDEN

Hare & Hounds

The Village Green, Old Warden, Biggleswade, SG18 9HQ (01767 627225). **Lunch served** noon-2pm Tue-Sat; noon-4pm Sun. **Dinner served** 6.30-9.30pm Tue-Sat. **Main courses** £9-£15. **Credit** MC, V.

A spruce-up at the end of 2003 has endowed this village pub-restaurant with a smart dining room – naturally textured walls and pinstriped and tartan chairs – that draws as many diners as the bar pulls drinkers. Food is unpretentious modern European: dishes such as tomato and basil risotto, caesar salad or mussels in white wine and tarragon are served as starters or mains. Or you could plump for a smoked duck breast pancake and chilli jam to start, and follow it up with fillet of venison, bubble and squeak and honey-roast vegetables. If you think a fish option might be better for your arteries, it ain't necessarily so: an alarming battered haddock appears the size of a whole tuna resting on chips the size of roast potatoes. If there's any room left try the ice-creams and sorbets, all of which are prepared here, or the cheese plate which offers a carefully picked range from Britain and Ireland.

STANBRIDGE

Five Bells

1 Station Road, Stanbridge, Leighton Buzzard, LU7 9JF (01525 210224/www.traditionalfreehouses.com). **Lunch served** noon-2.30pm, **dinner served** 7-9pm daily. **Main courses** £12.95-£21.50. **Credit** AmEx, DC, MC, V.

This 400-year-old village pub has been hauled into the 21st century with an impressive makeover – the restaurant has a real Gustavian feel to it with its wall of chopped wood surrounding the fireplace and distressed white chairs. The place comes into its own on warm summer weekends and in the evenings, but lunchtime custom gravitates towards the bar. There are two menus: Light Bites is a pretty loose term for offerings such as warm bread and olives, simple pasta puttanesca or a more substantial char-grilled Aberdeen Angus 7oz fillet steak. If you are hesitant about eating beef, full details of the meat and poultry suppliers are printed on the menu. The à la carte menu has a wider range of both starters and main courses, including delicious grilled haddock and baby spinach with roasted nutmeg butter. Raspberry and rum roulade promised much but its suet sponge gave it the texture of a more mundane roly-poly. Everything was immaculately presented and service was attentive.

Berkshire

BRAY

The Fat Duck ★

High Street, Bray, SL6 2AQ (01628 580333/ www.thefatduck.co.uk). **Lunch served** noon-2pm Tue-Sat; noon-3pm Sun. **Dinner served** 7-9.30pm Tue-Thur; 7-10pm Fri, Sat. **Set lunch** £35 3 courses. **Set meal** £65 8 courses, £90 12-course tasting menu. **Credit** AmEx, DC, MC, V.

Since 1995 the Fat Duck has attracted dizzying quantities of food lovers, restaurant reviewers, awards and column inches. In 2004 it was rated second best restaurant in the world (after the French Laundry, California, since you ask). So what can you expect? High drama and high prices, basically. The £35 lunch sounded promising but was quite ordinary, with soup, foie gras or the famous snail porridge for starters – the latter being like a nice herby, protein-studded oatmeal risotto – followed by roast chicken, salmon or poached halibut. Carrot toffee with butternut ice-cream for dessert was novel but not write-home-about good. The £60 and £90 menus, and little appetisers and refreshers which accompany any meal, is where you join Heston Blumenthal in his strange but uncannily appealing world of wacky flavours and combinations. Imagine poached oyster served in its shell under a passion fruit glaze and garnished with caramel, the acidic passion-fruitiness homing straight in on the sea-saltiness of the oyster, leaving a faint smudge of sweetness to echo around the palate like half-heard music. Memorable stuff. Be brave and try the likes of spiced cod with braised cockscombs, foie gras with crab and rhubarb, or mango and Douglas fir dessert from the à la carte and tasting menu.

Riverside Brasserie

Bray Marina, Monkey Island Lane, Bray, SL6 2EB (01628 780553/www.riversidebrasserie.co.uk). **Lunch served** noon-3pm Wed-Sun. **Dinner served** 6.30-10pm Wed-Sat. **Main courses** £13-£16. **Set lunch** (Sun) £23.50 2 courses, £28.50 3 courses. **Credit** AmEx, DC, MC, V.

For its doll's house portions and boatyard setting, the Riverside Brasserie is overpriced, despite Heston Blumenthal's interest. However, the Thames is undeniably attractive, the food you do get is mostly lovely, and if it's warm enough to dine outside on the decking, a good time will undoubtedly be had by all. If cooped up inside the Portakabin 'brasserie', try to ignore the smeary table tops and kitchen units (surely we are not supposed to believe that all the food is prepared here?), and the sound of metal chair legs scraping across the hollow floor, and just enjoy the food; potted pork and pickle, for instance, or chicken and goose liver mousse with sourdough toast and fig jam. Poached salmon is one perfectly cooked mainstay, but Caesar salad was drowned in its own dressing. Champagne, the obligatory waterside tipple, is £9.50 a glass, main courses around £12-£16. Do order the triple-fried chips.

Waterside Inn ★

Ferry Road, Bray, SL6 2AT (01628 620691/ www.waterside-inn.co.uk). **Lunch served** *Feb-Dec* noon-2pm Wed-Sat; noon-2.30pm Sun. **Dinner served** *Feb-May, Sept-Dec* 7-10pm Wed-Sun. *June-Aug* 7-10pm Tue-Sun. **Main courses** £36-£47. **Set lunch** (Mon-Sat) £40 3 courses; (Sun) £56 3 courses. **Set dinner** £85 5 courses. **Credit** AmEx, DC, MC, V.

Accept the sommelier's invitation of a champagne aperitif; you'll need something sustaining while absorbing the Waterside Inn's setting, and to take in the six-page menu while you map the culinary course of the next few hours – this is no place to be clock-watching. One wall of this square, compact room is made up of glass sliding panels and the outlook from any seat in the house is spellbindingly serene. Other diversions include chamfered glass panels, deep dark carpet and lots of sparkly glasses and gleaming silverware. The three course menu gastronomique includes canapés, petits fours and water. Consistency is the name of the game – seductively gorgeous mouthfuls from start to finish. Foie gras parfait with sauternes jelly, rhubarb compote, brioche toast and hazelnut salad played kaleidoscopic, beguiling games on the tongue, while pan-fried sea bream was accompanied by fresh pesto tagliatelle, a divinely filled courgette flower and sauce à la greque. Desserts are adorable pieces embellished with caramel, chocolate or feathery trellises for more textural adventure, but, unlike the Fat Duck along the road, the Waterside concentrates on re-creating classics (and excels at it) rather than making you work at every mouthful. Departing four hours later we overheard a lady telling chef Alain Roux (Michel's son) that her visit to the Waterside was a lifetime's wish come true.

COOKHAM DEAN

Inn on the Green

The Old Cricket Common, Cookham Dean, SL6 9NZ (01628 482638/www.theinnonthegreen.com). **Lunch served** noon-2pm Sat, Sun. **Dinner served** 7-9.30pm Tue-Sat. **Main courses** £14.50-£25.95. **Set meals** (lunch, dinner Tue-Thur) £14.95 2 courses, £23.95 3 courses. **Credit** AmEx, MC, V.

The setting may be verdant, but the Inn on the Green feels distinctly cosmopolitan, which comes as no surprise to those who know that London chef Gary

Dundas Arms

Hollihead is involved here (Embassy in Old Burlington Street, W1, is another of his interests). Secret and secretively lit gardens entice the inquisitive while another walled garden provides outdoor dining protected from winds that whip over the hills. The food's not bad either: roast free-range chicken on braised celery with broad bean mash was great, while scallops with julienne of vegetables and miso broth was vibrantly healthy. Treat someone.

HURST

Castle Brasserie

Church Hill, Hurst, RG10 0SJ (0118 934 0034/ www.castlerestaurant.co.uk). **Lunch served** noon-2.30pm, **dinner served** 7-10pm Mon-Sat. **Main courses** £11.95-£22.95. **Set lunch** £12.95 2 courses, £15.95 3 courses. **Credit** AmEx, DC, MC, V.
Hurst is a puny hamlet set in miles of flat, watery meadows. It's as dark as the devil at night, so rounding a sharp bend and falling into a pool of light where a sign announces your arrival at 'Castle' is a welcome surprise. Inside are open fires in a hip, exposed brick and beamed dining room with a small army of waitresses weaving in and out of a small army of cream chairs and properly set tables. Four years ago this opened as a fine dining restaurant, which downsized to a comfortable brasserie retaining an edge of glamour. We tucked into fabulous seared South American spiced tuna, tsatsiki and tabouleh, and risotto cakes with exceptional warm truffled and pickled mushrooms. Don't skimp on wine or dessert.

INKPEN

Swan Inn

Craven Road, Lower Green, Inkpen, RG17 9DX (01488 668326/www.theswaninn-organics.co.uk). **Lunch served** noon-2pm Mon-Fri; noon-2.30pm Sat, Sun. **Dinner served** 7-9pm Mon-Thur, Sun; 7-9.30pm Fri, Sat. **Main courses** £14-£21. **Credit** MC, V.
The Swan has firmly embraced the organic lifestyle since a local farmer saved it from becoming a private home. The surrounding farmland and attached farm shop have added their income and charm to this 17th-century inn and slightly smarter restaurant, both consistently popular with hordes of hungry walkers, cyclists and locals. It's best to book in advance if you want to get stuck into wholesome organic pasta dishes, hearty beefburgers, award-wining pies (meat is locally reared) and rib-sticking puddings, all at very reasonable prices. Seriously good beer is cool, expertly served and includes local Butts bitter; some is organic. No need to fear an over-zealous organic mob, though; things are down-to-earth, friendly and like a scene from *The Good Life*, in the nicest possible sense.

KINTBURY

Dundas Arms

53 Station Road, Kintbury, RG17 9UT (01488 658263/www.dundasarms.co.uk). **Open** 11.30am-2.30pm, 6-11pm Mon-Sat; noon-2pm Sun. **Lunch served** noon-2pm Mon-Sat. **Dinner served** 7.30-9pm Tue-Sat. **Main courses** £12-£14. **Credit** MC, V.

Your arrival at the Dundas Arms should be as sporting as possible. The River Kennet trickles along one side of the 18th-century pub, the Kennet and Avon Canal the other side and footpaths criss-cross the fields in all remaining directions, so most of those mingling around one weekend had got there by foot, bike, canoe or horseback. Cars? Pah! Food is no longer served on Sunday or Monday evening, but the rest of the time choose between the patio, the bar with its traditional beers and chalkboard menu of gutsy own-cooked pies, roasts and battered fish, or dine with more elegance in the tall-ceilinged, sparsely decorated river restaurant. Here you might be served pan-fried pigeon breast with celeriac purée, or chicken liver pâté with tequila and toast.

MARSH BENHAM

Red House

Marsh Benham, RG20 8LY (01635 582017). **Lunch served** noon-2.15pm Tue-Sun. **Dinner served** 7-9.30pm Tue-Sat. **Main courses** £13.95-£18.50. **Set lunch** (Sun) £16.95 2 courses, £19.95 3 courses. **Set meal** *Bistro* (Tue-Sat) £13.95 2 courses, £16.95 3 courses. **Credit** AmEx, MC, V.

A welcome red brick and thatched oasis in endless pastureland, the Red House is divided into a faux library-cum-restaurant and what the printed paper napkins call a gastropub, but either way the emphasis is on food rather than drink and punters are more likely to be supping champagne than beer. Indeed the dark red walls, long spotlit bar and towering vase of lilies are most un-publike. The gastro end of things is far less stuffy than the restaurant and was full to the brim one Sunday with birthday- and engagement-celebrating couples and kids, or those who were just celebrating an open pub in the middle of nowhere. Well cooked, interesting dishes such as tomato and parmesan crumble or duck and artichoke samosas sit alongside staples like roast rib of beef with Yorkshire pudding.

NEWBURY

Vineyard

Stock Cross, Newbury, RG20 8JU (01635 528770/ www.the-vineyard.co.uk). **Lunch served** noon-2pm, **dinner served** 7-9.30pm daily. **Set lunch** (Mon-Sat) £19 2 courses, £25 3 courses; (Sun) £26 3 courses. **Set dinner** £45 2 courses, £55 3 courses; (Fri, Sat) £65 7 courses. **Credit** AmEx, DC, MC, V.

Stretched out in a nook of rolling green downs, the Vineyard is a creamy mansion which wouldn't look out of place in California. As it happens the man behind this hotel and spa, Sir Peter Michael, owns vineyards in northern California, and Newbury has the unexpected good fortune to showcase the biggest and best collection of American wine in Europe. So leave the car behind and drink up. Classic cuisine in a pale, marble-clad split-level dining room is pure theatre and might include ambrosial herb risotto or 24-hour cooked veal cheeks with truffled macaroni, both sinfully rich and fabulously aromatic. A neutral, well-stuffed lounge takes the strain off your over-indulgence and a doorman will bring round the car if you're not staying the night.

READING

Loch Fyne

The Maltings, Bear Wharf, Fobney Street, RG1 6BT (0118 918 5850/www.loch-fyne.com). **Breakfast served** 10am-noon, **lunch served** noon-5pm, **dinner served** 5-10pm daily. **Main courses** £8.95-£24.95. **Set lunch** £9.95 2 courses. **Credit** AmEx, MC, V.

A few strides south of Reading's rejuvenated Oracle centre is the city's old brewery site, and still lapping at the Kennet and Avon Canal is a solid, three-storey malthouse where barley from the surrounding countryside was malted. This Victorian utility now houses a branch of Loch Fyne and it's pleasing to report that sound ingredients are worked as industriously these days as barley was then. Knowledgeable staff and regional drinks set the scene for well-sourced, simply prepared food. Born and bred in Scotland, Glen Fyne 42-day dry matured sirloin steak is fantastic (21 days is usually as good as it gets), smoked haddock chowder and moules marinière are light, flavour-packed and superb, while kiln-roasted salmon is a knockout dish of richly smoked, juicy fillet served with whisky sauce.

London Street Brasserie ★

Riverside Oracle, 2-4 London Street, Reading, RG1 4SE (0118 950 5036/www.londonstbrasserie.co.uk). **Meals served** noon-11pm Mon-Sat; noon-10.30pm Sun. **Main courses** £11-£20. **Set meal** (noon-7pm) £13.50 2 courses. **Credit** AmEx, MC, V.

Well frequented for good reason, this multi-roomed restaurant and bar at one end of Reading's Oracle centre is a stack of old red brick buildings shaped like wedges of cheese on the cusp of the River Kennet. Two or three tables (for two only) perch on a tiny deck area virtually overhanging the water – ask for one in summer. Staff clatter up and down from the kitchens with plates of steaming food, but the feel is relaxed and relaxing. Papers are strewn around the bar and you can slouch there ad infinitum, your champagne or coffee and petits fours within lazy arm's reach. A globetrotting menu full of instantly recognisable and lovable brasserie-style dishes doesn't change very often, but is long and supplemented by specials and Sunday menus. Decently priced wine, beer and cocktails are something of a passion here, so arrange for a taxi.

STREATLEY

Swan

High Street, Streatley-on-Thames, RG8 9HR (01491 878800/www.swanatstreatley.com). **Lunch served** 12.30-2pm daily. **Dinner served** 7-10pm daily. **Set lunch** (Sun) £16.95 3 courses; (Mon-Sat) £26.95 3 courses. **Set dinner** £26.95 3 courses. **Credit** AmEx, DC, MC, V.

Central

Like the French Horn further downstream at Sonning (0118 969 2204/www.thefrenchhorn.co.uk), the Swan occupies a truly exquisite position looking across a rippling, glittering expanse of the Thames, decorated by swans, dappled by willow trees and with a private launch at the ready to whisk you aboard at your whim. Both establishments are hotels above all else, with plush dining rooms contributing to the overall social well-being of guests rather than being the real gastro-magnets that bring food lovers flocking from across the globe. The Swan is less grand and the more modern of the two and also has the considerable benefit of being open all day to non-hotel residents. Formal meals are served in the Cygneture restaurant, while a fabulous terrace allows you to rest easy with a light meal, the watery world drifting slowly and seamlessly before you.

Central

TAPLOW

Cliveden ★

Taplow, SL6 0JF (01628 668561/www.cliveden house.co.uk). **Lunch served** noon-2pm, **dinner served** 7-9.30pm daily. **Set lunch** (Mon-Sat) £29.50 3 courses; (Sun) £47.50 3 courses. **Set dinner** £62.50 3 courses. **Credit** AmEx, DC, MC, V.

Think lavish and double it for a visit to Cliveden, which for 300 years has been dedicated to the pursuit of social and sporting pleasures, power, politics and intrigue. An army of uniformed footmen will park your car and welcome you into a stunningly grand hall filled with cascades of lilies, antique furniture, a cavernous carved stone fireplace and several suits of armour. There are numerous lounges in which to forget the real world and 300 acres of fabulous gardens in which to discover a new one, and that's before you even eat. The Terrace dining room is gently, approachably elegant with fine views down on to the River Thames. Food is light and of exceptional quality rather than overtly fancy, demonstrated in a noble fillet of beef with garden herbs and a courgette and potato gratin, or orange and coriander crusted sea bass with lobster raviolo. Adding to the occasion, staff are super-efficient, very correct but likeably human. Aside from the small matter of the bill, there can be no earthly reason why you wouldn't eat here – often.

WARGRAVE

Bull

High Street, Wargrave, RG10 8DD (0118 940 3120/www.thebullatwargrave.co.uk). **Lunch served** 11am-3pm Mon-Sat; noon-4pm Sun. **Dinner served** 6-11pm Mon-Sat; 7-10.30pm Sun. **Main courses** £7.50-£13.95. **Set lunch** £10 2 courses. **Set dinner** £10 2 courses; (Fri, Sat) £15 2 courses. **Credit** MC, V.

Wargrave is here and gone before you can register how chocolate-boxy it is, with the Bull and another pub, the Greyhound, midpoint. From the leaded bay window of the former, a languid trail of locals can be seen emerging from their swanky abodes and drifting between the two, idling in the road for conversation. Despite its riverine location – perfect but packed during Henley regatta – there's not a hint of pretension at the Bull and outsiders are as welcome as residents. In a very traditional setting the only nod to formality is a sign asking mobile phone users to take their calls outside, which they very courteously do, even in the rain. Brakspear beers and rustically enjoyable home-style food including 'proper' pies are part of the draw, with Sunday roast lunches starting at a remarkable £5.

WARREN ROW

Bistro at Warren Row

Warren Row Road, RG10 8QS (01628 825861/ www.warren-row-bistro.com). **Lunch served** noon-2pm Tue-Sun. **Dinner served** 7-9.30pm Tue-Sat. **Main courses** £12.50-£19.95. **Set lunch** (Tue-Sat) £12 2 courses, £16 3 courses; (Sun) £16.95 2 courses, £19.95 3 courses. **Set dinner** (Tue-Thur) £16.95 2 courses, £19.95 3 courses. **Credit** AmEx, MC, V.

Just the kind of place you wish was on your doorstep, the Bistro is so far down a leafy, field-flanked lane that it doesn't look to be on anybody's doorstep. In fact, it's only ten minutes from Henley, Wargrave, Twyford and Maidenhead, and word of hungry mouth about Adam and Lee Griffin has got around. In creating the kind of place they wanted to eat in themselves, this affable pair have renovated a characterful building to provide a mellow open-plan dining room with plenty of old pine and an ample bar decked with every libation you could desire, including numerous wines by the glass. Straightforward, appealing food is along the lines of smoked chicken in chilli batter with honeyed root vegetables, or hot smoked salmon with red onion jam.

WEST ILSLEY

Harrow

West Ilsley, RG20 7AR (01635 281260). **Lunch served** 11am-2pm daily. **Dinner served** 6.30-9pm Mon-Sat. **Main courses** £10-£15. **Credit** MC, V.

The microcosm of West Ilsley seems entirely self-sufficient, which is just as well given its remote location on Newbury Downs. A map of the horizon-spanning hills is criss-crossed with lines of gallops punctuated by occasional wooded patches, with names like Thorndown Folly, the Warren, Nine Acre Wood and Fox Covert. A sign asking drivers to 'Drive carefully, racehorses crossing' guards the clutch of well-to-do residences and conversation in the buzzing Harrow revolves around horses, stable gossip and, to the outsider, Dick Francis-esque intrigue. Smartened up in recent years with boldly coloured walls and warm staff, the character dining areas are full of guffawing locals tucking into robust, country crowd-pleasing food. Crown of wood pigeon with orange salad was one starter, and monkfish wrapped in parma ham a good main course. A beacon in fantastic walking country.

WINDSOR

Al Fassia

27 St Leonards Road, Windsor, SL4 3BP (01753 855370). **Lunch served** noon-2.30pm, **dinner served** 6.30-10.30pm Mon-Sat. **Main courses** £8.50-£11.95. **Set meal** £15.95 5 dishes. **Credit** AmEx, DC, MC, V.

St Leonards Road is an arty strip of ethnic shops and eateries, among which Al Fassia looks as inviting from the outside as it does from your Moroccan tiled table and wirework chair within. Authenticity is everything, from the furniture, wall hangings, filigree brass lamps and, most importantly, the menu. Skewers, tagines, pastries, veggie dishes, mint tea – all are fantastic. Beef tagine was steamily infused with celery, artichoke and fennel and served with couscous. Al Fassia salad has braised broad beans, baked aubergine, stewed tomato, garlic, carrot purée and more. Book ahead.

YATTENDON

Royal Oak

The Square, Yattendon, RG18 0UG (01635 201325). **Lunch served** noon-2.30pm, **dinner served** 7-9.30pm daily. **Main courses** £13.50-£19.50. **Set lunch** (Sun) £19.50 2 courses, £23.50 3 courses. **Credit** AmEx, DC, MC, V.

Looking at our Berkshire map, you could be forgiven for thinking we've not been doing our homework around here. That's because all that exists out this way are endless miles of woodland with few houses and even fewer restaurants or eateries of any nature dotted in between. Thank goodness, then, for the Royal Oak's successful combination of relaxed, bare-tabled pubbishness and formality of a sunny yellow, linen-clothed dining room, the two divided by an open-fired lounge. Locals and visitors from further afield tuck into superbly cooked meals such as slow-roasted guinea fowl on sweet potato and bacon risotto, or beautifully tender and fresh Cornish sole with crispy scallops and smooth tarragon and mustard velouté. The dining room is open only for evening meals although the same (pricey) menu is served in both. Rooms are available for romantic sojourns.

Also in the area

Chequers Brasserie Dean Lane, Cookham, Maidenhead, SL6 9BQ (01628 481232); **Loch Fyne** 70 London End, Old Beaconsfield, HP9 2JD (01494 679960); **Loch Fyne** 20 Market Place, Henley-on-Thames, RG9 2AH (01491 845780); **Prezzo** Cheap Street, Newbury, RG14 5DH (01635 31957); **Prezzo** 10-12 King Street, Reading, RG1 2HF (01189 596092); **Prezzo** 3 The Plaza, Denmark Street, Wokingham, RG40 2LD (01189 892090).

Buckinghamshire

AMERSHAM

Artichoke

9 Market Square, Old Amersham, HP7 0DF (01494 726611/www.theartichokerestaurant.co.uk). **Lunch served** noon-2pm, **dinner served** 7-10pm Tue-Sat. **Set lunch** £16.50 2 courses, £18.50 3 courses. **Set dinner** (Tue-Thur) £23.50 2 courses, £29.50 3 courses, (Fri, Sat) £29.50 3 courses. **Credit** MC, V.

Tiny but sleek, Artichoke is a crisply dressed restaurant that successfully blends with the fabric of an ancient oak-beamed cottage. The food has big ideas; Italian flavours complemented by a compact wine list. Grilled goat's cheese came with salad and two pestos, while caramelised scallops balanced a lightly curried plate of onions and salsify. Spinach cannelloni was excellent, ditto roasted halibut with wild mushroom velouté and puy lentils, although £29.50 for three courses, plus wine, coffee at £3 per head and service isn't a bargain. Watch also for a charmless policy of charging for three courses on Friday and Saturday nights, even if you order fewer.

BEACONSFIELD

Spice Merchant

33 London End Road, Beaconsfield, HP9 2HW (01494 675474/www.spicemerchantgroup.com). **Lunch served** noon-2.30pm, **dinner served** 6-11pm daily. **Main courses** £7.50-£22.95. **Set lunch** £12.50 5 dishes. **Set dinner** £22.50 14 dishes. **Credit** MC, V.

An ultra-modern refit and new menu have put Spice Merchant up there with some of London's best Indian restaurants. Set in Beaconsfield's Old Town, your view from the front of the restaurant will be of centuries-old shops and graceful townhouses. Further back is a lovely, glassed roof extension where light pours in from a professionally designed garden complete with ornamental bridge, groovy lights, fountains and summer dining space. Food is superbly presented and includes marinated and grilled rabbit with spinach and red onion pilaf, or Kerala crab-stuffed peppers with fenugreek sauce. The wine list has a superb affinity with spicy food, although beware the unadvertised price of soft drinks and beer.

DENHAM

Swan Inn

Village Road, Denham, UB9 5BH (01895 832085). **Lunch served** noon-2.30pm Mon-Sat; noon-3pm Sun. **Dinner served** 7-10pm daily. **Main courses** £9.75-£13.25. **Credit** AmEx, MC, V.

This country pub fulfils every criteria of the gastropub right down to the modern bistro fare on blackboards and bare floorboards. It's comfortable and perfectly chilled, and who can blame the Swan's owners for seizing the day and opening three more: this one, the Alford Arms in Frithsden, Hertfordshire, and the Royal Oak in Bovingdon Green, Buckinghamshire. Butternut soup was a yellow, mellow and deliciously gloopy affair with a whiff of roasted garlic about it, while tomato and mascarpone risotto came with a tasty tangle of deep-fried leeks; ribeye steak was sweetly bloody and served just as asked. Expect posh locals and thirtysomethings talking about other restaurants and politics.

EASINGTON

Mole & Chicken

Easington, HP18 9EY (01844 208387/www.moleand chicken.co.uk). **Lunch served** noon-2pm, **dinner served** 7-9pm Mon-Sat. **Meals served** noon-9pm Sun. **Main courses** £9-£16. **Credit** AmEx, MC, V.

Booking is essential at this country retreat. The old pub satisfies drinkers as well as diners with a good selection of draught ales, but things can get crowded at the bar. Tables tucked into corners provide privacy, and staff are reasonably adept at remembering the hidden and hungry. Down on last year was the unchanged menu and the tasteless disaster of a vegetarian option, under the scathing heading of 'chicken feed'. By contrast, a sirloin steak was pinkly gorgeous. Regulars to the Mole all order meat, which seems the surest route to satisfaction.

GERRARDS CROSS

Etcetera

14 Oak End Way, Gerrards Cross, SL9 8BR (01753 880888/www.etceterarestaurant.com). **Lunch served** noon-2.30pm Mon-Fri, Sun. **Dinner served** 6-9.30pm Mon-Sat. **Main courses** £10.95-£21.95. **Set meal** (lunch, 6-7.30pm) £8.95 2 courses. **Credit** MC, V.

Opened in 2002, this brasserie is invariably packed with your typical Gerrards Cross fiftysomething sporting his latest car or her latest diamonds. Still, they're a discerning lot when it comes to food and Etcetera meets much-needed local demand. A mix of classic and modern dishes include Atkins-friendly low-carb meals, sophisticated fish dishes and hearty meatier ones, all proficiently cooked and presented. No one batted an eyelid at a request for sirloin steak well done, and it arrived just as asked yet still tender and juicy. Pan-fried cod had an old-fashioned side order of cauliflower cheese (with strange dried pesto sprinkles) along with flavour-packed red wine and shallot jus. Desserts are pretty, coffee good and the bill reasonable, given the area.

Spice Merchant. *See p151.*

GREAT MISSENDEN

Annie Baileys

Chesham Road, Great Missenden, HP16 0QT (01494 865625/www.anniebaileys.com). **Lunch served** noon-2.30pm Mon-Sat; noon-3pm Sun. **Dinner served** 7-9.30pm Mon-Sat. **Main courses** £9.50-£15.95. **Set lunch** (Sun) £15 2 courses, £18.50 3 courses. **Credit** AmEx, MC, V.

Chilled is an overused word but one that nonetheless describes this subtly Italianate, rural restaurant and bar. Staff are calm and efficient, and wines of the week share a blackboard with specials above the bar. A cosy mix of tables, chairs, pews and worn-in Chesterfields are placed around interlinking rooms and an intimate walled garden gathers any lingering sunbeams. Al fresco dining is hugely popular in the summer and some say the service can suffer for it. Cooking generally shows flair, generosity and a good mix of British and Mediterranean dishes; fish, chips and mushy peas or herb-stuffed confit duck legs with sautéed potatoes and plum sauce, rounded off with classic bistro puds.

HADDENHAM

Green Dragon

8 Churchway, Haddenham, HP17 8AA (01844 291403/www.eatatthedragon.co.uk). **Lunch served** noon-2pm Mon-Sat; noon-2.30pm Sun. **Dinner served** 6.30-9.30pm Mon-Sat. **Main courses** £9.50-£18.50. **Set lunch** (Sun) £17.95 3 courses. **Set dinner** (Tue, Thur) £11.95 2 courses. **Credit** AmEx, MC, V.

Wearing its accolades on its sleeve is the done thing at the Green Dragon but, unlike many establishments, the plates and certificates adorning these colour-washed walls are all current. Food is the mainstay but real ale drinkers are equally at home in this relaxed, community-spirited pub. A long list of sandwiches are served on village-baked breads. Light lunches, starters and main courses can be swapped around without groans from staff. Unfussy combinations such as smoked halibut with olive oil and cracked pepper, harissa lamb shank with spicy couscous or soft chocolate tart with mandarin sorbet all exceed expectations.

KINGSWOOD

Crooked Billet

Ham Green, Kingswood, HP18 0QJ (01296 770239/ www.crookedbillet.com). **Lunch served** noon-3pm Mon-Thur; noon-6pm Fri-Sun. **Dinner served** 6-9.30pm daily. **Main courses** £10-£18. **Set meal** (Mon-Thur) £10 2 courses. **Set dinner** (Fri) £16.95 3 courses. **Credit** AmEx, MC, V.

Our country is awash with Crooked Billets and more ought to be like this one on the busy A41 between Banbury and Aylesbury. Once ensconced in this low-beamed, stripped pine pub, though, you could be anywhere in the green heart of the countryside. Staff were not overly cheerful on the day we visited, but plenty of locals were stopping off for a quick pint with lunch. Portions of typical gastropub fare are giant-size, freshly cooked and reasonably priced, as in starters of mushroom and leek frittata or welsh rarebit, both served with rounds of sourdough toast, zippy salad and jacket wedges.

LONG CRENDON

Angel

47 Bicester Road, Long Crendon, HP18 9EE (01844 208268). **Lunch served** noon-2.30pm daily. **Dinner served** 7-9.30pm Mon-Sat. **Main courses** £12.95-£19.75. **Set lunch** £11.75 1 course, £14.75 2 courses, £17.50 3 courses. **Credit** MC, V.

The Angel is an enduringly good place to relax over a meal. Service is less hurried during the week, when villagers and itinerant workers enjoy the airy, comfortable space to themselves. Fish is purchased daily. Delicately flavoured Thai fish cake on warm tomato fondue came as a starter, as did a courgette and red pepper soup packed with sweet flavours. Cod with herb crust teetering atop sliced tomatoes, shallots, green beans and charred baby potato halves was fresh and lovely but almost outdone by the just-baked honey-roast figs and crème fraîche in a brandy snap basket for dessert.

MARLOW

Crowne Plaza

Fieldhouse Lane, Marlow, SL7 1GJ (0870 444 8940). **Lunch served** noon-2.30pm Mon-Fri. **Dinner served** 6.30-10.30pm Mon-Sat; 6.30-10pm Sun. **Main courses** £9.50-£17. **Set lunch** £12.95 2 courses, £15.95 3 courses. **Set dinner** £17.95 2 courses, £19.95 3 courses. **Credit** AmEx, MC, V.

A mile from Marlow is the new über-modern Crowne Plaza. Located on the edge of a lake spouting fierce water jets, surrounded by expanses of green slate and grey pebbles and wildly at odds with the surrounding pastureland and old town of Marlow itself, the hotel only works because it so distances itself from these. A cavernous foyer of pink sofas gives way to a soft, dark lakeside bar illuminated by moody strips of purple and green, and a fusion restaurant called Glaze. Menus boast adventurous main courses such as sliced duck on a tangy plum and lavender tarte tatin with red wine jus, or braised squid stuffed with veal confit.

Marlow Bar & Grill

92-94 High Street, Marlow, SL7 1AQ (01628 488544). **Meals served** noon-11pm daily. **Main courses** £7-£16. **Credit** AmEx, MC, V.

Gutsy breakfasts extend the succour provided by this popular mainstay. Staff cover a lot of ground, from one end of the sleek bar-fronted room, down its cherry-floored length to a conservatory and walled garden. Bar and kitchen serve carefully prepared, tempting and reasonably priced food. Caesar salad and char-grilled chicken has rich, anchovy-flecked dressing; salmon teriyaki is pan-fried and sparkles on chilli-oiled snow peas and beansprouts.

Vanilla Pod ★
31 West Street, Marlow, SL7 2LS (01628 898101/ www.thevanillapod.co.uk). **Lunch served** noon-2pm, **dinner served** 7-10pm Tue-Sat. **Set lunch** £16.50 2 courses, £19.50 3 courses. **Set dinner** £40 3 courses, £45 7 courses. **Credit** AmEx, MC, V.
With just nine tables the Vanilla Pod is little but lively, and all credit is due to the remarkably polished food. Three lunchtime courses include an appetiser of button mushroom cappuccino, followed by asparagus risotto with fennel blossom cream. Roast monkfish was subtly spiced and accompanied by an exquisite mix of summer vegetables and buttery batons of crisp polenta. Sublime dessert could be a deliriously silky, elusively fragrant tonka bean panna cotta with toffee bananas and coconut sorbet. Gorgeous food, incredible value.

MENTMORE

Stag
The Green, Mentmore, LU7 0QF (01296 668423/ www.thestagmentmore.co.uk). **Lunch served** noon-2pm, **dinner served** 7-9pm daily. **Set meal** £22 2 courses, £28 3 courses. **Credit** MC, V.
The Stag is an imposing grey stone house in good walking and boating country. 'Fine dining' is the idea; the pub end is decisively separated from the restaurant. Light meals are served during the day, and a £22 two-course dinner is along the lines of individual cottage pie with Guinness gravy or tempura-fried buffalo mozzarella on delicious griddled vegetables with a piquant Malay spiced sauce. A modest number of bins on the wine list are well chosen and fairly priced. Although frequented by all ages, this is a great place to bring your mum.

MILTON KEYNES

Metro's Brasserie
319 Upper Fourth Street, Milton Keynes, MK9 1EH (01908 231323). **Lunch served** noon-5pm, **dinner served** 5-11pm Mon-Sat. **Meals served** 11am-7pm Sun. **Main courses** £10-£14.50. **Set lunch** £8.50 2 courses. **Set dinner** £12.50 2 courses, £15.95 3 courses. **Credit** MC, V.
This brasserie was once called Metro's Champagne Bar and Grill, and although the bubbly aspect has dropped from the name, it still exists aplenty on the ground. Food is simple and ample rather than spectacular, running from crab and noodle fritters with sweet chilli sauce (delicious), to chicken liver parfait and toasted brioche, sirloin steak and chips, smoked haddock fish cakes, and toffee cheesecake. Reliable and well situated for a bit of retail therapy.

NEWTON LONGVILLE

Crooked Billet ★
2 Westbrook End, Newton Longville, MK17 0DF (01908 373936/www.thebillet.co.uk). Bar **Lunch served** noon-2pm Tue-Sat. *Restaurant* **Lunch served** 12.30-3pm Sun. **Dinner served** 7-9.30pm Mon-Sat. **Main courses** £11-£20. **Set dinner** £50 8 courses, with wines £75. **Credit** AmEx, MC, V.
Friday and Saturday nights at the Crooked Billet are now booked weeks in advance and a credit card number is required to secure your table – £20 per person is deducted if you don't show; the price of success, country pub-style. Emma Gilchrist's food and John Gilchrist's wine list are the main reasons for being here; there aren't many pubs with 'a study of crab' on the menu, ham hock with foie gras, or the 'Nation's Best Cheeseboard'. Apart from leanings towards pretension – said study (two terrines, a claw and a cake) set in four corners of a vast glass platter – the food is exceptional. New season rack of lamb was pink and subtly flavoursome. The entire wine list is available by the glass.

SPEEN

Old Plow
Flowers Bottom, Speen, HP27 0PZ (01494 488300/ www.yeoldplough.co.uk). **Lunch served** noon-1.45pm Tue-Fri; noon-2pm Sun. **Dinner served** 7-8.45pm Tue-Sat. *Bistro* **Main courses** £9.50-£15. *Restaurant* **Set lunch** £22 2 courses, £26 3 courses. **Set dinner** £26 2 courses, £29.95 3 courses. **Credit** MC, V.
The idyllically located Old Plow combines the great food, wine and buzzing atmosphere of a French bistro with the roaring fires, lived-in sofas and low-beamed character of a British country pub. Michael Cowan has stayed true to the original intent of each dish to delicious effect. Cassoulet was a rib-sticking elixir of haricot beans, duck, venison sausage, black pudding and herbs with a mustard-dressed salad. Desserts are fantastic – toffee sponge, raspberry brûlée or chocolate torte with brandy sauce.

STOKE MANDEVILLE

Woolpack Inn
21 Risborough Road, Stoke Mandeville, HP22 5UP (01296 615970/www.woolpackstokemandeville.co.uk). **Lunch served** noon-2.30pm Mon-Sat; noon-4.30pm Sun. **Dinner served** 6-9.30pm Mon-Sat. **Main courses** £9.95-£15.95. **Credit** AmEx, MC, V.
You'll need to shoehorn yourself into this renovated pub at the weekends, despite its cavernous size. Ox-blood coloured walls complement limed panelling, open fires, copper tabletops, leather tub chairs and animal hide rugs tossed over terracotta floor tiles – it's snug, hip and fun. Food is simple: salads, stone-baked pizzas, and rotisseried mains such as garlic and lemon spit-roasted chicken with frites and aïoli.

STOKE POGES

The Park
Stoke Park Club, Park Road, Stoke Poges, SL2 4PG (01753 717171/www.stokeparkclub.com). **Lunch served** noon-3pm Sun. **Dinner served** 7-10pm daily. **Set lunch** £27.50 3 courses. **Set dinner** £31 2 courses, £36 3 courses. **Credit** AmEx, DC, MC, V.

Three hundred and fifty acres of vivid green turf roll around this cream palladian mansion. Sporting pastimes keep the place buzzing with healthy people and the interior of the main building, with its numerous lounges, sweeping staircases and galleried hallways, is pleasantly free of chintz. The Park has a well-padded art deco theme, decorated with giant posters of Monaco races and Paris bars. The man in the kitchen is Chris Wheeler, ex-Maison Novelli, and food is delicious. Expect tender beef fillet served with a crust of foie gras, a trio of fish as a main course, and an assiette of English desserts to send you off on your way.

TURVILLE

Bull & Butcher

Turville, RG9 6QU (01491 638283/www.bulland butcher.com). **Lunch served** noon-2.30pm Mon-Sat; noon-4pm Sun. **Dinner served** 7-9.45pm daily. **Main courses** £9.95-£14.95. **Credit** MC, V.

Situated in a picturesque valley, which ripples its way down to the River Thames, Turville contains just 30-odd houses and has featured as a backdrop to countless TV dramas in its time. The Bull & Butcher welcomes a constant stream of hungry walkers and cyclists, drawn by traditional ale and great platefuls of home-style food. Braised venison and orange casserole or rib-eye steak with fried onions and gigantic chips were as delicious as coffee and cognac crème brûlée or rhubarb crumble.

WADDESDON

Five Arrows Hotel

High Street, Waddesdon, HP18 0JE (01296 651727/ www.waddesdon.org.uk). **Lunch served** noon-2.15pm Mon-Sat; 12.30-2pm Sun. **Dinner served** 7-9pm Mon-Sat; 7.30-8.30pm Sun. **Main courses** £13-£19.50. **Credit** AmEx, MC, V.

Waddesdon was designed by an Aylesbury architect in the late 19th century. Elaborate brickwork, chequerboard roof tiles and mulberry-painted window-frames characterise most of the charming public buildings, including the Five Arrows Hotel, which is also lucky enough to possess a secluded courtyard for summer dining (complete with dancing elephant topiary). Food is generous and home-cooked in style, with British favourites such as braised beef and peppered swede or apple charlotte and custard complementing more radical dishes such as seared tuna on soy and walnut noodles or steamed mussels with ginger and bacon.

WESTON UNDERWOOD

Cowper's Oak

Weston Underwood, MK46 5JS (01234 711382). **Lunch served** noon-3pm Mon-Fri. **Dinner served** 5.30-11pm Mon-Thur; 5-11pm Fri. **Meals served** noon-11pm Sat, Sun. **Main courses** £6.95-£15.95. **Credit** MC, V.

Picture postcards don't come prettier than Weston Underwood, a Bucks Best Kept Village stuffed from one end to the other with expensive buff stone estate barns, thatched cottages, manicured lawns and a field of llamas (naturally). Cowper's Oak is the only brick building; a classy wisteria-clad inn with tables fronting the sleepy lane. Recently refurbished to a spick and span yet homely interior, there is also a games room and an orchard. Food is simple, flavour-packed and comforting: half pints of shell-on prawns with garlic mayo, for example, or steak and Guinness pie and soup of the day.

WINCHMORE HILL

Plough ★

The Hill, Winchmore Hill, nr Amersham, HP7 0PA (01494 721001). **Lunch served** noon-3pm, **dinner served** 6-10pm daily. **Main courses** £12.50-£16.95. **Credit** AmEx, MC, V.

Formerly a pub, this expansive old building has metamorphosed into a chic, pared down restaurant. The Plough is crisp, white and hovers on a sea of turf punctuated by two sentinel bay trees. Inside, too, is a lesson in restrained, putty-coloured paint, pewter wall lamps and acres of dark slate. Mellow wooden tables hold an appetite-whetting array of Riedel glassware and crisp white linen. Food is served in modest, stratified portions. Warm goat's cheese and asparagus tart covers all the texture and flavour bases possible, fish courses are expertly cooked, and a deep purple blueberry panna cotta with mango sorbet and elderflower escumé – foam to you and me – is top-notch.

WOOBURN COMMON

Chequers Inn

Kiln Lane, Wooburn Common, HP10 0JQ (01628 529575/www.chequers-inn.com). **Lunch served** *Restaurant* noon-2.30pm Mon-Fri. **Dinner served** 7-9.30pm Mon-Fri; 7-10pm Sat. **Main courses** £14.95-£23.95. **Set lunch** £18.95 3 courses. **Set dinner** (Mon-Fri) £23.95 3 courses, (Sat) £26.95 3 courses. **Credit** MC, V.

This beamed, flagstoned pub appears to have been hoarding paraphernalia for all its 300 years. Three closely scripted menus are difficult to pick out among the tankards, tables, pictures and people. But once found, they list roast sirloin with Yorkshire pudding, chicken kiev, sausages with mustard mash and onion gravy, and spotted dick with custard. French-inspired food is served in a more formal adjoining restaurant. Service can be overstretched but embodies the concept of the country pub, complete with fuggy atmosphere, honest cooking and real ale. Similar but less well trodden is sibling the Chequers Brasserie in Cookham Dean, Berkshire.

Also in the area

Loch Fyne 70 London End, Old Beaconsfield, HP9 2JD (01494 679960).

Gloucestershire

ARLINGHAM

Old Passage Inn

Passage Road, Arlingham, GL2 7JR (01452 740547/ www.fishattheoldpassageinn.co.uk). **Lunch served** noon-2pm Tue-Sun. **Dinner served** 7-9pm Tue-Sat. **Main courses** £10.80-£19. **Credit** AmEx, MC, V.

Sat on the banks of the Severn, the Old Passage Inn eschews the novelty piscine trappings beloved of lesser seafood restaurants in favour of cool mint colours and an elegant conservatory feel. Fish and crustaceans are confined to the menu… oh, and a couple of tanks of langoustine and wriggling lobster. To begin, provençale fish soup is epic, though a plate of oysters (there are six types) is an alternative. Typical mains might be Cornish fish stew or baked hake with garlic mash. After dessert, take advantage of the restaurant's other function – as a cigar club.

BARNSLEY

Barnsley House ★

Barnsley, GL7 5EE (01285 740000/www.barnsley house.com). **Lunch served** noon-3pm, **dinner served** 7-10pm daily. **Set lunch** £19.50 2 courses, £24.50 3 courses. **Set dinner** £34.50 3 courses, £46 4 courses. **Credit** AmEx, MC, V.

Renowned for its wonderful gardens, Barnsley House now has even more to commend it. The house was refurbished by the owners of the Village Pub (*see below*) and is now a gorgeous hotel. As for the food, consultant chef Franco Taruschio (the Walnut Tree, Abergavenny) and chef Graham Grafton (La Caprice, Bibendum) have created a menu that celebrates local produce in regional Italian dishes typified by the signature dish, vincisgrassi – a magnificent 18th-century lasagne of parma ham, porcini and truffles. Close to perfection.

The Village Pub ★

High Street, Barnsley, GL7 5EF (01285 740421/ www.thevillagepub.co.uk). **Lunch served** noon-2.30pm Mon-Fri; noon-3pm Sat, Sun. **Dinner served** 7-9.30pm Mon-Thur, Sun; 7-10pm Fri, Sat. **Main courses** £9.50-£15.50. **Credit** MC, V.

From the preliminary pints of local beer to the exquisitely bitter chocolates with the coffee, the Village Pub barely puts a foot wrong. Diners have a choice of five rooms, each decorated in a different style; subtle paint effects, wood panelling and flagstones are a common theme. The menu – now presided over by Michael Carr – makes a virtue of simplicity in flavour and presentation. A steaming bowl of sautéed scallops, clams and mussels with gremoulata was a generous starter; next chicken breast with tomato, olives and rosemary was impressive.

BIBURY

Bibury Court Hotel

Bibury, GL7 5NT (01285 740337/www.bibury court.com). **Lunch served** noon-2pm Mon-Thur; noon-2.30pm Fri-Sun. **Dinner served** 7-9pm daily. **Main courses** £10.95-£14.95. **Set dinner** £27 2 courses, £32.50 3 courses. **Credit** AmEx, DC, MC, V.

This Elizabethan manor house may be a tad old fashioned, but staff are friendly. Of the dining rooms – a study bar, a formal evening room and a sunny conservatory – the latter with natural woods and a high glass roof is the most preferable. The food is classic country house cuisine, a mix of French and British influences resulting in dishes like salmon terrine with pickled cucumber, and roast duck breast with orange sauce. Trout (caught in the River Coln that bounds the gardens) is a speciality.

BUCKLAND

Buckland Manor

Buckland, WR12 7LY (01386 852626/ www.bucklandmanor.com). **Lunch served** 12.30-1.45pm, **dinner served** 7.30-8.45pm daily. **Main courses** £23.75-£29.95. **Set lunch** (Mon-Sat) £19.50 2 courses, £25.50 3 courses; (Sun) £24.50 3 courses, £26.50 4 courses. **Credit** AmEx, DC, MC, V.

The epitome of formal dining, Buckland Manor requires the wearing of jacket and tie at table. Staff, in constant attendance, are young but trussed up severely. Such archaic posturings detract from food that deserves relaxed appreciation; this is a chef with ideas and the ability to carry them off with aplomb. Cooking is predominantly French in style; you could expect Cornish crab with honey and lime vierge to start, salt-baked sea bass with langoustine ravioli as a main. The 13th-century manor house is immaculately groomed and has some fine gardens.

CHELTENHAM

Beehive ★

1-3 Montpellier Villas, Cheltenham, GL50 2XE (01242 579443/www.slack.co.uk). **Open** noon-11pm Mon-Sat; noon-10pm Sun. **Lunch served** noon-3pm Sun. **Dinner served** 7-10pm Mon-Sat. **Main courses** £7.95-£12. **Credit** MC, V.

Landlord Scott Graff has created just about the perfect pub-restaurant. The well-worn bar is warm and welcoming, there's a garden out back, and upstairs is a great little restaurant (food is also served in the bar). Expect a nicely tuned menu that pays homage to the seasons and doesn't over-complicate dishes. Offerings might include peaches, parma ham and mint, or crab, anchovy, chunky tomato and couscous as starters, then braised rabbit with cider, rosemary and cream, or confit pork belly with pancetta and chorizo cassoulet. One to treasure.

Le Champignon Sauvage ★

24-26 Suffolk Road, Cheltenham, GL50 2AQ (01242 573449/www.lechampignonsauvage.com). **Lunch served** 12.30-1.30pm, **dinner served** 7.30-9pm Tue-Sat. **Set meal** (lunch, dinner Tue-Fri) £20 2 courses, £24 3 courses. **Set dinner** £36 2 courses, £44 3 courses. **Credit** AmEx, DC, MC, V.

A remarkable restaurant – despite its anonymous location and unpretentious decor. Le Champignon Sauvage could feel stuffy, were it not for the gracious service offered by Helen Everitt-Matthias. Since 1987, Helen's husband David has quietly built a towering reputation (and earned two Michelin stars) for cooking of a rare precision, verve and quality, resulting in perfectly judged dishes such as an earthy, melting daube of beef with spring onion risotto and water chestnuts, or tender breast of chicken with soft polenta and white raisins. A memorable experience was crowned with a cheese selection to die for and a perfect bitter chocolate parfait and beer ice-cream. *Formidable.*

Daffodil

18-20 Suffolk Parade, Cheltenham, GL50 2AE (01242 700055/www.thedaffodil.co.uk). **Lunch served** noon-2.30pm Mon-Sat. **Dinner served** *June-Aug* 6-10pm Mon-Sat; *Sept-May* 6.30-10pm Mon-Sat. **Main courses** £11.75-£19.50. **Set lunch** £12 2 courses, £14.50 3 courses. **Set dinner** (Mon) £15 2 courses; *June-Aug* (Mon-Fri before 7pm) £15 2 courses incl cocktail. **Credit** AmEx, MC, V.

Everyone in Cheltenham knows the Daffodil, and most love the place. Lunch offers the likes of steamed Evesham asparagus with poached egg and parmesan hollandaise, or deep-fried halloumi with rocket, red onion and caper salad. Mains might be a plump fillet of cod in beer batter with 'fat chips' and tartare sauce, or a warming confit pork with cassoulet and mustard and shallot sauce. The food is reliable, the service gracious, but it's the setting that's the star. A gem of an old cinema has been converted to preserve all its art deco glamour.

Lumiere

Clarence Parade, Cheltenham, GL50 3PA (01242 222200). **Dinner served** 7-8.30pm Tue-Sat. **Set dinner** £35 3 courses. **Credit** MC, V.

A well-groomed thoroughbred, the Lumiere looks sleek and metropolitan. Its neutral tones and abstract artworks create a calming atmosphere. Ingredients are high-quality and the execution is sure in dishes such as chicken and mushroom soup; baked goat's cheese and chive soufflé with salad; rack of lamb with dijon mustard jus and pan-fried rosemary potato cake; and tender chicken breast with spicy cabbage hash, gruyère potato and tarragon cream. Desserts are best: in a chocolate brownie and passion fruit brûlée torte, the two components – rich and sweet, sharp and light – complemented each other perfectly.

CHIPPING CAMPDEN

Cotswold House Hotel

The Square, Chipping Campden, GL55 6AN (01386 840330/www.cotswoldhouse.com). **Lunch served** noon-2.30pm, **dinner served** 6-9.45pm daily. **Main courses** £10-£15. **Credit** AmEx, MC, V.

Juliana's dining room is a paradigm of Georgian elegance: tall windows with views of the impeccable gardens, crisp linen and understated colours. Chef Simon Hulstone handles flavours with a delicate touch using local veg, meat and game: ballotine of foie gras with Earl Grey jelly, followed by pork belly with pea purée, say. At the more relaxed venue, the urbane Hicks brasserie, smart staff produce an efficient bustle. Standards such as caesar salad, tuna carpaccio and calf's liver are invigorated by the presence of vanilla-seasoned scallops or cassoulet of barbary duck leg, the latter an unctuous pleasure on a cold day. A further plus: 25 wines by the glass.

CIRENCESTER

Harry Hare's

3 Gosditch Street, Cirencester, GL7 2AG (01285 652375). **Meals served** 10.30am-9.30pm Mon-Thur; 10.30am-10pm Fri, Sat; noon-9pm Sun. **Main courses** £11.95-£18.95. **Credit** AmEx, MC, V.

The modern brasserie menu – thai crab cakes with lime pickle, or confit duck with beansprout stir-fry and lemongrass sauce – is decent enough here, but what's important is the atmosphere. A French-style café-bar in a medieval building (complete with arched windows on the shop front), Harry Hare's has massive appeal and a real buzz.

CLIFFORD'S MESNE

Yew Tree Inn

Clifford's Mesne, GL18 1JS (01531 820719/www.theyewtreeinn.co.uk). **Lunch served** noon-3pm Tue-Sun. **Dinner served** 6.30-9pm Tue-Sat. **Main courses** £13.75-£17. **Set dinner** £21.95 2 courses, £27 3 courses, £32 5-course tasting menu. **Credit** MC, V.

The building once housed a cider press; it's a little saggy inside, but the food is imaginative with an emphasis on local produce (Wiltshire venison terrine positively sung with flavour) and fresh fish from Brixham. In summer Roux-trained chef-cum-owner Paul Hackett makes a big deal of the sunny terrace and produces a specials menu of dishes running from straw-smoked haddock with poached duck egg, to grilled lobster with tomato and basil salsa.

COLN ST ALDWYNS

New Inn at Coln

Coln St Aldwyns, GL7 5AN (01285 750651/www.new-inn.co.uk). **Lunch served** noon-2pm Mon-Sat; noon-2.30pm Sun. **Dinner served** 7-9pm Mon-Thur, Sun; 7-9.30pm Fri, Sat. **Main courses** £8.95-£14.50. **Set dinner** £29 2 courses, £35 3 courses. **Credit** AmEx, MC, V.

There's a distinction between bar and restaurant here. The smoky bar with its fine bitter sees Hunter wellingtons and jodhpurs, whereas the restaurant is a mix of tweed jackets, twin sets and pearls. A slight exaggeration, of course, but the New Inn does well by the Cotswold set. The dining room's white tablecloths and discreet lighting create an intimate setting for luxurious dining. Food is epitomised by the clean flavours and presentation of swordfish and smoked salmon mousse with lemon aïoli.

CORSE LAWN

Corse Lawn Hotel

Corse Lawn, GL19 4LZ (01452 780771/www.corselawn.com). **Lunch served** noon-2pm daily. **Dinner served** 7-9.30pm Mon-Sat; 7.30-9.30pm Sun. **Main courses** £12.95-£19.95. **Set lunch** £17.50 2 courses, £19.50 3 courses. **Set dinner** £29.50 3 courses. **Credit** AmEx, DC, MC, V.

Diners can choose between the bistro and the more formal dining room of this impressive Queen Anne country house. The latter, with old-school elegance and polite service, is infinitely preferable; the former has the feel of the Crossroads Motel. Food is delivered with technical precision and rigorous attention to detail. Forget cutting-edge cuisine, focus instead on the virtues of classically derived dishes such as terrine of foie gras (a giant-killer both in flavour and size) or guinea fowl breast with Madeira sauce.

COWLEY

Cowley Manor

Cowley, GL53 9NL (01242 870900/www.cowleymanor.com). **Lunch served** noon-2pm, **dinner served** 7-10.30pm daily. **Main courses** £10.50-£19.50. **Credit** AmEx, DC, MC, V.

To lunch on the sunny terrace of Cowley Manor overlooking its beautiful gardens is splendid – a Jane Austen via Soho type of experience. This magnificent Georgian country pile has been transformed into an über-plush retreat for the loaded – all funky stylings and handsome staff. Food ranges from sausage and mash comfort cooking to pricey Med-style main courses such as swordfish with saffron risotto, ratatouille and tapenade. Non-residents are welcome Monday to Thursday and on Friday lunchtimes (and Friday evenings if not too busy).

DAYLESFORD

Daylesford Organic Farm Shop ★

Daylesford, GL56 0YG (01608 731700). **Open** 9am-6pm Mon-Sat; 10am-5pm Sun. **Lunch served** noon-3pm daily. **Main courses** £4.95-£10.95. **Credit** MC, V.

An extraordinary range of produce is stocked here – much of it from the farm and the sister estate of Wootton in Staffordshire. There's a pleasant café where you can sample the wares: dishes such as rillette of Wootton pork with Daylesford piccalilli and grilled sourdough. The future of food shopping? We hope so.

EWEN

Wild Duck Inn

Drakes Island, Ewen, GL7 6BY (01285 770310/www.thewildduckinn.co.uk). **Lunch served** noon-2pm Mon-Sat; noon-2.30pm Sun. **Dinner served** 6.30-10pm Mon-Sat; 6.45-9.30pm Sun. **Main courses** £5.95-£22.95. **Credit** AmEx, MC, V.

Moody dark reds, low beams and dried flowers give this busy pub a bawdy charm – enhanced by the loud music and occasionally raucous atmosphere of the bar. Diners spill through a series of interconnecting rooms with ample nooks and crannies. The menu runs from favourites such as beer-battered cod and roast belly pork to more adventurous offerings – whole red snapper with mango salsa, for example.

FAIRFORD

Allium

1 London Street, Market Place, Fairford, GL7 4AH (01285 712200/www.allium.uk.net). **Lunch served** noon-2pm Wed-Sat; noon-3pm Sun. **Dinner served** 7-10pm Wed-Sat; 7-9pm Sun. **Set lunch** £15 2 courses, £17.50 3 courses. **Set dinner** £25 2 courses, £29.50 3 courses; £42 10-course tasting menu. **Credit** MC, V.

An ambitious restaurant: stark white interiors, proactive service and discreet local art mark Allium out as a very different entity from the wealth of successful gastropubs in the area. Both poached breast of pigeon with tatin of endive, and confit shoulder of lamb with sweetbread and tongue were creatively executed, yet some dishes (a gazpacho of crab in jelly form, for instance) could be a step too far. Prices are reasonable and the wine list is interesting.

FRAMPTON MANSELL

White Horse

Cirencester Road, Frampton Mansell, GL6 8HZ (01285 760960/www.cotswoldwhitehorse.com). **Lunch served** noon-2.30pm Mon-Sat; noon-3pm Sun. **Dinner served** 7-9.45pm Mon-Sat. **Main courses** £9.95-£14.95. **Credit** MC, V.

Local contemporary art hangs on the walls, furniture is sleek and stylish, but behind the makeover there's still the warm glow of an exemplary English country pub. The food has a Mediterranean aspect – an antipasto of bresaola, milano salami and a delicious goose salami might be followed by whole grilled lemon sole with sun-dried tomato and saffron cream, though the menu changes daily. There's a good selection of wines too.

GUITING POWER

Hollow Bottom

Winchcombe Road, Guiting Power, GL54 5UX (01451 850392/www.hollowbottom.com). **Open** 11am-11pm Mon-Sat; noon-10.30pm Sun. **Lunch served** noon-2pm, **dinner served** 6-9pm daily. **Main courses** £8.95-£14. **Carvery lunch** (Sun) £9.95. **Credit** MC, V.

Barnsley House. *See p156.*

Hollow Bottom is unreasonably pretty. Inside, picture postcard exteriors give way to an equine celebration, jockey silks and numerous prints betraying a long-time association with Cheltenham races. There's plenty on the blackboard menu to keep hunger at bay. Exotic dishes (ostrich, wildebeest) sit alongside traditional fare such as collops of pork in a cider sauce.

LOWER ODDINGTON

Fox Inn

Lower Oddington, GL56 0UR (01451 870555/ www.foxinn.net). **Lunch served** noon-2pm daily. **Dinner served** 6.30-10pm Mon-Sat; 7-9pm Sun. **Main courses** £7.95-£12. **Credit** MC, V.

A creeper-clad Cotswold stone inn, the Fox has its origins in the 16th century, though nowadays it's a smart pub with a pleasing menu – baked sea trout with creamed fennel, or a comforting slab of sirloin steak. This is unfussy, well-priced eating, helped along by brisk, well-mannered staff, and a good selection of wine. The dining room, red-painted with age-worn flagstones, is half given over to hunting memorabilia, the other half to wine bric-a-brac.

NAILSWORTH

Mad Hatters

3 Cossack Square, Nailsworth, GL6 0DB (01453 832615). **Lunch served** 12.30-2pm Wed-Sat; 1pm Sun by appointment only. **Dinner served** 7.30-9pm Wed-Sat. **Main courses** £16.50-£19.50. **Set lunch** (Sun) £15 3 courses incl coffee. **Credit** MC, V.

With its sweet-shop frontage of Georgian bow windows, this restaurant is perhaps less *Alice in Wonderland* than *The Old Curiosity Shop*. The dining room has an intimate, friendly feel. There's a classic French influence to the food – fish with rouille (alive with flavour); chicken breast with a white wine cream sauce. Straightforward dishes are made extraordinary by the use of outstanding organic and free-range ingredients (many of them grown here). B&B accommodation is available.

NEWENT

Three Choirs Vineyards

Newent, GL18 1LS (01531 890223/www.three choirs.com). **Lunch served** noon-2pm Tue-Sun. **Dinner served** 7-9pm daily. **Main courses** £12-£16. **Set lunch** (Sun) £29.50 3 courses. **Credit** MC, V.

The wine list here is slightly biased. This is after all one of England's leading vineyards. There are few better ways to sample the wares than sitting on the vine-covered terrace of this converted farmhouse; the views are wonderful, and the wine's not bad either. The food fits in with the Mediterranean vibe: poached brill with courgette noodles and a grain mustard velouté, for example, followed by an indecently lovely hive honey mousse with orange syrup.

PAXFORD

Churchill Arms

Paxford, GL55 6XH (01386 594000/www.thechurchill arms.com). **Lunch served** noon-2pm, **dinner served** 7-9pm daily. **Main courses** £9-£17. **Credit** MC, V.

The no-bookings policy means it's first come first served here – and the Churchill is always busy. Photos and prints attest to local horsey connections but the clientele is mixed. The decor has a bistro feel. Chef Sonya Kidney and husband Leo Brooke-Little have run this pretty Cotswold stone inn since 1997, creating a genial atmosphere and garnering a reputation for good food. The menu changes regularly and offers such dishes as guinea fowl breast with rösti, braised cabbage and Madeira sauce, and a memorable sticky toffee pudding.

POULTON

Falcon

London Road, Poulton, Cirencester, GL7 5HN (01285 850844/www.thefalconpoulton.co.uk). **Lunch served** noon-2.30pm, **dinner served** 7-9pm daily. **Main courses** £8-£16. **Set lunch** (Sun) £15 2 courses, £20 3 courses. **Credit** MC, V.

In only two years the Falcon has been transformed into a contemporary pub-restaurant. Decorated in aubergine and sage, and with plenty of simple wooden furniture, it feels like a restaurant (though there's a comfy bar area). A heavenly starter of spiced prawn soup was followed by succulent duck breast with sauce jerez, and char-grilled ribeye steak with roasted garlic butter and superb chips.

SAPPERTON

Bell at Sapperton

Sapperton, GL7 6LE (01285 760298/www.foodat thebell.co.uk). **Lunch served** noon-2pm daily. **Dinner served** 7-9.30pm Mon-Sat; 7-9pm Sun. **Main courses** £9.50-£16. **Credit** MC, V.

Outside, the Bell is a typical Cotswold stone hostelry; inside, pine furniture and contemporary prints decorate a series of interlinking rooms, and tables are well spaced. The menu relies heavily on fish fresh from Cornwall (check the blackboard for daily specials) complemented by local produce. There's a strong Mediterranean influence in the likes of goat's cheese panna cotta with roast pimentos, or duck breast and confit leg with pickled endive and curried lentils. There's a decent wine list too.

SHURDINGTON

Greenway

Shurdington, GL51 4UG (01242 862352/862780/ www.thegreenway.co.uk). **Lunch served** 12.30-2.30pm, **dinner served** 7-9pm daily. **Set lunch** (Mon-Sat) £15.50 2 courses, £21 3 courses; (Sun) £25 3 courses. **Set dinner** £32-£45 3 courses. **Credit** AmEx, DC, MC, V.

Old-school formality predominates here (polished service, suited French staff, traditionally decorated dining room), but the ambience lacks modern verve. That said, the spacious conservatory is a delightful place in which to eat – and what food! Kenny Atkinson cooks with a mixture of classical precision and modern flair, delivering complex dishes such as pavé of Orkney salmon with braised beetroot cabbage, lobster sausage, and turnip fondant.

STOW-ON-THE-WOLD

Hamiltons Brasserie

Park Street, Stow-on-the-Wold, GL54 1AQ (01451 831700/www.hamiltons.br.com). **Lunch served** noon-2.30pm daily. **Dinner served** 6-9.30pm Mon-Sat. **Main courses** £9-£18.50. **Credit** AmEx, MC, V.

Stow is a buzzing destination for gastro-tourists. One reason for this is Hamilton's, with its light wood fittings, modern art on the walls and attentive staff. There's a menu to match. Fresh produce is brought to the fore in Mediterranean-style dishes: king prawns with spicy italian sausage, rocket, capers and lemon; or sea bass with brown shrimp butter.

King's Arms ★

Market Square, Stow-on-the-Wold, GL54 1AF (01451 830364/www.kingsarms-stowonthe wold.co.uk). **Open** 11am-11pm Mon-Sat; noon-10.30pm Sun. **Lunch served** noon-2.30pm daily. **Dinner served** 6-9.30pm Mon-Fri; 6-10pm Sat; 7-9pm Sun. **Main courses** £9-£14. **Credit** MC, V.

Behind the Cotswold stone façade, the King's Arms serves fine contemporary cooking. Eat downstairs and bask in the fireside glow of the cosy bar; or upstairs in a grander room with a medieval flavour. A blackboard menu features fish prominently – grilled Cornish scallop with spiced tomato salad, for example. Service is informal but impeccable.

Royalist

Digbeth Street, Stow-on-the-Wold, GL54 1BN (01451 830670/www.theroyalisthotel.co.uk). Eagle & Child **Lunch served** noon-2.30pm Mon-Sat; noon-3pm Sun. **Dinner served** 6-9.30pm Mon-Sat; 6-9pm Sun. **Main courses** £9-£14. *947AD* **Lunch served** noon-2.30pm, **dinner served** 7-9pm Tue-Sat. **Main courses** £16.75-£18. *Both* **Credit** MC, V.

The Royalist's Eagle & Child pub-bistro revels in rustic charm, whereas its 947AD restaurant is far more refined. Here, elegant, well-spaced tables, and slick staff are matched in sophistication on the menu by dishes like millefeuille of quail with apple and puy lentils, or blanquette of monkfish and king prawns with asparagus. Service can be careless, and some dishes arrived lukewarm; more consistent was food from the Eagle & Child – notably a starter of sea bass fillets with poached egg and spinach, and flawless vanilla panna cotta with raspberries.

TETBURY

Calcot Manor

A4135 north-west of Tetbury, GL8 8YJ (01666 890391/www.calcotmanor.co.uk). Gumstool Inn **Lunch served** noon-2pm, **dinner served** 5-9.30pm Mon-Fri. **Meals served** noon-9.30pm Sat; noon-9pm Sun. **Main courses** £8.75-£12.95. *Conservatory* **Lunch served** noon-2pm daily. **Dinner served** 7-9.30pm Mon-Sat; 7-9pm Sun. **Main courses** £15-£21. **Credit** AmEx, DC, MC, V.

Calcot Manor offers two dining choices alongside its accommodation and spa. The Gumstool serves high tea from 5pm (in line with an 'open arms' policy for children) and has a classic brasserie menu. The swimming pool acoustics and service are a bit rough and ready, but it's good for a family night out. The posher Conservatory has a sleek, modern look, with an open 'theatre kitchen' and a vintage champagne bar; here, scallops with watercress and lime salad could precede wood-roasted beef on the bone.

Trouble House

Nr Tetbury, GL8 8SG (01666 502206/www.troublehouse.co.uk). **Lunch served** noon-2pm Tue-Sat. **Dinner served** 7-9.30pm Tue-Sat. **Main courses** £12-£15.50. **Credit** AmEx, DC, MC, V.

The unassuming exterior of this whitewashed stone pub acts as camouflage for what is a top food destination. The pedigree of the owners couldn't be better – chef Michael Bedford was head chef at City Rhodes, while his wife Sarah attended to front-of-house duties at Le Manoir. His French-influenced style elevates dishes way beyond gastropub fare; roast scallops with chilli crab and linguini was sensual, while sole veronique revitalised a neglected classic.

UPPER SLAUGHTER

Lords of the Manor

Upper Slaughter, GL54 2JD (01451 820243/www.lordsofthemanor.com). **Lunch served** noon-2pm, **dinner served** 7-9.15pm daily. **Main courses** £20-£29. **Set lunch** £16.95 2 courses, £19.95 3 courses; (Sun) £26.50 3 courses incl coffee. **Set dinner** £65 8 courses. **Credit** AmEx, DC, MC, V.

The eight-course tasting menu is the ideal way to experience chef Toby Hill's well-conceived, imaginative creations – highlights being a sweetly earthy beetroot granité and a lemongrass crème brûlée with thyme ice-cream. Such sumptuous food is served in elegant surroundings with attentive and efficient service delivered by smart European staff.

WINCHCOMBE

No.5 North St

Winchcombe, GL54 5LH (01242 604566). **Lunch served** noon-2.30pm Wed-Sun. **Dinner served** 7-9.30pm Tue-Sat. **Main courses** £9.50-£18. **Set lunch** (Wed-Sat) £15.50 2 courses, £19.50 3 courses; (Sun) £23 3 courses. **Set dinner** £23.50-£33.50 3 courses, £48.50 10 courses. **Credit** MC, V.

With its Tudor sweetshop-style frontage, cheerful wood interiors and imaginative cooking, there's a fairytale feel to No.5. The food is impeccable, rightly lauded and perfectly delivered, with some unusually matched flavours – such as roasted turbot with braised oxtail, violet potato and chestnut velouté. The extras alone are almost worth a visit: an *amuse-gueule* of jerusalem artichoke soup with cep oil was simply delicious; own-made breads are exceptional.

Hertfordshire

BISHOP'S STORTFORD

Lemon Tree

14-16 Water Lane, Bishop's Stortford, CM23 2LB (01279 757788/www.lemontree.co.uk). **Lunch served** noon-2.30pm Tue-Sat; 1-4pm Sun. **Dinner served** 7-9.30pm Tue-Sat. **Main courses** £10-£16. **Set lunch** (Tue-Sat) £7.95 1 course incl glass of wine/soft drink, £12 2 courses, £15 3 courses. **Set dinner** (Tue-Sat) £17.50 2 courses, (Tue-Thur) £22.50 3 courses incl half bottle of wine per person. **Credit** MC, V.

Nestling in an attractive Georgian terrace close to the centre of this bucolic little town is the Lemon Tree, an incredibly popular, comfortable, slightly formal eaterie with a relatively new, less formal bar – both well worth a couple of hours of anybody's time. Lunch kicks off nicely with steamed mussels and pumpkin seed pesto followed by breast of chicken, black pudding, braised red cabbage and Cumberland sauce, before being rounded off by blueberry and almond tart. There's a greater selection on the dinner menu with particularly worthwhile starters being organic smoked salmon and savoury pancakes or bruschetta, vine tomatoes and buffalo mozzarella. You can follow these with oven-roast skate, veal and roast parsnips or crisp spinach, feta and date pancake, with rich and rewarding desserts to finish. Service is swift and the wine ranges from a tenner upwards.

BUSHEY

St James

30 High Street, Bushey, WD23 3HL (020 8950 2480). **Lunch served** noon-2pm, **dinner served** 6.30-9.30pm Mon-Sat. **Main courses** £14.95-£17.95. **Set lunch** £13.95 2 courses. **Set dinner** (6.30-7.30pm) £14.95 2 courses. **Credit** MC, V.

Situated on an otherwise uninteresting satellite town high street is St James, a smart, friendly, open and airy restaurant that is more spacious than its shop-front windows promise. Seating is sufficiently comfortable with enough space between tables to enable you to relax. The menu is a traditional mix of grilled meat and poultry and some slightly more challenging fish options. To kick off, make the tricky choice between vegetable bhajia with curry and coriander dressing or grilled tiger prawns with smoked chicken and bacon salad, before moving on to the poached haddock with prawn bisque and more prawns or the sea bass in a crunchy fennel crust. Alternatively hit the meat menu for a rich pork fillet wrapped in smoked bacon and try to ignore the doily-elaborate menu descriptions.

FRITHSDEN

Alford Arms

Frithsden, HP1 3DD (01442 864480/www.alfordarms.co.uk). **Lunch served** noon-2.30pm Mon-Sat; noon-3pm Sun. **Dinner served** 7-10pm daily. **Main courses** £9.75-£13.50. **Credit** AmEx, MC, V.

An increasingly popular country gastropub with loads of outdoor seating where you can watch cars manoeuvre for room in the narrow lane, while you examine the extensive menu and congratulate yourself on getting a table. Booking is a must, particularly at weekends – they were taking reservations in April for Saturday nights in August. The interior is comfortable with a large formal dining area and space round the bar where you can sink one of the guest ales, a glass of wine or bottle from the extensive list. Small plates (£3.50-£6.50) include oak-smoked bacon on bubble and squeak with a poached egg or warm roast beef salad. Mains include smoked haddock with mash, mustard sauce and another poached egg; rack of lamb; and pan-fried pork loin and fettuccine with asparagus and artichoke. Vegetables are extra, around £3, while puddings will set you back upwards of a fiver.

HERTFORD

Hillside

45 Port Hill, Hertford, SG14 3EP (01992 554556/www.thehillside.co.uk). **Lunch served** noon-2.30pm, **dinner served** 6.30-9.30pm daily. **Main courses** £9.75-£13.95. **Credit** MC, V.

Clinging to the side of the road on a steep, primarily residential hill is this one-year-old pub conversion with its mini wine bar and small restaurant. When dining rooms have tables so narrow you struggle to get your legs between those of the table, and if you rise to go you bump into the person sitting behind, it's usually a sign that space is an issue. That said, the food is excellent and of a quality that makes the menu great value. Starters include a delicious grilled goat's cheese, beetroot purée and mixed pesto or seared scallops with caramelised chicory, watercress and pancetta. Mains start at around £11 with the calf's liver, bacon, olive oil mash, oyster mushrooms and green beans only beaten into second place by the roast rump of spring lamb with spiced onion marmalade. A good bottle of plonk will dent your wallet by £15 to £20.

KINGS LANGLEY

La Casetta

18 High Street, Kings Langley, WD4 8BH (01923 263823/www.lacasetta.co.uk). **Lunch served** noon-2.30pm Tue-Fri; 12.30-3pm 1st Sun of mth. **Dinner served** 7-10.30pm Tue-Sat. **Main courses** £9.95-£16.95. **Set lunch** £11.95 2 courses. **Set dinner** £19.50 2 courses, £23.50 3 courses Fri, Sat. **Credit** MC, V.

While it's incongruous to find relatively modern European-influenced fare, listing heavily towards the Italian side, in the tiny uneven rooms of a 16th-century cottage, this place is more popular than sliced ciabatta. Starters range from roasted flat mushrooms with char-grilled aubergine, tomato and mozzarella to an absorbing own-cured gravadlax with cucumber salad and crème fraîche, or you could always try the diverting and extensive antipasto platter. Having negotiated the openers, you might want to move straight on to the tail – some refreshing lemon tart or lively plum and blackcurrant crumble with ice-cream – but that would be doing a disservice to a distinguished middle order. Plaice wrapped around asparagus, pan-fried calf's liver with parsnip mash or fillet steaks with dolcelatte cream all vie for a place in your final line-up. So go on, treat yourself.

REED

Cabinet

High Street, Reed, SG8 8AH (01763 848366/www.thecabinetinn.co.uk). **Lunch served** 12.30-2pm Tue-Fri; 12.30-2.30pm Sat; noon-5pm Sun. **Dinner served** 7-9.30pm Tue-Sat. **Main courses** £14-£25. **Set lunch** £20 3 courses. **Credit** AmEx, MC, V.

This freehouse pub, which has retained much of its original charm, contains an excellent white tablecloth restaurant, a bar and a garden, plus a lobster, steak and hog rotisserie – meaning that it pretty much covers all bases. Run enthusiastically by TV chef Paul Bloxham, this is a place to visit now before it becomes so popular that getting through the door proves absolutely impossible. The lunch menu is a surprisingly inexpensive sketch of the more expansive delights of the dinner menu, with a truly delightful duo of organic lamb, roasted and wrapped in a herb crust, weighing in at a paltry £14. Dinner sees greater choice and you'll be left in the quandary of wanting to try everything. A massive selection of wines, jazz with the rotisserie on Sundays and some good ale will keep most entertained, but if you want a real treat try the American-style beef short ribs in garlic mash.

ST ALBANS

Carluccio's Caffé ★

7-8 Christopher Place, St Albans, AL3 5DQ (01727 837681/www.carluccios.com). **Meals served** 8am-11pm Mon-Fri; 9am-11pm Sat; 10am-10pm Sun. **Main courses** £4.95-£10.50. **Credit** AmEx, MC, V.

Chains tend to be a bit of a drag, lacking the hands-on drive of the personality that made the original outlet a success. However, in this case the overriding philosophy is great ingredients in traditional Italian dishes that don't break the bank. So if you can block out the annoying electric-blue neon wall lighting you're in for a good time. The breakfast menu doesn't set the mind alight but scrambled free-range eggs with sautéed mushrooms and toasted ciabatta are well presented and the coffee excellent. Lunch and dinner tend to be more fun from a culinary point of view, with old favourites like calzone – filled with vegetables and melting cheese – vying for attention with penne giardiniera (a mix of pasta, courgette, chilli, deep-fried spinach balls, garlic and parmesan). It's all presented beautifully. What's more, this place is child-friendly without having dumbed down.

Conservatory

St Michael's Manor Hotel, Fishpool Street, St Albans, AL3 4RY (01727 864444/www.stmichaels manor.com). **Lunch served** 12.30-2pm daily. **Dinner served** 7-9.30pm Mon-Sat; 7-9pm Sun. **Set lunch** £22.50 2 courses, £26.50 3 courses. **Set dinner** £28.50 2 courses, £37.50 3 courses. **Credit** AmEx, DC, MC, V.

Grand old hotels sporting ivy immediately transport the mind to Agatha Christie murder mysteries, where people take tea and chomp on limp cucumber sandwiches with the crusts removed, but in this case any such assumptions about the food are unfounded. Lunch and dinner are three-course adventures including coffee and petits fours with a good deal more choice than you might expect. To begin you must pick between crab and lobster cake with fennel fondue or parmesan and Mediterranean crisps with ratatouille and basil mayo. Following this there are various options, the best of which are seared skate wing and zucchini spaghetti with a light curry sauce, cumin-crusted tuna or duck with crushed peppercorns, all described in a slightly too flowery manner on the menu. An extensive range of wine runs from £18 to £75.

Sukiyaki ★

6 Spencer Street, St Albans, AL3 5EG (01727 865009). **Lunch served** noon-2.15pm, **dinner served** 6.30-11.30pm Tue-Sat. **Main courses** £8.50-£17.50. **Set lunch** £7-£9.50 incl miso soup, rice & pickles. **Set dinner** £18.50-£24.50 5 courses. **Credit** AmEx, DC, MC, V.

The 1960s part-wood, part-frosted glass and part-clear glass front of this restaurant seems rather dull, but a peer through to the interior reveals one of those neat, well-ordered, unpretentious, minimalist spaces that seem typically Japanese. The menu is equally unshowy but its contents more than make up for any lack of designer flash. Deep-fried bean curd (agedashi) is a delight while skewered fried pork and onions in breadcrumbs (kushikatsu) is mouth-watering. Mains all come with salad and the abiding feeling is that not only are you pleasing your tastebuds, you're also eating healthily. Try chicken marinated in soya and ginger, king prawns and assorted vegetables in batter or Scotch beef sirloin, which is cooked impressively at your table.

TRING

Fornovivo ★

69 High Street, Tring, HP23 4AB (01442 890005/ www.fornovivo.com). **Lunch served** noon-3pm, **dinner served** 6-10.30pm Mon-Fri. **Meals served** noon-10.30pm Sat; noon-10pm Sun. **Main courses** £5.75-£11.95. **Credit** MC, V.

An efficient, roomy Italian café-cum-restaurant in the old post office, minus the usual fussy decor and obligatory red-and-white checked tablecloths but including the overly jolly, rumpy-pumpy, squeeze-box music along the lines of the trattoria in Disney's *Lady and the Tramp*. Romantically slurping one string of spaghetti until your noses meet is not really an option here – it's too bright and open-plan – but the food retains its comforting indulgent quality. Pizzas, pagnotelle (traditional Neapolitan round sandwiches) and calzone feature the usual toppings and fillings – the likes of mozzarella, sun-blushed tomatoes, porcini and pancetta. Lurking beside reasonably priced wines are tasty salads, inventive starters and traditional, great-value pasta dishes, as well as mains such as grilled best-end-of-lamb cutlets, salsa verde with fresh herbs or seared tuna marinated in chilli, garlic and lemon, with a warm salad of cherry tomatoes, rocket and potato.

Central

WELWYN

Auberge du Lac

Brocket Hall, Welwyn, AL8 7XG (01707 368888/ www.brocket-hall.co.uk). **Lunch served** noon-2.30pm Tue-Sun. **Dinner served** 7-10.30pm Tue-Sat. **Main courses** £23-£35. **Set lunch** (Tue-Fri) £28.50 3 courses incl 2 glasses of wine; (Sat, Sun) £35 3 courses. **Credit** AmEx, DC, MC, V.

Novelli is in the house, a beautiful rural spot where he's working his magic, so Auberge du Lac has to be worth visiting for anyone who loves unapologetically French fare and flair, described almost as elaborately on the menu as it is presented at the table. The à la carte has starters ranging from baby pumpkin soup (£6.50) to poached lobster, haricots and artichoke, asparagus and horseradish cream (£23). Mains start at £23 before going into orbit, but it's churlish to debate prices when you are being offered spiced spring Welsh lamb with Szechuan pepper, sea scallop and truffle, cream foie gras and tagliatelle or smoked and steamed monkfish with braised oxtail, caramelised onions and an osso bucco-style jus. King of the desserts is baby pineapple tatin and banana mousse.

Also in the area

Loch Fyne 12 Hadley Highstone, Barnet, EN5 4PU (020 8449 3674); **Wagamama** Unit 6, Christopher Place, St Albans, AL3 5DQ (01727 865122).

Oxfordshire

ARDINGTON

Boar's Head

Church Street, Ardington, OX12 8QA (01235 833254/www.boardsheadardington.co.uk). **Lunch served** noon-2pm Mon-Sat; noon-2.30pm Sun. **Dinner served** 7-9pm Mon-Thur; 7-10pm Fri, Sat. **Main courses** £13.95-£16.95. **Set lunch** (Sun) £18.95 3 courses. **Credit** AmEx, MC, V.

The Boar's Head remains enduringly popular. Enjoy a drink in the traditional bar area, a pub lunch in the cosy, central eating area, or treat yourself to the à la carte in the larger, modern extension. Cheery and discreetly welcoming, it can get busy at weekends. Menus are a sophisticated if pricey modern European mix. Starters include roast pepper brûlée with seared squid and chorizo or tempura of Cornish scallops with chilli jam. Try a main of fillet of Angus beef with kidneys in pastry or an onion and gruyère tart with foie gras sauce. Portions are generous, but leave space for pudding – toffee banana crumble with cream are worth it. They know their wines here too, and are happy to advise.

Trout

Tadpole Bridge, Buckland Marsh, Faringdon, SN7 8RF (01367 870382/www.trout-inn.co.uk). **Lunch served** noon-2pm daily. **Dinner served** 7-9pm Mon-Sat. **Main courses** £7.95-£15.95. **Credit** MC,V.

People come from far and wide to eat and drink here. Notwithstanding a somewhat unprepossessing location, the Trout has a very pretty interior. Beamed and flagstoned, it benefits from high ceilings and large rooms. Book a table and you'll arrive to find a slate with your name chalked on it at your allotted table, a personal touch in keeping with the friendly service and slightly quirky approach. The Trout's menu boasts some bold combos – so choose wisely. There's scallops with red onion marmalade and chicken liver mousse for starters, or chilled bacon and game terrine with cream compote and poached pear. We came a cropper with chicken with linguine and an anchovy sauce; roast loin of venison with vanilla risotto and chocolate sauce, or roast rump of Blenheim lamb with a sweet puy lentil and bacon casserole were better bets. Still, such invention always makes it worth a visit.

BURFORD

Jonathan's at the Angel

14 Witney Street, Burford, OX18 4SN (01993 822714/www.theangel-uk.com). **Lunch served** noon-2pm Tue-Sun. **Dinner served** 7-9.30pm Tue-Sat. **Main courses** £13.95-£18.50. **Set lunch** £14.50 2 courses, £18.50 3 courses. **Credit** MC, V.

Customers order food at the bar and are shown through to one of various cosy nooks to eat. With ancient flagstone floors, open fires in winter and classical sculptural reliefs, Jonathan's hums with appreciative consumption and conversation. From Gressingham duck with poached pear and pecorino rösti to steak with mash and scallions or a Billingsgate of fish options, this is first-class tuck in generous portions – soup comes in a large terrine with a ladle. On the downside, we watched our neighbours polish off two courses before our starter arrived – almost an hour after we'd ordered – and although some lovely *amuse-bouches* compensated, the bill included a bottle of wine that we hadn't drunk. Despite this, and the high prices, we'd return.

Lamb Inn

Sheep Street, Burford, OX18 4LR (01993 823155/ www.lambinn-burford.co.uk). **Lunch served** noon-2.30pm Mon-Fri; noon-3pm Sat, Sun. **Dinner served** 7-9.30pm Mon-Sat; 7-9pm Sun. **Main courses** £4.95-£15. **Set dinner** (Mon-Sat) £25 2 courses, £29.50 3 courses. **Credit** MC, V.

The large square restaurant is down a corridor from the cosy pub customers walk into. White linen tablecloths and wooden floors give a clean look, but the high ceilings make it most inviting in summer. And unless the restaurant is reasonably full, the acoustics can be oppressive. That said, the food really is excellent, despite over-fussy service. Stand-out dishes included bresaola with balsamic vinegar, potato bread and onions, and aged fillet of beef that almost sliced itself. Accompanying vegetables were a little dull and dripping in butter, but puddings were a journey into unknown territory. Light options such as Stowford cider granita sat alongside indulgences like a boozy chocolate St-Emilion. Own-made bread is almost too good – save some room. A warning: there's nothing here for vegetarians.

CHINNOR

Sir Charles Napier ★

Spriggs Alley, nr Chinnor, OX39 4BX (01494 483011/ www.sircharlesnapier.co.uk). **Lunch served** noon-2.30pm Tue-Sat; 12.30-3.30pm Sun. **Dinner served** 7-10pm Tue-Sat. **Main courses** £11.50-£17.50. **Set lunch** (Tue-Fri) £14.50 2 courses. **Set dinner** (Tue-Fri) £16.50 2 courses. **Credit** AmEx, MC, V.

We defy you not to question, at least twice, whether you've missed the Sir Charles Napier as you pass house after house along its unnervingly lengthy approach road until you finally see its large, welcoming sign to your right. This establishment has cachet, however, so it makes no apology for being off the beaten track. What makes it so irresistible? It may be the interesting art and sculpture on the walls, in the garden and on the tables (we had a bust nonchalantly lying beside the posy on our table), or it may be the extensive wine list. Most likely of all, of course, it's the food. The menu isn't extensive (about eight starters and mains), but the portions are generous, and the results impressive. Try a chilled Cornish crab salad with pineapple compote or seared foie gras with sweetcorn pancake. Mains include creamy wild mushroom, spinach and goat's cheese cannelloni, tender ribeye steak with shallots in a sweet red wine sauce and wild salmon with pea purée, mussel and saffron. Chocolate soufflé with pistachio ice-cream was superb. We wound our way home fully appreciative of why this place is so revered.

CRAY'S POND

White Lion

Goring Road, Goring Heath, Cray's Pond, RG8 7SH (01491 680471). **Lunch served** noon-2pm Tue-Sat; noon-2.30pm Sun. **Dinner served** 6-9.30pm Tue-Sat. **Main courses** £9-£14. **Credit** MC, V.

Cray's Pond is the tiny hamlet home of the White Lion, a pub remote but certainly well established on the local map. The character of this 300-year-old building hasn't been stripped away in the quest for modernity and half the space is still very much a relaxed pub, with newspapers for the taking and a fire in the hearth. The other end is laid-back too, but sports posh glasses on bare wooden tables and overlooks a lush garden. Food is knockout. Unusual beetroot, sage and pancetta tartlet had a light, deliciously creamy filling in fine golden baked pastry; char-grilled tuna, panzanella salad and tapenade was riotously colourful, expertly cooked and alive with fresh flavours of olive oil, lemon shreds and green peppercorns. Worth seeking out.

GORING

Leatherne Bottel

The Bridleway, Goring-on-Thames, RG8 0HS (01491 872667/www.leathernebottel.co.uk). **Lunch served** noon-2pm Mon-Fri; noon-2.30pm Sat; noon-3.30pm Sun. **Dinner served** 7-9pm Mon-Thur; 7-9.30pm Fri, Sat. **Main courses** £17-£20. **Set dinner** (Mon-Fri) £23.50 3 courses. **Credit** AmEx, MC, V.

A riverside setting really does mean riverside here, as the Leatherne Bottel nestles peacefully in an unspoilt crook of the Thames. Don't be fooled by the name, there is nothing crusty or olde worlde about this place; in fact, it is as sophisticated as it gets, and if you don't dress up you'll feel out of place. A BMW for the car park, if you can get your hands on one, wouldn't go amiss either. The most popular tables are those right on the riverbank. The extensive menu offers an interesting array: start with roast quail breast, handpicked crab or grilled marinated ostrich; move on to porcini dusted venison loin with a gratin of squash and celeriac or market-fresh fish. We enjoyed a generous cut of ribeye steak with sauce béarnaise and the most delicious chunky pont-neuf 'chips', and double lamb cutlets with a smooth white bean purée. With a peach melba and a creamy strawberry chocolate cheesecake to close, we left the water's edge having enjoyed a treat.

GREAT MILTON

Le Manoir aux Quat' Saisons ★

Church Road, Great Milton, OX44 7PD (01844 278881/www.manoir.com). **Lunch served** 11.45am-2.30pm, **dinner served** 6.45-9.30pm daily. **Main courses** £34-£40. **Set lunch** (Mon-Fri) £45 3 courses. **Set meal** £95 7 courses. **Credit** AmEx, DC, MC, V.

Raymond Blanc's Cotswold mansion oozes class – from its stately old grounds (walk around the landscaped ponds and the vegetable gardens) to the comfy lounge (for aperitifs and delectable *amuse-gueules*) and various dining areas. Top among the latter must be the conservatory, with its airy spaciousness and prime views. Eating options include a seven-course menu gourmande, a seasonal à la carte and a set lunch that offers a choice of two appetisers, three mains and two puds. For the set lunch, French country cooking is elevated to haute cuisine by Blanc's protégé Gary Jones's mastery of technique, his focus on superb ingredients, and his ability to balance strong flavours with the utmost delicacy. Thus an earthy terrine of duck confit was topped with a pungent foie gras parfait and sweetened by spiced pear chutney, while an intense wild mushroom and jabugo ham risotto was softened by mascarpone cream. To follow, fried sea bream and fricassee of squid was enlivened by salted cod brandade and a concentrated bouillabaisse jus, while an intricate rabbit leg confit

Central

The best Oysters

Butley-Orford Oysterage
A blast from the past, in Suffolk. *See p197.*

Bibendum Oyster Bar
Classy crustacea in art deco South Kensington surroundings. *See p47.*

Oyster Shack
Lunchtime bliss, Devon high tides allowing. *See p121.*

Silver Darling Seafood
Alfresco oysters in Aberdeen. *See p316.*

Wheelers Oyster Bar
Small but perfectly-formed Kent charmer. *See p92.*

had richness supplied by red wine jus and bitter harmonies added from braised endive. Iced lemon parfait with blood orange sorbet and an orange butter sauce completed the symphony, with a round of exquisite petits fours as an encore. The vast wine list is not for skimming. French chateaus are to the fore; there's a good choice of half bottles, yet little under £25. Staff are young, personable and expert at spotting where they're needed and where they're not. A party of kitchen staff sat down in their whites at a neighbouring table for lunch: an inspired touch that relaxed the assembly of business power-brokers and well-to-do families. Drawbacks? Price, of course – you could easily spend £150 a head on the carte, with wine – and we're puzzled where M Blanc found french beans and wild mushrooms in March. Nevertheless, our meal was memorable, and a joy.

KING'S SUTTON

White Horse

The Square, King's Sutton, OX17 6RF (01295 810843). **Lunch served** noon-2pm Mon-Sat; noon-3.30pm Sun. **Dinner served** 7-9.30pm Mon-Sat. **Main courses** £7.95-£14.95. **Credit** MC, V.

Set in an idyllic spot overlooking the green in a pretty village, this is a friendly pub, run efficiently and modernised in a pleasantly low-key, minimalist style with pine tables and warm-coloured walls. The lunch menu runs from generously filled sandwiches, to local specialties and a range of Mediterranean and oriental-themed dishes (Thai-style chicken with noodles and ginger jus, or peppered seared tuna with slow-roasted capsicums). To start there are grilled king prawns with garlic butter or Scottish mussels with white wine, garlic, cream and fries, or chicken and mushroom pâté with warm bread. Of the mains, the Oxfordshire sausage on mash with onion gravy was a winner, as was grilled whole baby lemon sole with lemongrass and chilli butter. An orange bread and butter pudding made a fine finish.

MIDDLE ASSENDON

Rainbow Inn

Middle Assendon, RG9 6AU (01491 574879). **Lunch served** noon-2pm, **dinner served** 7-9pm daily. **Main courses** £7.50-£12.95. **Credit** MC, V.

Deep in the countryside a few miles outside Henley, this unpretentious 17th-century inn oozes quiet country charm. Enjoy the fresh air as you dine in the attractive garden, supping a good pint and eating traditional pub meals. The food menu might not be long, but it contains some real gems. The beef and pork salads are something to behold, and hearty eaters will appreciate the steak and Guinness pie or scampi and chips. Other options include plump fish cakes and a homely chicken and mushroom pie. Refreshed with a pint of well-kept Brakspear or a very acceptable glass of house wine, you'll be delighted to discover that the down-to-earth atmosphere also comes at down-to-earth prices.

MOULSFORD

Beetle & Wedge

Ferry Lane, Moulsford, OX10 9JF (01491 651381/ www.beetleandwedge.co.uk). Brasserie **Lunch served** noon-2pm, **dinner served** 7-10pm daily. **Main courses** £12-£20. *Restaurant* **Lunch served** noon-2pm Sun. **Dinner served** 7-10pm Thur-Sat. **Main courses** £18-£21.50. **Set lunch** £37.50 3 courses incl coffee. **Credit** AmEx, DC, MC, V.

A hotel as well as a popular eating place, the Beetle and Wedge enjoys the loveliest of riverside settings and is a perennial favourite for wedding receptions and parties. Immaculately maintained, with pretty sitting rooms, florals and flagstones, the main building is classic and formal. The young, friendly staff, however (not to mention the selection of green wellies by the front door), ensure that the atmosphere can be as relaxed and homely as you wish. There is a choice of venues: the conservatory dining room with river views in the main house; the beamed boathouse, a larger, less formal venue with charcoal grill/cooking area; or the riverside terrace. The sophisticated menu is extensive (more so in the Boathouse), featuring starters such as foie gras terrine with toasted brioche, avocado and Cornish crab salad or a warm onion tart with sautéed foie gras and truffle sauce. Mains included a plump and pink Gressingham duck, saddle of venison, English lamb with provençal crust, and sea bass with asparagus. A banoffi pie to die for completed a very pleasant meal. All in all, well worth the mooring fee.

NETTLEBED

White Hart

28 High Street, Nettlebed, RG9 5DD (01491 641245/ www.whitehartnettlebed.com). Bistro **Lunch served** noon-2.30pm, **dinner served** 6-10pm daily. **Main courses** £8.50-£15. **Set meals** £10 2 courses, £15 3 courses. *Restaurant* **Dinner served** 7-10pm Thur-Sat. **Set dinner** £35 3 courses, £55 6-course tasting menu. **Credit** MC, V.

Nettlebed was a ghost town dissected by a busy B-road spraying old cottages and sleepy pubs with a dusty layer of neglect; ashes from which the White Hart has risen like a phoenix. Its 17th-century exterior looks nicely restored, with a private dining room conservatory added, but inside the building's aged contours and inglenooks have been sloshed with white paint, adorned with mismatched paintings and furnished in retro style to form a stark bar and bistro. Beyond a deeply buttoned white vinyl desk is Nettlebed restaurant, equally monotone but painted a fumblingly dark aubergine from floor to ceiling. Chris Barber's food claws the place out of its decorative nosedive. After 11 years as chef to Prince Charles, and then at the Goose, Britwell Salome, this is a man who loves earthy British ingredients and assembles them with a confident, light and satisfying touch: ribeye of local Charolais beef with onion purée, horseradish crust and truffle jus being just one example.

Liaison. *See p169.*

OXFORD

Bar Meze ★

146 London Road, Headington, Oxford, OX3 9ED (01865 761106/www.barmeze.co.uk). **Lunch served** 11.30am-5pm, **dinner served** 5-10.30pm daily. **Main courses** £10-£14. **Set lunch** £6 2 mezes incl drink. **Credit** AmEx, MC, V.

Firmly established as Headington's prime dining spot, this Turkish bar-restaurant has managed to cultivate a steady trade through the day and night. The long, attractive premises help. Ochre walls are matched with comfortable blue chairs; there's a bar along the middle, and an olive tree under a skylight at the back. Another draw is the drinks list, which includes cocktails, bottled beers and popular house wine. There's a long list of cold and hot meze, plus substantial main courses such as adana kebabs, incik (slow-roasted knuckle of lamb) and, moving away from Turkey, salmon with artichoke hearts in a white wine and pesto sauce. Most punters order meze and these range from marinated squid with chickpeas, via Albanian lamb's liver, to patlican tava (char-grilled aubergine with spicy tomato sauce). Many of the snacks seem bought in (and the bread is common pitta), but friendly service and attractive pricing keep the punters happy.

Branca

111 Walton Street, Oxford, OX2 6AJ (01865 556111/www.branca-restaurants.com). **Meals served** noon-11pm Mon-Thur, Sun; noon-11.30pm Fri, Sat. **Main courses** £8.25-£16.95. **Set lunch** (noon-5pm Mon-Fri) £5.95 1 course incl drink. **Set dinner** (5-7pm Mon-Fri) £10 2 courses incl drink. **Credit** AmEx, MC, V.

Branca – an olive oil and focaccia kind of place – exudes an appealing urban/urbane breeziness. Women, particularly, are attracted by the spacious, contemporary surroundings (the long, white interior is further brightened by spotlights, mirrors, a skylight and elaborate chandeliers in the bar area). They also like the wide choice of salads, and the fact that most dishes are available in two sizes. The food list also encompasses puffy-based pizzas, risottos (smoked haddock and herb risotto, topped by parmesan and a perfectly poached egg), and more substantial main courses such as roast duck breast, braised lentils and balsamic sauce. Specials might include a refreshing salad of fusilli with marinated octopus, spring onion, basil and chilli dressing. Hazelnut and praline semifreddo is one of many alluring desserts. The bill can mount here, which makes the set lunch deal – a risotto or pizza with a glass of wine for £5.95 – all the more attractive.

Brookes

Oxford Brookes University, Gipsy Lane, Headington, Oxford, OX3 0BP (01865 483803/www.brookes.ac.uk/restaurant). **Lunch served** noon-2pm Mon-Fri. **Dinner served** 6-8.30pm Fri. **Set lunch** £11.95 3 courses. **Main courses** £9-£14. **Credit** MC, V.

Ignore the unlovely architecture of Oxford Brookes University. Once inside the restaurant, showpiece of the Department of Hospitality, Leisure and Tourism Management, you'll find a stylish, light space split into bar, informal dining area (where quick meals – salmon with new potatoes, say – can be procured), and restaurant. Book and you can enjoy a classy three-course lunch for £11.95 from the weekly menu. There are generally three choices per course, including a vegetarian dish. Food is seasonal, mostly locally sourced, and cooked and served by students. The results are often extremely successful and beautifully presented. Lamb chump steak on red onion and mint risotto with Madeira and redcurrant sauce was the highlight of a meal that began with cream of cauliflower soup and concluded with a moist ginger cake and ice-cream. Service can be green, but is laudably keen. Academics and their guests predominate at lunch; seats for the twice-weekly themed dinners are highly prized.

Cherwell Boat House

Bardwell Road, Oxford, OX2 6SR (01865 552746/www.cherwellboathouse.co.uk). **Lunch served** noon-2.30pm, **dinner served** 6.30-9pm daily. **Set lunch** (Mon-Fri) £12.50 2 courses, £15.50-£19.50 3 courses; (Sat, Sun) £21.50 3 courses. **Set dinner** £23.50 3 courses. **Credit** AmEx, MC, V.

Somehow you don't expect to see the river down a side street off the Banbury Road. And what a serene stretch of river it is. Punts swish up and down, with laughter drifting through the tunnel of overhanging trees like a scene from a film. This mellow, exposed brick restaurant has completely shed its rustic, slightly grubby persona of not so many years ago, when it still looked like a carpenter's workshop, and is now airy and modern with plenty of windows overlooking the River Cherwell. Food is more conformist, with risottos, crab cakes, roasted black-leg chicken, meaty and non-meaty salads, and hearty puds. Punts, which are made in the boathouse next door, are for hire from 10am until dusk and the place is predictably heaving in summer.

Chiang Mai Kitchen

Kemp Hall Passage, 130A High Street, Oxford, OX1 4DH (01865 202233/www.chiangmaikitchen.co.uk). **Lunch served** noon-2.30pm daily. **Dinner served** 6-10.15pm Mon-Thur; 6-10.30pm Fri, Sat; 6-10pm Sun. **Main courses** £7-£10. **Credit** AmEx, DC, MC, V.

Set in a 14th-century English house, this restaurant blends the original charm of bare beams and stone fireplaces with Thai artefacts to achieve a relaxed, Zen-like atmosphere. The head chef, originally from Chiang Mai, is a stickler for ingredients. He flies in herbs and spices from Bangkok weekly, which are generously dispatched on each dish, along with purple orchids. The extensive menu is split logically, with seafood and fish the star attractions. Starters can be hot like the pak chup, vegetables dipped in batter for dipping into sweet chilli sauce, or cold like plar kung, a piquant salad of prawns. There's an array of beautifully flavoured main meat and fish dishes, plus additional lunchtime specials, all meals in themselves thanks to a generous mound of rice.

Edamame ★

15 Holywell Street, Oxford, OX1 3SA (01865 246916/www.edamame.co.uk). **Lunch served** noon-2.30pm Tue-Sat; noon-4pm Sun. **Dinner served** 5-8.30pm Thur-Sat. **Main courses** £6.50-£14; sushi £2.50-£8. **Credit** (dinner) MC, V.

On one of Oxford's most beautiful backstreets, Edamame is barely noticeable save for the lunchtime queues growing outside its door. Within lies the problem: it's a tiny Japanese restaurant, with only half a dozen polished pine tables that must be shared. A note on the white walls advertises the daily lunch special – perhaps chicken breast with onions cooked in egg on a bowl of rice with dried seaweed, served with miso soup. Otherwise, there's a list of eight noodle or rice meals plus side dishes such as edamame (boiled salted soya beans), crunchy pickles and natto (soya beans fermented to form a coating of white goo). Spicy miso ramen was an immense enjoyable bowlful of noodles, minced pork, crunchy vegetables, and resilient mushrooms in a salty stock. Sushi is served on Thursday evenings, while Friday and Saturday nights feature an extended version of the lunch menu, with more fish. A cup of green tea is free, service is swift and a meal rarely costs more than a tenner.

The Flame

1 The Parade, Windmill Road, Headington, Oxford, OX3 7BL (01865 760309). **Lunch served** noon-2.30pm Mon, Wed-Sun. **Dinner served** 6-11pm Mon, Wed-Sat; 6-10pm Sun. **Main courses** £6.50-£11. **Credit** AmEx, DC, MC, V.

An unexpected treat in suburban Headington, the Flame is a handsome and spacious Persian restaurant. Hidden behind a nondescript frontage and drab bar area (hubble bubble pipes available) is a long, light space decorated with Iranian tiles, paintings and artefacts. One section contains low tables and cushion seating. The menu embraces both the kebab and the stew facets of Persian cuisine, along with starters such as halim bademjan (a tasty purée of lamb, butter beans and aubergine) and mast-o-musir (creamy own-made yoghurt and garlic). To follow, the fruity stews like fesenjon (chicken with a puréed walnut and pomegranate sauce) are recommended, while the lamb shank cooked with parsley, coriander, dill, garlic and saffron was succulent but its sauce lacked oomph. Kebabs are invariably first rate: juicy, scorched, tender. The bread and rice are also excellent, and staff are helpful. This place deserves more custom.

Joe's ★

21 Cowley Road, Oxford, OX4 1HP (01865 201120/ www.joes-cafe.co.uk). **Meals served** 10am-11pm Mon-Sat; 10am-10.30pm Sun. **Main courses** £7.95-£11.95. **Set meal** (10am-7pm) £7.95 2 courses. **Credit** MC, V.

An informal little diner well-populated by students, Joe's is renowned for its brunches (10am-5pm). These include french toast with maple syrup and can be accompanied by smoothies, bottled beers or hangover-postponing cocktails. Otherwise, simple dishes such as bangers and mash (with a tangy onion and mustard gravy) or 'light bites' of the Caesar salad ilk (a serviceable, if parsimonious rendition) are supplemented by specials – perhaps char-grilled sardines with basil and tomato dressing and hand-cut chips, or spaghetti with asparagus and lemon. Staff are young, friendly and funky. There's modern art on the walls, Crosby, Stills & Nash on the sound system and a cramped courtyard garden at the back. This is somewhere to crank-up for, or wind-down from, the main event of the night.

Liaison ★

29 Castle Street, Oxford, OX1 1LJ (01865 242944/ 251481). **Lunch served** noon-3pm Mon-Thur; noon-2pm Fri, Sat; noon-4pm Sun. **Dinner served** 6.30-11.30pm Mon-Thur; 6.30pm-12.30am Fri, Sat; 7-11pm Sun. **Main courses** £6.50-£28. **Set dinners** £14.95-£18 3 courses. **Credit** MC, V.

Chinese restaurants serving genuine Chinese food are as rare as hen's teeth (or steamed hen's feet) outside Britain's major cities, so Liaison is a welcome surprise. Lunchtime dim sum is on a par with that found in London's Chinatown. At dinner, there are ingredients such as fish lips for the adventurous, but also hot-pot dishes full of wonderful, simmered flavours. Best among these is the classic belly pork with preserved vegetables: tender fat, juicy meat and luscious gravy. Chinese broccoli makes a good foil to this richness, while deep-fried oysters (plenty of little 'uns) add welcome crunch. Clear noodles and mixed vegetables with red beancurd in clay pot is one of several enticing vegetarian dishes. Liaison is a dark little place in a quaint old building; faux windows make some amends for the lack of natural light. Service on our trip veered between the scowling and the solicitous.

Old Parsonage

1 Banbury Road, Oxford, OX2 6NN (01865 310210/ www.oxford-hotels-restaurants.co.uk). **Breakfast served** 9-10.30am daily. **Lunch served** noon-2.30pm Mon-Sat; 12.30-2.30pm Sun. **Tea served** 3-5.30pm Mon-Sat; 3.30-5.30pm Sun. **Dinner served** 6-10.30pm Mon-Sat; 6.30-10.30pm Sun. **Main courses** £10-£15. **Credit** AmEx, DC, MC, V.

In a city of exceptionally beautiful buildings, the gorgeous Old Parsonage is easy to miss behind its high buff wall. Walking under a stone archway into a wisteria-stitched courtyard garden and up to an ancient studded oak door feels very *Alice in Wonderland*. Combining English charm with a streak of über-efficiency, every second of a visit here is enjoyable. The plush, fatly upholstered dining room is so relaxing that the term 'restaurant' hardly seems fitting, and on the day of our visit a group of diners as diverse as Oxford can conjure up tucked into broad platters of pasta, fish dishes, Angus beefburgers and elegant desserts. The same owners also run Gee's (61A Banbury Road, 01865 553540), Old Bank (92-94 High Street, 01865 799599) and Quod (92-94 High Street, 01865 202505).

Central

SHIPTON-UNDER-WYCHWOOD

Lamb Inn

Simons Lane, Shipton-under-Wychwood, OX7 6DQ (01993 830465). **Lunch served** noon-2.45pm, **dinner served** 6.30-9.45pm daily. **Main courses** £8-£15. **Credit** AmEx, MC, V.

Typically Cotswolds cute outside and tastefully bistro inside, you get the best of both worlds at this 16th-century inn. Its old-style charm coupled with efficient service and good food makes for a relaxing lunch. You can book the restaurant, but it's worth taking pot luck and eating in the attractive bar or outside in the garden. If you like good old-fashioned pub meals like beer-battered fish, hearty steaks and pies then you'll be more than satisfied. The chef also serves Mediterranean favourites like moussaka, lamb koftas and chicken provençal, and gives a nod to Asian cuisine with Thai fish cakes. If you just want a pint and a snack there's a formidable line-up of filled baguettes and sandwiches. They don't stint on portions, so leave space for one of the fabulous desserts – pancakes with cherries and clotted cream was well received. A good selection of wines by the glass completes the happy picture.

STADHAMPTON

Crazy Bear Hotel

Bear Lane, Stadhampton, OX44 7UR (01865 890714/ www.crazybearhotel.co.uk). English restaurant **Lunch served** noon-3pm, **dinner served** 7-10pm daily.

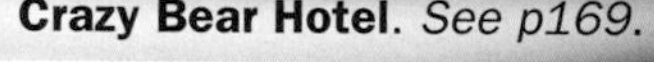

Crazy Bear Hotel. *See p169.*

Main courses £16.50-£18.50. **Set meal** (lunch Mon-Fri; dinner Mon-Thur) £12.50 2 courses, £15 3 courses. *Thai brasserie* **Lunch served** noon-3pm Mon-Sat. **Dinner served** 7-10pm Mon-Sat; 4-10pm Sun. **Main courses** £8.50-£18.50. **Credit** AmEx, DC, MC, V.
Perennial haunt of the hooray Henrys, the Crazy Bear belies its bucolic setting. Give your eyes time to adjust to the ancient, louche interior before letting them feast on zebra skins, beaten copper fittings, black and gold walls and stuffed bears hanging from the vaulted ceiling, all fingered by a lazy evening sun slanting through almost-closed blinds. Invisibly backlit by UV lights, the bar constantly shifts with glow-shirted staff, who weave to and fro between the iced oyster display, champagne bucket, chilled cabinet of flavoured vodkas and the till (the latter will become a significant feature for you too, upon leaving). Food is generally good, especially if you stick to organic British and French classics such as charred calf's liver with cep pomme purée, honey glazed parsnips and port jus; the Thai dishes are more problematic, and many taste more Chinese than Thai. Eclectic rooms are great for sleepovers, when you can linger longer in the twinkly palm garden.

STEEPLE ASTON

Red Lion

South Side, Steeple Aston, OX25 4RY (01869 340225/www.leorufus.co.uk). **Lunch served** noon-2pm Tue-Sun. **Dinner served** 7-9pm Tue-Sat. **Main courses** £9.50-£15.95. **Set lunch** £11.95 2 courses, £14.95 3 courses. **Credit** MC, V.
This freehouse north of Woodstock, with Hook Norton beer on tap and an impressive wine list, is a welcome watering hole in the deepest countryside. You can eat informally in the bar or move into the small but perfectly formed restaurant for a more refined experience. A conservatory extension was being built when we visited. The menu offers a wide selection of seductive dishes, from Gressingham duck to meat pies, fish specials and steaks. However the finished dishes don't quite live up to

expectations. A starter of smoked salmon was good but some basic prawns added nothing to the mix. A calamares special came in a tomato sauce instead of battered and fried, but this wasn't explained at the outset. Mains of coq au vin and lemon sole were good but not special. Stick to steaks and traditional fare for a more satisfying meal. Popular with locals, and with its excellent wines and well-kept beers, good service and friendly atmosphere it's easy to see why.

STOKE ROW

Crooked Billet

Newland Lane, Stoke Row, RG9 5PU (01491 681048/ www.thecrookedbillet.co.uk). **Lunch served** noon-2.30pm, **dinner served** 7-10pm Mon-Fri. **Meals served** noon-10pm Sat, Sun. **Main courses** £10.75-£19.50. **Set lunch** (Mon-Sat) £12.95 2 courses, £14.95 3 courses; (Sun) £17.95 3 courses. **Credit** MC, V.

This place – venue for Kate Winslet's wedding reception – is something of a one-off, an eclectic mix of pub, restaurant and music venue. You can sit outside (sometimes chokingly close to arriving cars) or inside, where the low snugs are so cool and dark they're practically subterranean. A larger dining room past the bar offers a brighter alternative, although its deep red walls and book-lined shelves give it a drawing room feel. The menu takes some reading with more than a dozen starters and mains (at least three of each were vegetarian). Quantities are also ample – a main of spring roll and bok choi noodles includes a half duck, while a huge rack of lamb came swimming in tomato and basil jus with a creamy fondant potato. With a pleasantly informal atmosphere and lovely woodland walks nearby, if you see out the afternoon, there's always the chance of some music in the evening. Note: no debit cards are accepted and credit cards incur a 3.9% fee.

TETSWORTH

Swan

High Street, Tetsworth, OX9 7AB (01844 281182/ www.theswan.co.uk). **Lunch served** noon-2.15pm Mon-Sat; noon-3.30pm Sun. **Dinner served** 7-9.30pm Tue-Sat. **Main courses** £12-£17.50. **Credit** MC, V.

This historic building turned from ugly duckling to beautiful Swan in the mid-1990s when it was restored to its former glory. It now combines a bar-restaurant (plus a large seating area outside) and antiques centre. Antiques are displayed to elegant effect in the restaurant, alongside some not-so-tasteful stuffed animal heads. Upstairs you can exercise your shopping urge in 40 rooms packed with antiques belonging to 80 collectors. Food and wine is geared to a discerning crowd who can afford upmarket prices. The menu is small, but everything is superbly prepared. Starters might be roast red tomato and basil soup, red pepper and mozzarella salad with anchovies, smoked Scottish salmon or pan-fried livers with spaghetti and sage. Mains easily surpass the pub food average and include seared scallops and black pudding with tarragon or guinea fowl breast with broad beans and pancetta. Desserts are recommended, notably the bread and butter pudding. Wines by the glass are also well above the norm. An excellent destination.

THAME

Old Trout

29-30 Lower High Street, Thame, OX9 2AA (01844 212146/www.theoldtrouthotel.co.uk). **Lunch served** noon-2.30pm, **dinner served** 6.30-9.30pm daily. **Main courses** £9.50-£16.95. **Set lunch** (Sun) £9 1 course, £12 2 courses, £16 3 courses. **Credit** AmEx, MC, V.

This thatched 16th-century inn and restaurant suits all seasons. Cosy up in the small rooms with log fires in winter and dine outdoors on the large patio in summer. The restaurant menu is a mix of traditional British with international strands. It's a little OTT at lunch – serious dishes and big portions, formally served in the small collection of dining rooms. Fricassee of wild mushrooms on fresh linguine was incredibly rich and filling. Ditto oriental-braised belly pork. Finish with one of the British puds and you will be done for the day. A better option might be a hearty sandwich such as hot roast beef with blue cheese fondant or char-grilled Mediterranean vegetables with pesto, glazed with mozzarella, both of which come with fat chips, coleslaw and potato salad. The wine list has some gems, including the Sancerre Domaine Michel Girard. Dinner is the best time to splash out in the restaurant, when you can settle down in the bar or book a room upstairs.

Central

WANTAGE

Thyme & Plaice

8 Newbury Street, Wantage, OX12 8BS (01235 760568). **Lunch served** noon-2pm Tue-Fri. **Dinner served** 7-9pm Thur-Sat. **Main courses** £14-£15.50. **Set dinner** (Thur, Fri) £18.50 3 courses. **Credit** AmEx, MC, V.

Just off Market Square in Wantage, the alleged birthplace of King Alfred, Thyme and Plaice remains the town's most agreeable place to dine. The interior of this traditional 18th-century townhouse has been sympathetically modernised to create a tranquil, almost oriental feel. Natural flooring, a subtle water feature, clean, simple lines, solid wood tables and splashes of deep red create a smart but cosy setting. Attentive service is matched by quiet efficiency in the kitchen. A choice of agreeable starters included pressed red mullet, basil and olive terrine, asparagus and butternut squash risotto with parmesan shavings, and duck terrine with celeriac and beetroot. Although a main of chicken and tiger prawns with pak choi was a tad heavy on the lime, the pepper sauce with ribeye steak was perfect in every way and the vegetables beautifully al dente. Servings were generous, so we passed on trifle with red fruit, champagne jelly, vanilla custard and sherry cream, but we vowed to try it when we returned in the not too distant future.

WITNEY

Fleece

11 Church Green, Witney, OX28 4AZ (01993 892270/www.peachpubs.com). **Open** 7.30am-11pm Mon-Sat; 8am-10.30pm Sun. **Breakfast served** 7.30-11am Mon-Sat; 8-10.30am Sun. **Lunch served** noon-2.30pm Mon-Sat; noon-3pm Sun. **Dinner served** 6.30-10pm Mon-Sat; 6.30-9.30pm Sun. **Main courses** £7.50-£14. **Credit** MC, V.

Modern, vibrant and stylish, the Fleece wouldn't be out of place in Fulham or Battersea. The trendy bar area was a bit loud, young and male for us (and it wasn't even a Friday), but once we'd successfully negotiated our way through the mêlée we found a much more congenial dining/restaurant area at the back. There is a deli board piled high with a vast array of cheese, charcuterie, antipasti and bread – ideal for those who don't want a huge meal. Big eaters are also well catered for, however, with a spread of dishes, ranging from salads and pizzas to the likes of Mediterranean vegetable and goat's cheese parcel, monkfish and prawn casserole with savoy cabbage, and plump duck breast with potato and carrot rösti in oriental juice. Portions were generous and the overall price very reasonable. A thoughtful and original place.

WOODSTOCK

Feathers Hotel

Market Street, Woodstock, OX20 1SX (01993 812291/www.feathers.co.uk). **Lunch served** 12.30-2.30pm, **dinner served** 6.30-9.30pm daily. **Set lunch** £17 2 courses, £21 3 courses; (Sun) £28 3 courses. **Set dinner** £28 2 courses, £35 3 courses. **Credit** AmEx, DC, MC, V.

The restaurant is a country mile ahead of what you'd normally associate with hotel food. Add elegant surroundings and exemplary service and it's the place to spoil yourself, though it's comfortably refined rather than prohibitively posh. You can eat in the bar, but for the full experience, book the restaurant. The kitchen produces British cooking by way of French haute cuisine, but no dish is heavy and overly rich. And you don't miss out if you don't go à la carte. The two well-priced set 'Market Menus' – one vegetarian – are just as lavish. They come with *amuse-bouches* such as oysters with horseradish and cucumber jelly and foie gras cream. Choice is limited to two starters and two mains on the set menus, but all the options are a treat, from the luxuriously creamy leek and potato soup to the meltingly gorgeous duo of lamb – a miniature shank and rump. To finish, an imaginative citrus soup with mint ice cream was refreshingly delicious. There is much to tempt on the wine list, with plenty to enjoy in the £20-£30 bracket.

WOOTTON

King's Head

Chapel Hill, Wootton, OX20 1DX (01993 811340/ www.kings-head.co.uk). **Lunch served** noon-2pm daily. **Dinner served** 7-8.30pm Mon-Sat. **Main courses** £9.95-£16.50. **Credit** MC, V.

Wootton is a serene Cotswold village and this old pub nestles in nicely, with its bare beams, wooden panelling and smell of wood smoke. Floral print sofas give it a touch of the Laura Ashley, but prissiness doesn't prevail. Outside is a small beer garden, where you can enjoy well-kept ales. Food is quite ambitious, with gastropub standards such as braised lamb shank being joined on the blackboard menu by the likes of vegetable mediterraneo (roast veg and goat's cheese with couscous: a hefty £14.95). There are also a few daily fish specials. Sichuan seared pigeon breast on shallots, with black bean and oyster sauce, was beautifully cooked and presented. To follow, whole plaice with coriander lime and butter sauce was small, but exquisitely fresh. We ended with an indecently luxurious sticky toffee pud. No slips with the food, then. Service can be prim (and children aren't welcome), but became friendly by dessert.

WYTHAM

Whyte Hart

Wytham, OX2 8QA (01865 244372). **Lunch served** noon-3pm daily. **Dinner served** 6.30-10pm Mon-Sat. **Main courses** £9.95-£18.50. **Credit** MC, V.

This pub-restaurant has a metropolitan air of efficiency and modernity that puts it firmly in gastropub territory. Despite being packed with families, you won't feel crowded and the smart furnishings stay the right side of trendy for a country pub. The small menu is not overly ambitious but makes an interesting collection of dishes. Starters, such as seared scallops, with crispy bacon, herb salad and tomato dressing, are all along main course proportions. Mains are pretty pricey but the quality ingredients justify the cost. Aberdeen Angus ribeye with coriander butter was tender and rich. Fish cake with hollandaise and herb salad had a generous ratio of salmon to spud. Strawberry tart with minted clotted cream had biscuity pastry and flavour-packed strawberries. Coffee is good and not overpriced, or there are fine teas and infusions. The only disappointment was the standard house wines, so aim a notch or two up the list.

Also in the area

Carluccio's Caffe Bicester Village, Bicester, Oxon OX26 6WD (01869 247651); **Livebait** 16 Turl Street, Oxford, OX1 3DH (01865 324930); **Loch Fyne** 20 Market Place, Henley-on-Thames, RG9 2AH (01491 845780); **Loch Fyne** 55 Walton Street, Jericho, Oxford, OX2 6AE (01865 292510); **Le Petit Blanc** 71-72 Walton Street, Oxford, OX2 6AG (01865 510999).

Wiltshire

BRADFORD-ON-AVON

Woolley Grange

Woolley Grange Hotel, Woolley Green, Bradford-on-Avon, BA15 1TX (01225 864705/www.woolley grange.com). **Lunch served** noon-2pm, **dinner served** 7-9.15pm daily. **Main courses** £19.50. **Set lunch** £15.50 2 courses, £20 3 courses. **Set dinner** £35.50 3 courses. **Credit** AmEx, DC, MC, V.

Just outside the former weaving town of Bradford-on-Avon, sits the picturesque Manor House Hotel. Set in several acres of grounds, complete with swimming pool, croquet lawn, football pitch, table tennis, swings, slides, bicycles, tricycles and crèche, you don't have to be a sleuth to deduce that this is a good place to bring children. Eat in the Orangery or one of the dining rooms and take your pick from the large menu. First courses include warm blue cheese soufflé, boneless quail with lemon and tarragon stuffing, and seared scallops with pea purée. For a main, try roasted guinea fowl with prunes and pancetta, a soft polenta of goat's cheese, roast vegetables and tapenade, or loin of Wiltshire Horn lamb with roast garlic purée and puy lentils. For a seasonal pudding, fruit salads, tarts and soufflés abound. If you bring the kids, there's an extensive Teenie Menu. Sourced from the highest quality ingredients, there's not a chicken nugget in sight and much of the fruit and veg is organically grown in the kitchen garden. There are also quiet nooks and cosy rooms where you can read the papers or chat, so don't let the child-friendly label put you off.

CASTLE COMBE

Bybrook

Manor House Hotel, Castle Combe, SN14 7HR (01249 782206/www.exclusivehotels.co.uk). **Lunch served** 12.30-2pm, **dinner served** 7-9.30pm daily. **Set lunch** £16.95 2 courses, £18.95 3 courses. **Set dinner** (Mon-Thur) £35 4 courses, (Fri-Sun) £45 4 courses, (Mon-Thur) £59 6-course tasting menu, (Fri-Sun) £65 6-course tasting menu. **Credit** AmEx, DC, MC, V.

Parts of the present building date back to the 14th century and it is surrounded by 365 acres of parkland that includes a Peter Alliss-designed golf course, Italian gardens and lawns that stretch down to the River Bybroo. The river lends its name to the baronial, L-shaped formal hotel dining room where the head chef has been in charge since 1991, offering high quality modern French food. Lunch could begin with a creamy velouté of white onions into which Sauternes has been incorporated to great effect, followed by crisp duck confit with braised cabbage and Madeira sauce, closing with rich chocolate tart with pistachio ice-cream. Dinner is more formal; four courses with fish and cheese as optional extras.

COLERNE

Lucknam Park Hotel ★

Lucknam Park, Colerne, SN14 8AZ (01225 742777/www.lucknampark.co.uk). **Lunch served** noon-3pm Mon-Sat; noon-2.30pm Sun. **Dinner served** 7-10pm daily. **Main courses** £18-£27. **Set dinner** £55 3 courses. **Credit** AmEx, DC, MC, V.

A fine Georgian manor house with a very grand dining room where chef Hywel Jones offers a short, very sophisticated menu where the liberal use of luxury ingredients is reflected in high prices. Among the starters are tian of Cornish crab with poached Cornish lobster, avocado salad and caviar vinaigrette, and his unmissable signature dish: roast diver scallops with fricassée of snails and ceps with turnip purée and creamed parsley. Among the main courses are loin of venison with beetroot tatin, crushed sweet potatoes, Alsace bacon and sloe gin sauce; and pan-fried turbot with provençal vegetables and baby fennel. For dessert, another signature dish: hot chocolate fondant with white chocolate cigarettes and whisky ice-cream, is irresistible. There's a good vegetarian menu too.

CORSLEY

Cross Keys

Lye's Green, Corsley, BA12 7PB (01373 832406). **Lunch served** noon-2.15pm Mon-Sat; noon-2.30pm Sun. **Dinner served** 7-9.30pm Mon-Sat; 7.15-9pm Sun. **Main courses** £8.25-£19. **Credit** MC, V.

The hamlet of Lye's Green stands midway between Frome and Warminster. Fraser Carruth and Wayne Carnegie moved here in September 2003 and offer their distinctive good food in this 400-year-old flint and brick pub. Bar snacks feature baguettes with a choice of fillings including rare roast beef with horseradish, own-smoked Wiltshire ham with apple chutney and oak-smoked chicken with avocado mayonnaise. In addition, there are fantastic burgers flavoured with garlic and thyme, and topped with stilton. More substantial, and equally excellent dishes are available either in the Garden Room restaurant, or in the no-smoking Front Room, both of which feature huge inglenooks.

CRUDWELL

Old Rectory

Crudwell, SN16 9EP (01666 577194/www.oldrectory crudwell.co.uk). **Lunch served** noon-2pm daily. **Dinner served** 7-9pm Mon-Thur, Sun; 7-9.30pm Fri, Sat. **Set lunch** (Sun) £13.95 2 courses, £16.95 3 courses. **Main courses** £12.50-£18.95. **Credit** MC, V.

Dating back to the 16th century, the Old Rectory is an elegant country house hotel. It's oak panelled dining room and conservatory overlook a large Victorian walled garden and ornamental pond, and the food suits the setting perfectly. The style of cooking is classically based with just the right modern notes. For dinner there's ravioli of goat's cheese with herb salad and sun-blushed tomato dressing; braised beef with glazed fondant potato, a miniature cottage pie and crispy pancetta; and baked white chocolate cheesecake with dark chocolate ice-cream. For a small supplement to the fixed-price menu, there's an excellent selection of about seven prime British cheeses. Friendly service takes place in impeccable surroundings.

DEVIZES

The Healthy Life

4 Little Brittox, Devizes, SN10 1AR (01380 725558/ www.thehealthylife.co.uk). Café **Meals served** 10am-4pm Mon-Sat. **Main courses** £3.95-£6. *Bistro (7 Little Brittox)* **Dinner served** 7-11pm Tue-Sat. **Set dinner** £14.95 2 courses, £19.95 3 courses. **Credit** AmEx, MC, V.

Peter Vaughan is an enthusiastic supporter of Wiltshire produce, and most of what he buys is organically grown, which he uses in both the all-day café and evening bistro (there's also a takeaway). The café is perfect for a light lunch of toasted pitta stuffed with warm falafel, freshly made houmous and mixed salad or a satisfying savoury crêpe filled with garlic mushrooms and cheese. In the continental bistro, the open kitchen allows diners to watch the action while enjoying well-made Mediterranean dishes such as bouillabaisse with garlic rye croutes, followed by grilled pork loin with parmesan and sage glaze, sautéed asparagus and crushed potatoes. Most dishes have vegetarian, vegan, dairy-free and wheat/gluten-free alternatives.

DONHEAD ST ANDREW

Forester

Lower Street, Donhead St Andrew, SP7 9EE (01747 828038). **Lunch served** noon-2pm daily. **Dinner served** 7-9.30pm Mon-Sat; 7-9pm Sun. **Main courses** £9.95-£15.50. **Credit** MC, V.

Alas no longer a pub for locals, but nevertheless an excellent place to eat. The low-key but professional hosts are attentive and offer a large selection of starters, main courses and puddings which are chalked up on a blackboard by the log fire. Starters include a delicious chicken's liver and foie gras parfait with onion marmalade or a tian of poached salmon and crab, while pan-roasted cod with a chilli and orange crust, or venison and red wine sausages served with onion gravy are among the main courses. As well as a choice of beers, five white and red wines are available by the glass (£2.95). You would be wise to book – and to look at a map before you set off, for this is in uncharted territory.

EASTON GREY

The Dining Room & Le Mazot at Whatley Manor ★

Easton Grey, SN16 0RB (01666 822888/ www.whatleymanor.com). Le Mazot **Lunch served** noon-2pm, **dinner served** 7-10pm daily. **Main courses** £11.50-£14.50. **Set lunch** £16.50 2 courses, £20.50 3 courses. *The Dining Room* **Dinner served** 7-10pm Wed-Sun. **Set dinner** £60 3 courses, £75 7-course tasting menu. **Credit** AmEx, DC, MC, V.

The combination of chef Martin Burge, formerly at John Burton-Race at the Landmark Hotel, London, and a stunning location, one of the county's newest and most exclusive hotels, sets very high standards. Diners have the choice of the formal Dining Room where reservations are required for non-residents, or the appealing Le Mazot, a brasserie styled on an original Swiss chalet (the hotel's owners are Swiss). Burge offers menus that are bang up to date but with a sound classical basis. In the brasserie, ballotine of duck pressed between foie gras came with honey pickled vegetables, while sea bream had boulangère potatoes, salt-water prawns and chicken jus flavoured with parsley and tomato. For dessert: a sensational orange crêpe soufflé with orange and Grand Marnier sauce.

FONTHILL GIFFORD

Beckford Arms

Fonthill Gifford, SP3 6PX (01747 870385). **Lunch served** noon-2pm, **dinner served** 7-9pm daily. **Main courses** £8.90-£15.95. **Credit** MC, V.

This handsome pub is justly popular with the local smart set. Log fires, a basking, aristocratic cat and mismatched antique collectibles create the shabby-chic effect so loved by style magazines, while interesting-looking people chat in dimly lit corners or dine in the chandeliered garden room. The food is bold and imaginative, but the service is so sharp that you can sometimes feel a little rushed. Duck and chorizo rillette, halibut with Bloody Mary sauce, and duck breast with chunks of rhubarb and ginger might feature, and the chef's interpretation will be entirely his own. Puddings include pecan pie and apple and cherry crumble; all delicious. Wines start at £14.50; there is a wide selection of other drinks.

GREAT HINTON

Linnet

Great Hinton, BA14 6BU (01380 870354). **Lunch served** noon-2pm Tue-Sun. **Dinner served** 6.30-9.30pm Tue-Sat; 7-9pm Sun. **Main courses** £10.95-£16.50. **Set lunch** £10.75 2 courses, £13.25 3 courses. **Credit** AmEx, MC, V.

The quiet village of Great Hinton, in the wilds of Wiltshire just a few miles from Bath, is home to this gem of a pub/restaurant. Small and understated, with a rather bijoux bar area and only about 12 tables, the Linnet offers a daily-changing lunch

The Rosemary. *See p177.*

Central

menu, a seasonal evening menu and a hugely popular Sunday lunch menu. Service is friendly and efficient. Starting with prawn sushi with avocado salsa, and peppered ham, leek and mango terrine, we moved on to confit of breast of chicken with creamy roasted tomato, basil mash and melting pesto butter, and a really exceptional steamed salmon with lemon and baby sweetcorn risotto and prawn sauce. Grilled asparagus, butternut squash, globe artichokes and olive pancake also caught the eye. Puddings included a 'fruit of the day', in our case banana, which featured in a trio of cheesecake, ice-cream and mousse. Well worth a visit.

HINDON

Angel Inn

Angel Lane, Hindon, SP3 6BJ (01747 820696/ www.theangelathindon.co.uk). **Lunch served** noon-2.30pm, **dinner served** 7-9.30pm Mon-Sat. **Meals served** noon-5pm Sun. **Main courses** £9.95-£14. **Credit** MC, V.

Having been voted among the top 50 gastropubs by the *Independent* in early 2004, the Angel is now under new management, although the chef remains the same. Very few people were there on a gloriously warm evening in June so it felt as though the place is still finding its feet despite the favourable publicity. A disappointing starter of own-smoked duck breast with melted goat's cheese was quickly forgotten when dressed crab salad with Jersey Royal potatoes and watercress mayonnaise appeared. It was simply summer on a plate and more than made up for anything that had gone before. Meals are served in the pleasingly uncluttered modern interior or, when weather allows, an ample outside dining area, and waiting staff are friendly and attentive.

HOLT

Tollgate Inn

Ham Green, Holt, BA14 6PX (01225 782326/ www.tollgateholt.co.uk). **Lunch served** noon-2pm Tue-Sun. **Dinner served** 7-9pm Tue-Sat. **Main courses** £10.50-£16.50. **Set lunch** £9.95 2 courses, £11.95 3 courses. **Credit** MC, V.

An award-winning pub on the B3107 between Melksham and Bradford-on-Avon. The licensees are both highly experienced, coming from hotel backgrounds, and this shows in the sophisticated food. Lunchtime sees a value-for-money set meal with delicious spiced tomato, aubergine and apricot soup followed by moreish salmon and haddock fish cakes with sweet and sour vinaigrette. In the evening the colourful restaurant is the setting for an imaginative selection of dishes ranging from Japanese-style belly pork with wasabi, to roast rack of Wiltshire lamb on a bed of fennel, spring onions and courgettes with rosemary and redcurrant sauce.

LACOCK

At the Sign of the Angel

6 Church Street, Lacock, SN15 2LB (01249 730230/ www.lacock.co.uk). **Lunch served** 12.30-2pm Tue-Sat; 1-2pm Sun. **Dinner served** 7-9pm daily. **Main courses** £8.95-£16.25. **Credit** AmEx, DC, MC, V.

This picturesque 15th-century wool merchant's house is in an equally pretty and unspoilt National Trust village. Ancient, half-timbered and gabled on the outside; welcoming log fires, oak panelling, low beams and creaking floor boards on the inside. There is an attempt to keep up with the times by offering Mediterranean dishes, but as if to complement the very traditional setting, the best of the food in the cosy dining rooms are the straightforward dishes – pork with apple sauce or lamb with lemon and mint stuffing. Other notable items are rabbit casserole with mash, fillet of beef, and treacle tart with clotted cream.

LITTLE BEDWYN

Harrow

Little Bedwyn, SN8 3JP (01672 870871/www.harrow inn.co.uk). **Lunch served** noon-2pm Wed-Sun. **Dinner served** 7-9pm Wed-Sat. **Main courses** £18-£24. **Set meal** £20 3 courses, £40 6-course tasting menu (£60 incl wine). **Credit** MC, V.

In a pretty village between Hungerford and Marlborough, this traditional inn has been thoroughly revamped and is now devoted to serving fine food and wine – with prices to match. Meat is free range, and fish is line caught. Every dish comes with a recommended wine and, when we were there, there was wine tasting and a free glass of wine with our meal. The menu favours fish, although there's 28-day hung Aberdeen Angus, Welsh lamb or roast milk-fed Anjou squab. Otherwise, pick from yellow fin tuna, baby red mullet, Torbay crab or king scallops for starters, with turbot, Cornish lobster, sea bass, or Torbay sole fillets as mains. Excellent dishes to match the sophisticated wine cellar.

MARTEN

Windmill

Salisbury Road, Marten, SN8 3SH (01264 731372). **Lunch served** noon-2pm Tue-Sun. **Dinner served** 7-9pm Tue-Thur; 7-9.30pm Fri, Sat. **Main courses** £15.50-£20. **Set dinner** (Tue-Thur) £19.95 2 courses. **Credit** MC, V.

Set in the heart of the Wiltshire countryside, with only the eponymous windmill and rolling hills for company, this recently refurbished restaurant-bar will take your breath away. Serious about service and serious about food, the patrons pride themselves on using only organic, home-produced and/or locally sourced ingredients. A full car park on a midweek evening spoke volumes. After an *amuse-gueule*, then a choice of three types of own-made bread, came seasonal asparagus salad with fine beans, tomato tartare and crispy polenta. This was followed by Gressingham duck in a foie gras sauce, and a braised shoulder and saddle of lamb with crushed rosemary potatoes – all expertly cooked and artfully presented. A delicious-sounding open ravioli of organic mushrooms and poached fillet of turbot were the only non-meat options. Puddings, each with a suggested wine to accompany it, included the Windmill banana split and a trio of crèmes brûlées.

ROWDE

George & Dragon

High Street, Rowde, SN10 2PN (01380 723053). **Lunch served** noon-2pm, **dinner served** 7-9pm Tue-Sat. **Main courses** £8.50-£19. **Set lunch** £11 2 courses, £13.50 3 courses. **Credit** MC, V.

The rather dull exterior belies a wonderful pub specialising in seafood from Cornwall. The interior has dark wood panelling and in the bar the huge stone inglenook creates a pleasant focal point. The main menu, which includes dishes like provençal fish soup with rouille, gruyère and garlic crouton, and baked cheese soufflé, plays second fiddle to a blackboard menu of daily-changing fish: roast razor clams with garlic and olive oil; fillet of turbot with hollandaise; pan-fried monkfish with couscous salad and tzatziki; Thai curry of hake, salmon and squid. For those preferring simpler food, there's whole grilled Dover or lemon sole. Among lovely puds are chocolate St-Émilion, and brown sugar meringues with Jersey cream.

SALISBURY

Bernières Tea Room

The Wardrobe, 58 Cathedral Close, Salisbury, SP1 2EX (01722 413666/www.thewardrobe.org.uk). **Meals served** 10am-5pm, **lunch served** noon-2pm daily. **Main courses** £6.75. **No credit cards**.

This place is named after Bernières-sur-Mer, a small Normandy coastal village on Juno beach, where the 5th Royal Berkshire Regiment landed on D-Day. The regiment later amalgamated with the Wiltshire Regiment. Now, a converted coach house in the Wardrobe Regimental Museum serves satisfying mid-morning and lunchtime bites. The food's homely and traditional; try buck rarebit muffin, smoked haddock tart with spicy tomato dressing, roast leg of English lamb with mint sauce, roast herb-crusted pork with apple sauce, cottage pie with cheesy parsnip topping or a memorable ham off-the-bone with fresh parsley sauce. Hazelnut meringue with lemon sauce and fresh raspberries, and bread and butter pudding with whisky and marmalade are two of the terrifically good sweets.

Haunch of Venison

1-5 Minster Street, Salisbury, SP1 1TB (01722 322024). **Lunch served** noon-2.30pm Mon-Sat. **Dinner served** 6-9.30pm Mon-Wed; 6-10pm Thur-Sat; 6-9.30pm Sun. **Main courses** £5.50-£12.50. **Set meal** (noon-1pm, 6-7pm) £5 1 course, £9.90 3 courses. **Credit** MC, V.

The city-centre pub dates back to 1320, but recently it's been smartened up and now has a more contemporary decor, with oak tables, leather seating and linen napkins. Complementing all this newness is some imaginative, well-prepared food that's fashionably Mediterranean: char-grilled garlic sausage with balsamic roast red onions and parmesan salad; wild mushroom millefeuille with roast pepper sauce; turbot, langoustine and chorizo broth with pearl barley and celeriac. Guinea fowl, veal and ham pudding with mash and mushroom velouté was excellent. There's a good choice of wines.

STANTON FITZWARREN

The Rosemary

Stanton House Hotel, The Avenue, Stanton Fitzwarren, SN6 7SD (01793 861777/www.stantonhouse.co.uk). **Lunch served** noon-2pm daily. **Dinner served** 6-10pm Mon-Sat; 6-9.30pm Sun. **Main courses** £5-£24. **Set lunch** £9.60 3 courses. **Set dinner** £17.50 3 courses. **Credit** AmEx, MC, V.

A Japanese restaurant is not quite what you would expect to find in a country house hotel in a sleepy village outside Swindon. But with a huge Honda factory just outside the village, there's plenty of Japanese custom to rely upon (as well as countless Hondas in the car park). Little effort seems to have been put into the decor – it's a rectangular open-plan room, dedicated to serving a huge choice of dishes. It's all here – miso soup, sushi, sashimi and udon (noodles) aplenty, not to mention the various methods of presenting meats – try a very successful pork katsu and a teriyaki chicken, both served in ample quantities. While you don't quite feel you've entered the home of another culture, you'll struggle to find such fine Japanese cuisine outside the capital (London, that is, not Tokyo).

TEFFONT EVIAS

Howard's House ★

Teffont Evias, SP3 5RJ (01722 716392/www.howardshousehotel.co.uk). **Lunch served** 12.30-2pm Tue-Thur, Sat, Sun. **Dinner served** 7.30-9pm daily. **Main courses** £13.95-£23.95. **Set lunch** £18.50 2 courses, £22.50 3 courses. **Set dinner** £23.95 3 courses. **Credit** AmEx, MC, V.

In an idyllic setting, this Jacobean stone farmhouse is now a charming hotel with exemplary standards of comfort. The smart dining room opens on to a terrace and very English garden. While the surroundings may be delightfully cushioned by the past, the food is very up to date. An unusual starter of salad of Brixham fish comes with chips and a brown shrimp dressing, while for a main course braised belly and roasted fillet of Wiltshire pork has accompaniments of mustard mash and apple and calvados sauce. Cherry and almond pithiviers with kirsch ice-cream makes a fitting finale.

WARMINSTER

Mulberry

Bishopstrow House, Warminster, BA12 9HH (01985 212312/www.bishopstrow.co.uk). **Lunch served** 12.15-2pm, **dinner served** 7.30-9pm daily. **Main courses** £6.50-£17. **Set dinner** £38 3 courses incl coffee. **Credit** AmEx, DC, MC, V.

The grand late-Georgian house stands in 28 acres of grounds about a mile outside the town centre. New owners are upgrading the property, and have also brought in a new head chef who has a modern English style of cooking with Mediterranean influences. There are seared scallops and tiger prawns with celeriac rémoulade and parma ham, and Caesar salad with grilled asparagus, avocado and quails' eggs to begin; honey roast duck, bok choi, noodles and oriental sauce, and char-grilled ribeye steak with fondant potato, ceps and salsa verde for mains. Lunch is a more relaxed affair, with superior snacks served in the lounge.

WHITLEY

Pear Tree

Top Lane, Whitley, SN12 8QX (01225 709131). **Lunch served** noon-2pm Mon-Sat; noon-2.30pm Sun. **Dinner served** 6.30-9.30pm Mon-Thur, Sun; 6.30-10pm Fri, Sat. **Main courses** £8.50-£19.50. **Set lunch** (Mon-Sat) £12.50 2 courses, £15 3 courses; (Sun) £13.50 2 courses, £16.50 3 courses. **Credit** MC, V.

Outward appearances are those of an old mellow stone farmhouse and the pub interior has a charming rusticity too. The rear dining area is an oak beamed barn conversion with conservatory doors that open on to a patio and lovely lawned garden. The menu is the same in both pub and restaurant. The set lunch includes very moreish sandwiches such as seared beef fillet with horseradish, red chard and crispy onion rings. More elaborate choices might be Cornish crab and own-cured salmon salad with rocket, beetroot relish, toast and sour cream followed by roast free range chicken breast with asparagus, grilled artichokes and potato salad with capers and olives. Desserts – fresh strawberry trifle with basil syrup and strawberry daiquiri sorbet, say – come with matching wine recommendations, or there are quality British cheeses (with an optional glass of port).

Also in the area

Prezzo 52 High Street, Salisbury, SP1 2PF (01722 341333).

East Anglia

East Anglia

North Sea
Hemsby Hole
Caister-on-Sea
Great Yarmouth
Gorleston on Sea
Lowestoft
Kessingland
Southwold
Walberswick
Dunwich
Beccles
Halesworth
Bramfield
St Peter South Elmham
Bungay
Earsham
Brundall
Hoveton
North Walsham
Overstrand
Cromer
Sheringham
Sprowston
NORWICH
Stoke Holy Cross
Harleston
Eye
Diss
Aylsham
Blicking
Itteringham
Drayton
Hellesdon
Wymondham
Attleborough
Cley-next-the-Sea
Blakeney
Holt
Blakeney Point
Morston
Swanton Morley
NORFOLK
East Dereham
Stanton
Thetford
Holkham Bay
Wells-next-the-Sea
Warham All Saints
Holkham
South Creake
Fakenham
Helhoughton
Swaffham
Brancaster Bay
Brancaster Staithe
Burnham Market
Thornham
Snettisham
Dersingham
Hunstanton
Heacham
Methwold
Brandon
Lakenheath
Mildenhall
Downham Market
Southery
Isleham
Littleport
Soham
Burwell
The Wash
King's Lynn
Skegness
Outwell
Wisbech
Ely
Manea
March
Chatteris
Sutton
Sutton Gault
Haddenham
Willingham
Cottenham
Doddington
Boston
Holbeach
LINCOLNSHIRE
Spalding
Whittlesey
Peterborough
Eye
CAMBRIDGESHIRE
Ramsey
Warboys
St Ives
Hemingford Grey
Godmanchester
Huntingdon
Little Stukeley
Brampton
Glinton
Orton Waterville
Stilton
Sawtry
Castor
Bourne
Sleaford
Stamford
Oundle
Keyston
Thrapston
Raunds

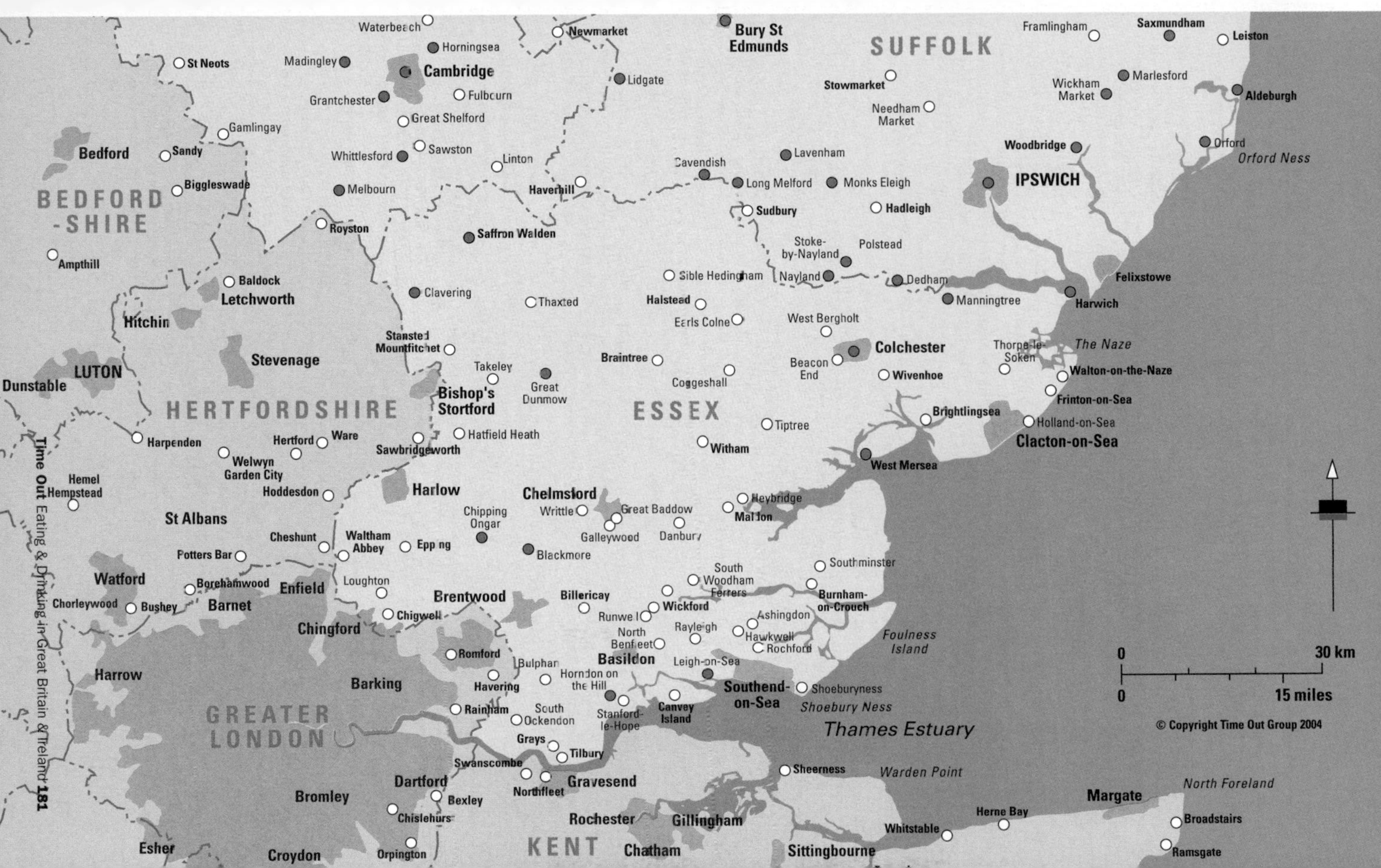

SUFFOLK
BEDFORD-SHIRE
HERTFORDSHIRE
ESSEX
GREATER LONDON
KENT
Waterbeach
Newmarket
Bury St Edmunds
Framlingham
Saxmundham
Leiston
St Neots
Horningsea
Madingley
Cambridge
Lidgate
Stowmarket
Marlesford
Wickham Market
Aldeburgh
Grantchester
Fulbourn
Needham Market
Gamlingay
Great Shelford
Bedford
Sandy
Whittlesford
Sawston
Linton
Cavendish
Lavenham
Woodbridge
Orford
Orford Ness
Biggleswade
Melbourn
Haverhill
Long Melford
Monks Eleigh
IPSWICH
Sudbury
Hadleigh
Royston
Saffron Walden
Ampthill
Stoke-by-Nayland
Polstead
Baldock
Letchworth
Clavering
Thaxted
Sible Hedingham
Nayland
Dedham
Felixstowe
Halstead
Manningtree
Harwich
Hitchin
Earls Colne
West Bergholt
Stansted Mountfitchet
Colchester
Thorpe-le-Soken
The Naze
Stevenage
Takeley
Braintree
Beacon End
LUTON
Great Dunmow
Coggeshall
Wivenhoe
Walton-on-the-Naze
Dunstable
Bishop's Stortford
Frinton-on-Sea
Brightlingsea
Holland-on-Sea
Tiptree
Harpenden
Hertford
Ware
Hatfield Heath
Clacton-on-Sea
Witham
Sawbridgeworth
Welwyn Garden City
West Mersea
Hemel Hempstead
Hoddesdon
Harlow
Chelmsford
Heybridge
Maldon
Chipping Ongar
Writtle
Great Baddow
St Albans
Cheshunt
Waltham Abbey
Galleywood
Danbury
Epping
Blackmore
Southminster
Potters Bar
South Woodham Ferrers
Watford
Borehamwood
Enfield
Loughton
Brentwood
Billericay
Burnham-on-Crouch
Chorleywood
Bushey
Barnet
Chigwell
Wickford
Runwell
Ashingdon
Chingford
North Benfleet
Rayleigh
Hawkwell
Foulness Island
Rochford
Romford
Basildon
Bulphan
Leigh-on-Sea
Harrow
Horndon on the Hill
Barking
Havering
Southend-on-Sea
Shoeburyness
Canvey Island
Shoebury Ness
Rainham
South Ockendon
Stanford-le-Hope
Thames Estuary
Grays
Tilbury
Swanscombe
Sheerness
Warden Point
Dartford
Gravesend
North Foreland
Northfleet
Margate
Bromley
Bexley
Rochester
Gillingham
Herne Bay
Broadstairs
Chislehurst
Whitstable
Esher
Croydon
Orpington
Chatham
Sittingbourne
Ramsgate
0
30 km
0
15 miles

Cambridgeshire

CAMBRIDGE

Graffiti

Hotel Felix, White House Lane, Huntingdon Road, Cambridge, CB3 0LX (01223 277977/www.hotelfelix.co.uk). **Lunch served** noon-2pm daily. **Dinner served** 6.30-10pm Mon-Thur; 6.30-10.30pm Fri-Sat; 6.30-9.30pm Sun. **Main courses** £11.95-£23.95. **Credit** AmEx, DC, MC, V.

The terrace here is beautiful, but inside the brown-on-brown decor is over-stylised, encouraging a hush even around the bar area. Chef Stuart Conibear learned his trade in London institutions the Ivy and the Dorchester; his Mediterranean menu has some British touches. Meat boasts its local origins wherever possible (braised belly of Denham Estate pork, pot-roasted haunch of Norfolk wild boar). The combinations of tastes and textures strive for surprises, but presentation is fussy. Witness salmon in a paper parcel – perfectly steam-poached, but what's the paper doily doing under the potatoes, all the better to get soggy with salad dressing? Bread is own-made and deliciously yeasty, although you do pay extra for the privilege. With puddings that look like American skyscrapers, there's a sense that Graffiti is trying too hard.

Midsummer House

Midsummer Common, Cambridge, CB4 1HA (01223 369299/www.midsummerhouse.co.uk). **Lunch served** noon-2pm, **dinner served** 7-10pm Tue-Sat. **Set lunch** £20 2 courses, £26 3 courses. **Set dinner** £48.50 3 courses, £60 8 courses. **Credit** AmEx, MC, V.

Occupying an enviable riverside spot with high-profile French food that rises to the occasion, Midsummer House is the ideal place for pushing the punt out. Service may be too fussy for some; expect plenty of coat-holding, chair-tucking and glass-filling, plus a lengthy explanation of each dish. But these factors are peripheral to the perfectly presented, painstakingly prepared food. Culinary extras – *amuse-bouches* such as champagne froth with pink grapefruit, plus own-made chocolates on departure – punctuate the meal. Our sole gripe is the atmosphere, or rather the lack of it; the plummy clientele on our latest visit spoke in hushed tones and rarely broke a smile. Still, on food alone this is Cambridge's finest restaurant. Prices are hard to swallow – a bottle of wine rarely slips through under £50 – but you're unlikely to leave disappointed.

Peking

21 Burleigh Street, Cambridge, CB1 1DG (01223 354755). **Dinner served** 6-10.30pm daily. **Main courses** £7-£14. **Set meals** £17-£25 per person (min 2 people). **No credit cards**.

In a mundane pedestrianised shopping street, the unassuming Peking fails to stand out. Even the long, narrow room with pine-clad walls, black banquettes and white cloth-clad tables is the very definition of basic. But don't be deterred. This is one of the best places in East Anglia for authentic Chinese cooking, and though prices might seem high (up to £14 for main courses), portions are more than generous. The high cooking standards came through in a meal that ranged from fresh, plump steamed scallops and spot-on crabmeat and beancurd, to delicate lamb and leeks with a subtle hit of chilli, and pork with aubergine in hot bean sauce. Quality food, served very pleasantly.

Restaurant 22

22 Chesterton Road, Cambridge, CB4 3AX (01223 351880/www.restaurant22.co.uk). **Lunch served** (Dec only) from noon. **Dinner served** 7-9.45pm Tue-Sat. **Set lunch** £17.95 3 courses. **Set dinner** £24.50 3 courses. **Credit** AmEx, DC, MC, V.

A white Victorian terraced house, set beside a parade of shops where the ring road becomes aggressively one-way, 22 is in a lousy location and parking is a nightmare. But once inside, the completely disarming, charmingly quirky house will soothe frazzled nerves with unpretentious service, and the modern food is a delight. It's a justifiably popular place, noted for value and a surprising degree of variety within the confines of a set menu: irresistible warm polenta and goat's cheese with olive tapenade and pecorino cream, then roast peppered monkfish with braised fennel and confit tomatoes. To finish, luscious baked lemon cheesecake.

Venue on the Roof

Cambridge Arts Theatre, 4th floor, 6 St Edward's Passage, Cambridge, CB2 3PJ (01223 367333/www.venuerestaurant.com). **Lunch served** noon-3pm, **dinner served** 5.30-11pm Mon-Sat. **Main courses** £10-£17. **Set lunch/pre theatre menu** £12.95 2 courses. **Credit** AmEx, MC, V.

Having moved from the first to the fourth floor of the Arts Theatre, this enjoyable restaurant nestles among the roofs between Market Square and King's College. The crisp decor of white walls, a wooden floor and brightly coloured chairs feels formulaic, but the relaxed service and abundance of natural light brings warmth to the experience. The regularly changing menu draws on broad international influences to offer ambitious dishes. A grilled cinnamon quail starter with roast carrot, ginger and pomegranate was beautifully presented but strangely dull. For mains, traditional dishes, such as pan-seared calf's liver and roast chump of English lamb, compete with the more eclectic fillet of beef

Graffiti. See p182.

with beetroot pesto, and wild monkfish with sautéed squid. Main ingredients were consistently superb, but seasoning and sauces did fail to deliver on occasion; herb risotto cake was one dimensional.

Volunteer

Trumpington Road, Cambridge, CB2 2EX (01223 841675). **Lunch served** noon 2pm daily. **Dinner served** 7-9pm Mon-Sat. **Main courses** £13-£18. **Credit** MC, V.

This converted roadside pub has a lot more to offer than outward appearance suggests. The open plan retains the informality of the building's former incarnation while eschewing the standard pub look. Instead the impression is of relaxed simplicity; cream walls are hung with abstracts. Food also comes with no unnecessary fuss or trimmings; just good materials lightly and confidently handled. It's assured cooking turning out a light leek and gruyère tart with a vivid roast red pepper dressing, followed by roast loin of Suffolk venison on a powerfully flavoured pancetta and sweet peppercorn sauce with creamed savoy cabbage. The no-smoking policy is another plus.

GRANTCHESTER

Red Lion

33 High Street, Grantchester, CB3 9NF (01223 840121). **Lunch served** noon-2.30pm, **dinner served** 6-9.30pm Mon-Thur. **Meals served** noon-9.30pm Fri, Sat; noon-8.30pm Sun. **Main courses** £7.25-£15.25. **Credit** AmEx, DC, MC, V.

A sprawling thatched pub-restaurant, with a glorious walk on the doorstep (beside the water meadows of the River Cam) and a menu that offers a useful assortment of popular snacks and a long list of more substantial offerings. From a bar menu listing pub standards, sirloin steak was not the best quality and a tad overcooked. But there's more of interest on the specials board: witness a huge helping of well-flavoured game casserole, and a decent if slightly bland Richmond venison wellington with port sauce. Offering less choice might tighten things up in the kitchen. Top marks, however, for atmosphere and service.

HEMINGFORD GREY

The Cock

47 High Street, Hemingford Grey, PE28 9BJ (01480 463609/www.cambscuisine.com). **Lunch served** noon-2.30pm daily. **Dinner served** 7-9.30pm Mon-Sat; 6.30-8.30pm Sun. **Main courses** £9.95-£16.95. **Credit** MC, V.

From the outside the Cock looks like a village local and that feeling is enforced by traditional benches and settles, low-beamed ceiling, log-burning stove and a strong line in real ale from East Anglian brewers like Adnams Bitter and Woodfordes Wherry. But the place has a dual role: while the bar remains unreformed, the restaurant next door sports a contemporary look of soft butter-coloured walls and polished wood floor that's matched by a fashionably breezy menu. Dishes can range from pubby (own-made Gloucester Old Spot sausages with spring onion mash and mustard sauce) to modish (monkfish steak with apple and thyme purée and smoked cheddar crisp). It's this latter style that has been followed at the Crown & Punchbowl, the sister establishment at Horningsea (High Street, 01223 860643), which is run as a restaurant-with-rooms.

HUNTINGDON

Old Bridge Hotel

1 High Street, Huntingdon, PE29 3TQ (01480 458410/www.huntsbridge.com). The Terrace **Lunch served** noon-2pm Mon-Sat; noon-2.30pm Sun. **Dinner served** 7-10pm Mon-Thur; 6.30-10pm Fri, Sat; 7-9.30pm Sun. **Main courses** £6-£20. **Set meal** (noon-2pm, 7-7.30pm Mon-Sat) £12 2 courses, £15.75 3 courses. *Dining Room* **Lunch served** noon-2.30pm Sun. **Dinner served** 7-10pm Wed-Sat. **Set dinner** £36 3 courses. **Credit** MC, V.

With all the style points of a boutique hotel, minus the pretension, the Old Bridge relies almost exclusively on local custom, whether it's tea in the lounge, a business deal in the lush Terrace restaurant with its striking Julia Rushbury murals, or a pint in the posh pubby bar. This is the flagship of the Huntsbridge Group and it deals in high standards, whether food, wine or service. A 'bargain lunch' of chicken liver parfait with red onion marmalade, grilled sardines with char-grilled new potatoes, wok-fried greens, coriander and lemon, then pineapple and coconut bakewell tart was very good value indeed, and the savvy wine list combines excellent quality with fair pricing.

MADINGLEY

Three Horseshoes ★

High Street, Madingley, CB3 8AB (01954 210221/ www.huntsbridge.co.uk). **Lunch served** noon-2pm Mon-Sat; noon-2.30pm Sun. **Dinner served** 6.30-9.30pm Mon-Sat. **Main courses** £9.50-£23. **Credit** MC, V.

A typically quaint thatched village pub that has upgraded itself to restaurant status. The soft-toned interior features strong contemporary details, which match the Italian-influenced, daily-changing menus perfectly. Eat casually in the bar, or book a linen-clad table in the restaurant or garden conservatory for a more formally paced meal that includes the best Portland crab salad in the world (with grilled baby leeks, dandelion, radicchio and saffron aïoli). And char-grilled Cumbrian rump steak with grilled Italian vegetable salad was a winner. Lovely too, also part of the Huntsbridge group, and run along the same lines, is the Pheasant (Keyston, 01832 710241).

MELBOURN

Pink Geranium

Station Road, Melbourn, SG8 6DX (01763 260215/ www.pinkgeranium.co.uk). **Lunch served** noon-2.30pm Tue-Sun. **Dinner served** 7-9.30pm Tue-Sat. **Main courses** £17.50-£26.50. **Set lunch** £16.50 2 courses, £21.50 3 courses. **Set dinner** £21.50 2 courses, £27.50 3 courses. **Credit** AmEx, DC, MC, V.

It's sugary pink, thatched and plays the 'olde' English look for all its worth: cottage garden, low beams, wonky wooden floors, open fires and swathes of chintz. Fortunately, the kitchen is firmly rooted in the present day, putting its own twist on classic French techniques and bright Mediterranean ideas. An intense wild mushroom soup with herb crème fraîche; plump, nutty seared scallops served with rösti potatoes, rich creamed mouli, baby carrots and beurre rouge; and delicate orange panna cotta with winter fruit compote lifted Sunday lunch out of the ordinary.

Sheene Mill

Station Road, Melbourn, SG8 6DX (01763 261393/ www.sheenemill.co.uk). **Lunch served** noon-2.30pm daily. **Dinner served** 7-10.30pm Mon-Sat. **Main courses** £13.50-£26. **Set lunch** (Sun) £25 3 courses. **Credit** AmEx, MC, V.

A pristinely restored white-clapboard mill, run as a restaurant-with-rooms. It's hard to pigeonhole the style. There's quite a buzz throughout, with a cosmopolitan feel to the smart conservatory bar and striking slate-floored restaurant, and a world-beat impulse behind the menu, especially in mains like tempura of organic salmon, soft noodle stir-fry and sweet chilli dressing. Local, organic ingredients are used, and care is taken over everything, from a delicious tian of white Cromer crabmeat to own-made Chelsea bun with spiced syrup and orange ice-cream.

SUTTON GAULT

Anchor Inn

Bury Lane, Sutton Gault, CB6 2BD (01353 778537/ www.anchor-inn-restaurant.co.uk). **Lunch served** noon-2pm daily. **Dinner served** 7-9pm Sun-Fri; 6.30-9.30pm Sat. **Main courses** £11.50-£16.50. **Set lunch** (Sun) £19.95 3 courses. **Credit** AmEx, MC, V.

The little white-painted cottage is set below a bridge and next to a raised dyke protecting it from the New Bedford River; above hangs the huge Fenland sky. Visit on a sharp-edged winter's day and you'll appreciate the blazing fires in the comfortable beamed bar. The kitchen gives due deference to small local suppliers, yet the daily changing menu looks beyond the back yard for inspiration, giving the food a cosmopolitan flavour. Smoked salmon risotto cake, fennel fondue and dill beurre blanc; and pan-fried fillet of pork, green peppercorn and calvados sauce, with caramelised apple were both honest and unfussy dishes underpinned by skill.

WHITTLESFORD

Tickell Arms

North Road, Whittlesford, CB2 4NZ (01223 833128). **Lunch served** noon-2pm Tue-Sun. **Dinner served** 7-9pm Tue-Sat. **Set lunch** £14.50 2 courses, £19.50 3 courses. **Set dinner** £27.50 2 courses, £34.50 3 courses. **Credit** AmEx, MC, V.

The fortunes of the Tickell have been mixed since the eccentric Kim Tickell died, but the standard of cooking is currently steady under chef Spencer Patrick. Things started well with a complimentary glass of champagne, soon followed with a meaty velouté of wild mushroom with white truffle oil. Favourite dish was tortellino of Scottish lobster with a perfectly seared scallop in an oriental beurre. Lean roast Barbary duck came atop creamy cabbage with a rich port jus. But an extensive wine list only had a few bottles under £25 and service was indifferent.

Also in the area

Chez Gérard 27-28 Bridge Street, Cambridge, CB2 1UJ (01223 448620); **Loch Fyne** The Little Rose, 37 Trumpington Street, Cambridge, CB2 1QY (01223 362433); **Loch Fyne** The Old Dairy, Elton, PE8 6SH (01832 280298); **Prezzo** 21-24 Northampton Road, Cambridge, CB3 0AD (01223 353110); **Prezzo** 2 Exeter Road, Newmarket, CB8 8LT (01638 669676).

Essex

BLACKMORE

Leather Bottle

The Green, Blackmore, CM4 0RL (01277 823538/ www.theleatherbottle.org). **Lunch served** noon-2pm Mon-Sat; noon-4pm Sun. **Dinner served** 7-9pm Mon-Sat. **Main courses** £7.25-£12.95. **Set lunch** (Mon-Sat) £8.95 2 courses; (Sun) £12.50 2 courses, £14.95 3 courses. **Credit** MC, V.

The sweet hamlet of Blackmore was one of the winners of the 2003 best-kept village in Essex award. The Leather Bottle has found such honours harder to come by, but this pub-restaurant generally does a decent job of keeping the locals fed and watered, at least those who choose carefully from the menu. While a crab and prawn starter was light and fresh, wild mushrooms on toast with a poached egg were less impressive, the former flavourless and the latter over cooked. A simple but successful dish of pan-seared scallops and prawns proved a better option than a timbale of skate and anchovy fillets, overwhelmed by caper butter. Sticky toffee pudding and Eton mess pavlova were as expected. Most diners sit in the not especially sympathetic conservatory, leaving the pub to drinkers spoiled by excellent ales.

CHIPPING ONGAR

Smiths Brasserie

Fyfield Road, Chipping Ongar, CM5 0AL (01277 365578/www.smithsbrasserie.com). **Lunch served** 12.30-3pm, **dinner served** 6.30-10.30pm Tue-Sun. **Main courses** £11.50-£23. **Set lunch** (Tue-Sat) £14.50 2 courses, £17.50 3 courses. **Credit** MC, V.

Consistency is the watchword here, as well it might for a family business with almost 50 years under its belt. Alec Smith is the third generation to have learnt his trade at Billingsgate, and although Smiths was founded just ten years ago, it was born from the family's chain of Chariot fish restaurants. A loyal customer base, the freshest fish and a smart, gleaming interior, have kept it popular. The style is unpretentious, typified by a substantial starter of sweet herring fillets with crème fraîche, fish soup, and haddock, cod, or plaice either grilled, or fried in batter, served with fat hand-cut chips. Everything is enthusiastically served by smartly dressed staff.

CLAVERING

Cricketers

Wicken Road, Clavering, CB11 4QT (01799 550442/ www.thecricketers.co.uk). **Lunch served** noon-2pm, **dinner served** 7-10pm daily. **Main courses** £11-£18. **Set dinner** £26 3 courses. **Credit** AmEx, MC, V.

With the pile of signed cookery books for sale by the entrance, there's no mistaking who grew up here; it was at the Cricketers that Jamie Oliver first discovered his passion for cooking. His dad's pub is an appealing place, all chintz with brass bits and lots of beams, but it's the modern British dishes served casually in the bar (or as a more formal fixed price menu in the restaurant) that draw the crowds. A perfect mix of comfort food (meatballs in a rich juniper and thyme gravy), tradition (a Sunday roast loin of pork with stuffing and apple sauce) and bold ideas (grilled fillet of bream with squid ink pasta and a tomato and shellfish bisque) means you're left in no doubt about the serious approach to cooking. Staff are lovely with zero attitude and maximum efficiency.

COLCHESTER

Lemon Tree

48 St John's Street, Colchester, CO2 7AD (01206 767337/www.the-lemon-tree.com). **Meals served** noon-10pm Mon-Sat. **Main courses** £7.95-£16.95. **Set lunch** (Mon-Fri) £6.50 1 course, £8.95 2 courses, £11.40 3 courses. **Set dinner** (Mon-Thur) £7.50 1 course, £10.95 2 courses, £14.40 3 courses. **Credit** AmEx, DC, MC, V.

The Lemon Tree is a bang-on-the-nail brasserie in a town not known for its culinary highlights. The former warehouse has scrubbed up well, offering an airy, clean look with high ceilings, supporting pillars, paddle fans and bare floorboards, with the back burrowing into the remains of the Roman city wall. It's a neighbourly spot with friendly staff happily turning out a bright list of modern British staples such as liver and bacon or bangers and mash. But there's a cosmopolitan streak too, with roasted hake, sautéed baby beetroot, red onions, french beans and salsa verde. Apple bread pudding with vanilla sauce keep standards high to the end. Wine tastings and jazz evenings make booking advisable.

DEDHAM

Fountain House

Dedham Hall, Brook Street, Dedham, CO7 6AD (01206 323027/www.dedhamhall.demon.co.uk). **Dinner served** 7-9.30pm Tue-Sat. **Set dinner** £25.50 3 courses. **Credit** MC, V.

The fixed-price dinner menu may not be cutting-edge, dealing as it does in melon salad with prawns and grapes, and mixed smoked fish hors d'oeuvres, but 15th-century Dedham Hall is a lovely, lived-in family house, and if the formula holds few surprises it's because that's what their loyal customers have come to expect. That's not to damn with faint praise, only to acknowledge that good cooking using quality ingredients is often to be preferred to high-risk experimentation under the guise of innovation. Beef fillet with wild mushrooms and red wine had great flavour; a light mustard sauce was a good background for some lamb's kidneys; and raspberry vacherin and lemon tart lived up to Wendy Sarton's reputation for great puddings. The wine list offers fair prices and a generous spread.

Milsoms ★

Stratford Road, Dedham, CO7 6HW (01206 322795/ www.tolbooth com). **Lunch served** noon-2.15pm daily. **Dinner served** 6-9.30pm Mon-Thur, Sun; 6-10pm Fri, Sat. **Main courses** £8.95-£14.95. **Set meal** £21 3 courses. **Credit** AmEx, DC, MC, V.

The sheer number of cars in the car park, plus the no-booking policy, seemed to suggest that we could forget lunch. Wrong! Past the local movers and shakers jostling cheerfully in the bar, and there was plenty of room in the smoking and no-smoking areas, the sheltered terrace and lush garden, to accommodate everyone. Milsoms, it seems, has a broad appeal. At heart it's a clubby country house brought up to date with lots of polished wood, modern leather chairs and industrial strength track lighting. A relaxed, wide-ranging brasserie menu keeps things simple – just order at the bar and cheerful staff bring good things like salt and pepper squid, teriyaki duck breast, wok-fried roots, shoots and leaves and hot and sour essence, and perfect Tuscan baked plum and almond tart with mascarpone and Vin Santo syrup.

Sun Inn

High Street, Dedham, CO7 6DF (01206 323351/ thesuninndedham.com). **Lunch served** noon-2.30pm Mon-Fri; noon-3pm Sat, Sun. **Dinner served** 7-9.30pm Mon-Thur; 7-10pm Fri, Sat. **Main courses** £7.50-£12. **Credit** MC, V.

Piers Baker's transformation of the Sun into a laid-back country inn with modern food and hip rooms is a huge success. Now the 15th-century inn is painted a sunny yellow, its ancient timbers, panelling, worn floorboards and open fires matched by pick 'n' mix antiques and hand-me-downs, creating a relaxed yet upmarket look. At heart it remains a local, but food is a major draw. The daily-changing menu is chalked on a board and reveals a penchant for fresh materials simply prepared. The contemporary repertoire reflects sunnier climes and a commendable air of restraint pervades the cooking, producing a talleggio cheese and red onion tart with slow-roasted tomato and rocket salad, grilled Tuscan sausages with mash and tomato chilli jam, and a light chocolate and almond cake.

Le Talbooth

Gun Hill, Dedham, CO7 6HP (01206 323150/ www.talbooth.com). **Lunch served** noon-2pm daily. **Dinner served** 7-9.30pm Mon-Sat. **Main courses** £15.50-£24.95. **Set lunch** (Mon-Sat) £20 2 courses, £24.50 3 courses; (Sun) £28 3 courses. **Credit** AmEx, DC, MC, V.

Great for a special occasion, Le Talbooth provides consistently high standards of cooking. Slickly orchestrated meals take place in surroundings verging on the bland, despite the attractions of the timber-framed 16th-century house and the setting on the banks of the River Stour. Menu descriptions are also muted, but dishes taste much better than they read. Straightforward comfort-leaning starters such as terrine of game in liver parfait are confidently done, while more adventurous mains like pan-fried supreme of turbot, braised oxtail and little gem with parsley mash and herb oil come off surprisingly well. For those with deep pockets, there's no questioning the quality of the wine list.

GREAT DUNMOW

Starr

Market Place, Great Dunmow, CM6 1AX (01371 874321/www.the-starr.co.uk). **Lunch served** noon-2pm daily. **Dinner served** 7-9.30pm Mon-Sat. **Set lunch** £13.50-£25 2 courses, £27.50 3 courses. **Set dinner** £27.50-£40 3 courses. **Credit** AmEx, DC, MC, V.

Step through the door of this four-square, sturdy sage-green former inn and breathe in the oak and wood smoke in the traditional bar. Then walk down the corridor and enter the 21st century. The cream dining room is an elegant space that blends ancient standing timbers and contrasts them with a light conservatory. The kitchen follows suit, harnessing flavours from the Med with occasional forays further afield. Tian of wild pigeon and beetroot with a zesty fennel and orange salad, followed by fillet of brill with salsify, creamed mash and beurre rouge made up a satisfying if pricey two-course lunch. This is a mature restaurant that knows how to care for its equally mature, well-dressed customers – the sort of place to take your prospective in-laws.

HARWICH

Pier Hotel

The Quay, Harwich, CO12 3HH (01255 241212/ www.milsomhotels.com). **Lunch served** noon-2pm, **dinner served** 6-9.30pm daily. *Restaurant* **Main courses** £9.95-£30. **Set lunch** (Mon-Sat) £17 2 courses, £20 3 courses; (Sun) £21. *Bistro* **Main courses** £8.95-£12.95. **Credit** AmEx, DC, MC, V.

This well-established hotel has a two-tiered operation that sees a pleasant, old-fashioned restaurant perched above a simple and lively bistro. Dress up to match the decor upstairs, and ask for a window seat to catch the view over the Stour and Orwell estuaries. Dishes split between a tried-and-tested repertoire of dressed local crab, moules marinière, fish and chips or Thai fish curry, and modern British ideas like soy-glazed salmon with coriander and chilli dressing or roasted sea bass with fennel and salsa verde. Meat appears in the guise of slow-braised shank of lamb or breast of duck with braised red cabbage, apple tartlet and

Madeira sauce. Accompany it with something French from the reasonably priced wine list, which has plenty of whites to match the cuisine.

HORNDON ON THE HILL

Bell ★

High Road, Horndon on the Hill, SS17 8LD (01375 642463/www.bell-inn.co.uk). **Lunch served** noon-1.45pm Mon-Sat; noon-2.15pm Sun. **Dinner served** 6.45-9.45pm daily. **Main courses** £11.95-£17.50. **Credit** AmEx, MC, V.

It's unusual to find an inn of this calibre in such a location – the centre of a triangular pocket of countryside bounded by Basildon, Tilbury Docks and the retail shopping park at Thurrock. It's a cross between a French brasserie and a country pub, with a panelled front bar and a clamorous bar-brasserie where customers mill around as they wait for tables (no booking). A rambunctious menu is chalked up on a blackboard-covered wall: chorizo ravioli with parsnip velouté and rhubarb, roast rib of beef or sauté of octopus with keta tempura and tomato juniper jelly, followed by poached pear en croûte with poppyseed cookies and quince paste. If you want to eat the same food in more sedate surroundings, book a table in the restaurant.

LEIGH-ON-SEA

Sand Bar

71 Broadway, Leigh on Sea, SS9 1PE (01702 480067). **Lunch served** noon-4pm, **dinner served** 6-10pm Mon-Sat. **Main courses** £7.95-£15.95. **Set dinner** £22.95 2 courses. **Credit** MC, V.

The Sand Bar is a sleek and trendy head-turner that stands out in this traditional estuary town. The interior is easy on the eye and does its level best to create a chic contrast to the macadamised gloom of the road outside. But an overlong fixed price menu delivers results that are no better than hit or miss. Potted cayenne spiced crayfish tails with lemon tartare and herb salad are good; Cajun roasted red snapper fillets served with a puy lentil and borlotti bean cassoulet and roasted vine tomatoes lack taste and muddle flavours. Less choice might focus the cooking, but staff are pleasant, there's a relaxed vibe and it fills a (relatively) upmarket gap.

MANNINGTREE

Stour Bay Café

39-43 High Street, Manningtree, CO11 1AH (01206 396687/www.stourbaycafe.com). **Lunch served** 12.30-2pm, **dinner served** 7-9.30pm Wed-Sun. **Main courses** £10-£16. **Set lunch** (Wed-Fri) £9.50 2 courses. **Set dinner** (Wed) £15 3 courses; (Thur) £6.50 fish and chips. **Credit** MC, V.

This is a user-friendly brasserie slap bang in the middle of Manningtree. Strong modern colours and atmospheric lighting lend a funky feel, and lots of bare wood means that even when half empty Stour Bay Café has a vibrant vibe. There's a strong emphasis on fish, and dishes can take a straight down-the-line international approach – chilli jam with plump salmon and coriander potato cakes – or march in tune with the seasons with steamed fillet of sea bass with English asparagus and jersey royals. Prices are reasonable, service likewise.

SAFFRON WALDEN

The Restaurant

2 Church Street, Saffron Walden, CB11 4LT (01799 526444/www.the-restaurantweb.com). **Lunch served** *Jan-Apr* 12.30-3pm Sun. **Dinner served** 7.30-10pm Tue-Sat. **Main courses** £10.95-£17.95. **Set dinner** (Tue-Thur) £12.95 2 courses, £15.95 3 courses. **Credit** MC, V.

Against the odds, the Restaurant has become a local legend, with eclectic cooking served in a converted cellar. Etched-glass tables, blue high-backed chairs and modern lighting divert the eye from the lack of natural light, while committed owners are on hand to ensure the menu responds to regulars' tastes. The kitchen mixes and matches in the modern way, and uses organic ingredients where possible. Fillet of sea bream poached in lemongrass and roasted garlic, served with a prawn and coriander butter, gratin potatoes and green vegetables had too many flavours; more successful was Italian green herb risotto with cream, parmesan and rosemary oil.

WEST MERSEA

The Company Shed

129 Coast Road, West Mersea, CO5 8PA (01206 382700). **Meals served** 9am-4pm Tue-Sat; 10am-4pm Sun. **Main courses** £8-£30. **No credit cards.**

The queue at this wooden hut is testimony to the fact that you can't fault the freshness or quality of the wet fish for sale on the slab. For those wishing to eat, the basic elements – proximity to fish and boats, cramped tables, kitchen paper for napkins – create a sense of adventure. But you need to brave the take-it-or-leave-it attitude of the staff and quirky blackboard-scrawled rules about what you can bring to supplement the two slivers of lemon that accompany the only thing served – strenuously worthy seafood platters. You're allowed bread, butter and wine, but the standard £16 platter for two (prawns, langoustine, mussels, smoked mackerel, smoked salmon, cockles and an undressed Cromer crab) cries out for more; well done the regular in the corner with the illicit jar of Hellmann's.

Also in the area

Loch Fyne 280-282 High Road, Loughton, IG10 1RB (020 8532 5140); **Prezzo** Charter Way, Chapel Hill, Braintree, CM7 8YH (01376 569022); **Prezzo** 129-129A High Street, Brentwood, CM14 4RZ (01277 216641); **Prezzo** Clements Road, Ilford, 1GI 1BA (020 8553 2351); **Prezzo** 69 High Street, Maldon, CM9 5EP (01621 842544).

East Anglia

Norfolk

BLAKENEY

White Horse Hotel

4 High Street, Blakeney, NR25 7AL (01263 740574/ www.blakeneywhitehorse.co.uk). Bar **Lunch served** noon-2pm, **dinner served** 6-9pm daily. *Restaurant* **Dinner served** 7-9pm daily. **Main courses** £10-£17. **Credit** MC, V.

It all comes together in this pleasant-looking former coaching inn a few steps up from the harbour. At heart it's a pub – charming bar, lots of dark wood, regional ales on handpump – but a glassed-in courtyard and simple restaurant in the former stables (evenings only) make sure all bases are covered. Everything is judged nicely, determinedly modern yet conscious of the coastal setting and rural tastes, and the result is good food, charming service and a short, balanced, reasonably priced wine list. Much emphasis is put upon local supplies, especially fish. Fantastic cockle chowder is served in the bar, alongside fresh local whitebait (a rare treat), and perfect cod and chips. More ambitious cooking in the restaurant delivers things like griddled scallops with tagliatelle and tomato and fennel broth, or loin of lamb with lentil, oyster mushroom and garlic casserole.

BRANCASTER STAITHE

White Horse

Main Road, Brancaster Staithe, PE31 8BY (01485 210262/www.whitehorsebrancaster.co.uk). **Lunch served** noon-2pm, **dinner served** 7-9pm daily. **Main courses** £13-£14. **Credit** MC, V.

The view sweeps over salt marshes to the distant sea in a blur of pastels and earth tones – a feature that's exploited to the full in the specially designed conservatory dining room and terrace. The kitchen picks up the coastal theme with the likes of dressed local crab with celeriac remoulade and rocket salad, local lobster with garlic butter, and the odd meaty dish like spring rump of lamb. Particularly impressive are the cockles, mussels and oysters from the 'beds' in the sea at the bottom of the garden. An ordinary looking pub from the outside, inside is a smart, urbane space delivering very polished food – ranging from sandwiches in the bar, a lunchtime salade niçoise on the terrace, to fillet of brill with wild mushroom and baby vegetables in the restaurant.

BURNHAM MARKET

Fishes

Market Place, Burnham Market, PE31 8HE (01328 738588/www.fishesrestaurant.co.uk). **Lunch served** noon-2pm Tue-Sun. **Dinner served** 7-9.30pm Tue-Sat. **Set lunch** £13.50 2 courses, £17.50 3 courses. **Set dinner** £27.50 2 courses, £32.50 3 courses. **Credit** MC, V.

Fishes is in a prime spot; the bay windows give a view across the green. While pine tables, rattan chairs and cork tile floors create a pleasant ambience, exotic mirrors in carved wooden frames reflect the presence of a tandoori oven. The friendly owner's enthusiasm for the food is wholly justified. Fish soup was just right and laced with red peppers, while smoked eel was extremely subtle yet still very intense. A good sized slice of roast halibut came with caramelised fennel and a subtle hollandaise. Bourride of hake, red gurnard and brill came in a creamy sauce plus tomato and raw courgette. Imaginative vegetables included carrot purée, roast courgettes and caramelised parsnips. When it came to desserts, we passed on sticky toffee pudding, dark chocolate fondant and bread and butter pudding in favour of sharing an excellent rhubarb tart and double cream. An extremely pleasing meal, worth taking slowly so that you can manage the full three courses.

Hoste Arms

The Green, Burnham Market, PE31 8HD (01328 738777/www.hostearms.co.uk). **Lunch served** noon-2pm, **dinner served** 7-9pm daily. **Main courses** £8.95-£16.50. **Credit** MC, V.

The Hoste Arms can lay claim to being the impetus behind Burnham Market's gentrification. This award-winning (it has garnered numerous prizes, including three times the Norfolk Dining Pub of the Year – most recently in 2000) 17th-century inn sits proud (and much extended) on the green. Tables outside soon fill in summer; inside the bar and restaurant are dark, woody and stylish. A light conservatory makes a relaxing venue for pre-prandial drinks. Smart staff – young, polite, well-trained – bring the menu. This entices with such creations as roast cod and artichoke salad with truffle oil dressing; and locally reared oysters served in a variety of styles (tempura, or grilled with parmesan topping, say). Execution is usually spot-on, typified by a succulent pot-roasted ham hock served with braised red cabbage and bitter orange compote, followed by an assiette of six desserts (good value for two at £7.95, given such delicacies as cardamom-spiced pineapple and papaya crumble). Plaudits also go to the local ales (try Woodforde's Great Eastern). The wine list runs to 200 choices from all over the world. The only detractions are the influx of Home County types, and the uninspired children's menu.

CLEY-NEXT-THE-SEA

George Hotel

High Street, Cley-next-the-sea, NR25 7RN (01263 740652/www.thegeorgehotelcley.com). **Lunch served** noon-2pm Mon-Fri; noon-2.30pm Sat, Sun. **Dinner served** 6.30-9pm Mon-Thur, Sun; 6.30-9.30pm Fri, Sat. **Main courses** £7.95-£14.95. **Credit** MC, V.

Still a pub, but stripped back to its bones with lots of polished wood, green walls and artwork, the George Hotel is a great addition to this hauntingly beautiful stretch of the coast. You can come here and stay a night, or just stop off for a plate of fresh, grilled, chillied squid with lemon dressing and wild rocket, or pan-fried halibut with roasted marinated vegetables (the burgers looked tempting, too); or you can pop in for a pint in the tiny village bar. Everyone's welcome – and it works: the atmosphere is buzzy because of it, with relaxed young staff and a happy mix of customers. The beer garden and view across salt marshes are other plus points.

CROMER

Mary Jane's Fish Bar ★

27-29 Garden Street, Cromer, NR27 9HN (01263 511208). **Meals served** 11.30am-9pm Mon-Thur; 11.30am-10.30pm Fri, Sat; noon-9pm Sun. **Main courses** £3-£5. **No credit cards**.

Centrally located and close to the pier, but hidden away on a narrow street corner, Mary Jane's can add cheer to the drizzliest day at the seaside. In fact, that's when the functional-looking restaurant next to the busy takeaway comes into its own. The choice of fish holds no surprises (cod, haddock, plaice, skate) but the quality is unmistakable. The chips are good, the mushy peas are worth ordering and you won't go wrong with one of their gherkins.

HOLKHAM

The Victoria

Park Road, Holkham, NR23 1RG (01328 711008/ www.victoriaatholkham.co.uk). **Lunch served** noon-2.30pm, **dinner served** 7-9.30pm daily. **Main courses** £11-£16.90. **Credit** MC, V.

The Victoria is exactly the kind of country bolt hole you dream of finding – gastropub casual with the seductive appeal of a glossy photo spread – where the British Raj rubs shoulders with the Conran Shop. The food is an unabashed combination of modern European ideas, local ingredients and oriental touches. As eclectic as it is, we were surprised that all the dishes worked. Deep-fried whitebait with garlic, lemon and parsley mayonnaise, and char-grilled tuna with white radish and wasabi sorbet, then grilled sea trout, gem lettuce, broad beans, tomato and mint vinaigrette, and venison burger with salad, chips and cranberry chutney were all hits. With its canopied terrace, sheltered courtyard and the sea just a stone's throw away, the Victoria is one of the best outdoor dining spots in the area.

HOLT

Yetman's ★

37 Norwich Road, Holt, NR25 6SA (01263 713320/ www.yetmans.net). **Lunch served** 12.30-2pm Sun. **Dinner served** 7-9.30pm Wed-Sat, bank hols. **Set meal** £26.50 2 courses, £32 3 courses, £36.75 4 courses. **Credit** AmEx, MC, V.

Dinner at Yetman's is a little like a romantic dinner at home. The setting – an attractive, cheery lemon yellow house on the edge of the village – is living-room cosy with its simple dining rooms of bare floorboards, fresh flowers and white clad tables. Peter Yetman's approach to front-of-house duties is as marvellously laid back as his attire. Heady scents waft from Alison Yetman's kitchen where she has a distinctive way with fresh seasonal produce, combining delicacy with expansive flavours. The prime quality may dictate high prices, but when you taste the food – hot gougère with local asparagus and crème fraîche, a fillet of local lamb poached in a broth of spring vegetables with lettuce and mint, and char-grilled fillet of local sea trout with fresh tomato and basil salsa – everything seems to sparkle.

ITTERINGHAM

Walpole Arms

The Common, Itteringham, NR11 7AR (01263 587258/www.thewalpolearms.co.uk). **Lunch served** noon-2pm Mon-Sat; 12.30-2.30pm Sun. **Dinner served** 7-9pm Mon-Sat. **Main courses** £8.95-£16. **Credit** MC, V.

With hens and a vocal rooster scratching around on the lawn outside, this off-the-beaten-track hostelry is very olde worlde in looks, but refurbishment has left it in superb condition with exposed brick walls, heavy timbers and an open fire. The bar functions superbly as a modern rural pub, with bright staff dispensing crab and rice curry with coriander flat bread. The same menu serves the more formal restaurant (salad of octopus stewed in red wine and chickpea fritters, mains of confit of duck leg with puy lentils, baked red cabbage and baby fig jus), a stylish area that makes the most of its setting, plus the option of eating out on a terrace in fine weather.

MORSTON

Anchor Inn

The Street, Morston, NR25 7AA (01263 741392). **Lunch served** noon-2.30pm, **dinner served** 6-9pm Mon-Sat. **Meals served** noon-8pm Sun. **Main courses** £7.95-£14.50. **Credit** MC, V.

Several small rooms with wood floors, open fires and an assortment of old furniture gives this pleasant pub a relaxed atmosphere so that, although the quality of the food is uneven, you'd probably go there anyway. Soft herring roes disappointingly came coated in batter, but inside were soft and succulent. Oysters were beautifully fresh. The long menu boasts classics like cod, chips and mushy peas, or crab salad and potatoes. The creamy sauce of seafood gratin, which contained cod, salmon, smoked haddock, lobster and prawns, was dried up, but steak and kidney pudding was kept moist by its suet pastry, so the meat remained tender and the gravy rich. Beers include Winton's and Old Speckled Hen and numerous wines can be had by the glass or the bottle. A pleasant place for a filling meal.

Morston Hall ★

The Street, Morston, NR25 7AA (01263 741041/ www.morstonhall.com). **Lunch served** 12.30-1pm Sun. **Dinner served** 7.30-8pm daily. **Set lunch** £24 3 courses. **Set dinner** £38 4 courses. **Credit** AmEx, DC, MC, V.

The porch is lined with awards; this country house hotel has been winning prizes since 1992, including a Michelin star in 1999. When you book, they'll ask if there is anything you don't eat. Take this question seriously, since the menu is fixed. Chef is Galton Blackiston and his wife Tracey runs front of house. A small glass of celeriac soup and truffle oil was followed by a pyramid of lasagne in a creamy sauce layered with wild mushrooms, leeks, tomatoes and decorated with a topknot of fine onions. Scallops came as two circles separated by a ridge of guacamole resting on a terrine of peppers and courgettes. With its rich jus, roast fillet of beef was thick and succulent. Chocolate in a mocha tart was perfectly offset by vanilla ice-cream and matched visually with a wafer the same size. Seven cheeses were accompanied by biscuits and olive and walnut bread, followed by coffee and petits fours. If you have one posh meal in Norfolk, choose Morston Hall.

NORWICH

Adlard's

79 Upper St Giles Street, Norwich, NR2 1AB (01603 633522/www.adlards.co.uk). **Lunch served** 12.30-1.45pm, **dinner served** 7.30-10.30pm Tue-Sat. **Main courses** £16-£22. **Set lunch** £21 3 courses. **Credit** AmEx, DC, MC, V.

David Adlard's attractive restaurant in a quaint quarter of the city has long been Norwich's prime exponent of haute cuisine. The local bourgeoisie (pressed linen, casual) dines here by night, though there's a relaxed feel to the split-level space, helped by simple furnishings and intense modern art. There's much intensity in the food too, with highly reduced sauces, caramelisation and the innovative juxtaposition of strong flavours being favoured on the concise menu. Often this works well, as in a main of rump of lamb with its sweetbreads, fèves and mousseron mushrooms and tangy creamed endive and mint. Sometimes it doesn't; a salted baked fillet of sea bass could, at a stretch, be paired with a cornet full of cold scallop segments, but the raisin and vanilla dressing was *de trop*. Onion royale, like a savoury crème brûlée, made a pleasing appetiser, and a starter of pungently garlicky ballottine of rabbit with rabbit rillette had welcome bitterness supplied by a dandelion salad. Puddings are similarly elaborate constructions. The wine list is huge, the à la carte prices stiff (starters and desserts about a tenner a throw, mains around £20). Service seemed to favour those throwing their money about.

Tatlers

21 Tombland, Norwich, NR3 1RF (01603 766670/ www.tatlers.com). **Lunch served** noon-2pm, **dinner served** 6.30-10pm Mon-Sat. **Main courses** £12-£16.50. **Set lunch** £16 2 courses, £20 3 courses. **Credit** AmEx, MC, V.

Tombland is a wide, tree-lined street running down from the main gate of the cathedral and it could lay claim to being Norwich's restaurant row. Standing out from the pavement cafés and casual eateries, Tatlers is a fine but formal-looking Georgian house, which eases up inside with a relaxed brasserie style of bare boards, wood tables, bright modern art and affable service. The market-driven menu shows a distinctive way with French-inspired Mediterranean dishes, but has the sense to keep things simple, be it cold duck breast with celeriac remoulade and bitter sweet dressing, or fillet of organic salmon with Cromer crab ravioli, crushed new potatoes, Norfolk asparagus and shellfish broth. The chocolate tart with crème de cassis sorbet is superb.

SNETTISHAM

Rose & Crown

Old Church Road, Snettisham, Norfolk, PE31 7LX (01485 541382/www.roseandcrownsnettisham.co.uk). **Lunch served** noon-2pm daily. **Dinner served** 6.30-9pm Mon-Thur, Sun; 6.30-9.30pm Fri, Sat. **Main courses** £8.75-£13.95. **Set lunch** (Mon-Fri) £10 2 courses. **Credit** MC, V.

Picture an old-fashioned, whitewashed country cottage dating from the 14th century, fill it with quirky bar and dining rooms (one of which is no-smoking) linked by a twisting passage, big open fires, settles, polished oak, heavy beams, and bold colours, and you have the Rose & Crown. Now match it with a kitchen delivering cooking with a metropolitan edge, and you have a place that is well worth a detour. The menu flits between tried-and-tested pub favourites (burger, red onion relish, bacon, monterey jack and fries; open-flamed ribeye with horseradish butter), and some modern, gutsy cooking of, say, scorched scallops Bloody Mary-style and roast halibut, courgette fritters and red pepper dressing. Bread is delicious, a side order of sage and olive potatoes was inspired. There's a genuinely local feel, due in no small part to the charming staff, while the wine list (including 20 by the glass) garners the praise it deserves.

SOUTH CREAKE

Ostrich Inn

1 Fakenham Road, South Creake, NR21 9PB (01328 823320/www.ostrichinn.co.uk). **Lunch served** noon-2.15pm, **dinner served** 7-9.15pm daily. **Main courses** £6.50-£16. **Credit** AmEx, MC, V.

Fishes. See p188.

With its dark red carpets, pool room and bare beams, the Ostrich still functions as a locals' boozer. Outside is a basic gravelled beer garden, and a converted barn (for hire or for overspill). Sunday lunch looks simple – roasts, beef and Guinness pie, chicken fajitas – but the food confounds expectations. Ingredients are fresh and of a high quality (many grown here), presentation is attractive and cooking skills are evident in roast stuffed lamb with sausage meat and thyme (great roast spuds, tender meat, glorious gravy); and asparagus and smoked salmon salad with pesto (though this came without the advertised bruschetta). Puddings might include classics like apple and fruit strudel. Woodforde's Wherry is one of four real ales at the bar, and there's an adequate wine list plus cocktails.

STOKE HOLY CROSS

Wildebeest Arms ★

82-86 Norwich Road, Stoke Holy Cross, NR14 8QJ (01508 492497). **Lunch served** noon-2pm, **dinner served** 7-9pm daily. **Main courses** £9.95-£18.50. **Set lunch** £11.95 2 courses, £14.95 3 courses. **Set dinner** £15 2 courses, £18.50 3 courses. **Credit** AmEx, DC, MC, V.

From the outside the Wildebeest Arms looks like any village pub, but it makes a rather more elegant statement of taste and style within. Modernised on an open plan, bold yellow walls contrast with polished wood floors, tables and sturdy beams. There are fresh flowers, a blazing fire, African tribal pieces plus other artwork on the walls. Food can take a while to arrive, but at least that suggests that everything is freshly prepared. Standouts include thyme roast pigeon breast with wild mushrooms, crispy pancetta and peanut vinaigrette, or roast fillet of brill and John Dory with brown shrimp risotto, leeks, fricassee of mussels, tomatoes and herbs – both dishes reflecting a cosmopolitan restaurant rather than rural pub approach. Expensive, but the cooking matches the cost.

SWAFFHAM

Strattons

4 Ash Close, Swaffham, PE37 7NH (01760 723845/ www.strattonshotel.com). **Dinner served** 7pm Mon-Sat by appointment. **Set dinner** £37.50 4 courses. **Credit** AmEx, MC, V.

You step from a market town square to a rural idyll in just two minutes. Les and Vanessa Scott's gently sprawling 18th-century farmhouse has shape-shifted into a funky private hotel with bags of theatrical swagger, lots of bold modern art and just a touch of kitsch. A commitment to environmental good practice is the driving force (hens on the front lawn), and the food follows suit – provenance, as much as local sourcing, is a key element. This all combines to make Strattons an unusual place to eat (or stay), though the cooking is more robust than the dining room suggests. Evening menus are a short, daily changing affair delivering hearty baked crab with mushrooms braised in port, baked monkfish in tomatoes with samphire and crushed new potatoes, and roasted peach and cranberry bread and butter pudding with peach apricot ice-cream.

THORNHAM

Lifeboat Inn

Ship Lane, Thornham, PE36 6LT (01485 512236/ www.lifeboatinn.co.uk). **Lunch served** noon-2.30pm, **dinner served** 6.30-9.30pm daily. **Main courses** £8.50-£15.95. **Set dinner** £26 3 courses. **Credit** MC, V.

The food might have florid descriptions (pan-fried marlin 'caresses' a salad niçoise), but the Lifeboat's Med-influenced repertoire features sound combinations rendered with a light touch. The printed menu is augmented by a varied list of specials that might start with bacon and pea soup. From the main menu, liver and smoked bacon (high-quality ingredients) comes with garlicky roast vegetables, olive mash and a rich red wine jus. Fish, especially, is cooked with delicacy – for example, a special of plaice baked under herb crumbs, or even the child's portion of fish and chips. Puddings are succulent and creamy, with glazed lemon tart, mango sorbet and chocolate bavarois all hitting the spot. At its kernel, the Lifeboat is a snug old pub with beams and nooks aplenty (along with beers from Adnams and Woodforde's, and cider from Aspall's). Popularity has been the impetus for various extensions, the best of which is the yellow-walled conservatory. Outside is a terrace, a children's play area and, beyond the car park, outstanding views of the marshes leading to the sea.

WARHAM ALL SAINTS

Three Horseshoes ★

Bridge Street, Warham All Saints, NR23 1NL (01328 710547). **Lunch served** noon-1.45pm, **dinner served** 6-8.30pm daily. **Main courses** £5.80-£8.20. **No credit cards.**

Would that more pub food were like this: unfussy, fairly priced and cooked with care. The Horseshoes is a lovely old place with a restful setting in a quiet village. Outside is a beer garden and a small courtyard; within, a clutch of old rooms feature ancient stone or tiled floors, gas lighting, sturdy furniture and an abundance of knick-knacks. Beer is local and sparklingly fresh. Soups and pies dominate the menu. Soused herrings might precede game and wine pie. Alternatively, choose from the blackboard menu by the bar. From here, creamy artichoke soup was followed by a seafood and salmon pie bountiful with fish, fresh mussels, cockles and prawns. Equally praiseworthy were the vegetables, the own-made puds (date and syrup pudding, marvellous) and the no-chips policy.

WELLS-NEXT-THE-SEA

Crown ★

The Buttlands, Wells-next-the-Sea, NR23 1EX (01328 710209/www.thecrownhotelwells.co.uk). Brasserie **Lunch served** noon-2.30pm, **dinner served** 6.30-9.30pm daily. *Restaurant* **Dinner served** 7-9pm daily. **Set dinner** £24.95 2 courses, £29.95 3 courses incl coffee. **Credit** AmEx, MC, V.

New Zealander Chris Moscrip Coubrough made waves at the Crown in Southwold before coming to this handsome old hotel in 2003. In the wooden-floored dining room – appealingly decorated with mustard-hued walls, white shutters and sea-themed artworks – he produces a set price menu that, though global in outlook, showcases many local ingredients. Thus after delicate canapés and a piquant pre-starter of spicy tomato soup, a meal might begin with eel, smoked at Cley and served on blinis with celeriac remoulade; or a bowl of soupy yet splendid watermelon curry with noodles, spring onions and prawn fried bread. Next pan-fried sea bass came on a pleasing pea and prawn risotto, while a juicy char-grilled beef fillet was accompanied by chicken liver parfait, morels (one-and-a-half of 'em), dauphinoise potatoes and (merely adequate) gravy. Don't miss the assiette of desserts, including lime brûlée, for dessert. Service is young, keen and Antipodean; the house red wine is a smooth winner.

Also in the area

Loch Fyne 30-32 St Giles Street, Norwich NR2 1LL (01603 723450; **Prezzo** 2-6 Thorpe Road, Norwich NR1 1RY (01603 660404).

Suffolk

ALDEBURGH

Golden Galleon ★

137 High Street, Aldeburgh, IP15 5AR (01728 454685). **Lunch served** noon-2pm Mon-Fri; noon-2.30pm Sat; noon-7pm Sun. **Dinner served** 5-8pm Mon-Wed; 5.30-8pm Fri, Sat. **Main courses** £5.50-£7.50. **No credit cards.**

If you prefer your fish and chips sitting at a table, then the upper-deck diner of the Golden Galleon is the place to go in the coastal town of Aldeburgh. Fresh local fish and chips with a good range of additional extras come from the fish shop downstairs and are served in a light and modern diner. The menu also includes burgers, pizzas and excellent pies for those not so keen on fish. Round off your meal, if you still have room, with a choice of traditional sponge puddings (jam, treacle, lemon) or an ice-cream. No children under four are admitted.

Lighthouse

77 High Street, Aldeburgh, IP15 5AU (01728 453377/www.thelighthouserestaurant.co.uk). **Lunch served** noon-2pm Mon-Fri; noon-2.30pm Sat, Sun. **Dinner served** 6.30-10pm daily. **Main courses** £8.15-£13.75. **Set meal** £13.25 2 courses, £16.50 3 courses. **Credit** AmEx, MC, V.

Sara Fox and Peter Hill's culinary beacon opposite Aldeburgh's cinema is the lynchpin of the town's impressive foodie scene. Sara runs the local cookery school and the couple have recently opened the Ikea-styled café Munchies further up the High Street, serving tea, coffee and all-day snacks. So the Lighthouse can now concentrate on serving up a reasonably priced two- or three-course prix fixe together with daily-changing lunch and dinner menus. To start there might be fish soup, Loch Fyne oysters or crayfish cocktail, followed by local cod fillet served on pea and bean risotto or a down-to-earth fillet steak with tomato confit, chips and salad. Service can be slow if you're upstairs, but the ambience is pleasantly informal and there's the added bonus of a garden at the back in fine weather.

152

152 High Street, Aldeburgh, IP15 5AX (01728 454594). **Lunch served** noon-3pm, **dinner served** 6-10pm daily. **Main courses** £10.50-£17. **Set meal** £16.50 3 courses. **Credit** AmEx, MC, V.

Under new ownership, 152 is still one of the best and most stylish places to eat in Aldeburgh. Tastefully refurbished in aubergine and cream, and close to the beach, the restaurant is a relaxing place for lunch or dinner. The emphasis is on high quality local produce, especially fish and seafood. Starters included fragrant fish cakes and a melt-in-the-mouth goat's cheese and caramelised onion tart. To follow there might be roast cod or rump of lamb with couscous. From a tempting list, iced banana parfait and summer pudding were winners. Service is helpful and friendly.

Regatta

171 High Street, Aldeburgh, IP15 5AN (01728 452011/www.regattaaldeburgh.com). **Lunch served** noon-2pm, **dinner served** 6-10pm daily. **Main courses** £8-£14. **Set dinner** (6-7pm) £9 2 courses, £12 3 courses. **Credit** AmEx, DC, MC, V.

Robert and Johanna Mabey's likeable, laid-back family restaurant has been going strong for more than 12 years. Luckily the formula hasn't changed much – a winning combination of sunny seaside decor, charming young staff and an excellent, adaptable menu. This is divided into nibbles, starters, own-smoked fish, mains and vegetarian dishes, all of which come in a starter or main size. For the kids, there's a range of crowd pleasing dishes such as sausages or fresh salmon and chips on a menu that doubles as a colouring book. Adult favourites are the specialities smoked over local oak in Regatta's own smoker: hot fillet of salmon served

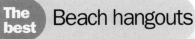

Beach hangouts

Beach Hut Bistro
Surfer-dude setting on Watergate Bay, near Newquay. *See p120.*

Porthgwidden Beach Restaurant
Moroccan themed food and decor, on a St Ives beach. *See p118.*

Porthminster Beach Café
Inspired cooking, also in St Ives, overlooking white sands. *See p120.*

Shell Bay Seafood Restaurant
Watch the boats go by at Studland beach's finest. *See p134.*

Start Bay Inn
The pebbled beach stretches out before this no-frills fish restaurant on Slapton Sands. *See p129.*

Whitstable Oyster Fishery Company
Cape Cod meets Kent in this warehouse on the shore. *See p91.*

with onion chutney, or plump prawns caught in Scotland and delivered fresh to Suffolk, where they're served with a wicked garlic mayonnaise.

BRAMFIELD

Queen's Head

The Street, Bramfield, IP19 9HT (01986 784214/ www.queensheadbramfield.co.uk). **Lunch served** noon-2pm daily. **Dinner served** 6.30-10pm Mon-Sat; 7-9pm Sun. **Main courses** £5.95-£14.95. **Credit** AmEx, MC, V.

Overlooked by the only separate, circular, 12th-century, flint church tower in the Blythe Valley, this pub's garden has a goodly number of seats for alfresco dining, but you might prefer to sit in the large open hall with its massive brick fireplace or the cosy no-smoking snug. Adnams provide the ale and the wines (£11.50-£20), and much is made of the organic local ingredients, combined cleverly to make filling, unpretentious meals. Starters double as light lunches with the Thai seafood salad, a combination of crayfish, herring and anchovies, topping the bill. It's run a close second by the own-cured gravadlax. Mains are traditional: the steak and kidney pie is topped by a thin shortcrust pastry lid beneath which bubbles ale-enriched gravy, and the cold rare roast Red Poll beef (trying saying that when you've had a few) with onion marmalade is mouth-watering – there's also local steak or venison.

BURY ST EDMUNDS

Maison Bleue at Mortimer's

30-31 Churchgate Street, Bury St Edmunds, IP33 1RG (01284 760623/www.maisonbleue.co.uk). **Lunch served** noon-2.30pm Tue-Fri; noon-2pm Sat. **Dinner served** 7-9.30pm Tue-Thur; 6.30-10pm Fri, Sat. **Main courses** £9.95-£27.95. **Set lunch** £9.95-£12.95 2 courses, £14.95 3 courses. **Set dinner** £21.95 3 courses. **Credit** AmEx, MC, V.

This local institution never fails to impress with its efficient and knowledgeable French staff, wide choice of the very freshest of fish and stylish but unpretentious interior. As well as the à la carte, there's also a very reasonable set dinner. No wonder

Farmcafe. *See p196.*

it's always full. Although Maison Bleue bills itself as a seafood restaurant – oysters, prawns, scallops, tuna, monkfish and mackerel, they're all here – the meat dishes are no slouch. Steak is cooked as only the French know how, and the rich lamb stew has meat that falls apart at the merest appreciative sigh. Puddings tip a nod to British classics as well as French. The word is confidence, found in the way the food is cooked, presented and served. A rare thing for restaurants in this price range.

CAVENDISH

George ★

The Green, Cavendish, CO10 8BA (01787 280248). **Lunch served** noon-3pm Tue-Sun. **Dinner served** 6.30-10pm Tue-Sat. **Main courses** £12. **Set meal** (Mon-Sat) £10.95 2 courses. **Credit** MC, V.

This yellow-painted inn overlooking the village green mixes the medieval (14th-century worm-eaten beams, timbered walls hiding daub and wattle, and an old stone fireplace) with contemporary chic (modern art, antique shop finds and neutral colours). It may have all the accoutrements of a smart country restaurant, but there is space for just having a pint, although most are here for the food. Jonathan Nicholson, former head chef at Conran's Bluebird, delivers food that is among the best in East Anglia. His menu is as generous in scope as it is spare in tone: crisp parma ham and rabbit with waldorf salad and orange dressing, roast guinea fowl, petit pois à la francaise and roast artichokes. Treatments are varied but never outlandish – it's proper food using ideas from a classical base that at its best will deliver a perfect French onion soup and rich game pudding.

DUNWICH

Flora Tearooms ★

Dunwich Beach, Dunwich, IP17 3DR (01728 648433). **Food served** *Mar-Oct* 11am-5pm daily. **Main courses** £5.95. **Unlicensed. Corkage** no charge. **Credit** MC, V.

The black weatherboarded shed-like building looks straight on to the beach car park, and with its serried rows of plain tables inside and picnic sets outside, there is no denying that the Flora Tearooms is extremely basic. But it has been battering for day trippers and holiday makers for years, touting a no-frills fish and chips menu of lemon sole, cod, haddock and plaice, with a few modern offerings like whole grilled brill or skate with salad. Freshness (everything is cooked to order) is its strength, all-day breakfasts ring the changes, and there could be good old treacle tart, knickerbocker glory or jelly and cream for afters. Wash it down with cups of tea.

Ship ★

St James Street, Dunwich, IP17 3DT (01728 648219). **Food served** noon-10pm, **lunch served** noon-3pm, **dinner served** 6-10pm daily. **Main courses** £7.95-£12. **Credit** MC, V.

The once thriving seaport is now a tiny hamlet (the last church crumbled into the sea in 1904). The attractions of modern-day Dunwich are bracing walks along gorse-and-heather-topped cliffs, a wide expanse of pebbly beach, the nearby RSPB reserve at Minsmere and fish and chips – it's the mainstay of menus both here at the Ship and at the Flora Tearooms on the beach (*see left*). The Ship is madly popular – the fish is local, the chips own-made, and Adnams Bitter is on tap – but don't be put off by the crowds or the slightly shabby, pubby interior. Head for the garden, courtyard or conservatory: there's plenty of room, and steak and ale casserole is a decent alternative to cod and chips.

EARSHAM

Earsham Street Café ★ ★

11-13 Earsham Street, Bungay, NR35 1AE (01986 893103). **Open** 9.30am-5pm, **lunch served** 11am-3.30pm Mon-Sat. **Dinner served** 7-9pm last Fri, Sat every month. **Main courses** £3.95-£11.50. **Credit** MC, V.

Walk in the door of Earsham Street Café and you feel instantly at home. With its cream and wood rough-hewn good looks, interesting art and greenery-filled back patio, it has the kind of simple, relaxed feel that lifts the spirits. Rebecca Mackenzie and Stephen David are passionate about what they do, with mornings and afternoons involving scones, chocolate cakes or Victorian fruitcake, as well as good sandwiches. Lunch keeps it simple, uses excellent local ingredients and puts a regional spin on roast breast of pigeon, black pudding and beetroot salad, or rare seared tuna, rocket and sun-blushed tomato, roast artichoke and Jersey Royal salad. The down-to-earth sensibility carries through to desserts and the wine list has plenty by the glass.

IPSWICH

Galley

25 St Nicholas Street, Ipswich, IP1 1TW (01473 281131/www.galley.uk.com). **Lunch served** noon-2pm Mon-Sat. **Dinner served** 6.30-10pm Mon-Thur; 6.30-11pm Fri, Sat. **Main courses** £13.95-£16.95. **Credit** AmEx, DC, MC, V.

Service here is quick and to the point with lobster, fresh fish and seasonal vegetables the order of the day and nearly all the ingredients local. The Gressingham duck liver pâté, Capel St Mary flat mushrooms and Tuddenham Hall asparagus really hit the spot, while the sauces are inventive, prices not disheartening and the wine list idiosyncratic but fun (that's down to the owner, Ugar). For meat-lovers, there's marinated venison with red onions, carrot, celeriac, juniper berries and red wine, on a bed of mustard seed mash. The restaurant is a leaning Elizabethan building decorated pink and aquamarine with a cosy downstairs section and little rooms upstairs – open between the wall beams to create light while the sloping floors add charm and a sense of adventure.

LAVENHAM

Great House

Market Place, Lavenham, CO10 9QZ (01787 247431/ www.greathouse.co.uk). **Lunch served** noon-2.30pm Tue-Sun. **Dinner served** 7-9.30pm Tue-Sat. **Main courses** £10.95-£18. **Set lunch** (Mon-Sat) £14.95 2 courses, £16.95 3 courses; (Sun) £21 3 courses. **Set dinner** £21.95 3 courses. **Credit** MC, V.

The pick of the bunch in Lavenham, the highly acclaimed Great House has been owned and run by Martine and Régis Crepy since 1985 (previous occupants include Sir Stephen Spender). The main dining room scores highly in atmosphere, with a huge inglenook fireplace and original beams. As for the food, it's full-on French fare, while the wine list leans the same way with prices starting at a very reasonable £2.10 for a glass of house wine. Not everything is spot on (a lukewarm starter, a soggy side order of veg), but minor niggles are more than made up for by beautiful calf's liver and bacon, moules poulette and tarte tatin with calvados sauce. If all the over-indulgence gets the better of you, you can stagger upstairs – it's a restaurant with rooms. Service is professional but not stuffy or intrusive.

Tickle Manor Tearooms ★

17 High Street, Lavenham, CO10 9PT (01787 248438). **Meals served** 10.30am-5pm daily. **Main courses** £3-£5.95. **No credit cards**.

These spotless tearooms, with their olde worlde atmosphere and friendly service, pack in a steady stream of tourists and locals. The two-storey, 16th-century premises is small, but provides a decent choice of basics that make a welcome change from the rich, hearty food offered by more upmarket places in the area. Choose from a selection of sarnies, salads, soups and spuds. Own-made cakes include chocolate, apple, honey and carrot. If all that sightseeing has taken its toll, go the whole hog and enjoy a full cream tea. Varieties of tea include decaf and several herbal options.

LIDGATE

Star Inn

The Street, Lidgate, CB8 9PP (01638 500275). **Lunch served** noon-2pm Mon-Fri; noon-2.30pm Sat, Sun. **Dinner served** 7-9.30pm Mon-Thur; 7-10pm Fri, Sat. **Set lunch** (Mon-Sat) £10.50 2 courses; (Sun) £15.50 3 courses. **Credit** AmEx, DC, MC, V.

Set in a sleepy village and exuding an unpretentious atmosphere, the 16th-century Star is the archetypal country inn. Recognisably pubby decor, with proper log fires and lots of wood, reinforces the image. The bar deals in Greene King beers and blackboard menus, and well-off locals treat this pub sensibly, popping in for a quick drink or evening meal without feeling the need to dress up. A quick perusal of the menu, however, hints that this is a cut above the ordinary. Landlady Maria Teresa Axon is Catalan, and food and wines show a strong Spanish influence. The cooking, in a homely yet modern vein, mixes scallops Santiago or paella Valenciana with carpaccio of venison or daube of beef, but puddings like treacle tart are resolutely British. Proximity to Newmarket brings in the racing fraternity (which probably explains the mobile-free zone notices).

LONG MELFORD

Black Lion

Church Walk, The Green, Long Melford, CO10 9DN (01787 312356/www.blacklionhotel.co.uk). Wine bar **Lunch served** noon-2pm, **dinner served** 7-9.30pm daily. *Restaurant* **Dinner served** 7-9.30pm daily. **Main courses** £7.95-£16.25. **Set lunch** (Sun) £18.95 3 courses. **Set dinner** £26.95 2 courses, £30.95 3 courses. **Credit** AmEx, MC, V.

At this Georgian hotel/restaurant overlooking the green, you might want to skip the restaurant, with its pricier, fancier dishes, and make a beeline for the bar area, with its interesting blackboard menu and relaxed atmosphere. Some items are a blast from the past (there are lots of sun-blushed tomatoes in evidence, plus old favourites like gammon steak, chips and fried egg), while others sound slightly too challenging (red mullet fillets with stir-fried vegetables and basil and cashew pesto). But there's some talent in the kitchen, preparing red pepper and tomato soup, salmon wrapped in parma ham with yoghurt, lentil and spinach sauce, and roast rib of beef with Yorkshire pud, which all hit the mark. Desserts might not quite maintain the high standards (chocolate and walnut pudding tasted more like a cake), but we'll be back for another instalment.

Scutchers of Long Melford ★

Westgate Street, Long Melford, CO10 9DP (01787 310200/www.scutchers.com). **Lunch served** noon-2pm, **dinner served** 7-9.30pm Tue-Sat. **Main courses** £12-£18. **Credit** AmEx, MC, V.

At Scutchers, ignore the bland (if inoffensive) decor and concentrate on the food. From basic to imaginative, with a nod to the Orient here and there, all dishes seem to work well. For starters, sesame prawn toasties with soy dip are ethereally light, while, at the other end of the scale, sautéed foie gras on a rösti with haggis, mushy peas and a port jus sounds like it should be an ingredient too far but manages to work brilliantly. Mains might be thinly sliced calf's liver with bacon (cooked to perfection), or grilled fillet of lemon sole with parmesan crust and a chive and vermouth sauce (ditto). Save room for dessert (bread and butter pudding with an apricot coulis, and other classics with a twist) and you won't be disappointed. Even with plenty of local competition, this place stands out from the crowd.

MARLESFORD

Farmcafe ★ ★

Main Road (A12), Marlesford, IP13 0AG (01728 747717/www.farmcafe.co.uk). **Breakfast served** 7am-noon, **lunch served** noon-5pm daily. **Main courses** £5.40-£7.90. **Credit** MC, V.

East Anglia

Looks can be deceiving. Many driving past this unprepossessing cream-coloured building set beside the A12 at Marlesford would not give it a second glance. Step inside, and you find a simple, compact space that leads on to a terrace protected against the elements, Parisian-style, by plastic walls and heaters, with chunky tables, modern art, stone floors and lots of touristy leaflets and local events posters. With a perfect Suffolk fry-up served from 7am, free range chicken, fresh fish, local dressed crabs, burgers and Suffolk ham and beef platters for lunch (with locally brewed Victoria Bitter from Soham Breweries tapped from the cask), and cakes and cappuccino at tea, this is a (posh) greasy spoon, pub, café and tourist information office rolled into one. Everything is prime quality, sourced from a local farmer or producer where possible, the kitchen keeps it simple, and staff are sweet. Don't drive past.

MONKS ELEIGH

Swan ★

The Street, Monks Eleigh, IP7 7AU (01449 741391). **Lunch served** noon-2pm, **dinner served** 7-9.30pm Wed-Sun. **Main courses** £9-£15. **Credit** MC, V.

The exterior may be textbook English 16th-century country pub complete with impeccably maintained thatched roof, but the Swan's interior has been modernised on an open plan, and the polished wood floor, cool shades of sage and contemporary lighting are definitely more restaurant than hostelry. But there's still a strong sense of local identity here with a dominant bar, log fire and excellent Adnams ales on tap. In the middle of all this, Nigel Ramsbottom cultivates a network of small producers to supply his intensely seasonal menus. From creamy cauliflower soup and poached egg, to apple and ginger pudding with sticky toffee sauce, there is scarcely a misstep. This is straightforward cooking that throws into relief skill, technique and perfect timing, whether it's a classic braised lamb's knuckle with mash and red cabbage, or fresh fillet of plaice with creamy leeks and new potatoes.

NAYLAND

White Hart Inn

11 High Street, Nayland, CO6 4JF (01206 263382/ www.whitehart-nayland.co.uk). **Lunch served** noon-2.30pm daily. **Dinner served** 6.30-9.30pm Mon-Fri; 6.30-10pm Sat; 6.30-9pm Sun. **Main courses** £9.90-£16. **Set lunch** (Mon-Fri)£12.95 3 courses; (Sun) £14.95 2 courses, £18.90 3 courses. **Set dinner** £21.50 3 courses. **Credit** AmEx, DC, MC, V.

Set in an old coaching inn in the sweet village of Nayland, this restaurant with rooms has built up a well-deserved reputation for its food in the five years since it opened. Both manager Frank Deletang and head chef Carl Shillingford trained at the Waterside Inn in Bray (*see p147*), and their expertise shows. Memorable dishes include grilled fillet of halibut with spinach, potato gauffrette and a herb nage, and escalope of veal milanese on fresh tagliatelle with tomato and tarragon sauce. Vegetarians are rewarded with the likes of millefeuille of baby spring vegetables with a tomato and basil butter sauce. When it came to desserts, a trio of white, milk and dark chocolate mousse was more pleasing than a very eggy crème brûlée. Try to get a table in the main dining room, which has a warmer decor than the tiled side area, or in summer, enjoy a barbecue in the lovely garden patio.

ORFORD

Butley-Orford Oysterage

Market Hill, Orford, IP12 2LH (01394 450277). **Lunch served** noon-2.15pm daily. **Dinner served** *Apr-Oct* 6.30-9pm Mon-Fri, Sun; 6-9pm Sat. *Nov-Mar* 6.30-9pm Fri; 6-9pm Sat. **Main courses** £3.90-£14.50. **Credit** MC, V.

Feeling very much like a blast from seasides past, the Oysterage is not just a restaurant but also a shop, smoking house and tiny fleet of fishing boats. From the freshest of local catches comes skate, sole, herring or sprats, and, of course, oysters from the creek, all of which make their way to the tables in the tiny, stripped-down dining room with the minimum of fuss or intervention. Most dishes from the blackboard menu are served simply, with bread and butter, new potatoes or a side salad as the only accompaniment. The eel and wild Irish salmon from the smokehouse are particular favourites. Don't forget to save time for a trip to Orford Castle next door for stunning views over Orford Ness and the surrounding Suffolk countryside.

The Trinity ★

Crown & Castle Hotel, Orford, IP12 2LJ (01394 450205/www.crownandcastle.co.uk). **Lunch served** noon-2pm daily. **Dinner served** *Apr-Oct* 7-9pm daily; *Nov-Mar* 7-9pm Mon-Sat. **Main courses** £9.50-£18. **Set lunch** (Sat, Sun) £15.50-£18.50 2 courses. **Set dinner** (Sat) £27.50 3 courses. **Credit** MC, V.

Combining a relaxed vibe with a huge dollop of urban chic, this restaurant with rooms fairly glows with the attention to detail lavished on it by proprietors Ruth and David Watson. The menu, like the rest of the operation, is flexible and eager to please. The majority of the ingredients are locally produced, including fresh cod, sea bass, skate and fish from the local smokehouse. Lunch is available from a one-, two- or three-course menu. At dinner there's properly hung sirloin steak and chips, spice-rubbed local cod with 'zippy' lentils and pak choi or Suffolk lamb served with garlic and spinach pilaf and salsa verde. Desserts – many of which feature in Ruth's much promoted cook book *Fat Girl Slim* – include the Sod it! hot bitter chocolate mousse with local Jersey cream. The wine list is a model of its kind, with around 20 choices by the glass. With a terrace for alfresco dining in summer and a log fire keeping the inside cosy in winter, who could ask for anything more?

SAXMUNDHAM

Bell Hotel

31 High Street, Saxmundham, IP17 1AF (01728 602331). **Lunch served** noon-2pm Tue-Sat. **Dinner served** 6.30-9pm Tue-Sat. **Main courses** £8-£15. **Set lunch** £10.50 2 courses, £13.50 3 courses. **Set dinner** £16.50 3 courses. **Credit** MC, V.

The intention was to re-create a provincial French country hotel in the centre of an increasingly prosperous Suffolk market town, and to a large extent it is done successfully. The decor in the small square dining room is reassuringly comfortable rather than exquisite, but the food is a delight. Rich beginnings pretty much sum up the menu: chicken liver parfait with sliced pears and toasted brioche vies with delicate grilled mackerel, salad and focaccia covered in tapenade for pure indulgence. Risotto with plump rice, asparagus and mint char-grilled vegetables will satisfy most vegetarians, while the excellent corn-fed chicken and assiette of pork with fondant potato, pea purée and apple sauce continues the French theme. Lastly, there was delicate baked custard tart with nutmeg and ice-cream. Coffee is best taken in the conservatory.

Harrison's

Main Road (A12 opposite the Kelsale turning), nr Saxmundham, IP17 2RF (01728 604444). **Lunch served** noon-2.30pm, **dinner served** from 7pm Tue-Sat. **Main courses** £10.50-£18. **Set lunch** (Tue-Fri) £11.95 2 courses, £13.95 3 courses. **Credit** MC, V.

There is almost no noise from the busy main road to disturb the monastic concentration on food here. It's an Elizabethan-style hall with uneven brick floors, open fireplaces, exposed beams and minimalist decor. The seating is comfortable, the dark-wood tables well spaced and the steamed mussel and chick pea broth as good a place as any to start on a simple menu. A decent selection of traditional, flavour-packed food – with local ingredients providing the key note – characterises the clever combination of tastes, including sea bass from nearby Walberswick served in a leek and butter sauce, and steamed haddock with a lively mix of cockles and chorizo. If it's meat you're after then an organic saddleback pork chop with mash and apple sauce is guaranteed to make you think of mother's cooking, as is the treacle tart and custard.

SOUTHWOLD

Harbour Inn

Black Shore, Southwold, IP18 6TA (01502 722381). **Open** 11am-11pm Mon-Sat; noon-10.30pm Sun. **Lunch served** noon-2.30pm, **dinner served** 6-9pm daily. **Main courses** £8-£11. **Credit** MC, V.

After a long day crabbing or walking against the biting North Sea winds that whip along the beach, this comfortable pub with atmospheric clutter-filled rooms and long dining room extension, provides an opportunity to indulge in some comfort eating. Portions are large by any standards, but the unpretentious food does not suffer from a lack of quality. Choose from crispy well-stuffed baguettes (around a fiver), a half-kilo of mussels steamed in white wine (£8.75) or trad fish and chips (cod or haddock). If you're feeling just slightly more cosmopolitan the own-made lasagne with beef bolognese sauce will do, and a bottle of vino (£11-£18) or a pint or two are guaranteed to induce a sleepy eyed riverside walk home.

The Trinity. *See p197.*

Mark's Fish Shop ★

32 High Street, Southwold, IP18 6AE (01502 723585). **Lunch served** 11.45am-2pm Mon-Sat; noon-2.30pm Sun. **Dinner served** 5-8pm Mon-Thur; 5-8.30pm Fri, Sat, 5-7.30pm Sun. **Main courses** £3.40-£4.20. **No credit cards.**

Situated on a street corner in central Southwold is Mark's, an unpretentious fish and chip shop cum cosy licensed restaurant. Formica-topped tables and moulded seats are fixed in a small space that is bedecked with fishing nets, evocative black and white photos, paintings and toy fish – all of which, despite sounding cheesy, provides a curious charm. The fish is generously portioned and presented in a steaming, crisp batter, fried in beef dripping, while the chips come by the net load. If the cod, haddock, plaice or skate don't excite it's worth checking the board to see if there is any locally caught rock or huss, which is same-day fresh, a treat that goes down well with a pint of the local Adnams.

Randolph ★

Wangford Road, Reydon, Southwold, IP18 6PZ (01502 723603). **Lunch served** noon-1.30pm Tue-Sun. **Dinner served** 6.30-9pm Tue-Sat. **Main courses** £15-£17. **Set lunch** (Sun) £15 3 courses. **Credit** MC, V.

East Anglia

Smartly decorated with bold modern colours, this renovated Victorian pub is a wake-up call for anyone who thought gastropubs had nothing new to say. The kitchen displays a passion for ingredients in their prime. Careful sourcing includes locally smoked 'Randolph cure' salmon that's a must-try, as is beautifully judged line-caught wild sea bass, herb-crusted and served with minted spuds, char-grilled asparagus, warm tomato and basil vinaigrette. There's also a perfect, healthy pick-me-up herb salad (from herbs grown in the Randolph's extensive herb and vegetable garden). And you must make room for stem ginger crème brûlée, rhubarb compote and lemon shortbread.

Swan Hotel

Market Place, Southwold, IP18 6EG (01502 722186/ www.adnams.co.uk). **Lunch served** noon-2pm, **dinner served** 7-9pm daily. **Set lunch** £18 2 courses, £22 3 courses. **Set dinner** £30 3 courses. **Credit** MC, V.

A grand country-house hotel restaurant with the elegant refined air and relaxed atmosphere of a bygone era; the Swan really does take some beating. The small bar offers a chance for a glass of the local brew while studying – and it rewards study – the extensive Adnams wine list and varied seasonal menu that takes local ingredients and enhances them with European flair. Once ensconced in the high-ceilinged, big-windowed comfort of the dining room, the warm spinach and gruyère tart kicks the taste buds into gear in preparation for confit of Aylesbury duck, with a glorious combination of roasted beetroot, shallots and garlic, or rabbit with savoy cabbage and red onion marmalade. To finish there's a difficult choice between Neal's Yard cheeses and comforting steam emanating from the sticky toffee pudding, followed by a languid slouch in the sofas of the lounge where you can sip coffee with lazy satisfaction. Adnams also own the Crown Hotel (90 High Street, 01502 722275).

ST PETER SOUTH ELMHAM

St Peter's Hall & Brewery

St Peter South Elmham, nr Bungay, NR35 1NQ (01986 782322/www.stpetersbrewery.co.uk). **Lunch served** noon-2.30pm, **dinner served** 7-9pm daily. **Main courses** £8.50-£15. **Set lunch** (Sun) £14.95 2 courses, £17.95 3 courses. **Credit** MC, V.

Parts of St Peter's Hall date back to 1280 and the main building is a splendid medieval sight as you approach through the flat Suffolk fields. The handsome rooms that form the bar and restaurant are decorated in a relaxed, small-scale baronial fashion, complete with wood panelling and huge fireplaces. Garden tables overlook the moat, which boasts a scenic pair of black swans. The flexible menu runs from simple bar meals (steak and ale pie, tuna steak) and afternoon teas, through to ice-creams and flapjacks. At dinner there might be salmon with a pecorino and pesto crust followed by caramelised pear tart. The quality is good rather than amazing, but the lovely setting and laid-back, child-friendly staff make St Peter's worth a detour. That, and the brewery shop (9am-5pm daily).

STANTON

Leaping Hare

Wyken Hall, Stanton, IP31 2DW (01359 250287). Café **Meals served** 10am-6pm daily. *Restaurant* **Lunch served** noon-2pm daily. **Dinner served** 7-9pm Fri, Sat. **Main courses** £9-£15. **Credit** MC, V.

Road signs for Wyken Vineyards lead to this county restaurant – converted with some flair from a 16th-century timbered barn. An industrious kitchen is committed to simplicity and artisanal ingredients. The first Suffolk asparagus of the season, the earliest rhubarb, or organic free-range chicken from Sutton Hoo all find their way on to the menu, served, perhaps, alongside organic salmon, pan-smoked over Wyken vine prunings, with cucumber salad and crushed new potatoes, or a gutsy dish of grilled saddle of rabbit with rosemary, polenta and black olives. Focaccia, baked in situ, is a must, as are the Wyken wines (served by the bottle or glass) – you can buy any you like from the adjoining craft-led gift shop. Teas, coffees, cakes and light snacks cater for those more interested in the garden and woodland walk, or customers at the weekly Farmers' Market.

STOKE-BY-NAYLAND

Angel Inn

Polstead Street, Stoke-by-Nayland, CO6 4SA (01206 263245/www.horizoninns.co.uk/theangel). **Lunch served** noon-2pm Mon-Sat; noon-5pm Sun. **Dinner served** 6.30-9.30pm Mon-Sat; 5.30-9.30pm Sun. **Main courses** £9.95-£14.50. **Credit** MC, V.

The setting of this 16th-century inn is apparently everything anyone could wish for (judging by the fully booked tables), with an outlook on to the broad street of a historic village, and beams, log fires and soft lighting within. The bar has cask-conditioned ales from Suffolk breweries and a blackboard menu, and the vaulted, understated dining room in the old brewhouse (complete with deep well) is marginally more formal. The modern repertoire is broad enough in scope to allow snacking or troughing, and as Mediterranean ideas lend themselves to this kind of treatment, expect to see dishes such as an excellent seared piperade of tuna served with black olive tapenade, or seared scallops well matched by a fricassee of artichokes and tomato dressing, served as either a starter or main course. Steak and kidney pudding or liver and bacon are there for traditionalists. Be prepared to share tables in the bar.

WALBERSWICK

Bell Inn

Ferry Road, Walberswick, IP18 6TN (01502 723109/ www.blythweb.co.uk/bellinn). **Lunch served** noon-2pm Mon-Sat; noon-2.30pm Sun. **Dinner served** 7-9pm Mon-Thur, Sun; 6-9pm Fri, Sat. **Main courses** £6.95-£11.25. **Credit** MC, V.

Every tiny, odd-shaped room of this 600-year-old Adnams pub has an eccentric table where you can stuff your face, and lots of people do just that, particularly at weekends. If you want to spread out, try the dining room at the back or one of the bench seats in the extensive garden overlooking the sea. The food may not be the most imaginative but it comes in agricultural portions and is, for the most part, tasty. Fish and chips are good value but the smoked haddock has a better flavour and the Walberswick fish pie, a mix of haddock, cod, prawns, a hard boiled egg and creamy spuds topped with cheddar will fill most people's boots. If you are watching the pounds try a starter, like the whitebait, which easily suffices as a light meal.

WICKHAM MARKET

Eat Inn ★

73 High Street, Wickham Market, IP13 0RA (01728 746361). **Lunch served** 11.30am-1.45pm, **dinner served** 4.30-10pm Mon-Sat. **Main courses** £2.80-£5.80. **No credit cards.**

In the centre of this unspectacular little ex-market town is a small unpretentious fish and chip restaurant with limited wooden-bench seating at fixed oblong tables, in an all-wood interior of little charm but great smells from the fryer next door. Along with the fish there are fried chicken, battered sausage and vegetarian options, all accompanied by a mountain of dark-gold chips and, if you so choose, a bucketload of mushy peas, gravy, curry sauce or Neill's own killer chilli sauce. Pound for pound the fish is the best option with meaty haddock, big white fluffs of cod and monstrous plaice, all in a crisp batter at between four and five quid, while the drinkable house wine is £6 a bottle.

WOODBRIDGE

Captain's Table

3 Quay Street, Woodbridge, IP12 1BX (01394 383145/www.captainstable.co.uk). **Lunch served** noon-2pm Wed-Sun. **Dinner served** 6.30-9.30pm Wed-Thur; 6.30-10pm Fri, Sat. **Main courses** £6.95-£15.50. **Credit** MC, V.

A narrow road beside this 16th-century house means that the wind from passing traffic nudges the building provocatively. After centuries of variant planning policy an eclectic mix of architecture overlooks the Captain's Table, while the arrangement of the four ground-floor dining areas perpetuates the theme of neighbourliness. The owners know their market: the local and weekending/holidaying crowd who demand, in a prosperous country town, conservative with a small 'c'. A solid wine list hints at release, but the broad selection of mildly adventurous starters merely allude to the exotic, without ever travelling far from home. Loch Fyne oysters and fried tiger prawns wrapped in pastry with a chilli dipping sauce give way to duck, Scotch fillet, ribeye steak and lamb kofta kebabs, with the 'Captain' presumably opting for lobster, sardines or sea bass. Basic vegetables are two quid extra, while the desserts avoid sophistication by being copious and sweet.

Also in the area

Galley 21 Market Hill, Woodbridge, IP12 4LX (01394 380055); **Prezzo** 1 Church Street, Woodbridge, IP12 1DS (01394 610401).

The Midlands

Midlands
Blackburn
Hebden Bridge
Halifax
Rothwell
LANCASHIRE
WEST YORKSHIRE
Chorley
Littleborough
Wakefield
Southport
Bolton
HUDDERSFIELD
GREATER
Barnsley
Wigan
Oldham
Crosby
Kirkby
Mossley
Liverpool Bay
Bootle
St Helens
MANCHESTER
Stocksbridge
Wallasey
MANCHESTER
MERSEYSIDE
Glossop
Birkenhead
LIVERPOOL
Warrington
Marple
SHEFFIELD
Widnes
Birch Vale
Runcorn
Chapel-en-le-Frith
Hathersage
Knutsford
Dronfield
Frodsham
Alderley Edge
Dove Holes
Tideswell
Holywell
Northwich
Froggatt
Ellesmere Port
Whittington
Flint
Macclesfield
Burbage
Buxton
Baslow
Ashford in the Water
Chesterfield
FLINTSHIRE
CHESHIRE
Bakewell
Denbigh
Chester
Middlewich
Mold
Buckley
Youlgreave
Matlock
Sandbach
Birchover
Hartington
Riber
Ruthin
Biddulph
DENBIGH-SHIRE
Crewe
Kidsgrove
Leek
DERBYSHIRE
Endon
Brassington
Wrexham
Nantwich
Audley
Baddeley Green
Wirksworth
Froghall
WREXHAM
Belper
STOKE-ON-TRENT
Ashbourne
Keele
Newcastle-under-Lyme
Cheadle
Whitchurch
Alton
Brailsford
Trentham
Blythe Bridge
Barlaston
DERBY
Ellesmere
Market Drayton
Stone
Doveridge
Littleover
Uttoxeter
Oswestry
Whittington
Sudbury
Alvaston
Wem
Eccleshall
STAFFORDSHIRE
Weston
Tutbury
Willington
Maesbury Marsh
Abbots Bromley
Burton upon Trent
Ruyton-XI-Towns
Stafford
Barton-under-Needwood
Llanfyllin
Newport
Acton Trussell
Rugeley
Yoxall
Swadlincote
Shrewsbury
Wellington
Donnington
Penkridge
Alrewas
Overseal
Ashby-de-la-Zouch
Cannock
Burntwood
Welshpool
Telford
Bridgtown
Lichfield
SHROPSHIRE
Shifnal
Summerhill
Swinfern
Madeley
Albrighton
Bloxwich
Brownhills
Dorrington
Broseley
Ironbridge
Tamworth
Aldridge
Montgomery
Much Wenlock
WOLVERHAMPTON
Walsall
Sutton Coldfield
Atherstone
Church Stretton
Sedgley
Wednesbury
Newtown
Bridgnorth
West Bromwich
Handsworth
Nuneaton
Dudley
BIRMINGHAM
Coleshill
Bedworth
Oldbury
WEST
Craven Arms
Stourbridge
Clun
Halesowen
MIDLANDS
Hagley
Solihull
Llanfair Waterdine
Bromfield
Kidderminster
Holy Cross
Cleobury Mortimer
Bewdley
Willenhall
Ludlow
Chaddesley Corbett
Lapworth
Knighton
Stourport-on-Severn
Alvechurch
Kenilworth
Royal Leamington Spa
Bromsgrove
Tanworth in Arden
POWYS
Brimfield
Hartlebury
Warwick
Mortimer's Cross
Tenbury Wells
Abberley
Redditch
Cutnall Green
Henley-in-Arden
Ombersley
Studley
Bishop's Tachbrook
Llandrindod Wells
Titley
Droitwich
Pembridge
WORCESTERSHIRE
WARWICKSHIRE
Leominster
Kington
Alcester
Luntley
Bromyard
Worcester
Stratford-upon-Avon
Builth Wells
Ullingswick
Malvern Link
Kempsey
HEREFORDSHIRE
Pershore
Great Malvern
Ilmington
Colwell
Evesham
Shipston on Stour
Hay-on-Wye
Dorstone
Eckington
Hereford
Ledbury
Upton upon Severn
Broadway
Great Wolford
Didley
Long Compton
Brecon
Sellack
GLOUCESTERSHIRE
Chipping Norton
Broad Oak
Ross-on-Wye
Cheltenham
Gloucester
Abergavenny

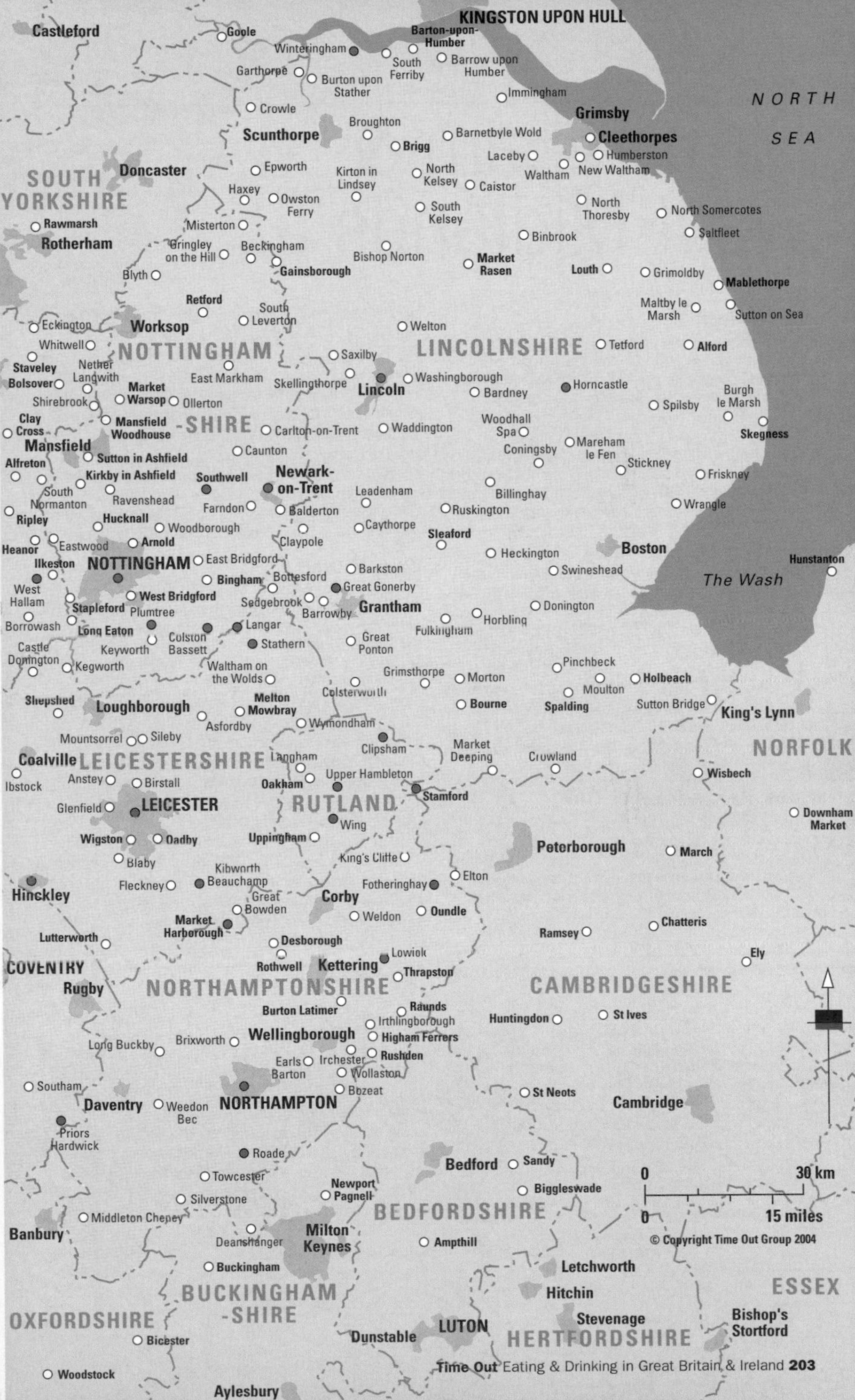
Castleford
Goole
KINGSTON UPON HULL
Barton-upon-Humber
Winteringham
South Ferriby
Barrow upon Humber
Garthorpe
Burton upon Stather
Immingham
Crowle
NORTH SEA
Broughton
Grimsby
Scunthorpe
Barnetbyle Wold
Cleethorpes
Brigg
Laceby
Humberston
Waltham
New Waltham
SOUTH YORKSHIRE
Doncaster
Epworth
Kirton in Lindsey
North Kelsey
Caistor
Haxey
Owston Ferry
South Kelsey
North Thoresby
North Somercotes
Rawmarsh
Misterton
Saltfleet
Rotherham
Binbrook
Gringley on the Hill
Beckingham
Bishop Norton
Market Rasen
Louth
Grimoldby
Gainsborough
Mablethorpe
Blyth
Retford
Maltby le Marsh
South Leverton
Sutton on Sea
Eckington
Worksop
Welton
Whitwell
NOTTINGHAM
Saxilby
LINCOLNSHIRE
Tetford
Alford
Staveley
Nether Langwith
East Markham
Bolsover
Skellingthorpe
Washingborough
Horncastle
Market Warsop
Lincoln
Bardney
Burgh le Marsh
Shirebrook
Ollerton
Spilsby
Clay Cross
Mansfield Woodhouse
-SHIRE
Carlton-on-Trent
Waddington
Woodhall Spa
Skegness
Mansfield
Caunton
Coningsby
Mareham le Fen
Alfreton
Sutton in Ashfield
Stickney
Kirkby in Ashfield
Southwell
Newark-on-Trent
Friskney
South Normanton
Ravenshead
Leadenham
Billinghay
Farndon
Balderton
Ruskington
Wrangle
Ripley
Hucknall
Woodborough
Caythorpe
Sleaford
Heanor
Eastwood
Arnold
Claypole
Ilkeston
NOTTINGHAM
East Bridgford
Heckington
Boston
Hunstanton
Barkston
Swineshead
West Hallam
Bingham
Bottesford
Great Gonerby
The Wash
Stapleford
West Bridgford
Sedgebrook
Grantham
Donington
Plumtree
Barrowby
Horbling
Borrowash
Long Eaton
Langar
Folkingham
Colston Bassett
Great Ponton
Castle Donington
Keyworth
Stathern
Pinchbeck
Kegworth
Waltham on the Wolds
Grimsthorpe
Morton
Holbeach
Moulton
Shepshed
Melton Mowbray
Colsterworth
Bourne
Spalding
Sutton Bridge
King's Lynn
Loughborough
Asfordby
Wymondham
Mountsorrel
Sileby
Clipsham
Market Deeping
NORFOLK
Coalville
LEICESTERSHIRE
Langham
Crowland
Ibstock
Anstey
Birstall
Upper Hambleton
Wisbech
Oakham
Stamford
Glenfield
LEICESTER
RUTLAND
Downham Market
Wing
Wigston
Oadby
Uppingham
Blaby
King's Cliffe
Peterborough
March
Kibworth Beauchamp
Elton
Hinckley
Fleckney
Fotheringhay
Corby
Great Bowden
Weldon
Oundle
Market Harborough
Chatteris
Lutterworth
Ramsey
Desborough
Lowick
Ely
COVENTRY
Rothwell
Kettering
Thrapston
Rugby
NORTHAMPTONSHIRE
CAMBRIDGESHIRE
Burton Latimer
Raunds
Irthlingborough
Huntingdon
St Ives
Wellingborough
Higham Ferrers
Long Buckby
Brixworth
Irchester
Rushden
Earls Barton
Wollaston
Southam
Bozeat
St Neots
Daventry
Weedon Bec
NORTHAMPTON
Cambridge
Priors Hardwick
Roade
Bedford
Sandy
Towcester
0
30 km
Newport Pagnell
Biggleswade
Silverstone
Middleton Cheney
BEDFORDSHIRE
0
15 miles
Banbury
Deanshanger
Milton Keynes
Ampthill
© Copyright Time Out Group 2004
Buckingham
Letchworth
ESSEX
BUCKINGHAM-SHIRE
Hitchin
OXFORDSHIRE
Stevenage
Bishop's Stortford
Dunstable
LUTON
HERTFORDSHIRE
Bicester
Woodstock
Aylesbury

Birmingham & West Midlands

Midlands

Adil's Balti ★

148-150 Stoney Lane, Sparkhill, B12 8AJ (0121 449 0335). **Lunch served** 11.30am-2.30pm, **dinner served** 4.30pm-midnight Mon-Fri. **Meals served** noon-midnight Sat, Sun. **Main courses** £4.39-£7. **Set lunch** (Mon-Fri) £7.95 4 courses. **Set dinner** (Mon-Tue) £7.95 4 courses. **Credit** AmEx, MC, V.

Balti houses may come and go in Balsall Heath and Sparkbrook, some inspirational, some fleetingly trendy, but only Adil's can lay claim to having been the first (in 1979, so legend has it) to save money on plates by serving up mix-and-match curries in the wok they were cooked in. The decor and menu have changed little since: clashing wood panelling and stripy wallpaper, with wipe-clean glass table tops. Try chilli bhaji starters for a quid or fish pakora, whose purple batter owes more to science than nature, all followed by hot, liquoricey balti chicken with a nan the size of a blanket. Also consider Imran's (264-266 Ladypool Road, 0121 449 1370) and Kababish (29 Woodbridge Road, Moseley, 0121 449 5556) – plus the Milan Sweet Centre (191 Stoney Lane, Balsall Heath, 0121 449 1617) for astonishing farsan (fresh-made, deep-fried mixed bhajia snacks to take away).

Bank Restaurant & Bar

4 Brindleyplace, B1 2JB (0121 633 4466/www.bankrestaurants.com). **Breakfast served** 7.30-10am Mon-Fri. **Lunch served** noon-2.45pm Mon-Fri; 11.30am-3pm Sat, Sun. **Dinner served** 5.30-11pm Mon-Sat; 5-9.30pm Sun. **Main courses** £9.50-£18. **Set meals** (lunch, 5.30-7pm daily; 10-11pm Mon-Sat) £11.50 2 courses, £14 3 courses. **Credit** AmEx, DC, MC, V.

Big, bold and buzzy, Bank is one of Birmingham's most popular venues, with a bar that's as stylish and as packed as the restaurant. The dining room can seem a little on the cavernous side – it's not a place you'd pick for a romantic meal à deux – but if it's good, straightforward, modern food you're after, this is the place; balconies make the most of the setting right on the canalside. It's a slick operation too, with young staff and a large open kitchen. You can't go far wrong with lobster, asparagus and mango salad or chicken and shrimp nam rolls. Puds are excellent, especially the warm Valrhona chocolate cake with white chocolate ice-cream.

Bar Epernay

The Mailbox, 171-172 Wharfside, B1 1RL (0121 632 1430/www.utopiainns.co.uk). **Meals served** noon-9pm Mon-Thur; noon-10pm Fri, Sat; noon-8pm Sun. **Main courses** £11.75-£14.50. **Credit** AmEx, MC, V.

Bar Epernay seems to have pitched itself just right, with its mood of non-fussy quality. While the Mailbox, Birmingham's premier shopping mall, can seem quiet at times, there's always a crowd here. The decor is a little airport lounge-like but it's comfortable. The large space has been carved up and made more human with smaller seating areas. The food is straightforward but as upmarket as the Epernay (capital of the Champagne region) name suggests: quality meat (ribeye, tournedos) or fish and seafood (Dover sole, lobster). Champagne is a speciality with an excellent selection by the glass.

Blue Mango

5 Regency Wharf, Broad Street, B1 2DS (0121 633 4422). **Lunch served** noon-2pm Mon-Fri. **Dinner served** 6-11pm Mon-Sat. **Main courses** £6.45-£25. **Set lunch** £7.95 2 courses, £9.95 3 courses. **Set dinner** £16.95 2 courses, £25.95 3 courses. **Credit** AmEx, MC, V.

Blue Mango is actually one half of a strange double act. Upstairs is Jimmy Spices, its alter ego, a mega buffet place offering more than 100 dishes from China, Thailand, India and Italy. Both chic, big spaces but Blue Mango is the better bet, with its light, inventive approach to Indian food. The upmarket twists and turns include a starter of golden chunks of paneer with pineapple and pomegranate-scented wild rice or lamb dum ki biryani, which arrives in three separate bowls – meat and rice in one, roast garlic yoghurt in another and 'gravy' in the third. There are more traditional dishes, but the real fun is trying something different. Service can be slow.

Café Ikon

1 Oozells Square, Brindleyplace, B1 2HS (0121 248 3226/www.ikon-gallery.co.uk). **Lunch served** noon-3pm Tue-Sun. **Dinner served** 5-10pm Tue-Sat. **Main courses** £4-£12.50. **Credit** AmEx, MC, V.

Little Café Ikon may not enjoy quite the reputation it once had but it's still a feelgood place to while away an hour or three. In fine weather, this section of the beautifully converted old school throws open its doors to make the most of its position overlooking one of the prettier squares in Brindleyplace. Inside it's pretty smart, all stylish white walls and neat arty pieces befitting its role as the café of the cutting-edge Ikon Gallery. The food is Spanish with a decent range of tapas, raciones and paellas. This sort of down-to-earth fare offers more comfort than elegance – the opposite, in fact, of the hard café-style chairs. Service is youthful and matey.

Café Lazeez

The Mailbox, 116 Wharfside Street, B1 1RF (0121 643 7979). **Meals served** 11am-midnight Mon-Sat; 11am-10.30pm Sun. **Main courses** £6.95-£16.60. **Set meals** £17.95-£24.95 5 courses. **Credit** AmEx, DC, MC, V.

Well and truly bouncing back after a temporary closure, Lazeez is once again a see-and-be-seen hot spot. Competing head-on with Lasan (*see p207*) in the upscale post-Indian restaurant stakes, Lazeez is marginally more expensive and self-consciously funky; but as the open kitchen exemplifies, 'if you've got it, flaunt it'. Head chef Parvinder Multani has undeniably got it: trained at the House Oberoi in Cairo, his signature dish of badami talapia features fish pan-fried in almond slivers, served in cheesey veg spaghetti. Other innovations run to coriander and peppercorn lamb chops, and hot malabari pepper prawns served up in coconut with banana wafers. Smoothly geared to thrill and charm.

Café Soya ★

Unit B106, Cathay Street, Arcadian Centre, B5 4TD (0121 683 8350). **Meals served** noon-10pm Mon, Tue, Thur-Sun. **Main courses** £4.80-£9.90. **Set meals** (noon-5pm) £5.45 2 courses, (5-10pm) £10.95 3 courses. **Unlicensed. No credit cards.**

Tucked away in the Arcadian Centre, Café Soya is a bargain corner of Chinatown and always packed. If you're after stylish decor, forget it – the orange and yellow colour scheme of this tiny room would give Laurence Llewelyn-Bowen a sleepless night or two. And the kitchen is an itsy-bitsy, rough and ready space screened off in the corner. But the food is great and very cheap. Most of the dishes are Chinese but there are also Thai and Vietnamese offerings on the lengthy, laminated menu.

Jessica's. *See p207.*

China Red

193-194 Broad Street, B15 1AY (0121 632 6688). **Dinner served** 6-11.30pm Mon-Thur; 6pm-midnight Fri, Sat. **Meals served** (buffet) noon-1am Sun. **Main courses** £8.50-£12.50. **Set dinner** £16-£28 per person. **Credit** AmEx, DC, MC, V.

While many of the bars on Broad Street have earned a questionable reputation, restaurants such as Shimla Pinks (*see p209*) and China Red make sure the quality of the food on offer remains high. China Red wallows in the plush feel beloved of the Strip, with leather banquettes and the buzz of a busy brasserie. There's a wide variety of dishes compared to the average Chinese. Yes, there are prawn crackers, spring rolls, crispy duck and the rest, but the mains offer a few curiosities. There's an extensive and dependable fish menu, but more timid tastes won't be disappointed by tried-and-tested dishes. Service is attentive.

Cielo

6 Oozells Square, Brindleyplace, B1 2JB (0121 632 6882/www.cielobirmingham.com). **Meals served** noon-11pm Mon-Sat; 11am-10pm Sun. **Main courses** £10.95-£19. **Set meal** £11.95 2 courses, £14.95 3 courses. **Credit** AmEx, MC, V.

Modern, exciting Italian restaurants are a bit of a rarity in Brum – most are the traditional suburban variety offering bistecca and pollo with Chianti bottles round the window. Cielo (Italian for 'heaven') aims to put that right. A large, wide-open place occupying a corner spot in this buzzy area, it oozes sleek contemporary style and has service to match. The food's not bad either. Italian/Mediterranean, it offers an attractive mix of risottos, pastas, charcuterie and fish. A rich squash, chorizo, chestnut and sage risotto, and fried sea bass with spinach come highly recommended. But there are more adventurous dishes on offer too – confit of rabbit leg with beetroot risotto, puy lentils and Barolo jus or fillet of red mullet with mango and pawpaw pickle, caramelised fennel, and lemon and dill dressing.

City Café

City Inn, Brindleyplace, B1 2HW (0121 643 1003/ www.cityinn.com). **Lunch served** noon-2.30pm Mon-Sat; 12.30-2.30pm Sun **Dinner served** 6-11pm Mon-Sat; 7-9.30pm Sun. **Main courses** £10.50-£16.95. **Set lunch** £9.95 2 courses, £12.50 3 courses. **Set dinner** £12.95 2 courses, £16.50 3 courses. **Credit** MC, V.

Like many of Birmingham's new wave of restaurants, City Café – the dining room of the City Inn – is a cavernous place and can seem an atmosphere-free zone if there aren't enough people around to fill its chic monochrome interior. But it has the edge on many of its competitors with a menu that's lively and imaginative, and delivers. The enterprising dishes don't always have appeal on the page – a Shropshire blue cheese and cabbage risotto for instance – but they actually work well. Expect

Midlands

lots of global touches, including some welcome Caribbean dishes rarely seen even in a city with Birmingham's ethnic mix. If you spot the seared Jamaican jerk hake with fried plantain and coconut sauce, try it – it's a winner.

Denial Bar & Restaurant

The Mailbox, 120-122 Wharfside Street, B1 1RQ (0121 632 1232/www.denialrestaurant.co.uk). **Meals served** noon-10pm Mon-Fri; 10am-10.30pm Sat; 10am-5pm Sun. **Main courses** £12.75-£19.25. **Set meals** (noon-3pm, 5-7pm Mon-Fri) £11.95 2 courses, £13.95 3 courses. **Credit** AmEx, DC, MC, V.

Denial can come over as a little schizophrenic – the bar and restaurant seem to be appealing to two different markets. At weekends, when a young crowd hits the bar, the music gets a little loud for the more mature crowd who have the taste and money for food of this calibre. So if quiet conversation is your thing, avoid Friday and Saturday nights to make the most of this venue's canalside location. The bar may give you the impression that the menu will be all burgers and pizzas, but that's not the case. It's direct, contemporary fare – risotto, carpaccio, escabeche et al – competently executed. Char-grilled sardines, pressed pigeon terrine provide excellent starter options, while mains can include satisfying roast rump of lamb, guinea fowl or loin of pork.

Jessica's ★

1 Montague Road, Edgbaston, B16 9HN (0121 455 0999/www.eat-the-midlands.co.uk/jessicas). **Lunch served** 12.30-2pm Tue-Fri. **Dinner served** 7-10pm Mon-Sat. **Set lunch** £15 2 courses, £21.50 3 courses. **Set dinner** £29.95 3 courses. **Credit** MC, V.

Jessica's only opened in summer 2003 but the pedigree of its head chef, Glynn Purnell, is beyond doubt (one previous workplace being Hibiscus in Ludlow). It's not a big place but it is clever – with a dining room and conservatory that offer two different but equally stylish spaces, both light, airy and decidedly smart. It's comfortable and relaxed, despite the fact that the service is rather aloof, and the food is full of creative flair. Expect dishes that play around a little with standard flavour combinations. Sautéed scallops may get a salad of crispy mackerel, cauliflower, coconut and truffle cream; loin of French veal is made outstanding by squid and white beans, tomato confit and shallot purée. There's a real passion at work here.

Lasan Restaurant & Bar ★

James Street, St Paul's Square, B3 1SD (0121 212 3664/www.lasan.co.uk). **Dinner served** 6-11pm Mon-Sat. **Main courses** £8-£14. **Credit** AmEx, MC, V.

If the stripped, groovy look and acrobatic menu twists are becoming no more than par for the course in Brum's trendier Indian eateries, it's certainly worth bearing with Lasan's modern north Indian conceit, which barely even touches the curry house base. Reached through a smart St Paul's Square front bar, the whole operation – from winning welcome to swish table settings and clattering ambience – is instantly impressive. This delicate trio of hors d'oeuvres are samosas only in name. Lamb shank in fenugreek sauce could never be mistaken for common methi gost. Interesting too, how Indian vermicelli pudding and fruit crumbles close the circle and recall British comfort food.

Liaison

1558 Stratford Road, Hall Green, B28 9HA (0121 733 7336/www.liaisonrestaurant.co.uk). **Lunch served** noon-2.30pm Tue-Fri. **Dinner served** 6.30-10pm Tue-Sat. **Main courses** £8.95-£16.95. **Set lunch** £11.50 2 courses, £14.90 3 courses. **Credit** MC, V.

The original Liaison was in Stratford-upon-Avon and the move to Birmingham by the couple who run this smart, ambitious restaurant was eagerly anticipated by their old fans. It's a good-looking place and the food is seriously cheffy, impressively presented and very labour-intensive. The menu-speak reflects its aspirations as home-spun dishes get the treatment, such as chicken and leek pie with a parmesan and tarragon crust 'scented with the essence of lemongrass'. This is complex, ostentatious fare, whether a marinated pork loin with celeriac and sage rösti and chorizo-flavoured ratatouille or mosaic of foie gras and chicken with a salad of sweetened grapes, toasted brioche and citrus butter.

Mechu

45 Summerrow, B3 1JJ (0121 212 1661/ www.summerrow.com). Bar **Open** noon-midnight Mon-Wed, Sun; noon-2am Thur-Sat. *Restaurant* **Meals served** noon-10.30pm Mon-Thur; 10am-1am Fri, Sat; noon-4pm Sun. **Main courses** £10.95-£14.25. **Set meal** (Mon-Thur) £11.95 2 courses. **Credit** AmEx, MC, V.

There are little hotspots of nightlife development dotted around Birmingham, and Summerrow – home of Mechu – is one of them. It promises a 'new way of drinking, dining and dancing', and is a slightly odd mix of kitsch (glitter balls, throwback music) and chic (smart, Japanese-style dining area) but it seems to hit the spot. The food majors on fish and seafood – whole platters if you want, all decent and not too messed about with. Then there's a hearty array of meaty main courses – roast rump of peppered lamb with fondant potato, or 10oz Scottish ribeye steaks. Mechu sets itself high targets but hits them.

Metro Bar & Grill

73 Cornwall Street, B3 2DF (0121 200 1911/ www.themetrobarandbar.co.uk). **Lunch served** noon-2.30pm Mon-Fri. **Dinner served** 6.30-9.30pm Mon-Fri; 6.30-10pm Sat. **Main courses** £9-£17. **Credit** AmEx, MC, V.

It doesn't seem to matter how many wannabe competitors come along, Metro (all curved walls, long stylish bar and a spacy atrium dining room) still rides high as a perennial fave of the drinking, dining and chattering classes. The menu has the confidence and ease that its time-tested reputation brings – a selection of well-combined and competently cooked modern flavours, from the

Midlands

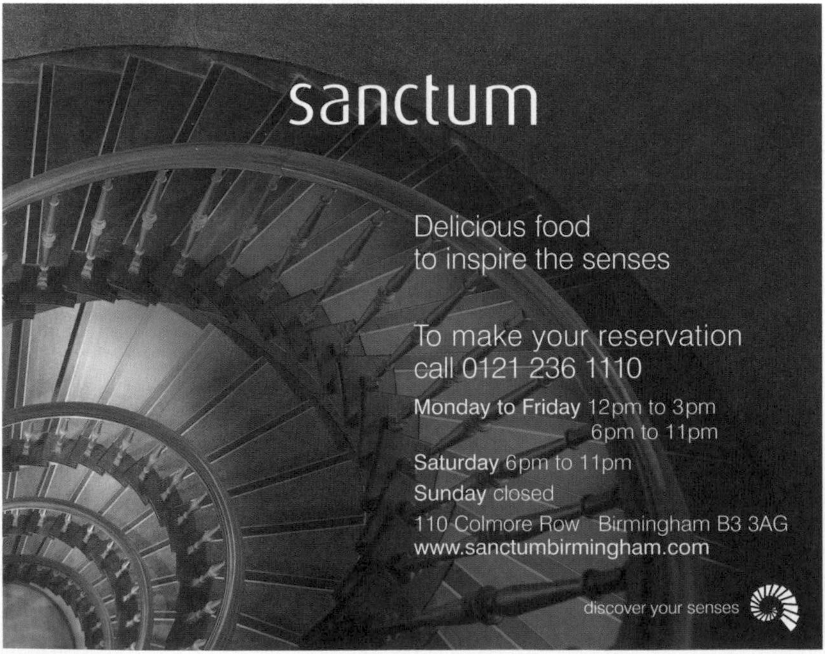

rotisserie selection to a variety of fish specials, along with bang bang chicken, salads and pasta. Nothing too fussy but always appealing, direct, fresh cooking. Air-conditioned, feel-good and buzzy, it can get hectic at times (and the bar can get very smoky), but the young staff seem to stay on top of things.

Paris

109-111 Wharfside Street, The Mailbox, B1 1RF (0121 632 1488/www.restaurantparis.co.uk.) **Lunch served** noon-2.30pm Tue-Sat. **Dinner served** 7-9.30pm Tue-Thur; 7-10pm Fri, Sat. **Main courses** £17.50-£26.50. **Set lunch** £16.50 2 courses. **Set dinner** £60 7 courses. **Credit** AmEx, MC, V.

A mighty impressive restaurant. With no natural light, it can feel rather cave-like but it's undeniably swish: lots of chocolatey browns, modern art and a stylish staircase linking the two levels. Prices are high and put it firmly at the top end of the city's restaurant scene. There's a gourmet menu available too. Expect to pay about £60 a head if you don't give the hefty wine list too much of a hammering. This is serious, high-minded stuff, whether it's squab pigeon, roast shallot, pomme fondant and Madeira jus or an upmarket vegetarian special of confit of cep mushrooms with roast shallots, parsnip purée and truffle vinaigrette. Wear your posh frock or break out the tie and collar for this one.

Primitivo

10-12 Barwick Street, B3 2NT (0121 236 6866). **Lunch served** noon-3pm Mon, Fri. **Meals served** noon-9pm Tue-Thur. **Dinner served** 6-9pm Fri. **Main courses** £9-£15. **Credit** AmEx, DC, MC, V.

The status of Primitivo as one of the suits' favourite watering holes dipped a little some time ago but it is now firmly back as a must-visit lunching and after-work haunt. It's rare and welcome in the city now to find somewhere not the size of an aircraft hangar. Primitivo offers two rooms – bar and restaurant – that are on the cosy side of bijou, but they are welcoming, attractive places with a great atmosphere. The Med-biased menu isn't long, but the dishes do have bags of appeal, featuring lots of fish and pasta. Try mussels with linguine in a tomato and chilli sauce, perhaps, or serrano ham-wrapped chicken.

Shimla Pinks

214 Broad Street, B15 1AY (0121 633 0366/ www.shimlapinks.com). **Lunch served** noon-2.30pm Mon-Fri. **Dinner served** 6-11pm daily. **Main courses** £10.95-£14.95. **Credit** AmEx, MC, V.

A glam buzz pervades the spacious pine interior of Shimla Pinks, where circular semi-private padded leather booths are set aside for Bond baddie parties. Despite all the expense accounts, there's no watered-down 'Anglo-friendliness' in this cuisine: witness the innovative brill in a hot coconutty Goan-style sauce. Try the rich Mughlai speciality koh-e-avadh, tender lamb in a gingery onion sauce 'flavoured with mace, sunflower seed, green cardamom and kewda wate'. Named after the Indian equivalent of Sloane Rangers, the place has suffered problems with accusations of arrogance in the past. Yes, it's pricey, and rather noisy with 250 covers; but right now on Birmingham's contemporary Indian scene it's firing on all cylinders.

Midlands

Bar crawl: Birmingham

The hottest new arrival on Birmingham's bar scene is **Chi** (61 Newhall Street, 0121 233 3150) – or to give it its cumbersome full title, Chibarloungerestaurant. This slick oasis of modern cool offers three floors of stylish space that include a jacuzzi and a giant bed, which can house up to 60 people. Soft jazz keeps the atmosphere laid-back during the day, while the evening speeds up with hip hop and jazz funk. Food is kept simple and the service is friendly and clued-up.

Nearby **One Ten** (110 Colmore Row, 0121 236 1110) offers another perfect home to those out to impress, with its marble and leather, chrome and glass. Its many levels include a roof terrace, smart restaurant and a luscious private members' bar (including a cigar room) called Alhambra, a nod to its Moroccan theme. All very Moorish.

If an Alpine lodge is more your thing, the award-winning bar **Apres** (45 Summerrow, 0121 212 1661) over on Summerrow offers an update on après-ski style with pine, cosy nooks and wood-burners. Shoppers ready to drop may prefer **Red** (Temple Street, 0121 643 0194), a popular oasis offering a snacky menu during the day as well as a good-looking haunt by night.

Over in the buzzing nocturnal Arcadian centre, **Poppyred** (Arcadian Centre, Hurst Street, 0121 687 1200) packs a young crowd into its brown leather banquettes, as do many of its neighbours, including **Sobar** (Arcadian Centre, Hurst Street, 0121 693 5084) – great for noodles – and **Indi** (Arcadian Centre, Hurst Street, 0121 622 4858), a minimalist white space offering wacky Asian tapas.

Fonteyns (17 Thorp Street, 0121 622 5757) and **Dial** (17 Thorp Street, 0121 622 5659) both located next to the Hippodrome are perfect destinations for pre-theatre drinks and meals. Dial has a great pubby feel while Fonteyns goes more for a much more upmarket style.

St Martin's Arts Café

St Martin's Centre, The Bullring, B5 5BB (0121 643 5428). **Meals served** 10am-6pm. **Main courses** £4.95-££8.95. **Credit** AmEx, DC, MC, V.

The Bullring is the latest shops and food development to get not only Birmingham talking but the national London-centric press too. The venue that has won over the locals is in the building that gives the Bullring its focus and heart – St Martin's church. A stylish new development has been added to the venerable, spruced-up building and it includes an excellent arts café. It's a fairly basic dining room with an open kitchen; a short menu offers panini and baguettes, tapas, filling pasta dishes and rustic fare such as lamb's liver with roast garlic mash.

Thai Edge

7 Oozells Square, Brindleyplace, B1 2HL (0121 643 3993/www.thaiedge.co.uk). **Lunch served** noon-2pm Mon-Sat; (buffet) noon-3pm Sun. **Dinner served** 5.30-11pm Mon-Sat; 6-10.30pm Sun. **Main courses** £7-£28. **Credit** AmEx, DC, MC, V.

While Thai restaurants abound, Thai Edge can still claim to be not only the best but also the best-looking. That white space, broken up with twiggy screens and feathered dados, remains a tranquil spot. The staff, wreathed in purple, are gracious; the menu has something for everyone. Its ethnic authenticity has been challenged by some (one complaining that a religious icon had been put in the loo) but that's unlikely to trouble its regulars, who feast on a range of top-quality soups, salads and the many traditional curries. Handy for the Symphony Hall and the Rep.

La Toque d'Or ★

27 Warstone Lane, Hockley, B18 6JQ (0121 233 3655/www.latoquedor.co.uk). **Lunch served** 12.30-1.30pm Tue-Fri. **Dinner served** 7-9.30pm Tue-Sat. **Set lunch** £16.50 2 courses, £19.50 3 courses. **Set dinner** £24.50 3 courses. **Credit** AmEx, MC, V.

With all the talk in Birmingham over recent months about who is going to get the city's first Michelin star, it seems a real pity that this excellent independent outfit seems destined to be continually overlooked. La Toque d'Or is the *bébé* of French chef-patron Didier Philipot. It's a cosy but romantic place, bare brick walls, stained-glass windows and pretty globe lights. The high open ceiling stops it feeling claustrophobic. The menu is kept short but there's always an appealing range of specials, though these often carry supplements that can seriously bump up the fixed price. Quality and real flair come as standard here. A starter of generous, juicy scallops comes with ceps and a hazelnut oil dressing; the main courses may sound hefty – Scotch beef fillet with crushed potatoes and a dreamy wild mushroom sauce – but the deft handling of flavours ensures that nothing feels out of kilter.

Wing Wah ★

278 Thimble Mill Lane, Nechells, B7 5HD (0121 327 7879). **Meals served** 11am-11pm daily. **Main courses** £6.80-£16. **Credit** AmEx, MC, V.

A giant green pagoda marks the entrance; inside, it's as spacious as the Wing Yip superstore next door, with a large circular central bar and plate glass windows affording panoramic views of the car park and A47. Best eschew the à la carte menu for the £7.50 'eat all you can' buffet. Pile your plate high with crispy seaweed, prawn toast and curry samosas – but go easy, big fella. Leave room for succulent crispy duck; robust, garlicky chilli beef; ginger-brimming stir-fried squid with leek and spring onions, and spicy veg vermicelli on the side. Forget romance – this is a splendid venue for a no-nonsense blow-out.

OLDBURY

Saffron ★

909 Wolverhampton Road, Oldbury, B69 4RR (0121 552 1752). **Lunch served** noon-2.30pm Mon-Fri. **Dinner served** 5.30-11.30pm daily. **Main courses** £5.50-£6.25. **Set lunch** £5.95 2 courses. **Credit** MC, V.

An unglamorous Black Country location, offering classy ambience and food of real quality. Dishes are sourced from all over the Indian subcontinent, with occasional culinary seasons dedicated to particular regions. But at base this is a curry house with a nouvelle twist, presentation being every bit as important as preparation. Bengal fish curry basks in a thin, hot sauce, while machli tikka ajwani – hake cubes dipped in sugar cane and steeped in a cream cheese marinade – is full of surprising flavours. Expect a beaming chef to check that everything is to your satisfaction.

WOLVERHAMPTON

Bilash

2 Cheapside, Wolverhampton, WV1 1TU (01902 311 991). **Lunch served** noon-2.30pm, **dinner served** 6-11pm Mon-Sat. **Main courses** £9-£23. **Set lunch** £10.90 2 courses. **Credit** AmEx, DC, MC, V.

Contemporary art and subdued lighting make this a stylish venue. From a vast menu, try murghi tok – chicken with shatkora, a sour Bangladeshi fruit – or the excellent murghi diya donia, chicken cooked in coriander. The key is the richness and subtlety of the Bangladeshi sauces, which even in a tangy tomato kofta accompaniment, achieve alchemical flavours way beyond the sum of their parts. Justifiably proud, Mr Khan can sometimes be persuaded to share hints from the kitchen.

Also in the area

Living Room Unit 4, Regency Wharf Two, Broad Street, B1 2JZ (0870 442 2539); **Loch Fyne** Bank House, High Street, Knowle, B93 0JU (01564 732750); **Malmaison** The Mailbox, 1 Wharfside Street, B1 1RD (0121 246 5000); **Petit Blanc Brasserie** 9 Brindleyplace, B1 2HS (0121 633 7333); **Shimla Pinks** 44 Station Road, Solihull, B91 3RX (0121 704 0344); **Tin Tin** 9F The Water Edge, Brindleyplace, B1 2HL (0121 633 0888); **Wing Wah** 188 Causeway Green Road, Oldbury, B68 8LQ (0121 552 0041).

Derbyshire

ASHBOURNE

Bramhall's

6 Buxton Road, Ashbourne, DE6 1EX (01335 346158/ www.bramhalls.co.uk). **Lunch served** noon-2.30pm daily. **Dinner served** 6-9.30pm Mon-Sat; 7-9pm Sun. **Main courses** £9.95-£14.95. **Credit** MC, V.

An informal brasserie within a converted 250-year-old coaching inn, Bramhall's offers Derbyshire diners a no-nonsense approach to modern, fusion cooking. The weekly changing menu is augmented by a daily specials board featuring fresh fish, always popular. It's a buzzy place, with friendly staff who make you feel as welcome as regulars. Presentation is a touch over-fancy, but the skill is evident. Try seared king scallops with pak choi and mild coconut – just the right amount of seasoning made the meaty scallops mouthwateringly good. Steaks are fabulous – fillet of Derbyshire beef, fondant potato, fine beans, crispy onions and green peppercorn sauce was judged to perfection. For afters, you'd be a fool not to try the almond tart with crème anglaise.

ASHFORD-IN-THE-WATER

Riverside Rooms

Riverside House Hotel, Fennel Street, Ashford-in-the-Water, DE45 1QF (01629 814275/www.riverside househotel.co.uk). **Lunch served** noon-2pm, **dinner served** 7-9.30pm daily. **Set lunch** (Mon-Sat) £18.95 2 courses, £26.95 3 courses; (Sun) £28.95 3 courses. **Set dinner** £44.95 3 courses incl coffee. **Credit** AmEx, DC, MC, V.

A delightful, mellow stone village, Ashford is a fine destination in itself. That it has one of the area's most imaginative restaurants only adds to the appeal. A compact menu shows that the Riverside kitchen likes to stay in control, never trying to dazzle with an overambitious range. Starters may feature terrine of confit organic chicken with baby artichoke, piquillo peppers and a salad of girolle. Mains are similarly uncomplicated: slow roasted confit of leg of lamb, braised vegetables and mint and rosemary gnocchi. Desserts are more elaborate – chef John Whelan obviously likes to end with a flourish.

BAKEWELL

Renaissance

Bath Street, Bakewell, DE45 1BX (01629 812687/ www.renaissance-restaurant.com). **Lunch served** noon-1.30pm Tue-Sat; 1st 2 Suns of mth. **Dinner served** 7-9.30pm Tue-Sat. **Set dinner** (Tue-Thur) £14.95 3 courses incl coffee. **Set meal** £20.45 2 courses, £25.95 3 courses. **Credit** AmEx, MC, V.

By far the best restaurant in this busy tourist town, Renaissance occupies the ground floor of a sturdy Victorian townhouse and has both a formal, French-leaning restaurant and a more relaxed (lunchtime only) brasserie. Poached egg filo pastry with wild mushroom sauce is a deliciously simple starter, while mains feature local and French ingredients, which results in winning combinations such as rack of lamb with herb crust, lentils and rosemary jus. The Renaissance's dark and white chocolate gateau will knock your socks off but if you'd rather keep your feet warm, plump for the retro-chic fab crêpe suzettes. Advance booking is advisable.

BASLOW

Gallery, Cavendish Hotel ★

Church Lane, Baslow, DE45 1SP (01246 582311/ www.cavendish-hotel.net). **Lunch served** noon-2pm, **dinner served** 6.30-10pm daily. **Main courses** £16.50-£19.95. **Credit** AmEx, DC, MC, V.

A stunningly situated hotel stuffed with fine antiques and oil paintings, the Cavendish is an elegant choice for a special occasion. The Gallery interestingly offers a table within the kitchen itself, allowing one curious couple to see the inner workings of a busy, first class restaurant. For those who are happy just to have the end results, the Cavendish won't disappoint. Service is unobtrusive but efficient, and the menu offers plenty to tempt. Seafood features prominently, and is precisely handled. Starters may feature pan-seared scallops with scallop roe risotto, fresh asparagus and a lemon and dill butter. Mains are more substantial, though no less delicate. We'd happily have ordered warm tart of langoustines and quail eggs, with rocket, parmesan and a tarragon dressing twice. That we didn't meant we could enjoy Thai coconut rice pudding, and sample a few slices from the excellent British cheese board.

Fischer's ★

Baslow Hall, Calver Road, Baslow, DE45 1RR (01246 583259/www.fischers-baslowhall.co.uk). **Lunch served** noon-2pm Tue-Sun. **Dinner served** 7-9pm daily. **Set lunch** £17.50 2 courses, £22.50 3 courses. **Set dinner** £35 3 courses, £59 5 courses. **Credit** AmEx, DC, MC, V.

Excellent dining in rarefied surroundings – that's the Fischer's experience. Smooth service, a comfortable dining room and a well-balanced menu create an expectation of something special. Menus follow the seasons, capturing the best of local produce: veal kidneys, pancetta and mustard sauce to start followed by pig's trotter stuffed with chicken and morel mushrooms. Fish is skilfully grilled and simply served; desserts are followed by hand-rolled chocolates and petits fours. The wine list isn't as scary as you'd imagine, with a good range under £20. Head and shoulders above anything for miles around.

BIRCHOVER

Druid Inn

Main Street, Birchover, DE4 2BL (01629 650302). **Lunch served** noon-2pm, **dinner served** 7-9pm Tue-Sat. **Meals served** noon-8pm Sun. **Main courses** £7.90-£14.90. **Credit** MC, V.

The Druid is a hit with locals and walkers alike, and the resulting atmosphere is buzzy and infectious. The dining room is cream, cool and maybe a touch too stiff; the restaurant takes up most of the pub, but there's a flower-filled terrace too. Food is delightfully free-thinking, ranging from starters of slow roasted pork spare ribs with hoisin sauce to baked mushrooms in a cream sauce with chopped smoked bacon and mozzarella. Mains include beef and venison casserole with orange and sherry dumplings. Vegetarians might try a filling vegetable wellington. Wines are excellent value.

BIRCH VALE

Waltzing Weasel

New Mills Road, Birch Vale, SK22 1BT (01663 743402/www.w-weasel.co.uk). **Lunch served** noon-2pm, **dinner served** 7-9pm daily. **Main courses** (lunch) £6.95-£12.50. **Set dinner** £23.75 2 courses, £27.75 3 courses. **Credit** MC, V.

Honest English cuisine served in a busy High Peak pub – the Waltzing Weasel knows how to keep folk happy. And, for those wanting their taste buds to travel a little further, the menu always features a strong selection of influences from the Umbrian region of Italy, thanks to their 'Umbrian scout', Simon White. It's in the starters that this touch is most evident – black olive pâté is aromatic and bursting with Mediterranean flavours. Game, when in season, regularly appears. We loved the pheasant – woody, rich and roasted to perfection. Pasta is delicate and as good as you'd get in Amalfi. It's a noisy place, but this is food worth shouting about.

CHESTERFIELD

Old Post

43 Holywell Street, Chesterfield, S41 7SH (01246 279479). **Lunch served** noon-2pm Tue-Fri; 12.30-2.30pm Sun. **Dinner served** 7-9.30pm Tue-Sat. **Main courses** £13.50-£19.50. **Set lunch** £8.50 1 course, £11.25 2 courses. **Set dinner** £23.50 4 courses. **Credit** MC, V.

One of the oldest buildings in Chesterfield, the Old Post is one of those places that makes you glad the world hasn't been entirely taken over by interior designers. The dining room is homely, with tables set at a comfortable distance from each other. Walls are cream-painted wood panelling. Menus feature five or six choices at each course, and the chef is more than happy to tweak, or prepare something else, ingredients permitting. Starters include tartare of mackerel, beetroot and rhubarb with fennel salad – a robust palette of flavours. For mains, corn fed chicken, carrot suet pudding, lightly scented garlic and lemon thyme velouté. Cooking is assured, wines and service excellent. One to return to.

FROGGATT

Chequers Inn

Froggatt Edge, Hope Valley, S32 3ZJ (01433 630231/www.chequers-froggatt.com). **Lunch served** noon-2pm, **dinner served** 6-9.30pm Mon-Fri. **Meals served** noon-9.30pm Sat; noon-9pm Sun. **Main courses** £7.75-£15.50. **Credit** AmEx, MC, V.

A lovely pub. Despite being more than 200 years old, Chequers was quick to move with the times, becoming one of the area's first dependable gastropubs. Banish thoughts of plush armchairs, swags and orchid arrangements; this is a real pub with great food. Try smoked duck with caramelised kumquats and redcurrant dressing for starters, pork fillet with apple and plum marmalade for mains, or perhaps fluffy salmon and crab fish cakes. Lunches are great value, and there's a lovely walled beer garden at the back for those occasional warm summer evenings.

HATHERSAGE

George Hotel

Main Road, Hathersage, Hope Valley, S32 1BB (0845 4560581/www.george-hotel.net). **Lunch served** noon-2.30pm, **dinner served** 6.30-10pm daily. **Main courses** £11.50-£18.50. **Set dinner** (6.30-7.30pm Mon-Fri) £12 2 courses, £14.95 3 courses. **Credit** AmEx, DC, MC, V.

A smart, well-presented restaurant within a traditional stone Peak hotel, the George offers exuberant cooking in a plush setting. The bar is rich and inviting, while the dining room is more Scandinavian cool. Both attract their fair share of passing trade and loyal regulars. Precise modern cooking is the motif – no meddling, no flourishes where none are needed. Starters include smoked haddock and watercress with a roquefort cream while the mains offer a difficult choice between pasta, fish and meat. We loved 'steak and kidney pudding' of Castlegate lamb, and seared Australian red mullet with gruyère. Desserts – chocolate and hazelnut brownies served with Baileys – are superb, as are the decently priced wines.

Also in the area

Bramhall's at the Crown Inn Rigg Lane, Marston Montgomery, Ashbourne, DE6 2FF (01889 590541).

Herefordshire

BRIMFIELD

Roebuck Inn

Brimfield, SY8 4NE (01584 711230/www.theroebuckinn.com). **Lunch served** noon-2.30pm Mon-Sat; noon-3pm Sun. **Dinner served** 7-9.30pm Mon-Sat; 7-8.30pm Sun. **Main courses** £9.95-£17.95. **Set lunch** (Sun) £16.95 3 courses incl coffee. **Credit** MC, V.

'We don't do rush,' says the man serving us with a note of reproof for anyone daft enough to want to eat at speed. Quite right too – places like this merit savouring. Although the floor-to-ceiling wood panels in the dining room are not of any great age, the walls are 15th century. A few miles south of culinary over-achiever Ludlow, the Roebuck holds its own with dishes like fillet Roebuck, a miniature Martello tower of immaculately cooked, succulent beef wrapped around a hunk of stilton and drizzled in a luscious red wine sauce. Most of the ingredients are sourced locally. Starters might run to salad niçoise or pan-seared scallops served on carrot and cumin purée, to be followed by fish pie (with salmon, cod and prawns) or steamed steak and mushroom suet pudding. The one failing was a flavour-free side of boiled vegetables. Facilities include two lounge bars (serving Shropshire Lad bitter, from the local Woods brewery, on draught), a no-smoking dining room and three bedrooms.

HEREFORD

Café @ All Saints ★

High Street, Hereford, HR4 9AA (01432 370415/www.cafeatallsaints.co.uk). **Food served** 8.30am-5.30pm, **lunch served** 11.30am-3pm Mon-Sat. **Main courses** £5.50-£6. **Credit** MC, V.

Give us this day our daily quiche (or Thai pancake salad, or fruit juice, or chocolate cake)? We've heard of broad churches, but this is something else: a still-operational place of worship that also houses an award-winning purveyor of drinks and light meals. Owner Bill Sewell's other gastrochurch venture, the Place Below in London, occupies a crypt; here, your table is a bun's throw from the altar. The sleek, curvy steel-and-wood balcony works well amid the stained glass and medieval stonework of its host, and scores tradition points for its use of English oak. When it comes to feeding the 5,000 (well, 50-odd, at a squeeze), there's a daily lunch menu of hot and cold dishes (pasta with asparagus and garlic, perhaps, or a 'healthbowl' salad with wholegrain rice, puy lentils and fresh leaves) or an all-day array of sarnies and sweets, all made on the premises. A blessing in a city not oversupplied with good snack stops.

La Rive at Castle House ★

Castle Street, Hereford, HR1 2NW (01432 356321/www.castlehse.co.uk). **Lunch served** 12.30-2pm daily. **Dinner served** 7-10pm Mon-Sat; 7-9.30pm Sun. **Main courses** £18.45-£22.45. **Set lunch** £21.95 3 courses. **Set dinner** £49.95 7 courses. **Credit** AmEx, DC, MC, V.

The dining room is a warm and sophisticated yellow, and the immaculate table linen and cutlery do this luxuriously appointed country hotel more than justice. Far better, though, if the sun is smiling, to take a meal in the garden – and best of all to take it on the lower terrace by the duck pond, a last remnant of Hereford Castle's moat. A basket of still-warm, fancy breads – scented with garlic, studded with olives – preceded the meal. We followed on with a lovely starter cappuccino of wild mushroom and truffle and an accomplished pot roast pork loin with creamed cabbage and pancetta. Staff are formal though not stiff; the menu still lists its lavish dishes in encyclopedic detail; and the kitchen still offers, by way of dessert, so-called 'studies in' various ingredients. La Rive's brand of culinary earnestness can all too easily provoke mirth, but keep a straight face: the results generally live up to the ambition. And in any case, as the menu says, 'if you would prefer something simpler' they're happy to oblige.

KINGTON

Penrhos Court

Kington, HR5 3LH (01544 230720/www.penrhos.co.uk). **Dinner served** 7.30-8.45pm by arrangement only. **Set dinner** £33.50 4 courses. **Credit** MC, V.

This lovely 700-year-old farm building, all black and white façades and ancient stonework, operates as hotel, a venue for cookery courses and, for a quarter of a century now, a restaurant serving great organic food. What a pity it doesn't open more often. Steered by chef/nutritionist Daphne Lambert, the short menu starts with soup and leads on with an interim course of, say, nettle ravioli, followed by a choice of four mains – vegetarian, vegan, poultry and fish – and four desserts. There's nothing fancy about the fare, but it's reliably well made, flavourful and nourishing. Desserts might include apricot and almond tart or blackcurrant and vanilla ice-cream. Winner of various organic awards and with lovely architectural features such as its fantastic 13th-century crook hall and large main courtyard, Penrhos Court is a lovely setting for a country dinner. Note that booking is essential (doing so well ahead is advisable).

Cafe @ All Saints. See p213.

PEMBRIDGE

Cider House Restaurant at Dunkertons

Pembridge, HR6 9ED (01544 388161/ www.dunkertons.co.uk). **Open** *Easter-30 Sept* 10am-5pm, **lunch served** noon-2.30pm Wed-Sat (& bank hol Mon). **Main courses** £9.85-£14. **Credit** MC, V.

Bloody Turk, Sheep's Nose, Foxwhelp, Strawberry Norman: just a handful of the more resonant apple varieties that go into the celebrated Dunkertons ciders. This is cider country and apples are a recurring feature of the food served in the mill's adjoining restaurant. Co-founder Susie Dunkerton (husband Ivor is the other) presides in the kitchen, and her concise, hand-written seasonal menu lines up onion and tarragon soup with parsley dumplings, or a satisfying cottage pie made with Hereford beef, marjoram and cider, and served with red onion relish and assorted vegetables; the dessert list runs to own-made ice-cream and a local cheese selection. Vegetarians have the choice of at least one starter and main course. The staff will gladly show you round their traditionally run mill, while the organic cider and perry (they claim, incidentally, to be the only makers of organic perry in the country) can be bought from the shop or had on draught at the bar.

ROSS-ON-WYE

Pheasant at Ross

52 Edde Cross Street, Ross-on-Wye, HR9 7BZ (01989 565751). **Dinner served** 7-10pm Fri, Sat; also by appointment. **Main courses** £14.90-£18. **Credit** AmEx, DC, MC, V.

This first-rate country restaurant may no longer be open on a regular basis by the time you read this. However, although still feeling the after-effects of the foot and mouth crisis, the many times award-winning (and name-changing) Pheasant is not wholly out of the running. Its two genii loci, Eileen Brunnarius in the kitchen and genial Kiwi Adrian Wells at front of house, are diversifying into superior organic pork pies, and even if they stop opening their cosy 20-seat dining room to a fixed timetable, they promise to keep up a programme of 'private dining' events to which anyone is welcome. If you're in the area, it's well worth ringing up to find out what's what. Wines are a strong point – Wells's wine list comes in three volumes, and his down-to-earth manner ('if you don't like it, we'll change it') is engaging and still all too rare. Food-wise, the Pheasant has nothing to be ashamed of: delicious breast of Gressingham duck, perhaps, cashew nut wellington for the vegetarians, and local varietal apple juices for those driving. Here's hoping there's squawk in the old bird yet.

SELLACK

Lough Pool Inn

Sellack, HR9 6LX (01989 730236). **Lunch served** noon-2pm, **dinner served** 7-9pm daily. **Main courses** £10.50-£15. **Credit** MC, V.

The menu at the Lough Pool has been shaken up since our previous visit – it's now shorter and less overarchingly international – but the standards are still high. Set on its own at the edge of Sellack, the pretty 16th-century black and white timbered inn has a pleasant cottage feel – beams, low ceilings, warm yellow walls – and there are three rooms for dining, including a cosy bar area. Chef-proprietor Stephen Bull swapped advertising for the rural restaurant trade, and is now turning out the sort of solidly English fare which seems so essential to such a setting. Roast breast of guinea fowl with swede and carrot mash was succulent. He also experiments with overseas influence: Spanish charcuterie, or an open lasagne with mushrooms and leeks. The dessert menu features the much-lauded Tuscan orange cake with maple syrup and clotted cream, and eton mess with rhubarb, orange and ginger.

TITLEY

Stagg Inn ★

Titley, Kington, HR5 3RL (01544 230221/www.thestagg.co.uk). **Lunch served** noon-2pm Tue-Sun. **Dinner served** 6.30-9.30pm Tue-Sat. **Main courses** £12.50-£16.50. **Set lunch** (Sun) £13.50 3 courses. **Credit** MC, V.

Peckish wayfarers have been coming to this spot for sustenance since medieval times. True to form the Stagg won the Best Restaurant gong in the prestigious Flavours of Herefordshire awards in 2003. Local boy and Gavroche alumnus Steve Reynolds runs the place. His focus is hand-picked ingredients from nearby producers, careful presentation and an excellent wine list. Kick off with the gorgeous local goat's cheese and fennel tart, and follow up with the breast of Gressingham duck with rhubarb purée. Desserts, if you have space, might include passion fruit jelly and panna cotta or a swish trio of crèmes brûlées – vanilla, coffee and elderflower. Accommodation is available.

ULLINGSWICK

Three Crowns Inn

Bleak Acre, Ullingswick, HR1 3JQ (01432 820279/www.threecrownsinn.com). **Lunch served** noon-2pm, **dinner served** 7-9.30pm Tue-Sun. Closed 2 wks from 24 Dec. **Main courses** £14.25. **Set lunch** (Tue-Sat) £10.95 2 courses, £12.95 3 courses. **Credit** MC, V.

This multi-award-winning gastropub is deep in the heart of some of the finest countryside in England – and we mean deep. You'll need a good map to find the place, and the journey will take longer than you expect. Thank goodness that the food is so good. Starters like sublime blue cheese soufflé, solid but perfectly executed mains like roast rump of Buccleuch beef with feather-light Yorkshire pud and vegetables, imaginative desserts along the lines of hibiscus flower and red berry soup with basil ice-cream. The cheese board is replete with local produce, and the rest of the menu is also locally sourced. Chef-proprietor Brent Castle puts his 'simple sophistication' watchword to excellent use, and the pricing is simple to understand as well: £6 for starters, £14.25 for mains and £4.25 for sweets.

Leicestershire

HINCKLEY

Watergate

Trinity Marinas Complex, Wharf Farm, Coventry Road, Hinckley, LE10 0NB (01455 896827/www.trinitymarinas.co.uk). **Open** 11am-11pm Mon-Sat; noon-10.30pm Sun. *Bar* **Lunch served** 11am-2.30pm, **dinner served** 6-8.30pm Mon-Thur. **Meals served** 11am-8.30pm Fri-Sun. *Restaurant* **Lunch served** 11am-2.30pm, **dinner served** 6-10pm Tue-Sat. **Main courses** £9.95-£13.95. **Credit** MC, V.

Hats off to Hinckley for notching two of the top five restaurants in the latest Leicestershire Tourism Awards. While the King's Hotel's Anglo-Hungarian flavours are duly noted, the buzz of the new surrounds the Watergate, a great wedge-shaped construction on the Grand Union Canal that offers waterside decking, prices set not to intimidate and a post-prandial stroll around the bijou marina. The ocean-liner chic – all air and glass and steel guide-ropes – is complemented by clean pine furniture and fresh, light food. The latter was faultless, from baked Thai sea bass on a bed of spiced saffron vegetables through to the audacious cream and mint brandy sauce accompanying the char-grilled lamb steak. A balti dish – another surprising chef's special – met with promising 'oohs' of delight from the neighbours.

KIBWORTH BEAUCHAMP

Firenze ★

9 Station Street, Kibworth Beauchamp, LE8 0LN (0116 279 6260/www.firenze.co.uk). **Lunch served** noon-2pm Tue-Fri. **Dinner served** 7-10pm Tue-Sat. **Main courses** £7-£17. **Set lunch** £10 incl water, coffee. **Set dinner** £15 2 courses. **Credit** MC, V.

Sarah Poli is instantly welcoming, hands-on and impressively expert in all the seasonal, authentic fare magicked up by partner Lino. From the second you open the door, you're caught in the happy buzz reverberating around the sunny walls subtly hung with great Italian images. Antipasti: goat's cheese, hazelnut and rocket salad was simple and exceptional. Primi: no room for pasta! Secondi: local steak and lamb cutlets were tender, complemented by generous dishes of ratatouille, roast artichokes and oiled and minted potatoes. Dolci: own-made ice cream, chocolate and almond-jewelled DeliFirenze treats were every bit as tempting as the startling wine list. Even the delicate Italian breadsticks are a joy. A must-visit.

LEICESTER

Bobby's ★

154-156 Belgrave Road, Leicester, LE4 5AT (0116 266 0106/www.eatatbobbys.co.uk). **Meals served** 11am-10pm Tue-Fri; 11am-10.30pm Sat, Sun. **Main courses** £3.99-£4.75. **Set thali** £6.49-£7.99. **Credit** MC, V.

First and foremost in the provision of pure veg southern Indian fare to the people of Leicester, Bobby's fully deserves its status as an institution. If there's any problem at all, it's reconciling the legendary care and energy head chef Mrs Lakhani puts into lavish farsan starters with the relatively plain main courses, while fending off both multiple taste explosions and the generosity of the chirpy waiters to leave room for bread and vegetable curry or a dhosa. Go large on a £4.99 bhajia platter – dalwada lentil balls coated in coconut chutney, batetawada potato balls in chickpea batter, aubergine bhajia fritters, dhokla spongecake with mustard and sesame seeds and cascades of other elusive flavours to dip in your chutneys – bliss.

Case Restaurant & Champagne Bar

4-6 Hotel Street, Leicester, LE1 5AW (0116 251 7675/www.thecase.co.uk). **Open** 11.30am-10.30pm Mon-Sat. **Lunch served** noon-2.30pm Mon-Fri; noon-3pm Sat. **Dinner served** 7-10.30pm Mon-Thur; 6.30-10.30pm Fri, Sat. **Main courses** £6-£19. **Credit** AmEx, DC, MC, V.

Set in the reclaimed shell of a bygone luggage factory, the retro mood of the Case's cool, clean interior is enjoyable, especially as the sun angles through its acreage of first-floor window. The menu is agreeably open ended, suitable for a shopper's lunch or the longer haul, which could also take in the ground-floor champagne bar. Warm duck and oriental veg pancakes with redcurrant and spring onion prove an appetiser worthy of the name. Mains range between salmon fish cakes with grilled veg and basil pesto through to a more extravagant loin of venison with rabbit, apple and thyme sausage. If pan-fried tuna is available, snap it up: it's a winner.

Curry Fever ★

139 Belgrave Road, Leicester, LE4 6AS (0116 266 2941/www.curryfever.com). **Lunch served** noon-2pm Tue-Sat. **Dinner served** 6-11pm Tue-Thur, Sun; 6-11.30pm Fri, Sat. **Main courses** £4.90-£13.90. **Credit** AmEx, MC, V.

An old school curry house from the name down, the passing fads of frenchified Indian cuisine and the cool pine interiors of the new wave are not for the Curry Fever. What you do get here is the real deal: sizzling sizzlers, fragrant bread, tangy sauces. Tellingly, butter chicken doesn't involve tandoori cubes in creamy almond sauce, but salty, succulent cuts of chicken on the bone, swimming in ghee. The Kenyan influence on Punjabi cuisine is best exemplified by the hot, dry pili pili chicken, unspoilt by progress since Anil and Sunil Anand opened for business in 1978.

Friends Tandoori ★

41-45 Belgrave Road, Leicester, LE4 6AR (0116 266 8809). **Meals served** noon-midnight Mon-Sat. **Main courses** £6-£11.50. **Credit** AmEx, MC, V.

So much of the great give-and-take of Indian culture is exemplified by a night out at Friends. Meat features heavily in the rich, decadent cuisine and there's plenty of saucy flesh in the Kama Sutra-style art that dates back unabashed to '70s beginnings. On the menu, words of wisdom from the likes of Vikram Seth and Mahatma Ghandi vie for attention with murg sheek gilafi (sizzling minced chicken kebabs, hot on ginger and coriander) and fish goanese (hot coconut creamy with mustard seeds). Children aren't just tolerated, they're welcomed. Service is a breeze. And what a pleasure to discover a large fridgeful of selected English real ales alongside the Indian-brand Anglo lagers. The manifold pleasures of the lightness of food, freshness of oil, and simplicity of menu make this arguably the highlight of the 'golden mile'.

Jones' Café Bistro

93 Queens Road, Leicester, LE2 1TT (0116 270 8830). **Lunch served** 10am-2pm daily. **Dinner served** 6.30-9.30pm Mon-Thur; 6.30-10pm Fri, Sat. **Main courses** £7.95-£13. **Credit** MC, V.

Close by the University, the Clarendon Park area of Leicester enjoys a low-key cosmopolitan atmosphere that's redolent of comfortable post-grad timelessness. In a neighbourhood served by a chatty boozer, two tremendous continental delis, tapas bars and a fine Indian, Jones' is the undoubted highlight. Seafood specialities are sourced at the city's superb fish market, with whole menus devoted to mussel bowls (the Thai liquor was irresistible), pasta and risotto. The joys of mod Brit are tapped but never forced, with old favourites – Cumberland sausage, crab cakes, red leicester mash – given a welcome wake-up call. Service is relaxed and friendly, the ambience intimate and agreeably noisy. You'll need to book.

Opera House

10-12 Guildhall Lane, Leicester, LE1 5FQ (0116 223 6666/www.theoperahouserestaurant.co.uk). **Lunch served** noon-2pm, **dinner served** 7-10pm Mon-Sat. **Main courses** £15-£19.50. **Set lunch** £7.75 1 course, £11.75 2 courses, £13.50 3 courses. **Set dinner** £29.50 2 courses, £34.50 3 courses, £39.50 4 courses. **Credit** DC, MC, V.

Ask a cross-sample of Coritanians to name their splashiest home-town restaurant, and a good few will be able to recount stories of tremulous dates, anniversaries and other celebrations in the brick-vaulted cellars at the Opera House. Over five centuries these atmospheric nooks fell into use as a jail overspill, a knocking shop, a pub cellar and a sewing machine factory. Now special occasion is the aim of the game, with food and service living up to the ambience. Bresola is own-cured, rare beef local and mushroom gnocchi wild. If slow roast pork belly with scallops and black pudding sounds sexy, wait till you taste the twice-baked three-cheese soufflé with mixed leaf salad and olive tapenade.

Sayonara Thali ★

49 Belgrave Road, Leicester, LE4 6AR (0116 266 5888/www.eatcon.co.uk). **Meals served** noon-9.30pm Mon-Fri, Sun; noon-10pm Sat. **Main courses** £1.95-£4.95. **Set meals** £6.50-£7.50 3 courses, £12.50 4 courses. **Credit** AmEx, DC, MC, V.

There's no shortage of guidance on hand here to make sure you get your south Indian snack-staple-curry ratio right, and sample the awesome range of flavours that have somehow gone undiscovered in carnocentric cuisine. If you find taking the leap from generic 'bread' to a list of seven offerings (bhatura: a deep-fried balloon of a bread; paratha, puri, rotla…) troubling, the starting point might be an all-in thali combo that includes two veg curries, a soupy dahl sambhar, breads, rice and a lassi. The real Gujerati Anglo-pleaser is the paneer tikka masala, a straight cheese-for-chicken swap; but it's probably more rewarding to take a chance on specialities such as cheese uttapam and the various filled dosa.

Sharmilee ★

71-73 Belgrave Road, Leicester, LE4 6AS (0116 261 0503/www.sharmilee.co.uk). **Lunch served** noon-2.30pm, **dinner served** 6-9pm Tue-Fri. **Meals served** noon-9.30pm Sat; noon-9pm Sun. **Main courses** £3.90-£7.15. **Set thali** £6.90-£8.95. **Credit** AmEx, DC, MC, V.

Now a newbie of some 16 years, it's all too easy to overlook Sharmilee, situated Mr Benn-style above a sweet shop opposite Bobby's (*see p216*) on the Belgrave Road. Waiters are all togged up in grey, blending in efficiently with the rather '80s decor. South Indian hare bhare kebab and mix chaat proved well up to the sky-high local standard. From the extensive 'Selection of Chinese Dishes with Indian Style', we plumped for mushroom bhajee, a 'mushroom curry in thick sauce', which neither sounded nor tasted Chinese but was nonetheless a subtly spiced alt-Burmese hit. The cashew-sprinkled veg pilau had more than a hint of the Chinese about it; likewise the dry, spring onion-strewn paneer and chilli peppers. It's brilliant value overall, with Gosai family specialities and curiosities all under a fiver.

Tiffin

1 De Montfort Street, Leicester, LE1 7GE (0116 247 0420/www.the-tiffin.co.uk). **Lunch served** 11am-2pm Mon-Fri. **Dinner served** 6-11pm Mon-Sat. **Main courses** £7-£12. **Set thali lunch** £7.50. **Credit** MC, V.

Currently, the pick of south Leicester's London Road curry quarter comes down to the Tiffin and Shimla Pinks, both brashly appealing to vibe-seekers. Truly, the 'future-retro' style and menu at Shimlas pale slightly in comparison with their Brummie franchisors, and while the Tiffin's take on sumptuous Raj living is just as historically confused, at least it's pure Leicester – all frilly pink curtains in the conservatory, Gentlemen's Club bars and no-nonsense Route One curry. The power resides in its lack of surprises – often an underrated attribute as increasingly obvious 'twists' prevail. When in Madras, Ceylon, Kashmir… shashlik, korma, bhuna.

MARKET HARBOROUGH

Shagorika

16 St Mary's Road, Market Harborough, LE16 7DU (01858 464644/www.qfol.co.uk). **Lunch served** noon-2pm daily. **Dinner served** 6-11.30pm Mon-Thur, Sun; 6pm-midnight Fri, Sat. **Main courses** £5.50-£13.95. **Credit** AmEx, DC, MC, V.

Noticeably pricier than any other Indian restaurant in the area, but customers know where they stand when they've been served nothing but quality ingredients and spices for 24 years. For starters, we plucked the nargis kebab from the tandoori platter: a rich lamb scotch egg draped in an omelette, served with side salad and mint sauce. What the menu lacks in fads it makes up for in unexpected fishy treats such as machali kofta balls, eyre khana and the Bangladeshi boal baza. Morchee chicken is tandoori-baked, served in a chopped green chilli, onion and fresh coriander sauce. Worth travelling for.

Midlands

STATHERN

The Red Lion

2 Red Lion Street, Stathern, Melton Mowbray, LE14 4HS (01949 860868/www.therutlandinn company.co.uk). **Lunch served** noon-2pm Mon-Sat; noon-3pm Sun. **Barbecue** (weather permitting) noon-5pm Sat. **Dinner served** 7-9.30pm Mon-Sat. **Main courses** £8.50-£14.25. **Set lunch** (Mon-Sat) £11.50 2 courses, £13.50 3 courses. **Credit** MC, V.

With the reputation of the Olive Branch in Rutland (*see p225*) threatening to bring it to a standstill, Marcus, Ben and Sean decided to keep the peace and open this second outfit 20 miles away. The same solid cornerstones of organic renovation, cosy ambience and a reliance on first-class local produce apply. Game specialities, sourced direct from the Belvoir Estate, are perhaps best taken in the smart dining room, while half a local pork pie and prized local stilton wedges might wash down nicely with a warm hunk of Rearsby loaf in the lounge or pubby snug. Abbey Parks Farm asparagus and pub smoked duck are highly recommended.

Also in the area

Shimla Pinks 69 London Road, LE2 0PE (0116 2471 471).

Lincolnshire

GREAT GONERBY

Harry's Place ★

17 High Street, Great Gonerby, NG31 8JS (01476 561780). **Lunch served** 12.30-2pm, **dinner served** 7-9.30pm Tue-Sat. **Main courses** £30. **Credit** MC, V.

Harry and Caroline Hallam do everything themselves in this tiny three-table Michelin-starred restaurant. That may mean that service is a touch slow at times, and the handwritten menu is short, but there's fabulous attention to detail and you're guaranteed that everything is lovingly and expertly prepared by Harry, using carefully sourced ingredients. Dinner could include locally grown asparagus in a heavenly soup, a whole sparklingly fresh Cleethorpes lobster on a tangy salad of mango and avocado, or delicately flavoured North Esk salmon. Puddings might be airy apple and calvados soufflé or own-made prune and armagnac ice-cream with passion fruit. Buzzy it isn't, but there's a gentle calm about this elegant, unpretentious place, largely due to Caroline's quiet competence front of house. She enjoys discussing the classy, if pricey, wine list, which is as just as carefully selected as the food. As for Harry: there can't be many award-winning chefs who'll see you to your car and wave you off into the night.

Midlands

HORNCASTLE

Magpies

71-75 East Street, Horncastle, LN9 6AA (01507 527004). **Lunch served** noon-2.30pm Sun. **Dinner served** 7-9.30pm Wed-Sun. **Set dinner** £26.50 3 courses. **Credit** MC, V.

Andrew Gilbert (chef) and Caroline Ingall (front of house) took over Magpies in January 2004, with the intention of serving modern dishes, using local produce where possible. The refurbished restaurant has proved very popular. Once you've sampled curry and lemongrass soup with seared monkfish tail followed by orange and honey pot-roasted guinea fowl with fondant potato and spring greens, you'll see why. The vegetarian option is an imaginative must-try – sweet potato and butternut squash kebab with spiced couscous and kohlrabi pear and watercress salad. Puds are the likes of espresso crème brûlée and frozen latte with pecan biscotti. Lucky Horncastle.

LINCOLN

Cheese Society ★

1 St Martins Lane, Lincoln, LN2 1HY (01522 511003/ www.thecheesesociety.co.uk). **Meals served** 10am-4.30pm Mon-Sat. **Main courses** £4.95-£8.95. **Set lunch** £7.95 2 courses, £9.95 3 courses. **Credit** MC, V.

It may only be a small café plus an even tinier cheese shop, but it's still one of the nicest places to eat in Lincoln. They keep things simple – with cheese at the heart of the operation – but use quality ingredients: so try melted raclette over new potatoes, Boston sausage tartiflette, croque mademoiselle (with the addition of chilli jam), or one of a handful of non-cheese dishes. It's a lovely place to have coffee and cake (baked vanilla cheesecake, say, or sachertorte) – cream walls, blond wood furniture and lots of windows make for a light room with a sunny feel. Staff are friendly and on the ball too.

Restaurant at the Jews House

15 The Strait, Lincoln, LN2 1JD (01522 524851). **Lunch served** 11.30am-2pm, **dinner served** 6.30-9.30pm Tue-Sat. **Main courses** £12.50-£16.95. **Set lunch** £10.95 2 courses, £12.95 3 courses. **Credit** MC, V.

Lincoln's most upmarket restaurant is housed in one of the city's oldest buildings, a cottage-like affair with low beams and restrained decor. It attracts a range of diners, so the atmosphere isn't stuffy, and staff are very welcoming. Typical dishes on the modern European menu might be frothed mushroom soup with wild mushrooms and truffle oil or carpaccio of beef with parmesan and wild rocket, followed by rack of Lincolnshire lamb with celariac purée and rosemary jus or pan-fried halibut fillets with coarse grain mustard sauce and stir-fried leeks. Finish with white chocolate cheesecake or crème brûlée. A dependable, quality establishment in a charming setting.

Wig & Mitre

30 Steep Hill, Lincoln, LN2 1TL (01522 535190/ www.wigandmitre.com). **Meals served** 8am-11pm Mon-Sat; 8am-10.30pm Sun. **Main courses** £8.50-£19.50. **Set meals** (noon-6pm daily) £9.50 1 course, £11 2 courses, £13.95 3 courses. **Credit** AmEx, DC, MC, V.

The bar/brasserie bit of this sprawling, faintly ecclesiastical looking establishment is the best bet for a decent meal; excellent breakfasts and simpler dishes such as pan-fried fillet steak with mushrooms in toasted bread are served in relaxed surroundings. In the restaurant, everything is a little more ambitious, and some dishes suffer as a result, notably a spring vegetable tart tatin – a badly conceived dish made worse by the lack of any spring vegetables (aubergine, red pepper, leek and tomato instead). Best of the bunch were medallions of pork with sage, parma ham, bubble and squeak and cider sauce, and a hot fondant pudding with thyme-scented ice-cream. Tables are too close together, and on this most recent visit, one of the waitresses really

Cheese Society. *See p218.*

couldn't be bothered. It seems harsh to carp, when few places in the area have this much ambition and energy (note the gourmet and wine evenings), but something was lacking this time around.

STAMFORD

The George

71 St Martins, Stamford, PE9 2LB (01780 750750/ www.georgehotelofstamford.com). Bistro **Meals served** noon-11pm daily. *Restaurant* **Lunch served** noon-2.30pm, **dinner served** 7-10.30pm daily. **Main courses** £15.50-£24. **Set lunch** (Mon-Sat) £17.50 2 courses. **Credit** AmEx, DC, MC, V.

You won't get the finest food you've ever eaten at the George, but what this busy 17th-century coaching inn lacks in culinary finesse, it makes up for in atmosphere and charm. In summer, try the platters of langoustines or lobster from the all-day bistro menu, eaten outside in the cobbled courtyard, surrounded by chatter and tubs of flowers. Winter days lend themselves to a stomp through nearby Burghley Park, followed by pre-dinner drinks in squashy chairs by the roaring log fire. You'll need to change out of your rambling gear if you want to try the formal panelled dining room with its pricier menu, as there's a strict dress code. Highlights are the roast beef and punchy horseradish (around £17) or rack of lamb. There's an adventurous wine list, which changes four times a year. It's not trendy, but the chintz, heavy silver and thick napkins have a comfortable allure. The main disappointments are desserts and cakes served at afternoon tea; it appears the pastry chef has a seriously heavy hand. Service is efficient, if a trifle harried.

WINTERINGHAM

Winteringham Fields ★

Winteringham, DN15 9PF (01724 733096/ www.winteringhamfields.com). **Lunch served** noon-1.30pm, **dinner served** 7-9.30pm Tue-Sat. **Main courses** £29-£33. **Set lunch** £27 2 courses, £31 3 courses. **Set dinner** £38 3 courses, £70 6 courses. **Credit** AmEx, MC, V.

Germain and Annie Schwab almost sold up last year on health grounds, but now health and restaurant have bounced back in scintillating style. Beyond any sober debate, this is one of the very best restaurants in Britain on the best form of its life. Surrender to the exquisitely calibrated service. Choose from 18 different mineral waters and you're off. One version of a spring set lunch could give a procession of the following: scallop and black truffle wrapped in spring cabbage; a foam of jerusalem artichoke with a miniature brioche studded with truffle and an intoxicating truffle butter; sautéed cod cheeks, succulently served with risotto and foam of scallop roe; loin of pork set on leek and prunes, with shards of sage, crackling and black pudding set in sweet potato; a pre-pudding of strawberry granita and perfect hot lemon soufflé pierced by a cone of vanilla ice cream; a pure white lavender sorbet, contrasting with the deepest, darkest chocolate tart. That's one selection without a duff note. Ingredients and cooking are impeccable. More amazingly for such a celebrated destination, it pulls off the most elaborate creations without being remotely snobby. You can actually relax at Winteringham Fields. If the £70 dinner menu is twice as good as the £31 lunch, raid the piggy bank now.

Northamptonshire

FOTHERINGHAY

Falcon

Fotheringhay, PE8 5HZ (01832 226254/www.huntsbridge.com). **Lunch served** noon-2.15pm daily. **Dinner served** 6.30-9.30pm Mon-Sat; 7-9pm Sun. **Main courses** £9.75-£19.50. **Set lunch** £11.75 2 courses, £14.75 3 courses Mon-Sat. **Credit** AmEx, DC, MC, V.

In this freehouse with its stable courtyard at the back and slightly more formal dining conservatory, the bars are the most atmospheric features – the snug is suitable for recreational drinking, while the other, larger bar adjoining the conservatory is ideal for intimate dining. Tandoori chicken weighs in at £4.75, while the teriyaki chicken costs £7.95 and will do nicely for a light lunch, as will the crispy duck spring rolls. A mix of Mediterranean veg goes surprisingly well with a Barnsley chop, but the best deals are the spicy Moroccan pork kebabs with couscous and harissa aïoli or the roast pepper, red onion, aubergine, feta and filo torte with roast pine nut salad, followed by sticky toffee pudding with rum and raisin ice-cream. Wine is available by the glass; bottles cost from £12 to £29.

LOWICK

Snooty Fox

16 Main Street, Lowick, NN14 3BH (01832 733434). **Lunch served** noon-2pm daily. **Dinner served** 6.30-9.30pm Mon-Sat; 7-9.30pm Sun. **Main courses** £7.95-£16.95. **Credit** MC, V.

Specialising in food and fitting perfectly into an idyllic village made up of buildings with the same thick stone walls, the Snooty Fox has a formal dining room, a couple of spacious dining nooks either side of a converted fireplace and a bar. It's a freehouse so there are excellent guest ales and an extensive wine list. Fish is fresh from Cornwall and meat is cut to size at the counter: £1.50 for 25 grams of sirloin, £2.10 for 25 grams of fillet and £10.50 for a Barnsley chop. The pork pies look great, the bangers and mash tempt, but top of the menu is the fish pie, stuffed with haddock, salmon, prawns and mackerel, topped with creamy mash and cheddar.

NORTHAMPTON

Academy Coffee Haus ★

1 College Street Mews, Northampton, NN1 2QF (01604 232111). **Meals served** 10am-4pm Mon-Wed; 10am-10pm Thur-Sat. **Main courses** £6.95-£9.95. **Set meal** (5.30-7.30pm Thur-Sat) £11.50 2 courses. **Credit** MC, V.

This stylish, licensed coffee shop is pleasing on the eye with barred windows, wooden floors and tables, pale walls, a steel bar and food counter, all enhanced by the work of local artists on the walls. A full breakfast is £3.95 and there's a veggie alternative. Waffles, crêpes, sandwiches, baguettes, salads, spuds and pasta suffice for the lunchtime crowds. A pre-theatre menu starts at £11.50 for two courses and includes warm breads and stuffed olives, followed by a combination of buffalo mozzarella, rocket and beef tomatoes or local pâté. Mains feature tray-baked salmon or chicken, or brie and redcurrant tart with spinach and french fries. For dessert you could go for vanilla fudge truffle or chocarocha cream pie, difficult to spell but easy to digest.

The best One-offs

Island Cottage
A trip in a tiny boat brings diners to this restaurant on a remote island. *See p354.*

Mud Dock Café
Mountain bike shop meets atmospheric bistro. *See p111.*

Wimborne St Giles Village Hall
Home-made Sunday teas from a vanished era. *See p135.*

ROADE

Roade House

16 High Street, Roade, NN7 2NW (01604 863372/www.roadehousehotel.co.uk). **Lunch served** 12.30-2pm Tue-Fri. **Dinner served** 7-10pm Mon-Sat. **Main courses** £15.50-£19. **Set lunch** £17 2 courses, £20 3 courses. **Credit** AmEx, MC, V.

Originally a village pub from the 18th century, Roade House is now a country hotel and restaurant with a broad dinner menu and limited lunchtime options. Among the starters that catch the eye are a smoked haddock and tomato tartlet with a poached egg and cheese sauce, seared scallops or a ricotta and mint ravioli. Mains – between £17 and £19 – and include steamed halibut with leeks, roast monkfish, roast guinea fowl breast with braised leg or venison steaks – all of which points to the traditionally rural and slightly staid atmosphere that dominates. Portions are generous, without being overwhelming, while the service is attentive without being intrusive, but prices are no bargain.

Nottinghamshire

COLSTON BASSETT

Martin's Arms

School Lane, Colston Bassett, NG12 3FD (01949 81361). Bar **Open** noon-3pm, 6-11pm Mon-Sat; noon-3pm, 6.30-10.30pm Sun. **Lunch served** noon-2pm daily. **Dinner served** 6-10pm Mon-Sat. **Main courses** £9-£15. *Restaurant* **Lunch served** noon-1.30pm daily. **Dinner served** 6-9pm Mon-Sat. **Main courses** £9.50-£19. **Credit** AmEx, MC, V.

Located in the quaint village of Colston Bassett (which is justly famous for its stilton), the Martin's Arms is a quintessential country pub with a strong local reputation for its gourmet menu. The small dining room (separate from the main part of the pub) feels rather formal although service is generally good. Highlights from an interesting menu include char-grilled zucchini with tempura halloumi and chilli crab dressing; seared fillet of beef with roasted root vegetables, foie gras samosa and wilted watercress; and sweet stilton cheesecake with caramelised figs. This is high-end pub grub – but it certainly doesn't come cheap. Budget for at least £70 for a modest meal for two. You're paying for both the idyllic rural setting (cosy in winter, gorgeous in summer) and the superb food.

LANGAR

Langar Hall

Langar Hall, Church Lane, Langar, NG13 9HG (01949 860559/www.langarhall.com). **Lunch served** noon-1.45pm daily. **Dinner served** 7-8.45pm Mon-Thur, Sun; 7-9pm Fri, Sat. **Main courses** £13-£21. **Set lunch** (Mon-Thur) £13.50 2 courses, £16.50 3 courses; (Fri, Sat) £17.50 2 courses, £20 3 courses; (Sun) £24.50 3 courses. **Set dinner** £30 3 courses. **Credit** MC, V.

As you reach the end of a long avenue of lime trees near the tiny village of Langar, stunning Langar Hall comes into view. From Cliff Richard to Jools Holland, Langar Hall has hosted some famous guests, and as a posh country house hotel and restaurant, it plays its part to perfection. But thankfully it's far from stuffy. Owned and run by the well-known local restaurateur Imogen Skirving, the small restaurant is located in an elegant pillared hall. The seasonal menus, described as 'Classical English Country with a twist', vary daily but favour meat-lovers – veal, beef and lamb figure heavily – so vegetarians may struggle a little. Nevertheless, both the watercress and potato soup, and mushroom and spinach risotto options were excellent.

Bar crawl: Nottingham

Nottingham can be a raucous city, especially at night. But avoiding the rampaging hordes of lads and ladettes isn't a problem if you know where to go. One of the best bets in recent years has been the rejuvenated Lace Market district, where dozens of trendy late-night bars have appeared to service the needs of penthouse apartment owners and design agency staff. High Pavement, a historic street at the edge of the Lace Market, is a boozer's utopia with everything from chainy theme pubs to a clutch of Nottingham's finest drinking dens – **Brass Monkey** (11 High Pavement, 0115 840 4101), where the city's most cutting-edge cocktails are served from the long, Manhattan-style bar; **Cock & Hoop** (25-27 High Pavement, 0115 852 3231) a real ale enclave given a stylish makeover by the adjoining fancy Lace Market Hotel; and the cosmopolitan **Saint Bar** (31 High Pavement, 0115 852 3236) within the hotel itself, an oasis of style and sophistication with a cocktail list (and prices) to match.

Nearby recommendations include the industrial chic of **Bluu** (5 Broadway, 0115 950 5359) where punters chill-out on the comfy leather sofas in its basement DJ bar; **Brownes** (17-19 Goosegate, 0115 958 0188), a huge café-bar that's a Nottingham fixture and lively throughout the day; **Dogma** (9 Byard Lane, 0115 988 6830) where DJs and bands entertain an up-for-it crowd in its basement; and the **Social** (23 Pelham Street, 0115 950 5078), the northern outpost of London's Social, which is always worth checking for hot new bands.

Meanwhile, two venues perfect for meeting friends of all ages are the **Broadway Cinema Café-Bar** (Broad Street, 0115 952 6611), for its range of European beers and video installation art, and the **Dragon** (67 Long Row, 0115 941 7080) at the other end of town, which has been renovated into a quietly stylish bar.

Cast.

NEWARK

Café Bleu

14 Castlegate, Newark, NG24 1BG (01636 610141/ www.cafebleu.co.uk). **Lunch served** noon-2.30pm Mon-Sat; noon-3pm Sun. **Dinner served** 7-9.30pm Mon-Fri; 6.30-10pm Sat. **Main courses** £9.50-£14.95. **Credit** MC, V.

Despite the rather garish decor (slightly reminiscent of a 1980s wine bar), the great and the good flock here for gourmet cuisine that enjoys showing off its upmarket credentials. Hence the potted crab and shrimps with chilled gazpacho, caviar and truffle oil or the chicken liver and foie gras parfait with apricot chutney and toasted brioche. Clearly this is a place that loves to impress and it doesn't come cheap, so bank on at least £30 per head for a three-course dinner. With regular jazz sessions also on the menu, Café Bleu sees itself as a destination restaurant – and that's just what its well-heeled clientele expects.

NOTTINGHAM

Alley Café Bar ★ ★

1a Cannon Court, Long Row West, Nottingham, NG1 6JE (0115 955 1013/www.alleycafe.co.uk). **Meals served** 11am-6pm Mon, Tue; 11am-9.30pm Wed-Sat. **Main courses** £3-£4.60. **Set breakfast** (11am-noon) £4. **Set meals** (3-5pm) £4.50 incl soft drink, (5.30-6.30pm) £5 pizza and one drink. **Credit** MC, V.

A real favourite with the Nottingham cognoscenti, this tiny venue is well worth seeking out. Intimate, bohemian and friendly, the Alley hosts funky events such as beat poetry slams and percussive beat nights. The excellent vegetarian and vegan food is also a huge incentive – black bean burrito, tandoori tofu kebabs and halloumi salad come in generous portions. This is a multi-purpose venue – serving everything from all-day breakfast specials to lunchtime sandwiches, afternoon coffees (Fairtrade, naturally) and late-night cocktails. So it's a favourite with everyone from trendy students to discerning office workers and veggie enthusiasts of all persuasions. Not surprisingly, it's constantly busy.

Cast

Nottingham Playhouse, Wellington Circus, Nottingham, NG1 5AS (0115 852 3898/www.cast restaurant.co.uk). **Lunch served** noon-2.30pm Mon-Sat; noon-4pm Sun. **Dinner served** 6-10pm Mon-Wed; 6-10.30pm Thur-Sat; 6-9pm Sun. **Main courses** £9-£12. **Set lunch** (Sun) £12.50 2 courses, £15 3 courses. **Set dinner** (6-8pm) £10.50 2 courses, £13 3 courses. **Credit** MC, V.

Designed by architect Peter Moro (partly responsible for the Royal Festival Hall), Nottingham Playhouse – thanks to a lottery grant of £1.2 million – now boasts a new delicatessen, restaurant and café-bar. Although the restaurant's minimalist design feels rather clinical, this is a venue that can't fail – it has a constant turnover, from panto-ing parents to drama queens. The food, though yet to win universal acclaim, is reasonably priced – a three-course set menu might include cauliflower soup; roast chicken breast, new potatoes and spinach; and banana mousse for £15. Such an important venue obviously takes time to find its feet. But with staff in Paul Smith-designed uniforms, a view that includes the huge 'Sky Mirror' designed by Anish Kapoor and a regular supply of punters, it should run and run.

Chino Latino ★

41 Maid Marion Way, Nottingham, NG1 6GD (0115 947 7444/www.chinolatino.co.uk). **Lunch served** noon-3pm, **dinner served** 6-11pm Mon-Sat. **Main courses** £7-£22. **Set lunch** £9.95 2 courses. **Set dinner** £25-£37.50 per person (minimum 4). **Credit** AmEx, DC, MC, V.

Far-East fusion cuisine arrived with a bang in March 2003 when Chino Latino opened its doors. The exciting mix of Asian and South American flavours is just what you'd expect from a chef who's worked at London's Nobu. This is a place to enjoy nijisaki-infused saké shots before dinner – perhaps those addictive endamame beans to start with, followed by grilled shrimp with Peruvian pesto potato or black cod in miso sauce, then hot fig tatin with sambuca ice-cream. If you enjoy culinary experimentation and dark interiors, you'll love it here.

Fresh

15 Goosegate, Hockley, Nottingham, NG1 1FE (0115 924 3336/www.freshjuicebar.co.uk). **Lunch served** noon-3pm, **dinner served** 6-9.30pm Mon-Sat. **Main courses** £5.95-£11.95. **Credit** AmEx, DC, MC, V.

Housed above the trendy juice and sandwich bar of the same name, Fresh is a 40-seater restaurant that has proved a big hit. With innovative veggie dishes such as roasted aubergine with a rarebit crust and tomato salad, or chickpea and broccoli curry with coriander rice alongside Cromer crab in tagliatelle with chive and cream sauce, the menu is consistently strong. Service can be rather patchy but there seems little danger of Fresh's popularity wilting just yet.

Hart's

Standard Court, Park Row, Nottingham, NG1 6GN (0115 911 0666/www.hartsnottingham.co.uk). **Lunch served** noon-2pm daily. **Dinner served** 7-10.30pm Mon-Sat; 7-9pm Sun. **Main courses** £11.50-£18.50. **Set lunch** (Mon-Sat) £11 2 courses, £14.95 3 courses; (Sun) £18 3 courses. **Set dinner** (Sun) £14.95 3 courses. **Credit** AmEx, MC, V.

Some find Hart's clinical and slick; others believe it has the best kitchen and service in town. It has certainly been a huge success since opening in 1997 – evidenced by the fancy Hart's Hotel that opened in 2003. Located in the old A&E department of the former Nottingham General Hospital, the restaurant's contemporary interiors and modern British menu attract visiting business types and locals with fat wallets. Dishes include smoked duck breast and orange and hazelnut salad, roasted turbot with steamed clams, and beef fillet with rösti potato. Vegetarians have little room for manoeuvre – only one main option at dinner. With dinner for two reaching £100, Hart's is an aspirational choice.

Mozart's

153 Wollaton Street, Nottingham, NG1 5GE (0115 950 9044/www.mozarts.co.uk). **Dinner served** 6-9.30pm Tue-Sat. **Main courses** £8.95-£15.95. **Set dinner** (6-7pm) £9.95 2 courses, £11.95 3 courses. **Credit** MC, V.

Something of an old-school experience, Mozart's is a small family-run restaurant housed in an industrial building. Personal service is the name of the game with an extensive menu of mainly traditional English fare. Portions are generous and there's certainly no rush to finish your meal (the table is yours for the night). Mozart's is not particularly fashionable, but this cheery diner attracts a loyal following who enthusiastically tuck into '70s-style dishes like prawn cocktail, fillet steak, beef stroganoff and cherry brandy duck. Retro chic? Not exactly. But do take your mum – she'll love it.

Opium

25 Warser Gate, Lace Market, Nottingham, NG1 1NU (0115 988 1133). **Lunch served** noon-2.30pm Mon-Sat. **Dinner served** 6-10.30pm Mon-Thur; 6-11pm Fri, Sat; 6-10pm Sun. **Main courses** £6.50-£10.50. **Set meals** £17-£22.50 per person (minimum 2). **Credit** AmEx, MC, V.

By revolutionising Nottingham's Chinese dining scene, Opium has done the city a great service. This three-floored bar/restaurant/chill-out lounge is located in a listed building decorated with traditional Chinese fabrics and prints. For such a large operation, it can still feel intimate, and the food is excellent Chinese with a sprinkling of Far-East influences. There's also a good choice for veggies – a three-course set menu at £17. With bands on Thursdays and Fridays and Ibiza-style ambient DJs playing in the top-floor Zen-like lounge, it's really no wonder that Opium is proving such a stayer.

Saltwater

The Cornerhouse, Forman Street, Nottingham, NG1 4AA (0115 924 2664/www.saltwater-restaurant.com). **Lunch served** noon-2.30pm Mon-Fri; noon-5pm Sat, Sun. **Dinner served** 6-10pm Mon-Thur; 6-10.30pm Fri, Sat; 6-9pm Sun. **Main courses** £11-£16. **Set lunch** (Mon-Sat) £9 2 courses, £12 3 courses; (Sun) £12 2 courses, £15 3 courses. **Credit** AmEx, MC, V.

The management at Saltwater, one of the last additions to the Cornerhouse entertainment complex, have gone for a modern British and Mediterranean menu. The lunchtime fast service menu is a welcome introduction, but prices for dinner remain on the high side – £17 for sirloin steak and £16 for duck breast, for instance. Perhaps they're still attempting to recoup the fortune (a rumoured £800,000) that was spent on the decor of fashionable timber and glass panels. The impressive penthouse location features a roof terrace overlooking the city that is a great draw in summer. With a rooftop conservatory planned for autumn 2004, Saltwater could prove an equally attractive proposition in winter too.

Sat Bains ★

Old Lenton Lane, Nottingham, NG7 2SA (0115 986 6566/www.hoteldesclos.com). **Lunch served** noon-2pm Tue-Fri. **Dinner served** 7-9.30pm Tue-Sat. **Set lunch** £20 2 courses, £25 3 courses. **Set dinner** £45 3 courses, £55 dégustation menu, £75 surprise menu. **Credit** AmEx, DC, MC, V.

After retaining his Michelin star (the city's first and only), Sat Bains remains a local culinary hero at his eponymous restaurant in the Hotel des Clos. After making an effort to find it (the converted farm outbuildings are a ten-minute drive from the city), most diners put themselves in Sat's capable hands with the nine-course dégustation menu (£55). This has recently included scallop curry, ham hock and foie gras, and veal gnocchi with asparagus and summer truffles; all punctuated by palette cleansers like rocket shots and beetroot sorbet. For vegetarians and seafood lovers, Sat also creates imaginative dishes. At around £150 for two (with modest wine from the glamorous list), many an expense account and credit card is hammered. The benchmark for Nottingham's gourmet scene.

Shaw's ★

20-22 Broad Street, Hockley, Nottingham, NG1 3AL (0115 950 0009/www.shawsrestaurant.co.uk). **Meals served** 10am-11pm Mon-Sat. **Main courses** £9-£13. **Set meal** (*restaurant* noon-2.30pm; *bar* 2.30-11pm) £9 2 courses, £11.95 3 courses. **Credit** AmEx, MC, V.

With just a hint of Left Bank panache, Shaw's is a rather bohemian bistro-style restaurant. Housed over two floors in a beautiful industrial building (next to the Broadway, an arthouse cinema), Shaw's offers some of the best food – and value – in this thriving area. A recent set lunch offered cauliflower soup with black truffle oil, baked chicken supreme with a warm salade niçoise and an orange and thyme crème brûlée. Service befits the laid-back vibe. The upstairs room operates as a bar-restaurant and is furnished with a collection of antique fittings, red lamps, wicker chairs and comfortable sofas. This is a place you'll want to adopt as your own.

La Toque

61 Wollaton Road, Beeston, Nottingham, NG9 2NG (0115 922 2268). **Lunch served** noon-2pm Tue-Fri. **Dinner served** 7-10.30pm Tue-Sat. **Main courses** £13-£19.50. **Set lunch** £10 2 courses, £13 3 courses. **Credit** AmEx, MC, V.

The first surprise is its location – a scruffy main road in the studenty suburb of Beeston. The second is its ambition – from the urban chic of its chocolate brown aesthetic to the sophistication of its French menu. The food here is devilishly decadent, from lobster brûlée to venison medallions with pancetta ham. Some of the dishes, particularly extravagant desserts, are certainly on the rich side. Another couple of caveats: La Toque can feel slightly claustrophobic and prices are steep (among the most expensive in Nottingham). That said, it's a class act.

World Service ★

Newdigate House, Castlegate, Nottingham, NG1 6AF (0115 847 5587/www.worldservicerestaurant.com). **Lunch served** noon-2.15pm Mon-Sat; noon-3pm Sun. **Dinner served** 7-10pm Mon-Sat, 7-9pm Sun. **Main courses** £11.50-£19. **Set lunch** (Mon-Sat) £10.50 2 courses, £14 3 courses; (Sun) £17 3 courses. **Credit** AmEx, MC, V.

Discreetly located in a side alley near Nottingham Castle, this historic 17th-century building has been skilfully converted into a super-chic restaurant. Signature dishes include Thai beef salad with crispy noodles, monkfish tail with Indian rice and curry sauce, and strawberry and crème fraîche tart. This doesn't come particularly cheap – although the Light Lunch menu (£10.50 for two courses) is top value. For urbanites who have outgrown nightclubs, don't mind paying premium prices for premium drinks and relish exciting food, World Service delivers.

PLUMTREE

Perkins

The Old Station, Station Road, Plumtree, NG12 5NA (0115 937 3695/www.perkinsrestaurant.co.uk). **Lunch served** noon-2pm Tue-Sat; noon-2.30pm Sun. **Dinner served** 6.45-9.30pm Tue-Sat. **Main courses** £9-£14. **Set lunch** (Tue-Sat) £9.75 2 courses; (Sun) £13.50 2 courses, £16.95 3 courses. **Set dinner** (Tue-Thur) £17.50 3 courses. **Credit** AmEx, MC, V.

This converted railway station feels like a happy place to be. In summer, the outside tables adjacent to the abandoned railway line offer a wonderful place to chill out. Or there's the conservatory area built on the station's platform where you half expect a steam train to arrive any minute. Winner of numerous awards, the quality of Perkins' European menu rarely disappoints. Sample dishes include guinea fowl and pistachio nut terrine, devilled sea bass with sweet potato cake, and grilled duck supreme. Service is patient, prices are reasonable.

SOUTHWELL

Filbert's Bistro

1 Westgate, Southwell, NG25 0JN (01636 815678). **Lunch served** noon-2.30pm Tue-Sun. **Dinner served** 7-9.30pm Tue-Sat. **Main courses** £7.95-£15.25. **Set lunch** (Sun) £14.95 3 courses incl coffee. **Credit** AmEx, MC, V.

Tucked inconspicuously down a tiny alley, this beautiful Georgian townhouse has been converted into an oak-panelled dining room adjoined by a couple of intimate private rooms for larger groups. The food is exemplary, despite the slightly eccentric range of dishes – featuring everything from beef wellington to Thai vegetable curry – on a rather baffling system of menus and 'specials' blackboards. Fish and seafood is particularly good. No surprise that Filbert's has attracted a loyal following.

Also in the area

Living Room 7 High Pavement, The Lace Market, Nottingham, NG1 1HF (0870 442 2716); **Loch Fyne** 17 King Street, Nottingham, NG1 2AY (0115 988 6840); **Shimla Pinks** 38-46 Goose Gate, Nottingham, NG1 1FF (0115 958 9899); **Sonny's** 3 Carlton Street, Nottingham, NG1 1NL (0115 947 3041); **Wagamama** The Courthouse, Burton Street, Nottingham, NG1 4DB (0115 924 1797).

Rutland

CLIPSHAM

Olive Branch ★

Main Street, Clipsham, LE15 7SH (01780 410355/ www.rutlandinnco.co.uk). **Lunch served** noon-2pm Mon-Sat; noon-3pm Sun. **Dinner served** 7-9.30pm Mon-Sat. **Main courses** £8.25-£17. **Set lunch** (Mon-Sat) £12.50 2 courses, £15 3 courses; (Sun) £15 3 courses. **Credit** MC, V.

Arriving soon after midday at a village pub set in the quiet heart of the Rutland countryside, you might not expect to have to grab the last free table in the entire place. A pub since three labourers' cottages were knocked together in 1890, the Olive Branch is very much part of the local community and more besides. The Rutland Inn Company, who also run Stathern's Red Lion (*see p217*) puts cosiness, quality and local ingredients first, safe in the knowledge that news of a Michelin star travels fast. It might be a mystery where all these smart-but-casual diners come from, but it's no mystery why: local cheeses, trout and warm Rearsby loaves, Grasmere Farm gammon and sausage, own-made piccalilli. Try honey-roast pork belly with sweet potato mash and hot red cabbage, followed by olde English Olive Branch pudding in a fab-value £12.50 set lunch. In response to a neighbour's mix-and-match menu query, one of the smart young waiters smiled: 'Madam, you can have absolutely *anything*.'

UPPER HAMBLETON

Finch's Arms

Oakham Road, Upper Hambleton, LE15 8TL (01572 756575/www.finchsarms.co.uk). **Lunch served** noon-2.30pm, **dinner served** 6.30-9.30pm Mon-Sat. **Meals served** noon 9pm Sun. **Main courses** £8.95-£13.50. **Set lunch** (Mon-Fri) £9.95 2 courses, £11.95 3 courses. **Credit** MC, V.

Tastefully geared for quality food and accommodation, one of the Finch's Arms prime pleasures is its easygoing hangover of having been a simple village pub for 300 years. Hikers and bikers are welcome to drop in for a pint of local Oakham Grainstore and a lunchtime ciabatta, while diners can take their pick between the cosy old bar, the airy nouveau dining room or the patio with sweeping views over Rutland Water. Waitresses, perhaps surprisingly, are all French; but they're far from overattentive. The lunch menu leans a little too much toward comfort – confit of duck leg wrapped in parma ham cries out for zest; likewise the fillets of lemon sole embedded in a cheese, potato and spinach bake – but we are assured the chef's sauces come out in the evening.

Hambleton Hall ★

Upper Hambleton, LE15 8TH (01572 756991/ www.hambletonhall.com). **Lunch served** noon-1.30pm, **dinner served** 7-9.30pm daily. **Main courses** £15-£20. **Set lunch** (Mon-Fri) £18.50 2 courses. **Set dinner** £35 3 courses. **Set meal** (Sat, Sun) £35 3 courses. **Credit** AmEx, MC, V.

'*Fay Que Voudras*' – 'do as you please' – is the invitation carved in stone over the portal at Hambleton Hall, a strangely synchronous throwback to Regency days of aristocratic decadence. This impressive pile was transformed into a country hotel and restaurant in 1979 and has been impressing diners ever since. If truth be told, the trick once inside is to allow yourself to relax sufficiently amid the respectful hush, grandeur and precision pampering to genuinely enjoy the Michelin-vaunted morsels offered up like religious relics. Mercifully, fantastic food and wine are great levellers. Hors d'oeuvres and amuse-gueules alone are marvellous, and from there it's all uphill via crab ravioli with crab and ginger bisque or clear essence of tomato with goat's cheese tortellini and a small purple flower. When it comes to confit duck leg or poached fillet of organic salmon, delight is in the detail: soya roasted leeks like baby spring onions; an extraordinary hollandaise sauce, and an amazing lemon tart. Tim and Stefa Hart's self-styled 'Lunches For Less' are a fine entry point, although don't expect chef Aaron Patterson to flash his *whole* hand for just £30 or £40 per head.

WING

King's Arms

13 Top Street, Wing, LE15 8SE (01572 737634/ www.thekingsarms-wing.co.uk). **Lunch served** noon-2pm, **dinner served** 6.30-9pm daily. **Main courses** £6.95-£15.50. **Credit** AmEx, MC, V.

After a saunter around Wing's mysterious pre-Christian turf maze, any right-minded Rutland Water explorer will next head on to the King's Arms for fine food and accommodation. From the atmospheric flagstone bar dating from 1649 to the upstairs eaterie given light and air just a couple of years ago, this bears all the hallmarks of a winning enterprise. Head chef Allan Sinkinson is an ingredients hard-liner, concentrating on quality local produce (including Bisbrook ostrich) cooked 100% to order: expect a short wait while every last pea is prepared and freshly cooked. Cutlets of pork with plum compote, cider cream sauce and poached apple proved hard to beat; pear, orange and Archers parfait was similiarly splendid. Service and presentation were perfect.

Shropshire

BROMFIELD

Cookhouse

Bromfield, SY8 2JR (01584 856565/www.thecookhouse.org.uk). Bar **Open** 11am-11pm Mon-Sat; noon-10.30pm Sun. *Brasserie & Restaurant* **Lunch served** noon-2.30pm, **dinner served** 6.30-9.30pm daily. **Main courses** £12.95-£15.95. **Set lunch** £12.50 2 courses. **Credit** AmEx, DC, MC, V.

A roadside halt of superior credentials, this large, slightly severe-looking building (it boasts a plain Georgian brick frontage, though the main structure is almost certainly older) provides wayfarers with 15 rooms, an accomplished restaurant, a bar with two distinct areas and a modern brasserie. Its restaurant, the Clive, serves sophisticated meals that might start with chicken and chorizo terrine and continue with roast fillet of Shropshire beef in a wild mushroom sauce, or decent vegetarian options like fennel and sun-dried tomato risotto. Less formal, the Cookhouse brasserie is relaxingly low-lit, with brown paper tablecloths (you're encouraged to draw on them) and sleek modern furniture. Prices are good and the food several notches above most rest-stop fare. The bar has some good traditional ales (Hobson's) and local ciders.

Midlands

DORRINGTON

Country Friends

Dorrington, SY5 7JD (01743 718707). **Lunch served** noon-2pm, **dinner served** 7-9pm Wed-Sat. **Set meals** £29.50 2 courses, £31.90 3 courses. **Credit** MC, V.

Idiosyncratic as foodie havens go, Country Friends is housed in detached mock-tudor premises where decor is not a priority; with its brown velvet curtains, carpets, brown paint over embossed wallpaper (there's even a dubious attempt at a trompe l'oeil wood-panelled fireplace in one of the rooms) you could be in a slightly faded B&B. Food, on the other hand, is prepared with commitment, passion and skill. Flavours range from the delicate (a twice-baked sweet potato, spring onion and gruyère soufflé) to the very bold (queen of puddings with lime and gin ice-cream; bitter ice-cream packed a punch and clashed beautifully with the hot, sweet meringue of the pudding). Main courses tend toward the robust: a good, tender venison steak in raspberry vinegar sauce and duck leg with celeriac purée in a red wine sauce. Vegetables come in generous portions on the side. Tables are well spaced and the place doesn't cater for many diners so it's pretty quiet. Staff are attentive, but not overwhelmingly so. This is a generous-spirited restaurant.

LLANFAIR WATERDINE

The Waterdine ★

Llanfair Waterdine, LD7 1TU (01547 528214). **Lunch served** noon-2pm Tue-Sun. **Dinner served** 7-9.30pm Tue-Sat. **Main courses** £10.50-£16.50. **Set lunch** (Sun) £16 3 courses. **Set dinner** (Sat) £26 3 courses. **Credit** MC, V.

For the vista alone, it would be hard to beat the rear dining room at this 16th-century drover's inn: from nearest to furthest, a flowery garden, green fields, the River Teme doing duty as the England-Wales border, and a steep hill from which, meteorological conditions permitting, mist rises in an Arthurian fashion. We got a faultless welcome, even though we were late. Head chef Ken Adams used to run a restaurant (now Hibiscus) in Ludlow, and his short, seasonal three-course menu is formed from local ingredients (some very local – herbs, vegetables and fruit come from the garden) and imaginative twists on traditional fare. Fillet of brill wrapped in smoked salmon was perfectly done, as was herb risotto with balsamic roast vegetables. Desserts might include strawberry and elderflower mousse or – our choice – ginger pudding with lemongrass cream, a scrummy nursery treat. There are rooms here too, and an attractive church to explore across the road.

LUDLOW

Hibiscus ★

17 Corve Street, Ludlow, SY8 1DA (01584 872325/www.hibiscusrestaurant.co.uk). **Lunch served** 12.15-1.30pm Wed-Sat. **Dinner served** 7-10pm Tue-Sat. **Set lunch** £19.50 2 courses, £25 3 courses. **Set dinner** £38 3 courses, £45 7-course tasting menu, £55 9-course tasting menu. **Credit** MC, V.

With its award-winning French double act – Claude Bosi in the kitchen and his wife Claire at front of house – at the helm, Hibiscus has been steered into exalted company: it's regularly spoken of as one of the best restaurants in the country. The decor is simple but classy – bare stone, wood panels, mellow lighting and a constantly changing selection of contemporary artworks – and the mood pleasantly relaxed. Fresh local ingredients go without saying, and the seasonal food is as sophisticated and impressively executed: in summer, exquisite ravioli of white onion and lime, roast whole lobster with baby plum tomato confit; in the colder months, tartare of langoustine and saddle of Mortimer Forest venison. By way of dessert, three mini crème brûlées – pea and marjoram, elderflower and peach, cherry tomato and brown sugar – gave the perfect measure of the kitchen's imagination and talent.

Koo

127 Old Street, Ludlow, SY8 1NU (01584 878462/ www.koo-ook.com). **Lunch served** noon-2pm, **dinner served** 7-10pm Tue-Sat. **Set lunch** £10.95 2 courses. **Set dinner** (Tue, Wed) £16.95 3 courses; (Thur-Sat) £22.50 4 courses. **Credit** MC, V.

'Authentic', proclaims the menu. That's pushing it a bit. For sure, we're glad there's a Japanese restaurant in Ludlow (every town should have one), but a liberal scattering of sesame seeds over nearly every dish in sight does not textbook *nihon no ryori* make. And the soundtrack was Latino! Overlook the eccentricities, though, and you'll find much to like. The aquamarine walls and ceiling set an unpretentious note, the staff – especially the mama-san – are lovely, and the ingredients are grade A. OK, so we'd never seen maki sliced so thin, and our gyoza turned out, with no prior warning from the menu, to be a veggie variety; but, all in all, our meal – agedashi tofu, gyu don – was tasty and nicely presented; and the dessert plate, in a move that was by then familiar, included a sesame biscuit. Good value; they also do bento boxes to take away.

Les Marches

Overton Grange Hotel, Old Hereford Road, Ludlow, SY8 4AD (01584 873500/www.overtongrangehotel.co.uk). **Dinner served** 7-9pm daily. **Set dinner** £37.50 3 courses, £49.50 7-course tasting menu. **Credit** MC, V.

This is a gourmet grandee in a luxury country hotel. Where most restaurants around these parts plough a furrow that could broadly be described as English Country Cooking, head chef Olivier Bossut and his underlings produce food in unabashed French haute cuisine tradition, not that anyone's complaining. Dining options run from à la carte to a three-course set menu and a push-the-boat-out tasting menu, and whatever course you take, the presentation of the food will be of the kind that's so painstaking you almost feel bad about disturbing the artful dabs of sauce and the delicate arrangement of leaves. So, for starters: chocolate raviolis of game in a fresh girolle mushroom velouté. Then, as a main, paupiette of wild sea bass with a red mullet farce. And, to conclude, pear tart bourdaloue in the company of cinnamon ice-cream. All delicious, and all prepared with a masterful hand.

Merchant House ★

62 Lower Corve Street, Ludlow, SY8 1DU (01584 875438/www.merchanthouse.co.uk). **Lunch served** 12.30-2pm Fri, Sat. **Dinner served** 7-9pm Tue-Sat. **Set lunch** £29 3 courses. **Set dinner** £35 3 courses. **Credit** MC, V.

One of Ludlow's most accomplished restaurants has one of its most discreet entrances; blink and you'll miss it. As it turns out, modesty is a Merchant House hallmark: the dining room seats just over 20, and the mood here (no dress code, a relaxed approach to food and wines, however splendid) is marvellously unstuffy. Husband and wife Shaun and Anja Hill officiate in and in front of the kitchen (respectively).

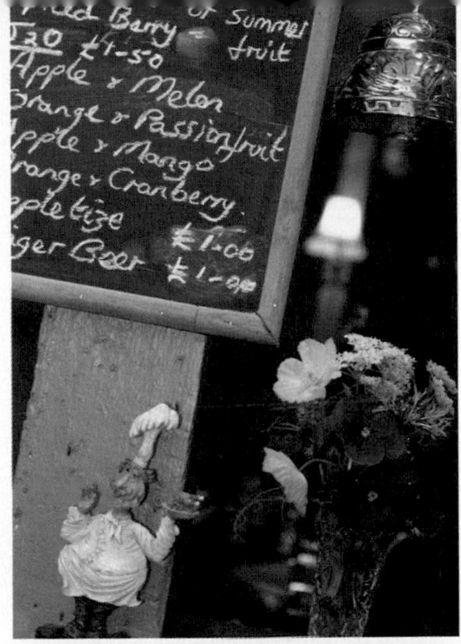

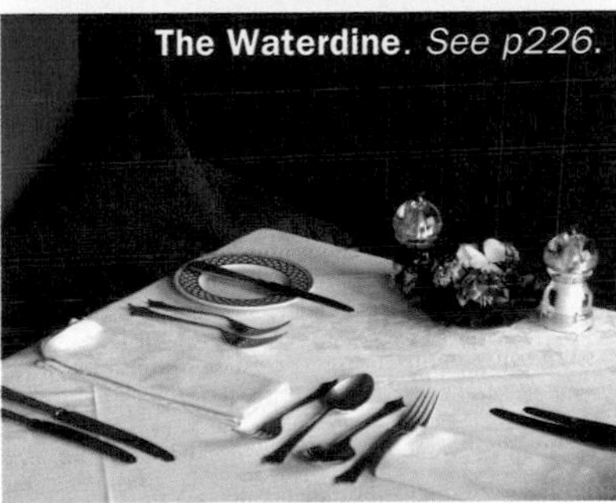

The Waterdine. *See p226.*

There's no fixed theme or style: the short, three-course fixed menus are guided by whim, the availability of ingredients and culinary excellence rather than by party line: calf's sweetbreads with potato and olive cake, maybe, followed by roast squab pigeon with parsley risotto and crème caramel with prunes in armagnac. Vegetarian dishes need to be requested in advance. In matters of good cheer, there's an award-winning wine list (fancy a 1949 Château Pontet-Canet, perhaps?) and, in the winter, an invigorating log fire. Be warned: the Merchant House is often booked up months ahead.

Mr Underhills

Dinham Weir, Ludlow, SY8 1EH (01584 874431/ www.mr-underhills.co.uk). **Dinner served** 7.30-8.15pm Mon, Wed-Sun. **Set meals** £36 5-course tasting menu incl coffee. **Credit** MC, V.

For location, this place certainly trumps its local rivals: down by the babbling weir just a short lob from the castle walls. The long dining room, decked out with linen-draped tables and wicker-backed chairs, has subdued, attractive lighting, and food is more than satisfactory: asparagus cream with parmesan crisp to start with, perhaps, and a roasted rack and slow cooked shoulder of Marches lamb with garden sorrel and mint. They also serve a daily tasting menu. It's a hotel too, and parking is at something of a premium.

SHREWSBURY

Drapers

Drapers Hall, 10 St Mary's Place, Shrewsbury, SY1 1DZ (01743 344679). **Lunch served** 10.30am-3pm Mon-Sat; noon-3pm Sun. **Dinner served** 7-9.30pm Mon-Sat. **Main courses** £12.50-£20. **Set meals** (Mon-Fri, Sun; lunch Sat) £12.50 2 courses, £14.50 3 courses. **Credit** AmEx, DC, MC, V.

The atmosphere-laden Tudor surroundings define Drapers: dark oak-panelled walls; high, beamed ceilings; ancient paintings; a huge fireplace. There's no creepy butler, though, just friendly staff who are happy to welcome families (though most diners are more middle aged). Food is relatively contemporary, however: starters were simple – Greek salad and moules marinière. Mains were more inventive. Seared spiced monkfish with Chinese-style noodles was a firm piece of fish with subtle accompaniments. An asparagus and parmesan risotto with rocket salad was a creamy success. In addition to separate vegetables, mains were accompanied by incongruous dollops of parsnip and potato mash (on top of the risotto, beneath the fish). We mused at this anomaly over good puds of iced hazelnut parfait and tiramisu.

Also in the area

Tin Tin Wellington Road, Donnington, Telford, TF2 8AJ (01952 608688).

Staffordshire

ACTON TRUSSELL

Moat House

Lower Penkridge Road, Acton Trussell, ST17 0RJ (01785 712217/www.moathouse.co.uk). **Lunch served** noon-2pm, **dinner served** 7-9.30pm daily. **Set lunch** £14.95 2 courses. **Set dinner** £29.50 3 courses. **Set meal** £27.95 2 courses, £34.50 3 courses. **Credit** AmEx, DC, MC, V.

A grade II-listed moated manor house in pretty countryside by a canal? That could only be the Moat House, one of Staffordshire's culinary high spots. Though the building has been added to considerably under its present owners, this 15th-century place is still a destination venue, popular with the wedding biz, but with a great deal to offer to the hungry diner too. There's a brasserie bar and restaurant proper, and standards are high in both, with a laudable reliance on local producers. It's all quite fancy – there's a bourgignon garnish with the Staffordshire beef fillet, as well as rösti potato and braised oxtail. An excellent loin of lamb is accompanied by black pudding, confit shallots, wilted spinach and a cassoulet of lentils. It could all be too much but it's expertly handled and flavours work well together.

BRIDGTOWN

Zafroni

Fourth & fifth floors, Virage Point, Walsall Road, Bridgtown, WS11 3NH (01543 505023/ www.zafroni.com). **Lunch served** noon-12.30pm Sun. **Dinner served** 5.30pm-midnight daily. **Main courses** £5.95-£12.95. **Set lunch** £8.95 3 courses. **Set dinner** £15.95 5 courses. **Credit** AmEx, DC, MC, V.

Downtown Bridgtown near Cannock may not be Manhattan, but the view from Zafroni's windows can still be impressive, especially at night. This is an Indian restaurant with style and it aims just as high as its outlook. Dotted in among the expected favourites are some more unusual 'connoisseur' dishes. A salmon starter (machli tikka malika) was made special by a rich and lively marinade of dill, fennel, ginger and mustard oil; a Durdesh main course of braised lamb (kaddie korai ghosth) was another winner. Service is effortlessly attentive.

LEEK

Cottage Delight at No.64

64 St Edward Street, Leek, ST13 5DL (01538 381 900/www.number64.com). **Lunch served** noon-2pm Tue-Sun. **Dinner served** 7-9pm Tue-Sat. **Main courses** £14.95-£23.50. **Set dinner** £25 2 courses, £35 3 courses. **Credit** AmEx, MC, V.

Cottage Delight is a box of surprises. Behind its elegant Georgian exterior is a 'unique speciality food emporium', including a restaurant, private dining room, cellar wine bar, delicatessen and pâtisserie. As if all that weren't enough, it's also a B&B and has a terrace garden. It's all a little self-consciously grand, with food that is rich and complicated. Roast Warwickshire pork comes with poached william pear crumble, Wiltshire ham, cabbage dumplings and watercress cream; Devon lamb in a confit pavé gets overloaded with creamed leek, apple and baby spinach suet pud, caramelised garlic cloves, fondant potato and woodland mushroom stock fumet. Well done, if a little overpowering.

LICHFIELD

Chandlers Grande Brasserie

Corn Exchange Building, Conduit Street, Lichfield, WS13 6JU (01543 416688/www.chandlers restaurant.co.uk). **Lunch served** noon-2pm, **dinner served** 6-10pm daily. **Main courses** £8.50-£12.95. **Set lunch** £8.95 2 courses, £11.95 3 courses. **Set dinner** £12.50 2 courses, £16 3 courses. **Credit** AmEx, MC, V.

Chandlers seems to have created a cosy little niche for itself and regularly packs them in. The place can take it – the listed building has an airy interior, lots of tables and masses of room. The menu concentrates mainly on European fare. Things are pretty straightforward – starters of Scottish salmon, fish cakes or mushrooms on toast with mascarpone and Dijon mustard. Mains add little tweaks – brill with leek and asparagus fricassée – but if you want to rev your meal up a bit, try roast suckling pig with savoury apple cake and cider gravy. This was an elegant dish with lots of taste. Desserts lean heavily on the comfort factor, with blueberry bread and butter pud. Paper napkins and cloths add a naff touch and children are not particularly welcome.

Thrales

40-44 Tamworth Street, Lichfield, WS13 6JJ (01543 255091/www.thrales.co.uk). **Lunch served** noon-1.30pm Tue-Fri; noon-2.30pm Sun. **Dinner served** 7-9.30pm Mon-Fri; 7-9.45pm Sat. **Main courses** £12.50. **Set dinner** (Mon-Fri) £13.95 3 courses. **Credit** AmEx, MC, V.

Renowned local chef Simon Smith is the culinary brains behind this quaint and homely restaurant in one of Lichfield's many pretty old buildings. It didn't have a particularly romantic past though – it was once an abattoir. Smith also provides the catering at nearby Tutbury Castle and his busy life may explain why Thrales doesn't always have a 100% success rate, pleasant though it is. The menu plays it straight with starters such as stilton pâté followed by good milk-fed pigeon or sea bass. Pre-dinner drinks may find you sitting in a corridor and odd touches of whimsy – such as blue sea salt on a starter of scallops – don't always come off, but this place has a loyal local fan base so it's always best to book.

SUMMERHILL

Oddfellows in the Boat

Walsall Road, Summerhill, WS14 0BU (01543 361692/www.oddfellowsintheboat.com). **Lunch served** noon-2.30pm, **dinner served** 6-9.30pm Mon-Sat. **Meals served** noon-8pm Sun. **Main courses** £5.95-£14.50. **Credit** MC, V.

The pub-restaurant distinction is a little blurred at this smart and welcoming venue. It probably errs on the pub side but it doesn't really matter too much, as the quality of the dishes is generally decent, if not entirely consistent. Where so many menus list every last ingredient, descriptions here are kept almost tantalisingly brief – bacon-wrapped char-grilled chicken or pigeon breast with artichoke mash don't tell you a huge amount about what will finally arrive on your table, but they do at least include decently cooked side veg. These are always a highlight, along with ace desserts; lemon posset and chocolate raspberry fondant winning special praise. Service is generally good but can get a little absent-minded.

SWINFEN

Swinfen Hall

Swinfen, WS14 9RE (01543 481494/www.swinfen hallhotel.co.uk). **Lunch served** noon-2.30pm Mon-Fri, Sun. **Dinner served** 7-9.30pm daily. **Set meal** £35 3 courses. **Credit** AmEx, MC, V.

This is a real special occasion venue; a grand 18th-century hotel with sweeping drive and impressive grounds. But though it aims high, the feel is relaxed with staff who are eager to please. Enjoy a pre-dinner drink in a chintzy drawing room with giant fireplace and views of the gardens before feasting in the formal restaurant on high-minded fare. If it's lunchtime and the weather's good, the grand terrace may take your fancy. They genuinely care about food here and it shows. The classically based dishes are skilfully updated with plenty of modern touches and it's also the perfect home for local game, cheeses, asparagus and raspberries. There may be, for instance, local Innes goat's cheese in a fondant with a sable of roast vegetables and pesto, alongside lively dishes such as pressed ham hock terrine with piccalilli-marinated vegetables. Elsewhere, the feel is flavour-packed classic – fillet of brill with lobster ravioli and vanilla sauce or roast chump of lamb with sautéed kidneys and rosemary jus.

Warwickshire

BISHOP'S TACHBROOK

Mallory Court ★

Harbury Lane, Bishop's Tachbrook, CV33 9QB (01926 330214/www.mallory.co.uk). **Lunch served** noon-1.45pm, **dinner served** 7-9.30pm daily. **Main courses** £16-£26. **Set lunch** (Mon-Sat) £19.50 2 courses, £25 3 courses; (Sun) £29.50 3 courses. **Set dinner** £37.50 3 courses. **Credit** AmEx, DC, MC, V.

A classic country house hotel in a grand Arts and Crafts mansion amid magnificent gardens (with terrace tables in summer, plus tennis courts and a pool), Mallory Court provides everything necessary for a sybaritic treat. To eat here in the evening is wildly expensive, but the lunch menus are reasonable, with no drop in quality. And the food, by Michelin-starred chef Simon Haigh is impeccable. Brawn terrine with mustard dressing and a mushroom and bean salad had just the right blend of meatiness and subtlety; asparagus risotto with poached egg and parmesan was rich and smooth. Ingredients are outstanding and well handled whether in a deliciously satisfying main like pan-fried cod fillet with basil potatoes, or in just-right desserts like a beautifully tangy raspberry crème brûlée – we've all got pretty used to tasteless polytunnel raspberries, but these were the real thing. Service is charming, and there are comfortable lounges in which to study the impressive wine list, or cogitate over coffee. A seductive experience.

GREAT WOLFORD

Fox & Hounds Inn

Great Wolford, CV36 5NQ (01608 674220). **Lunch served** noon-2pm Tue-Sun. **Dinner served** 7-9pm Tue-Sat. **Main courses** £9.50-£17. **Credit** MC, V.

The quality of the flagstone floor alone will have interiors fans drooling before they even get to the menu at this quintessentially 16th-century inn. Low ceilings and soft light create a cosy setting. You can eat in the bar area, or the separate restaurant, but there is little to choose between them. The daily changing blackboard is packed with tempting combinations that revolve around local and seasonal foods. You may balk at paying restaurant prices when you have to order at the bar, but the meals are a cut above. Leek and mascarpone tart had a rich filling with light pastry, while asparagus wrapped in prosciutto with parmesan shavings was delicious. Mains of sea bass fillet with a lemon dressing was beautifully cooked as was calf's liver with its accompanying black pudding mash. After meals this size, you'd be stretched to fit in a pud, so go easy on starters if you want to indulge at the other end.

HENLEY-IN-ARDEN

Edmunds ★

64 High Street, Henley-in-Arden, B95 5BX (01564 795666). **Lunch served** noon-2pm Tue-Fri. **Dinner served** 7-9.45pm Tue-Sat. **Set meal** £10 2 courses, £15 3 courses, £26.95 3 courses. **Credit** MC, V.

One of Warwickshire's Michelin-starred restaurants, this doesn't look at all like one if you associate that gong with grand, stuffy places. In an old house with wildly sloping roof and low beams on Henley's pretty main street, it feels a bit like a comfortable country pub. The tone set by chef-owner Andy Waters is easygoing; staff are charmingly attentive. Dishes are an ideal balance of enjoyable and subtle. Char-grilled Mediterranean vegetables with feta, rocket and a gazpacho dressing was refreshing; langoustine spring rolls with a ginger and cress salad were less successful, but still intricately flavoured and very pleasant. To follow, pavé of Loch Duart salmon with a scallops and lobster brochette and shellfish nage featured salmon of a flavour we thought no longer existed, while with rosette of beef with a cep forestière and truffle jus the high point was the delicious, rich gravy. Desserts included an irresistible Valrhona chocolate tartlet with pistachio ice-cream. Prices are very reasonable overall, while for value the set-lunch menu is positively mind boggling.

ILMINGTON

Howard Arms ★

Lower Green, Ilmington, CV36 4LT (01608 682226/www.howardarms.com). **Lunch served** noon-2pm Mon-Sat; noon-2.30pm Sun. **Dinner served** 7-9pm Mon-Thur; 7-9.30pm Fri, Sat; 6.30-8.30pm Sun. **Main courses** £9.50-£15. **Set lunch** (Sun) £18.50 3 courses. **Credit** MC, V.

This inn-restaurant is textbook perfect and well worth the detour. It overlooks the prettiest village green, is quaint but light and airy inside, has a log fire and blackboard menu, and more than enough room to cope with its loyal clientele and passing trade. Whether you want to eat or stay it is best to book in advance. You get just as good a meal and service if you turn up at 2pm as you do if you eat at 1pm. What sets the food apart is the quality of ingredients used, the chef who cooks them simply but superbly, and prices which are fairly pitched. The Sunday roast Herefordshire beef was beautifully cooked and came with fresh greens and red cabbage. The halibut fillet with its pesto dressing was also exquisite. The selection of wines by the glass is a match for any top restaurant and the polite service isn't intrusive. Bag a table by one of the pretty bow windows if you can.

LAPWORTH

Boot Inn

Old Warwick Road, Lapworth, B94 6JU (01564 782464/www.thebootatlapworth.co.uk). **Open** noon-11pm Mon-Sat; noon-10.30pm Sun. **Lunch served** noon-2pm, **dinner served** 7-10.30pm daily. **Main courses** £8.95-£16.95. **Credit** AmEx, MC, V.

This attractive pub-restaurant draws the rich crowd that lives along this idyllic country corridor south of Birmingham. The low-ceilinged bar is filled with stripped wood tables and scented with the heady fragrance of lilies, or there's the equally smart restaurant. Whichever you choose make sure you book, as it's popular for celebrations and there's a real buzz in the evenings. The menu offers something for everyone and tours the world to include international, fusion, modern European and traditional British. You can start with crispy oriental duck, move on to calf's liver and mash with caramelised onions or have pan-fried yellow fin tuna with a pineapple feta and pesto. If there's any criticism it is that some of the dishes are over embellished, and the simpler dishes, like the whole roasted fish, or fish cakes, work best. Starters are large, so share if you're planning a dessert such as American cheesecake or sticky toffee pudding. Its reputation has grown, and an offshoot, the Saxon Mill, opened in Warwick in spring 2004.

LEAMINGTON SPA

King Baba ★

58 Bath Street, Leamington Spa, CV31 3AE (01926 888869). **Food served** 6pm-midnight Mon-Thur, Sun; 6pm-2.30am Fri, Sat. **Main courses** £4.75-£6.50. **Credit** AmEx, MC, V.

If you want to try balti dishes without hitting the hustle and bustle of downtown Birmingham, then this friendly restaurant in Leamington Spa hits the spot. It's in the least nice part of town, but cheap prices and good food make it worth downgrading for the night. The decor is old-fashioned Indian –

Edmunds. *See p230.*

heavy wallpaper and dark interiors, but welcoming and friendly staff offer distraction. A comprehensive menu covers all the balti favourites, curries that come sizzling in their metal dishes. Each balti sauce – there are 14 in all – come with six options of meat or fish. And if you're feeling creative you can devise your own balti using the basic sauce and adding extras. None of the dishes are particularly spicy, so it you want your curry hot it might be well to choose the madras or vindaloo. The vegetable sides were disappointing, but the breads and popadoms first rate. Cobra, the perfect accompaniment, comes on draught or in bottles.

Love's ★

15 Dormer Place, Leamington Spa, CV32 5AA (01926 315522). **Lunch served** noon-1.45pm, **dinner served** 7-9.30pm Tue-Sat. **Set lunch** £14.50 3 courses. **Set dinner** £25 2 courses, £29.50 3 courses, £37.50 6 courses; (Tue-Thur) £25 3 courses incl glass of wine. **Credit** AmEx, MC, V.

Chef-owner Steve Love – Roux brothers- and French-trained – is a star in the Midlands' culinary world, with a growing national reputation. The restaurant, where his wife looks after front-of-house, is neat, comfortable and simply decorated, with no design fussiness to distract from the food. Love's style is adventurous and intricate, and menus change frequently; both set dinner and lunch are generously priced (despite an odd practice of not including VAT in the listed prices). Grilled goat's cheese with tomato sorbet and balsamic dressing provided a refreshing contrast of warm and cold; mushrooms in batter oreilles with parmesan, leeks, lardons and cep sauce was a bravura presentation. Love has a particularly fine touch with pastry and batter: roast saddle of lamb came with an explosive deep-fried anchovy in batter. Fillet of brill with Swiss chard, baby squid and a celery velouté was equally fine, and there was no letting up in our dessert, a delicious exploration of everything apple: a baked braeburn apple with apple and lemongrass sorbet, apple and cinnamon fritter and a little apple jelly. In between came a steady stream of impressive niceties: appetisers of parmesan pastry trumpets and a cup of broccoli velouté, a pre-dessert of passion fruit crème brûlée. These distracted a little from our one complaint – disappointingly slow service, perhaps due to the kitchen having to keep up the flow of such elaborate dishes

PRIORS HARDWICK

Butcher's Arms

Church End, Priors Hardwick, CV47 7SN (01327 260504/www.thebutchersarms.com). **Lunch served** noon-2pm Mon-Fri; noon-3pm Sun. **Dinner served** 7-9.30pm Mon-Sat. **Main courses** £12-£20. **Set lunch** (Mon-Fri) £18 3 courses; (Sun) £27.75 3 courses. **Credit** AmEx, MC, V.

This 14th-century inn has certainly got the wow factor, especially in summer when its outdoor hanging baskets are in bloom. The interiors might not live up to expectation – more old fashioned than traditional – but that doesn't spoil the welcoming atmosphere. It's been run by the ebullient Portuguese owner Lino Pires for more than 30 years, but don't think you'll be tucking into grilled sardines here. The Butcher's Arms is renowned and revered for its top quality retro food. The menu could be straight out of *Abigail's Party*. Starters of egg mayonnaise, prawn cocktail and avocado filled with prawns set the scene, before moving on to steak diane or Dover sole mornay. Vegetarians are well catered for with a choice of five mains that includes vegetarian moussaka and mushroom and stilton tart. There's even the ubiquitous desserts trolley and fancy liqueur coffees. The wine list is strong on French wine – from basic to blow-the-budget – and Pires should be applauded for offering drivers and teetotallers a selection of non-alcoholic wines.

STRATFORD-UPON-AVON

Callands

13-14 Meer Street, Stratford-upon-Avon, CV37 6QB (01789 269304). **Lunch served** noon-2pm Tue-Sun. **Dinner served** 6-9.30pm Tue-Sat. **Set lunch** £6.50 2 courses, £8.95 3 courses. **Set dinner** £19.95 2 courses, £23.95 3 courses. **Credit** AmEx, MC, V.

In a town where tourists are here one day, gone the next, it's good to find a restaurant that offers consistently good cooking aimed at locals and repeat business rather than the quick buck. The emphasis in this cheery brightly decorated restaurant is on good quality and exceptionally good value. At lunch choose from the well-priced set menus; short but without stinting on flavours. Start with soup such as tomato and paprika with a choice of breads or Thai fish cakes with a chilli dipping sauce, then move on to crab risotto, Moroccan-spiced chicken or a hearty steak and kidney pudding. In the evenings, try succulent grilled prawns, followed by grilled whole lemon sole or fillet steak. On Friday, there's a lobster menu, which you will need to book a week in advance. If you don't have time to eat in, get some goodies from the deli downstairs.

Fox & Goose Inn

Armscote, off A3400, Stratford-upon-Avon, CV37 8DD (01608 682293/www.aboveaverage.co.uk). **Lunch served** noon-2.30pm, **dinner served** 7-9.30pm daily. **Main courses** £8.95-£14.95. **Credit** AmEx, MC, V.

It's off the beaten track, but the Fox & Goose has plenty of enticements on its chalked blackboards to lure you down country lanes. The terracotta painted bar rooms and boudoir-style private dining room with zebra cover seats are a sight to behold for a pub in a sleepy village. The food is equally extravagant, but with the emphasis on home-style food using local ingredients. The own-cured salmon gravadlax starter was tasty, not too moist, but a little over salty. Alongside trad dishes such as chicken liver parfait and leek and potato soup are more exotic recipes such as saffron risotto cakes and fillet of grouper with orange and coriander tagliatelle – a winning combination. Curiously, the slow-roasted lamb kleftico, while rich and tender, was more English lamb shank with jus rather than the Greek original with herbs and onions, while the chocolate orange panna cotta was more of a mousse. But even if dishes might not resemble the original, they are always superbly cooked. You also can't fault the service or the nice little touches of chocs with coffee, and own-made chutneys and recipe books to buy.

Lamb's of Sheep Street

12 Sheep Street, Stratford-upon-Avon, CV37 6EF (01789 292554/www.lambsrestaurant.co.uk). **Lunch served** noon-1.45pm daily. **Dinner served** 5-9.45pm Mon-Fri; 5-10pm Sat; 6-9pm Sun. **Main courses** £9.25-£15.95. **Set meals** (lunch, 5-7pm) £11.95 2 courses, £14.50 3 courses. **Credit** MC, V.

You could easily dismiss Lamb's as part of an anonymous chain, albeit in one of Stratford's most attractive and oldest buildings. But once inside, the cosy charm of this venture grows on you. What its setting lacks in individuality, its cooking makes up in imagination, and at good prices. The unchanging menu offers popular dishes, plus there's a supplementary menu of daily specials: all fish the day we visited. The starter of grilled sardines was good, although the skins could have been crispier the light dressing was excellent. Next, chicken with Thai green curry sauce was a cut above the norm and came as a whole breast with a light and fragrant sauce. Leave room for puddings as the chef clearly has a talent for sweet things. The baked lemon tart was a masterpiece, its brûléed top a pleasant contrast to the soft, lemony filling and rich raspberry sorbet that came with it. This restaurant is popular with locals and visiting Shakespeare fans, so book around pre-theatre times.

Restaurant Margaux

6 Union Street, Stratford-upon-Avon, CV37 6QT (01789 269106/www.restaurantmargaux.co.uk). **Lunch served** noon-2pm, **dinner served** 6-10pm Tue-Sat. **Main courses** £8.95-£18. **Credit** AmEx, MC, V.

If you can't get tickets for the theatre, fear not: proprietor Maggie Margaux will keep you entertained at her eponymous restaurant. Her friendly and entertaining floorshow in the upstairs bistro will see you through from starter to pud, but if you are after a more intimate dining experience head for the whitewashed basement. Food is based around British ingredients but with French flair. Start with beautifully cooked seared scallops with lemon cinnamon, or equally rich and satisfying duck terrine with confit leg and balsamic dressing. The main courses offer eight thoughtful combinations: braised collar of pork with potato purée and mustard sauce was excellent as was pan-fried halibut on clam and mussel chowder. The well-balanced meals leave room for dessert; Thai rice pudding with mascarpone cream hits the spot.

TANWORTH IN ARDEN

The Bell

The Green, Tanworth in Arden, B94 5AL (01564 742212). **Open** noon-11pm Mon-Sat; noon-10.30pm Sun. **Lunch served** noon-2pm Mon-Sat; noon-3pm Sun. **Dinner served** 6.30-9pm Mon-Sat. **Main courses** £8.95-£14.50. **Credit** AmEx, MC, V.

Makeovers of historic pubs in classically pretty villages rarely avoid ye olde rusticky touch, but the owners of the Bell, in one of the most desired spots in the Birmingham commuter belt, have branched out with a positively metropolitan modern gastro-pub look: pale walls, metal bar, leather sofas and so on. There are equally stylish hotel rooms, plus a deli on the premises. Service is youthful, a bit scatty and, since mains are cooked to order, often slow (order from the bar rather than wait at your table). The menu promises 'English cuisine fused with Mediterranean and Middle Eastern influences'. Goat's cheese bruschetta with basil and pine nut pesto was pleasant, and wild mushroom, brandy and duck liver pâté rich and excellent. Mains from the dinner menu are generous to the point of over-busy: in roast monkfish tail with sautéd fennel and bacon and smoked potatoes, and pan-fried lamb with mint mash, roast veg and a port and currant sauce, the main ingredients were overwhelmed by masses of veg and other flavours. There's a simpler (and speedier) lunch menu, sandwiches and smaller dishes, plus a quality wine list. This is a modish departure from the country-pub norm, which might be better if the kitchen tried less hard to impress.

WARWICK

Findon's

7 Old Square, Warwick, CV34 4RA (01926 411755/ www.findons-restaurant.co.uk). **Dinner served** 6.30-9.30pm Mon-Sat. **Main courses** £10.95-£18.95. **Credit** MC, V.

An especially pretty restaurant in a Georgian house in the middle of old Warwick, with a fresh, snug dining room decorated in yellows and blues and with an eclectic range of artwork. It was quiet on a Friday evening, but deserves to be more widely known. Chef-owner Michael Findon's frequently changing menus are rich and ambitious. The style is modern English with global influences, combinations that sound overintricate, but are skilfully done. Among the starters, seared scallops with tagliatelle and a sambuca and lobster broth were both a smooth, delicate mix. Of the mains, fillet of beef with ratatouille and oregano sauce and an excellent roast pork with Italian honey glaze and pancetta were original and enjoyable. There are equally fine fish dishes and decent vegetarian options, such as a roast vegetable and pesto tartlet with wild mushrooms and a red pepper coulis. To finish, there are suitably elaborate and alluring desserts. The wine list is brief and to the point. Prices are high, but dishes are immaculate, and service is charming.

Worcestershire

ABBERLEY

The Elms ★

Stockton Road, Abberley, WR6 6AT (01299 896666/www.theelmshotel.co.uk). **Lunch served** noon-2.30pm, **dinner served** 7-9.30pm daily. **Set lunch** £12.50 2 courses, £16.50 3 courses; (Sun) £21.95 3 courses incl coffee. **Set dinner** £32.50 3 courses. **Credit** AmEx, DC, MC, V.

Deep in the prettiest corner of rural Worcestershire lies this beautiful country house hotel, nestling into the Abberley hills. It looks old fashioned, but inside the chintzy Brooke restaurant the food is bang up to date. The five choices at each course look deceptively effortless, with flavours that are appealing and expertly combined, cooked and presented. You just can't go wrong here and – untypically – it's actually worth the country house prices. Try starting with gravadlax of salmon with soused cucumber linguini and pumpernickel bread, and follow it deliciously with cannon of Cornish lamb with ratatouille and cashew nut pesto.

CHADDESLEY CORBETT

Brockencote Hall

Chaddesley Corbett, nr Kidderminster, DY10 4PY (01562 777876/www.brockencotehall.com). **Lunch served** noon-1.30pm Mon-Fri, Sun. **Dinner served** 7-9.30pm daily. **Main courses** £19.50-£22.50. **Set lunch** (Mon-Fri) £13 2 courses, £17 3 courses; (Sun) £24.50 3 courses. **Set dinner** £29.50 3 courses incl coffee, £46.50 5-course tasting menu incl coffee. **Credit** AmEx, DC, MC, V.

Truly a special occasion venue, this French-style mansion out in the wilds keeps the Gallic feel throughout. Chef Jerome Barbancon is from Brittany; here he cleverly puts a native twist into local produce, including Herefordshire snails in the starter selection or a Worcestershire sauce dressing with an assiette of game. There's rightly no fear of cheaper cuts given an upmarket treatment either. Feast on stuffed pig's trotter with onion and sage mashed potato or try a medley of rabbit – sausage, roast saddle, stuffed leg and bolognese with Madeira and Dijon mustard jus. Grand stuff, and if the credit card won't take the à la carte, try the set lunches.

COLWALL

Colwall Park Hotel

Walwyn Road, Colwall, WR13 6QG (01684 540000/ www.colwall.com). **Lunch served** noon-2pm, **dinner served** 7-9pm daily. **Main courses** £15.95-£19.95. **Set lunch** (Mon-Sat) £10 2 courses, £15 3 courses, (Sun) £17.95 3 courses. **Credit** AmEx, MC, V

A mere hop, skip and a jump from lovely Great Malvern is this half-timbered genteel hotel, which prides itself so much on its food that it offers regular gourmet breaks to sample its award-winning meals. The wood panelled, fancy linened and theatrically curtained dining room is old-school fine dining but don't let that put you off. There's some very good food here with lots of luxury additions. The grand à la carte includes plenty of fish and some own-made specialities such as boudin blanc. Mostly it plays to the classics, with Scottish beef fillet (served with a wild mushroom charlotte and foie gras), roast duckling and lemon sole possibly featuring among the main courses. Wonderful bread comes fresh from the kitchen oven each morning and local and seasonal ingredients are favoured where possible. For a more casual meal out, try the Lantern bar, which has masses of equally good, more homely fare at sensible prices.

CUTNALL GREEN

Chequers

Kidderminster Road, Cutnall Green, WR9 0PJ (01299 851292). **Lunch served** noon-2pm daily. **Dinner served** 6.30-9.15pm Mon-Sat; 7-9pm Sun. **Main courses** £10.50-£12.50. **Credit** MC, V.

This bijou village is dominated by the sizeable Chequers. As gastropubs go, this is one of the best – thanks to its owner, Roger Narbett, who also happens to be chef to the England football team. Fortunately, his able staff here ensure that things don't fall apart when he's jetting around the world keeping the squad well fed. The interior is divided into a large bar and a roomy restaurant, both beautifully done up, with the sand-blasted pale beams sitting nicely alongside the colourful walls. Traditional fare such as eggs benedict or ribeye steaks is served alongside the likes of bruschetta with niçoise vegetables and melted brie (a hearty beginning) or lime and black pepper cod with saffron and ginger potato chutney.

HOLY CROSS

Bell & Cross

Belbroughton Road, Holy Cross, Clent, DY9 9QL (01562 730319). **Lunch served** noon-2pm daily. **Dinner served** 6.30-9pm daily. **Main courses** £10.25-£12.75. **Credit** MC, V.

The interior of this listed building sitting at the foot of the Clent Hills has managed to hang on to its old pubby feel while updating the decor so it doesn't feel all horse brasses and swirly carpets. The Bell & Cross retains its maze of separate rooms and has real

Venture In

character – though people-watchers may feel a little cheated. The food is excellent – swish modern stuff that wouldn't be out of place in a smart bistro. Ribeye steaks with chips are a regular menu item, as are quality fish cakes. There's just one veggie main course option, but the willing chef can usually suggest another if the place isn't too frenetic. And be warned – it can get very, very busy.

OMBERSLEY

Venture In ★

Main Road, Ombersley, WR9 0EW (01905 620552). **Lunch served** noon-2pm Tue-Sun. **Dinner served** 7-9.30pm Tue-Sat. **Set lunch** (Tue-Sat) £16.95 2 courses, £19.95 3 courses; (Sun) £19.95 3 courses. **Set dinner** £30.50 3 courses. **Credit** MC, V.

Young chef-patron Toby Fletcher quietly goes about his business in this smart yet cosy little place in this quaint, half-timbered village. There are no airs and graces here; instead the food available in the ancient beamed and stone-walled dining room is bursting with generosity – both in flavour and in the size of the portions. You have been warned. Expect deeply satisfying, superbly cooked and hearty dishes that may leave you feeling like you need to be stretchered out to the car. Fletcher excels in getting maximum taste out of everything he prepares and his bountiful approach (the menu is great value too) has won him legions of fans. Prepare yourself first with a fortifying drink by the real fire in the bar before you venture in for the feast.

WORCESTER

Browns

24 Quay Street, Worcester, WR1 2JJ (01905 26263). **Lunch served** 12.30-2pm Tue-Fri, Sun. **Dinner served** 7-9.45pm Tue-Sat. **Set lunch** £20.50 3 courses. **Set dinner** £18.95 2 courses, £22.50 3 courses, £38.50 4 courses incl coffee. **Credit** AmEx, MC, V.

The huge advantage of Browns is its location – in the middle of Worcester yet right on the River Severn, with armies of swans sailing gracefully by (so get a window table if you can). Indeed, the river can feel a bit too close for comfort if the water level is high but inside is a haven of calm, those high cream-painted brick walls and pillars betraying its origins as a corn mill. Browns' new owners have added a splash of deep red colour here and there but the staff remain largely the same. The £38.50 menu includes cheese as an extra course and some more upmarket options (langoustine, Gressingham duck, fillet steak instead of sirloin). The cooking has occasional weak moments but mostly hits the spot. A tart of mushrooms, roast shallots and goat's cheese was particularly good.

North West

North West

NORTHUMBERLAND
Catlowdy
Roughsike
Butterburn
Gretna
Bowness-on-Solway
Kirkbride
Brampton
Carlisle
Castle Carrock
Wetheral
Silloth
Abbeytown
Solway Firth
Wigton
Thursby
Sebergham
Renwick
Alston
Allonby
Allonby Bay
Maryport
Plumpton
Melmerby
Bassenthwaite
Cockermouth
CUMBRIA
Penrith
Workington
Applethwaite
Tirril
Portinscale
Watermillock
Pooley Bridge
Keswick
Whitehaven
Frizington
Cleator Moor
St Bees Head
St Bees
Egremont
Grange-in-Barrowdale
Howtown
Helton
Appleby-in-Westmorland
Bampton
Shap
Ravensworth
Rothay Bridge
Haweswater
Grasmere
Kirkby Stephen
Ambleside
Seascale
Santon Bridge
Troutbeck
Hawkshead
Windermere
Coniston
Bowness-on-Windermere
Torver
Broughton in Furness
Crosthwaite
Kendal
Sedbergh
Bootle
Newby Bridge
Witherslack
Silecroft
Millom
Cartmel
Grange-over-Sands
Burton-in-Kendal
Kirkby Lonsdale
Ulverston
Dalton-in-Furness
Silverdale
Flookburgh
Bardsea
Warton
Barrow-in-Furness
Carnforth
Morecambe Bay
Vickerstown
Bolton-le-Sands
Isle of Walney
Morecambe
Hest Bank
Ashington
Morpeth
Newbiggin-by-the-Sea
Bedlington
Blyth
NORTH SEA
Ponteland
NEWCASTLE UPON TYNE
South Shields
Hexham
Prudhoe
TYNE & WEAR
Gateshead
Sunderland
Stanley
Consett
Durham
Peterlee
Crook
DURHAM
Shildon
Hartlepool Bay
Sedgefield
Bishop Auckland
Newton Aycliffe
Stockton-on-Tees
CLEVELAND
MIDDLESBROUGH
Barnard Castle
Darlington
Thornaby-on-Tees
Richmond
Northallerton
NORTH
YORKSHIRE
Ripon

IRISH SEA
Hilpsford Point
Heysham
Lancaster
Scotforth
Harrogate
Knaresborough
York
Skipton
LANCASHIRE
Pilling
Fleetwood
Sawley
Barnoldswick
Chatburn
Earby
Ilkley
Otley
Wetherby
Garstang
Cleveleys
Thornton
Thornton-le-Fylde
Poulton-le-Fylde
Clitheroe
Foulridge
Barrowford
Colne
Trawden
Keighley
Guiseley
Longridge
Nelson
Bingley
Shipley
BLACKPOOL
Great Harwood
Padiham
Brierfield
BRADFORD
LEEDS
Garforth
Rothwell
Selby
Kirkham
Fulwood
Burnley
Hebden Bridge
WEST YORKSHIRE
Lytham St Anne's
Freckleton
PRESTON
Accrington
Castleford
Blackburn
Halifax
Haslingden
Rawtenstall
Bacup
Leyland
Darwen
Wakefield
Pontefract
Southport
Wrightington Bar
Chorley
Ramsbottom
Rochdale
Littleborough
HUDDERSFIELD
Bispham Green
Adlington
Horwich
Bury
Standish
Bolton
Formby
Ormskirk
Skelmersdale
Wigan
GREATER MANCHESTER
Middleton
Barnsley
Hindley
Farnworth
Oldham
Atherton
Doncaster
Maghull
Rainford
Ashton-in-Makerfield
Mosssley
SOUTH YORKSHIRE
Leigh
Salford
Stocksbridge
Crosby
Kirkby
St Helens
MANCHESTER
Ashton-under-Lyne
Rawmarsh
Liverpool Bay
Bootle
Newton-le-Willows
Wallasey
LIVERPOOL
Prescot
Hyde
Glossop
SHEFFIELD
Maltby
MERSEYSIDE
Rotherham
Hoylake
Altrincham
Birkenhead
Warrington
Cheadle
Stockport
Marple
Great Ormes Head
Allerton
Widnes
Hale
Prestatyn
Bebington
Handforth
Llandudno
Rhyl
Heswall
Runcorn
Wilmslow
Whaley Bridge
Colwyn Bay
Knutsford
Alderley Edge
Worksop
Frodsham
Conwy
Abergele
Holywell
Neston
Ellesmere Port
Prestbury
Penmaenmawr
Helsby
Northwich
Staveley
Flint
Buxton
Chesterfield
CHESHIRE
Davenham
Macclesfield
Little Barrow
Market Warsop
Bolsover
FLINT-SHIRE
Kelsall
Bakewell
Tarvin
Winsford
Holmes Chapel
Mansfield Woodhouse
Denbigh
CONWY
DERBYSHIRE
Chester
Middlewich
Mold
Buckley
Congleton
Llanrwst
Tarporley
Hightown
Matlock
Sandbach
Mansfield
Bunbury
Alfreton
Ruthin
Biddulph
Burwardsley
Crewe
Leek
Alsager
Kidsgrove
Wirksworth
Kirkby in Ashfield
DENBIGH-SHIRE
Wrexham
Ripley
Tilston
Nantwich
Shavington
STOKE-ON-TRENT
Blaenau Ffestiniog
Hucknall
Belper
Heanor
Arnold
Malpas
WREXHAM
Ashbourne
Newcastle-under-Lyme
Ffestiniog
Audlem
Ilkeston
NOTTINGHAM
Whitchurch
STAFFORDSHIRE
DERBY
Stapleford
GWYNEDD
Beeston
Ellesmere
Stone
0 30 km
0 15 miles

Cheshire

ALDERLEY EDGE

Alderley Edge Hotel

Macclesfield Road, Alderley Edge, SK9 7BJ (01625 583033). **Lunch served** noon-1.45pm, **dinner served** 7-9.45pm daily. **Main courses** £22.50-£24.50. **Set lunch** £17.95 3 courses. **Set dinner** £29.50 3 courses. **Credit** AmEx, DC, MC, V.

Justifiably proud of its restaurant, the Alderley Edge Hotel is fast becoming one of the best places to sample dramatic modern British cooking in Cheshire. The dining-room conservatory setting doesn't set the heart a-flutter, though, coming halfway between urban loft and country tea-room. Food is consistently exciting and revelatory. Starters of lasagne of seared foie gras, braised calf's tongue and celeriac with sherry reduction, or poached and deep-fried horseshoe farm egg with wild mushrooms à la crème and truffle sauce have real flair. Mains up the ante: roast fillet of beef with oxtail mash and sauce perigeaux, say, or roast fillet of sea bass, chorizo crushed potatoes and cappuccino of fennel.

The Wizzard

Macclesfield Road, Alderley Edge, SK10 4UB (01625 584000). **Lunch served** noon-2pm Tue-Sun. **Dinner served** 7-9.30pm Tue-Sat. **Main courses** £9-£19. **Set lunch** (Sun) £12.95 1 course, £15.95 2 courses, £18.95 3 courses. **Credit** AmEx, MC, V.

Up on the Edge itself, the Wizzard is a cut above much else on offer in this prosperous corner of the county. The comfortable, restrained interior exudes calm, even during busy times. Meals are well prepared and often feature a surprise ingredient or two amid the traditional building blocks of well-cut steaks, fresh fish and seafood. You could enjoy cod with buttered spinach and salsa verde or sautéed chicken livers with thyme jus and red cabbage marmalade. Puddings are more traditional – sticky toffee pudding is a delight.

ALTRINCHAM

Juniper ★

21 The Downs, Altrincham, WA14 2QD (0161 929 4008). **Lunch served** noon-2.15pm Tue-Fri. **Dinner served** 7-9.30pm Tue-Sat. **Main courses** £19-£23. **Set lunch** £17.50 2 courses, £21.50 3 courses. **Credit** AmEx, MC, V.

It's hard to find a chef who enjoys pushing the boundaries of taste as much as Juniper's Paul Kitching. Juniper's kitchen must be a terrifically exciting place to work – more akin, we think, to a laboratory than anything – as disparate ingredients are coaxed together to form fabulous, inspired and truly memorable meals. The dining room is unfussy and cool, with attentive staff and a buzz of expectation born of a far-reaching reputation. Many diners opt for the full Juniper experience by choosing the gourmet menu (a succession of up to 20 mini-plates of impromptu wonder). Be prepared to experience anything from curried chocolate to scallops with Horlicks. Nimble cooking pervades the carte too, with seafood and fowl spectacularly handled. Wines are first rate, but pricey.

BIRKENHEAD

Station

24-8 Hamilton Street, Birkenhead, CH41 1AL (0151 647 1047). **Open** 8am-4pm Tue; 8am-9pm Wed-Fri; 10am-9pm Sat. **Lunch served** 11.30am-2.30pm Tue-Sat. **Dinner served** 5.30-9pm Wed-Sat. **Main courses** £8-£14.50. **Set lunch** £6.95 2 courses. **Set dinner** (5.30-7pm) £15 2 courses. **Credit** AmEx, DC, MC, V.

Birkenhead's stylish (and only) contemporary dining option has had a rocky few years – its delicatessen has closed, and ambitious extensions to the business (such as its restaurant-with-rooms scheme) saw the Station's competent urban, brasserie-style cooking wane somewhat, with diners noticing haphazard service. But things are looking up again with the restaurant offering a safe bet in a neglected corner of Merseyside. Succulent ribeye steaks, tortellini with ricotta, spinach and pine nuts, and fillet of Dover sole all passed the taste test, as did the well-stocked, and decently priced wine list.

BUNBURY

Dysart Arms

Bowes Gate Road, Bunbury, CW6 9PH (01829 260183/www.dysartarms-bunbury.co.uk). **Lunch served** noon-2.15pm, **dinner served** 6-9.30pm Mon-Fri. **Meals served** noon-9.30pm Sat; noon-9pm Sun. **Main courses** £6.95-£13.95. **Credit** MC, V.

A trad Cheshire pub with an off-beat, welcoming character, the Dysart has long been a favourite place to while away an afternoon. The pub was once a farm, later an abattoir, but little has changed here for well over a hundred years. And, thankfully, that goes for the hearty British fare served inside. Starters may include ham hock terrine with piccalilli or grilled black and white pudding skewer with couscous. Mains feature grilled trout with toasted almonds, or Bunbury bangers (made by a local butcher) with mash and onion gravy. Cheeses are particularly well selected and well kept, as is the range of cask ales and wines. A characterful pub with lots to recommend it.

Smokehouse Café. See p242.

CHESTER

Arkle

Chester Grosvenor and Grosvenor Spa, Eastgate, Chester, CH1 1LT (01244 324024/www.chester grosvenor.com). **Lunch served** noon-2.30pm Tue-Sun. **Dinner served** 7-9.30pm Tue-Sat. **Set lunch** £30 3 courses. **Set dinner** £47.50 2 courses, £55 3 courses, £65 5 courses. **Credit** AmEx, DC, MC, V.

Elegant and unashamedly old school, the Arkle is the perfect bolt-hole, and that rare thing in these parts – a truly great hotel restaurant. You're entering another world – gentlemen are requested to wear a jacket and to take their cigars in the lounge. Decor is cool marble offset by warm mahogany, simple and reassuring. The menu offers a surprisingly strong contemporary mixture of flavours and styles – steamed halibut, crab ginger and pak choi, for example, manages to be complex and clean at the same time. Traditionalists will love the saddle of venison with boudin blanc. The extensive wine list is on the pricey side, but the Arkle really isn't a place to come to penny-watch.

Blue Bell

65 Northgate Street, Chester, CH1 2HQ (01244 317758/www.bluebellrestaurant.co.uk). **Lunch served** noon-2.30pm Mon-Sat. **Dinner served** 6-9.30pm Mon-Fri; 5.30pm-9.30pm Sat. **Main courses** £10-£17. **Set lunch** £7 2 courses; £10 3 courses. **Set dinner** (until 7pm) £9.95 2 courses. **Credit** MC, V.

Thought to be the oldest surviving structure in the city, the Blue Bell refreshingly builds an unfussy atmosphere around a building which, in the wrong hands, could have become twee and chintzy. Starters may include a meaty duck liver and olive pâté served with a simple basil chutney, while mains favour locally reared meat in dishes such as chive-crusted beef fillet with wild mushrooms. Desserts bring berries and fruity sauces to the fore. A dependable choice if you're seeking an efficient, buzzing bistro in the city.

Brasserie 10/16

10-16 Brookdale Place, Chester, CH1 3DY (01244 322288/www.brasserie1016.com). **Lunch served** noon-2.30pm, **dinner served** 5.30-10pm Mon-Sat. **Meals served** noon-10pm Sun. **Main courses** £6.95-£18.25. **Credit** AmEx, DC, MC, V.

Bright and confident, Brasserie 10/16 offers diners a modern British selection with Mediterranean twists. The interior is a little less than inspired (light, stripped wood, cream walls, clutter-free). The lack of local competition means that the Brasserie can get busy – very busy. Try the towering creations: poached egg on ham hock atop bubble and squeak: great to dismantle and devour. A vegetarian option might be penne with sunblush tomatoes, broccoli and goat's cheese. Wines offer a solid global range.

Old Harker's Arms

1 Russell Street, Chester, CH3 5AL (01244 344525). **Lunch served** noon-2.30pm, **dinner served** 5.30-9.30pm Mon-Fri. **Meals served** noon-9.30pm Sat, Sun. **Main courses** £6.50-£13. **Credit** AmEx, MC, V.

A relaxing city centre pub, just far enough away from the hustle, on the canalside (under an antique shop). Once you've found it, you can enjoy their great food and well-kept beers. The menu changes daily (always a good sign in pubs) and includes fresh local produce – steamed mussels in cream and pink peppercorn sauce maybe, or wild mushroom and spinach pancakes with pine nuts and cheese sauce. That the menu never overreaches itself is also to be commended. Especially popular with younger visitors.

CREWE

Les's Fish Bar ★

49-51 Victoria Street, Crewe, CW1 2JG (01270 257581). **Meals served** 11am-5pm Mon-Sat. **Main courses** £3-£5.50. **No credit cards**.

Giving a much needed jolt of life to the traditional English chippy, Lee's locally famous fish bar is worth a detour if you're a fan of fish and chips the way they used to be. There are no plans, alas, to keep this fantastically unreconstructed fish bar open past 5pm. Come for fabulously fresh haddock (served with the skin off) and golden brown chips. You might even be tempted to try a bag of 'batter bits'.

HALE

Amba

106-108 Ashley Road, Hale, WA14 2UN (0161 928 2343/www.amba.uk.com). **Lunch served** noon-2.30pm, **tapas served** noon-6pm, **dinner served** 6-10.30pm daily. **Main courses** £7.95-£14.95. **Tapas** £1.75-£3.95. **Credit** AmEx, MC, V.

The ultimate in casual neighbourhood dining, or so the PR jargon attests. But, for once, it's a mission statement that's bang on the money. Fabrics are rich and earthy in the front bar section. Here diners can place their orders before being seated in the naturally lit, unfussy dining area to the rear. Cooking is a reassuring mix of the inventive and familiar, with more than a nod to the Mediterranean and the East. Starters include marinated sardines with avocado and pesto drizzle, or griddled asparagus with baby leeks and vine tomatoes. Mains feature a healthy selection of salads (the chef's salad of satays, goujon, deep-fried brie, prawns and avocado is a real winner). More substantial offerings include Cumbrian fell-bred steaks with 'big chips'.

HIGHER BURWARDSLEY

Pheasant

Higher Burwardsley, CH3 9PF (01829 770434/ www.thepheasant-burwardsley.com). **Lunch served** noon-2.30pm Mon-Sat; noon-4pm Sun. **Dinner served** 6.30-9.30pm daily. **Main courses** £10.95-£18.95. **Set lunch** (Sun) buffet £13.95 3 courses. **Credit** AmEx, DC, MC, V.

This sprawling, brick, traditional pub has been steadily honing its skills, and fine tuning its portfolio over the past five or so years. Now, a tasteful, contemporary interior leads to a stone-flagged, bright dining conservatory. The views from here are stunning – Wales on one side, Liverpool on the other. Daily specials could include game terrine, monkfish brochettes or poached seafood sausages with creamed leeks. In fact, surprisingly, seafood is more popular here than the excellent Cheshire reared beef. Desserts are homely and stodgy (in a good way): try toffee and date pudding. A great spot for a summer evening and, in winter, a huge open fire ensures an equally warm welcome.

KNUTSFORD

Belle Epoque

60 King Street, Knutsford, WA16 6DT (01565 633060/www.belleepoque.co.uk). **Lunch served** noon-2pm daily. **Dinner served** 6-11pm Mon-Sat. **Main courses** £10.50-£18.95. **Credit** AmEx, DC, MC, V.

A flourishing, ebullient art nouveau encrusted restaurant, Belle Epoque has had a chequered culinary history. The building's curlicues and turrets have often provided more drama than the rather hit-and-miss creations inside. A new menu and a re-invigorated kitchen staff have put paid to this. Essentially an upmarket brasserie, Belle Epoque fuses local produce with international influences – thus you could sample braised frogs' legs with watercress salad or Bury black pudding with mustard seed oil and smoked bacon for starters, and 'proper' fish and chips or Gressingham duck with candied clementines to follow.

LITTLE BARROW

Foxcote Arms

Little Barrow, CH3 7JN (01244 301343/www.thefoxcote.com). **Lunch served** noon-2.30pm, **dinner served** 6-10pm Mon-Sat. **Meals served** noon-4pm Sun. **Main courses** £11-£18. **Credit** MC, V.

A stunning seafood-strong gastropub in the hills, the Foxcote doesn't look much from the outside (to be honest, it doesn't look much from within, but no matter). Fish is sourced twice weekly from Manchester's excellent market – and is treated with creativity and flair. If the range is daunting, take advice from the proprietors, or plump for the tempura starters – something of a house speciality – or own-made fish cake. Desserts are inspired too – check out the apple and pear crumble. Wines (especially the whites) are well sourced.

WILMSLOW

Smokehouse Café ★

Cheshire Smokehouse, Vost Farm, Morley Green Road, Wilmslow, SK9 5NU (01625 548499/ www.cheshiresmokehouse.co.uk). Shop **Open** 8.30am-5pm Mon; 8.30am-6pm Tue-Thur; 8.30am-7pm Fri; 9am-5pm Sat. *Café* **Lunch served** 11.30-2.30pm, **tea served** 2.30-4pm Tue-Sat. **Main courses** £6.95-£8.95. **Corkage** £3. **Credit** AmEx, DC, MC, V.

A bright new addition to Wilmslow's popular Smokehouse, the Café serves great food. The own-smoked salmon pâté with cream cheese and horseradish is perfect, not too salty, not too chewy. Gourmet sandwiches are served on the Smokehouse's own bread and are noteworthy. Main meals are imaginative: smoked timbale of trout is divine, and the all-day breakfast is equally good if you fancy taking a break from the smoked stuff. Though it's licensed, wines can be brought in from the adjoining wine shop, with a small corkage charge (cheeky).

Also in the area

Living Room 13 St Werburgh Street, Chester, CH1 2DY (0870 442 2805); **Les's Fish Bar** 172 Widnes Road, Widnes, WA8 6BL (0151 424 2444); **Les's Fish Bar** 15 Dingle Walk, Winsford, CW7 1BA (01606 556425); **Piccolino Knutsford** 95 King Street, Knutsford, WA16 6EQ (01565 751402).

Cumbria

AMBLESIDE

Drunken Duck Inn

Barngates, Ambleside, LA22 0NG (015394 36347/ www.drunkenduckinn.co.uk). **Lunch served** noon-2.30pm, **dinner served** 6-8.45pm daily. **Main courses** £9.95-£16.95. **Credit** AmEx, MC, V.

This 400-year-old stone pub stands in splendid isolation on a crossroads in wild and scenic countryside. It's a magnet to tourists and ramblers – for the surroundings, but also for the four beers from the on-site Barngates microbrewery, the well-prepared, lunchtime bar snacks and elaborate dinner menus. The latter could include a starter of spring onion pancake with wild smoked salmon and baked goat's cheese, followed by lamb cutlets with sweet roast onion, parsnip dauphinoise and rosemary jus. Desserts such as warm walnut tart with honey-roast pears and caramel crunchy ice-cream could follow. Food is enjoyable, but dishes tend to have too many ingredients, resulting in confused flavours.

Glass House

Rydal Road, Ambleside, LA22 9AN (015394 32137). **Lunch served** noon-5pm daily. **Dinner served** 6.30-9.30pm Mon-Fri, Sun; 6.30-10pm Sat. **Main courses** £11.75-£27. **Set dinner** £15 2 courses, £18 3 courses. **Credit** MC, V.

Following an appearance on TV's culinary makeover show, *Ramsay's Kitchen Nightmares*, this became a Cumbrian hotspot. The clever conversion of the listed 15th-century mill has created a smart, attractive, oak-beamed restaurant, with a varied and imaginative menu. Lunch sees delicious light bites such as a BLT; Morecambe Bay shrimps and taramasalata on rye bread; Lakeland confit duck with caper potato cake; and fish cakes with fat chips, salad and lemon mayo. There's a varied, regularly changing carte at dinner.

Lucy's on a Plate

Church Street, Ambleside, LA22 0BU (015394 31191/ www.lucysofambleside.co.uk). **Meals served** 10am-9pm daily. **Main courses** £6-£19. **Credit** MC, V.

A gem of a place. Lucy's is a café by day and a restaurant in the evening, with a deli next door. The decor is rustic chic, with scrubbed pine tables and chapel chairs creating a relaxed setting made even more inviting by the friendliness of the staff. As well as quirkily named dishes such as Bantry beauties (Irish mussels), rumpy pumpy (Lakeland lamb rump steak), and pancetta piggy wig (stuffed pork fillet), there are proper, own-made puddings: crumbles, sticky toffee pudding, pavlovas, trifles, tortes and tarts – the list reads like school dinner dream time. Lucy 4 just across the road in St Mary's Lane has a great tapas menu to accompany a choice of 60 wines.

Rothay Manor

Rothay Bridge, Ambleside, LA22 0EH (015394 33605/www.rothaymanor.co.uk). **Lunch served** 12.30-2pm Mon-Sat; 12.45-1.30pm Sun. **Dinner served** 7.30-9pm daily. **Main courses** (lunch) £9.50. **Set lunch** (Mon-Sat) £16 3 courses, (Sun) £18.50 3 courses. **Set dinner** £30 3 courses, £34 5 courses. **Credit** AmEx, DC, MC, V.

This attractive Regency building set in secluded grounds has been run as a friendly country house hotel by the Nixon family for 37 years. It's a thoroughly traditional set-up, from the buffet lunch during the week (roasts on Sunday), afternoon tea served daily (3.30-5.30pm), to dinner in the elegant dining room with its polished, candlelit mahogany tables. The menu, though varied, holds no surprises, offering starters like chicken livers with bacon, croûtons and fresh asparagus with tomato and thyme salsa, and mains such as breast of guinea fowl with wild mushrooms and champagne and cream sauce, or medallions of beef fillet with creamy peppercorn sauce and spinach. There's lemon tart and chocolate parfait among the desserts. A good-value wine list has several choices by the glass.

Zeffirelli's

Compston Road, Ambleside, LA22 9AD (015394 33845/www.zeffirellis.co.uk). **Meals served** 10am-9.30pm daily. **Main courses** £5.95-£7.85. **Credit** MC, V.

A winning combination of a stylish pizzeria with four cinema screens – two in-house, and now a further two just 200m away. The art deco interior allows you to dine in comfort before moving to the cinema to enjoy a film. Food is vegetarian with an Italian edge, including starters like bruschetta and hot toasted ciabatta. The wholemeal pizza bases come with toppings like the Zeffirelli: Zeff sauce (tomatoes, garlic, basil and virgin olive oil), cheddar and mozzarella; and Quattro Formaggi: Zeff sauce, goat's cheese, taleggio, cheddar and mozzarella topped with red onions. End with great locally made ices, or even better, sundaes, for dessert.

APPLETHWAITE

Underscar Manor

Applethwaite, nr Keswick, CA12 4PH (01768 775000). **Lunch served** noon-1pm, **dinner served** 7-8.30pm daily. **Main courses** £19-£21. **Set lunch** £28 3 courses. **Set dinner** £38 5 courses. **Credit** AmEx, MC, V.

Set on the slopes of Skiddaw, with striking views over Derwentwater, this Victorian Italianate house

Holbeck Ghyll. See p247.

has a serene atmosphere. A formal conservatory dining room, its windows festooned with chiffon drapes, is the setting for a modern French menu. The carte is available for lunch and dinner, with an abbreviated version as a set lunch. Dish descriptions are detailed and demonstrate the complexity of the presentation: pan-fried medallions of calf's liver with onion and apple puff pastry tart, mushroom risotto and finished with calvados sauce is a typical first course, while char-grilled duck breast on a cassoulet with beans, spring cabbage, herb sausage and creamed potato with a red wine sauce could follow. Desserts include a delicious hot soufflé.

BOWNESS-ON-WINDERMERE

Linthwaite House

Crook Road, Bowness-on-Windermere, LA23 3JA (015394 88600/www.linthwaite.com). **Lunch served** 12.30-1.30pm daily. **Dinner served** 7.15-9pm daily. **Main courses** (lunch) £5.95-£14.95. **Set lunch** (Mon-Sat) £14.50 3 courses; (Sun) £17.95 3 courses. **Set dinner** £42 4 courses. **Credit** AmEx, DC, MC, V.

Set in 14 acres of grounds, with the Langdale fells as a backdrop, and views down to Windermere from the terrace and conservatory, Linthwaite House is both a stylish and relaxing hotel. The elegant dining rooms are formal but unstuffy, with well-spaced, highly polished mahogany tables. The four-course fixed-price dinner offers modern European cooking from a talented young chef. Seared scallops with cauliflower purée and crisp pancetta is a wonderful starter. Next, a fine white bean soup, then a truly delicious assiette of pork for main: roasted fillet, confit belly, sage and onion sausage, black pudding bon bon and port jus. For dessert, the chocolate fondant is worth the 12-minute wait, especially as it comes with hot chocolate ice-cream.

Porthole Eating House

3 Ash Street, Bowness-on-Windermere, LA23 3EB (015394 42793/www.porthole.fsworld.co.uk). **Lunch served** noon-2pm Sun. **Dinner served** 6.30-10.30pm Mon, Wed-Sun. **Main courses** £11.50-£25. **Credit** AmEx, DC, MC, V.

A younger generation of the Berton family has taken over the running of this quaint little restaurant in a 17th-century cottage, but high standards are being maintained. Food is a mix of enjoyable restaurant classics, mainly Italian with a dab of the French: chicken liver pâté with Madeira-soaked raisins; escalope of veal ai funghi (wild mushroom, Marsala and cream sauce). A few innovations are creeping in: crispy fish cakes with sautéed leeks and coconut mash, for instance. There's a great wine list, particularly strong on Germany and Alsace.

CARTMEL

L'Enclume ★

Cavendish Street, Cartmel, LA11 6PZ (015395 36362/www.lenclume.co.uk). **Lunch served** noon-1.45pm, **dinner served** 7-9.30pm Tue-Sun. **Main courses** £18-£26. **Set lunch** £25 3 courses. **Set dinner** £50 8 courses, £75 14 courses, £95 23 courses. **Credit** AmEx, MC, V.

Once a smithy, this is now a UK foodie destination of some style and originality. Chef-patron Simon Rogan, inspired by French chefs like Marc Veyrat, ensures that a meal here involves embarking on an extraordinary voyage of gastronomic discovery. Sourcing unusual flavours, textures and fragrances gathered from the wild, he assembles them into dishes that challenge preconceptions. Though there is a carte, the best way to participate in the experience is to order one of the tasting menus, of which there are three, culminating in the Gourmand, of 23 suitably tiny courses. Be prepared to be amazed by the likes of brushed tuna, smoky flavour, lovage squirt, apple wash in plastic, cubes from land and sea, eucalyptus hollandaise-style and roasted sea bass with calamint flavours and nutty nougatine.

Uplands

Haggs Lane, Cartmel, LA11 6HD (015395 36248/ www.uplands.uk.com). **Lunch served** 12.30-1pm Fri-Sun. **Dinner served** 7.30-8pm Tue-Sun. **Set lunch** £16.50 3 courses. **Set dinner** £31 4 courses. **Credit** AmEx, MC, V.

A lovely country house – more a relaxing restaurant with rooms than a hotel – set in two acres of gardens with views to the Leven Estuary. Tom Peter has created a wonderful, well-balanced fixed-price menu. Freshly baked bread heralds a meal prepared with great attention to detail. Dinner began with hot salmon soufflé wrapped in smoked salmon with watercress sauce, followed by a tureen of roasted red pepper and tomato soup. Next came roast loin of lamb with redcurrant and caper sauce, accompanied by butternut squash, baked spiced red cabbage, and potatoes with cream and cheese. Dessert was a rich chocolate Grand Marnier mousse.

COCKERMOUTH

Quince & Medlar

13 Castlegate, Cockermouth, CA13 9EU (01900 823579/www.quinceandmedlar.co.uk). **Dinner served** 7-9.30pm Tue-Sat. **Main courses** £12.75. **Credit** MC, V.

Q&M is something of a northern rarity: it's vegetarian but licensed, and offers diners an evening out in an attractive no-smoking setting. Located in a Georgian building, the cosy dining room is wood panelled and candlelit, a perfectly informal backdrop to a varied, imaginative carte. Start with tasty baked watercress and cheese soufflé, followed by wild and button mushroom casserole with aduki beans in a rich tomato and paprika sauce, with courgette and potato cakes. Chocolate truffle terrine is a great finale. The wines, beers and cider are organic and mostly vegan.

CROSTHWAITE

Punch Bowl Inn

Crosthwaite, LA8 8HR (015395 68237/www.punchbowl.fsnet.co.uk). **Lunch served** noon-2pm, **dinner served** 6-9pm Tue-Sat. **Main courses** £9.95-£15.75. **Set lunch** (Tue-Sat) £12.95 2 courses, £14.95 3 courses; (Sun) £14.95 2 courses, £16.95 3 courses. **Set dinner** (6-7pm) £15.95 2 courses, £18.95 3 courses. **Credit** MC, V.

Steven Doherty used to be head chef at London's Le Gavroche (*see p26*), and the walls of this gastropub are crowded with menus and photos from there, and other famous restaurants. The place has a friendly atmosphere, with service that's on the ball. Food is enjoyable, and not at all highbrow. Typical starters are black pudding and haggis terrine with spiced pickled damsons, or pea and asparagus soup. Mains could be roast rib of beef with mashed potatoes, caramelised onions and beer gravy, or pan-fried sea bass on crushed new potatoes. Finish, perhaps, with coffee bean crème brûlée. The short interesting wine list has lots of choice by the glass.

GRASMERE

White Moss House

Rydal Water, Grasmere, LA22 9SE (015394 35295/ www.whitemoss.com). **Dinner served** 7.30-8pm Mon-Sat. **Set dinner** £34.50 5 courses. **Credit** MC, V.

A tiny hotel built as a private house in 1730. It was once owned by William Wordsworth and is a quiet, intimate place with views over Rydal Water. Residents have preference, so booking is essential for the five-course dinners, served in a little cottagey room. Menus change daily; meticulous care is taken in sourcing and preparation, but there's no choice until dessert. Soup comes first, perhaps baby fennel and apple, then a fish dish: Coniston Water char and smoked sea trout soufflé, perhaps. Fell-bred beef fillet marinated in real ale is served with wild mushroom sauce and stir-fried leeks with Pernod. Dessert might be Mrs Beeton's chocolate pudding, with British cheeses as the finale.

MELMERBY

Village Bakery ★ ★

Melmerby, CA10 1HE (01768 881811/www.village-bakery.com). **Meals served** *Apr-Nov* 8.30am-5pm Mon-Sat; 9am-5pm Sun. *Dec-Mar* 8.30am-4.30pm Mon-Sat; 9am-4.30pm Sun. **Main courses** £4.50-£8. **Credit** MC, V.

A pioneer of wholefood and organic cuisine, in a converted barn with a bright airy conservatory. From a wood-fired brick oven come wonderful breads and cakes for the restaurant. The all-day menu kicks off with breakfast (till 11am), which includes the famous raspberry porridge, free-range eggs and home-cured bacon. Later tuck into vegetable soup, or savoury snacks like steak and kidney pie or cheese pasty, then date and walnut scones or teabread.

PENRITH

Scott's ★ ★

34 Burrowgate, Sandgate, Penrith, CA11 7TA (01768 890838). **Lunch served** 11.30am-2pm, **dinner served** 4.30-8pm Tue, Wed; 4.30-9pm Thur-Sat. **Main courses** £5.75-£12. **No credit cards**.

Phill and Janet Jarvis bought this licensed town centre fish and chip shop in July 2003, and they have since smartened up the decor. Fish is of a prime quality. As elsewhere, haddock and cod are the two most popular choices. These are fried to a golden crispness in lovely batter, with mushy peas the classic accompaniment. Salmon is often available and, like other fish, can be poached to order.

POOLEY BRIDGE

Sharrow Bay

Pooley Bridge, CA10 2LZ (01768 486301/www.sharrowbay.co.uk). **Lunch served** 1-1.45pm, **dinner served** 8-8.45pm daily. **Set lunch** £38.25 4 courses incl coffee. **Set dinner** £49.25 5 courses incl coffee. **Credit** AmEx, MC, V.

The lakeside dining room of this magnificent country house hotel is a study in elegance, while the adjacent Victorian panelled room retains a genteel air. Head chefs, Johnny Martin and Colin Akrigg, have been here for 40 and 36 years respectively. The daily-changing lunch and dinner menus have kept pace with trends and now offer lighter options, but the cooking and presentation are still benchmarks of skill and artistry. 'Luncheon' might be terrine of venison and duck with pear and saffron chutney and toasted brioche, followed by fillet of sole, then a sorbet, then sea bass on ratatouille with a red pepper coulis and finally apple charlotte with vanilla sauce.

TIRRIL

Queens Head Inn

Tirril, CA10 2JF (01768 863219/www.queenshead inn.co.uk). **Lunch served** noon-2pm daily. **Dinner served** 6-9.30pm Mon-Sat; 7-9pm Sun. **Main courses** £8.50-£13.95. **Credit** MC, V.

Built in 1719, this popular, whitewashed, village pub attracts all ages and types. There's a maze of small cosy rooms with open fires, low oak beams and high-back settles. Other attractions are the excellent beers from landlord Chris Tomlinson's brewery (at nearby Brougham Hall); and the wide choice of filling bar food. The menu runs from filled jacket potatoes, baguettes and stuffed pitta breads for lunch, to more substantial dishes like braised shoulder of lamb with redcurrant gravy, and brewer's pudding – a rich suet pudding filled with steak and Tirril ale.

TROUTBECK

Queens Head

Townhead, Troutbeck, LA23 1PW (015394 32174/www.queensheadhotel.com). **Lunch served** noon-2.30pm, **dinner served** 6.30-9pm daily. **Main courses** £7.25-£14.25. **Set meal** £15.50 3 courses. **Credit** MC, V.

This 17th-century inn stands in the Troutbeck valley. Inside are log fires, stone flag floors, solid oak beams and a bar counter made from an Elizabethan four-poster bed. While the setting oozes antiquity, the menu is more modern, with good vegetarian choices, as well as fish and meat dishes with a certain originality in their make-up. Salmon fillet comes with a chive risotto and pink peppercorn and lemongrass cream; breast of chicken is stuffed with stilton wrapped in bacon on a grape compote with cream. The mayor's chair used in the annual mayor-making ceremony (February) is now in the bar.

ULVERSTON

Bay Horse

Canal Foot, Ulverston, LA12 9EL (01229 583972/www.furness.co.uk/bayhorse). **Lunch served** noon-2pm Tue-Sun. **Dinner served** 7.30pm for 8pm daily. **Main courses** (lunch) £9-£13; (dinner) £22.50-£24.50. **Set dinner** £28.50 3 courses.
Credit AmEx, MC, V.

The pub stands at the water's edge of the Leven Estuary, with views of the fells. Its conservatory restaurant makes the most of the scenery and offers an imaginative weekly-changing menu that makes good use of local ingredients. Fresh shrimps potted with butter, gin and nutmeg is a delicious starter, followed by pink, tender roasted rack of salt marsh lamb with dijon mustard and herb crust. To follow, try brown sugar meringue with mango and paw-paw. Booking is essential for afternoon tea (3-5pm).

WATERMILLOCK

Rampsbeck Country House Hotel

Watermillock, CA11 0LP (01768 486442/www.rampsbeck.fsnet.co.uk). **Lunch served** noon-2pm daily by appointment only. **Dinner served** 7-8.30pm daily. **Set lunch** £26 3 courses. **Set dinner** £38 3 courses, £44.50 4 courses incl coffee. **Credit** MC, V.

North West

Standing in parkland sloping towards Ullswater, this 18th-century country house enjoys stunning views. The terrace, which opens from the bar, is the perfect summer spot for light lunches and afternoon cream teas. At dinner the cooking from long-serving chef Andrew McGeorge is accomplished and imaginative. Try the amazing poached pear with seared foie gras and cinnamon flavoured jus. Follow that with a delicious assiette of spring lamb with globe artichoke and sweet potato fondant. Top marks for desserts too: chocolate and mocha flavoured mousse, with (a great retro touch) iced advocaat snowball.

WHITEHAVEN

Zest

Harbourside, West Strand, Whitehaven, CA28 7LR (01946 66981). **Food served** 11am-9.30pm Mon-Thur, Sun; 11am-10pm Fri, Sat. **Main courses** £2.50-£7. **Credit** MC, V.

This friendly café-bar overlooks the quay, with pavement tables for drinks. London-born Ricky Andalcio's career has included time spent at Langan's Brasserie and with the Roux brothers. His menu is a long list of well-prepared light bites, served in generous portions and at kind prices. There are blinding butties; penne with mushrooms and garlic; four-hour lamb; mussels in Hoegaarden; and spicy bean and tomato hot-pot. The other Zest (01946 692848) is a mile away on Low Road and offers more serious, but unpretentious, modern cooking in a smart, relaxed setting.

WINDERMERE

Gilpin Lodge

Crook Road, Windermere, LA23 3NE (015394 88818/www.gilpinlodge.com). **Coffee served** 9am-noon, **lunch served** noon-2.30pm, **tea served** 3-5.30pm, **dinner served** 7-9.15pm daily. **Set lunch** £14.75 2 courses, £19.50 3 courses. **Set dinner** £42.50 5 courses. **Credit** AmEx, DC, MC, V.

There are four beautiful, cosy dining rooms here, including the Garden Room with french doors opening on to a terrace, and the bright conservatory-roofed Courtyard Room – both perfect for summer dining. The fixed-price dinner menu is sophisticated and modern, featuring ravioli of langoustines with cep, mushroom froth and baby leeks; consommé of vine tomatoes with tapenade tortellini; pink champagne sorbet; fillet of fell-bred beef with wild mushrooms, roast shallots and cabernet sauvignon jus; and hot raspberry ripple soufflé with raspberry crumble ice-cream. For lunch, as well as the set-priced options, light meals are served in the lounges.

Holbeck Ghyll ★

Holbeck Lane, Windermere, LA23 1LU (015394 32375/www.holbeckghyll.com). **Lunch served** noon-2pm, **dinner served** 7-9.30pm daily. **Set lunch** £22.50 2 courses, £27.50 3 courses. **Set dinner** £45 6 courses. **Credit** AmEx, DC, MC, V.

The view to Lake Windermere is a corker. Inside this former hunting lodge there's an air of lived-in elegance, enhanced by Arts and Crafts details, mullioned windows and fine oak panelling. Chef David McLaughlin's modern French menus possess a sublime simplicity that highlights the flavours and textures of ingredients. For Sunday lunch, perfectly timed roast scallops came with celeriac and a balsamic dressing, tender best end of lamb with shallot purée and rosemary jus, and to finish, nougat glacé with mango parcels and passion fruit sorbet.

Jerichos

Birch Street, Windermere, LA23 1EG (015394 42522). **Dinner served** 6.45-9.30pm Tue-Sun. **Main courses** £13.50-£16.95. **Credit** MC, V.

For ten years before opening this colourfully decorated town-centre restaurant, Chris Blaydes was head chef at Miller Howe. That experience has been distilled into a short well-constructed menu. A satisfying smoked haddock, spinach, pea and mature cheddar risotto with warm virgin oil vinaigrette was followed by full-flavoured dark soy and honey marinated char-grilled pork fillet with horseradish mash, puy lentil fondue, glazed greens and port wine reduction. Lavender crème brûlée with fresh sugared fruit makes for a delicious last mouthful. Value-for-money wines are usefully matched to food styles.

Miller Howe

Rayrigg Road, Windermere, LA23 1EY (015394 42536/www.millerhowe.com). **Lunch served** 12.30-2pm, **dinner served** 8pm daily. **Set lunch** (Mon-Sat) £19.50 3 courses; (Sun) £21 4 courses. **Set dinner** £42.50 6 courses. **Credit** AmEx, MC, V.

One of the Lake District's best-known and most idiosyncratic hotels, the Miller Howe continues to enchant; camp decor is just one of the many attractions. A split-level dining room makes the most of the fantastic views over the lake and is the setting for a feast of flavours from the fixed-price dinner menu. This comes in six elaborate stages (lunch is a simpler, multi-choice three-parter). The start of the single sitting is signalled by a theatrical dimming of the lights before the arrival of courses that might include roast quail, followed by seared turbot fillet and loin of Lakeland lamb.

Samling

Ambleside Road, Windermere, LA23 1LR (015394 31922/www.thesamling.com). **Lunch served** 1pm Sun by appointment. **Dinner served** 7-9.30pm daily by appointment. **Set lunch** £45 4 courses. **Set dinner** £45 4 courses, £60 9 courses. **Credit** AmEx, MC, V.

Set in 67 acres above Lake Windermere, this mansion is almost the antithesis of the typical country house hotel in that any formality is low key. Comfort levels remain high, however. In the stylish, unfussy dining room the food hits all the right modern notes with simple, well-considered combinations such as boudin of pigeon and foie gras followed by pan-fried halibut with seafood nage. The nine-course tasting menu (£60) is a succession of exquisite little creations.

Lancashire

BISPHAM GREEN

Eagle & Child

Maltkiln Lane, Bispham Green, L40 3SG (01257 462297). **Lunch served** noon-2pm Mon-Sat. **Dinner served** 6-8.30pm Mon-Thur; 6-9pm Fri, Sat. **Meals served** noon-8.30pm Sun. **Main courses** £8.50-£14. **Credit** MC, V.

This is a cracking village pub where they've got everything right. From the outside all is traditional – whitewashed, stone built and sturdy, yet, inside, the textures, lighting and ambience are altogether more stylish. Staff bustle about, smiling and joking with customers creating a refreshingly informal atmosphere. Food is dependable – a mix of traditional and modern. So you can enjoy spicy sausage and mash, olive- and tomato-bread pizza, or fabulous haddock and chunky chips. The pub's cask ales are great – and as perfect an accompaniment to the hearty grub as you could get. But, for those who prefer the grape, there is plenty of choice, including interesting varieties such as English fruit wines.

BLACKBURN

Millstone Hotel

Church Lane, Mellor, Blackburn, BB2 7JR (01254 813333/www.shirehotels.co.uk). **Lunch served** (bar snacks) noon-2pm Mon-Sat. **Dinner served** 6.30-9.15 Mon-Thur; 5.30-9.30pm Fri, Sat. **Meals served** noon-9pm Sun. **Set dinner** £20.95 2 courses, £24.95 3 courses. **Credit** AmEx, DC, MC, V.

A former coaching inn, the Millstone at Mellor is passionate about its food, and it shows. You can join in the evangelical mood by opting for the restaurant – with its leaded windows, chandeliers and exuberant floral displays – or take things a little easier in the cosy bar, with a pint of hand-pulled Thwaites. Whatever you choose, there's little room for error on the short seasonal menus. Starters feature pressed chicken with local black pudding – a solid, no-nonsense wedge of meaty textures. Mains are slightly more elaborate, and may feature pork tenderloin with chorizo mash served with oyster mushroom and chickpea gravy. There's a great selection of English cheeses and a good wine list.

Northcote Manor ★

Northcote Road, Langho, Blackburn, BB6 8BE (01254 240555/www.northcotemanor.com). **Lunch served** noon-1.30pm Mon-Fri; noon-2pm Sun. **Dinner served** 7-9pm Mon-Thur, Sun; 7-9.30pm Fri; 7-10pm Sat. **Main courses** £18.50-£24.50. **Set lunch** (Mon-Fri) £18.50 3 courses incl coffee; (Sun) £23 3 courses. **Set dinner** £50 5 courses incl coffee. **Credit** AmEx, MC, V.

This is a special place. Excellent cooking, a bright, stylish restaurant and a brigade of well-informed staff . It's an exciting place to eat too, with a constantly changing carte of inspired, locally sourced ingredients handled with precision. The black pudding and buttered trout starter is just such an example of how traditional Lancashire delicacies can be transformed into something special. Organically grown greens and herbs (there are over 100 grown in Northcote's grounds) go into making fine salads. Fish, such as wild Lytham sea bass with Formby asparagus (arguably the best in the land) is stunning. Meat shows a similarly deft eye for cuts, with the fillet of Bowland Forest beef just perfect. Desserts are reassuringly over the top, while the wine list is confidently chosen to provide a perfect match.

BLACKPOOL

Seniors ★

106 Normoss Road, Blackpool, FY3 8QP (01253 393529/www.seniorsfishexperience.com). **Lunch served** 11.30am-2pm Mon-Sat. **Dinner served** 4.30-8pm Mon-Fri; 4-7.30pm Sat. **Main courses** £3-£7. **Credit** MC, V.

That there aren't more excellent fish bars in Blackpool is a constant source of amazement and, frankly, disappointment. Seniors is an exception to the rule and is not only the best in Blackpool but one of the best in Britain. Inside the bright blue and yellow bar, wonderfully fresh fish (13 varieties) is simply served. Fish cakes are fluffy and filling, and chips are golden and as fresh as the fish. Own-made ice-cream is another highlight here, as is the fact that champagne is sold. Bubbly and sea bass, anyone?

CLITHEROE

Inn at Whitewell ★

Whitewell, Forest of Bowland, nr Clitheroe, BB7 3AT (01200 448222). **Lunch served** noon-2pm, **dinner served** 7.30-9.30pm daily. **Main courses** £12.50-£22. **Credit** MC, V.

Perched above the River Hodder with stunning views across to the fells, the Inn at Whitewell has a romantic, lush and captivating location. Hospitality is first rate, service is as crisp as the linen, and food is first class. Goosnargh chicken is plump and juicy, beef is divine and veggies will go mad for goat's cheese cannelloni with sweet pepper sauce. Black pudding also gets rave reviews from regulars. Wines are a careful selection of old and New World producers. Despite the opulent surroundings, the Inn at Whitewell remains a refreshingly unstuffy place to enjoy great, carefully presented food.

DENSHAW

Rams Head Inn

Denshaw, OL3 5UN (01457 874802). **Lunch served** noon-2.30pm, **dinner served** 6-9.30pm Tue-Sat. **Meals served** noon-8.30pm Sun. **Main courses** £8.95-£16.90. **Set lunch** £10.95 3 courses. **Credit** MC, V.

Unreconstructed and all the better for it, the Rams Head is a border pub with an equal smattering of white and red roses to keep punters from both counties happy. But we're in Lancashire here – high up on the moors – and Lancashire food features strongly on the blackboard's selection of hearty, own-cooked food. Seasonal ingredients are fresh, never frozen, and portions are suitably solid. Game, venison and locally reared beef are all startlingly good – as are bread and ice-cream. Cask ales are superb. In winter, log fires warm the small rooms, and you'll be glad of this, as the Rams Head is one of the highest pubs in the county, with great views.

Nutters. See p250.

HORNBY

Castle Barns

Castle Hotel, 49 Main Street, Hornby, LA2 8JT (01524 221204/www.diningroomhornby.co.uk). Bistro **Meals served** noon-9pm daily. **Main courses** £6.95-£9.95. *Dining Room* **Dinner served** 7-9.30pm Wed-Sat. **Set dinner** £39.95 3 courses. *Both* **Credit** MC, V.

Tucked neatly on the elegant High Street, the Castle is a sparkling hotel with an eye for presentation. The hotel's popular restaurant is equally enticing, an informal, chatty bistro with metropolitan cooking, employing fast grills and confident use of locally sourced ingredients. Service is impeccable and headed by a team of French waiting staff. The dining room is a refined setting offering excellent meals served with care and precision. Try smoked haddock and shrimp risotto followed by rack of English lamb with curried courgettes.

LONGRIDGE

Longridge Restaurant ★

104-106 Higher Road, Longridge, PR3 3SY (01772 784969/www.heathcotes.co.uk). **Lunch served** noon-2.30pm Tue-Fri. **Dinner served** 6-10pm Tue-Fri; 5-10pm Sat. **Meals served** noon-9pm Sun. **Main courses** £12-£22. **Set lunch** £14 2 courses, £17 3 courses. **Set dinner** £25 3 courses incl half bottle of wine. **Credit** AmEx, DC, MC, V.

Paul Heathcote's empire now includes Simply Heathcotes, the Olive Press and the Longridge – this perhaps his flagship operation. Sharp styling, a clutch of awards and an impressive (frustrating?) waiting list means this carries all the hallmarks of a serious foodie hotspot. A restrained menu offers a selection of Heathcote signatures – pressed terrine of duck, chicken liver and foie gras is as good as it gets. Mains too are simple lessons in inventive cooking with everyday ingredients – whether that's a herb-crusted fillet of turbot or Goosnargh chicken. Strawberry shortcake with strawberry sorbet was a delicious end to an excellent evening.

LYTHAM ST ANNES

Greens Bistro

3-9 St Andrew's Road South, Lytham St Annes, SY8 1SX (01253 789990/www.greensbistro.co.uk). **Dinner served** 6-9pm Tue-Sat. **Main courses** £11.95-£16.50. **Set dinner** (Tue-Fri) £12.95 2 courses, £15.50 3 courses. **Credit** MC, V.

Tucked away in prosperous Lytham, this rustically styled bistro is winning lots of friends. They come for the intimate lively atmosphere, the excellent value and the effusive service. From a short menu, rack of lamb, spinach and ricotta tortellini and Goosnargh duck all scored top marks. This is how a seaside bistro should be – atmospheric, with a vigorous menu that never over-reaches itself, and an unselfconscious decor – stone floors, gingham linen and subtle lighting. Wines are decently priced too. And sticky toffee pudding? So good we ordered it twice.

North West

PRESTON

Inside Out

100 Higher Walton Road, Preston, PR5 4HR (01772 251366/www.insideoutrestaurant.co.uk). **Lunch served** noon-2pm Tue-Fri. **Dinner served** 6.30-9.30pm Tue-Fri; 6-10pm Sat. **Meals served** noon-8pm Sun. **Main courses** £8.75-£15.75. **Set lunch** £12.50 2 courses, £14.50 3 courses. **Set dinner** (Tue-Thur) £15 3 courses. **Credit** MC, V.

Husband and wife Mark and Anne Wilkinson are ebullient hosts, and this bright, modern restaurant captures a house party atmosphere, with its infectious, feel-good vibe, and lively customers. In summer, a decked terrace forms the 'out' (with views over the restaurant's trim gardens) while 'inside' all is smart and uncluttered. Mark has created a confident, exciting menu that is not afraid of mixing and matching influences to create something a little different. Try the starter of 'butter pie' – gruyère served with onion gravy – to see what we mean. Mains of pan-fried sea bass with roasted fennel, or glazed Goosnargh duck breast with chestnuts are also good. Desserts don't let the side down, as evidenced in baked white chocolate cheesecake.

RISHTON

Auberge

106 High Street, Rishton, BB1 4LQ (01254 882343/www.aubergerestaurant.co.uk). **Lunch served** *Summer* 2.30-6pm Sun. *Winter* noon-2pm Sun. **Dinner served** 5.30-9pm Tue-Fri; 6-9.30pm Sat. **Main courses** £10.75-£17.95. **Set lunch** (Sun) £10.95 3 courses. **Set dinner** (5.30-7pm Tue-Thur) £6.95 2 courses. **Credit** MC, V

Rishton's old bank has turned into a trendy restaurant serving modern British food with continental leanings. Some original features, notably the bank's ornate wood panelling, have been retained and, together with high ceilings and a generously proportioned dining space, give the place a calming sense of sobriety. Food is consistently good, and often includes a flash of the dramatic – a nice touch amid the formality of the setting. Starters are well judged: smoked salmon and sardine parcels, perhaps, or chicken liver pâté. Mains may feature ostrich or pheasant, but also more traditional staples such as excellent steaks or goujons of monkfish. Bread and butter pudding with strawberry chutney makes for a delicious end. House wines, at under £9, are remarkably good value.

ROCHDALE

Nutters ★

Edenfield Road, Norden, Rochdale, OL12 7TY (01706 650167). **Lunch served** noon-2pm Tue-Sat; noon-4pm Sun. **Tea served** 3-5pm Tue-Sat. **Dinner served** 6.30-9.30pm Tue-Sat; 6.30-9pm Sun. **Main courses** £14.80-£16.95. **Set lunch** £12.95 2 courses, £15.95 3 courses; (Sun) £19.95 3 courses. **Set dinner** £32 6 courses (gourmet menu). **Credit** AmEx, MC, V.

Recently dramatically restyled, Nutters has lost none of its charm. Indeed, it looks a lot better in its new home (an old manor house) and the whole experience has taken a sharp upward turn. Modern British food, with bags of imagination and a healthy dose of eccentricity is the Nutters formula. But rest assured, all the surprises are good ones. Take the Gourmet Menu for example. You won't know what you're getting, but each of the six courses will delight and satisfy. Opt for a more traditional way of dining and you can choose from wonderful seafood, locally reared meats and well-presented vegetables and salads. The attention to detail and evident love of food is as good as it's always been.

SAWLEY

Spread Eagle ★

Sawley, BB7 4NH (01200 441202/www.the-spread eagle.co.uk). **Lunch served** noon-2pm Tue-Sun. **Dinner served** 6-8.45pm Tue-Sat. **Main courses** £5.25-£10.50. **Set lunch** (Tue-Fri) £9.25 2 courses. **Set meals** (6-7pm Tue-Thur) £10.25 2 courses, (after 7pm Tue-Thur) £11.50 2 courses; (Fri-Sun) £12.50 2 courses, £15.75 3 courses. **Credit** MC, V.

Undoubtedly one of Lancashire's best restaurants, Sawley's Spread Eagle doesn't have an ego problem – it's a charming, welcoming place. The setting is superb – the restaurant was a 17th-century coaching inn – floors creak, fires crackle and the rest of the world seems a long way away. Food is never short of stunning. Goat's cheese niçoise is poised and packed with flavour, as is the salad of duck leg confit. Mains feature venison haunch steaks, or seared salmon with gnocchi. A carrot and cashew nut pavé was simple but successful – as are the desserts, like the layered chocolate truffle cake. Ice-creams and sorbets are fantastic. A class act.

WRIGHTINGTON BAR

Mulberry Tree

9 Wood Lane, Wrightington Bar, WN6 9SE (01257 451400). **Lunch served** noon-2pm Mon-Sat; noon-3pm Sun. **Dinner served** 6-9.30pm Mon-Thur, Sun; 6-10pm Fri, Sat. **Main courses** £9.50-£17.95. **Set lunch** (Sun) £19.50 3 courses. **Credit** MC, V.

A thriving gastropub that's in the perfect spot for those who savour long leisurely lunches or more relaxed, unstructured eating at evening time. Despite the relaxed atmosphere, cooking is always ambitious, and a notch or two higher than you'd expect from a place like this – wood pigeon and duck terrine being a prime example of the chef's bravura. Vegetarians have a limited choice, however. A decent bottle of red will set you back £18, but there are good cask beers to enjoy with your game pie.

Also in the area

Olive Press 23 Winckley Square, Preston, PR1 3JJ (01772 252732); **Simply Heathcotes** 23 Winkley Square, Preston PR1 3JJ (01772 252732).

Liverpool & Merseyside

LIVERPOOL

L'Alouette

2 Lark Lane, L17 8US (0151 727 2142/www.lalouette restaurant.co.uk). **Lunch served** noon-2.30pm Tue-Fri; 12.30-3.30pm Sun. **Dinner served** 7-10pm Tue-Sun. **Main courses** £14.95-£17.50. **Set lunch** (Sun) £12.95 2 courses, £15.95 3 courses. **Credit** AmEx, DC, MC, V.

Two or three restaurants are always vying for the status of best Scouse French in Liverpool's increasingly gentrified environs, and after 20 years the 'lark of Lark Lane' is still a fave. This bistro serves outstanding chive crêpes, braised oxtail and spinach tart, roast cod and monkfish and, crucially, a mean onion soup. The specialities are luxurious. Wines range from a £10 litre of half-decent Paul Bouchard house to a long list of fine wines for £30 to £50. Desserts are all own-made and include a tasty mix of ice-cream, nougat, crispy meringue, raisins and rum as well as a nicely tangy pear and chocolate tart.

Floor One, Baltic Fleet

33A Wapping, L1 8DQ (0151 709 3116). **Open** noon-11.30pm Mon-Thur; 11.30am-11.30pm Fri, Sat; noon-11pm Sun. **Lunch served** noon-2.30pm Mon-Fri; noon-3pm Sat; noon-4pm Sun. **Dinner served** 6-9.30pm Tue-Sun. **Main courses** £6.25-£11. **Credit** AmEx, DC, MC, V.

The 800th birthday (2007), the capital of culture (2008), renovation and reinvention (now)... sometimes, Liverpool's leisure-obsessed renaissance can be a bit wearying. This lonely tug-shaped inn opposite Albert Dock (opposite in mood as well as location) is where you should come to sail away from the hectic shopping hub and booming dining districts. The beer is award winning, but the food is pretty fine too. Welsh black beef sausage, black pudding, Sunday roasts with crispy veg, spuds and gravy are staples. Portholes, ships' compasses and the like theme the place quietly, and soft indie rock or the TV are all you get for background buzz. But listen carefully: beyond the hammering rain, you might just catch the lapping of the icy waves off Lithuania. As far as anyone knows, the Beatles never drank here so come 'ed and enjoy.

Café Number Seven ★

15 Falkner Street, L8 7PU (0151 709 9633). **Food served** 8am-5pm Mon-Fri; 10am-5pm Sat. **Main courses** £1.65-£3.80. **No credit cards.**

Owned by the same people who manage ultra-posh Ziba (*see p255*), this is at the opposite end of the market. Basically a walk-in upmarket deli-café, it's a grotto of fantastic pastas, cheeses, oils, juices, sweets and snacks that is particularly popular with vegetarians and vegans. Many of the items on offer are turned into bites to be eaten on site, either at the slate tables in the small, cosy side room, or on the pavement. Jarlsberg cheese, ploughman's, chicken and poached salmon sarnies are all winners, but the gooey sweets are even better. Standards such as roast vegetable pasta bake and the Spanish omelette are always light and tasty. Loads of organic sodas and juices are on sale too. Best of all, you feel as if you're miles away from the city centre. Liverpool's best café.

Colin's Bridewell ★

Campbell Street, off Duke Street, L1 5BL (0151 707 8003/www.colinsbridewell.co.uk). **Lunch served** noon-5.45pm Mon-Sat; noon-6.45pm Sun. **Dinner served** 7-10pm Mon-Wed; 7-10.30pm Thur-Sat. **Main courses** £12.95-£22.50. **Set dinner** (Mon, Tue) £12.95 2 courses, £14.95 3 courses; (Wed) £19.95 2 courses. **Credit** MC, V.

It's hard to get a table at this stylish restaurant because, while the old police bridewell provides plenty of space, the owners have gone for intimate, attentive service and numbers are kept down. Dining in refurbished cells adds to the cosiness, though many clients opt to eat in the bright, airier piazza in the centre. Ignore the joke names for some meals – Usual Suspects, First Offenders – because this is great food, whether you fancy a light tuna salad or Greek meze or prefer a serious steak sandwich. Other small but savoury numbers include onion and feta cheese tart, herb muffin with poached egg, cannon of lamb and asparagus risotto. Desserts worth dipping into are lemon tart and mango coulis, and apple pie and cream. Good Spanish wines on a decent list, jazz on Wednesdays and special events for the likes of Burns' Night and St Paddies.

Don Pepe

Union House, 19-21 Victoria Street, L1 6BD (0151 227 4265). **Lunch served** noon-3pm, **dinner served** 5.30-10.30pm Mon-Sat. **Main courses** £11-£14. **Tapas** £1.95-£6.50. **Set tapas** £11.95 6 tapas, £13.95 7 tapas (per person, minimum 2). **Credit** MC, V.

This convivial Castilian cellar in the business district continues to serve up the best tapas and à la carta (sic) main courses in town. It's the sourcing that does it, as all the chorizos, hams and oils are brought from the old country, along with bold and bouncy Riojas. Among the many impressive main dishes, the empanada gallega (tuna and tomato pie), chicken and tarragon and the house lamb special stand out. Staff are always friendly. By sticking to classic, Old World Spanish dishes and concentrating on atmosphere, it's still the don.

Everyman Bistro ★

5-9 Hope Street, L1 9BH (0151 708 9545/www.everyman.co.uk). **Meals served** noon-midnight Mon-Wed; noon-1am Thur; noon-2am Fri, Sat. **Main courses** £4.90-£7.50. **Credit** MC, V.

Posher places seem to be ganging up around the Everyman, but the combination of theatre, cheap food and a basement setting fit for clandestine anarchist reunions continues to draw regulars. Food doesn't get very fancy, but specials might include Chinese roast duck with cabbage and noodle broth or pork casserole and curried pasta (not as offensive as it sounds), with chocolate and mincemeat pudding to wrap up. If you're just filling a corner, try the quiches, pizzas, or herby salads. Cakes and pastries are great. With a menu changing twice daily, a keen eye on local produce and a regular range of gluten and meat-free dishes, this buffet bar probably deserves to call itself bistro. Cask cider, Belgian beers and local Cains ale keep the bar end kicking. There are free folk nights on Tuesdays.

Gulshan

544-8 Aigburth Road, L19 3QG (0151 427 2273/www.gulshan-liverpool.com). **Dinner served** 5-11pm daily. **Main courses** £6.95-£12. **Set menu** £14.80 (vegetarian), £16.95-£17.60 (minimum 2), £16.45 per person (minimum 3). **Credit** AmEx, DC, MC, V.

While most of the city curry houses marinate their lamb, prawns and chicken with the outpourings of three standard reddish-coloured buckets, Gulshan uses spice and ghee with craft and subtlety. Original items like the tandoori trout, murgi mossaka (minced meat, cooked with wine and cream) and the fish and yoghurt maaskorma will impress even specialists. The Gulshan special (a mild but massive dish of king prawns, chicken tikka, lamb tikka, mushrooms, paneer and wine, crowned with scrambled egg) is only for diners with largesse in all areas. Desserts, from jams to kulfi, are an after thought. Rivalling the best of Brum and Bradford, Gulshan cooks fine food without even a nod in the 'new curry restaurant' direction. It's all substance.

Bar crawl: Liverpool

When Cream closed its doors to regular Saturday night hedonists, Liverpool lost a venue so crucial to the city's nightlife, pessimistic punters thought the Superclub had called time on the city's newly invigorated night-time economy.

They were wrong. Liverpool has never offered so much, or been such an attractive proposition for a friendly, stylish and safe (yes, safe) night out. The DJ bar has replaced the nightclub as a destination rather than just a pre-club stop off – resulting in a more eclectic, all-embracing and democratic night out.

The Albert Dock used to be a daytime attraction for coach parties keen to gawp at *This Morning*'s weather map. Now it's a thriving after dark location with bars like **Panamerican club** (*see p254*), red leather banquettes and fab cocktails; **Blue** (Edward Pavillion, 0151 709 7097), exposed brickwork, low sofas. Hollyoaks stars optional; and **Baby Cream** (Atlantic Pavillion, 0151 709 7097), excellent DJ nights – as you'd expect from this club offshoot – and a stylish crowd.

Walk into town from here and you'll pass the **Newz Bar** (18 Water Street, 0151 236 2025) a glitzy, perma-busy stop en route between the Mersey and the city centre. Alternatively, newly opened **Anderson's Bar** (26 Exchange Street East, 0151 243 1330) offers a slightly calmer, cooler environment – a good choice for a lunchtime drink.

Matthew Street is a boisterous enclave, much as it was 40 years ago when those four lads appeared at the Cavern (now demolished – the Cavern you see today is a replica across the road from the original site). This area is best avoided if you don't want to play sardines in theme pubs.

Head instead for Concert Square, a European-like cloister of stylish bars, parasols and buzzing crowds. Some say its best days are behind it (primarily because the cool venues now rub shoulders with Walkabout and Lloyd's Number 1 outlets) but, on a summer's evening this is still the place to be.

Try **Modo** (23-25 Fleet Street, 0151 709 8832), with its hidey-hole kiosks – great for a romantic tete-à-tête, or newly opened **Mood** (18-20 Fleet Street, 0151 709 8181) with video screens, party mad crowds and dazzling lights.

Head north to St Peter's Square if you're in need of an altogether calmer experience: next-door neighbour **Bluu** (St Peter's Square, Fleet Street, 0151 709 8462) and **Tea Factory** (78-82 Wood Street, 0151 708 7008) offer a similar vibe: Bluu is slightly more showy, Tea Factory more chilled.

Then, when you've had your fill, end your drinking session in a police cell. **Colin's Bridewell** (*see p251*) is a renovated police station with individual cells that offer a private, if somewhat sobering way to enjoy a quiet pint.

Everyman Bistro. See p253.

The Living Room

15 Victoria Street, L2 5QS (0870 442 2535/ www.thelivingroom.co.uk). **Meals served** noon-11pm Mon-Wed; noon-11.30pm Thur; noon-midnight Fri, Sat; noon-10pm Sun. **Main courses** £7.95-£15.95. **Credit** AmEx, MC, V.

Too classy to be confused with all those replica settee-and-zinc wine bars. At lunch it's a bright and airy refuge for Victoria Street's younger, smarter set; at night it's a choice venue for clubbers and cocktail drinkers. The seasonal menu ranges from seasoned thyme and garlic potato cakes and rustic croutes to mains of pan-fried veal, Chinese crispy duck and whole plaice. Food is prepared and presented with care. New World and Italian wines are good value, and the Belgian waffles are delicious. A pioneer, and still one of the city's best informal venues.

London Carriage Works ★

40 Hope Street, L1 9DA (0151 705 2222/ www.hopestreethotel.co.uk). Brasserie **Lunch served** noon-3pm Mon-Sat. **Dinner served** 5-9pm Mon-Sat; 4-9pm Sun. *Restaurant* **Lunch served** noon-2.30pm Mon-Sat; noon-4pm Sun. **Dinner served** 5.30-9pm Mon-Sat. **Set lunch** £16.95 2 courses, £21.95 3 courses. **Set dinner** £23.95 2 courses, £29.95 3 courses. **Credit** AmEx, DC, MC, V.

Adding weight to Hope Street's claim to be Liverpool's ultimate gourmet thoroughfare, the LCW is arguably the hippest new space in town. Housed in an old workshop, the lounge bar/lunch spot and main restaurant are divided by vertical shards of crystal. Big, tasty salads in bucket bowls, nibbles and half a dozen mains are on the noon menu, with modern European mains in the evening. Cheffed by Paul Askew, who is doing good things at the once weary Lower Place opposite, nothing can be faulted. By evening, explore crab farcie and prawn brochette, Welsh beef, assiette of caramel; by day don't miss colcannon (mash and herby cabbage), the pepper-packed salads and the charcuterie selection. Aiming to edge slowly into the high-end market, LCW's fame has spread so book early.

Monro

92-94 Duke Street, Liverpool, L1 5AG (0151 707 9933/www.themonro.com). **Lunch served** noon-3pm, **dinner served** 6-9pm Mon-Sat. **Meals served** noon-8pm Sun. **Main courses** £9.55-£15. **Credit** AmEx, DC, MC, V.

'Liverpool's latest gastropub' might not sound like much of a headline, but even fans of the city's loveliest real ale inns will admit that there is a shortage of decent food in the centre. This brewery pub has based its menu on trips to farmers' markets to find the best wild boar, rabbit and Welsh buffalo – the latter has become a speciality. Local artist Rachel Hunter was recruited to paint murals to enhance the Renaissance-style stencilling and Georgian and Regency portraits – the result is regal.

Panamerican Club

Unit 22, Britannia Pavillion, Albert Dock, L3 4AD (0151 702 5849/www.lyceumgroup.co.uk/ panamerican). Deli **Meals served** noon-10.30pm Mon-Thur; noon-11.45pm Fri; noon-midnight Sat; noon-9.30pm Sun. *Restaurant* **Lunch served** noon-2.30pm daily. **Dinner served** 6-10.30pm Mon-Thur; 6-11.45pm Fri; noon-midnight Sat; noon-9.30pm Sun. **Main courses** £8.95-£16. **Set dinner** £25 3 courses. **Credit** AmEx, MC, V.

All things to all its fashionable people, the Panam continues to impress with its confidence and creative cocktails. The drinks are vastly palatable, tidily punctuating the various platters of bowl foods on offer round the clock. This is more stylish snack bar than designer diner, theming its dishes according to US regions. All are abundant and carbo-superpowered but best for taste are the Cajun tiger prawns, Dixie sausages and American-style major league salads. Unashamedly unsubtle, it's great for party feasts.

Pod ★

137-9 Allerton Road, Mossley Hill, L18 2DD (0151 724 2255). Bar **Open** noon-11pm Mon-Sat; 6-10.30pm Sun. *Restaurant* **Lunch served** noon-3pm Mon-Sat. **Dinner served** 6-9.30pm daily. **Credit** AmEx, MC,V.

Everybody raves about Pod. Laid-back and suburban, it draws a trendy crowd who lunch on wraps, toasted sandwiches and pastas, with an evening menu of tapas-y tasters. Quality mains include the Moorish marinated lamb and Lebanese chicken with almonds, mint and pomegranate molasses. Run by graduates from Hope University, it's a magnet for bright young things.

St Petersburg

7A York Street, L1 5BN (0151 709 6676/ www.russiancuisine.co.uk). **Lunch served** noon-3pm daily. **Dinner served** 4pm-2am Mon-Sat; 4pm-midnight Sun. **Main courses** £7.95-£14.95. **Set meals** £15.95-£25 3 courses. **Credit** AmEx, MC, V.
St Petersburg is built in honour of old, imperial Russia, with plush, decadent decor, silver candelabras, a handsome old samovar and fine tableware. Most people dine here in suits and smart frocks. Try tasty Tsarist dishes such as farsh po patarsky, a lavish (and at almost £50, pricey) platter of raw fillet, egg yolk, potatoes, pickles, black bread and frozen Russian vodka, which comes with a serving of black caviar. There's also chicken blini, chinaxi (lamb baked in a traditional pot) and stroganoff. Coffee, like most things, is served with vodka, and then you can sit back and listen to the balalaika player. There's jazz on Thursday nights.

Simply Heathcotes ★

Beetham Plaza, 25 The Strand, L2 0XL (0151 236 3536/www.heathcotes.co.uk). **Lunch served** noon-2.30pm daily. **Dinner served** 6-10pm Mon-Fri; 6-11pm Sat; 6-9.30pm Sun. **Main courses** £9.75-£21.50. **Set meal** (lunch, 6-7pm) £13.50 2 courses, £15.50 3 courses. **Credit** AmEx, MC, V.
Unfazed by upstarts on its block, people flock to taste Bolton-born masterchef Paul Heathcote's food amid radical metallic architecture. There's little dull or dusty here: try the watercress soup, terrine of black pudding, or fish in beer batter, mushy peas and chips if you want to eat at the edge of Modern British classics. This is audacious food, with Heathcote's agents sourcing from Accrington or Tuscany, depending on his whim and what local farmers make available. The six or so pasta dishes make for excellent lunches, and for a fiver you can feast on bread and butter pudding, lemon curd sponge, knickerbocker glory or a tray of English cheeses. It might sound like a visit to the land of northern irony à la Martin Parr, but there's no cynicism in the production. The best place in town for pure eating.

60 Hope Street ★

60 Hope Street, L1 9BZ (0151 707 6060/www.60 hopestreet.com). Café & Bar **Open** 11am-10.30pm Mon-Sat. *Restaurant* **Lunch served** noon-2.30pm Mon-Fri. **Dinner served** 7-10.30pm Mon-Sat. **Main courses** £13.50-£20. **Set lunch & pre-theatre** (café) 5-7pm £12.95 2 courses, £15.95 3 courses. **Credit** MC, V.
60 Hope Street has become something of a benchmark, both for tasteful decor and for the food that's cooked up here. Gary Manning's superb front-of-house team and brother Colin's well-travelled suitcase of British-based fusions make a night out a treat. King prawns and Piedmontese peppers, pheasant and cabbage, salmon and risotto and tomato and mozzarella soup indicate a liking for basic Italian ingredients. It's often an elementary twist that makes every taste interesting, like chives in the spuds and tarragon lacing the butter for frying. Service is fast and unfussy, and there's a serious wine list.

Valparaiso

4 Hardman Street, L1 5AX (0151 708 6036/ www.valparaiso-restaurant.co.uk). **Dinner served** 5.30-10.30pm Tue-Sat. **Main courses** £8.80-£17.50. **Credit** AmEx, DC, MC, V.
This Chilean stalwart has been serving up prime steaks, fresh sea fish and a range of seafood platters since 1985. Paellas, slow-cooked stews, fish soups, anything with prawns – the kitchen only serves what it can obtain fresh. Alternatively, try papas chorreadas ('dripping spuds' – potatoes in cheese, tomato and onion sauce) or pastel del choclo (minced beef topped with minced sweet corn). While service is slow, it's worth the wait. The bulk of the wines are from Santiago and its surround, and they are excellent value, especially the reds. There's even a story as heartwarming as the food: the owner, Julio Arellano sends part of the proceeds back to poor neighbourhoods in Chile.

Yuet Ben

1 Upper Duke Street, L1 9DU (0151 709 5772/ www.yuetben.co.uk). **Dinner served** 5-11pm Tue-Sun. **Main courses** £6-£9.50. **Set meals** £10-£17.50 per person (min 2). **Credit** AmEx, DC, MC, V.
Taller and older than its many challengers, Yuet Ben's strength is its authenticity. The staff strive to treat diners as 'honoured guests' (which is what the restaurant's name means). The menu is poetry – try tomato and egg-flower soup, gon bay chon seaweed, lamb with leeks or cherry chicken if you want to rediscover why Chinese cuisine is the most exquisitely perfumed in the world. Other fantastic dishes are kwo-ta chicken, which uses a red wine reduction, and the house special spare ribs. Vegetarian options have won acclaim. Nothing here is over-sweetened or made solely to explore a chef's fascination with the red and orange sections of the spectrum, and the set menus are a steal.

Ziba (Racquet Club) ★

5 Chapel Street,L3 9AG (0151 236 6676/ www.racquetclub.org.uk). **Breakfast served** 7-10am Mon-Sat; 8-11am Sun. **Lunch served** 11.30-2.30pm, **dinner served** 6.30-10pm Mon-Sat. **Main courses** £9.95-£15.95. **Set lunch** £15 2 courses, £18 3 courses. **Credit** AmEx, MC, V.
The Racquet Club's in-house eaterie is a gaudy, glamorous lounge given over to perfect cooking. Whitebait, scallops and raviolis are the smalls you get on the lunch and starter menus. Lamb stuffed with black pudding, grilled salmon with crab cakes,

chicken with bubble and squeak, and rhubarb for dessert give some idea of the British flavouring in the kitchen, but this is artful, cosmopolitan cooking and everything is presented with great panache. Expect to blow about £40 per person here – fairly pricey for Liverpool. You could then spend another £100 on one of the eight hotel rooms in the building.

ST HELENS

Colours

St Helens College, Water Street, St Helens, WA10 1PZ (01744 623295). **Lunch served** noon-1pm Tue-Fri; noon-2pm Sun. **Dinner served** 6.30-8pm Wed, Thur; 6.30-8.30pm Fri; 6-9pm Sat. **Main courses** £9.95. **Set lunch** (Tue-Fri) £7 2 courses, £8.60 3 courses; (Sun) £10.25 3 courses. **Set dinner** (Sat) £21 5 courses. **Credit** MC, V.

Colours is staffed by catering students from the local FE college, so every meal is likely to be the loving masterwork of three or four wannabe chefs working hard to impress. Award-winning ex-army chef Jeff Nugent has his students explore a range of Mediterranean, East Asian and British dishes. Whether you go for the lightweight pastas and oriental-influenced options, or the steak and sea fish dishes, expect fresh, quality ingredients and fine cooking. Colours is the new, sophisticated face of this noble town. Utterly original.

SOUTHPORT

Warehouse Brasserie

30 West Street, Southport, PR8 1QN (01704 544662/www.warehouse-brasserie.co.uk). **Lunch served** noon-2pm, **dinner served** 5.30-10pm Mon-Sat. **Main courses** £7.95-£38. **Set lunch** £9.95 2 courses, £11.95 3 courses. **Set dinner** (5.30-7pm Mon-Thur) £10.95 2 courses, £13.95 3 courses. **Credit** AmEx, MC, V.

Breaking the beach-resort mould of Ye Hearty British Stodge, the split-level Warehouse has been an absolute success. Not that you can't get a plate of Southport shrimps, but you can also enjoy ham hock, grilled grouper, Cornish crab and mango tian, or Moroccan lamb meatballs – with garlic mash, thick chips or a pungent anchovy salad to dress them up. Michelin-starred chef Marc Verité is doing a fine job, but for all that the owners work hard to make this Southport's most serious restaurant, the youngish crowd are drawn mainly by the cosmopolitan buzz and smart decor. Don't expect Merseyside gentry or any stiff upper lips.

Also in the area

The Other Place Restaurant 141-143 Allerton Road, Liverpool, L18 2DD (0151 724 1234); **Tai Pan** WH Lung Building, Great Howard Street, Liverpool, L5 9TZ (0151 207 3888).

Manchester

The Bridge

58 Bridge Street, Deansgate, M3 3BW (0161 834 0242/www.thebridgemanchester.co.uk). **Lunch served** noon-3pm Mon-Fri; noon-4pm Sun. **Dinner served** 5.30-10.30pm Mon-Fri. **Meals served** noon-10.30pm Sat. **Main courses** £6.95-£11.50. **Set lunch** (Mon-Fri) £10.50 2 courses incl coffee. **Credit** AmEx, MC, V.

Dark and inviting and full of charm, the Bridge was not always thus. A recent makeover has transformed this once rather ordinary-looking city centre pub into a winning and richly atmospheric gastropub. Candles, swags and wood panelling give the place a real gentlemen's club feel. But the food isn't nearly as stuffy. Lunches (the likes of grills and filling baguettes) offer good value. Dinners are more opulent – starters include duck egg omelette with smoked bacon and spring onion; mains feature herb-crusted fillet of wild salmon with creamed leeks and watercress. Afters feature a truly impressive cheese board and a scrummy, local Eccles cake, served warm, with double cream.

Café Istanbul

79-81 Bridge Street, off Deansgate, M3 2RH (0161 833 9942/www.cafeistanbul.co.uk). **Meals served** noon-11pm Mon-Thur; noon-11.30pm Fri, Sat; 5.30-10pm Sun. **Main courses** £9-£12. **Set dinner** (5.30-7pm, 10-11pm Mon-Fri) £9.90 2 courses incl coffee. **Credit** MC, V.

Perma-busy and always buzzing, Café Istanbul is as popular for lunch as it is during the evenings. Exotic, meze-style meals bursting with flavour might include shredded chicken breast served with walnut sauce, or tabouleh; hot starters include a divine lamb filo pastry roll. Mains include a greatest hits creation of char-grilled lamb fillet, spit-roasted lamb and Istanbul chicken served with tomato sauce and yoghurt. There's a decent selection of wines.

La Casona

27 Shaw Road, Heaton Moor, Stockport, SK4 4AG (0161 442 5383). **Dinner served** 5.45-10.30pm Mon; 5.45-10.45pm Tue-Sat. **Meals served** 1-10.15pm Sun. **Main courses** £12.95. **Credit** MC, V.

A little out of town, but with a fiercely supportive local crowd, La Casona is richly atmospheric and always alive with conversation. Popular, authentic tapas include moreish calamares, and truly memorable gambas al ajillo (king prawns cooked in garlic and olive oil), brought to the table still sizzling in an earthenware dish. Unlike other chain tapas restaurants nearby, everything is fresh and served with pride.You can tell there's a real Spanish chef hard at work in La Casona's little kitchen.

Choice Bar & Restaurant ★

Castle Quay Building, off Deansgate, Castlefield, M15 4NT (0161 833 3400/www.choicebarandrestaurant.co.uk). **Meals served** noon-11pm Mon-Sat; noon-9.30pm Sun. **Main courses** £12.95-£14.95. **Set lunch** (noon-4pm, Mon-Fri) £13.95 2 courses, £16.95 3 courses. **Credit** AmEx, DC, MC, V.

Castlefield's looking a bit neglected these days, but Choice proves that, if the food's great, the location can take a back seat. So, as ever, this waterside restaurant is busy with after-work imbibers in the piano lounge, and evening diners in the restaurant. Choice's menu is a relatively controlled affair, with the occasional well-placed flourish matching the elegantly restrained interior perfectly. Try a starter, perhaps, of smoked trout salad with quails' eggs and piccalilli, or black pudding and pork meatballs (local produce is allowed to shine here). Mains may feature rack of fell-bred Cumbrian lamb with mint butter or slow cooked cottage pie with beef fillet, root veg and thyme gravy. Ginseng and heather honey jelly served with stem ginger scone and jasmine cream is an inspired dessert. Top marks.

Croma ★

1 Clarence Street, M2 4DE (0161 237 9799/www.cromamanchester.co.uk). **Meals served** noon-11pm Mon-Sat; noon-10.30pm Sun. **Main courses** £4.45-£7.20. **Credit** AmEx, MC, V.

Perhaps the busiest Italian in town, and rightly so. Croma is cool: it's not the most strikingly designed – although it is stylish, with chrome, mirrors and exotic planting – but it's certainly the most upbeat and infectious modern Italian. Pizzas are textbook stuff – crispy bases, fresh toppings, utterly delicious. Salad niçoise with dough balls, and sticky toffee pudding are also worth trying. The house wine is very drinkable, the crowd is a vibey, good-natured lot, and the place is great value, especially considering just how sought after tables are.

8th Day ★

107-109 Oxford Road, M1 7DU (0161 273 1850). **Meals served** 9.30am-7.30pm Mon-Thur; 9.30am-9.45pm Fri, Sat. **Main courses** £4.50-£5.75. **Set dinner** (7.30-9.45pm, Fri, Sat) £15 5 courses. **Credit** MC, V.

A superior veggie restaurant in Manchester's student land, 8th Day remains popular. Food quality is high; prices are low. Even though expanded opening times now offer tweaked and posher cuisine of an evening, the 8th Day has lost none of its buzzy, canteen feel. Cranberry wellington with red wine sauce (available as a starter or a main) is a fantastic concoction, with veggies, nuts and lemon wedges tumbling about around a meaty nut-roast parcel. Cooking is simple, but flavours suffer not a bit for it – pancakes filled with mushrooms and broccoli are heavenly. Desserts, such as chocolate and pear sponge cake with vanilla sauce, are too good to miss.

The Establishment

43-45 Spring Gardens, M2 2BG (0161 839 6300/www.establishmentrestaurant.co.uk). **Lunch served** noon-2.30pm Mon-Fri. **Dinner served** 7-10pm Mon-Sat. **Main courses** £15.50-£18. **Set lunch** £13.95 2 courses, £16.50 3 courses. **Credit** AmEx, MC, V.

The one most likely to: the newest addition to the city's business district knows all about show. It's situated in a fabulously Gothic old bank and has courage enough to fill half its traditional, hushed interior with a walloping great purple, circular enclosure. Food is just a few steps behind the high standard we're sure this place is capable of, but is still passionate stuff and full of twists. Corned beef, globe artichokes and deep-fried egg makes for a punchy starter. Sea bass with buttered spinach and white bean clam chowder is deftly handled, as is rare roast beef fillet. Portions aren't huge, flavours are.

Greens ★

43 Lapwing Lane, West Didsbury, M20 2NT (0161 434 4259). **Lunch served** noon-2pm Tue-Fri; 12.30-3.30pm Sun. **Dinner served** 5.30-10.30pm daily. **Main courses** £10.25. **Set lunch** (Sun) £12.50 3 courses. **Set dinner** (Mon, Sun; 5.30-7pm Tue-Fri) £12.50 3 courses. **Credit** MC, V.

Following a refurb, a new menu and application for an alcohol licence, many regulars held their breath in fear. They needn't have worried, because Greens is still the place other vegetarian restaurants have to beat. Flavours are a revelation – rarely have vegetables tasted so diverse or inspired. Perhaps it's the fact that recipes are sourced from all corners of the globe, so you may have a filo pastry strudel (with cream cheese, tomato and leeks) followed by red Thai vegetable curry with green rice, the latter as colourful as it sounds. Service can be impersonal.

Gurkha Grill ★

198 Burton Road, West Didsbury, M20 1LH (0161 445 3461). **Dinner served** 6pm-midnight Mon-Thur, Sun; 6pm-1am Fri, Sat. **Main courses** £4.95-£15. **Set dinner** £10-£11.99 3 courses incl coffee. **Credit** AmEx, MC, V.

An institution that's recently increased its covers capacity, the Gurkha looks much like any other smart suburban restaurant. But its food sets it apart. Intriguing is the word, especially if you're relatively new to Nepalese cuisine. Highlights include starters of prawn sandeko – hot, juicy prawns with coriander and green chilli. Mains of lobster chilli curry and a Nepalese vegetable medley with cream, mango and coconut, or the fabulous gurkhali chicken with an aromatic, intense gravy are memorable.

Harvey Nichols Second Floor Brasserie

Cateaton Street, M1 1AD (0161 828 8898/ www.harveynichols.com). **Lunch served** noon-3pm Tue-Fri; noon-4pm Sat; noon-6pm Sun. **Dinner served** 6-10pm Tue-Fri; 6-10.30pm Sat. **Main courses** £9-£12. **Set dinner** £9.50 2 courses, £13.50 3 courses. **Credit** AmEx, DC, MC, V.
A dramatic black and white dining space within Manchester's newest, swankiest department store, Harvey Nichols delivers modern European cuisine with flair: waiting staff are handsome, lighting is dramatic. Spring pea, asparagus and mint risotto or niçoise salad with teriyaki tuna might be followed by rump of lamb, Turkish spiced aubergine and minted yoghurt. Finish with Yorkshire curd tart with vanilla nutmeg ice-cream. Wines are surprisingly good value, with a decent chardonnay weighing in at £17.

Hurricane Bar & Grill

King Street, Spring Gardens, M2 4ST (0161 835 2785/www.hurricanerestaurants.com). Bar **Meals served** noon-6pm Mon-Sat. *Restaurant* **Lunch served** noon-2.30pm, **dinner served** 6.30-11pm Mon-Sat. **Main courses** £9-£19. **Credit** AmEx, MC, V.
A bit of a posh place this, right in the heart of Manchester's high-finance district, where every other building is either a bank or a designer clothes emporium. Or a smart bar and grill. This is one of the nicest. The interior cleverly imposes stark modern fittings within the building's ornate frame. Starters feature plump oysters, ham hock terrine with lentils or a sea bream fillet with artichoke. Mains offer Gressingham duck with beetroot (it works) or juicy steaks – nothing too fey: this is where the city makes its money. The wine list is just as you'd expect in a place where the expense account rules.

Koreana ★

40A King Street West, M3 2WY (0161 832 4330/www.koreana.co.uk). **Lunch served** noon-2.30pm Mon-Fri. **Dinner served** 6.30-10.30pm Mon-Thur; 6.30-11pm Fri; 5.30-11pm Sat. **Main courses** £6.50-£13.50. **Set lunches** £5.50-£8 2 courses. **Set dinner** £12.40 3 courses. **Credit** MC, V.
A smashing little restaurant, this, tucked away off Deansgate amd with an inviting atmosphere. The hosts are keen – nay, evangelical – to spread their love of Korean cuisine. Traditionally, all dishes arrive together, with side dishes, pickles and main dishes placed in the centre of the table and shared.

Bar crawl: Manchester

For those who doubt Manchester's bullish claim to be considered England's second city, a weekend here should set you straight. Every flavour, every quirk and every kink is catered for in this city that manages to stay essential, cutting edge and, most importantly, remarkably inclusive. Revellers between the ages of 18 and 50 can rub shoulders in some of the cooler spots without either party feeling out on a limb.

Newest (and, therefore coolest) hang outs include **Bluu** (Thomas Street, Northern Quarter, 0161 839 7195), a low slung, dark wood achingly trendy bar with decent food and a friendly, new media vibe. For more glamour, **Prohibition** (6-8 St Mary's Street, 0870 220 3026) offers candlelight, black and gold decor and lots of very glam people.

The Northern Quarter isn't just a fancy name dreamed up by an eager tourism officer, this richly atmospheric, gritty part of town feels very NYC, and is home to a clutch of lively drinking dens. **Centro** (74 Tib Street, 0161 835 2863) is a stripped down, friendly joint with a 'democratic jukebox' – bring your own MP3 player, and get the party started! Over the road, **Cord** (Dorsey Street, off Tib Street, 0161 832 2863) is a narrow, no-nonsense bar attracting ex-students, musos and groups of mates set for a night on the town. It's a good-natured crowd.

Matt and Phreds (85 Oldham Street, 0161 661 7494) bills itself as a jazz club but, on most nights, entrance is free and the vibe is noticeably more chilled than some of this area's frenetic offerings.

Deansgate Lock's succession of über-cool (and über-posey) bars are not for everyone. Style sometimes wins out over content here but, at **Loaf** (Deansgate Locks, Whitworth Street West, 0161 819 5858), **Baa Bar** (Deansgate Locks, 0161 832 4446) and the **Sugar Lounge** (Sunhouse, 2-4 Little Peter Street, 0161 834 6500) meaty sound-systems pump out quality tunes and the bling factor is never less than 11.

Hotel bars shouldn't be avoided in a city where every new boutique hotel tries to out design and out manoeuvre its rivals. The **Radisson Edwardian**'s (Peter Street, 0161 835 9929) bar wisely has its own entrance – step inside for an island bar surrounded by dark red swags, jazzy music and opulent pieces of Asian art. The **Terrace Bar** at the Lowry (Pier 8, Salford Keys, 0870 787 5790) is more Scandinavian in feel, with low beige sofas and teak screens. All a far cry from Travelodge.

Choice Bar & Restaurant. See p257.

North West

It all makes for a great social occasion, and one you can replicate if you order from the recommended Korean special menu. We loved shallow-fried dumplings, potato and beef pancakes, and chicken gang jung – chicken and potato crisply deep fried and sautéed in a sharp, spicy sauce.

Little Yang Sing

17 George Street, M1 4HE (0161 228 7722/ www.littleyangsing.co.uk). **Meals served** noon-midnight Mon-Fri; noon-12.30am Sat; noon-10.45pm Sun. **Main courses** £7.50-£15. **Set meals** (noon-6pm Mon-Fri, Sun; noon-5.30pm Sat) £8.50 2 courses, £10.50 3 courses. **Set dinner** £16 3 courses; £19.50-£26 banquets. **Credit** AmEx, MC, V.

Bigger than before but no less intimate and welcoming, Little Yang Sing is no lightweight. Decor is clean and bright, and service is effusive. Food is carefully prepared, flavours clean and fresh, with staff ready and willing to help you find what you're after. Sui mai (prawn and meat dumplings) are excellent, as is fried wun tun. Banquets are great value, and feature specialities such as fish fillet in spicy Sichuan sauce. For Yang Sing, *see p263*.

Love Saves the Day ★

Unit G18, Smithfields Buildings, Tib Street, M4 1LA (0161 832 0777/www.lovesavestheday.co.uk). **Food served** noon-3pm Mon-Wed; noon-9pm Thur, Fri; noon-4pm Sat. **Main courses** £4.95-£6.95. **Credit** AmEx, MC, V.

Coffee is the real draw here. It's almost worshipped by the good folks at LSTD. But there's even more to this place than the bean. Fabulously fresh salads, quiches and pastas make this a serious foodie venue too. The vibe is very New York deli. Sandwiches are big – stuffed with cheeses, farm-made pâtés and speciality meats. It's great for breakfast or brunch, and there's a surprisingly cosmopolitan wine list.

The Market Restaurant

104 High Street, Northern Quarter, M4 1HQ (0161 834 3743/www.market-restaurant.com). **Lunch served** noon-2.30pm Wed-Fri. **Dinner served** 6-10pm Wed-Sat. **Main courses** £12.95-£15.95. **Credit** AmEx, DC, MC, V.

Like a stage set for *The Forsyte Saga* or *Hancock's Half Hour*, the interior here resembles a grandmother's lounge, circa 1950. And all the more fantastic for it: homely, intimate and welcoming. And, in a city where style occasionally overtakes content, it's a real tonic. The food is eclectic: local specialities include Cheshire air-dried ham with figs; otherwise you might find peppered fillet of beef with deep-fried potato wedges or toasted cashew nut roulade with ratatouille filling. Puddings are scrumptious: try chocolate pavlova with whipped Jersey cream and raspberries.

Mr Thomas's Chop House

52 Cross Street, M2 7AR (0161 832 2245/www.toms chophouse.com). **Lunch served** noon-3pm Mon-Fri; noon-4pm Sat, Sun. **Main courses** £8.95-£14.95. **Credit** AmEx, MC, V.

A richly atmospheric pub serving top-notch British food with a 21st-century twist. The dining room – actually just the rear end of this ornate Victorian boozer – is always busy (especially at lunch) with business folk tucking into corned beef hash, haddock and chunky chips or steak sandwiches. There are occasional skirmishes into modern flavours, such as dim sum and bhajis, but stick to the traditional dishes for best results. Cask beers are well conditioned, and wines are keenly priced. Service is genuinely friendly – if a little hassled.

Le Mont

Urbis Museum, Cathedral Gardens, M4 3BG (0161 605 8282/www.urbis.org.uk). **Lunch served** noon-2.30pm Mon-Fri. **Dinner served** 7-10.30pm Mon-Sat. **Main courses** £13.50-£29.95. **Set lunch** £14.95 2 courses. **Set dinner** £24.95 3 courses. **Credit** AmEx, MC, V.

Urbis, the museum of the urban landscape, has had a troubled few years. But that doesn't seem to have affected one of the city's coolest restaurants (complete with some of the best views). Meals are imaginative and exciting – try warm goat's cheese with walnut and parsley gratin, or terrine of foie gras, smoked chicken and vegetables, followed by pan-fried (or poached) Dover sole with wine sauce. The cheese board is fantastic. While the museum is free, the restaurant is a pricey affair, with mains reaching just short of £30.

Olive Press

4 Lloyds Street, off Deansgate, M2 5AB (0161 832 9090/www.heathcotes.co.uk). **Meals served** 11.45am-10pm Mon-Fri; 11.45am-11pm Sat; 11.45am-9.30pm Sun. **Main courses** £6.75-£14.50. **Credit** AmEx, DC, MC, V.

Paul Heathcote's cool new mini-chain, the Olive Press is a fun place to eat. There are two areas here, a bar/brasserie lounge with squishy chairs and a more formal dining space with chunky tables and an open kitchen galley. Both are busy. Food is straightforward, offering a Mediterranean palette of flavours that's heavy on the homely vibe. Starters feature rustic chicken and pork pâté with red onion marmalade. Mains might be pappardelle with mushrooms and artichokes, or the Olive Press lasagne – if you haven't had lasagne for a while, rediscover how good it is here. Stone-baked pizzas are delicious. Wines, averaging around £15 a bottle, offer a brief, but exciting selection.

The Ox

71 Liverpool Road, Castlefield, M3 4NQ (0161 839 7740/ww.theox.co.uk). **Lunch served** noon-2.45pm Mon-Thur; noon-5.45pm Sun. **Dinner served** 5.30-9.45pm Mon-Thur. **Meals served** noon-10pm Fri; noon-10.15pm Sat. **Main courses** £9.25-£16.95. **Credit** AmEx, MC, V.

Now very much a gastropub (the drinking section has been reduced to a mere handful of tables) the Ox continues to pull the crowds. And with good reason. Food is confident – bullish, even – and the cheer is good. The global menu leans towards the east, with spicy Thai fish cakes, to Europe with chicken piri piri, and then north for fresh seared Scottish salmon. Decor is dark, with crimson swags, dark wood tables and lighting kept to a minimum. As you'd hope, ales are from the cask and well kept.

Pacific

58-60 George Street, M1 4HF (0161 228 6668/ www.pacific-restaurant-manchester.co.uk). Thailand **Lunch served** noon-3pm daily. **Dinner served** 6-11.30pm Mon-Fri, Sun; 6pm-midnight Sat. **Main courses** £7.90-£12.90. **Set lunch** (buffet) £6.95. **Set dinner** £25-£38 3 courses (minimum 2). *China* **Meals served** noon-11.30pm daily. **Main courses** £7.50-£16. **Set lunch** (Mon-Fri) £5.50-£7.50 2 courses, £9.50 3 courses. **Set dinner** £20 3 courses, £35 4 courses (minimum 2). **Credit** AmEx, DC, MC, V.

The most innovative Chinese restaurant in Chinatown? Probably. In double quick time, it's earned itself a reputation as one of the city's most consistently exciting venues. The Pacific actually offers two restaurant experiences – Thai and Chinese (Cantonese) dishes are served in two separately themed rooms. The one thing the two floors have in common is the quality of the dishes – food is clean-flavoured and well cooked. Dim sum, Sichuan chicken and baked lobster with noodles all hit the mark, ditto stir-fried bean sprout with mixed pork and sea curd. Service, though, is hit and miss.

Le Petit Blanc Brasserie

55 King Street, M2 4LQ (0161 832 1000/www.petit blanc.co.uk). **Lunch served** noon-3pm, **dinner served** 5.30-11pm Mon-Sat. **Meals served** noon-10pm Sun. **Main courses** £9.25-£17.25. **Set meals** (noon-7pm, 10-11pm daily) £12 2 courses, £14.50 3 courses. **Credit** AmEx, MC, V.

Refurbished and far more confident than it was before, Le Petit Blanc is a buzzing, stylish choice. Blanc is still involved in this small chain and in this particular overhaul. The new menu is sharp and focused, and the decor similarly strident and less minimalist than before. Service too (once a gripe) is swift and courteous. Fish is always a rewarding choice – char-grilled squid with rocket, perhaps, or moules marinière served simply with bread. Signature mains include confit of guinea fowl and pan-fried calf's liver cooked with finesse.

Piccolino

8 Clarence Street, M2 4DW (0161 835 9860/ www.individualrestaurants.co.uk). **Meals served** 8am-11pm Mon-Fri; noon-11pm Sat; noon-10pm Sun. **Main courses** £10.50-£20. **Credit** AmEx, DC, MC, V.

Big wooden tables, a flurry of smart and attentive young staff, and big people-watching windows help make this Italian an attractive proposition. Dishes are competent, but good enough for a fun, casual meal. Pastas, grills and seafood are all worth ordering. Piccolino is as much about atmosphere as food.

Punjab Tandoori ★

177 Wilmslow Road, M14 5AP (0161 225 2960). **Dinner served** 5pm-midnight Mon. **Meals served** noon-midnight Tue-Thur, Sun; noon-1am Fri, Sat. **Credit** MC, V.

Bright neon (the brightest in a street of neon) lights the way to this curry house. The Punjab is renowned for its dosas – south Indian rolled pancakes stuffed with mouthwatering spicy fillings and served with perfectly judged curries. These great value specialities set the Punjab apart, but mains such as tandoori pomfret make good alternatives.

Rajdoot ★

Carlton House, 18 Albert Square, M2 5PR (0161 834 2176). **Lunch served** noon-2pm, **dinner served** 6.30-11.30pm Mon-Sat. **Main courses** £7.25-£8.25. **Set lunch** £8.95 3 courses. **Credit** AmEx, DC, MC, V.

A popular and dependable Indian in the heart of the city. Quality cooking is served in a stylish, calm atmosphere. Duck tikka with garlic and honey is an assured starter that will have your mouth watering – as it smells divine. Mains feature classic sauces made with fresh spices and chunky, generous cuts of meat. Vegetarians won't be disappointed: bhindi mushroom is justifiably popular. Service is attentive.

El Rincon

244 Deansgate, M3 4BQ (0161 839 8819). **Meals served** noon-11pm Mon-Thur, Sun; noon-11.30pm Fri, Sat. **Tapas** £1.95-£4.95. **Main courses** £8.75-£13.95. **Credit** AmEx, MC, V.

This corner of town is rapidly becoming a Spanish enclave and El Rincon is among the best. A cavernous bar/restaurant below ground, it feels incredibly Andalucian. Sevillian even. Tapas, El Rincon's speciality, are strident and served when they're ready with no fuss or pretension. Try albondigas – bullishly meaty meatballs in a thick tomato sauce – crab claws, or the classic tortilla. Paella is also superb. A lively, echoey place where the Rioja flows with the conversation. Great fun.

River Room

The Lowry Hotel, 50 Dearmans Place, Chapel Wharf, Salford, M3 5LH (0161 827 4000/www.thelowry hotel.com). **Lunch served** noon-2.30pm Mon-Sat; 12.30-4pm Sun. **Dinner served** 6-10.30pm Mon-Sat; 7-10.30pm Sun. **Main courses** £8.95-£30. **Set meal** (Mon-Sat) £18.50 2 courses £20.50 3 courses; (Sun) £17.75 3 courses. **Credit** AmEx, DC, MC, V.

Contemporarily styled, and bathed in natural light Marco Pierre White's graceful River Room restaurant is a big hit with those who put quality assurance above all else. Relaxing, and with superbly charming waiting staff, the whole experience is impressive without ever being intimidating. A confident menu lists the likes of cow's liver with caramelised cauliflower or MPW's signature Dover sole with lemon. Pig's trotters are treated with tenderness too. Some criticise the restaurant's clinical look and hushed atmosphere, but sometimes a little peace is just perfect.

Stock

4 Norfolk Street, M2 1DW (0161 839 6644/ www.stockrestaurant.co.uk). **Lunch served** noon-3pm, **dinner served** 6-10pm daily. **Main courses** £14.65-£17.10. **Set meal** (before 7pm) £12.50 2 courses, £15.50 3 courses. **Credit** AmEx, MC, V.

If it's not the best Italian restaurant in the city (and it's a close run thing), it's certainly the swankiest – its home being a grand old former stock exchange. Chef Enzo Mauro is passionate to the point of obsessiveness about the delights of his native cuisine. Nothing too outlandlish, just classic cooking, simple ingredients and excellent wines. Try exquisite tiger prawns in garlic butter with lemon arborio rice. Gnocchi served with walnuts and pancetta is masterly, as is ravioli of any variety.

Tampopo ★

16 Albert Square, M2 5PF (0161 819 1966). **Meals served** noon-11pm Mon-Sat; noon-10pm Sun. **Main courses** £5.95-£8.95. **Set meal** £6.95-£15.95. **Credit** AmEx, MC, V.

A quirky, appealing chain (Manchester owned) that's the venue of choice for South-east Asian and Pacific Rim cooking. Diners sit on benches along rows of stripped and simple tables. Gyozo dumplings are little parcels of heaven – whether you opt for the pork or vegetable options – dipped in soy sauce, they're perfect. Mains are cooked in a flash, and presented with no fuss. Nasi goreng brings a moreish rice, spice and meat combo, and the soup-based noodle ramen dishes have a kick that you'll remember for quite some time.

39 Steps

39 South King Street, M2 6DE (0161 834 9155/ www.39stepsrest.co.uk). **Lunch served** noon-2.30pm, **dinner served** 6.30-10pm Tue-Sat. **Main courses** £9.95-£16.95. **Set lunch** £15.95 2 courses incl a glass of wine. **Credit** AmEx, MC, V.

It's been around for some time now – more than 20 years if you're counting – and still there are some who've not been. Indeed, there are probably some who've never even heard of the place. That's a shame, because 39 Steps really is a little gem. Try scallops with black pudding to see what we mean. Seafood is treated with respect and flair: sea bass with smoked salmon and lime for example, or the signature dish of spicy fish hotpot with fresh chilli, white wine and tomato.

This and That ★

3 Soap Street, M4 1EW (0161 832 4971). **Meals served** 11am-5pm Mon-Fri; 11am-4pm Sun. **Main courses** £2.70-£4.50. **No credit cards.**

Cheap, dependable and totally pretension free, This and That is only open during the day, serving fresh fast Indian food. Dahls are the speciality: take a tray and queue to be served from a selection. Pilaf rice, mutter paneer, lassi – all are first rate. And you'll get change from a tenner. An increasingly difficult trick to pull off in this city. Great for vegetarians.

Yang Sing

34 Princess Street, M1 4JY (0161 236 2200/ www.yang-sing.com). **Meals served** noon-11.30pm Mon-Thur; noon-midnight Fri, Sat; noon-10.30pm Sun. **Main courses** £8.60-£50. **Set meals** £17.50 per person; £22-42 banquets. **Credit** AmEx, MC, V.

Probably one of Britain's finest Chinese restaurants, the Yang Sing is the one others must follow – although its little cousin, Little Yang Sing (*see p260*) might contend this – with world class Cantonese cooking. Meticulously prepared and sourced ingredients are transformed into something special. Dim sum is a case in point – there's even a vegetarian selection (spicy dumpling with vegetable and nut, for example) as well as the likes of steamed bun with roast pork filling. Surroundings more than match the menu – which is vast; staff will help you navigate its pages.

ZenZero

55 Backbridge Street, M3 2PB (0161 831 7277). **Lunch served** noon-5pm Mon-Sat. **Dinner served** 5-10.30pm Mon-Thur, 5-11pm Fri, Sat. **Main courses** £6-£15. **Set lunch** £5.50 1 course. **Set dinner** (5-7pm) £10.99 2 courses, £12.99 3 courses. **Credit** MC, V.

Imaginative cooking with a strong Amalfi-coast bias is on offer at this new, basement restaurant just off Bridge Street. Lunch is a brisk affair, but in the evening you can linger over starters such as butter-fried tiger prawns sautéed with white wine and garlic, or carpaccio dressed in olive oil. Pasta and pizza dishes are assured creations, or there are mains such as escalope of veal rolled in Parma ham and served in a Marsala sauce.

Zinc

Unit 12A, Hanging Ditch, M4 3ES (0161 827 4200/ www.conran.co.uk). **Meals served** 10am-10pm Mon-Sat; 11am-9pm Sun. **Main courses** £7.50-£15.50. **Set meal** (before 7pm, Mon-Fri) £12.50 2 courses, £15 3 courses. **Credit** AmEx, DC, MC, V.

Conran's classic formula of fast, competent cooking, minimalist surroundings and stylish service is paying dividends in the newly relaunched Triangle area of the city. Zinc's ebullient creations feature zesty salads, tapas and eastern-infused small plates (the crispy duck spring rolls are highly recommended), which make lunchtimes more fun than most places in town. Take your time over dinner and enjoy ribeye steaks, chicken Caesar salads and the best chips in town. Desserts might be a lovely lemon tart, or excellent vanilla poached pears. Cocktails are taken very seriously here. Monday nights are fast gaining a reputation for chilled beats: it's a dinner dance, in other words (just don't let them hear you calling it that).

Loves Saves The Day. *See p260.*

Also in the area

Chez Gerard 43A Brown Street, M2 2JJ (0161 214 1120); **Livebait** 22 Lloyd Street, M2 5WA (0161 817 4110); **Living Room** 80 Deansgate, M3 2ER (0870 442 2537); **Malmaison** Piccadilly, M1 3AQ (0161 278 1000); **Nawaab** 1008 Stockport Road, M19 3WN (0161 224 6969); **Nawaab** 47 Rochdale Road, M4 4HT (0161 839 0601); **Shimla Pinks** Dolefield, off Bridge Street, M3 3EN (0161 831 7099); **Simply Heathcotes** Jacksons Row, Deansgate, M2 5WD (0161 835 3536); **Tampopo** 126 The Orient, The Trafford Centre, M17 8EH (0161 747 8878); **Tampopo** 62 Beech Road, M21 9EG (0161 861 8862); **Wagamama** 1 The Pineworks, Corporation Street, M4 4DG (0161 839 5916).

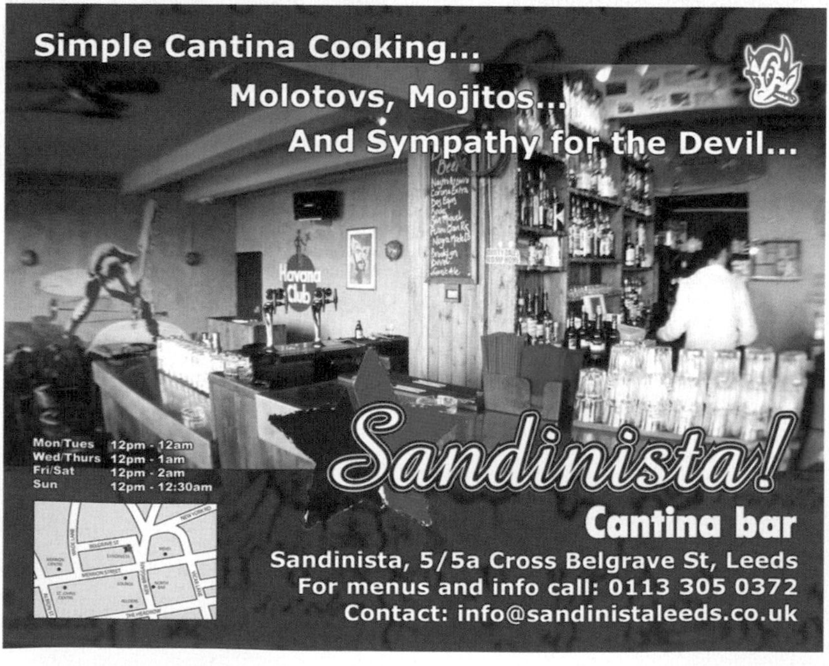

North East

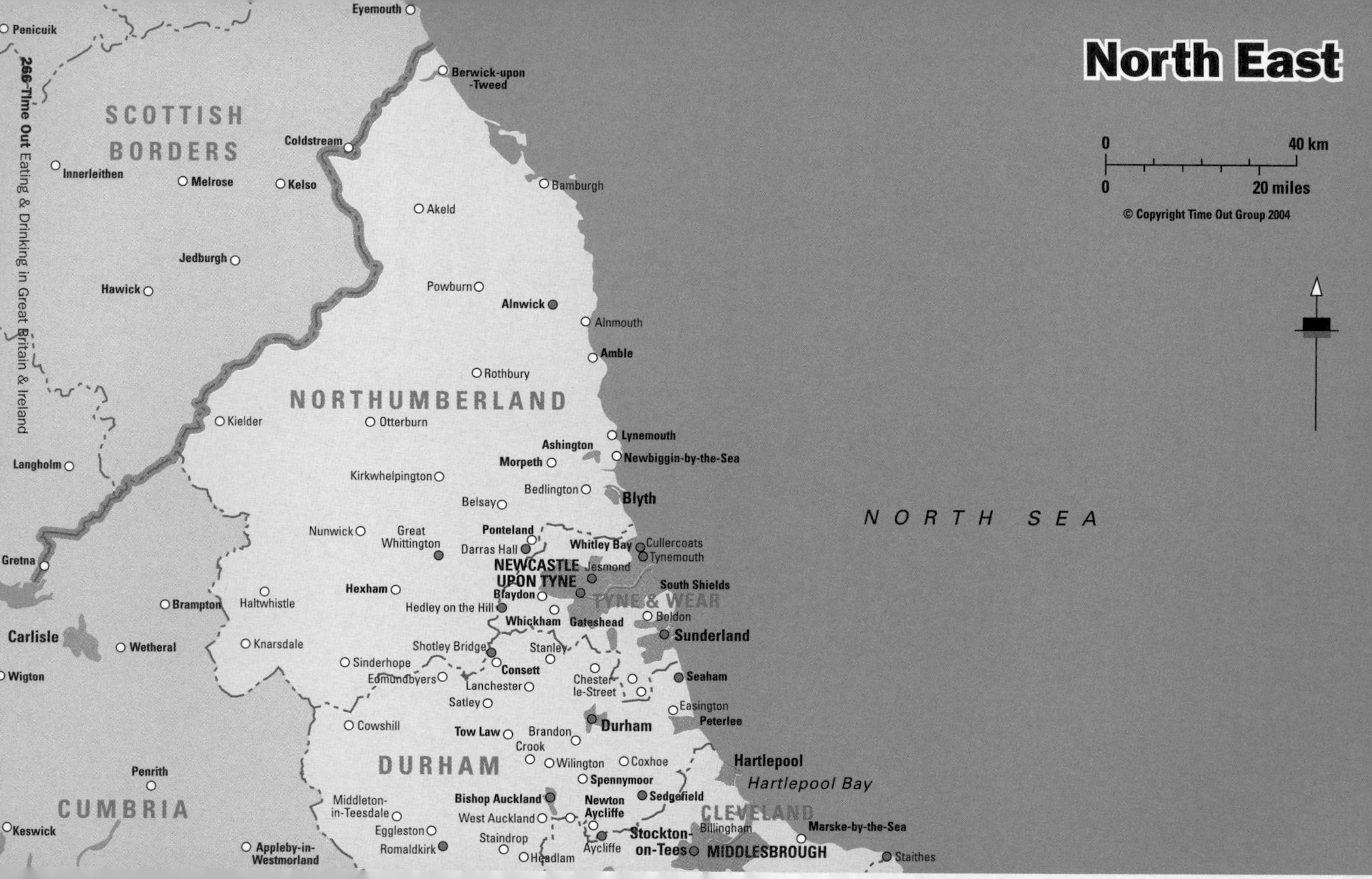
North East
0
40 km
0
20 miles
© Copyright Time Out Group 2004
NORTH SEA
SCOTTISH BORDERS
NORTHUMBERLAND
DURHAM
CUMBRIA
TYNE & WEAR
CLEVELAND
Hartlepool Bay
Penicuik
Eyemouth
Berwick-upon-Tweed
Coldstream
Innerleithen
Melrose
Kelso
Bamburgh
Akeld
Jedburgh
Hawick
Powburn
Alnwick
Alnmouth
Amble
Rothbury
Kielder
Otterburn
Lynemouth
Ashington
Morpeth
Newbiggin-by-the-Sea
Langholm
Kirkwhelpington
Bedlington
Blyth
Belsay
Nunwick
Great Whittington
Ponteland
Darras Hall
Whitley Bay
Cullercoats
Tynemouth
Gretna
NEWCASTLE UPON TYNE
Jesmond
South Shields
Hexham
Blaydon
Brampton
Haltwhistle
Hedley on the Hill
Whickham
Gateshead
Boldon
Carlisle
Wetheral
Knarsdale
Shotley Bridge
Stanley
Sunderland
Sinderhope
Consett
Wigton
Edmundbyers
Lanchester
Chester-le-Street
Seaham
Satley
Easington
Cowshill
Tow Law
Brandon
Durham
Peterlee
Crook
Wilington
Coxhoe
Hartlepool
Penrith
Spennymoor
Middleton-in-Teesdale
Bishop Auckland
Newton Aycliffe
Sedgefield
West Auckland
Billingham
Marske-by-the-Sea
Keswick
Eggleston
Staindrop
Stockton-on-Tees
Appleby-in-Westmorland
Romaldkirk
Headlam
Aycliffe
MIDDLESBROUGH
Staithes

Bridlington Bay
NORTH YORKSHIRE
EAST RIDING
WEST YORKSHIRE
SOUTH YORKSHIRE
LANCASHIRE
GREATER MANCHESTER
MERSEYSIDE
CHESHIRE
DERBYSHIRE
NOTTINGHAM-SHIRE
LINCOLNSHIRE
Scarborough
Whitby
Bridlington
Filey
Darlington
Northallerton
Harrogate
Ripon
York
KINGSTON UPON HULL
Beverley
Grimsby
Cleethorpes
Scunthorpe
Doncaster
Selby
Goole
LEEDS
BRADFORD
HUDDERSFIELD
Halifax
Wakefield
Castleford
Pontefract
Barnsley
Rotherham
SHEFFIELD
Chesterfield
Worksop
Lincoln
Gainsborough
Skipton
Keighley
Burnley
Blackburn
Bolton
Oldham
Rochdale
MANCHESTER
Stockport
Macclesfield
Wigan
St Helens
LIVERPOOL
Birkenhead
Chester
Southport
PRESTON
BLACKPOOL
Lytham St Anne's
Fleetwood
Lancaster
Morecambe
Kendal
Windermere
Ambleside
Ulverston

County Durham

AYCLIFFE

The County

13 The Green, Aycliffe, DL5 6LX (01325 312273/ www.the-county.co.uk). **Lunch served** noon-2pm Mon-Sat; noon-2.45pm Sun. **Dinner served** 6-9.15pm Mon-Sat. **Main courses** £10.95-£16.95. **Credit** AmEx, MC, V.

Andrew Brown, the licensee, was the first person to win a Raymond Blanc scholarship. That was in 1995, and after further experience with Gary Rhodes he took over this pretty village pub. The bar menu sticks mainly to the familiar: from sausages with mash and onion gravy, to Chinese crispy beef with stir-fried peppers, mushrooms and noodles in oyster sauce. The restaurant carte, on the other hand, is more ambitious: char-grilled smoked salmon on red pepper couscous, with spiced fruit chutney, mixed leaves and sweet potato chips, and roast chump of lamb, with braised puy lentils, smoked bacon and red wine and thyme jus. Don't miss out on the puds.

BISHOP AUCKLAND

Morley's ★

12 Fore Bondgate, Bishop Auckland, DL14 7PF (01388 606239). **Lunch served** 11am-1.30pm Mon-Wed; 11am-2pm Thur, Fri; 11am-2.30pm Sat. **Main courses** £2.90-£5.50. **No credit cards.**

Cod, haddock, and occasionally hake feature on the menu of this traditional and well-liked chippie. Boneless fillets of skinless cod and fresh skin-on haddock are matched by Maris Piper spuds (for the major part of the season). Frying is in vegetable oil, the fish cooked separately in big square pans, the chips in round pans, where they are first fried to blanch, allowed to cool then flash-fried as required. The results are the perfect chip, with a wonderful golden, crisp exterior and soft, fluffy middle. Simple accompaniments include authentic mushy peas.

DURHAM

Almshouses Café ★

Palace Green, Durham, DH1 3RL (0191 386 1054). **Meals served** *Sept-May* 9am-5pm daily. *June-Aug* 9am-8pm daily. **Main courses** £4.95-£6.20. **Credit** MC, V.

Though facing the cathedral and housed in a terrace of ancient stone buildings, the restaurant interior is cheerfully bright and modern. Blackboards list the menu, which changes daily. The daily selection usually offers a couple of soups, a salad bowl with various dressings, a pâté or two, a vegetarian and a meat dish, as well as an array of delicious puddings and cakes. All (apart from bread) are prepared on the premises. A full-flavoured yellow pea, roast tomato and rosemary soup preceded a slice of moist cotherstone cheese, watercress and red pepper quiche. Lemon and almond polenta cake to finish was superb.

Bistro 21

Aykley Heads House, Aykley Heads, Durham, DH1 5TS (0191 384 4354). **Lunch served** noon-2pm Mon-Sat. **Dinner served** 7-10.30pm Mon-Fri; 6-10.30pm Sat. **Main courses** £10.50-£16.50. **Set lunch** £13 2 courses, £15.50 3 courses. **Credit** AmEx, DC, MC, V.

Housed in part of a converted farmhouse, Terry Laybourne's landmark bistro has a minimalist yet cosily rustic decor, and a menu of simple dishes that punch well above their weight for flavour. The good-value set lunch menu includes ham knuckle and parsley terrine with plum chutney, a superb signature dish that also appears on the carte. Outstanding char-grilled pork chop with black pudding mash and apple sauce is another favourite. There's a short but varied wine list, with a good selection under £20. *See also p276* Café 21.

Hide Café Bar & Grill

39 Saddler Street, Durham, DH1 3NU (0191 384 1999/www.hidebar.com). **Meals served** 9.30am-4pm Mon-Sat; 10.30am-4pm Sun. **Dinner served** 6-9.30pm daily. **Main courses** £8-£16. **Credit** MC, V.

A stylish café-bar with cool music and smart modern décor. The food's eclectic and imaginative, and runs from traditional breakfasts, and an all-day café menu of pizzas, salads and stir-fries, through to a three-course affair in the grill, where advance bookings are required. It's a cut above average: bruschetta with rocket, goat's cheese and vine tomatoes followed by roast line-caught cod with crushed potatoes and beurre blanc. The drinks list encompasses shooters, cocktails, champagnes and wines.

ROMALDKIRK

Rose & Crown

Romaldkirk, DL12 9EB (01833 650213/www.rose-and-crown.co.uk). **Lunch served** noon-1.30pm daily. **Dinner served** *Bar* 6.30-9.30pm daily. *Restaurant* 7.30-9pm Mon-Sat. **Set lunch** £15.95 3 courses. **Set dinner** £26 4 courses. **Credit** MC, V.

Built in 1733 as a coaching inn, the impressive stone-building occupies a commanding position at the heart of this unspoilt Teesdale village. Under its current ownership it has blossomed into an inviting establishment with high standards of hospitality, attracting in the process a smart clientele. There are two dining options: the restaurant, with its elegant, upmarket look and formal, fixed-price menus; or the

Bistro 21. See p268.

more laid-back brasserie, where the choice is similar, but individually priced. Black pudding with poached egg, grilled bacon and hollandaise delivered plenty of flavour, as did slow-baked confit of lamb with haricot bean cassoulet and mint pesto.

SEAHAM

White Room at Seaham Hall

Lord Byron's Walk, Seaham, SR7 7AG (0191 516 1400/www.seaham-hall.com). **Lunch served** noon-2pm, **dinner served** 7-10pm daily. **Main courses** £25-£32. **Set lunch** £17.50 2 courses, £20 3 courses. **Set dinner** £40 3 courses. **Credit** AmEx, DC, MC, V.
The classical beauty of the original Georgian mansion has been enhanced by a 21st-century makeover. Perched on the edge of the North Sea, it's surrounded by wild countryside. This is an all-suite hotel with a cool, chic dining room whose menus of modern European dishes complement the sophisticated ambience. The fixed-price lunch offers two choices per course with a fabulous chicken liver parfait served with grape chutney and brioche preceding perfectly cooked roast rump of Cumbrian fell-bred lamb. Tiramisu with mocha sorbet and coffee anglaise was a marriage made in heaven. Sister restaurant to the Samling (*see p247*).

SEDGEFIELD

Dun Cow

43 Front Street, Sedgefield, TS21 3AT (01740 620894). **Lunch served** noon-2pm daily. **Dinner served** *Bar* 6.30-9.30pm Mon-Sat; 7-9.30pm Sun. *Restaurant* 7-9.30pm Mon-Sat; 7-9pm Sun. **Main courses** £7.95-£16. **Credit** AmEx, MC, V.
During his 2003 state visit, George W Bush stopped off here for a lunch of fish and chips at this attractive flower-bedecked inn. The simple bar menu offers Whitby cod or scampi, and grilled gammon with egg or pineapple, as well as baguettes and jacket potatoes. In the restaurant there's a little more style, with a menu that lists dressed crab with lemon and olive oil, followed by overambitious combos like honey and chilli-glazed pork fillet with king prawn kebab and Moroccan rice. The simpler dishes work best.

SHOTLEY BRIDGE

Manor House Inn

Carter Way Heads, nr Shotley Bridge, DH8 9LX (01207 255268). **Meals served** noon-9.30pm Mon-Sat; noon-9pm Sun. **Main courses** £10.95-£15.95. **Credit** AmEx, DC, MC, V.
The inn's position on this remote, and in winter bleak and windswept, section of the A68 makes it a welcoming beacon of good accommodation and food. A rustic public bar with scrubbed wood floor, and smarter, comfortably furnished lounge bar offer the same daily-changing menu. An imaginative choice runs from simple bar snacks (Cumberland sausage, mash and mustard gravy), to more elaborate, well-executed mains such as roast duck breast with sugar-roasted plums and piquant sauce, or lamb cutlets with port and cranberry, garlic and rosemary mash. Fish, all from North Shields (locally smoked kippers with crème fraîche, say), is a strong point.

STOCKTON-ON-TEES

Moby Grape

Calverts Lane, Stockton-on-Tees, TS18 1SW (01642 611311). **Meals served** 11am-4.30pm Mon-Sat. **Main courses** £3-£10. **Credit** MC, V.
One of the town's trendiest after-hours music and dancing venues attracts the hip and wannabes for club nights starting at 10pm, but meal times have been severely curtailed. The place is popular at lunch with the local business community who flock in for well-made American-style snacks. Sandwiches include a generous Moby Club: char-grilled chicken breast with grilled bacon, tomato, crisp lettuce and lemon mayo on toasted granary bread. Other options are jacket potatoes, gigantic burgers, wraps, salads, and noodles with mussels in a Thai green sauce. The terrace offers alfresco dining with riverside views.

Leeds

Anthony's ★

19 Boar Lane, LS1 6EA (0113 245 5922). **Lunch served** noon-2.30pm Tue-Sat. **Dinner served** 7-9.30pm Tue-Thur; 7-10pm Fri, Sat. **Main courses** £15.95-£17.95. **Set lunch** £18.95 2 courses, £22.95 3 courses. **Credit** MC, V.

A truly stunning new addition to the very top drawer of the Leeds restaurant scene. With his dad as business manager, his sister behind the bar and his Spanish girlfriend running the dining room, Tony Flinn is creating gorgeously innovative dishes from this 25-cover basement. The initially austere setting melts away with the arrival of roast duck breast with olive oil and chocolate bonbons or risotto of white onion with espresso and parmesan air. Never mind the exotic fusions, relish the quality. Flinn's cooking is new, different and exceptionally good. His inspiration comes directly from El Bulli, the famously avant-garde eaterie near Barcelona regularly touted as the best restaurant in the world. Flinn cooked there for two seasons. He clearly learned well because everything – from starters of white loaf with fluffy parmesan butter, intensely flavoured roast scallops and a velvet-textured soup of butternut squash, to a main of roast suckling pig and a pudding of chocolate fondant and black sesame seed ice-cream – was just terrific.

Art's Café Bar

42 Call Lane, LS1 6DT (0113 243 8243/www.artscafe bar.co.uk). **Open** noon-11pm Mon-Sat; 10am-10.30pm Sun. **Meals served** noon-10pm Mon-Wed; noon-10.30pm Thur-Sat; noon-10pm Sun. **Main courses** £7.50-£14.50. **Set lunch** £5. **Credit** AmEx, DC, MC, V.

Easygoing Art's barely bothers competing in the design stakes for the coolest café-bar in the Calls. It's still all rough-hewn floors, rickety chairs, student art and daily papers but it does have the confidence of being the oldest kid on the block – and its calling card, Art's Lunch Plates, does the rest. For £5, try combination dishes of roast vegetables, houmous, potato salad and lemon couscous or grilled red mullet, calamares, smoked salmon and pasta salad. Open sandwiches are packed with steak and horseradish, or prawns with coriander and lime. Pick up the pace at night with steak and tomato confit on rocket and red onion salad, and pot-roast chicken with cabbage and pancetta.

Bibi's Criterion

Criterion Place, off Sovereign Street, LS1 4AG (0113 243 0905/www.bibisrestaurant.com). **Lunch served** noon-2pm Mon-Sat; noon-3.30pm Sun. **Dinner served** 6-11pm Mon-Wed; 6-11.30pm Thur, Fri; 5.30-11.30pm Sat; 5.30-10.30pm Sun. **Main courses** £7.25-£18.50. **Credit** AmEx, MC, V.

The most bombastic opening of the year. Ever-popular, Bibi's began life as a cheerful backstreet trattoria, traded up in Roman Empire style and has now gone right over the top with its third home, a purpose-built 300-cover art deco temple to chrome, mirror, marble, chandeliers, plasma screens, glitter balls and enough wattage to fuse the National Grid. For all the ersatz glamour, the place is bursting with parties, young bloods and families, happily buying into the fantasy. Sadly, the food plummets you back to earth. It's an overpriced production line. Mediocre steaks come in at £18, wine mark-ups are eye-watering and anything that can be charged as an extra is. Worth a gawp, but stick to pizza and pasta.

Brasserie 44

44 The Calls, LS2 7EW (0113 234 3232/www.brass erie44.com). **Lunch served** noon-2pm Mon-Fri. **Dinner served** 6-10.30pm Mon-Thur; 6-11pm Fri, Sat. **Main courses** £10-£16. **Set meals** (lunch, 6-7.15pm) £11.50 2 courses, £14 3 courses. **Credit** MC, V.

This landmark brasserie in a warehouse-turned-boutique hotel was the launch pad in the early 1990s for chef Jeff Baker's ascent to Michelin-dom. (Baker is head chef here and at the hotel's other restaurant, Pool Court; *see p273.*) It still has the unmistakable energy of a restaurant in the prime of life – smartly kept and smartly staffed, live with a sense of occasion – but the menu and cooking feel just a little tired. Starters are internationally inspired (lamb meatballs with houmous, celeriac soup with poached egg, duck wun tuns) and mains are more pub/grill: steak and kidney pie, cauliflower Thai curry, steaks. A Whitby smokehouse provides smoked cod and salmon, and feta for pizza. There are two distinct seating areas: a narrow, atmospheric hairpin of coffee and cream decor, plus a more formal room with large riverview windows.

Brio

40 Great George Street, LS1 3DL (0113 246 5225/ www.brios.co.uk). **Lunch served** noon-2.30pm, **dinner served** 6-10.30pm Mon-Sat. **Main courses** £5.75-£14.50. **Credit** AmEx, MC, V.

Leeds lacks a truly inventive new-wave Italian but Brio is holding up well as the city centre's next best thing. What might otherwise be a conventional room of blond wood and etched glass is lifted by splashes of colour; and so are the starters, pasta and main course standards. Smear your focaccia with the best tapenade in town. Lively starters include bresaola with a rocket salad or fried squid, or a pear and dolcelatte salad. From the pasta menu, linguine with Sardinian bottarga (dried tuna roe) and courgettes or farfalline with fagioli beans and pancetta both pack a real punch. Mains and desserts are reliable if familiar. For pizza try Brio Pizza, their compact outlet round the corner in the Light shopping centre.

Bryan's

9 Weetwood Lane, Headingley, LS16 5LT (0113 278 5679). **Meals served** noon-9pm Mon; noon-9.30pm Tue-Thur; noon-10pm Sat; 12.30-7pm Sun. **Main courses** £6.80-£12.99. **Credit** MC, V.

Surreal local sighting of the year in Leeds' most famous chippie was Monica Lewinsky dropping by for a jumbo haddock in between book signings. More shocking to regulars was the makeover; the expensive suede and leather seating, the champagne and latte, the Thai fish cakes and 'market price' lobster salads. Bryan's says it's setting its sights at the 'younger professional market'. Seventy years of tradition will take some shifting, though, and 5,000 portions of battered fish per week are still wolfed down via the café and takeaway. Golden haddock, chunky chips and lush mushy peas, all washed down with a mug of Yorkshire tea, is a winning formula that is still not ready for downsizing.

Casa Mia Millennium

Millennium Square, Great George Street, Leeds LS1 3DP (0113 245 4121/www.casamiaonline.co.uk). **Meals served** 7am-midnight Mon-Wed; 7am-2.30am Thur-Sat; 8am-midnight Sun. **Main courses** £5.95-£19.95. **Credit** MC, V.

Casa Mia has spread its wings yet again. It begun as a deli in suburban Chapel Allerton that grew into a bistro and spawned a big sister Casa Mia Grande. Now the granddaddy of them all and the flagship of the Casa Mia chain has opened in the old Electric Press Building in Millennium Square. Deep red walls, marble topped tables and great views over the square, the formula for Millennium is the same as its siblings: a deli selling pasta, oils, olives and prepared takeaway dishes. A restaurant serving pizza, pasta, charcoal-grilled steaks and good fish. New to this branch is early opening, Italian coffee, croissants and brioche for city breakfast.

Dine China Chinese & Herbal Restaurant

4 New Station Street, LS1 5DL (0113 243 8866). **Meals served** 11.30am-9.30pm Mon-Thur; 11.30am-10.30pm Fri, Sat. **Main courses** £2.99-£12.99. **Credit** MC, V.

Cramped and untidy at the upstairs takeaway, unevenly orientalised downstairs, there's no external clue that Dine China has cut interesting new ground in the moribund local Chinese scene. Crispy daikon cake, skewers of Mongolian lamb, lotus seed and almond broth, roast duck with mango sauce and a run of specials contain 'active herbal ingredients to re-establish your body to health and fitness', blessed by Elder Pa Pa Wu. Hay fever, arthritis, 'women's problems', sexual potency and even cancer can all allegedly be helped by crocodile meat with reishi or coley gingseng reishi in garlic sauce. A brain-power boosting 'chicken with intelligent reishi mushroom' has yet to deliver, however. No scoffing, though, for a policy of free range eggs, own-made tofu, no animal fats, no monosodium glutamate, no GM and plenty of vegan and vegetarian dishes.

Dough Bistro

Dough Bistro ★

293 Spen Lane, West Park, LS16 5BD (0113 278 7255). **Dinner served** 7-10pm Tue-Sat. **Set dinner** (Tue-Thur) £16.95 2 courses; (Fri, Sat) £21.95 4 courses. **No credit cards.**

Wayne Newsome is Leeds' most restless, maverick, loveable chef. He's survived a string of crashed ventures to bounce back with what is hopefully his most viable yet. On the front line between council tower blocks and posh West Park, Dough is a terrific little 12-table BYO bistro. Its no credit card, low-choice menu delivers four bright and rewarding courses for £21.95, including crisp belly of pork with soy dressing, saffron and spring onion risotto with tempura battered vegetables. Piquant little additions arrive at every turn – aubergine dip, pimento coulis, tomato salsa – and the puddings are super. How about warm chocolate fondant with caramel ice-cream or pineapple tatin? Newsome's enjoyment is infectious. Every neighbourhood should have a Dough.

Flannels ★

68-78 Vicar Lane, LS1 7JH (0113 242 8732). **Open** 10am-6pm Mon-Sat; 11am-5pm Sun. **Lunch served** noon-4pm, **afternoon tea served** 4-5pm daily. **Main courses** £9-£12. **Set lunch** (Sun) £12 2 courses, £15 3 courses. **Credit** AmEx, MC, V.

This upmarket fashion store on Vicar Lane has quietly spawned a little treasure of a café-restaurant. It's a great breakfast spot with the papers, freshly squeezed oranges, muesli, croissants or full English. Mid morning brings smoked salmon and cream cheese bagels. And beyond the cool of the Damien

North East

Hirst installations, contemporary lighting, leather chairs and massive oak beams, there is real substance at lunch: roast tomato soup with pesto, or parma, rocket and parmesan salad, followed by mains of smoked haddock, seared tuna, shepherd's pie or calf's liver and mash. Currently the restaurant operates shop hours only with a few special functions, but watch for regular evening openings.

Fourth Floor Café & Bar

Harvey Nichols, 107-111 Briggate, LS1 6AZ (0113 204 8000/www.harveynichols.com). **Meals served** 10am-6pm Mon-Wed; 10am-10pm Thur, Fri; 9am-10pm Sat; noon-4pm Sun. **Main courses** £10.50-£15. **Set lunch** (Mon-Sat) £15 2 courses, £18 3 courses. **Set brunch** (Sun) £15 2 courses incl one drink. **Set dinner** (Thur-Sat) £10.95 2 courses, £14 3 courses. **Credit** AmEx, DC, MC, V.

No ordinary department store caff, this, and don't let the Formica and banquette seating fool you: it's not so very casual either. In keeping with the character of Harvey Nichols restaurants, Fourth Floor nails contemporary food and mood with enjoyable ease. The staff in the open kitchen turn out a short list of modern international dishes: chargrilled ox tongue, pan-fried scallops with purple crushed potato, calf's liver with caramelised shallot tart and chilli-glazed duck are typical. A new brunch menu is filling the place at weekends: £10 for two courses, £15 for three, including a Bloody Mary or one of several rather beautiful fruity virgin cocktails. Ask for a window table for a sweeping rooftop view.

Fuji Hiro ★

45 Wade Lane, Merrion Centre, LS2 8NJ (0113 243 9184). **Meals served** noon-10pm Mon-Thur, Sun; noon-11pm Fri, Sat. **Main courses** £5.50-£6.95. **Set meals** £10.95 vegetarian, £11.95 non-vegetarian. **No credit cards.**

Still the city centre's best equation of quality, nutrition and cost. There are far cooler Eastern temples elsewhere, but little Fuji Hiro is the real deal. Actors and students, office workers and family shoppers all pile in along the bare Formica tables for a steaming bowl of ramen noodles in a miso broth topped with prawns, squid, chicken and vegetables. Or a filling plate of fried soba noodles mixed with leeks, beansprouts, onions and chilli. The ingredients and cooking are exemplary, and most main dishes are around £5. It's a steal.

Leodis

Victoria Mill, Sovereign Street, LS1 4BJ (0113 242 1010/www.leodis.co.uk). **Lunch served** noon-2pm Mon-Fri. **Dinner served** 6-10pm Mon-Sat. **Main courses** £9-£17. **Set meal** £16.95 3 courses. **Credit** AmEx, DC, MC, V.

Bold and innovative when it opened among the decaying warehouses and neglected river basin a generation ago, Leodis straddles the market between the thrusting suits that dominate this quarter, and the casual crowd that keeps the place young. New innovations are a lunchtime tapas menu – duck pancakes with chilli dip, mussels, king prawn, marinated octopus – and sandwiches and light meals, taken at the bar or on the plaza. The main menu upholds Leodis's strength in fish, with swordfish steak and tuna carpaccio, and vegetarian plates like rösti with asparagus and wild mushroom, and tomato and mozzarella tart.

No.3 York Place

3 York Place, LS1 2DR (0113 245 9922/www.no3yorkplace.co.uk). **Lunch served** noon-2pm Mon-Fri. **Dinner served** 6.30-10pm Mon-Sat. **Main courses** £12.95-£19.95. **Set meals** (lunch, 6.30-7.30pm, Mon-Fri) £14.50 2 courses, £18.50 3 courses. **Set dinner** £45 7 courses. **Credit** AmEx, MC, V.

This sophisticated dining room is emerging smoothly from under the shadow of the mercurial Simon Gueller to sustain its place as one of the classiest restaurants in town. Chef Martel Smith is one of Yorkshire's hottest talents. His menu du jour delivers three precision dishes for £18.50. For £45, the top end offers ballotine of foie gras with truffle vinaigrette, poached oysters with noodles and Avruga caviar, and a fêted signature dish of pig's trotter stuffed with ham hock and black pudding. Desserts are edible sculptures: a pyramid of passion fruit sorbet and nougat ice, or a warm fondant of dark chocolate and coffee with milk ice-cream and espresso syrup. Serious stuff but not too precious.

Old Police Station

106 Harrogate Road, Chapel Allerton, LS7 4LZ (0113 266 8999/www.theoldpolicestation.co.uk). **Open** noon-11pm Mon-Thur; noon-midnight Fri, Sat; noon-10.30pm Sun. **Lunch served** noon-2pm, **dinner served** 6-10pm Mon-Sat. **Meals served** noon-8pm Sun. **Main courses** £9-£16. **Set meals** (lunch, 6-7pm) £9.99 2 courses, £12.99 3 courses. **Credit** AmEx, DC, MC, V.

Outside the city centre, Chapel Allerton now has the best concentration of restaurants in Leeds and the Old Police Station has been a popular part of the surge. A cell complete with peephole and graffiti is retained – this nick saw serious action in the Chapeltown riots. Starters include crab and chilli spaghetti or squid tempura with lime, chilli and soy dip. Mains of rack of lamb and suckling pig all demand good cooking – and generally get it. There's a short pudding list, sandwiches and snacks in the bar, and decent value from the £12 lunch and early evening set menus. Not much for veggies, though.

Pool Court at 42

42 The Calls, LS2 7EW (0113 244 4242/www.poolcourt.com). **Lunch served** noon-2pm Mon-Fri. **Dinner served** 7-10pm Mon-Thur; 7-10.30pm Fri; 7-8.30pm Sat. **Set meals** (chef's menu) £25 2 courses, £30 3 courses; £39.50 2 courses, £49. 3 courses. **Credit** MC, V.

One chef, two kitchens: Jeff Baker runs Pool Court and its sister restaurant Brasserie 44 (*see p270*) on the riverside. Pool Court is like an exclusive private club with streamlined decor, impeccable service and a connoisseur's wine list. The cooking is sumptuous.

Bar crawl: Leeds

Students new to Leeds are soon initiated into the ritual of the Otley Road Run – a drink in every pub from **Woody's** (104 Otley Road, 0113 278 4393) in Far Headingley to the edge of the city centre. About a dozen if you can keep a straight line. In Headingley, the **Skyrack** (2-3 St Michael's Road, 0113 278 1519) and the **Original Oak** (2 Otley Road, 0113 275 1322) are established student pubs. Of the modern bars, **Arc** (19 Ash Road, 0113 275 2223) has balcony tables, **Trio** (44 North Lane, 0113 203 6090) has a top floor lounge for niche beers and tapas, the **Box** (8 Otley Road, 0113 224 9266) is Headingley's busiest sports bar. **Arcadia** (32 The Arndale Centre, Otley Road, 0113 274 5599) is the city's first no-smoking bar.

Head into town via the **Hyde Park** (Hyde Park Corner, Headingley Lane, 0113 274 5597), the **Library** (229 Woodhouse Lane, 0113 244 0794) and the **Fenton** (161 Woodhouse Lane, 0113 245 3908), student haunts all, but none can touch the **Faversham** (1-5 Springfield Mount, 0113 243 1481). Embedded in the University campus it has served every passing student. On a Saturday night, the Fav still bounces like nowhere else.

Fringing the city centre, **Joseph's Well** (Hanover Walk, 0113 203 1861) pulls in skateboarders with live music. **Dry Dock** (Woodhouse Lane, 0113 203 1841), an old barge beached on a traffic island opposite Leeds Met University, has a late licence until 2am. **Wardrobe** (6 St Peter's Buildings, St Peter's Square, 0113 383 8800) near the Playhouse and the Music College rolls out bands for funk and soul.

Then it's into the mass of ever-evolving bars around Call Lane. In its latest refurb **Norman** (36 Call Lane, 0113 234 3988) has defrosted enough to put a sign up while dealing martinis, sake and noodles to older trendies. **Oporto's** (33 Call Lane, 0113 243 4008) refit is adding a new menu and **Jakes Bar and Grill** (27-29 Call Lane, 0113 243 4008) is an old favourite. Chain bars that wear it well include **BRB** (37 Call Lane, 0113 243 0315) and **Mook** (Hirsts Yard, 0113 245 9967).

Expensively dressed graduates gravitate to **Townhouse** (Assembly Street, 0113 219 4004). It's DJ led with retro funk and a late licence. **Oslo** (174 Briggate, 0113 245 7768) is a trendy cave that can take two or two hundred and stay intimate with music that veers between techno and house. Another smart basement, off Boar Lane, houses the **HiFi Club** (2 Central Street, 0113 242 7353), which flicks nightly through world music, hip hop, blues, jazz and comedy. **Elbow Room** (64 Call Lane, 0113 245 7011) is a much loved barn with pool tables. Live music begins early at **Dr Wu's** (35 Call Lane, 0113 242 7629), blaring out from 5pm on a Friday afternoon. Friendly retro **Milo's** (10-12 Call Lane, 0113 245 7101) is a magnet for long hair and sports jackets.

Going north, **Harvey Nichols Café Bar** (Fourth Floor, 107-111 Briggate, 0113 204 8888) is cool for expensive cocktails. **North Bar** (24 New Briggate, 0113 242 4540) is a popular long narrow bar with continental beers and local art. **Mojo's** (18 Merrion Street, 0113 244 6387) is where Chris Moyles and Fat Boy Slim hang out when they're in town. A Leeds classic, it's loud, fun and rock 'n' roll. When the crush gets too much, head for the **Reform** (12-14 Merrion Street, 0113 244 4080) for show-off cocktails and obscure spirits. **Sandinista** (5-5a Cross Belgrave Street, 0113 305 0372) has big windows that are taken out on hot summer nights.

For gay bars, plush and chandeliered **Velvet** (11-13 Hirst's Yard, 0113 242 5079) does good food and good party. So too does **Fibre** (168 Lower Briggate, 0870 120 0888). Less lipstick is **Queens Court** (167 Lower Briggate, 0113 245 9449). A vast, white vested, tattooed body builder doorman tells you plenty about the **New Penny** (57-59 The Calls, 0113 243 8055), famous from the 1950s as the first gay bar outside London.

When the fizz fades from the import lagers and you crave a proper Yorkshire pint, real ale abounds. The **Regent** (15-17 Regent Street, 0113 293 9395) in Chapel Allerton has a pleasant beer garden. Gastropub **Reliance** (76-78 North Street, 0113 295 6060), supplies Med food, newspapers and sofas. Architectural gems include the stained glass of the **Guilford** (115 The Headrow, 0113 244 9204), the period interior of the **Victoria Commerical Hotel** (28-38 Great George Street, 0113 245 1386), the curvaceous **Adelphi** (3-5 Hunslet Road, 0113 245 6377) and the classic marble, mahogany and mirrors of the legendary **Whitelocks** (Turk's Head Yard, Briggate, 0113 245 3950).

The smoothest soup of petits pois, mint and caviar; a rich duck foie gras with poached rhubarb; Dublin Bay prawns in a crisp batter; spring lamb with a ravioli parcel stuffed with ratatouille; brie laced with truffles; classic crêpe suzette filled with Seville orange and soused in cognac and Grand Marnier.

Raja's ★

186 Roundhay Road, LS8 5PL (0113 248 0411). **Lunch served** 11-2pm, **dinner served** 5-10.30pm Mon-Fri. **Meals served** 3.30-10.30pm Sat, Sun. **Main courses** £5.25-£7.95. **Credit** MC, V.

This year Raja's celebrates 20 years of supplying excellent north Indian food from this red-brick end terrace on Roundhay Road. It has smartened up, but the authentic tandoor oven remains, producing sharply flavoured chicken, lamb, sheekh kebab and wonderfully blistered naan straight off its clay sides. All the usual Punjabi dishes are here plus a new lobster masala. Trusty specials include makhan chicken and handi gosht. Plenty of vegetarian choices and an excellent takeaway service.

Room

Bond House, The Bourse Courtyard, Boar Lane, LS1 5DE (0113 242 6161/www.roomrestaurant.com). **Open** 11am-11pm Mon-Wed; 11am-2am Thur-Sat; noon-6pm Sun. **Meals served** 11am-6pm, **dinner served** 6-10.30pm Mon-Sat. **Brunch** served noon-6pm Sun. **Main courses** £14. **Pre theatre menu** (6-7pm, Mon-Sat) £15 2 courses, £18 3 courses incl one drink. **Credit** AmEx, DC, MC, V.

Almost too cool for its own good when it opened, Room has been generating more warmth amid its purple banquettes, glass bricks, split-level dining and atmospheric lighting. The menu turns junk food on its head with posh pie 'n' peas, duck pot noodle or turbot fish and chips, and while Dean Sowden's cooking has its rough edges, the whole package is driven along with great verve by owners John Pallagi and Simon Wright. Each month sees some new food event: North African night, Mother's Day lunch, champagne tasting. A welcome meltdown.

Salvo's

115 Otley Road, Headingley, LS6 3PX (0113 275 5017/www.salvos.co.uk). **Lunch served** noon-2pm Mon-Sat. **Dinner served** 6-10.45pm Mon-Thur; 5.30-11pm Fri, Sat. **Main courses** £6.90-£16.50. **Set lunch** £5 2 courses. **Set dinner** (6-7pm Mon-Thur; 5.30-7pm Fri) £10 2 courses, £12.95 3 courses. **Credit** AmEx, DC, MC, V.

It just rolls on. During the last 28 years the Dammone dynasty has barely missed a beat at this buzzing neighbourhood trattoria with its menu of Italian staples that invariably pleases all ages and all pockets. Bring the kids for Early Doors or go for the Rapido menu, two courses for a fiver might be spicy bean stew followed by pasta with meatballs. The carte has rump steak, venison steak, sea bass, calf's liver and plenty more. Everything comes in generous portions with heaped salads and vegetables. Equally traditional are the evening queues. Arrive early or be prepared to wait.

Sami's ★

49 Harrogate Road, Chapel Allerton, LS7 3PD (0113 262 1676). **Food served** 8am-3pm daily. **Dinner served** 6-11pm Mon-Sat. **Main courses** £6-£7. **Unlicensed. Corkage** no charge. **No credit cards.**

Quite a split personality, this place. By day it's a greasy spoon. At night out come the hookah pipes, decorative lanterns and ethnic cushions and we're in Sami's, in a Moroccan souk. It's still cheerful and, with nothing over £7, it's cheap. Begin with caponata or filo parcels of spiced mince. Follow up with a tagine of chicken and preserved oranges served with saffron rice, or couscous with marinated lamb, spiced chicken or vegetables.

Sous le Nez en Ville

The Basement, Quebec House, Quebec Street, LS1 2HA (0113 244 0108). **Lunch served** noon-2.30pm Mon-Sat. **Dinner served** 6-10pm Mon-Fri; 6-11pm Sat. **Main courses** £8.95-£17.50. **Set meal** (lunch Sat; 6-7.30pm Mon-Sat) £19.95 3 courses incl half bottle wine. **Credit** DC, MC, V.

The leisurely and alcoholic business lunch has never fallen out of fashion at this engaging dive. For 13 years a sharp wine list and a bargain of six plates of tapas for £9.50 has kept the bar buzzing long past a strict interpretation of the lunch hour. There's less character in the dining room but moules marinière, game, steak and pig's cheek cassoulet are reliably delivered. There's also good choice for vegetarians.

Tin Tin

Ground Floor, Minerva House, 29 East Parade, LS1 5PS (0113 245 1245). **Lunch served** noon-2.30pm daily. **Dinner served** 6-11.30pm Mon-Thur, Sun; 6pm-midnight Fri, Sat. **Main courses** £6.50-£22.50. **Set meals** £13-£26 (min 2 people). **Credit** AmEx, MC, V.

A long-awaited quality upmarket Chinese for Leeds' prosperous business district. The long Cantonese menu was disappointingly familiar so try one of the half dozen Malaysian dishes: 'special chicken' was sweetly spiced strips of chicken in coconut milk served in a hollowed-out coconut husk, while the crab curry brought on a roll-your sleeves-up whole shell-on crab drenched in a fiery sauce. It needed a small armoury of picks and crackers, plus finger bowls, napkins and hot towels, to complete a messy job and douse the fires – but it was worth it.

Also in the area

Brio Pizza The Courtyard, The Light, LS1 243 5533; **Casa Mia** 10-12 Stainbeck Lane, LS7 3QY (0113 266 1269); **Casa Mia Grande** 33-35 Harrogate Road, LS7 3PD (0113 239 2555); **Livebait** 11-15 Wharf Street, Shears Yard, The Calls, LS2 7EY (0113 244 4144); **The Living Room** 7 Greek Street, LS1 5RW (0870 442 2720); **Malmaison** Sovereign Key, LS1 1DQ (0113 398 1000); **Simply Heathcote's** Canal Wharf, Water Lane, LS11 5PS (0113 244 6611); **Tampopo** 15 South Parade, LS1 5QS (0113 245 1816); **Thai Edge** New Portland Place, 7 Calverley Street, LS1 3DY (0113 243 6333).

Newcastle

Barluga

35 Grey Street, NE1 6EE (0191 230 2306). **Lunch served** noon-4pm Mon-Sat; noon-5pm Sun. **Dinner served** 6-10pm Mon-Thur; Sun. **Main courses** £9-£15. **Set meal** £11.95 2 courses, £14.95 3 courses. **Credit** AmEx, DC, MC, V.

One of the best bars in town just got better. There's style in buckets at this city-centre bar-café, from the classical simplicity of the John Dobson exterior, to the bright, airy ground-floor bar area, and smartly contemporary decor of the lounge and dining areas. The snacks also have a fashionable edge: Cumberland sausage with spring onion and mustard mash; mussels and chips; tempura prawns with ponzu dipping sauce. Between 8pm and midnight every Friday and Saturday, caviar (not beluga) flows freely, offered on wafers by 'caviar hostesses'.

Barn @ the Biscuit

16 Stoddart Street, Shieldfield, NE2 1AN (0191 230 3338). **Lunch served** noon-2pm, **dinner served** 7-10pm Mon-Sat. **Main courses** £9-£16. **Credit** AmEx, MC, V.

In 2003, Barn Again relocated lock stock and cooker to the ground floor of the Biscuit Factory, Europe's largest commercial art gallery. Apart from the change to more spacious premises and a decor that's not quite as quirky as in the original bistro, the staff, chef and concept remain unchanged. French, Mediterranean and oriental flavours combine in an eclectic fusion that's about as exciting as it gets, foodwise, in this city. Blue swimmer crab spring roll with a cashew and shaved fennel salad and lime dressing will kick things off brilliantly; follow with pan-roasted chicken breast with Singapore laksa sauce, rice noodles, lime leaf and chilli. The daytime menu is a cheaper version of the evening carte.

Billabong Bistro & Bar

Caledonian Hotel, 68-72 Osborne Road, Jesmond, NE2 2AT (0191 281 7881). **Meals served** 10am-9.45pm daily. **Main courses** £8-£18. **Credit** AmEx, DC, MC, V.

The Caledonian Hotel is a popular and busy destination particularly at weekends. The Billabong, with its cool pastel decor, cheerful ambience and friendly staff, forms part of the attraction, its menu offering a wide choice of cosmopolitan dishes from light bites to more serious food. As well as the regular carte, look out for the specials, which might include duck and chicken liver terrine with apple and maple syrup preserve, followed by char-grilled medallions of fillet steak on sautéed leeks with stilton sauce. In addition to a comprehensive beer and cocktail list, the majority of the wines are available by the glass or 250ml pichet, with most bottles priced under £20.

Café Royal

8 Nelson Street, NE1 5AW (0191 231 3000). **Meals served** 11.30am-6pm Mon-Wed, Fri, Sat; 11.30am-8pm Thur; 10am-4pm Sun. **Main courses** £6.50-£11.50. **Credit** AmEx, MC, V.

A popular and modish daytime café, that's housed in an elegant listed building, contrasted by an up-to-date and stylish interior that wouldn't be out of place in Milan. The menu too, has that essential touch of continental chic, with flavoursome Mediterranean-influenced light bites. Choose from all-day faves such as grilled chicken club with crispy pancetta, roast tomatoes and avocado mayo, or salmon fish cakes with wilted greens and garlic cream. Just as tempting are blackboard specials like grilled sea bass with herb-crusted potatoes and tapenade.

Café 21 ★

19-21 Queen Street, Princes Wharf, Quayside, NE1 3UG (0191 222 0755). **Lunch served** noon-2.30pm, **dinner served** 6-10.30pm Mon-Sat. **Main courses** £11-£22. **Set lunch** £13.50 2 courses, £15.80 3 courses. **Credit** AmEx, DC, MC, V.

Terry Laybourne's stylish invocation of a smart French bistro wouldn't be out of place on one of the Left Bank boulevards, except that here the food is probably better and more imaginatively diverse than any similar place from Calais to Cannes. Choice is a real dilemma, and the addition of blackboard specials further complicates matters, but nicely so. A salad of ham knuckle with piccalilli and endive with soft-poached egg and mustard dressing is a truly outstanding starter. And as for the slow-cooked shoulder of pork with braised cabbage, black pudding mash and crackling – cracking! For a funkier experience from the same stable, there's Café Live, 27 Broad Chare, Quayside, NE1 3DF (0191 232 1331).

Caffè Zonzo

83-89 Goldspink Lane, Sandyford, NE2 1NQ (0191 230 4981/www.caffezonzo.com). **Lunch served** noon-2pm, **dinner served** 5.30-9.45pm Mon-Sat. **Main courses** £5.60-£12.65. **Set lunch** £4.50 1 course. **Credit** MC, V.

Cheerfully decorated, and airy, this is a popular neighbourhood bistro with a mean line in modern Italian food. The short regular menu is supplemented by specials, projected on to the walls instead of the usual blackboards. Starters come with own-baked rustic bread and are light and appetisingly assembled: cured meat or vegetable based antipasto; or toasted garlic-rubbed bread topped with sautéed chicken livers, sage and white wine. There's a short selection of excellent salads, imaginative pasta dishes and mains like pink-roasted duck breast with chestnuts, mushrooms and Marsala – but no pizzas.

The Cluny

36 Lime Street, Ouseburn, NE1 2PQ (0191 230 4474). **Meals served** noon-9pm Mon-Sat; noon-5pm Sun. **Main courses** £4-£6. **Credit** AmEx, MC, V.

Officially known as the Head of Steam, though everyone calls it the Cluny. Forming part of what was an old whisky bottling plant, it's now home to some of the region's top arts and crafts people. As well as having a gallery, it's also a major music venue. The kitchen keeps energy levels suitably high with daily-changing blackboard selections: there's everything from sandwiches (made to order) to lamb chilli and salsa burgers; and real chips with dip and side salad. Sunday roasts are very popular.

Fisherman's Lodge

Jesmond Dene, Jesmond, NE7 7BQ (0191 281 3281/ www.fishermanslodge.co.uk). **Lunch served** noon-2pm, **dinner served** 7-10.30pm Mon-Sat. **Main courses** £21-£36. **Set lunch** £22.50 3 courses. **Credit** AmEx, MC, V.

The location, in quiet wooded parkland, gives the impression of an idyllic rural retreat, yet Newcastle's most serious and formal restaurant is minutes from the city centre and is as classy and polished an act as ever. There's a definite contemporary edge to the cooking; menus feature sophisticated modern French dishes, with seafood from North Shields fish quay a major force. For dinner, beautifully presented roast quail breast with pancetta, tarte tatin of caramelised shallots and barolo sauce precedes flavoursome roast fillet of sea bass with basil tortellini, stuffed morels, asparagus, broad beans and thyme velouté. From the same stable as the Samling (*see p247*), Seaham Hall (*see p268*), and Treacle Moon (*see p278*).

King Neptune

34-36 Stowell Street, NE1 4XQ (0191 261 6657). **Lunch served** noon-1.45pm daily. **Dinner served** 6-10.45pm Mon-Fri; 6-11.30pm Sat; 6-10.30pm Sun. **Set lunch** £8 4 courses. **Set dinner** £13 2 courses, £17-80-£20.80 3 courses, £23.80-£30.80 4 courses. **Credit** AmEx, MC, V.

The restaurant name is a strong clue that seafood is a speciality on the extensive and varied menu. Among the starters, the most popular items are the Peking-style spare ribs and deep-fried squid with garlic and spiced salt, while classic aromatic crispy duck with steamed pancakes, spring onion and cucumber salad is excellent. With a sharing cuisine like Chinese, the fresh whole lobster, or Northumbrian crab stir-fried with ginger and spring onions, are great value. Staff are friendly; booking is essential.

McCoys at the Baltic ★

South Shore Road, Gateshead, NE8 3BA (0191 440 4949). **Lunch served** noon-1.45pm daily. **Dinner served** 7-9.30pm Mon-Sat. **Set lunch** £14.95 2 courses, £16.50 3 courses. **Set dinner** £28.50 2 courses, £33.50 3 courses. **Credit** MC, V.

Located on level six of the main building, this is now the only McCoy-run operation at the gallery. With a huge expanse of glass, the restaurant (the Rooftop) is wonderfully bright and the views amazing. Those familiar with the McCoy style will appreciate the terrifically eclectic food that's their hallmark. The food's a riot of colour and a feast of tastes: a starter of beetroot-cured salmon with char-grilled octopus, avocado purée and blood orange vinaigrette is out-of-this-world, as is char-grilled beef fillet with bacon and onion rösti, roast banana shallots, pancetta and port jus to follow. For dessert, a near-perfect white chocolate and Tia Maria soufflé comes with a fabulous morello cherry sorbet. There's a great wine list too.

The Cluny.

Pani's

61 High Bridge, NE1 6BX (0191 232 4366/ www.pani.net). **Meals served** 10am-10pm Mon-Sat. **Main courses** £5-£10. **Credit** MC, V.

A genuine touch of Italian magic in almost every respect, with more than a hint of Sardinia. During the day, fill up on deliciously satisfying ciabatta bread sandwiches: numero quattordici is a toasted number with meaty Italian sausage, tomato sauce and salad. Other choices include hot dishes like lasagne, or various salads. The evening menu is more ambitious.

Paradiso

1 Market Lane, NE1 6QQ (0191 221 1240). **Meals served** 11am-11pm Mon-Sat; 11.30-6pm Sun. **Main courses** £6-£14. **Set lunch** £6.95 2 courses, £8.95 3 courses. **Credit** MC, V.

A favourite destination for the city's bright young things. The ground floor is a popular New York-style lounge bar with a horseshoe bar counter, intimate corners and leather sofas. Climb the stairs to Paradiso and you're greeted with a devilishly stylish setting, with great alfresco dining options. The menu runs from lamb brochette with houmous, herb salad and coriander flat bread to a moreish royal thai fish casserole.

Treacle Moon

5-7 The Side, Quayside, NE1 3JE (0191 232 5537/ www.treaclemoonrestaurant.com). **Dinner served** 5.30-10pm Mon-Sat. **Main courses** £14.95-£23.95. **Set dinner** £14.95 2 courses, £19.95 3 courses. **Credit** AmEx, MC, V.

An intimate restaurant made even more romantic by soft lighting and a lilac and purple colour scheme. The unusual name comes from Byron, who, when asked how his honeymoon went, replied, 'Call it rather a treacle moon,' such was its sweetness. The short menu is a fashionably up-to-date mix of global influences. Start with thai confit duck salad before moving on to marinated lamb rump with baby leeks, red dahl and Madeira and tarragon jus. Under the same ownership as Fisherman's Lodge (*see p277*).

Valley Junction 397

Old Jesmond Station, Archbold Terrace, Jesmond, NE2 1DB (0191 281 6397). **Lunch served** noon-2pm Tue-Sat. **Dinner served** 6-11.30pm Tue-Sun. **Main courses** £6.95-£14.50. **Credit** AmEx, MC, V.

The No.397 Pullman railway carriage, which is part of this unusual Indian restaurant, was built for the Great Northern Railway at Doncaster in 1912. The interior provides a fun setting for well-prepared specialities from the sub-continent. There's choice in abundance, from vegetable pakora to salmon with fresh herbs, spices and sliced green chillies with a hint of orange zest.

Vujon

29 Queen Street, Princes Wharf, Quayside, NE1 3UG (0191 221 0601/www.vujon.demon.co.uk). **Lunch served** noon-2.30pm Mon-Sat. **Dinner served** 6-11.30pm daily. **Main courses** £7.90-£16.90. **Set meal** £20-£22 3 courses. **Credit** AmEx, DC, MC, V.

The smartest Indian restaurant in the north has a menu to match the elegant surroundings. Staff in brilliantly colourful waistcoats add to the allure. Foodwise, the emphasis is on subtle spicing, and flavours derived from fresh herbs and seasonings. Pakoras supreme is a starter selection of fish, chicken and vegetables. Although main courses major on lamb and chicken, there's also roast duck and boneless pheasant, plus salmon and monkfish.

Also in the area

Hide Bar The Gate, Newgate Street, NE1 5RF (0191 243 5558); **Malmaison** The Quayside, NE1 3DX (0191 245 5000).

Northumberland

ALNWICK

Carlo's ★

7-9 Market Street, Alnwick, NE66 1SS (01665 602787). **Meals served** 11.30am-10pm Mon-Sat. **Main courses** £3.05-£3.25. **No credit cards.**

Spread over two floors, this friendly town-centre chippy has been run by Italian Carlo Biagioni and his wife Laura for the past 15 years. With laminate-topped tables and clean, simple, modern lines, it's a typically informal fish and chip set-up with a thriving takeaway trade. All the fish comes from suppliers in the region, and though cod, battered and fried in vegetable oil is the most requested item that they sell, the menu also features a long list of alternatives: for example, smoked sausage; various pies (from steak and kidney to Scotch); sausages and hot dogs. There's even haggis available. Overall, however, it's the simpler, less manufactured things that taste best, and their exquisite chip butty can definitely be included among them.

GREAT WHITTINGTON

Queen's Head

Great Whittington, NE19 2HP (01434 672267). **Lunch served** noon-2pm Tue-Sun. **Dinner served** 6.30-9pm Tue-Sat. **Main courses** £10-£17. **Set lunch** (Tue-Sat) £10 2 courses; (Sun) £16 3 courses incl coffee. **Credit** MC, V.

Dating from 1615, the solid stone pub stands in an attractive village north of Hadrian's Wall. The emphasis is very much on food, served in the cottagey, candlelit dining room. Though ambitious, dishes are uncomplicated and enjoyable. Among the starters, deep-fried king prawns come with a sweet chilli and garlic sauce, and for a main herb-crusted rack of lamb has roast vegetables with redcurrant and rosemary jus. Their own Queens Head bitter is an alternative to wine.

Also in the area

Café 21 33-35 The Broadway, Darras Hall, NE20 9PW (01661 820357).

Tyne & Wear

CULLERCOATS

Bill's Fish Bar ★

4A Victoria Crescent, Cullercoats, North Shields, NE30 4PN (0191 253 5003). **Meals served** 11.30am-9.30pm daily. **Main courses** £3-£3.50. **No credit cards.**

The town's most notable restaurant is also one of the most famous fish and chip shops on Tyneside. Customers come from far and wide to eat here and enjoy the additional bonus of a great location overlooking the sea. It stands in a parade of shops right on the seafront, with a ground floor dedicated to supplying takeaways, while up on the first floor the simply furnished restaurant offers a more pleasant environment for the two most popular items on the short menu – prime cod and haddock. Fish comes from North Shields and is, as per tradition, cooked in beef dripping. The result is a wonderfully light crisp batter encasing moist, delicately flavoured fish. And to accompany, a portion of mushy peas is just the ticket.

HEDLEY ON THE HILL

Feathers Inn ★

Hedley on the Hill, NE43 7SW (01661 843607). **Open** noon-3pm Sat, Sun; 6-11pm Mon-Sat; 6-10.30pm Sun. **Lunch served** noon-2.30pm Sat, Sun, bank hol Mon. **Dinner served** 7-.30pm Tue-Sun. **Main courses** £7.50-£9.95. **Credit** MC, V.

High up in the hills, the Feathers requires good navigational skills to find, but it is worth the effort. Meals are served in both bars, but the lounge, comprising two small cosy rooms, is quieter; there are open fires in winter. Choose with confidence from the daily-changing blackboards as everything produced is own-made and truly excellent. The arrangement is that you can enjoy anything from a snack to three courses. Sweet potato, tomato and coconut soup, and Greek salad are typical starters. To follow, try goat's cheese and red onion tart, or chicken casserole in white wine with fennel. And don't miss out on sticky toffee pudding or chocolate brandy torte among the desserts.

SUNDERLAND

The Place Restaurant

11 Tavistock Place, Sunderland, SR1 1PB (0191 514 5000). **Lunch served** noon-2pm, **dinner served** 6-10pm Tue-Sat. **Main courses** £11.25-£17.50. **Set lunch** £9.95 2 courses, £11.95 3 courses. **Set dinner** (Tue-Fri) £11.95 2 courses, £13.95 3 courses. **Credit** MC, V.

A classy basement restaurant in a central location. The decor is cool, bright and contemporary with polished wood floor, modern art on the plain walls, and a laid-back ambience. Inspiration for the uncomplicated food comes from France, the Med and Far East. Flavours that hit all the right notes are found in Chinese duck salad with oriental dressing and prawn crackers, and parma ham, artichokes and seasoned greens with balsamic dressing. Grilled fillet steak, fine beans, thick-cut chips and Madeira sauce stood out among the mains. Bailey's cheesecake is a very moreish dessert.

Throwingstones

National Glass Centre, Liberty Way, Sunderland, SR6 0GL (0191 565 3939). **Lunch served** noon-2.45pm daily. **Dinner served** 7-8.30pm Fri, Sat. **Main courses** £4.95-£12.50. **Set meal** (5-6.45pm Fri, Sat) £7.95 2 courses incl tea or coffee. **Credit** MC, V.

Wearside and Teesside are running way behind Tyneside in the North-east's regeneration stakes but Sunderland can genuinely shout about the innovative National Glass Centre – and the neatly named restaurant that comes with it. Spacious and flooded with light from the wall of glass that gives views of the once mighty industrial landscape across the Wear, Throwingstones is gently pushing the envelope for a city with no gourmet traditions. Tomato and mozzarella salad with basil dressing, brie, bacon and caramelised onion tart to start; char-grilled steak, braised lamb hock or stuffed mushrooms with asparagus and brie to follow; plus plenty of popular puddings, sandwiches and snacks.

TYNEMOUTH

Sidney's

3-5 Percy Park Road, Tynemouth, NE30 4LZ (0191 257 8500/www.sidneys.co.uk). **Lunch served** noon-2.30pm Mon-Sat. **Dinner served** 6-9.45pm Mon-Sat. **Main courses** £10-£16. **Set lunch** £8.50 2 courses, £10.95 3 courses. **Set dinner** (6-7pm Mon-Fri) £9.95 2 courses, £12.95 3 courses. **Credit** AmEx, MC, V.

Close to the ancient ruins of Tynemouth Castle and Priory, this is a thoroughly up-to-date and smartly decorated bistro with burnt orange and purple walls, stripped wood floors, light wood furniture and a brushed stainless-steel bar counter. The short, imaginative menu lists dishes like cumin-rubbed lamb with sweet potato and feta salad; seared scallops with watermelon, pear and honey vinaigrette; pan-fried monkfish with chunky chips and garlic aïoli, and confit leg and pan-fried duck breast with carrot purée and game chips. Finish with turkish delight and chocolate parfait with raspberry compote.

Yorkshire

North Yorkshire

ASENBY

Crab & Lobster

Dishforth Road, Asenby, North Yorkshire YO7 3QL (01845 577286/www.crabandlobster.com). **Lunch served** noon-2.15pm daily. **Dinner served** 7-9.30pm Mon-Fri; 6.30-9.30pm Sat; 7-9pm Sun. **Main courses** £13.50-£35. **Set lunch** (Sun) £16.50 2 courses, £21.50 3 courses. **Credit** AmEx, MC, V.

Forty miles from the coast, the Crab & Lobster's fishing nets are filled with a self-conscious jumble of puppets, sheet music, race tags and old menus. Antique clutter invades every corner of this thatched pub, but the seafood tastes fresh: oysters, mussels, fish soup, deep-fried Thai crab cakes and a justly 'famous' club sandwich (hot and cold layers of prawn, salmon and white fish between toast and mayo). Mains include a £35 lobster thermidor with king prawn and scallops. Bargains are few, but that never deters people from packing out the place.

BOLTON ABBEY

Burlington

Devonshire Arms Country House Hotel, Bolton Abbey, North Yorkshire BD23 6AJ (01756 710441/ www.devonshirehotels.co.uk). **Lunch served** noon-2pm Sun. **Dinner served** 7-9.30pm daily. **Set meal** £58 5 courses. **Credit** AmEx, DC, MC, V.

The Duke of Devonshire's estate includes a stately home, two hotels, three restaurants and a farm shop. At the top of the Devonshire food chain, the Michelin-starred Burlington ticks all the right boxes for a sumptuous night out. Venison, pigeon, veal, turbot, duck and guinea fowl are the cornerstones for a deluxe sporting country hotel. Chef Phil Phillips artfully converts them into labour intensive, high-end dishes laced with langoustines, foie gras, ceps and truffles. With numerous *amuse-bouches* along the way, you can see where your money goes.

Devonshire Brasserie & Bar

Devonshire Arms Hotel, Bolton Abbey, North Yorkshire BD23 6AJ (01756 710710/www.devonshirehotels.co.uk). **Lunch served** noon-2.30pm Mon-Sat; noon-3.30pm Sun. **Dinner served** 6.30-10pm Mon-Sat; 5-9pm Sun. **Main courses** £9.75-£16.95. **Credit** AmEx, DC, MC, V.

Where the Burlington (*see above*) next door is hushed high church, the Brasserie sheds pomp in favour of a relaxed atmosphere, easy food and a dazzling Mediterranean blue colour scheme. All dishes are available as starters or main courses. The list roams cheerfully around sausage and mash, Thai fish cakes with lime and coriander mayonnaise, grilled goat's cheese and roast vegetables, and smoked haddock and pea risotto. Puddings are in the sticky toffee pudding mould. One criticism: the children's menu should grow out of its chicken nugget rut.

BOROUGHBRIDGE

Dining Room

20 St James's Square, Boroughbridge, North Yorkshire YO51 9AR (01423 326426). **Lunch served** noon-2.30pm Sun. **Dinner served** 7-9.30pm Tue-Sat. **Main courses** (Sun) £15. **Set meals** £19.95 2 courses, £23.50 3 courses. **Credit** MC, V.

This husband and wife operation works hard for a spotless, house-proud ethos that might be a touch prissy. Pre-dinner drinks are in a plush bar; the cream dining room keeps it formal with starched linen and smart service. Pleasant starters include a salad of celeriac remoulade and parmesan, or prawns with Thai flavourings. Mains of steak, guinea fowl and chicken served with vegetables were conventional but rescued by a super spring dessert of poached Yorkshire rhubarb and liquorice ice-cream. A welcome local restaurant that could benefit from undoing a button or two.

BURNSALL

Devonshire Fell Hotel & Restaurant

Burnsall, North Yorkshire BD23 6BT (01756 729000/ www.devonshirehotels.co.uk). **Lunch served** noon-3pm daily. **Dinner served** 6.30-10pm Mon-Sat; 6.30-9pm Sun. **Main courses** £10.50-£15. **Set dinner** £16 2 courses, £20 3 courses. **Credit** AmEx, DC, MC, V.

Once a country club for Victorian mill owners, then a sturdy hotel, the Fell is now the third restaurant in the Duchess of Devonshire's Wharfedale group (*see left*). The impressive setting (on the descent into Burnsall) and the vivid art play well alongside a menu that inhabits the middle ground between the Fell's two siblings. The first two courses are best, with a lively choice embracing roast fig galette with Sicilian ham, and a frothy watercress soup to start. Nidderdale lamb; or crab, sweetcorn and mange tout risotto typify the capably cooked mains.

CRAYKE

Durham Ox ★

Westway, Crayke, North Yorkshire YO61 4TE (01347 821506/www.thedurhamox.com). **Lunch served** noon-2.30pm Mon-Sat; noon-3pm Sun.

Dinner served 6-9.30pm Mon-Fri; 6-10pm Sat; 6-8.30pm Sun. **Main courses** £8.95-£14.50. **Set lunch** (Sun) £14.95 2 courses, £16.95 3 courses. **Set meals** (6-7pm Mon-Fri, 6-8.30pm Sun) £9.95 2 courses, £13.50 3 courses. **Credit** AmEx, MC, V.
The lovely whitewashed country inn looks timeless, but there's a refreshing restlessness within, as the carte changes monthly and the blackboard daily. Jason Plevey's assured British cooking works with the seasons and region. You could find asparagus with poached egg and spring onion mash, rack of new season lamb, pigeon salad on toasted brioche, or smoked haddock with poached egg and black pudding. Eat in a mezzanine bar amid inglenook and leather, outside on the deck or in the vivid blue more formal restaurant. After one of the fruity desserts, emulate the Grand Old Duke of York's men who reputedly marched up and down the hill outside.

FERRENSBY

General Tarleton

Boroughbridge Road, Ferrensby, North Yorkshire HG5 0PZ (01423 340284/www.generaltarleton.co.uk). Brasserie **Lunch served** noon-2.15pm, **dinner served** 6-9.15pm daily. **Main courses** £11-£17. **Set lunch** (Mon-Sat) £9.95 2 courses. *Restaurant* **Lunch served** noon-2.15pm Sun. **Dinner served** 6-9.15pm daily. **Set lunch** (Sun) £17.50 3 courses. **Set dinner** £29.50 3 courses. **Credit** AmEx, DC, MC, V.
Once a run-down roadside inn, the General was agreeably transformed by the folk behind the Angel at Hetton (*see p282*). Fish dishes stand out, with a grand fruits de mer for four at £49.50, king scallops with black pudding, cullen skink and Thai crab cakes. The fish soup is excellent. Meat eaters also fare well with Goosnargh duck breast, slow-roast saddle back pork, or Yorkshire lamb. The children's menu offers proper sausage and mash, own-made goujons, or pasta. All ages can indulge in treacle tart or Hetton mess for pudding. Eat in the spacious bar or more formally in the dining room.

HAROME

Star Inn ★

Harome, North Yorkshire YO62 5JE (01439 770397/www.thestaratharome.co.uk). **Lunch served** 11.30am-2pm Tue-Sat; noon-6pm Sun. **Dinner served** 6.30-9.30pm Tue-Sat. **Main courses** £9-£17. **Credit** MC, V.
If you want to eat in the Michelin-starred dining room, then stay in the luxury accommodation, you'll need to save up and book early. But if you turn up on spec at pub opening time you can eat in the lovely old polished oak bar, the best room on the premises. Either way it's a treat. Feast on Ryedale roe deer, Whitby crab, Fadmoor beetroot with Ragstone goat's cheese, or beef fillet reared on a village farm. For pudding, order Andrew Pern's signature dish of baked ginger parkin with rhubarb ripple ice-cream and hot spiced treacle. Throughout, the commitment to local, regional and seasonal ingredients is for real.

HARROGATE

Attic

62A Union Street, Harrogate, North Yorkshire HG1 1BS (01423 524400/www.attic-harrogate.co.uk). **Lunch served** noon-2pm, **dinner served** 6.30-10pm Mon-Sat. **Main courses** £10.95-£14.50. **Set meal** (noon-2pm Mon-Sat; 6.30-7.30pm Mon-Thur) £9.50 2 courses, £11.50 3 courses. **Credit** AmEx, DC, MC, V.
White sofas, a sleek bar, a big skylight and a vase of lilies set the mood at this smart bistro in a rejuvenated backstreet warehouse off swanky Parliament Street. There have been wobbles in consistency for the food, but generally it represents good value bistro cooking. Start with roquefort and chicory salad, lamb's kidney with girolles, or pea soup with ham hock. Main courses include steak, roast poussin, duck confit and a vegetarian dish such as chickpea and spinach curry.

Betty's Café Tea Rooms

1 Parliament Street, Harrogate, North Yorkshire HG1 2QU (01423 502746/www.bettysandtaylors.co.uk). **Meals served** 9am-9pm daily. **Main courses** £3.85-£9.50. **Credit** MC, V.
A queue is inevitable at Betty's, but the place is vast and the line moves quickly. A shop sells tea, coffee, chocolates and baked goods at the front of this handsome Edwardian building; the tea rooms are further in and continue into the basement. Once settled, you can succumb to the charms of the comforting food. Savouries are given as much importance as sweet stuff in a menu that features Swiss as well as Yorkshire specialities (Betty's was established by a Swiss chocolatier). So spring onion and mushroom rösti topped with raclette cheese shares space with Masham sausages. For afters there are Yorkshire curd tarts, but also Swiss tortes. Prices are highish – yet so is the quality.

Courtyard

1 Montpellier Mews, Harrogate, North Yorkshire HG1 2TQ (01423 530708). **Lunch served** noon-2.30pm, **dinner served** 6.30-9.30pm Mon-Sat. **Main courses** £10.95-£17. **Set meal** (noon-2.30pm, 6.30-7.30pm) £11.95 2 courses, £14.95 3 courses. **Credit** AmEx, MC, V.
Currently the best of the bistros and wine bars that dot Harrogate's antiques quarter, the Courtyard has had several incarnations. Wayne Benson is the latest chef. His bright, modern dishes complement a fresh, smart interior. Lunch could start with Whitby crab and salmon fish cake, with a leek and blue cheese fondue flavoured with truffle oil; followed by confit of duck leg, saffron potatoes and baby beetroot with a sharp tamarind sauce. Dinner, more expansive and expensive, deals in Nidderdale beef, poached sea bass, asparagus and wild mushroom torte.

Drum & Monkey

5 Montpellier Gardens, Harrogate, North Yorkshire HG1 2TF (01423 502650). **Lunch served** noon-2.30pm Mon-Sat. **Dinner served** 6.30-10.15pm Mon-Sat. **Main courses** £8.30-£21.50. **Credit** MC, V.

Despite new ownership, Harrogate's blazered colonels still order their oysters and Chablis over the slate bar – as they've done for 25 years. Nothing's changed except that Jan Fletcher, doyenne of Headingley's Bryans, has repaired the crumbling ceiling and electrics. So upstairs and downstairs, the lobster thermidor, plaice with prawn and brandy sauce, fish pie and other English ways with seafood march out to the same institutional beat. Time-warp or treasure? Either way, it looks indestructible.

Sasso ★

8-10 Princes Square, Harrogate, North Yorkshire HG1 1LX (01423 508838). **Lunch served** noon-2pm Tue-Sat. **Dinner served** 6.30-10pm Mon-Sat. **Main courses** £6.95-£16. **Set lunch** £6.95 2 courses. **Credit** MC, V.

Stefano Lancelotti's modest basement trattoria is seriously underrated. Pasta is made fresh here, and the difference shows. Try cannelloni filled with parsley and ricotta topped with gorgonzola and walnuts, ravioli stuffed with spinach and ricotta with wild mushroom and truffle sauce, or tagliatelle bolognese: three great bowls. Alternatives include roast chicken powered with fennel chutney, pork fillet wrapped in prosciutto, or duck breast with dried plums; proper panna cotta and tirasimu are for afters – high quality for a £6.95 lunch menu.

Villu Toots

Balmoral Hotel, Franklin Mount, Harrogate, North Yorkshire HG1 5EJ (01423 705805/www.villutoots.co.uk). **Lunch served** noon-2.30pm Sun. **Dinner served** 5-9pm Mon-Thur, Sun; 5-9.30pm Fri, Sat. **Set lunch** (Sun) £14.95 3 courses. **Set dinner** £15.95 2 courses, £19.95 3 courses. **Credit** AmEx, MC, V.

The Balmoral has fashioned a light contemporary dining room of blond wood and etched glass within its staid Harrogate shell. The Modern European cooking presses all the right buttons: carpaccio of tuna, a salad of shredded duck confit, roast scallops or goat's cheese with roasted vegetables. Mains might be red snapper, turbot, calf's liver or squab pigeon. Half a dozen desserts complete an elegant meal. It's suave but not snooty; Sunday lunches see plenty of kids perched on the Philippe Starck chairs.

HETTON

Angel at Hetton

Hetton, North Yorkshire BD23 6LT (01756 730263/www.angelhetton.co.uk). Bar **Lunch served** noon-2.15pm daily. *Bar & restaurant* **Dinner served** 6-9.30pm Mon-Sat; 6-9pm Sun. **Main courses** £12-£15. **Set lunch** (Mon-Sat) £8.75 2 courses. **Set dinner** (6-7pm Mon-Fri) £19.25 3 courses incl glass of wine. **Credit** AmEx, MC, V.

The Angel first took flight in this Dales village 21 years ago. Its popularity means there can be a scramble for tables among the oak-beamed nooks and crannies. But it's worth the scrap for a menu skewed towards fish, or comfort food like braised belly pork with black pudding and seared foie gras, calf's liver with Timothy Taylor's beer sauce, or braised oxtail on horseradish mash. Well-judged specials may include sea bass with red wine, cod with clams, monkfish with wild mushrooms, and sea bream with pesto. The terrific wine list is big on France. Atmosphere: green wellies.

INGLEBY ARNCLIFFE

McCoy's Bistro

The Tontine, Staddlebridge, nr Ingleby Arncliffe, North Yorkshire DL6 3JB (01609 882671/www.mccoysatthetontine.co.uk). Bistro **Lunch served** noon-2pm daily. **Dinner served** 7-9.30pm Mon-Thur, Sun; 7-10pm Fri, Sat. **Main courses** £17-£20. **Set lunch** (Mon-Sat) £12.95 2 courses, £14.95 3 courses; (Sun) £17.95 3 courses. **Set dinner** (7-8pm Mon-Thur, Sun) £16.95 2 courses, £18.95 3 courses. **Credit** AmEx, DC, MC, V.

The McCoy brothers are the patron saints of good food in the north-east. The upstairs dining room is now only open for private functions, as the basement and conservatory bistro has taken centre stage, but kitchen standards still impress. Oysters, mussels with chorizo, crab mayo, seafood pancake and wild mushroom tart are among a sharp-edged starter list. Mains offer sea bass with pak choi, noodles and coconut broth; halibut and wild mushroom gnocchi; rack of lamb with a herb crust; and foie gras and beef wellington: robust cooking.

MARTON

Appletree Country Inn

Marton, North Yorkshire YO62 6RD (01751 431457/www.appletreeinn.co.uk). **Lunch served** noon-2pm Wed-Sun. **Dinner served** 6.30-9.30pm Mon, Wed-Sun. **Main courses** £10-£16.90. **Credit** MC, V.

For a rural gastropub, the gaudy decor and highly ambitious food could benefit from loosening up a little. But Trajan Drew is wowing critics and customers with plates like venison with red wine and chocolate jus, sea bass on samphire, and truffled wild mushroom risotto. A test dish of deep-fried monkfish and bananas was no easy combination in its 1970s heyday; it still isn't today. Desserts aim high and score better. A marbled pyramid of white and dark chocolate filled with chocolate mousse, and a boozy griottine of cherry crème brûlée were show-stoppers.

OSMOTHERLEY

Golden Lion

6 West End, Osmotherley, North Yorkshire DL6 3AA (01609 883526). **Lunch served** noon-2pm, **dinner served** 6-9pm daily. **Main courses** £6.50-£13.95. **Credit** MC, V.

It looks so simple. Whitewashed walls, polished oak tables, big mirrors, a peat fire and an unchanging menu of sensibly priced, well-cooked food. Fish starters star mussels in wine and cream, crab mayonnaise, or grilled sardines. There are soups, a

Star Inn. *See p281.*

goat's cheese and red pepper terrine, a lovely lemon risotto, and spicy pork spare ribs. Hearty mains include beef stroganoff, cod and chips, lentil burgers or superb char-grilled poussin dripping in buttery rosemary and garlic juices. Seemingly simple, but Peter McCoy's back-to-basics pub makes it special.

RAMSGILL

Yorke Arms Country Inn

Ramsgill, Harrogate, North Yorkshire HG3 5RL (01423 755243/www.yorke-arms.co.uk). **Lunch served** noon-2pm daily. **Dinner served** 7-9pm Mon-Sat. **Main courses** £18-£21. **Set lunch** (Mon-Sat) £17.50 3 courses; (Sun) £29 3 courses. **Set dinner** £45 7-course tasting menu. **Credit** AmEx, DC, MC, V.

This 18th-century creeper-clad inn is home to some of Yorkshire's finest cooking. Frances Atkins uses excellent, often local, produce. She may contrast cheap and luxury materials in one dish, as with Yorkshire potted beef, ham hock and foie gras terrine with asparagus velouté and beetroot relish, or allow the flavour of one or two ingredients to shine – as in a glorious spinach and nutmeg soup. The setting for this quiet creativity is a calm, elegant room with an open fire for cold winter evenings. Service is professional and unobtrusive.

RIPLEY

Boar's Head Hotel

Ripley Castle Estate, Ripley, North Yorkshire HG3 3AY (01423 771888/www.boarsheadripley.co.uk). **Lunch served** noon-2pm, **dinner served** 7-9pm daily. **Set lunch** £13 2 courses, £16 3 courses. **Set dinners** £18.95-£33 3 courses. **Credit** AmEx, DC, MC, V.

The estate village of Ripley has history to spare. Sir Thomas Ingilby owns the castle, plus a hotel and bistro. The main dining room is all sparkling silver and glass, set against deep-red walls. Here the upmarket menu includes crab and scallop with mango and chilli salsa; tiger prawn and avocado mousse with 'spice of angel' sorbet; spring lamb with stuffed figs; and Jaffa Cake soufflé. In the bistro, staff dress down in polo shirts to serve ham hock and parsnip terrine, salmon on creamed leeks, and duck breast with chorizo for a good-value lunch.

SANDSEND

Estbek House

East Row, Sandsend, North Yorkshire YO21 3SU (01947 893424/www.estbekhouse.co.uk). **Dinner served** 6-9pm daily; *July, Aug* 4-9pm daily. **Main courses** £10-£16. **Credit** MC, V.

New management has reinvigorated the Estbek's attractive two-storey dining rooms, which are less formal than the hotel's smart black and yellow decor might suggest. Plus points were the child-friendly welcome for kids in sandy shoes, own-made burgers, big bowls of mussels and grilled local fish at very reasonable prices. There was room for improvement in sloppy service and dull desserts. The front courtyard offers a pleasant eating area in summer.

STAITHES

Endeavour ★

1 High Street, Staithes, North Yorkshire TS13 5BH (01947 840825/www.endeavour-restaurant.co.uk). **Dinner served** 7-9.30pm Tue-Sat. **Main courses** £10-£16. **Credit** AmEx, DC, MC, V.

Nonna's. *See p289.*

A small, homely restaurant fitting snugly into a cobbled fishing village, Endeavour delivers the freshest, most sophisticated seafood on Yorkshire's coast. The menu adapts daily to the region's catches with the 'crab tower' and whole lobster grilled with hazelnut butter reliably Staithes' finest. There's ray wing, fish cassoulet, roast sea bass served with a plum and star anise compote, and sea is steamed over seaweed. Look out for original desserts like a paperweight of Skinningrove orange wine jelly.

WATH

Sportsman's Arms

Wath-in-Nidderdale, Pateley Bridge, North Yorkshire HG3 5PP (01423 711306). Bar **Lunch served** noon-2pm daily. **Dinner served** 7-9pm Mon-Sat; 7-8pm Sun. *Restaurant* **Dinner served** 7-9pm Mon-Sat. **Main courses** £11.50-£15. **Set lunch** (Sun) £20 3 courses. **Credit** MC, V.

The Sportsman's is a 17th-century hotel and restaurant run for by the Carter family. The kitchen uses local produce: trout from the river, perhaps served with beurre noisette, and locally raised lamb roasted on spring cabbage with its juices. Starters might include smoked salmon on rösti or a goat's cheese camembert on roasted peppers. The dining room gleams; service shows corresponding polish.

WEST TANFIELD

Bruce Arms

Main Street, West Tanfield, North Yorkshire HG4 5JJ (01677 470325/www.brucearms.com). **Lunch served** noon-2pm Fri-Sun. **Dinner served** 6.30-9.30pm Tue-Sat. **Main courses** £10-£16. **Credit** MC, V.

The accent on the food at this Georgian country pub/bistro-with-bedrooms is as much English as French. Classical roots show in the fine hollandaise that puddles a slice of seared organic salmon, in the intense red wine sauce with the guinea fowl, and in a silky crème caramel. Modern touches come in dishes like confit of duck with shiitake mushrooms and lemon couscous. Much of the meat is reared close to this Dales village. Cheerful, not always swift service. Attractive outside terrace.

WHITBY

Finley's Café-bar

22-23 Flowergate, Whitby, North Yorkshire YO21 3BA (01947 606660). **Open** 10am-11pm Mon-Sat; 10am-10.30pm Sun. **Food served** 10am-10pm Mon-Sat; 10am-9.30pm Sun. **Main courses** £6.95-£9.95. **Credit** AmEx, DC, MC, V.

Lead planters, a split-level layout, leather sofas and a blackboard of tapas show this café-bar to be a sight more modern than the usual tea shop. Drop in for bacon and egg breakfast, a brie and bacon sandwich lunch, or early evening tapas of houmous, grilled peppers and feta. Mains include spicy chicken breast with tortilla, guacamole and sour cream, or proper burgers. Mellow and welcoming, with music at night.

Greens of Whitby

13 Bridge Street, Whitby, North Yorkshire YO22 4BG (01947 600284/www.greensofwhitby.com). **Lunch served** noon-2pm, **dinner served** 6-10pm daily. **Main courses** £11-£17. **Credit** MC, V.

Candlelight, old panels and a dark burgundy colour scheme make Greens a haven from busy harbour-side streets. Added comfort comes from Rob Green's

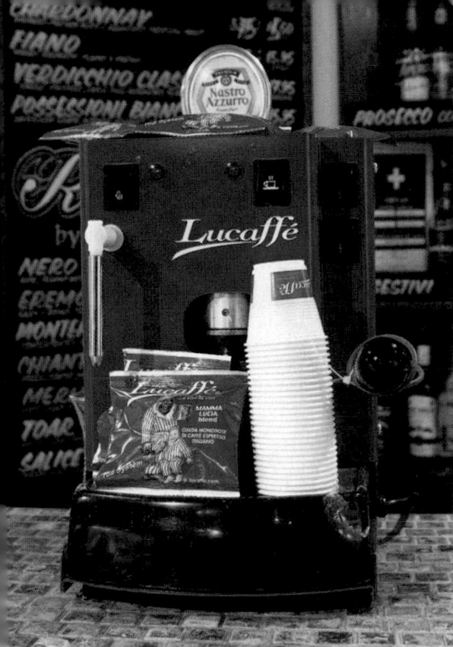

ham hock terrine with beetroot relish, char-grilled aubergines with tomatoes, local rump steak, crisp belly pork, Yorkshire lamb, and a simple but exceptional spaghetti and lemon. Fish, fresh from the quayside market, lines up with salt and pepper squid and grilled Whitby crab. Desserts – own-made ices, bitter chocolate and raspberry torte – sustain the quality. The best restaurant in town.

Magpie Café

14 Pier Road, Whitby, North Yorkshire YO21 3PU (01947 602058/www.magpiecafe.co.uk). **Meals served** 11.30am-9pm daily. **Main courses** £7.95-£17.95. **Credit** MC, V.

With the fish quay directly across the road, the monkfish, plaice, skate, lemon sole and catfish ('woof' on a Yorkshire menu) could hardly be fresher. These days the cod will probably come frozen from the Faroes or the Baltic, but the Magpie's ladies still serve it up sweet, flaking and crisply battered, alongside chunky chips. Though the fish menu is wide-ranging, cod and haddock dinners are the mainstays that have for decades spawned queues outside this old, whitewashed, seafarers' house.

North Beach Café

Sea Wall, North Promenade, Whitby, North Yorkshire YO21 3JX (01947 602066/www.northbeachcafe.co.uk). **Meals served** *June-Aug* 9am-9pm daily; *Sept-May* 9am-5pm Mon-Wed, Sun; 9am-9pm Fri, Sat. **Main courses** £7.95-£9.95. **Credit** MC, V.

This was last summer's dream location. Sandwiched between beach huts on Whitby sands was a spirited regeneration of a faded art deco café. The rooftop was all modern decking, glass bricks, barbecues and beer. Lively local and internationally inspired fish dishes were served in the aquamarine dining room downstairs. Sadly, summer 2004 arrived with an urgent need for a lick of paint; worse, all ambition drained from the menus under the new management. Sandwiches and jacket potatoes are available during the day, with the likes of grilled marlin steak in Cajun marinade, sausages on mustard mash, and daily specials in the evening. It's still a great spot on a sunny day. Let's hope things improve.

YARM

Chadwick's

104B High Street, Yarm, North Yorkshire TS15 9AU (01642 788558). **Meals served** 10am-5pm Mon-Sat. **Dinner served** 5.30-9.30pm Mon-Thur; 5.30-10pm Fri, Sat. **Main courses** £11.95-£16.50. **Credit** MC, V.

Although its Georgian setting is typically English, Chadwick's describes itself as 'a licensed continental café'. It certainly feels like one. There's good coffee at the zinc bar, sparky service, a globe-hopping wine list and a menu that offers sandwiches, continental meats, salads and tapas (black pudding and chickpeas, say). At dinner the aubergine dining room is buzzing, and the kitchen shifts up a gear to produce well-presented dishes like panna cotta of goat's cheese, and calf's liver on bubble and squeak. A pity that puddings don't quite reach this level.

YORK

Bengal Brasserie

York Business Park, Millfield Lane, Poppleton, North Yorkshire YO26 6PQ (01904 788808/www.bengal-brasserie.com). **Lunch served** noon-2pm Sat. **Dinner served** 6-11.30pm Mon-Sat. **Meals served** noon-10.30pm Sun. **Main courses** £4.95-£12.95. Set buffet (Sun) £10.95. **Credit** AmEx, DC, MC, V.

Set by a petrol station and the office blocks of a trading estate, the BB does its best by going for bright colours, contemporary design and modern art. Instead of the usual curries, try Bengali starters like stuffed green pepper, or nchar c kebab (deep-fried potato with lentil and coriander). The Bengali fondness for fish can be witnessed in specials of spicy marinated salmon, and macher salan – cod, cooked with the chef's 'secret' mix of spices.

Blakehead Vegetarian Café ★

Blakehead Bookshop, Micklegate, York, North Yorkshire YO1 6JX (01904 623767/www.blakeheadcafe.co.uk). **Meals served** 9.30am-3.30pm Mon-Sat; 10am-3.30pm Sun. **Main courses** £3.50-£5.95. **Credit** MC, V.

Blakehead Bookshop serves excellent vegan and vegetarian dishes in its art-filled conservatory: waffles with maple syrup for breakfast; scones mid-morning; and for lunch lentil and sorrel soup. Savouries include filo parcel of arami seaweed, carrot, ginger and shoyu. Cakes feature pear and ginger loaf. Quality can waver – our espresso was poor – but this isn't a production line.

Blue Bicycle

34 Fossgate, York, North Yorkshire YO1 9TA (01904 673990/www.thebluebicycle.com). **Lunch served** noon-2.30pm daily. **Dinner served** 6-9.30pm Mon-Sat; 6-9pm Sun. **Main courses** £14.50-£22. **Credit** MC, V.

It's the one with the old blue bicycle propped outside. Inside, a rustic dark wood floor, mismatched chairs and paint-effect walls make for intimacy in winter but a more oppressive enclosure at summer lunches. Asparagus soup with truffle oil, dressed crab, or beef fillet on leek and bacon mash were spring offerings. Fried halloumi with citrus salad, grilled sardines and crab ravioli, followed by swordfish or cajun chicken stood out from the main menu. End with Yorkshire cheeses, or white chocolate and pistachio nut parfait. Good enough, but not as hot as some critics suggest.

Café Concerto

21 High Petergate, York, North Yorkshire YO1 7EN (01904 610478/www.cafeconcerto.biz). **Meals served** 10am-10pm daily. **Main courses** £9.95-£15. **Credit** MC, V.

A cosy café-bar quietly thriving on simple food well done. There's ageing sheet music on the walls, old wooden floorboards and a relaxed clientele. Thick, chunky tomato soup comes with a dollop of pesto and a grating of parmesan. Warm baguettes are brimming with bacon and brie, or cold with spiced chicken. Hot dishes include a wedge of frittata and soothing sausage and mash. Round off with a carrot, honey and walnut cake.

The Ivy

The Grange Hotel, 1 Clifton, York, North Yorkshire YO30 6AA (01904 644744/www.grangehotel.co.uk). **Lunch served** noon-2pm Sun. **Dinner served** 7-10pm Mon-Sat. **Main courses** £17-£23. **Set lunch** (Sun) £12.95 2 courses, £15.95 3 courses. **Set dinner** £28 3 courses. **Credit** AmEx, DC, MC, V.

In a charming Regency townhouse hotel, the Ivy is dressed with starched linen and polished silver. There's a choice of six dishes at every course, with seasonal, local ingredients given a French accent. Thus: Whitby crab mayonnaise, loin of Swaledale lamb fillet with wild garlic leaves; Yorkshire pork stuffed with Agen prunes; and a plate of rhubarb-themed desserts. Lunches are served in the more casual brick-vaulted basement brasserie. Try chorizo scotch egg with buttery couscous and sweet chilli salsa (surprisingly successful). There's also a fish bar and a sumptuous lounge for afternoon teas.

Melton's Too ★

25 Walmgate, York, North Yorkshire YO1 9TX (01904 629222/www.meltonstoo.co.uk). **Meals served** 10.30am-10.30pm Mon-Sat; 10.30am-9.30pm Sun. **Main courses** £6.90-£11.90. **Credit** MC, V.

A lively offspring of the more grown-up Melton's, Too is a clever act. It is open all day, in an historic street, and staff don't seem to mind if you dawdle over a coffee at lunchtime or order a dinner mid-afternoon. You can have vegetarian full English breakfast, tapas, sandwiches, salads, fish cakes or orange cakes; main dishes include lamb and apricot tagine, Thai green curry or duck cassoulet with Toulouse sausage. The house wine is organic. There's a warren of bare brick rooms to choose from, prices are sensible and the kitchen delivers well.

Middlethorpe Hall

Bishopthorpe Road, York, North Yorkshire YO23 2GB (01904 641241/www.middlethorpe.com). **Lunch served** 12.30-1.45pm, **dinner served** 7-9.30pm daily. **Set lunch** (Mon-Sat) £16.50 2 courses, £19.50 3 courses; (Sun) £23.50. **Set dinner** £37.95 3 courses. **Credit** MC, V.

This impeccable Queen Anne house, set in parkland by the racecourse, delivers textbook country house living: embedded antiques, panelled dining room, well-oiled service. Dinner's a candlelit extravaganza, from red mullet with courgette flowers and slow-roast beef with asparagus and wild mushrooms, to chocolate fondant with iced cherry yoghurt and pistachio jelly. Leave the wine list to the racehorse owners. For an each-way bet, pop in for afternoon tea in one of many elegant drawing rooms or on the lawns and sip Tippy Assam with cucumber sandwiches, toasted teacakes, scones, cream, cakes, biscuits, and a glass of champagne: £21.50.

Rish ★

7 Fossgate, York, North Yorkshire YO1 9TA (01904 622688/www.rish-york.co.uk). **Lunch served** noon-2.30pm daily. **Dinner served** 7-10pm Mon-Thur, Sun; 6.30-10pm Fri, Sat. **Main courses** £11.75-£23.75. **Set lunch** £15 2 courses, £18.50 3 courses. **Credit** AmEx, DC, MC, V.

The creamy smooth two-floor dining room already looked sleek, but this year Rish made a dramatic new signing in Gavin Aitkinhead (ex-Winteringham Fields). His silky skills were displayed in a three-course lunch: delicately spiced sautéed squid with black olives, preserved lemon and sweet chilli pepper; grilled sea bass with caramelised chicory and orange sauce; and a superb chocolate fondant with pistachio ice-cream. The à la carte has some of the priciest dishes in Yorkshire: Swaledale lamb and aubergine purée costs £22.50; roast lobster with beignet of courgette flower is £23.50.

St William's

5 College Street, York, North Yorkshire YO1 7JF (01904 634830). **Lunch served** noon-2.30pm, **dinner served** 5.30-10pm daily. **Main courses** £14.25-£15.45. **Set dinner** (5.30-6.45pm Mon-Fri, Sun) £12.50 2 courses, £15 3 courses. **Credit** AmEx, DC, MC, V.

Some setting. By York Minster and with tables outside in the courtyard of a fine medieval hall, St William's could be truly special. It isn't, but is a cut above most cafés on the tourist route. The self-service counter can be let down by poor coffee and a humdrum choice. Roast vegetables and couscous, and chicken casserole were the pick of the hot lunches. There are tempting cakes too. At night, candlelight and tablecloths come into play, and food includes competently served duck confit with pancetta and haricot beans, and roast vegetable galette with goat's cheese. Desserts (brûlée, sticky toffee pudding, cheesecake) are strictly mainstream.

Tasting Room

13 Swinegate Court East, York, North Yorkshire YO1 8AJ (01904 627879/www.thetastingroom.co.uk). **Lunch served** 11.30am-3pm daily. **Dinner served** 6-9.30pm Tue-Thur; 6-10pm Fri, Sat. **Main courses** £9.95-£18.50. **Credit** MC, V.

A year after opening the Tasting Room, Sally Robinson and Nigel Stacey's commitment to quality food is coming good. Bread is from Ottavio Bocca's excellent deli in High Petergate; try it with soup, as sandwiches, or with a light plate such as smoked haddock rarebit on garlic crostini. In the evening, the bustling lunch room turns into a calm, candlelit restaurant and the menu stretches to beef fillet carpaccio, bouillabaisse with garlic rouille, or chicken with tarragon. Vegetarians get four mains, including wild mushroom and asparagus steamed pudding with herb and garlic broth.

Also in the area

Aagrah York Road, Steeton, Tadcaster, North Yorkshire LS24 8EG (01937 530888); **Aagrah** Unicorn House, Devonshire Place, Keighley Road, Skipton, North Yorkshire BD23 2LR (01756 790807); **Bengal Brasserie** 21 Goodram Gate, York, North Yorkshire YO21 2LW (01904 613 131); **Bengal Brasserie** 4 High Street, Market Weighton, North Yorkshire YO43 3AH (01430 876 767/768); **Betty's Cafe Tea Rooms** 188 High Street, Northallerton, North Yorkshire DL7 8LF (01609 775154); **Betty's Café Tea Rooms** 6-8 St Helens Square, York, North Yorkshire YO1 8QP (01904 659142); **Bizzie Lizzie's** Albion Yard, Otley Street, Skipton, North Yorkshire, BD23 1ED (01756 793785); **Brio Pizza** 44 Commercial Street, Harrogate, North Yorkshire, HG1 1TZ (01423 529933); **Hide Bar** 32 High Street, Yarm, North Yorkshire TS15 9AG (01642 355558); **Hotel du Vin & Bistro** Prospect Place, Harrogate, North Yorkshire, HG1 1LB (01423 856800); **Little Bettys** 46 Stonegate, York, North Yorkshire YO1 8AS (01904 622865); **Living Room** 1 Bridge Street, York, North Yorkshire YO1 6DD (0870 220 3001); **McCoys in Yarm** At Strickland & Holt, 44 High Street, Yarm, North Yorkshire TS15 9AE (01642 791234); **Loch Fyne** Town Centre House, Cheltenham Parade, Harrogate, North Yorkshire HG1 1DD (01423 533070); **Miller's Famous Fish & Chips** 77 Main Street, Fulford, York, North Yorkshire YO10 4PN (01904 637301).

South Yorkshire

SHEFFIELD

Blue Moon Café ★

2 St James' Street, Sheffield, South Yorkshire S1 2EW (0114 276 3443). **Open** 8am-8pm Mon-Sat. **Main courses** £5.25. **Credit** AmEx, DC, MC, V.

For good vegetarian (and vegan) food (GM-free) in friendly surroundings, this is the place. Although busy at times, the high barrel-vaulted ceiling – rediscovered during renovation work – and huge windows mean that the feel remains airy and peaceful. Breakfast, snacks and full meals are offered at the counter. Soup of the day is served with hearty bread, while daily specials such as summer roasted vegetable casserole are served with a choice of up to six salads. A selection of cakes, such as pear upside-down cake are always available; the daily papers, organic soft drinks, wines and beers complete the welcome. Centrally located next to Sheffield cathedral.

Blue Room Brasserie

798 Chesterfield Road, Sheffield, South Yorkshire S8 0SF (0114 255 2004). **Dinner served** 6-9.45pm Mon-Thur; 6-10.30pm Fri, Sat. **Main courses** £6-£17. **Credit** MC, V.

Lively at weekends, this stylish, modern restaurant offers substantial British dishes (plus oriental sizzlers) in a spacious pillared dining area next to a relaxed and welcoming bar. All are made welcome, with children also in evidence early evening. There are limited vegetarian options on a menu centred on traditional dishes such as suckling pig with red cabbage, though fish also features. Puddings – nut brownie with honey ice-cream – are substantial. The exterior and location remain unprepossessing but it's a great place for a big night out.

Curator's House Restaurant & Tea Rooms

Botanical Gardens, Clarkehouse Road, Sheffield, South Yorkshire S10 2LN (0114 268 7788). **Lunch served** 11.30am-2.30pm daily. **Dinner served** 7-9.30pm Tue-Sat. **Main courses** £12.50-£15. **Credit** MC, V.

This intimate restaurant in a converted lodge building overlooks the Botanical Gardens (currently flourishing after years of restoration work). Tearoom by day, the menu changes in the evening to one of Sheffield's most inventive. Starters might be roast fennel and lemon soup or seared scallops with beetroot crisps and houmous; mains the likes of seared sea bass on crab and shellfish linguine or roast fillet of beef with potato, artichoke and tarragon. Puddings include chocolate hazelnut tart with crushed hazelnut ice-cream and banana tarte tatin. The wine list is helpfully descriptive and there are some nice touches, such as the speciality bread and own-made petits fours with coffee. Larger groups can be seated in the modern extension.

Kashmir Curry Centre ★

121-125 Spital Hill, Sheffield, South Yorkshire S4 7LD (0114 272 6253). **Dinner served** 5pm-midnight Mon-Sat. **Main courses** £4-£6.50. **Set dinner** £8-£11 3 courses. **No credit cards**.

The walls may now show art for sale, and the chairs might have floral fabric covers, but this remains one of Sheffield's legends, a cheap and cheerful curry café. Freshly cooked ingredients are combined to the customer's taste. Starters include the usual mushroom and onion bhajis as well as masala chops and poppadoms. Breads are delicious and freshly cooked: peshwari or garlic naans are particularly good. A small selection of desserts, including pistachio kulfi, and a choice of sweet lassis satisfy the sweetest tooth. It's not licensed but hand-pulled beer and lager can be brought over by the glass or jug from the pub opposite.

Lion's Lair

31 Burgess Street, Sheffield, South Yorkshire S1 2HF (0114 263 4264). **Meals served** noon-8.45pm Mon-Thur; noon-8.15pm Fri, Sat; noon-7pm Sun. **Main courses** £7.50-£11.95. **Credit** MC, V.

That rare thing, a city centre pub with good food. Booking is advisable in busy periods, though attentive service ensures that all-comers are accommodated if possible. A compact front room, plus a small beer garden out back. A full menu and daily specials that focus on fresh seafood and traditional-with-a-twist dishes are not particularly cheap, though puddings such as rum and truffle bread and butter pudding are delicious and good value. Drinks include guest ales, decent wines (many by the glass) and cocktails (£5).

Nonna's

537-541 Ecclesall Road, Sheffield, South Yorkshire S11 8PR (0114 268 6166/www.nonnas.co.uk). **Lunch served** noon-3.30pm Mon-Thur; noon-4pm Fri, Sat; noon-5pm Sun. **Dinner served** 6-9.45pm daily. **Main courses** £7.95-£13.95. **Credit** MC, V.

This immensely popular Italian enterprise now comprises a restaurant, espresso bar, bar and wine shop. At Saturday lunchtime the place was soon packed. The low-ceilinged space is pleasantly cluttered, the staff well-meaning but disorganised. The lengthy menu is authentically Italian and portions generous, but cooking is variable: farfalle puttanesca came with a meagre, oily sauce; risotto of the day (wild mushroom with thyme and lemon) was unexciting. But a hefty slab of salt cold was excellent, served with creamy minted peas and good mash. Top marks for the olives, own-made bread and chips too. Puds include a moist, fluffy almond, pine nut and orange cake. Prices rise a bit at dinner.

Rafters ★

220 Oakbrook Road, Nether Green, Sheffield, South Yorkshire S11 7ED (0114 230 4819/www.rafters restaurant.co.uk). **Dinner served** 7-9.30pm Mon, Wed-Sat. **Set dinner** £27.50 3 courses. **Credit** AmEx, MC, V.

A restaurant with a respected history in the area, Rafters has been taken over in the past year by the former chef, who still mucks in on the food front. Subtle changes in the upstairs dining room have modernised the interior and new, young staff are friendly and efficient. The menu remains a serious food experience and is pretty much the same as before, with starters such as crab millefeuille or roast asparagus, rocket and parmesan salad, and main courses of canon of Derbyshire lamb herbed and served with a vegetable purée. Traditional puddings and cheeses are particularly good. The wine list varies from good basic wine by the glass to some pricey bottles and vintages. One of Sheffield's finest.

Thyme

32-34 Sandygate, Crosspool, Sheffield, South Yorkshire S10 5RY (0114 266 6096/www.thymefor food.co.uk). **Lunch served** noon-2pm daily. **Dinner served** 6-9.30pm Mon-Sat; 6-9pm Sun. **Main courses** £10-£20. **Set lunch** (Mon-Sat) £12 2 courses, £16 3 courses; (Sun) £20 3 courses. **Set dinner** £24.50 3 courses. **Credit** AmEx, MC, V.

This modern bistro has developed greatly since chef proprietor Richard Smith opened here as Smiths Restaurant some years ago. Now also open upstairs (which can be booked for private dining), both floors are light, bright and somewhat noisy. This is not the place for an intimate discussion, but it has a loyal clientele. The ingredients are sourced carefully and local products featured where possible; for example, canon of Derbyshire lamb from the local Chatsworth estate. Fish is fresh and excellently cooked; puddings are divine. Service is friendly and helpful.

Thyme Café

490 Glossop Road, Sheffield, South Yorkshire S10 2QA (0114 267 0735/www.thymeforfood.co.uk). **Lunch served** 11am-3pm daily. **Dinner served** 5-9.30pm Mon-Sat. **Main courses** £4-£15. **Credit** MC, V.

Thyme Café, sibling to the posher Thyme (*see above*) in Crosspool, is the most intelligent café to open in Sheffield for years. It is located in the university district, and though some students might struggle to afford own-made cheeseburger and fries at £8, there are other less pricey goodies like fish and chips, plus a knockout meat and potato pie. Cutlery comes in a bucket on the table along with a bottle of HP sauce; service comes with a smile. But for all the jokiness and fizzy atmosphere, food is serious.

Also in the area

Aagrah Great North Road, Woodlands, Doncaster, South Yorkshire, DN6 7RA (01302 728888); **Hide Bar** 3 Wood Street, Doncaster, South Yorkshire, DN1 3LH (01302 760777).

West Yorkshire

ADDINGHAM

Fleece ★

152-154 Main Street, Addingham, West Yorkshire LS29 0LY (01943 830491). **Lunch served** noon-2.15pm, **dinner served** 6-9.15pm Mon-Sat. **Meals served** noon-8pm Sun. **Main courses** £5.75-£13. **Credit** MC, V.

There's no booking, just grab a pint of Black Sheep and a seat in the stone-flagged bar, choose from the blackboard above the fireplace, and tuck into hearty

North East

English dishes. Food is satisfying rather than subtle. There's roast loin of Gloucester Old Spot, slow-cooked shoulder of lamb, saddle of hare, and lots of fish. For once, kids aren't palmed off with junk; their menu has mussels, goat's cheese salad, fish and chips, minute steak, and roast chicken with rosemary and lemon. Puds include apple and plum crumble, and calvados and apple bread and butter pudding. Tables outdoors and barbecues in summer.

BRADFORD

Akbar's ★

1276 Leeds Road, Thornbury, Bradford, West Yorkshire BD3 8LF (01274 773311/www.akbars.co.uk). **Dinner served** 5pm-midnight Mon-Thur; 4.30pm-midnight Fri; 4pm-midnight Sat; 2-11pm Sun. **Main courses** £4.50-£8.25. **Credit** MC, V.

Shabir Hussain's Kashmiri restaurant has grown in size and scope since it began nine years ago. There are now 200 seats, most filled every night, often by families. The decor is sleek and modern, and service is quick. Baltis feature, but best is the 'Indian food cooked as we would eat at home'. Karahi keema and peas owes its verve to chilli and fresh lemon, while tarka dahl has a subtlety not always associated with the dish. For accompaniment there's fine cinnamon-scented rice or naans the size of duvets.

Karachi ★

15 Neal Street, Bradford, West Yorkshire BD5 0BX (01274 732015). **Meals served** 11am-1am Mon-Thur; 11am-2am Fri, Sat. **Main courses** £3.40-£5. **No credit cards**.

Not the smartest Asian café in the city, but one of the oldest and certainly the most quirky. A job lot of repro Regency chairs and faux-marble tables has nudged it upmarket, but the formula's still the same. Bag a seat, choose from the peg-board menu, order at the kitchen hatch and expect swift service. Crisply fried onion pakora, cardamom-rich chicken and spinach, and zingy keema and peas are cooked in a domestic style refreshingly different from that of a curry house. Don't expect anything more elaborate than a chapati to mop up the food.

Mumtaz Paan House ★

286-300 Great Horton Road, Bradford, West Yorkshire BD7 3HS (01274 571861/www.mumtaz.co.uk). **Meals served** 11am-midnight daily. **Main courses** £5.99-£9.50. **Credit** AmEx, DC, MC, V.

The Victorian cottages that housed Mumtaz when it opened in 1979 have all but disappeared under a swathe of contemporary steel and glass. The latest innovation is a cutting-edge deli, containing goodies from kebabs to ready-cook curries, and a paan bar. The place has grown glitzier, yet the food is still punchy, and the restaurant remains alcohol free. Crisp pakora, rich in garlic and fresh coriander, may be followed by on-the-bone lamb and spinach karahi, and aromatic chicken methi. Some main portions come as regular or large, for which read large or giant. Rice and breads are reliably fresh.

Nawaab ★

32 Manor Road, Bradford, West Yorkshire BD1 4QE (01274 720371/www.nawaab.net). **Lunch served** noon-2pm Mon-Fri. **Dinner served** 5.30-11.30pm Mon-Thur; 5.30-12.30am Fri, Sat; 4-11pm Sun. **Main courses** £5-£11. **Set lunch** £7.95 3 courses. **Set dinner** £10-£22 3 courses. **Credit** AmEx, DC, MC, V.

Head chef Pervez Akhtar created his award-winning nirali special ten years ago; the diced chicken arrives in a silver-topped casket, the creamy sweetness of its tomato-based sauce lifted by fresh chilli heat and the muskiness of cloves. Nawaab now has branches from Manchester to Majorca, but standards remain high back at this opulently attired former bank. Don't miss the dahl, memorable for its pungent tarka of scorched onions and garlic.

CLECKHEATON

Aakash ★

Providence Place, Bradford Road, Cleckheaton, West Yorkshire BD19 3PN (01274 878866/870011/www.aakashrestaurant.com). **Dinner served** 6-11pm Tue-Sun. **Main courses** £6.95-£11.95. **Credit** AmEx, DC, MC, V.

'Cleckheaton is a town where the carnival begins when both street lights are turned on', runs a local joke. Iqbal Tabassum changed all that with the conversion of a chapel into a mammoth Indian restaurant. With its cloud-painted ceilings and pastel pulpit and organ pipes it must be the most kitsch. The food can be good – raan-e-changezi is braised lamb fizzing with ginger, and you can expect fresh-flavoured muttar paneer and chilli-rich bindi dopiaza – but buffet dishes can tire. Try the carte first. Service is concerned and attentive.

DENBY DALE

Aagrah ★

250 Wakefield Road, Denby Dale, Huddersfield, West Yorkshire HD8 8SU (01484 866266/www.aagrah.net). **Dinner served** 6-11.30pm Mon-Sat; 6-10.30pm Sun. **Main courses** £4.75-£8.95. **Set dinner** £14-£15 2 courses (minimum 4 people). **Credit** AmEx, MC, V.

Now run by Mohammed Aslam's Shipley-based Aagrah chain, this roadside restaurant (and former pub) is buzzing again. Good-value Indian food can be eaten in the ground-floor bar or upstairs. Stand-out dishes include marinated chicken liver tikka, kashmiri kebabs, chicken hyderabadi and keen-edged lamb achar (with fenugreek and mustard seeds). Service is mostly quick and friendly.

ELLAND

La Cachette

31 Huddersfield Road, Elland, West Yorkshire HX5 9AW (01422 378833). **Lunch served** noon-2.30pm Mon-Sat. **Dinner served** 6-9.30pm Mon-Thur;

Shibden Mill Inn. *See p293.*

6-10pm Fri, Sat. **Main courses** £8.95-£15.95. **Set lunch** £8.95 2 courses. **Set dinner** (Mon-Thur; 6-7pm Fri, Sat) £15.95 3 courses incl half bottle wine. **Credit** AmEx, MC, V.

New head chef, Jonathan Nichols, has brought fresh fizz to the impressively long menu at this Gallic-inspired bistro. There's an uptown feel to the place, an impression unhindered by a long, bright, interesting, fairly priced wine list, and an owner-manager who has worked as a sommelier at some swanky places. The kitchen can dish up a perfectly fried fish cake, robustly dressed salad leaves, zinging Dover sole, and a fine ribeye with peppercorn sauce. Puddings are lively too. For intimate dining there are candlelit corners, while for those of a more sociable nature or in large groups, dining booths extend off the bar.

HAWORTH

Weaver's

15 West Lane, Haworth, West Yorkshire BD22 8DU (01535 643822/www.weaversmallhotel.co.uk). **Lunch served** noon-2pm Wed-Fri, Sun. **Dinner served**

6.30-9pm Tue-Sat. **Main courses** £9.95-£16.95. **Set meals** (lunch; 6.30-7.30pm Tue-Thur, 6.30-7pm Fri) £12.95 2 courses, £15.95 3 courses. **Credit** AmEx, DC, MC, V.

Catering can reach its wuthering depths in Haworth but this restaurant-with-rooms is a beacon. Care is evident in the cooking and sourcing of local food. Weaver's is a cosy warren in which to enjoy mushroom tart with ribblesdale cheese, Lune Valley lamb shank, chicken glazed with moorland honey, or dales beef with skin-on chips. Staff are obliging.

HONLEY

Mustard & Punch

6 Westgate, Honley, West Yorkshire HD9 6AA (01484 662066/www.mustardandpunch.co.uk). **Lunch served** noon-2pm Tue-Fri. **Dinner served** 6-9.30pm Mon-Thur; 6-10pm Fri, Sat. **Main courses** £9.95-£15.95. **Set lunch** £10.50 2 courses incl coffee. **Set dinner** (6-9.30pm Mon-Fri; 6-7pm Sat) £16.95 3 courses. **Credit** AmEx, DC, MC, V.

Bright combinations on the carte of this smart local restaurant range from soused mackerel with grilled black pudding, pickled vegetables and jus xeres, to rabbit with braised lettuce and chorizo. The set dinner boasts juicy sirloin with exemplary fries, calf's liver on braised cabbage, and a stonking rhubarb crumble with crème anglaise. A routine house white lets down the good wine list.

ILKLEY

Box Tree

37 Church Street, Ilkley, West Yorkshire LS29 9DR (01943 608484/www.theboxtree.co.uk). **Lunch served** noon-2.30pm Tue-Sun. **Dinner served** 7-9.30pm Tue-Sat. **Main courses** £12.50-£22. **Set meal** £19.50 2 courses. **Credit** AmEx, DC, MC, V.

Once a stellar restaurant, the Box Tree has lived in the past over recent years: the grandiose wine list, the gilded antiques, the ballotine of rabbit with foie gras and truffles, and the smoked salmon mousseline with caviar and pickled cucumber. There has been a revolving door of chefs, but at the time of writing, chef Simon Gueller (ex Rascasse and 3 York Place) had arrived and the place had closed for a refurb, so it's possible the glory days could return.

Farsyde

1-3 New Brook Street, Ilkley, West Yorkshire LS29 8DQ (01943 602030/www.thefarsyde.co.uk). **Lunch served** 11.30am-2pm, **dinner served** 6-10pm Tue-Sat. **Main courses** £10.95-£14.95. **Set lunch** £12.95 3 courses. **Set dinner** (6-7.15pm Tue-Thur) £12.95 2 courses. **Credit** MC, V.

Farsyde's new premises are big, bright and sophisticated and the food has lost nothing in the move. Gavin Beedham confidently produces a menu of British fare with Mediterranean flourishes: pig's cheek with black pudding, grilled mackerel with new potatoes and bacon, well-judged risottos and pastas. Own-made ices make satisfying finales.

KIRK DEIGHTON

Bay Horse

Main Street, Kirk Deighton, Wetherby, West Yorkshire LS22 4DZ (01937 580058). **Lunch served** noon-2pm Tue-Sun. **Dinner served** 6-9.15pm Mon-Sat. **Main courses** £9.95-£18.95. **Set lunch** (Sun) £13.50 2 courses, £15.50 3 courses. **Set dinner** (6-7pm) £13.95 2 courses. **Credit** MC, V.

Chef Karl Mainey now runs this village pub off the A1. The gastropub conversion peeved a few locals shorn of their favourite alehouse, but the stone-flagged entrance doubles as a snug and the kitchen still does sandwiches. Calm decor and gentle service go down well with the professional crowd. The menu ranges from comfort food such as fish pie and black pudding salad, to nicely pink char-grilled tuna over rocket with tomato and lemon chutney, and daily specials like tempura oysters. There's also a good wine list with 16 by the glass.

MARSDEN

Olive Branch

Manchester Road, Marsden, West Yorkshire HD7 6LU (01484 844487/www.olivebranch.uk.com). **Lunch served** noon-2pm Wed-Fri. **Dinner served** 6.30-9.30pm Tue-Sat. **Meals served** 1-8.30pm Sun. **Main courses** £10.50-£17.50. **Set meal** (noon-2pm Wed-Fri; before 7pm Tue-Thur, Sun) £13.95 2 courses, £16.95 3 courses. **Credit** MC, V.

Proprietor John Lister may have handed the kitchen to Paul Kewley, but the menu is still written on cards pinned to every surface. The contemporary dining space at the back of this 17th-century former inn has stunning moorland views, yet most diners prefer the open-fire, beams and scrubbed pine tables of the bar, where they can expect exciting cooking of first-rate ingredients. Try the wild sea bass with mixed leaves, vanilla oil and tapenade, or the roast duck with chillies, ginger and coriander. Sunday lunch is a bargain. Extensive wine list; good-natured service.

MILL BANK

Millbank

Mill Bank, West Yorkshire HX6 3DY (01422 825588/www.themillbank.com). **Lunch served** noon-2.30pm Tue-Sat; 12.30-4.30pm Sun. **Dinner served** 6-9.30pm Tue-Thur; 6-10pm Fri, Sat. **Main courses** £8.95-£17.95. **Set meal** (noon-2.30pm Tue-Sat; 6-7pm Tue-Fri) £10.95 2 courses incl coffee. **Credit** MC, V.

This Pennine pub has a new conservatory, a new owner, and a revamped outdoor dining area – but Glen Futter's cooking glides along unfazed. The Millbank aims to bring city-cool to the country. It does this with sharp service, a savvy wine list and a classy brasserie menu. Futter's take on staples like belly pork (served with linguini and oriental sauce) and shoulder of lamb (braised with white beans, smoked bacon, pine nuts and basil) works well and the beehive lemon meringue shows wit in its rehab of a classic. Real ales are served in the snug.

ROYDHOUSE

Three Acres Inn

Roydhouse, Shelley, Huddersfield, West Yorkshire HD8 8LR (01484 602606/www.threeacres.com). **Lunch served** noon-1.45pm, **dinner served** 7-9.30pm daily. **Main courses** £10-£16. **Set meal** (Sun) £17.95 3 courses. **Credit** AmEx, MC, V.
This 19th-century village inn has been extended sideways, backwards and upwards to incorporate a bistro, fish bar, deli, terrace, private dining room and bedrooms. The dining areas, filled with antiques, are constantly busy. The menu is stuffed with comfort food like potted shrimps, or steak, kidney and mushroom pie with mustard shortcrust. But there's also space for sprightly cooking of feuilleté of wild mushrooms in a tarragon and truffle cream, and fresh mackerel fish cakes with sorrel and spiced ratatouille salsa. Staff cope well with the crowds.

SALTAIRE

Old Tramshed ★

Saltaire Roundabout, Saltaire, West Yorkshire BD18 4DH (01274 582111). **Lunch served** noon-2.30pm, **dinner served** 5.30-9.30pm daily. **Main courses** £4.95-£10. **Set lunch** £8.95 2 courses. **Credit** MC, V.
Don't be deterred by the theme pub clutter and Victoriana that wastes this fantastic lofty space. Happily the food is far from off-the-peg, including a perfectly pitched Caesar salad and asparagus with lobster, fried egg and parmesan. The restaurant and bar menu ranges through mussels, mackerel with mustard sauce, halibut and saffron mash, Dover sole or sea bass, steak and chips, lamb with corned beef hash, roasts and pastas. There are also homely puds, Yorkshire cheeses, live jazz and gourmet evenings.

Salts Diner ★

Salts Mill, Saltaire, West Yorkshire BD18 3LB (01274 530533). **Open** 10am-5.30pm, **meals served** 10am-4.30pm daily. **Main courses** £7-£10. **Credit** MC, V.
The funky Salts Diner is set in the heart of a huge Victorian Italianate mill brilliantly converted into a gallery for the work of David Hockney. The food from a bustling open-plan canteen never quite lives up to the location, but this is a great spot for coffee or a relaxed lunch of salmon kebab, wild mushroom risotto or Caesar salad. Different in style is the third-floor fish bar. Among its heavy drapes, chandeliers and bottle-green walls staff serve herring salad, smoked haddock rarebit, seafood salad, and grilled cod. All pretty unbeatable by Bradford's standards.

SHELF

Bentley's

12 Wade House Road, Shelf, West Yorkshire HX3 7PB (01274 690992/www.bentleys-foodand wine.co.uk). **Lunch served** noon-2pm Tue-Fri. **Dinner served** 6.30-9pm Tue-Sat. **Main courses** £10.50-£18. **Set lunch** £5.95 1 course, £9.25 2 courses, £10.25 3 courses. **Credit** MC, V.
The dining room at this family-run bistro lies down stone steps past the kitchen. Here, Paul Bentley and his team make almost everything on the menu, from bread to pasta to ice-cream. The stone-flagged, vaulted cellar lends a traditional feel, but dishes like flash-fried goat's cheese with two syrups, and duck breast with noodles and spicy fruit are of the moment. The brio continues in breasts of wild pigeon on roast saffron bread with wild mushroom and tarragon gravy, and a compelling toffee and banana bread and butter pudding. Friendly service.

SHIBDEN HEAD

Shibden Mill Inn

Shibden Mill Fold, Shibden Head, West Yorkshire HX3 7UL (01422 365840/www.shibdenmillinn.com). **Lunch served** noon-2pm Mon-Sat; noon-7.30pm Sun. **Dinner served** 6-9.30pm Mon-Sat. **Main courses** £6.95-£15. **Credit** AmEx, MC, V.
Time will tell how damaging the loss of chef Adrian Jones will be after he breathed new life into this sprawling old whitewashed pub-hotel near Halifax. An early visit suggested the food was holding up better than the welcome. Eat in the candlelit dining room, the beamed bar or outside Jones bequeathed a menu of English classics with a twist: ham and eggs with own-made pineapple chutney; macaroni cheese with smoked mackerel fritter; slow-roast pork shank with a spicy sauce of chorizo, cabbage and new potatoes; rice pudding with jam sauce.

SOWERBY

Traveller's Rest

Steep Lane, Sowerby, Halifax, West Yorkshire, HX6 1PE (01422 832124). **Lunch served** 12.30-2.30pm Sat; noon-8pm Sun. **Dinner served** 6-9.30pm Wed-Fri; 6-10pm Sat. **Main courses** *bar* £8.50, *restaurant* £15.95. **Set meal** (Sun) £12.95 2 courses, £15.95 3 courses. **Credit** MC, V.
Sitting in isolated splendour, this gastropub is divided into bar and restaurant. Handsome use is made of exposed stone in the bar; the restaurant is modern, in line with Darren Collinson's cooking. He goes for zesty flavours and complex alliances like pan-fried sea bass on slow-roasted red pepper filled with roasted artichoke and tomato confit with basil oil; and crab cocktail with Bloody Mary dressing and aubergine fritter with chive crème fraîche.

Also in the area

Aagrah Aberford Road, Garforth, Leeds, West Yorkshire, LS25 2HF (0113 287 6606); **Aagrah** 483 Bradford Road, Pudsey, West Yorkshire, LS28 8ED (01274 668818); **Aagrah** 4 Saltaire Road, Saltaire, Shipley, West Yorkshire, BD18 3HN (01274 530880); **Aagrah** Barnsley Road, Sandal, Wakefield, West Yorkshire, WF1 5NX (01924 242222); **Betty's Cafe Tea Rooms** 32 The Grove, Ilkley, West Yorkshire LS29 9EE (01943 608029); **Nawaab** 35 Westgate, Huddersfield, West Yorkshire, HD1 1NY (01484 422775).

Scotland

Scotland
0
75 miles
0
120 km
© Copyright Time Out Group 2004
North Ronaldsay
Westray
Sanday
Rousay
Stronsay
Stromness
Kirkwall
Hoy
St Margarets Hope
South Ronaldsay
Pentland Firth
Thurso
John O' Groats
Durness
Skerray
Portskerra
Port of Ness
Balchrick
Tongue
WESTERN ISLES
Mybster
Wick
North Minch
Culkein
Unapool
Altnaharra
Stornoway
Drumbeg
Kinbrace
Lybster
Outer Hebrides
Isle of Lewis
Lochinver
Achiltibuie
Taransay
Lairg
Brora
Ullapool
Dornoch Firth
Pabbay
Harris
Berneray
Kincardine
Dornoch
Braemore Junction
Gairloch
North Uist
Moray Firth
Invergordon
Lossiemouth
Little Minch
Macduff
Buckie
Fraserburgh
Cromarty
Elgin
Colbost
Achnasheen
Forres
Benbecula
Nairn
Applecross
Skye
Keith
Inverness
Mintla
Kishorn
Peterhead
Grantown-on-Spey
Craigelliachie
Huntly
Inner Hebrides
South Uist
Kyle of Lochalsh
Drumnadrochit
Inverurie
Ellon
Canna
Invermoriston
Aviemore
Dyce
Ardvasar
Aberdeen
Barra
Invergarry
Kingussie
Mallaig
Newtonmore
Banchory
Braemar
Eigg
Stonehaven
Spean Bridge
Dalwhinnie
Fort William
Laurencekirk
Johnshaven
Coll
Pitlochry
Brechin
Tobermory
Montrose
Glencoe
Forfar
Aberfeldy
Tiree
Port Appin
Blairgowrie
Arbroath
Mull
Dundee
Carnoustie
Oban
Firth of Tay
NORTH SEA
Iona
Auchterarder
Perth
Cairndow
Callander
Cupar
St Andrews
ATLANTIC OCEAN
Glenrothes
Colonsay
Dunblane
Alloa
Jura
Stirling
Dunfermline
Cowdenbeath
Crinan
Helensburgh
Firth of Forth
Denny
North Berwick
Tarbert
Dunoon
Dumbarton
South Queensferry
Gullane
Dunbar
Tighnabruaich
Greenock
Glasgow
Falkirk
Linlithgow
Islay
Livingston
Edinburgh
Rothesay
Paisley
Bute
Eyemouth
Sound of Jura
Hamilton
Berwick-upon-Tweed
Dalry
Peebles
Arran
Galashiels
Kilmarnock
Biggar
Melrose
Coldstream
Brodick
Troon
Muirkirk
Kelso
Prestwick
Cumnock
Campbeltown
Ayr
New Cumnock
Rathlin I.
Maybole
Sanquhar
Turnberry
Moffat
Thornhill
Kielder
Ballantrae
Morpeth
New Galloway
NORTHUMBERLAND
Londonderry (Derry)
Lockerbie
Kirkcolm
Newton Stewart
Dumfries
Newcastle-upon-Tyne
Crossmichael
Gretna
Annan
Stranraer
Glenluce
Kirkcudbright
Dalbeattie
Carlisle
TYNE & WEAR
Larne
Solway Firth
Whithorn
Alston
Durham
Antrim
Luce Bay
Wigtown Bay
DURHAM
Drummore
BELFAST
Bangor
Workington
Penrith
Keswick
CUMBRIA
Darlington
Armagh
Windermere
Monaghan
Ramsey
Northallerton
Kendal
Hawes
Isle of Man
Douglas
Dundalk
Castletown
LANCS
NORTH YORKSHIRE
Morecambe

Edinburgh

The Atrium ★

10 Cambridge Street, EH1 2ED (0131 228 8882/ www.atriumrestaurant.co.uk). **Lunch served** noon-2pm Mon-Fri. **Dinner served** 6-10pm Mon-Sat. **Main courses** £16-£21. **Set lunch** £9.50 1 course, £13.50 2 courses, £17.50 3 courses. **Set dinner** £25 3 courses. **Credit** AmEx, DC, MC, V.

A top-end dining experience often equates with linen as crisp as the waiter's manner, and a table so cluttered with crystal that you're scared to look sideways. Not here. Andrew Radford opened the Atrium back in 1993, setting a new benchmark for fine dining in the Scottish capital. There's an enduring modern design that still looks good after more than a decade, low lighting, a skilled kitchen and professional but approachable staff; it all adds up to Edinburgh's most relaxed destination restaurant. In recent years it has introduced a bargain lunch menu, which might bring salt cod fish cake with a perfect poached egg to start; breast of maize-fed chicken with artichoke and mushroom ragoût as a main; then a zingy glazed lemon tart with crème fraîche for dessert. The full lunch and dinner menus are in a similar modern European vein, and there's an award-winning wine list.

Centotre

103 George Street, EH2 3BS (0131 225 1550/ www.centotre.com). **Lunch served** 11.45am-3pm Mon-Sat. **Dinner served** 6-9pm Mon-Wed; 6-10pm Thur-Sat. **Meals served** 11am-6pm Sun. **Main courses** £10-£22.95. **Credit** AmEx, MC, V.

Victor and Carina Contini are part of the Valvona and Crolla dynasty (*see p306*) but after years with the family business wanted to try something different – Centotre followed in spring 2004. It's an all-day Italian eaterie sympathetically introduced into a classic Georgian space: a former bank with pillars and delicate cornicing way up there; enthusiasm and modernity down where the people eat. The approach – from breakfast through to dinner – is simple food with good ingredients. A typical appetiser would be prosciutto de parma with roasted trevisana lettuce, balsamic, rocket, and parmigiano reggiano; pastas come as starters or mains (tortelloni with pumpkin and ricotta, butter and sage sauce); and Centotre will run to a 400g chargrilled T-bone, Florentine style, with salt and lemon. Pizza is a real feature however, and truly excellent (fior di latte, italian greens, pancetta, and tomato perhaps). The choice for a final course would include classics like crema cotta, ice-creams that actually taste Italian and a couple of very good cheeses. Initially, excitement generated by the opening meant occasionally scatty service, but that didn't preclude deserved and laudatory reviews. What's more, the wine list is compact but exceptional, and the grappa list truly educational.

Channings

12-15 South Learmouth Gardens, EH4 1EZ (0131 315 2225/www.channings.co.uk). **Lunch served** 12.30-2.30pm Tue-Sat. **Dinner served** 7-10pm Tue-Thur; 6.30-10pm Fri, Sat. **Set meal** £39.50 7 courses, £59.50 7 courses with wine. **Credit** AmEx, DC, MC, V.

This is a smart suburban hotel about 15 minutes' walk from the west end of Princes Street. It feels much more out of the way than that, though, so it's good for anyone who likes a bit of peace but wants to stay relatively close to the pulse. There are two basement restaurants: a Mediterranean bistro (Ochre Vita) and a fine dining room. The latter has come to prominence since the appointment of Hubert Lamort as chef in autumn 2002. He worked at the now-defunct (fitz)Henry in Leith and has brought a modern European flair to his new environment: foie gras 'bonbon' with poached baby pear, vanilla and pear compote; braised pork cheeks with spices, creamed quinoa and stuffed cabbage; banana and date samosa with blood orange sorbet, mint and citrus salad. Discreet dining to a high standard.

David Bann ★

56-58 St Mary's Street, EH1 1SX (0131 556 5888/www.davidbann.com). **Meals served** 11am-10pm Mon-Thur, Sun; 11am-10.30pm Fri, Sat. **Main courses** £9.50-£10.50. **Credit** AmEx, MC, V.

There are Indian vegetarian restaurants in Edinburgh, considerate upmarket establishments that offer a separate meat-free menu, even vegetarian eateries doing meat dishes on the side, but David Bann is still the best vegetarian restaurant in the city by some way. He opened here in 2002 after establishing a reputation at the now-closed Bann UK in Hunter Square. There's a flexible approach, so if you want a quick coffee (from 11am) or a light snack that's fine. But you could also have a good lunch or dinner: Thai courgette and sweetcorn fritters with papaya salad, hot garlic sauce and mango relish to start; an elaborate filo parcel as a main, stuffed with artichoke heart and gubbeen artisan cheese from Ireland; then meringue with lime and ginger parfait to finish. The wine list is short and affordable, and there's a great weekend brunch.

Dusit

49A Thistle Street, EH2 1DY (0131 220 6846/ www.dusit.co.uk). **Lunch served** noon-3pm, **dinner served** 6-11pm Mon-Sat. **Meals served** noon-11pm Sun. **Main courses** £7.95-£17.95. **Set lunch** £9.95 2 courses. **Credit** AmEx, MC, V.

If an Edinburgh resident of the 1990s had taken a few years out then returned early in 2004, their first statement would surely have been: 'Where did all the Thai restaurants come from?' Many of these new arrivals have been fairly unimaginative in terms of decor, but not Dusit. The dining room is up some steps to the rear of the premises and adorned with Thai masks in glass cases. Buddhas abound, the floor is tiled, and the effect echoes a cross between an upmarket restaurant and an arty museum. The menu is fairly extensive – and far from cheap – with everything from traditional tom yum soup to curries, wok dishes, seafood and vegetarian options. Stand-outs include the char-grilled duck starter with shallots, cashews, coriander, mango and garlic-chilli dressing (ped chom yong); crispy sea bass with soy, ginger and spring onion from the seafood list (pla si-el); and the wonderful coconut cream rice (kao mun kati). Wines are generally under £20.

Ecco Vino

19 Cockburn Street, EH1 1BP (0131 225 1441).
Meals served noon-10pm Mon-Sat; 12.30-10pm Sun. **Main courses** £5.95-£8.50. **Credit** AmEx, MC, V.
Between the main railway station and the Royal Mile, Ecco Vino sits in the middle of Edinburgh's tourist country. Fortunately, this wine bar is far from a tourist trap. It opened in 2001 with a simple formula: an affordable wine list, Italian providing the ballast, and some straightforward but laudable food. The space is oblong with leather banquette seating and tables along one wall (wine bins above), the bar opposite. The decor now looks a little lived-in, but no one minds. There are 44 wines, the vast majority under £20 and with 19 by the glass. The menu offers simple starters (bruschetta, antipasti), assorted focaccia (chorizo, vegetables and mozzarella), various frittata, excellent tarts (goat's cheese, basil and tomato) and robust pasta dishes. There's always a meat stew as a daily special (Italian sausage, say) and some simple desserts. So it's possible to do one course, three courses or just drink the wine. A dependable refuge.

First Coast

99-101 Dalry Road, EH11 2AB (0131 313 4404/www.first-coast.co.uk). **Lunch served** noon-2pm, **dinner served** 5-11pm Mon-Sat. **Main courses** £6.95-£12.95. **Set meal** (lunch, 5-6.30pm) £5.95 1 course, £10 2 courses, £12.50 3 courses. **Credit** MC, V.
In Edinburgh the best restaurants are very good, while the cheap 'n' cheerful are legion. What the city has traditionally lacked (in comparison to London, for example) are neighbourhood eateries with reliably high standards but reasonable prices. Thankfully, in spring 2003 along came the MacRae brothers from Skye with First Coast: Allan does front of house, Hector is the chef. It has a bistro atmosphere with white and light blue decor, a touch of bare stone, dark wood tables and cheerful staff. On offer are starters such as spicy fish cakes with coriander and chilli dip, or steamed mussels with garlic and parsley cream. There are accomplished vegetarian and meat choices, but the kitchen does wonders with unfashionable fish: try ling fillet with pea, potato, olive and tomato stew as a main. Puddings are crowd-pleasers; wine is affordable.

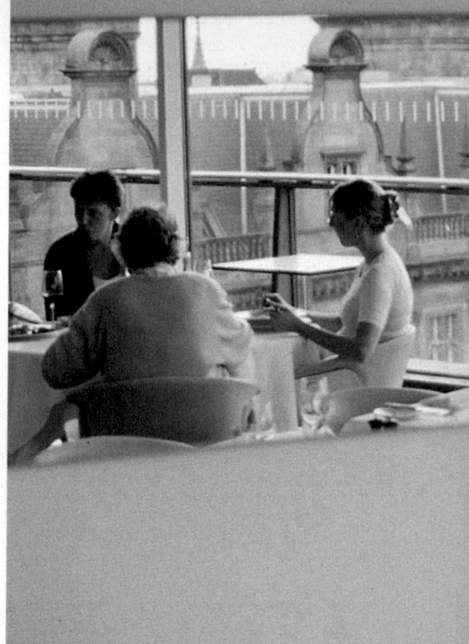

Harvey Nichols Forth Floor.

Fishers in the City

58 Thistle Street, EH2 1EN (0131 225 5109/ www.fishersbistros.co.uk). **Meals served** noon-10.30pm daily. **Main courses** £9-£26.95. **Credit** AmEx, MC, V.
The original Fishers dates back to 1991 and is well established as one of the city's best seafood bistros (1 The Shore, Leith, EH6 6QW, 0131 554 5666). So it made absolute sense to open this city centre version in 2001. It's a smart eaterie which blends a seafood theme with a modern touch. The menu is ever-changing, apart from a short list of hardy perennials like the brilliant creamy fish soup. You might be lucky enough to visit when Lindisfarne oysters are available (poached), or fresh halibut (pan-fried on a mixed herb salad). Otherwise dinner could involve grilled half-shell queenie scallops glazed with sun-dried tomato and mint butter; seared tuna on braised leeks with rocket gnocchi and a gravy made from red wine, mushroom and truffle; then chocolate truffle cake with wild berry coulis for pudding. Lively atmosphere, decent wine list.

La Garrigue

31 Jeffrey Street, EH1 1DH (0131 557 3032/ www.lagarrigue.co.uk). **Lunch served** noon-2.30pm Mon-Sat. **Dinner served** 6.30-10pm Mon-Sat;

5.30-10pm Sun. **Main courses** £12.50-£18. **Set lunch** £9.50 2 courses, £13.50 3 courses. **Set dinner** (Mon-Thur, Sun) £15.50 2 courses, £19.50 3 courses; (Fri, Sat) £17.50 2 courses, £21.50 3 courses. **Credit** AmEx, MC, V.

Sneaking quietly on to the scene in summer 2001, La Garrigue has settled into the role of Edinburgh's specialist Languedoc restaurant. Sitting on the sweep of Jeffrey Street, the front of the premises has a grand open view over to Calton Hill, while decor is in keeping with the restaurant's food philosophy: rustic but with a touch of quality (tables and chairs by the late Tim Stead, English sculptor and furniture-maker). Chef Jean Michel Gauffre was once at the Sheraton Grand in Festival Square, but here he's focusing on the cuisine of southern France – country food with a contemporary twist: duck and apricot terrine, a rich cassoulet with walnut salad, a simple but neat lemon tart. With some great regional wines available as well, it's almost like being back in Castelnaudary.

Haldane's ★

39A Albany Street, EH1 3QY (0131 556 8407/ www.haldanesrestaurant.com). **Lunch served** noon-1.45pm Mon-Fri. **Dinner served** 5.45-9pm Mon-Thur, Sun; 6-9.30pm Fri, Sat. **Main courses** £16.95-£24.50. **Set meal** (lunch, 5.30-7pm) £17.50 2 courses. **Credit** DC, MC, V.

Haldane's has been around since the mid-1990s when George and Michelle Kelso decided to up sticks from the hotel they ran in Kentallen (round the corner from Glencoe) and establish their own country house-flavoured restaurant in the Scottish capital. Housed in a basement on the eastern fringes of New Town, there's lots of white linen and a traditional drawing room feel to the dining areas (overlooking a small garden at some tables, an open fire at others). George Kelso is the chef and his menu focuses very much on high-quality Scottish ingredients in a Franco-Caledonian style: tian of Shetland crab and smoked trout; saddle of Highland venison with celeriac and bacon mousse; a fine mixed berry parfait with roast strawberries for dessert. The wine list is as serious as the food.

Harvey Nichols Forth Floor

Harvey Nichols, 30-34 St Andrew's Square, EH2 2AD (0131 524 8350/www.harveynichols.com). Brasserie **Meals served** 10am-6pm Mon; 10am-10pm Tue-Sat; noon-6pm Sun. **Main courses** £9-£12. **Set lunch** £14 2 courses, £17.50 3 courses. **Set dinner** £10 2 courses, £13.50 3 courses. *Restaurant* **Lunch served** noon-3pm Mon-Fri; noon-3.30pm Sat, Sun. **Dinner served** 6-10pm Tue-Sat. **Main courses** £12-£18. **Set lunch** (Sun) £18.50 2 courses, £22.50 3 courses. **Credit** AmEx, DC, MC, V.

The famous posh shop touched down in Edinburgh's New Town towards the end of 2002. Since then, even anti-fashion sceptics have admitted that its fourth-floor restaurant and bar-brasserie are pretty good. The views are tremendous (including north to the Firth of Forth, hence the punning name), the decor is modern and funky, and the kitchen has already won awards. During the day shoppers can snack, but at night there's a real buzz under the red,

recessed ceiling lights. The restaurant has a slightly more elaborate menu than the bar-brasserie – and better sightlines – but it's effectively one space, discreetly divided by a glass partition. Highlights include asparagus wrapped in pancetta with black pudding and roquefort dressing to start; pan-fried duck breast with beetroot risotto and roast fig as a main; then a generous apple crumble cheesecake with toffee sauce for dessert.

Henderson's Salad Table & Wine Bar ★

94 Hanover Street, EH2 1DR (0131 225 2131/ www.hendersonsofedinburgh.co.uk). **Lunch served** 11.30am-3pm, **dinner served** 4.30-10pm Mon-Sat. **Main courses** £5.50-£6.75. **Set lunch** £7.95 2 courses. **Set dinner** £9.50 2 courses. **Credit** AmEx, MC, V.

Back in 1963, the year it opened, the idea of a vegetarian canteen in the city must have seemed astonishingly radical – but over the decades Henderson's has thrived. Basically it's a self-service restaurant with seating on counter level (eat 'n' go) or in a cellar space down a few stairs, where lingering feels more appropriate. There are various soups, salads that seem like a meal in themselves and assorted hot dishes such as aubergine pasta with olives and peppers, or spinach and cauliflower dahl with rice. Puddings can hit the spot (sour cream with dried fruit and ginger), there are good cheeses, a short wine list and a few bottled beers. Some evenings a pianist might be playing *A Nightingale Sang in Berkeley Square*. Staring into your organic red, and thinking about all the water under the bridge, it can sometimes get a little too poignant for words.

Home Bistro

41 West Nicolson Street, EH8 9DB (0131 667 7010). **Lunch served** noon-3pm Tue-Fri. **Dinner served** 5-9.30pm Tue-Sat. **Main courses** £7.50-£12.95. **Set lunch** £7.95 2 courses. **Set meal** (5-7pm Tue-Sat) £9.95 2 courses. **Credit** MC, V.

Although Edinburgh isn't traditionally well served in terms of really decent neighbourhood bistros, spring 2003 brought a brace: First Coast (*see p298*) and Home. This is a one-room establishment, one block away from Edinburgh University's George Square campus, with arty, minimalist decor save for a small camp concession to ceramic kitsch. The menu focuses on hearty home-style food, so starters might include a hefty country terrine with spicy lemon chutney or a competent mushroom soup. Mains offer a quite brilliantly done fish and chips (battered coley), or a tender and ample game casserole with shallots, mushrooms, thyme and a splendid creamy mash. The vegetarian alternative would be goat's cheese salad and spiced orange marmalade to start, then wild mushroom stroganoff as a main – perfectly fine if not wildly exciting. Dessert might be a comforting apple pie with a very accomplished cinnamon and vanilla ice-cream. The wine list runs to just nine choices, all under £19 except for a token bottle of bubbly.

Jasmine

32 Grindlay Street, EH3 9AP (0131 229 5757). **Lunch served** noon-2pm daily. **Dinner served** 5-11.30pm Mon-Thur, Sun; 5pm-12.30am Fri, Sat. **Main courses** £7.60-£19.90. **Set lunch** £6.90 3 courses. **Set dinner** £18.50 3 courses, £25 4 courses. **Credit** MC, V.

Edinburgh isn't a centre for cutting-edge Chinese restaurants, but this is one of the better examples. Opposite the Royal Lyceum Theatre, the Jasmine is loved by locals as well as luvvies. It's been around for years, but an early 2004 revamp saw it emerge looking more spruce: lemon walls, dark wood floor and comfortable banquettes on three sides of the room. (Some nice *objets* in the window too.) There's a cheap lunch menu for the office crowd, but the full menu is awesome in scope and there's even a respectable vegetarian list. Hot and sour soup is a good way to start: nice texture and a spicy bite. For mains, regulars rave about the likes of almond chicken with orange sauce or aromatic crispy duck. Meanwhile, the seafood specials include steamed monkfish or steamed turbot – so there's certainly more to the Jasmine than generic pork curry.

Kalpna ★

2-3 St Patrick Square, EH8 9EZ (0131 667 9890/ www.kalpnarestaurant.com). **Lunch served** noon-2.30pm Mon-Sat. **Dinner served** 5.30-10.30pm daily. **Main courses** £4-£7.50. **Set buffet** (lunch) £5.50, (dinner Wed) £10.50. **Set dinner** £12.50 2 courses, £15 3 courses. **Credit** MC, V.

The Kalpna has been around since the 1980s and it hasn't changed much over the years. It was the first Indian vegetarian restaurant in Edinburgh the bright yellow signage with paintings of vegetables above the door and the slogan 'You do not have to eat meat to be strong and wise' give it away. A cast of regular customers have been eating here for years. It's also close to Edinburgh University and bargain hunters come for the buffets (lunch and Wednesday evening). Otherwise, a thali is always a good option with a sample mix of tastes. Archna thali, for instance, includes aloo tikka (potato cutlets stuffed with coconut, sultanas, nuts and coriander), some aubergine-based baingan barta, a mixed vegetable navratan korma, lentil dahl, rice, deep-fried puri bread, raita, popadom, pickles and even dessert.

Marque Central

30B Grindlay Street, EH3 9AX (0131 229 9859). **Lunch served** noon-2pm Tue-Sat. **Dinner served** 5.30-10pm Tue-Thur; 5.30-11pm Fri, Sat. **Main courses** £10.95-£16.50. **Set meal** (lunch, 5.30-7pm) £12.50 2 courses, £15 3 courses. **Set dinner** £14 2 courses, £17 3 courses. **Credit** AmEx, MC, V.

Marque Central appeared in 2001 as a sister to Marque in Causewayside. But early in 2004, the original was up for sale with the planned departure of founding partner and chef Glyn Stevens; fortunately that still leaves the talented John Rutter in the kitchen. You enter on the ground floor to a sparse bar, but there are more satisfying and modish

Scotland

designer surroundings upstairs in the main dining space. The menu changes regularly but could offer chicken Caesar salad and crispy pancetta, followed by grilled salmon with basil crumble and crushed vine tomato and pea beignet. The crème brûlée is one of the city's best (passionfruit, with lemon curd ice-cream and biscotti) and although the wine list has some serious choices, there are lots under £20. The restaurant is next to the Royal Lyceum Theatre and has a pre- and post-theatre menu.

Martins

70 Rose Street North Lane, EH2 3DX (0131 225 3106). **Lunch served** noon-1.30pm Tue-Fri. **Dinner served** 7-9.30pm Tue-Sat. **Main courses** £17-£23. **Set lunch** £15 2 courses. **Credit** AmEx, DC, MC, V.

Martin and Gay Irons opened this excellent restaurant back in 1983. It's a neat little space: white walls, wicker chairs and wooden blinds to shut out the backstreet view. Trends and infrastructure have changed around it – more snackers in chic café-bars at lunchtimes these days and a couple of years when building works on the lane discouraged casual custom – but Martins has endured. The evening menu tends to be a touch more elaborate, but even at lunch the kitchen can turn out a creamy wild mushroom soup, world-beating halibut and langoustine risotto with baby spinach and surround of port jus, plus puddings such as iced raspberry parfait or cappuccino panna cotta. Then there's the cheeseboard. Martin Irons' presentation of Scottish and Irish artisan cheeses is one of life's most fulfilling experiences, and he can even source varieties available virtually nowhere else (errington's special for instance). Only two minutes' walk from Princes Street: go eat.

9 Cellars

1-3 York Place, EH13EB (0131 557 9899). **Lunch served** noon-2.30pm Mon-Sat. **Dinner served** 5.30-11pm Mon-Thur; 5.30-11.30pm Fri, Sat. **Main courses** £6.50-£7.70. **Set meal** (lunch, 5.30-7pm) £7.50 3 courses. **Credit** MC, V.

This establishment has been easy to miss since its autumn 2003 opening. Down a few steps from pavement level, the signage is nothing special and the interior design not to everyone's taste. It's bright with lilac walls and bland furniture, hardly capitalising on the old alcoves and dining spaces that inspired its name. That said, food-wise it's the freshest Indian to arrive on the scene in ages. An eclectic menu offers starters like pan-cooked quail marinated in yoghurt and spices (bhuni batter), or spinach and lentil medallions stuffed with cheese and mint (palak kebab). Stand-out mains include a Goan fish curry, strong on coconut, and a rich vegetarian dish of potatoes stuffed with nuts and cheese in cashew sauce (dum aloo banarsi). The side dish of black lentils cooked with tomato, ginger, butter and cream is fabulous (dahl makhani) and the desserts are the best of their type in Edinburgh.

Oloroso.
See p303.

Scotland

Number One ★

The Balmoral Hotel, 1 Princes Street, EH2 2EQ (0131 557 6727/www.thebalmoralhotel.com). **Lunch served** noon-2pm Mon-Fri. **Dinner served** 7-10pm Mon-Thur, Sun; 7-10.30pm Fri, Sat. **Main courses** £20-£25. **Set lunch** £16.50 2 courses, £19.50 3 courses. **Set dinner** £55 3 courses, £85 with wine. **Credit** AmEx, DC, MC, V.

The east end of Princes Street with its bus stops, shopping mall, railway station and burger branch is far from placid. Sitting above all this, however, is the Balmoral Hotel with its landmark clock tower. Number One is its flagship restaurant. You sip drinks while scanning the menu and bulky wine list in the bar area, then it's off into a spacious dining room that pulls off the trick of being contemporary and classic at the same time. The standard is very high indeed and might include langoustine in maccheroncini with langoustine broth to start; marinated Gressingham duck breast, creamed polenta and black olive compote as a main; then creamed rice pudding with apricot compote for dessert. Under executive chef Jeff Bland, Number One has gained, and retained, a Michelin star. And although à la carte isn't cheap, budget diners could try the excellent-value lunchtime 'market menu'.

Off the Wall ★

105 High Street, EH1 1SG (0131 558 1497/www.off-the-wall.co.uk). **Lunch served** noon-2pm, **dinner served** 6-10pm Mon-Sat. **Main courses** £19.95-£22. **Set lunch** £16.50 2 courses, £19.95 3 courses. **Set dinner** (pre-book only) £65 6 courses. **Credit** AmEx, MC, V.

There's a theory that says if you're going to hide, it's best to do it somewhere obvious – hence up a narrow flight of stairs on Edinburgh's main tourist street would be ideal. In among the tartan shops and backpacker hostels of the Royal Mile, where cameras flash and 90% of pedestrians in August are 'doing the Festival', the blessed counterpoint is Off the Wall. Originally situated in nearby South College Street, it moved here in 2000. The place has understated, contemporary decor, and thanks to chef David Anderson has built a solid reputation for its menu. All meat, game and seafood come from Scottish sources, but the style leans towards France. That means seared scallops with crab risotto, cep cream and shellfish vinaigrette; acclaimed fillet of Scotch beef with all the trimmings as a main; then coconut parfait to finish. A great restaurant – and it still feels wonderfully discreet despite the location.

Oloroso

33 Castle Street, EH2 3DN (0131 226 7614/ www.oloroso.co.uk). **Lunch served** noon-2.30pm Mon-Sat; 12.30-2.30pm Sun. **Dinner served** 7-10.30pm daily. **Main courses** £17-£49. **Credit** AmEx, MC, V.

Oloroso was one of the most important restaurant openings in the city in 2001 and since then, under chef Tony Singh, it has consolidated its position as a cosmopolitan bar and food hub for the beautiful people. Sited on top of a city centre office building, its fourth-floor location (lift to the third, then stairs) has excellent views. The bar area buzzes with atmosphere and many come just to drink, although there are excellent bar meals and snacks to be had (try cold Punjabi salmon with warm turmeric rice). In the adjacent dining room, the grill menu is a big feature (ribeye steak with sauce au poivre) while the à la carte could bring sweet potato and lime leaf soup; seared seabass with butternut squash purée, chicory and white bean sauce; then chocolate and prune terrine for dessert. Sharp contemporary decor, a lengthy international wine list and excellent chips.

Palourde

78 Commercial Street, Leith, EH6 6LX (0131 555 7663/www.palourde.co.uk). **Lunch served** noon-2.30pm, **dinner served** 6.30-10.30pm Tue-Sat. **Meals served** noon-6pm Sun. **Main courses** £12-£17.50. **Set lunch** £14.50 2 courses, £17.50 3 courses. **Credit** AmEx, DC, MC, V.

When this part of Leith was redeveloped in the mid-1990s, a row of conservatory premises were built into an old warehouse on the north side of Commercial Street, opposite the gargantuan Scottish Executive building. Many restaurants have tried and failed here; the latest to have a go is Palourde. Chef Joe Taggart has worked in some distinguished kitchens (including Restaurant Martin Wishart, *see p304*) and the food on offer is French with an emphasis on seafood. The mixed seafood platter is excellent, from the steamed mussels and smoked salmon right down to the accompanying green salad. Three courses might involve chicken and puy lentil terrine to start; sea bream with barley risotto, pancetta and vegetable broth to follow; then egg custard tart with cinnamon ice-cream for dessert. On early showings, let's hope Palourde sticks around.

Pompadour

Caledonian Hilton Hotel, Princes Street, EH1 2AB (0131 222 8888/www.hilton.com). **Lunch served** 12.30-2.30pm, **dinner served** 7-10pm Tue-Sat. **Main courses** £19-£23.95. **Set lunch** £15.95 2 courses, £19.95 3 courses. **Set dinner** £25.50 2 courses, £29.50 3 courses. **Credit** AmEx, MC, V.

Faddish eateries come and go, but the Pompadour endures (it recently celebrated its 75th birthday). Housed in a former Edwardian railway hotel, the room is effortlessly traditional in a dainty rococo manner, with the odd concession to modernity (long, fluted glass vases on the tables). Equally traditional is the food, in the elaborate French sense – in early 2004, executive chef Paul Newman advertised a new signature dish of chateaubriand served from a carving trolley. Yes there are tourists, yes there are young couples on that special weekend break. But you might also see an elderly lady and gent sitting at the table with the castle view, looking as if they've been there since VE Day and browsing a menu offering duck rillettes; roast chicken breast with boudin noir; and a frangipane and cherry tart. A genteel and reassuring presence.

Restaurant Martin Wishart ★

54 The Shore, EH6 6RA (0131 553 3557/ www.martin-wishart.co.uk). **Lunch served** noon-2pm Tue-Fri. **Dinner served** 7-10pm Tue-Sat. **Main courses** £22.50-£24.50. **Set lunch** £18.50 3 courses. **Set dinner** £48 5 courses, £55 6 courses. **Credit** AmEx, MC, V.

You start off with partridge and venison tartlet with plum compote; the main is roast monkfish with shallot cream, langoustine and red wine jus; dessert is mandarin jelly, blood orange granite and passionfruit salad. This is all happening in a simple, neat room near Edinburgh's docks, separated from the Water of Leith (the city's small river) by the width of a cobbled street. The wine list stretches to more than 300 bins and the exemplary front of house service is supervised by Cecile (Mrs Wishart). Mr Wishart is in the kitchen, drawing on his experience from working with Michel Roux and Marco Pierre White in London, and Albert Roux in Amsterdam. He came back to Edinburgh to set up this eponymous eaterie in 1999 and won a Michelin star within a couple of years (still retained). One of the very best restaurants in Scotland, and it has a separate vegetarian menu as well.

Rhubarb

Prestonfield, Priestfield Road, EH16 (0131 225 7800/ www.rhubarb-restaurant.com). **Lunch served** noon-3pm, **dinner served** 6-11pm daily. **Main courses** £12.95-£24.95. **Set meal** (lunch, 6-7pm, 10-11pm) £12.95 2 courses. **Credit** AmEx, DC, MC, V.

James Thomson is Edinburgh's star restaurateur. The Witchery by the Castle and the Secret Garden are his (*see p306*), as is the Tower (*p305*), but in 2003 he really got into opulent mode with the refurbishment of Prestonfield House Hotel (a 17th-century mansion in the shadow of Arthur's Seat, now simply Prestonfield). To say the makeover has been sumptuous is a bit of an understatement: late period Stuart with a hint of restrained Gaultier. Although there's a traditional country house feel, there's also a decent vibe; consequently the hotel's restaurant, Rhubarb, is unlike anything else in the city. The wine list is large and impressive, while a typical dinner might involve seared scallops on horseradish pomme purée; peppered lamb loin with polenta and bell pepper jus; topped by an inventive chestnut mousse. The two-course menu (lunch, pre- and post-theatre only) affords the whole jaw-dropping experience at bargain prices.

Santini/Santini Bistro

Sheraton Hotel, 8 Conference Square, EH3 8AN (0131 221 7788). **Lunch served** noon-2.30pm Mon-Fri. **Dinner served** 6.30-10.30pm Mon-Sat. **Main courses** (bistro) £6.95-£16.50, (restaurant) £15-£24. **Credit** AmEx, DC, MC, V.

Milano, Londra, Edimburgo: not a bad trio of locations for a restaurant business. Santini and Santini Bis arrived in the Scottish capital in 2001 – both in the same building as the terminally swish One health spa, behind (but attached to) the Sheraton. Their sister eateries are in Milan's Via San Marco and London's Ebury Street. Edinburgh's Santini is a very contemporary European space with cold, clean lines bang in the middle of the city's financial services district. Hint? Dress smart; urban wear will mis-identify you as one of Conference Square's skateboarding fraternity. The menu is the opposite of Italian cliché with starters such as pan-fried red mullet with saffron on sweet pickled vegetables, and mains like herb-crusted carpaccio of swordfish with crab meat and asparagus. There's still a classic tiramisu for dessert, of course, with espresso sauce. The adjacent Santini Bis is more bistro-style and even does pizza. As you'd expect, there are some very nice Italian wines.

Scalini

10 Melville Place, off Queensferry Street, EH3 7PR (0131 220 2999/www.scaliniristorante.com). **Lunch served** noon-2pm, **dinner served** 6-10pm Tue-Sat. **Main courses** £7.95-£16.50. **Set lunch** £10.95 2 courses. **Credit** AmEx, DC, MC, V.

There are various reasons why Scalini has been successful since it opened towards the end of the last decade. For one thing, descending the stairs into its soothing basement space, away from the hustle of the city's West End, is a blessed relief – especially in the middle of the day. Secondly, proprietor Silvio Praino is one of Edinburgh's more voluble and friendly restaurateurs. Then there's a wine list that ranges from generally affordable sub-£20 varieties to vintage Italian reds dating back to the 1940s. These ain't cheap, and you're almost surprised to find them in such a seemingly modest eaterie. Finally, there's the food – far from fussy but prepared with real care and attention. Three courses could bring a simple polenta al gorgonzola to start, or a great antipasti mediterraneo; then fegato di vitelo as a main (pan-fried calf's liver with onions and wine); and a pine nut and custard cake to finish (pinolata). Interesting dessert wines too.

Skippers Bistro

1A Dock Place, EH6 6LU (0131 554 1018/ www.skippers.co.uk). **Lunch served** 12.30-2pm Mon-Sat; 12.30-2.30pm Sun. **Dinner served** 7-10pm daily. **Main courses** £12-£19. **Set lunch** £7.50 2 courses, £10.50 3 courses. **Set dinner** £15.50 2 courses, £19.50 3 courses. **Credit** AmEx, MC, V.

Once upon a time Leith was home to salty pubs, streets of ill repute and merchant mariners looking for assorted 'recreations'. Actually it still is, but over the last couple of decades there has also been a move towards dinky designer flats and creative white collar businesses (not to mention Sir Terence Conran shopping malls). One of the first decent eateries to appear, blazing a trail way back in the 1980s, was Skippers and it has lasted the course (under the charge of Gavin and Karen Ferguson since 1999). Its dinner menu could give you half a dozen Loch Etive oysters to start; char-grilled tuna steak as a main; then a simple sticky toffee pudding – but the ever-changing seafood specials are the main event (roast

The Tower

sea bream with fennel, garlic and lemon or grilled halibut with asparagus, prosciutto and white truffle oil). Legendary fish cakes, cosy red walls, maritime decor and some very good white wines to complement your chosen *poisson*.

Suruchi

14A Nicolson Street, EH8 9DH (0131 556 6583/ www.suruchirestaurant.com). **Lunch served** noon-2pm Mon-Sat. **Dinner served** 5-11.30pm daily. **Main courses** £8-£13. **Set dinner** (5.30-7pm) £9.95 2 courses incl glass of wine. **Credit** AmEx, DC, MC, V.

Under the direction of Herman Rodrigues, Suruchi has consolidated its position as one of Edinburgh's very best Indian restaurants. Here you'll find jazz gigs, food festivals, cultural displays and some great dishes with the odd nod to the Scottish larder (starters like vegetarian haggis pakora or salmon tikka). The menu (with some copies written in a generic Scottish dialect) does have typical favourites such as king prawn masala or lamb korma, but you could also try butter chicken, which is popular back on the subcontinent (it involves more herbs and spices than you can count). Meanwhile, vegetarians are catered for with the likes of a rich palak kofta makhani: spinach and potato dumplings in cashew and tomato sauce. On the side, a dahl tarka lentil dish is homely, while rice can be sublime (coconut or lemon). Restrained decor, nice atmosphere. The kind of place Indian tourists choose to eat.

Thaisanuk ★

21 Argyle Place, EH9 1JJ (0131 228 8855). **Lunch served** noon-3pm Fri-Sun. **Dinner served** 6-11pm daily. **Main courses** £3.15-£8.95. **No credit cards.**

In among the new wave of Thai restaurants that have hit Edinburgh in the last few years there are examples with high prices, punning names and self-conscious gentility. But there's nowhere like funky little Thaisanuk, in the student ghetto of Marchmont. It's a tiny dining room that barely holds 30, has no drinks licence (BYOB) and doesn't accept credit cards. An effort has been made with the decor (browns, creams and hessian-style flooring), while the food could certainly be described as generous and robust. Starters include tempura, steamed lemongrass mussels, and a tom yum soup vivid with flavour (with chunks of ginger, galangal, chilli and all its other constituent spices). Popular noodle dishes come in hefty portions and various styles from all over east Asia (Vietnamese, Malaysian, Japanese, Thai), while chicken dishes, crispy whole fish (sea bass or trout), Thai green curry and other main courses cater for the noodle-phobic. Homely, hand-knitted and cool as Phuket.

The Tower ★

Museum of Scotland, Chambers Street, EH1 1JF (0131 225 3003/www.tower-restaurant.com). **Lunch served** noon-4.30pm, **dinner served** 5-11pm daily. **Main courses** £13-£20. **Set meal** (noon-6.30pm) £12.50 2 courses. **Credit** AmEx, DC, MC, V.

It's contemporary, cosmopolitan and sits atop Scotland's premier museum; the Old Town views are incomparable and the food's not half bad either. No wonder that since local restaurateur James Thomson opened the Tower in 1998, it has been on everyone's list of best Edinburgh eateries. Access is via the main museum entrance; once inside you take a lift to the top floor. In the evenings, security staff are on hand to make sure you don't get 'lost' among the nation's priceless artefacts. There's a light lunch and pre-theatre menu, while the à la carte offers all kinds of choices, from oysters and langoustines to Aberdeen Angus fillet steak and chips. The dinner menu could bring terrine of ham hough and chicken livers, followed by guinea fowl coq-au-vin style and then an assiette of citrus puddings. Further assets are a good international wine list and a terrace for Scotland's brief summer.

Valvona & Crolla Caffè Bar ★

19 Elm Row, off Leith Walk, EH7 4AA (0131 556 6066/www.valvonacrolla.com). **Breakfast served** 8am-11.45am Mon-Sat. **Lunch served** noon-3pm daily. **Main courses** £8.95-£13.95. **Credit** AmEx, MC, V.

Simply put, this is Scotland's best delicatessen; its caffè bar is a tasteful space at the rear of the shop, a former stable block with white walls and wooden beams. The food draws on the quality of raw materials sold in the deli, shipped in fresh from Italian markets. In the morning, there's an excellent breakfast menu, brilliant panatello sandwiches (prosciutto, parmesan, roast artichoke and rocket, for example) or you can have just a coffee. The main menu is available at lunch, with the likes of lamb shank and pasta broth; venison stew or a neat pizza margharita; then lemon tart for dessert. A simpler menu becomes available again in the late afternoon until closing. The deli doubles as a prize-winning wine merchant so you can pull any bottle off the shelf (for retail price plus reasonable corkage) and drink it here. Amazing value from a peerless establishment. A combined wine bar, caffè and shop – the Valvona & Crolla VinCaffè – is scheduled to open just off St Andrew's Square in autumn 2004.

Vermilion

Scotsman Hotel, 20 North Bridge, EH1 1YT (0131 556 5565/www.thescotsmanhotelgroup.co.uk). **Dinner served** 7-9.30pm Tue-Sat. **Main courses** £19-£22. **Set dinner** £35 3 courses, £50 5 courses (Fri, Sat). **Credit** AmEx, DC, MC, V.

Once upon a time this grand building resonated with the sound of typewriters and printing presses. It was constructed between 1899 and 1904 as the imposing home of *The Scotsman* – now moved to Holyrood Road. In its stead, in 2001, came an upmarket hotel. The following year, Vermilion opened for business as the hotel's dining room. You reach it down a marble staircase, entering a world of low lighting and oenophile decor (wine bottles in translucent wall cases). Starters bring out a sense of adventure from the kitchen (civet of rabbit with Granny Smith jelly and wasabi cream); mains can be similarly inventive (vegetarian puff pastry tartlet of artichoke and tomato, with shiitake custard and sweetcorn) or more orthodox (seared tuna with parmesan broth and truffled herb risotto). Chocolate marquise with pistachio ice-cream makes a fine dessert.

Vintners Rooms

The Vaults, 87 Giles Street, EH6 6BZ (0131 554 6767/www.thevintnersrooms.com). **Lunch served** noon-2pm Tue-Sat; noon-2.30pm Sun. **Dinner served** 7-10pm Tue-Sat. **Main courses** £15-£19. **Set lunch** (Tue-Sat) £13 2 courses, £16.50 3 courses; (Sun) £14.50 2 courses, £18 3 courses. **Credit** AmEx, MC, V.

The current Vaults building dates from the late 18th century, although its roots as a wine warehouse can be traced back to the late 16th. So when dining at the Vintners Rooms (ground floor, off the courtyard), you're sitting on over four centuries of Scotland's love affair with the grape. It's fitting then that this is a French-slanted establishment (Patrice Ginistière in the kitchen, Laure Pagès front of house). Diners can eat in the attractive wine bar area or a more formal, stucco-to-the-max room – not so good in harsh daylight but better when candlelit. Highlights are tuna tartare with courgette velouté to start; a char-grilled sirloin steak with olive oil béarnaise as a main; then a gratin de fruits exotiques to finish. The wine list is largely, but not exclusively, French with a selection of Bordeaux in the £50-£100 range.

The Witchery by the Castle/ The Secret Garden ★

Castlehill, EH1 2NF (0131 225 5613/www.the witchery.com). **Lunch served** noon-4pm, **dinner served** 5.30-11.30pm daily. **Main courses** £14-£22. **Set meal** (noon-4pm, 5.30-6.30pm) £9.95 2 courses. **Credit** AmEx, DC, MC. V.

It's just turned 10.30pm and the cobbles on the ancient Royal Mile are glistening. You turn to your other half, look deep into their eyes and say: 'Fancy late supper in a 16th-century building up by the castle?' Works every time. The Witchery opened in 1979 and has since developed a reputation as a destination restaurant in world terms, let alone Scottish ones. The original dining room is rich and atmospheric (wood panelling, red leather, candles, tapestries), while the Secret Garden, added in 1989, is even more so. The menu is the same in both and features starters such as a small Aberdeen Angus steak tartare with fried quail's egg; mains like venison poached in red wine and juniper; then the unmissable dessert selection (pistachio brûlée, chocolate torte, white peach parfait and verbena ice-cream). There's a huge and distinguished wine list.

Also in the area

Fishers Bistro 1 The Shore, Leith, EH6 6QW (0131 554 5666); **Living Room** 113-115 George Street, Edinburgh, EH2 4JN (0870 442 2718); **Malmaison** 1 Tower Place, EH6 7PB (0131 468 5000); **Suruchi Too** 121 Constitution Street, Leith, EH46 7AE (0131 554 3268).

Glasgow

Arisaig

24 Candleriggs, G1 1LD (0141 552 4251). **Meals served** noon-midnight daily. **Main courses** £9.95-£16.95. **Set dinner** (5-7pm Mon-Thur, Sun) £12.95 2 courses. **Credit** AmEx, MC, V.

Named after that little coastal chunk of the country south of Mallaig, this fine restaurant comes with an interesting Scottish menu, plus very good staff. (Some lipstick noticed on the rim of the glass while tasting a chosen wine? Back comes not only a clean glass, but also a replacement bottle.) The excellent fish cakes, served with lemon cheese and dulse leaf sauce as a starter, are not the potato-heavy nightmares you get elsewhere. Care is given to the sourcing of raw materials while a main of vegetarian honey-roast sausages with kale mash, rocket and tomato sauce makes you sit up and take notice. Good whiskies feature in some sauces (Cragganmore to go with roast venison sausages; Lagavulin and peppercorn alongside the fillet of Scotch beef), and the fruit dumpling dessert is wonderful. Arisaig has been so successful, they have opened a second branch on Byres Road with a bar attached.

Ashoka

108 Elderslie Street, G3 7AR (0141 221 1761/ www.currykareoke.com). **Meals served** noon-midnight Mon-Sat; 5pm-midnight Sun. **Main courses** £7-£15. **Set lunch** £6.95 3 courses. **Set dinner** (from 5pm) £10.95 4 courses. **Credit** AmEx, DC, MC, V.

As you go down the steps to the Ashoka's entrance, there are several tables outdoors, patio heaters and a well-tended plant bed. Strangely, this throws off any assumptions about the basement interior, which by contrast looks warm, sumptuous and very, very red. This friendly establishment has been going since 1982. Syrus Bavarsagh knows the Glasgow market well and offers the usuals like pakora to start, jalfrezi or bhoona for mains – but that's not all. The kitchen is proud of its 'abpaz' technique, flash-frying to seal in flavour. ('I give it more love,' says the head chef.) This yields dishes such as chicken in lemon sauce with coconut. Certainly one of the better Indian options hereabouts, and not related to the local chain with the same name. The Ashoka also has a buffet karaoke space – to be embraced or evaded depending on preference.

Babbity Bowsters

16-18 Blackfriars Street, G1 1PE (0141 552 5055). **Dinner served** 6.30-9.30pm Mon-Sat. **Main courses** £14-£15. **Credit** AmEx, MC, V.

This pub is found at the edge of Merchant City, just as contemporary affluence splits off from the structurally disadvantaged East End. It has a 'proper' restaurant upstairs for those who feel the need (Schottische, 0141 552 7774), but the bar food is fine. There's a beer garden for lazy days, and every Saturday afternoon a few musicians break out their fiddles and bodhrans. Inside, the decor is eggshell blue walls and wipe-clean tablecloths in chunky plaid. In keeping with the trad-Scottish theme, you can get a plate of stovies or haggis with neeps and tatties. There are also more refined choices like a Loch Fyne salmon platter, Kilbrandon Seil oysters or Cullen skink. Vegetarians are catered for (cauliflower and mung bean moussaka perhaps), and the menu has a French section with the likes of roast duck leg or Toulouse sausage.

Brian Maule at le Chardon d'Or ★

176 West Regent Street, G2 4RL (0141 248 3801/ www.lechardondor.com). **Lunch served** noon-2.30pm Mon-Fri. **Dinner served** 6-10pm Mon-Sat. **Main courses** £16.50-£19.50. **Set meal** (until 7pm) £14.50 2 courses, £17.50 3 courses. **Credit** AmEx, MC, V.

The life of Brian: Ayrshire lad trains in France, then becomes head chef at Le Gavroche in London. Returns to Scotland to open 'the golden thistle' in 2002 where his name features to such an extent on the signage that you're never in doubt who's in charge. But given the standards, you can forgive the branding. The interior is tasteful, if not cutting edge, while the French-style cooking is confident enough not to over elaborate. Three courses could start with cream of leek and potato soup; then own-made black pudding with rillettes of pork, shallot confit and Bayonne ham crisp; and chocolate fondant and mascarpone ice-cream to finish. Affordable lunch and pre-theatre menus are a good alternative to a full-blown dinner. With Gordon Ramsay's Amaryllis having closed in early 2004, Maule is the leader at the *haute* end of the market.

Buttery ★

652 Argyle Street, G3 8UF (0141 221 8188). **Lunch served** noon-2pm Tue-Fri. **Dinner served** 6-9pm Tue-Fri; 6-10pm Sat. **Set lunch** £16 2 courses. **Set dinner** £34 2 courses, £38 3 courses. **Credit** AmEx, MC, V.

The Buttery has been trading in one form or another at its current premises since 1869 (save for a short hiatus in 2002) on the ground floor of a traditional tenement. It was such a haunt for the city's great and good, goes the story, that when Glasgow was redeveloped in the 1960s and 1970s, the tenement was left alone while the surrounding area was devastated. Now its neighbours include grotesque blocks of flats and a motorway flyover. But once inside there's a classy, old-school feel with dark wood panelling. Three courses could involve an assiette of wild boar with creamed barley scented with apple and cider to start; roast halibut fillet on truffled pea purée with scallop and white wine and herb infusion; iced fudge and marshmallow parfait with Agen prunes for dessert. Excellent Scottish cooking in an unlikely urban setting.

Café Gandolfi

64 Albion Street, G1 1NY (0141 552 6813/www.cafegandolfi.co.uk). **Meals served** 9am-11.30pm Mon-Sat; noon-11.30pm Sun. **Main courses** £7-£14. **Credit** AmEx, MC, V.

Café Gandolfi is a Glasgow legend, going since 1979 – these days it even has merchandise like T-shirts and umbrellas. It's an L-shaped room with wooden furniture you want to stroke – many fall in love with the place at first sight. The dark aquamarine ceiling is high, the windows have stained-glass fish, the wines are good and the mood is informal. It does breakfast, sandwiches, pasta, then light meals, standards and desserts – specials are chalked up on the blackboard. So if you want to dash in for a bacon and avocado salad, then you can – or take your time over smoked venison with gratin dauphinoise, followed by walnut tart. At the end of 2002, Bar Gandolfi appeared upstairs – smaller, with more sexy wood furniture and skylights. It has similar eats in a more vibrant atmosphere, and is the city's top gastropub – although the Liquid Ship (*see p311*) offers serious competition.

Café Ostra

The Italian Centre, 15 John Street, G1 1HP (0141 552 4433/www.cafeostra.com). **Meals served** 11am-10pm Mon-Thur; 11am-10.30pm Fri, Sat; noon-10pm Sun. **Main courses** £4.95-£17.95. **Set meal** (until 6pm) £12.95 2 courses incl glass of wine. **Credit** AmEx, MC, V.

The Italian Centre is a mini-mall with Versace and Armani stores: Café Ostra is its latest occupant. This seafood eaterie is under the same ownership as Gamba (*see p310*) and shares elements of its menu. The approach is more informal with no starters and mains (as such) but soups, salads and a fish/shellfish list including dishes of various sizes – anything from a snacky half pint of prawns to a very rich dressed crab. If you want three courses, though, you could try the excellent fish soup with stem ginger and prawn dumplings; then goujons of sole with fries in a wooden bowl lined with greaseproof paper; and finish with a populist slice of Bakewell tart. Slick service takes place amid modern decor (dark wood, black and white tiling) in various dining spaces (including a mezzanine and tables outside). A hit.

Chinatown

42 New City Road, G4 9JP (0141 353 0037). **Meals served** noon-11.30pm daily. **Main courses** £9. **Set meal** £16 3 courses. **Credit** AmEx, DC, MC, V.

On first impressions Chinatown isn't promising. It's on the ground floor of a red-brick warehouse on the northern edge of the city, near the M8 flyover. Once inside it's very different: tropical fish tanks and a chandelier like a great diamanté squid. The fact that so many of the customers are Chinese tells you something about this establishment's authenticity and there's a typically enormous Cantonese menu. The seafood is good (lobster with black beans and chilli, crispy oysters, sea bass with spring onion, satay king prawns, squid of course); grandstand dishes include deep-fried stuffed whole duck with yam paste; there's even stewed duck's web with fish lips in pot for the adventurous. Decent dim sum too.

The Corinthian

191 Ingram Street, G1 1DA (0141 552 1101/www.g1group.co.uk). **Lunch served** noon-5pm daily. **Dinner served** 5-9.30pm Mon-Thur; 5-10pm Fri, Sat. **Main courses** £9.50-£19.95. **Set dinner** (also all day Sat) £10.50 2 courses, £12.50 3 courses. **Credit** AmEx, DC, MC, V.

They don't come much more flash than this: a restaurant-plus-bars complex in an ornate 19th-century Merchant City building. Originally it was a bank, later the High Court, then it opened as the Corinthian in 1999. The two main spaces are the Lite Bar (area of a five-a-side pitch, huge glass dome above) with its more informal eats and the restaurant (smaller floor space, also fairly vertiginous). At the outset, with many customers looking at the design – and each other – the food disappointed. More recently, socks have been pulled up. Try scallops with lemon risotto and cauliflower purée; a solid roast fillet of beef with fondant potato, tomato chutney and red wine sauce; then orange rice pudding with strawberry and orange salsa for dessert. However, the main selling point remains the wow factor of the interior.

Dragon-i

311-313 Hope Street G2 3 PT (0141 332 7728/www.dragon-i.co.uk). **Lunch served** noon-2pm daily. **Dinner served** 5-11pm Mon-Sat; 5-10pm Sun. **Main courses** £10-£22. **Set lunch** £9.95 2 courses. **Credit** AmEx, MC, V.

Dragon-i arrived in spring 2003 and binned all notions of *Madame Butterfly* interior design cliché for a spacious modern look. The floor is dark wood, the walls blue and red, while big windows look over to the Theatre Royal opposite. Complimentary prawn crackers arrive as you order and the wine list is 50-strong. Mains include wok-fried tiger prawns in sweet chilli sauce with onion, courgette and aubergines or beef simmered in stout with cherry tomatoes and onion. Both come with garlic butter fried rice that actually tastes of garlic butter. Desserts are delicious The extensive à la carte is even more adventurous and eclectic.

étain

Princes Square, Buchanan Street, G1 3JX (0141 225 5630/www.etain-restaurant.co.uk). **Lunch served** noon-2.30pm Mon-Fri; noon-3pm Sun. **Dinner served** 7-11pm Mon-Thur; 6.30-11pm Fri, Sat. **Set lunch** £16 2 courses, £18.50 3 courses. **Set dinner** £29 3 courses. **Credit** AmEx, MC, V.

Arisaig.
See p307.

Since 2003, there have been rumours of a very posh Conran restaurant on the second floor of the Princes Square shopping mall. People duly troop up there and find another Conran creation: Zinc Bar & Grill (same address and phone number). Ask a staff member and they'll lead you through the back saying something about 'Glasgow's best-kept secret'. So étain does actually exist; it even has a separate entrance at the Springfield Court side of the mall. Where Zinc has warm wooden fittings and red, pink and purple furnishings, étain looks light and minimal. They operate from a single kitchen, but at the more formal étain three courses could bring wild mushroom soup with soft poached quail's eggs to start; crab risotto with seared scallops and fennel cream as a main; hot raspberry soufflé with coconut sorbet for dessert. An impressive space.

Fanny Trollope's ★

1066 Argyle Street, G3 8LY (0141 564 6464/ www.fannytrollopes.com). **Lunch served** noon-3pm Mon-Sat; noon-6pm Sun. **Dinner served** 5.30-10.30pm Tue-Sat. **Main courses** £10-£14. **Set lunch and pre-theatre** (5.30-7pm) £8 2 courses, £12 3 courses. **No credit cards.**

Frances Trollope ran away from an arranged marriage in Brazil in the 1920s, headed for Lisbon but arrived in Glasgow by accident, where she worked in a café in Finnieston and married a man from Skye called McKay. Thus a legend was born, the inspiration for Fanny Trollope's café-bistro which opened in 2003. It's basic – no credit cards, school chairs, brown vinyl tablecloths – but there are artworks and prints all over the walls. Food is ambitious. You could start with roast quail, garlic and mushroom salad, and beetroot sauce; move on to pan-fried fillet of sea bass with potatoes, smoked salmon and prawn salad, lemon butter and chive sauce; then finish with a raspberry and lemon crème brûlée. The dishes might lack a little finesse, but the portions are generous and since it's BYOB, you can afford a decent wine – the cooking deserves no less.

Firebird

1321 Argyle Street, G3 8TL (0141 334 0594). **Meals served** 11.30am-10.30pm Mon-Thur; 11.30-11pm Fri, Sat; 12.30-10.30pm Sun. **Main courses** £8.50-£17.95. **Credit** MC, V.

Not far from Kelvingrove Park, this unpretentious café-bar is a bright, open room with big windows, yellow walls and the odd funky painting. The menu has starters, salads, pasta, pizza and mains – daily specials too – but there's no formulaic assembling of dishes: everything's made to order. The pizza is the best in Glasgow with a light, crispy base and toppings such as sunblushed tomato, olives and buffalo mozzarella. The salads (avocado and peppers with blue cheese, pine nuts, mixed leaves and herbs) are also pretty decent. Some people just come for a bowl of olives and glass of wine; others for a more elaborate meal – maybe lemon sole baked with cream and parmesan, followed by homely fruit crumble. A great place to linger – livelier later.

Fratelli Sarti

42 Renfield Street, G2 1NE (0141 572 7000). **Meals served** noon-10.30pm daily. **Main courses** £5.95-£20. **Pre-theatre menu** (4.30-6.30pm) £8.95 2 courses, £10.95 3 courses. **Credit** AmEx, MC, V.

The original Fratelli Sarti is the Wellington Street version – a deli-and-trat combination where you'd stop for a plate of pasta and glass of wine. Next came the more polite premises round the corner in Bath Street with the stained-glass windows. (These two are actually linked within the interior of the block they occupy.) More recently they've added another couple. The Renfield Street branch is more upmarket than its predecessors with relief sculptures, marble and wood panelling but the menu is similar: antipasti, pizza, pasta, plus classic dishes like salt cod in herbs and spices. The specials can be simple but fabulous, allowing the constituent ingredients to shine through: primi like mixed leaf salad with red onion, peppers and ripe gorgonzola layered with mascarpone; secondi like tortellini filled with parma ham in four cheese sauce. Meanwhile, Il Piccolo Sarti in Sauchiehall Street has a more truncated menu but a nice space upstairs. No gimmicks – just the best informal Italians in the city.

Gamba ★

225A West George Street, G2 2ND (0141 572 0899/ www.gamba.co.uk). **Lunch served** noon-2.30pm, **dinner served** 5-10.30pm Mon-Sat. **Main courses** £12-£22.50. Set lunch £15.95 2 courses, £18.95 3 courses. **Pre-theatre menu** (5-6.15pm) £15 2 courses, £18 3 courses. **Credit** AmEx, MC, V.

This is an upmarket seafood restaurant co-owned by Alan Tomkins and head chef Derek Marshall. They recently opened Café Ostra (*see p308*) in Merchant City as a more informal sister establishment and Tomkins also owns Papingo (*see p312*), so there's a lot of experience of the local scene, particularly at the top end. Gamba itself is a basement affair with an ornamental fountain by the door and an understated, modern interior. Three courses might bring sashimi (tuna and scallop) with soy dip, wasabi and pickled ginger; seared swordfish with spiced salsa relish, mango and prawns with mint; then Valhrona chocolate tart with maple syrup and mascarpone. It's not all this elaborate – alternatives include half a dozen oysters followed by excellent grilled lemon sole. The house wine is affordable, most of the others pricey.

Grassroots Café ★

93-97 St George's Road, G3 6JA (0141 333 0534/ www.grassrootsorganic.com). **Meals served** 10am-10pm daily. **Main courses** £5.75-£7.65. **Credit** AmEx, DC, MC, V.

Serving up decent vegetarian and vegan dishes since 1999, Grassroots is a simple establishment in an unlikely location: one room adjacent to the M8. The floor is black flagstone, the walls off-white, there are a few sofas, also tie-dye curtains separating the tables opposite the open kitchen. It's homely, though, with an art college feel, and all the food is GM-free (also organic and free-range where possible). There are some organic wines and beers available, while the menu runs from breakfast (full-on version, or just a couple of poached eggs on toast with chilli jam) via sandwiches and salads through to the more substantial. Tempura, chickpea fritters, or Greek dips are typical starters; there might be bangers and mash, Thai green curry, pizza or pasta for mains and puddings along the lines of apple and rhubarb pie or orange poppyseed cake. Far from elaborate, but they do care about food here – so diners benefit.

Brian Maule at le Chardon d'Or. *See p307.*

Horse Shoe ★
17 Drury Street, G2 5AE (0141 229 5711). **Meals served** noon-7.30pm Mon-Sat; 12.30-5pm Sun. **Main courses** £2.60-£3.50. **Set lunch** (12.30-2.30pm) £3.20 Mon-Sat. **Credit** AmEx, MC, V.
This Victorian pub is said to have the longest bar in the world, curved to fit the space, and measuring over 100ft (34 metres), and it serves a three-course lunch for £3.20. Yes, the decimal's in the right place: three pounds and twenty pence. For this you get soup or fruit juice to start; roast beef salad or macaroni cheese as a main; jelly and fruit for pudding. The parsimonious could opt for a mutton-filled scotch pie with beans or peas (90p) to accompany their lunchtime pint instead. The TV screens show football, the gold and platinum discs behind the bar were presented by Travis (who rehearsed a couple of floors up before they were famous), and football fans congregate here before Scotland games. There is a spartan dining room on the first floor (pakora starter, farmhouse stew main, then cheesecake – £6.45 all in), but the bar's livelier. Haute cuisine no; essence of Glasgow yes.

Liquid Ship
171 Great Western Road, G4 9AW (0141 331 1901). **Meals served** 11am-8pm Mon-Sat; 12.30-8pm Sun. **Snacks served** 8-10.30pm Mon-Thur; 8-11.30pm Fri, Sat; 8-10.30pm Sun. **Main courses** £3.95-£6.75. **Credit** MC, V.
The latest venture from the people behind Stravaigin (*see p315*), the Liquid Ship arrived in early 2004 and instantly became a contender for title of Glasgow's top gastropub. It has a fairly cosy red-brick basement with chunky wooden furniture; the ground floor is lighter and brighter. Even a choice from its 'wee bits' menu can bring a Spanish platter on an oblong glass plate with four ramekins containing a lump of decent manchego, dukkah (billed as an Australian mix of nuts, seeds and spices), olive oil and balsamic, and thick romesco. The main menu includes a seafood platter with soused herring, smoked salmon and taramasalata; there are also sandwiches with assorted fillings such as smoked trout, coriander, fresh chillies and citrus mayo. Good staff, nice space, superior snacks.

Mono ★
12 King's Court, King Street, G1 5RB (0141 553 2400). **Meals served** noon-10pm daily. **Main courses** £5.65-£6.75. **Credit** MC, V.
In among the architectural disasters between the Trongate and the Clyde, there are some railway arches featuring a small shopping centre of rare ugliness. This is home to Mono – not just a vegan eaterie, but also a bar and music store (the kind where you find rare Japanese tunes on vinyl). On the inside, it looks like a drop-in centre created by urban culture enthusiasts: there's a large open bar area with wicker chairs, tables and a row of silver brewing vessels; the dining area is up three steps to the side – also spacious with whitewashed walls, grey wooden tables and street art. The menu is short but offers breakfast (smoked tofu with mushroom on toast) and light meals (veggie burger and chips), though it could run to three courses: bruschetta to start, then chestnut and vegetable loaf, and fruit crumble. A comprehensive antidote – antithesis even – to nearby Argyle Street.

Mother India ★
28 Westminster Terrace, off Sauchiehall Street, G3 7RU (0141 221 1663). **Lunch served** noon-2pm Wed-Fri. **Dinner served** 5.30-10.30pm Mon-Thur; 4.30-10pm Sun. **Meals served** 1-11pm Sat. **Main courses** £6.10-£12. **Set lunch** (Wed-Fri) £10.50 2 courses. **Set dinner** (5.30-6.30pm Mon-Fri; 5.30-6pm Sat, Sun) £10.50 2 courses. **Credit** AmEx, MC, V.
It's not unusual for people to eat here then declare it's the best Indian meal they've ever had. From the outset you know you're not dealing with subcontinental cliché – the downstairs dining space looks more like a Scottish bistro than a typical curry house with stone walls, fleur-de-lys wallpaper, photographs of old Glasgow and a chequered stone-tiled floor. Upstairs is a little more opulent – the premises once housed a very polite tearoom. The menu isn't huge and everything is made to order: generic sauces aren't just thrown on top of separately cooked meats, so even a familiar chicken dhansak has the opportunity to shine. There are good house specials, vegetarian options, and the haddock cooked in foil with Punjabi spices is a rare treat. In spring 2004, after a decade of success, the owners opened a sister venue nearby. Same standards but with a small-dish tapas approach.

No.16
16 Byres Road, G11 5JY (0141 339 2544). **Lunch served** noon-2.30pm daily. **Dinner served** 5.30-10pm Mon-Sat; 5.30-9pm Sun. **Main courses** £11.50-£16.50. **Set lunch and pre-theatre menu** (5.30-6.30pm Mon-Fri, Sun). **Credit** MC, V.
With its vaguely distressed light grey frontage and driftwood-style installation in the window, No.16 could almost pass for a relaxed seaside bistro. The reputation of this place had been growing steadily for years but wasn't even dented when a new regime took over towards the end of 2001 (the Campbells). It keeps edging up that fantasy list of 'best eats in Glasgow', gathering accolades along the way for its creative approach – even the most demanding critics have been fairly generous with their praise. Three typical courses could bring pan-fried scallops with green pea dahl, coconut chapati, yoghurt and lime dressing to start; pan-roast chump of lamb with dauphinoise, ratatouille and basil pesto as a main; passion fruit and vanilla iced terrine with soft fruits for dessert. The wine list isn't bad either.

OKO
68 Ingram Street, G1 1EX (0141 572 1500/www.okorestaurants.com). **Lunch served** noon-3pm Tue-Fri. **Dinner served** 6-11pm Tue-Thur; 5-11pm Sun. **Meals served** noon-11pm Fri, Sat. **Main dishes** £1.70-£4.25. **Lunch box** £7.90 noon-3pm Mon-Sat. **Credit** AmEx, DC, MC, V.

Scotland

Restaurateur Stephen Ellis and Simple Minds singer Jim Kerr set up Scotland's first conveyor-belt sushi bar in summer 2000. It looked swish, modern and interesting – a cut above Yo! Sushi – and proved to be a big hit. But after four years, Ellis and Kerr decided to sell the place to head chef Colin Barr, who introduced a new menu, including a few dishes of Korean inspiration. The conveyor belt still trundles along with sashimi, nigiri and maki, and you can order assorted tempura, various types of teriyaki, all kinds of noodles and gyoza (small Japanese dumplings). But now there are also bulgoki (marinated char-grilled beef or pork) or pajeon (a kind of pancake with spring onion, seafood and vegetables). The upstairs bar – OKO-hi – is still a decent option if you want to slow down a little.

Otago

61 Otago Street, G12 8TQ (0141 337 2282). **Lunch served** noon-4.30pm, **dinner served** 5-9pm daily. **Main courses** £9.95-£11.95. **Set dinner** (5-7.30pm Mon-Thur, Sun; 5-6.30pm Fri, Sat) £10.95 2 courses. **Credit** MC, V.

For anyone who has been stomping along the Great Western Road in rush hour, adjacent Otago Street seems serene: a whiff of bohemianism, trees and sandstone tenements. In the middle of all this sits the eponymous bistro and delicatessen. Decor is contemporary and straightforward: light wood floor, off-white walls, artworks and small but chunky wooden tables. Starters might include a simple bruschetta with buffalo mozzarella, cherry tomatoes and rocket pesto – or perhaps asparagus and borlotti bean risotto depending on appetite. Mains can get quite fruity: pan-fried duck breast with Seville orange and green peppercorn sauce or medallions of Scotch beef with merlot and blackberry sauce. Roasted almond rice pudding with mango compote makes for a decent finish. A popular, likeable neighbourhood diner.

Papingo

104 Bath Street, G2 2EN (0141 332 6678/ www.papingo.co.uk). **Lunch served** noon-2.30pm Mon-Sat. **Dinner served** 5-10.30pm Mon-Sat; 5-10pm Sun. **Main courses** £12-£19. **Set dinner** (5-6.30pm Mon-Thur, Sun; 5-6pm Fri, Sat) £11.95 2 courses, £13.95 3 courses. **Credit** AmEx, MC, V.

Papingo – French for 'parrot' – is a well-established and dependable presence on the local scene: a smart, modern restaurant in the city centre grid. With blue chairs and banquettes, and a light wood floor, it even has a bright and airy feel despite the basement location. The old bird sticks to a fairly tried and tested formula: French-slanted food with some sense of international adventure. There is a decent choice of wines under £20, plus bargain lunch and pre-theatre menus, but an evening meal could bring smoked duck breast salad with kumquat marmalade dressing; corn-fed chicken breast with Stornoway black pudding mash and caraway gravy; then milk chocolate and orange cheesecake. (An alternative vegetarian main might be something like beetroot and pine nut risotto with parmesan and crispy onions.) Owner Alan Tomkins also has an interest in Gamba (*see p310*) and Café Ostra (*see p308*).

La Parmigiana

447 Great Western Road, G12 8HH (0141 334 0686/www.laparmigiana.co.uk). **Lunch served** 10am-2.30pm, **dinner served** 5.30-10.30pm Mon-Sat. **Main courses** £15-£20. **Set lunch** £10.50 3 courses. **Set dinner** £11.50 2 courses, £13.50 3 courses. **Credit** AmEx, DC, MC, V.

When every other Italian in Glasgow was up to its ears in trattoria-style decor and pizza – many still are – La Parmigiana ran directly upmarket and stayed there. Since 1978, it has been the city's 'posh Italian' par excellence – which means tasteful yellow

The Corinthian. *See p308.*

Scotland

walls, dark wood furniture, white linen, polite service and a traditionally aspirational menu. Starters could include lobster ravioli in a cream and basil sauce. There's a seafood dish of the day, plus rich mains like pan-fried beef fillet with crushed peppercorns and tarragon cream sauce. Desserts can also be fairly toothsome – maple syrup cheesecake with sautéed bananas. The wine list has some rare Italians around the £200 mark, but also a fair choice under £20. An old dependable.

Quigley's

158-166 Bath Street, G2 4TB (0141 331 4060).
Dinner served 5-10.45pm Mon-Sat. **Main courses** £12.50-£19.50. **Set dinner** £24.50 3 courses. **Credit** AmEx, MC, V.

They do like their complexes in Glasgow. Quigley's is one of three establishments in the same building: there's a smart basement café-bar called Lowdown, Quigley's on the ground floor and the Kelly Cooper Bar adjacent. Quigley's is where it's at food-wise – the creation of local celeb chef John Quigley. It's a long room with dark wood tables, light walls, banquettes and recessed lighting – a refurbishment of a Victorian auction house. The cooking is accomplished, with an Asian flourish. Dinner could bring ceviche of scallops, wild salmon and avocado with hot and sour dressing; smoked ham hock with baby carrots, bubble and squeak cake, and parsley sauce; then chilled coconut rice pudding with a tropical fruit kebab. There's an affordable wine list.

No.16. See p311.

Scotland

Rococo ★

202 West George Street, G2 2NR (0141 221 5004/ www.rococoglasgow.com). **Lunch served** noon-2.30pm Mon-Sat. **Main courses** £15-£24. **Dinner** 5-9.30pm Mon-Thur; 6.30-10pm Fri, Sat. **Set lunch/ pre-theatre menu** (5-6.30pm) £14 2 courses, £18 3 courses. **Set dinner** £36.50 3 courses. **Credit** AmEx, DC, MC, V.

One of the more self-consciously chic and upmarket restaurants in the city, Rococo is the fine dining option in the Bouzy Rouge Group, a small chain of eateries in central Scotland. However, where the average Bouzy Rouge advertises itself in 'casual gourmet' terms, has decor involving bright primary colours and farmhouse pâté or 10oz steak on the menu, Rococo – under head chef Mark Tamburrini – is pushing for something altogether different. Its basement premises are plush, modern and restrained – even the fairy lights on the ceiling seem low-key. The wine list runs to around 400 choices, while a three-course dinner could bring escabeche of red mullet with saffron-marinated vegetables to start. Follow this with a fine fillet of Buccleugh beef with roasted root vegetables, gnocchi, caramelised garlic and thyme jus, then close the deal with baked alaska with praline and raspberry coulis.

Rogano ★

11 Exchange Place, off Buchanan Street, G1 3AN (0141 248 4055/www.rogano.co.uk). **Meals served** *Bar* 11am-11pm Mon-Sat; 12.30-11pm Sun. *Café* noon-11pm Mon-Thur, Sun; noon-midnight Fri, Sat. **Lunch served** *Restaurant* noon-2.30pm, **dinner served** 6.30-10.30pm daily. **Main courses** £17.95-£33.50. **Set lunch** £16.50 3 courses. **Credit** AmEx, DC, MC, V.

In the summer, Rogano has a terrace on the pedestrianised thoroughfare outside. Despite the fact this is subject to the visual intrusion of teen goths as they pass by to congregate in nearby Royal Exchange Square, the establishment still exudes old-style class. Even an espresso on the terrace will bring a couple of petits fours on the side. Indoors there's a 1935 art deco interior, plus a bar, seafood restaurant and downstairs café. You get snacks at the bar and good meals in the café space which has a late menu for the post-theatre crowd (daily except Saturday). The restaurant is beautiful and more formal: three courses could include smoked haddock and leek terrine to start; baked halibut with fennel and mango salsa as a main; lavender crème brûlée for dessert. It's not all seafood though: there are meat (peppered roe deer perhaps) and vegetarian options too, while the wine list leans towards French whites.

Saint Jude's

190 Bath Street, G2 4HG (0141 352 8800/ www.saintjudes.com). **Lunch served** noon-2.30pm Mon-Fri. **Dinner served** 6-10.30pm daily. **Main courses** £11.50-£18.50. **Set lunch** £11.50 2 courses. **Set dinner** (6-7.15pm) £11.50 2 courses. **Credit** AmEx, DC, MC, V.

This is actually a boutique hotel that landed in Bath Street back in 1999 as an outpost of London's Groucho Club, but that association has long gone. It has a designer basement bar – a relaxing space but showing a few signs of age these days. The ground-floor restaurant still looks as fresh as ever though, with its muted colours, grey banquettes and signature nude (painting) opposite the door. In the bar, you can snack on the likes of linguine with tiger prawns, a decent burger with fries or just a baguette with poached salmon and lemon mayonnaise. The restaurant is more formal with fusion cooking to the fore. Three courses at dinner could bring mussels poached in tomato, chilli and lemongrass broth; lemon sole with tempura oysters, pak choi and fragrant rice; dark chocolate soufflé to finish.

Stravaigin ★

28 Gibson Street, G12 8NX (0141 334 2665/ www.stravaigin.com). **Lunch served** *Restaurant* noon-2.30pm Fri, Sat; 12.30-2.30pm Sun. **Dinner served** 5-11pm Tue-Sun. **Meals served** *Café* 11am-10.30pm Mon-Sat. **Pre-theatre menu** *Restaurant* (5-7pm) £13.95 3 courses. **Credit** AmEx, DC, MC, V.

Stravaigin opened on Gibson Street in the mid-1990s and fast became a Glasgow favourite. It's a basement space with simple modern decor, red-brick walls and a food philosophy of 'think global, eat local'. Rated among the city's top five restaurants, Stravaigin offers three courses like pomegranate-marinated venison with grape couscous to start, then roast halibut with basil-dressed roast peppers and pommes purées, followed by bitter chocolate velouté with pink grapefruit and cinnamon ice-cream. Gibson Street also has the bijou ground-floor Stravaigin Café-Bar, a more informal eating area featuring home-grown items (steak, fish and chips, haggis) as well as dishes with a more international influence. The new millennium addition to the empire was Stravaigin 2 (8 Ruthven Lane, off Byres Road, 0141 334 7165) – a converted townhouse with decorative greenery outside, a contemporary bistro interior and a good reputation for burgers (including ostrich). The global approach takes full effect here: Kashmiri chicken and cauliflower curry with roasted cashews, orange basmati and a Rajasthani relish is a typical and delicious main course.

Thai Fountain

2 Woodside Crescent, G3 7UL (0141 332 1599). **Lunch served** noon-2.30pm, **dinner served** 5.30-midnight daily. **Main courses** £11-12. Half-price main courses 5.30-7pm. **Set meal** £26 5 courses. **Credit** AmEx, DC, MC, V.

Where conservative Edinburgh has around 20 Thai restaurants these days – from the mannered and traditional to the small and funky – Glasgow has largely demurred. Thai Fountain was the first to arrive in Glasgow in the mid-1990s and with the pioneer status came an overwhelmingly oriental-exotic approach: staff are very formal, all dressed up in traditional costume; the interior aims upmarket with ethnic touches; and on the grounds that more means more the à la carte runs to a disconcerting 151 choices, although that does include starters, sides and sundries. Suits haunt the place at (business) lunchtimes, while smart diners take advantage of the pre-theatre offer of half-price mains before 7pm weekdays. But if you're in the city and gagging for a zingy plate of tom yam soup, followed by some prawns with lemongrass, chilli, lime leaf and coconut rice, you really should head here. There are very few competitors.

Two Fat Ladies

88 Dumbarton Road, G11 6NX (0141 339 1944/ www.twofatladies.5pm.co.uk). **Lunch served** 12.30-2.30pm Mon-Sat. **Dinner served** 5.30-10.30pm daily. **Main courses** £14.50-£17. **Pre- and post-theatre menu** (5.30-7pm; 9.30-10.30pm) £10.95 2 courses, £12.95 3 courses.

The internal configuration here means that the kitchen backs on to the main shopfront window. It does have a decorative grille with fish motifs over the glass, but that fails to disguise the food processor, boxes and other working bric-a-brac. It's not the most appealing introduction, but don't let that deter you – Two Fat Ladies (number 88 Dumbarton Road, bingo, geddit?) is actually one of the best seafood eateries in the city. Some of the dishes double as starters or mains (king prawns sautéed in garlic, chilli and coriander butter with focaccia for example). Otherwise you could kick off with some Loch Etive mussels with white wine, garlic and cream; follow that with fine whole lemon sole and chive butter; then finish with a mixed berry pavlova. With affordable white wines to pick from, it's an altogether friendly and informal experience.

The Ubiquitous Chip ★

12 Ashton Lane, G12 8SJ (0141 334 5007/ www.ubiquitouschip.co.uk). **Lunch served** noon-2.30pm Mon-Sat; 12.30-3pm Sun. **Dinner served** 5.30-11pm Mon-Sat; 6.30-11pm Sun. **Meals served** *Brasserie* noon-11pm Mon-Sat; 12.30-11pm Sun. **Set lunch** £21.80 2 courses, £26.80 3 courses. **Set dinner** £32.80 2 courses, £37.80 3 courses. **Credit** AmEx, DC, MC, V.

Monday evening in the covered, cobbled courtyard at the Chip, a space teeming with greenery (there's an upstairs bistro, bars and formal indoor dining room). The menu appears and the waiter explains they've run out of rocket velouté with tomato beignet (starter) and Scrabster-landed lythe (cod cousin). He describes the alternative starter fulsomely (walnut brioche with asparagus, salsify and orange mayonnaise). Main? Organic Orkney salmon with salmon beignet, vanilla-lime mash, red pepper and vermouth sauce. The walnut bun doesn't thrill, the kitchen cranking out a quick menu replacement; the fish is great, the vanilla and vermouth flavours pretty vestigial though; a neat cheese platter third course involves fruit bread, savoury wafers and four cheeses; coffee to finish. Without wine? That's £37.80 sir. But there are Alasdair Gray murals, habitual excellence and a real sense that Scotland has happened here. Let lapses go, you'll be back.

Also in the area

City Cafe Finnieston Quay, G3 8HN (0141 240 1002); **Fratelli Sarti** 133 Wellington Street, G2 2XD (0141 204 0440); **Fratelli Sarti** 404 Sauchiehall Street, G2 3AH (0141 572 3360); **Fratelli Sarti** 121 Bath Street, G2 2SZ (0141 204 0440); **Malmaison** 278 West George Street, G2 4LL (0141 572 1000); **Mother India Café** 1355 Argyle Street, G3 8AD (0141 339 9145).

Rest of Scotland

Aberdeenshire

ABERDEEN

Silver Darling Seafood ★

Pocra Quay, North Pier, Aberdeen, AB1 5DQ (01224 576229). **Lunch served** noon-2pm Mon-Fri. **Dinner served** 7-9.30pm Mon-Fri; 6.30-9.30pm Sat. **Main courses** £18-£20. **Credit** AmEx, DC, MC, V.

Didier Dejeans' French seafood restaurant at the entrance to Aberdeen harbour goes from strength to strength. In 2003 a ground-floor oyster bar was added: neat, small and modern with a more informal approach (moules, steak frites). It only opens in summer, but has tables outside – a welcome option on those days sufficiently warm to offset the North Sea breeze. Meanwhile, the main conservatory-style dining room upstairs (much glass, great views of the working port and the beach) provides perhaps the best food in the city. Three serious courses like woodland mushroom and langoustine minestrone with mascarpone dumplings and truffle oil to start; pan-fried medallions of monkfish with squid, spinach, fish roe and squid ink sauce as a main; then filo layers filled with cinnamon-flavoured pear, maple sauce and pecan nuts for dessert. Well-executed and complex French cooking.

Angus

DUNDEE

Metro Brasserie & Restaurant

Apex City Quay Hotel and Spa, 1 West Victoria Dock Road, Dundee, DD1 3JP (01382 202404/www.apex hotels.co.uk). Brasserie **Lunch served** noon-2.30pm, **dinner served** 6-10pm daily. **Main courses** £6.50-£13.55. **Set lunch** £14 3 courses. **Set dinner** £14 3 courses. *Restaurant* **Dinner served** 7.30-9.30pm Tue-Sat. **Main courses** £14-£19.50. **Set dinner** £25-£32 5 courses. **Credit** AmEx, MC, V.

This hotel is part of a small Scottish chain and arrived with a flourish in spring 2003. It looks like the jewel in the Apex crown, with rave reviews from the outset and one of its younger chefs picking up an award within months of the opening. The wood panelling on the mod-Scandinavian exterior already looks a little sad and weathered (dockside location), but inside both the brasserie and the adjacent restaurant have spacious, contemporary design. The brasserie does pasta, grills, burgers or the full three courses: prawn and avocado cocktail with harissa and coriander dressing; free-range chicken breast with Moroccan spices, couscous and lime; then passion fruit and white chocolate parfait. The restaurant is appreciably more elaborate with three tasting menus of veggie, fish and meat options. Nowhere in Dundee has such chutzpah or scope.

Argyll & Bute

CAIRNDOW

Loch Fyne Oyster Bar

Clachan, Cairndow, PA26 8BL (01499 600264/ www.lochfyne.com). **Meals served** *Winter* 9am-6.30pm daily (times vary; booking advisable). *Summer* 9am-8.30pm daily. **Main courses** £4.95-£25. **Credit** AmEx, DC, MC, V.

Described as a 'sister business' to the namesake chain of Loch Fyne restaurants in England (but not part of the limited company that operates them), this was the original that spawned the whole enterprise. It's also the closest to the raw materials, eco-conscious and actually owned and run by its staff. Getting here involves a beautifully scenic drive of not much more than an hour from Glasgow. The premises are simple (whitewashed walls, wooden booths and tables) and although it may be too bright and busy for a romantic encounter, it's an ideal stopover for seafood lovers. The menu breaks down into starters and light dishes (local kippers), mains (skewered king scallops in bacon), specialities (Loch Fyne oysters in chilli and coriander), or the daily specials (char-grilled halibut with parsley butter). The seafood platter is spectacular and there's an adjacent shop if you want to take anything home.

CRINAN

Crinan Hotel ★

Crinan, PA31 8SR (01546 830261/www.crinan hotel.com). Bar **Lunch served** noon-3pm, **dinner served** 6-8.30pm daily. **Main courses** £11.95-£14.50. *Restaurant* **Dinner served** 7-8.30pm daily. **Set dinner** £42.50 5 courses. **Credit** MC, V.

The Crinan Canal runs nine miles from Loch Gilp to the Sound of Jura. It opened in 1801 and was a vital part of Scotland's 19th-century infrastructure – now mostly used by pleasure craft. At the canal's west end is the tiny hamlet of Crinan where the hotel is a social hub. The setting is picturesque (the Isle of Jura lies only five miles over the water), while dining options, courtesy of chef Ben Tish, are excellent – even the bar menu has dishes such as grilled mackerel fillet or handmade lamb and rosemary sausages. The more formal Westward Restaurant could offer four courses such as terrine of Argyll rabbit and foie gras with Gewürztraminer jelly and toasted brioche, langoustine velouté, Loch Crinan jumbo prawns, and lemongrass panna cotta with marinated fennel and citrus consommé for dessert. Interesting wines and fresh seafood add to the appeal.

OBAN

Ee-usk

North Pier, Oban, PA34 5QD (01631 565666). **Lunch served** noon-2.30pm, **dinner served** 6-9.30pm daily. **Main courses** £3.95-£16.95. **Credit** MC, V.

Oban is a busy little port that largely grew up in the 19th century – and it has the architectural styles to match. The intrusive, modern white edifice on the north pier, with its orange-red roof, does look like an anomaly – but since summer 2003 it has been home to seafood restaurant Ee-usk (phonetic spelling of the Gaelic for fish). Hit this place on a busy night and it's like walking into an Edinburgh or Glasgow café-bar: packed, high noise levels, waitresses speeding around like pinballs and clean, contemporary decor on both floors. Seafood is the big feature with locally caught white fish and langoustine, Lismore oysters, Loch Etive mussels and more. The cooking doesn't over elaborate and three courses could see seared scallops with mornay sauce to start, haddock and chips with pea and pancetta purée as a main, then a very moist and decent bread and butter pudding for dessert. The wine list is short, affordable and mainly white.

PORT APPIN

Airds Hotel ★

Port Appin, PA38 4DF (01631 730236/www.airds-hotel.com). **Lunch served** noon-2pm, **dinner served** 7.30-9pm daily. **Set lunch** £17.95 2 courses, £21.95 3 courses. **Set dinner** £45 5 courses. **Credit** MC, V.

The reputation of this excellent hotel was built up over many years by the celebrated Allen family, but they moved on in 2002. Shaun and Jenny McKivragan took over, retaining chef Paul Burns. Has Airds lost its lustre? No. The hotel is in a beautiful setting 20 miles north of Oban, by the pier for the ferry to Lismore. The dining room view is gorgeous, service is excellent and a three-course lunch could entail seared tuna with artichoke salad and aged balsamic dressing to start; baked cod with tapenade crust, wild garlic mash, fine beans and chive velouté as a main; then an inspired coconut and cardamom mousse on pineapple with mango purée for dessert – it's a talented kitchen. There's a French ballast to the wine list, and sitting in the conservatory on a summer evening, dividing your attention between the Argyll panorama and the menu, is one of the great Scottish dining experiences.

TARBERT

The Anchorage

Harbour Street, Tarbert, PA29 6UD (01880 820881). **Dinner served** *Winter* 6.30-9.30pm Tue-Sat. *Summer* 6.30-9.30pm daily. **Main courses** £10-£17. **Credit** MC, V.

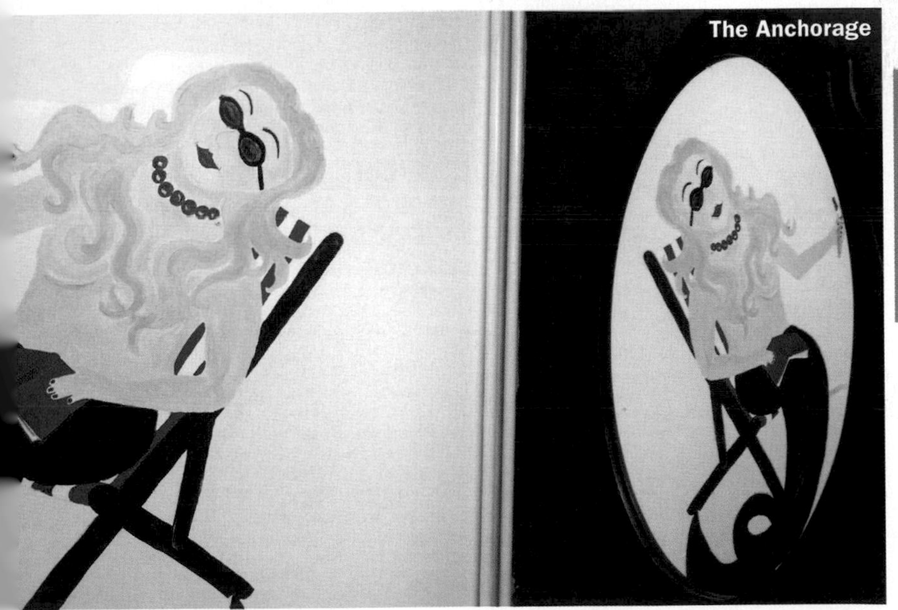

The Anchorage

Scotland

It wasn't all that long ago when eating out in provincial Scotland entailed microwaved scampi and the impossibility of finding a decent coffee in the afternoon ('Aye, we turn the machine aff efter lunchtime ye ken'). Sadly, this approach is still all too common so it's important to laud those whose personality and enthusiasm stand between diners and oven chip armageddon. One such angel is Clare Johnson, kitchen doyenne at the Anchorage, bang on the harbour front in the scenic village of Tarbert. This is a small, neat room where three courses could see queenie scallops toasted with ginger and lemongrass; cod roasted with white bean and parsley purée; then molten chocolate babycake and vanilla ice-cream. Don't miss the mermaid in the Gents.

TIGHNABRUAICH

Royal Hotel

Tighnabruaich, PA21 2BE (01700 811239/www.royalhotel.org.uk). The Deck **Lunch served** noon-3pm, **dinner served** 6-9pm daily. **Main courses** £11.95-£26. *Crustacean* **Dinner served** 7-9pm Wed-Sat. **Set dinner** £30 5 courses. **Credit** MC, V.

The Royal has been run by the McKie family since 1997, transformed from just another Argyll hotel to a tasteful and civilised destination with the best kitchen on the Cowal peninsula (if not beyond). There's a pub round the back with bar food, then two more serious eating options to the front with views to the Isle of Bute; well-sourced ingredients are paramount in both. The Deck is an informal bistro space (jumbo langoustine with creamed garlic, ribeye steak or the Royal burger with fries) while the fine-dining area (the Crustacean) sits on the other side of the entrance foyer. Here, chef Claire McKie offers her 'crustacean menu,' which could bring Jerusalem artichoke soup with truffle oil; a tian of scallops and salmon; some carrot sherbet; a main like local venison, rosemary barley risotto, kale and cocoa reduction; then Valrhona chocolate tart for dessert. Around 60 wines are listed by grape variety.

Ayrshire

DALRY

Braidwoods ★

Drumastle Mill Cottage, Dalry, KA24 4LN (01294 833544/www.braidwoods.co.uk). **Lunch served** noon-1.45pm Wed-Sun. **Dinner served** 7-9pm Tue-Sat. **Set lunch** (Wed-Sat) £16 2 courses, £19 3 courses; (Sun) £25 3 courses. **Set dinner** £32 3 courses, £36.50 4 courses. **Credit** AmEx, DC, MC, V.

Take a couple of talented chefs, a husband-and-wife team as it happens, put them in a tidy little country cottage in rural Ayrshire (only about 25 miles south-west of central Glasgow), let them get on with it, then watch the accolades roll in. Keith and Nicola Braidwood have been cooking up a storm since the mid-1990s and won a Michelin star in 2000, putting them right up with Scotland's elite. The restaurant doesn't hold that many diners and it's not that easy to find – so book beforehand and ask for directions. The cuisine style is Franco-Caledonian (French style, local material) with starters of seared scallops on herb risotto and mains such as roast turbot with truffle crust and chanterelle sauce. After that, there might be a fantastic chocolate soufflé pudding with ice-cream. A decent wine list contains some gems.

Dumfries & Galloway

CROSSMICHAEL

Plumed Horse ★

Crossmichael, DG7 3AU (01556 670333/www.plumed-horse.co.uk). Brasserie **Dinner served** 7-8.30pm Tue-Sat. *Restaurant* **Lunch served** 12.30-1pm Tue-Fri, Sun. **Dinner served** 7-8.30pm Tue-Sat. **Main courses** £19. **Set lunch** £20 3 courses. **Credit** MC, V.

Chef Tony Borthwick and manager Charles Kirkbride opened this restaurant in 1998, instantly transforming an unfashionable location north of Castle Douglas into a two-horse town. The urban masses in Edinburgh and Glasgow (and attendant media) tend to look north for recreation so it took a while to click that things were stirring in the south-west. But 'the Horse' picked up a Michelin star by 2001, currently retained, and people started to take note. Kirkbride has since left, Borthwick is now firmly in charge and the establishment has the original, small restaurant on ground level or, since 2003, an upstairs brasserie. The cooking is accomplished, offering a downstairs dinner of moist smoked haddock and smoked salmon quiche with spinach, parmesan and lemon dressing to start; a much-eulogised breast of guinea fowl with loads of accessories as a main; then chocolate sorbet with apricot soufflé for dessert.

East Lothian

GULLANE

La Potinière ★

Main Street, Gullane, East Lothian, EH31 2AA (01620 843214/www.la-potiniere.co.uk). **Lunch served** 12.30-2pm, **dinner served** 7-9pm Wed-Sun. **Set lunch** £15.50 2 courses, £18 3 courses. **Set dinner** £35 4 courses. **Credit** MC, V.

This establishment was a beacon of good food from the 1970s right through until 2000 when its respected proprietors, the Browns, called it a day. But after an 18-month hiatus, new owners Mary Runciman and Keith Marley picked up the torch in summer 2002. Since then, the general foodie public in the area has been readjusting to the fact that La Potinière is back – and very good indeed. The restaurant itself remains very small and neat (it barely seats 20), with an obvious French influence in both the cooking and the relatively short wine list.

The four-course set evening menu only offers a couple of choices at each stage, but diners enthuse about dishes like duck and foie gras terrine with fig and plum relish as a starter, and roast fillet of beef with horseradish crust as a main, then go into total overdrive about the desserts (coffee amaretto crème brûlée perhaps) and the cheeseboard.

Fife

CUPAR

Peat Inn

Peat Inn, nr Cupar, KY15 5LH (01334 840206/www.thepeatinn.co.uk). **Lunch served** 1pm, **dinner served** 7-9.30pm Tue-Sat. **Main courses** £17-£22. **Set lunch** £22 3 courses. **Set dinner** £32 3 courses, £48 6 courses. **Credit** AmEx, MC, V.

David and Patricia Wilson opened as a gastropub in 1972 before the term was even coined, progressed into fine dining in 1979 and haven't looked back. Open fire and comfy sofas in the lounge still? Check. That classic chocolate rosemary pot on the dessert menu? Check. The list goes on. White fish and lobster come from fishing villages nearby, wildfowl from a local farmer, a lot of fruit and vegetables from Fife smallholders. The cooking has an avowedly French style, and three courses could bring lobster salad with avocado to start; cassoulet with lamb, pork, duck and flageolet beans as a main; then iced lemon parfait dessert. The Peat Inn is friendly and enduring with a serious wine list; there are even rooms so you can stay over.

ST ANDREWS

The Seafood Restaurant

Below the Scores, St Andrews, KY16 9AB (01334 479475/www.theseafoodrestaurant.com). **Lunch served** 12.30-2.30pm, **dinner served** 6.30-9.30pm daily. **Set lunch** £18 2 courses, £20 3 courses. **Set dinner** £30 2 courses, £35 3 courses, £40 4 courses. **Credit** MC, V.

The original Seafood Restaurant overlooks the old harbour at St Monans, a pretty fishing village on the south-east tip of Fife. It's a tidy establishment in a traditional whitewashed building, which has been under its current management since 1993 and picked up accolades along the way. Indeed it proved such a success that the team, including head chef Craig Millar, decided to try a second restaurant just ten or so miles away: a modern, purpose-built, glass-sided pavilion perched above the West Sands at St Andrews. This opened in August 2003 and people tend to love or loathe the look. Cooking-wise, it's up to the standard of its St Monans sibling with a not dissimilar menu; three courses at the new one could bring crab and langoustine risotto with avocado ice-cream and shellfish sauce to start; seared fillet of cod with chorizo, sun-blushed tomatoes, beans and garlic in herb butter as a main; then a highly accessorised walnut tart for dessert.

Highland

ACHILTIBUIE

Summer Isles Hotel ★

Achiltibuie, IV26 2YG (01854 622282/www.summer isleshotel.co.uk). Bar **Meals served** noon-9pm daily. **Main courses** £7.50-£30. *Restaurant* **Lunch served** 12.30-2pm, **dinner served** 8pm daily. Closed mid Oct-Easter. **Set dinner** £46 5 courses. **Credit** MC, V.

Thanks to chef Chris Firth-Bernard, the Summer Isles Hotel has been recognised for some years as one of the pinnacles of Scottish dining. Dinner comes as a set menu, always served at 8pm. It might start with fish soup, move on to stilton soufflé, offer a main of grilled halibut fillet, then tempt diners with the dessert trolley before the celebrated cheeseboard appears. These dishes may sound simple but the execution is more than dextrous. The wine list is highly respected and the setting is simply beautiful – miles off the main A835, through the Inverpolly National Nature Reserve and sitting right on the coast overlooking those eponymous isles. If you get too hungry for dinner at 8pm, there's a decent pub attached. It's friendly, there are wooden booths to the front, a tiny bar space at the back, and at lunch it serves sandwiches, soup, light dishes (like a rich, creamy mackerel pâté), seafood (an enormous langoustine platter) and desserts.

APPLECROSS

Restaurant at the Walled Garden

Applecross House, Applecross, IV54 8ND (01520 744440). **Meals served** 10am-5pm daily. **Dinner served** 6.30-9pm Thur-Sat. **Main courses** £4.95-£13.75. **No credit cards.**

This is a potting shed. Not like a potting shed, it actually is one, albeit fairly roomy and well-appointed. It's in the walled garden at Applecross House and has been going since 2001. Chef Robert Macrae joined in 2003. It does brilliant snacks and light meals by day then gets more formal in the evenings when three courses could bring roast asparagus and avocado salad with poached egg to start, then local estate venison casserole, apple and mustard mash, and savoy cabbage, followed by fig and brioche pudding. Applecross, a coastal hamlet, is beautiful and remote; the fun way of getting here involves the most dramatic single-track road in the British Isles (from sea level at Loch Kishorn to 2,000 feet through the mountains and back down again in ten miles). The nearby Applecross Inn where Macrae used to work (Shore Street, Applecross, 01520 744262) still does the best pub food for miles.

COLBOST

Three Chimneys

Colbost, Isle of Skye, IV55 8ZT (01470 511258/ www.threechimneys.co.uk). **Lunch served** *Apr-mid Oct* 12.30-2pm Mon-Sat. **Dinner served** 6.30-9.30pm daily. Closed 13th-19th Dec 2004 & last 3 wks Jan. **Set lunch** £17.50 2 courses, £24 3 courses. **Set dinner** £42 3 courses, £48 4 courses. **Credit** AmEx, DC, MC, V.

The Three Chimneys is on the far-flung side of a particularly dramatic nowhere – a distant island with mountains of Wagnerian imposition – and that's a major part of its appeal. Even if you've driven all the way up the crinkly west coast from Glasgow, then remortgaged the house to pay the bridge toll over to Skye, there are still more than 50 miles to go to Shirley and Eddie Spear's multiple-award-winning 'restaurant with rooms' by Loch Dunvegan. People come here to get away from it all – and also for the food. The establishment has a tasteful crofter cottage style, Shirley is the chef, and local seafood is a big feature. A typical four courses could start with baked highland blue cheesecake with blueberry, mint, and honey dressing; six local oysters to follow; grilled lobster and langoustine with vanilla sauce, spiced lemon rice timbale, and salad leaves as a main; then gooseberry and elderflower fool with home-made shortbread for dessert. The wine list runs to around 150 choices.

DRUMBEG

Drumbeg Hotel & Seafood Restaurant ★

Drumbeg, nr Lochinver, IV27 4NW (01571 833236/ www.drumbeghotel.com). **Lunch served** 12.30-2pm Mon, Tue, Thur-Sun. **Dinner served** 7-9pm daily. **Main courses** £9-£17. **Credit** MC, V.

Michel and Carolyn Hédoin took over this modest establishment in summer 2002; their love of food shines through in everything they do. The polite and quiet dining room has a great view overlooking Loch Drumbeg, and three courses at dinner could start with oysters from the north coast at Tongue, or perhaps some Eddrachillis Bay langoustine served on a bed of bladderwrack with bagnarotte sauce. A typical main might be halibut (landed at Kinlochbervie) with potatoes and beurre blanc, or gnocchi à la romaine as a vegetarian alternative. To finish, the dark chocolate mousse is surely the best in Scotland (chunky, intense, but not too sweet). Attention to detail is amazing: the coffee is splendid (an Ethiopian-Javan blend) and in the morning even the eggs seem to have extra flavour, but they do come from a croft down the road at Achmelvich. Food-wise, the Hédoins have created something quite exceptional in the far north-west.

FORT WILLIAM

Inverlochy Castle Hotel

Torlundy, Fort William, PH33 6SN (01397 702177/ www.inverlochycastlehotel.com). **Lunch served** 12.15-1.30pm, **dinner served** 7-9pm daily. **Set lunch** £23.50 2 courses, £28 3 courses. **Set dinner** £52.50 5 courses. **Credit** AmEx, MC, V.

It's Queen Victoria's fault; her purchase of Balmoral Castle (1852) set society abuzz. The Highlands was no longer a barren wasteland full of troublesome Gaels. Now it was trendy, with opportunities for rich people to shoot things, or do watercolours! Hurrah! Against this recherché background the first Lord Abinger built Inverlochy Castle in 1863, just four miles from Fort William and the slopes of Ben Nevis. These days, it's the most sumptuous, Scottish-by-dint-of-constructed-identity country house hotel in the land; the kitchen, under the charge of Matthew Gray, has accolades coming out of its *oreilles* (très classic French with local ingredients). Dinner, in one of three dining rooms, might involve saddle of rabbit with roast Loch Linnhe prawns and bisque-style sauce to start; then a white bean and celery soup; venison loin poached in gin with braised little gem lettuce and caramelised figs as a main; caramel poached pear with toffee mousse and vanilla ice cream for dessert. Dress smart.

GAIRLOCH

Mountain Restaurant

Strath Square, Gairloch, IV21 2BX (01445 712316). **Meals served** 10am-6pm daily. **Main courses** £4.25-£6. **Credit** MC, V.

This is more a café than a restaurant and the environment is its big theme. (It's also attached to a New Age bookshop – handy if you're gripped by a need to discover feng shui while travelling in Wester Ross.) The decor is wooden and rustic, with a few tables by the counter, but also a conservatory where it's possible to slump on a sofa and contemplate the view over Gairloch Bay to the mountains. Since many people head for this part of the world to mess around in those mountains, they need stoking up. The food therefore tends to be of the baked potato or hearty soup variety, desserts are rich (cheesecake, chocolatey things), and the scones are both legendary and enormous (cheese and herb or fruit). There are all kinds of teas (even Ayurvedic) and perhaps the best roadside coffee between Glasgow and Reykjavik. The California Blue entails a double espresso with steamed milk, guarana and cinnamon.

INVERNESS

Mustard Seed

16 Fraser Street, Inverness, IV1 1DW (01463 220220/www.themustardseedrestaurant.co.uk). **Lunch served** noon-3pm, **dinner served** 6-10pm daily. **Main courses** £9.95-£14.50. **Set lunch** £5.95 2 courses. **Set dinner** £11.95 2 courses. **Credit** AmEx, DC, MC, V.

The Mustard Seed (not a sackcloth and lentil café as its name might suggest) is among the very best stand-alone restaurants in this burgeoning northern city. It appeared in 2001 – a conversion of an old church – with modern decor, mustard-yellow walls, artworks and a good sense of space. (Get a window seat and you've got a nice view of the River Ness

Mustard Seed. *See p320.*

making its way from loch to sea.) The food is good without being over-elaborate and a typical three-course dinner could bring a filling wild mushroom risotto with parmesan biscuit and truffle oil, followed by pan-fried monkfish with crushed potatoes and sauce vierge, then a lemon-lime bavarois for dessert.

Rocpool

1 Ness Walk, Inverness IV3 5NE (01463 717274/ www.rocpool.com). **Lunch served** noon-2.30pm Mon-Sat. **Dinner served** 6-10pm Mon-Sat; 5-9pm Sun. **Main courses** £8.90-£16.90. **Set lunch** £7.95 2 courses. **Credit** MC, V.

Scotland may be shrinking population-wise but Inverness, with just over 50,000 souls, is bucking the trend with people attracted by affordable property, countryside and quality of life (if not guaranteed sunshine). Bars and restaurants are opening to cater to the new buoyancy and the most chic is Rocpool, which arrived in 2002. Bang in the centre, on the west side of the Ness Bridge, it buzzes. The menu ranges from the creative and ambitious (king prawn, pineapple and halloumi skewer with couscous) to the very simple (spaghetti with mushrooms, garlic, chilli and rocket or T-bone steak and chips). The wine choice runs to around 35, with a dozen by the glass. For a night out in a cosmopolitan environment with youthful staff, this is the place.

KISHORN

Kishorn Seafood Bar ★

Kishorn, IV54 8XA (01520 733240). **Meals served** *Apr-Oct* 10am-5pm Mon-Sat; noon-5pm Sun. Closed Sept-Mar. **Main courses** £3.50-£15.75. **Credit** MC, V.

Around 50 miles west of Inverness, on the A896 between Lochcarron and Shieldaig, the hamlet of Kishorn isn't really near anything except spectacular scenery and big sea lochs. Its claim to fame is a basic roadside lodge selling great seafood – courtesy of Viv Rollo. She's been opening her establishment from Easter to September every tourist season since 1996. Although the menu extends to baked potatoes and bacon rolls, fish and crustacea are the main event. It's all very simple: steamed mussels, scallops in butter, smoked salmon or trout, squat lobster tails and more. Anything that needs to be cooked is made to order, while Viv also has a licence (one red wine, three whites and some bottled beers). It's more of an airy daytime café than a dinner destination, but it usually stays open as late as 9pm in July and August.

NAIRN

Boath House Hotel

Auldearn, Nairn, IV12 5TE (01667 454896/ www.boath-house.com). **Lunch served** 12.30-2pm, **dinner served** 7-8.30pm daily. **Set lunch** £27.50 3 courses, £32.50 4 courses. **Set dinner** £45 5 courses. **Credit** AmEx, DC, MC, V.

After several years of hard work and careful restoration, Don and Wendy Matheson opened the Boath House as a hotel in 1998. It was a new lease of life for this grade A listed mansion, designed by the renowned Archibald Simpson in 1825. (It has amazing bedrooms, over 20 acres of grounds, a trout loch, and more besides.) Food-wise, the kitchen is in the able and experienced hands of Charles Lockley – a man who spends his spare time reading antique French cookery books. The ingredients are well-sourced – including some from the kitchen garden. A typical table d'hote dinner could start with sweetcorn soup with Parma ham; then an entrée of seafood tortellini poached in lobster bisque with pea velouté; fillet of sea bass as a main with puy lentils, caper berry olive oil dressing, and potatoes; some very good Scottish artisan cheese; finishing with rich chocolate tart and mascarpone sorbet. There's a French-slanted wine list with lots of choices under £20.

SPEAN BRIDGE

Old Pines

Spean Bridge, PH34 4EG (01397 712324/ www.oldpines.co.uk). **Lunch served** 12.30-2.30pm Tue-Sun. **Dinner served** 8pm Tue-Sun by appointment only. **Main courses** £3.50-£10.50. **Set dinner** £34 5 courses. **Credit** MC, V.

Champany Inn. *See p324.*

Scotland

Old Pines is more than just a restaurant – often it seems more like a mission, on the part of proprietors Sukie and Bill Barber, to promote a lifestyle featuring family-friendliness and a love of good food. There's an undoubted talent at work here though – Sukie won Rural Chef of the Year at the 2003 Scottish Chef Awards, and Bill's pretty good with his wines. The establishment has a well-appointed cabin-in-the-woods look and a typical set dinner could involve Isle of Muck crab soup to start; then a fruit, walnut, and cheese salad with deft dressing; duck breast with fried parsnips and a Madeira, Seville orange, garlic, and coriander sauce for a main accompanied by other vegetables of interest; rhubarb and banana brûlée for pudding; and finally some Scottish artisan cheese. Vegetarians are more than welcome at dinner, but should call ahead so Sukie can plan. Meanwhile the more informal snacky day menu features the likes of soup, sandwiches, and own-smoked fish.

ULLAPOOL

Ceilidh Place

14 West Argyle Street, Ullapool IV26 2TY (01854 612103). **Meals served** *Bar* noon-6pm daily. **Dinner served** *Restaurant* 6.30-9pm daily. **Main courses** £11.50-£17.50. **Credit** MC, V.

Once north of the Great Glen, towns of any size are few and far between – so Ullapool, despite having a population of around only 1,700, is quite a centre of activity. One of its main features is the Ceilidh Place which can trace its roots back to 1970: a hotel, bar, restaurant, bunkhouse and music venue rolled into one. There's a formal dining area (a long white-walled room with artworks and seating for around 30), plus a much larger café-bar space. One menu serves all from the full-on breakfast (meat or veggie), through to a decent plate of mince and tatties for lunch, and afternoon coffee and scones (soda farls with dunsyre blue). The seafood here is fresh from the water and a more extensive meal could bring three courses of fish soup with tomato, orange and saffron, pan-roasted prawns with lemon and garlic, plus poppyseed and apricot parfait for dessert. There are decent beers too.

Orkney Islands

ST MARGARETS HOPE

The Creel

Front Road, St Margarets Hope, South Ronaldsay, KW17 2SL (01856 831311/www.thecreel.co.uk). **Dinner served** *Apr-Oct* 7-8.30pm daily (phone to check Apr, Sep, Oct). **Main courses** £17.80. **Credit** MC, V.

Orkney is very far away. Even from Aberdeen a flight takes just under an hour, or the ferry six hours. Only 16 of its many islands are inhabited and the total population is just under 20,000. Not exactly a hotbed of high-class eateries then, but a great source of raw materials: white fish, mussels, scallops, lobster, lamb and beef, even raspberries and strawberries in season. All the same, The Creel on South Ronaldsay is a much better restaurant than anyone would dare expect in its setting. It's neat, unpretentious and chef Alan Craigie uses the best of the local produce to create straightforward dishes to high and consistent standards. That means three courses like North Ronaldsay mutton terrine with rhubarb chutney and salad to start; a trio of perfectly steamed fish as a main with tomato and basil salsa (sea trout, wolf fish, and lemon sole maybe); then the ever-popular own-made ice-cream for dessert. And there's Highland Park to finish.

Perth & Kinross

AUCHTERARDER

Andrew Fairlie at Gleneagles ★

Gleneagles Hotel, Auchterarder, PH3 1NF (01764 694267/www.gleneagles.co.uk). **Dinner served** 6.30-10pm Mon-Sat. **Main courses** £27. **Set dinner** £55 3 courses, £75 6 courses. **Credit** AmEx, DC, MC, V.

Gleneagles was originally a grand railway hotel that appeared in 1924 and almost immediately became a big hit with people lacking both a Scottish accent and a chin. It opened seasonally for many years until a multi-million pound investment in the 1980s went a long way to creating the 24/7 modern McXanadu (it now has an equestrian school, shooting school, three championship-standard golf courses and much more). But anyone with the requisite slack on their credit card can enjoy Andrew Fairlie's restaurant – embedded in the hotel but run as a separate business. It opened in 2001 and introduced understated cosmopolitan design and modern French cooking to rural Perthshire. A three course dinner could entail smoked lobster with herb and lime butter sauce to start; roast entrecôte of Strathearn beef with oxtail parmentier as a main; hazelnut pithivier with ginger ice-cream for dessert. The pricing of the wine list is in keeping with the surroundings and service is formal. One of Scotland's very top eateries though? Surely.

PERTH

Let's Eat

77-79 Kinnoull Street, Perth, PH1 5EZ (01738 643377/www.letseatperth.co.uk). **Lunch served** noon-2pm, **dinner served** 6.30-9.45pm Tue-Sat. **Main courses** £9-£17.50. **Credit** AmEx, MC, V.

It's hard to remember what the restaurant scene was like in Perth prior to 1995, but it's fair to say that the arrival of Let's Eat that year completely changed the rules of the game. Head chef Tony Heath and front-of-house doyenne Shona Drysdale brought a modern, informal style to bear that immediately established their eaterie as the best in town. Now there's a modern, relaxed interior with sofas while you browse the menu, warm colours, a

Scotland

relatively hefty wine list, a great focus on good Scottish ingredients and a real confidence about the place. Dinner could bring hand-dived scallops, seared and served with a parsnip purée, white truffle oil and parsnip crisps to start; grilled pavé of Scotch beef fillet on the bone with a puff pastry 'casket' of braised oxtail and mushrooms, celeriac purée and Madeira jus as a main course; finished off by apple tarte tatin with caramel sauce, crème fraîche and vanilla ice-cream.

63 Tay Street

63 Tay Street, Perth, PH2 8NN (01738 441451/ www.63taystreet.co.uk). **Lunch served** noon-2pm, **dinner served** 6.30-9pm Tue-Sat. **Main courses** £14.95. **Set lunch** £13.45 2 courses, £18.40 3 courses. **Credit** AmEx, MC, V.

Jeremy and Shona Ware are not a brand. They don't have bankers queueing up to finance expansion into the major metropolitan UK markets, and it's unlikely that they'll ever appear on television swearing at some semi-competent cook as freakshow entertainment. But they have application and talent – taking premises by the River Tay in sleepy old Perth and turning them into a neatly appointed, modern restaurant with all the wooden flooring, chic blue seats and artworked walls that you might expect to find somewhere more populous. Jeremy's the cook, Shona does front of house, and even a bargain three-course lunch could bring a decent smoked haddock with creamed leeks and poached egg to start; medallions of pork fillet with chive mash, greens and grain mustard sauce as a main; then date and fig pudding. Good modern cooking with affordable wines listed in an intelligent manner. Long may they run.

PITLOCHRY

Port-Na-Craig

Pitlochry, PH16 5ND (01796 472777/www.portna craig.com). **Lunch served** 12.30-2pm Tue-Sat; 1-2.30pm Sun. **Dinner served** 6-9pm Tue-Sat. **Main courses** £9-£15. **Credit** MC, V.

The Thewes family took over this pleasant 17th-century riverside inn back in 2002. It sits on the other side of the Tummel from the centre of Pitlochry (handy for the Festival Theatre) and although the old place had been a fixture on the town's restaurant circuit for many years, they have instituted some bold and welcome changes. In came an improved and brighter interior as well as a modern bistro menu drawing on good Scottish ingredients (some of the produce even sourced from their own garden): warm caramelised salad of chicken livers; Aberdeen Angus fillet with béarnaise sauce; lemon and lime tart with crème fraîche. There's a good vegetarian selection too. Not content to rest on their laurels, in spring 2004 they opened part of the premises as a bar. This does light meals and has seating outside: the perfect place to sit and watch the river flow by.

West Lothian

LINLITHGOW

Champany Inn ★

Nr Linlithgow, EH49 7LU (01506 834532/ www.champany.com). Chop & Ale House **Lunch served** noon-2pm, **dinner served** 6.30-10pm Mon-Fri. **Meals served** noon-10pm Sat; 12.30-10pm Sun. **Main courses** £7.95-£19.95. *Restaurant* **Lunch served** 12.30-2pm Mon-Fri. **Dinner served** 7-10pm Mon-Sat. **Main courses** £19.50-£35.50. **Set lunch** (Mon-Fri) £16.75 2 courses. **Credit** AmEx, DC, MC, V.

This complex of buildings – run since 1983 by Clive and Anne Davidson – includes two restaurants as well as rooms for overnight guests. The more informal diner is the Chop and Ale House, farmstead-like and offering high-class burgers, steak, lamb and ample desserts. It doesn't take bookings – you just turn up (and wait with a drink if it's busy). The main dining room is much grander: octagonal, with polished wood, portraiture and shining glassware. There's a rockpool in the bar with live oysters and lobsters, but the main attraction is the steak: Aberdeen Angus hung for three weeks and cooked on a specially designed grill. Ribeye, fillet, porterhouse and more. With a decent sauce (black pepper perhaps) and really great chips, it's a carnivore's delight. The wine list meanwhile runs to over 900 choices. Quite an experience but not one for the faint of wallet.

SOUTH QUEENSFERRY

Orocco Pier

17 High Street, South Queensferry, EH30 9PP (0131 331 1298/www.oroccopier.co.uk). **Meals served** 10am-10pm daily. **Main courses** £7.50-£16.95. **Credit** AmEx, DC, MC, V.

Formerly this was a simple 17th-century coaching inn in the middle of a cobbled street in the heart of old South Queensferry. Then, in 2003, the owners reinvented the place as a boutique hotel and café-bar. The decor is in the modern Edinburgh café-bar mould (the city is less than ten miles to the east) – clean lines, dark wood tables, banquettes and booths – but the view is unparalleled. The dining area to the rear of the ground floor sits right above the shoreline and affords a giddy panorama of the Forth and its iconic bridges. The flexible menu could include falafel-like Moroccan salmon cakes with lime mayonnaise, decent smoked haddock with poached egg and cheese on spring onion mash, then glazed lemon tart with cardamom cream for dessert. The wine list is short with tasting notes designed to amuse.

Also in the area

Loch Fyne Clachan, Cairndow, PA26 8BL (01499 600236); **Shimla Pinks** 4 William Street, Johnstone, Renfrewshire, PA5 8DS (01505 322588).

Wales

Wales

Lytham St. Anne's
Irish Sea
LANCASHIRE
Southport
Ormskirk
Wigan
Liverpool Bay
Bootle
St Helens
MERSEYSIDE
LIVERPOOL
ISLE OF ANGLESEY
Amlwch
Llanerchymedd
Holyhead
Benllech
Llandudno
Colwyn Bay
Rhyl
Prestatyn
Birkenhead
Holy Island
Gwalchmai
Llangefni
Beaumaris
Conwy
Dyserth
Rhuddlan
Holywell
Ellesmere Port
Rhosneigr
Penmaenmawr
Abergele
Flint
Connah's Quay
Queensferry
Menai Bridge
Bangor
Llanfairfechan
St Asaph
FLINTSHIRE
Ty'n-y-Groes
Denbigh
Chester
Bethesda
Caernarfon
Llansandffraid
CONWY
Llanrwst
Ruthin
Mold
Buckley
CHESHIRE
Caernarfon Bay
Llanberis
Capel Curig
Betws-y-coed
Capel Garmon
DENBIGHSHIRE
Llandegla
Penygroes
Wrexham
Beddgelert
Blaenau Ffestiniog
WREXHAM
Malpas
Nefyn
Morfa Nefyn
Porthmadog
Ffestiniog
Corwen
Llangollen
Overton
Ruabon
Penley
Criccieth
Llandrillo
Pwllheli
Talsarnau
Trawsfynydd
Bala
Glyn Ceiriog
Chirk
Harlech
Llanrhaeadr-ym-Mochnant
Oswestry
Abersoch
Llanbedrog
Wem
Llanbedr
Llanuwchllyn
Dyffryn Ardudwy
GWYNEDD
Bardsey Island
Llanfyllin
Barmouth
Dolgellau
Shrewsbury
Welshpool
SHROPSHIRE
Cardigan Bay
Llanbrynmair
Tywyn
Montgomery
Machynlleth
Church Stretton
Aberdyfi
Pontdolgoch
Eglwysfach
Newtown
Bishop's Castle
Llanidloes
Aberystwyth
Devil's Bridge
POWYS
Knighton
Ludlow
Llanrhystud
Rhayader
Aberaeron
CEREDIGION
Presteigne
New Quay
Llandrindod Wells
Tregaron
Leominster
Kington
Aberporth
Builth Wells
HEREFORDSHIRE
Lampeter
Cardigan
Dinas Head
Newcastle Emlyn
Llanwrtyd Wells
Goodwick
Llandysul
Hay-on-Wye
Newport
Fishguard
Llyswen
Hereford
Llandovery
Felin Fach
Talgarth
Portgain
St David's
Welsh Hook
CARMARTHENSHIRE
Brecon
PEMBROKESHIRE
Llanfrynach
Llanthewy Skirrid
Skenfrith
Carmarthen
Llandeilo
Crickhowell
St Bride's Bay
Whitland
Nantgaredig
Haverfordwest
Abergavenny
Rockfield
St Clears
Glanaman
Llanvihangel
St Brides
Narberth
Laugharne
BLAENAU GWENT
MONMOUTHSHIRE
Monmouth
Johnston
Ammanford
Merthyr Tydfil
Milford Haven
Neyland
Kidwelly
Clytha Hill
Pendine
Pontardawe
NEATH & PORT TALBOT
Nant-y-derry
Whitebrook
Pembroke Dock
Saundersfoot
Pontardulais
MERTHYR TYDFIL
Aberdare
TORFAEN
Llandenny
Llandogo
Pembroke
Tenby
Burry Port
RHONDDA CYNON TYDFIL
Gorseinon
CAERPHILLY
Pontypool
Tintern Parva
Carmarthen Bay
Llanelli
Neath
Cwmbran
Caldey Island
Oldwalls
Llanrhidian
Chepstow
St. Govan's Head
Reynoldston
SWANSEA
Maesteg
Pontypridd
Port Talbot
Tredunnock
Wentlooge
NEWPORT
BRIDGEND
Caerphilly
Swansea Bay
Bridgend
Talbot Green
CARDIFF
Portishead
Porthcawl
Cowbridge
CARDIFF
VALE OF GLAMORGAN
Penarth
BRISTOL
Nash Point
Barry
Weston-super-Mare
Bristol Channel
Lynton
Burnham-on-Sea
Lundy
Ilfracombe
Minehead
Wells
Watchet
DEVON
Glastonbury
Bridgwater
SOMERSET
Bideford

0 50 km
0 25 miles

Wales

Bridgend

LALESTON

The Great House

Laleston, Bridgend CF32 0HP (01656 657644/ www.great-house-laleston.co.uk). **Lunch served** 11.45am-2pm daily. **Dinner served** 6.45-9.30pm Mon-Sat. **Main courses** £6.95-£23.95. **Set lunch** (Mon-Sat) £6.95 2 courses. **Credit** AmEx, DC, MC, V.

Built in the 1550s, the Great House is an historic hotel in miniature. The original structure – now the bar – was added to meet the demands of aristocratic and royal residents. The clientele may not be quite so celebrated nowadays but the food still justifies a visit. Evening light through ancient windows, muted yellow walls and clothed chairs give a vaguely French feel to this relaxing dining room. Start with carpaccio of Welsh lamb served with baby vegetable ratatouille and sweet anchovies or confit of salmon crêpe with french beans and a light vanilla jus. Brandade of own-salted cod is served with a creamy vegetable and potato chowder and reinforced with sweet, fresh scallops and slices of chorizo. Gnocchi with gorgonzola and sage sauce or orecchiette with roast Mediterranean vegetables and feta keep pasta fans happy. Preparation was of a very high quality and timing was exact. Polite, smart staff do an excellent job, moving with skill along the narrow ancient passageways. All this and sea air too.

Cardiff

Armless Dragon

97 Wyeverne Road, Cathays, Cardiff, CF24 4BG (029 2038 2357/www.thearmlessdragon.co.uk). **Lunch served** noon-2pm Tue-Fri. **Dinner served** 7-9pm Tue-Thur; 7-9.30pm Fri, Sat. **Main courses** £12-£20. **Set lunch** £10 2 courses, £12 3 courses. **Credit** MC, V.

Located in the student quarter of Cathays, the old shopfront of this excellent restaurant has been sympathetically renovated to retain a vaguely bohemian feel. Inside, the comfortable dining area is divided in two and decked out with simple wood furniture. The set lunch is not only one of the best in quality but also great value. Start with a wonderfully fresh tian of light and dark Gower crab meat served with a simple, well-dressed salad. Main courses can include salt marsh lamb from Laugharne accompanied with samphire or a skate wing (usually the bigger thornback ray) served with blanched summer vegetables and samphire and roast potatoes. Puddings are traditional and the selection of cheese always includes something interesting from Wales. The wine list is well chosen and service is Cardiffian: bold, friendly and efficient. This place is very popular, so book in advance.

Da Venditto ★

7-8 Park Place, Cardiff, CF10 3DP (029 2023 0781/ www.vendittogroup.co.uk). **Lunch served** noon-2.30pm, **dinner served** 6-10.45pm Tue-Sat. **Main courses** £18.50. **Set lunch** £14.50 2 courses, £18 3 courses. **Set dinner** £27.50 2 courses, £32.50 3 courses. **Credit** AmEx, DC, MC, V.

The interior of this expensively refurbished basement opposite Cardiff's New Theatre may scream *Footballers' Wives* but the menu is a different matter altogether, with accomplished and thoughtful cooking by Ifan Duff and his team. Packed with wonderful Italian regional dishes, there's enough here to keep you coming back again and again. A starter of hand-made tagliatelle is cooked perfectly and served with meltingly enriched duck and concasse with a dusting of parmesan. Main courses are equally impressive, whether it's spaghetti with lobster and lemongrass or risotto of spring veg. Puddings are just as well made if a little less adventurous. Panna cotta with spiced poached pear, tiramisu, and lemon, ricotta and almond cake with mascarpone lead the calorific charge. The wholly Italian wine list is a joy to read – the Tuscan and Venetian wines alone would justify a visit – and service is informed, helpful and efficient.

Le Gallois

6-10 Romilly Crescent, Canton, Cardiff, CF11 9NR (029 2034 1264/www.legallois-ycymro.com). **Lunch served** noon-2.30pm, **dinner served** 6.30-10.30pm Tue-Sat. **Main courses** £20. **Set meal** £30 2 courses, £35 3 courses. **Credit** AmEx, MC, V.

Cardiff-born chef Padrig Jones heads a kitchen team that produces well thought-out and flavoursome dishes from the best ingredients. Meat, game and seafood is from Wales; offal, poultry, cheese and wine from France. The suburban setting is misleading as behind the blue canopies and engraved glass frontage lies a metropolitan interior of polished wood surfaces and yellow and ochre walls. An appetiser of intense cold consommé with chives and tomato prepares you for starters of sautéed scallops with belly pork, boudin noir, quail's egg, confit tomato and honey jam. Presentation is excellent, whether you choose a main of goujons of calf's liver with braised bok choi and fondant potatoes or the confit duck leg with green lentils and roast pumpkin. Puddings are light: try thyme-roasted peach with ricotta ice-cream. House wines are good value, service is professional.

Old Post Office

Greenwood Lane, St Fagan's, Cardiff, CF5 6EL (029 2056 5400/www.old-post-office.com). **Lunch served** noon-2pm Thur-Sun. **Dinner served** 7-9.30pm Wed-Sat. **Set lunch** £12.50 2 courses, £15.95 3 courses. **Set dinner** £27.50 2 courses, £32.50 3 courses. **Credit** AmEx, MC, V.

Comparatively out in the sticks, the original post office building has been radically modernised, with dazzlingly lit conservatory dining areas, modern British dishes and young, enthusiastic staff. Expect starters of pan-fried pigeon breast with grape chutney or ham hock terrine with onion marmalade. Main courses include Welsh Black beef with seared foie gras or John Dory with red pepper and truffle sauce. Pistachio crème brûlée concludes. This is the flagship restaurant of a group of three that also includes Woods Brasserie (Stuart Street, Cardiff, CF10 5BW, 029 2049 2400). On the waterfront, it's housed in an old slate and stone built port building. Again, clean modern interiors combine with a take on brasserie classics such as Thai green curry with rice noodles, or fresh yellowfin tuna in a niçoise salad. The other member of the trio is Cutting Edge (Discovery House, Scott Harbour, Cardiff Bay, CF10 4PJ, 029 2047 0780), opposite the Welsh National Assembly with food catering to the meat and two veg mentality of the local politicos.

Carmarthenshire

LAUGHARNE

The Cors

Newbridge Road, Laugharne, Carmarthenshire SA33 4SH (01994 427219). **Lunch served** *May-Sept* noon-2pm, **dinner served** 7-9.30pm Wed-Sun. *Nov-Apr* 7-9.30pm Thur-Sat. Closed Oct. **Main courses** £12.50-£17. **No credit cards.**

Laugharne is the town where Dylan Thomas lived, worked and drank. The marsh along the town brook is the setting for the Cors (bog in Welsh), a restaurant with rooms run by vivacious chef and owner, Nick Priestland. The marsh has been turned into a wonderful water garden and this Victorian villa has been decorated in a bohemian style. Starters include bruschetta with grilled local goat's cheese, smoked haddock crème brûlée and dressed crab with a basil mayonnaise. Mains feature local specialities such as rack of salt marsh lamb raised on the nearby marshes. Fish from the local market can include Towy sewin perfectly fried with crispy skin and pale pink flesh served with asparagus and a light lemon hollandaise. The wine list is excellent value.

NANTGAREDIG

Four Seasons

Nantgaredig, Camarthenshire SA32 7NY (01267 290238/www.fourseasonsleisure.co.uk). **Dinner served** 7.30-9pm Tue-Sat. **Set dinner** £27.50 3 courses and coffee. **Credit** AmEx, MC, V.

Situated in the heart of rural Camarthenshire, the Four Seasons comprises a series of old farm buildings that have been renovated to offer comfortable accommodation as well as a spacious, open-kitchen restaurant. Owned and run by sisters Charlotte Pasetti and Maryann Wright, the style is modern British with Mediterranean overtones. Starters of tomato and garden herb soup, Carmarthen ham with cherry tomatoes and crumbled feta were more successful than over-cooked hot smoked haddock tart with warm potato salad. Main courses include fresh salmon with watercress, cucumber and salsa, or a more robust hake fillet with basil crust and red pepper sauce. Desserts are filling. This isn't sophisticated food but it is locally sourced and the preparation is straightforward and honest, allowing ingredients to sing. The wine list includes a good list of half bottles.

Ceredigion

ABERAERON

Harbourmaster

The Quay, Aberaeron, Ceredigion SA46 0BA (01545 570755/www.harbour-master.com). **Lunch served** noon-2pm Tue-Sun. **Dinner served** 6.30-9pm Mon-Sat. **Main courses** £12.50-£17.50. **Credit** MC, V.

With its purple frontage and prominent position, the Harbourmaster is easy to find in this Georgian-squared harbour town. Owners Glyn and Menna Heulyn have transformed a rather charming if down at heel pub into a cool, modern mini-hotel with nine rooms. A meal here is always a bit of an occasion. An appetiser of pea soup with basil oil can be followed by starters of Penclawdd cockles, perfectly cleaned, crisply fried in batter and served with a freshly made sauce tartare, or a rich smooth chicken liver parfait with red onion marmalade and wholemeal toast. Welsh Black sirloin is served alongside a lattice of chunky chips and fillet of Finish with the best cup of coffee in west Wales.

Conwy

CAPEL GARMON

Tan-y-Foel

Capel Garmon, Conwy LL26 0RE (01690 710507/ www.tyfhotel.co.uk). **Dinner served** 7.30-8.15pm daily by appointment only. **Set dinner** £34 3 courses. **Credit** MC, V.

There is a real feeling of achievement as you sit down for dinner here. Not only have you managed to book a table, you've managed to find the place. High up above Betws-y-Coed, this 16th-century farmhouse has been renovated to a high standard. Drawing room and dining room are surprisingly modern in style with a French feel to the decor. You'll never have more than a dozen fellow diners so the meal takes on a special intimacy. The

Plas Bodegroes. See p331.

daily-changing menus are restricted to two options for each course and focus on local produce. Wild rabbit confit on a base of cassoulet or a tempura of red mullet was precisely prepared. Marinated Welsh pork with kale and vegetable fritters was fabulously rich; tender veal arrived with oven-crisped parsnip and beetroot fritters reinforced with liquorice sauce. The long wine list has an impressive array of halves.

LLANDUDNO

St Tudno Hotel

North Parade, The Promenade, Llandudno, Conwy LL30 2LP (01492 874411/www.st-tudno.co.uk). **Lunch served** 12.30-1.45pm Mon-Sat; 12.30-1.30pm Sun. **Dinner served** 7-9.30pm Mon-Sat; 7-9pm Sun. **Main courses** £16-£19. **Set lunch** (Mon-Fri) £14 2 courses, £17.50 3 courses; (Sat, Sun) £17.50 3 courses. **Credit** AmEx, DC, MC, V.

This hotel has wonderful views across the bay and along the seafront. The Garden restaurant to the rear is light and comfortable. There's a long carte with seven or eight choices per course. Mint and pea broth as an appetiser is followed by crab risotto with shellfish glaze, or seared king scallops with tomato and basil salad and saffron dressing. Salad of mozzarella and plum tomato with roast pine nuts, rocket and olive oil was refreshingly bold and unfussy. Roast fillet of salmon with cherry tomatoes, couscous and deep-fried courgettes was more effective in presentation and taste than fricassee of scallops in puff pastry case with lobster velouté and carved vegetables. Finally, try white chocolate mousse served between thin wafers of crisp milk chocolate accompanied by a zingy passion fruit jelly.

LLANSANDFFRAID

Old Rectory

Llanrwst Road, Llansandffraid, Glan Conwy, Conwy LL28 5LF (01492 580611/www.oldrectorycountryhouse.co.uk). **Dinner served** 7.30pm for 8pm. **Set dinner** £39.50 3 courses. **Credit** MC, V.

Owners Michael and Wendy Vaughan have spent two decades creating a relaxing environment at this Georgian country home. Aperitifs and appetisers are served in the drawing room; a good opportunity to survey the menu before entering a sumptuous dining room with mahogany tables and expensive glassware. Local seasonal produce is a priority. Fish is strongly represented, together with white meats and game when it is in season. Start with local brill with sweet potato purée, fig and lemon compote or Lady Llanover salt duck with a delicious egg and olive sauce. Mains include turbot or Conwy salmon, but also mountain lamb roasted to perfection with fondant potato and cabbage ratatouille parcel. Roast breast of guinea fowl is accompanied by a spinach, goat's cheese and wild mushroom risotto.

Denbighshire

LLANDEGLA

Bodidris Hall

Llandegla, Denbighshire LL11 3AL (08707 292292/www.bodidrishall.com). **Lunch served** noon-4pm, **dinner served** 7-9.30pm daily. **Set lunch** (Mon-Sat) £9.95 2 courses, £14.95 3 courses, (Sun) £14.95 4 courses. **Set dinner** £29.95 5 courses. **Credit** AmEx, DC, MC, V.

A 15th-century mansion house that stands in the beautifully maintained remains of the once massive Denbighshire estate. With a laudable refusal to develop the site, it's amazing that such a place can prosper. Go easy on the appetisers; dinner here is several courses. Starters include a delicate langoustine cappuccino with horseradish and chives or exotica like steamed courgette flowers filled with fish mousse and tomato reduction. A sorbet or soup is followed by a meaty shark steak served with fine green beans, or rack of North Wales lamb. Finish with iced pistachio terrine with raspberry coulis.

LLANDRILLO

Tyddyn Llan ★

Llandrillo, Denbighshire LL21 0ST (01490 440264/ www.tyddynllan.co.uk). **Lunch served** 12.30-2.30pm Thur-Sun. **Dinner served** 7-9pm daily. **Set lunch** £19.50 2 courses, £24.50 3 courses; (Sun) £19.50 3 courses. **Set dinne**r £29.50 2 courses, £35 3 courses, £40 4 courses. **Credit** MC, V.

Bryan and Susan Webb have swapped one award-winning restaurant (Hilaire) in South Kensington for another in North Wales. Tyddyn Llan, a stone-built farmhouse, has been converted into a rural retreat with a dining room and ten bedrooms. Canapés of fish cakes and parmesan biscuits are followed by an appetiser of curried pea soup. Starters include firm, rich parfait of foie gras and chicken livers with rich onion chutney. Main courses include brill with leek risotto and a red wine sauce or wild salmon with a watercress sauce. Puddings are fab and the wine list has an impressive choice by the glass.

Gwynedd

ABERDYFI

Penhelig Arms

Aberdyfi, Gwynedd LL35 0LT (01654 767215/ www.penheligarms.com). Bar **Lunch served** noon-2pm, **dinner served** 6-9.15pm daily. *Restaurant*

Dining South Wales-style

Le Monde threw open its doors to an unsuspecting Cardiff public some 25 years ago with its winning formula of lavish displays of fresh fish and meat simply but effectively prepared in an open central kitchen. Diners immediately took this fast, furious and fun dining style to their hearts. So much so that it has virtually invented a local dining style.

The Le Monde site (62 St Mary's Street, Cardiff CF10 1FE, 029 2038 7376) houses three restaurants. Don't expect fizz at Champers (029 2037 3363), but this rather inappropriately named tapas bar does do a good line in tortilla, patatas bravas and delicately pickled anchovy. La Brasserie (029 2023 4134) may like to think of itself as more French than its sister establishment – starters of frogs' legs with garlic mayonnaise, for instance – but these do little to mask the Spanish influence. Main courses include hake cutlet, Dover sole or darne of salmon with an array of steaks, kebabs, veal and venison. Le Monde's menu is seafood-oriented, with deep-fried whitebait, fish soup, mussels and king prawns, followed by sea bass baked in rock salt, grilled crayfish tails and Cornish lobster. Excellent value for money, comfortable surroundings and engaging service that ranges from the charming to the quixotic are factors in the success of this venture.

With these successes in place, the Le Monde group continues to open new eateries around Cardiff. La Fosse (9-11 The Hayes, Cardiff, CF10 1AH, 029 2023 7755) is situated in the old fish market basement. An absolutely huge venue with subdued lighting, it relies on fabulous fixed-price lunch deals (£7.95 for two courses) to keep the place filled with passing shoppers. The oysters are especially good.

The group's most recent venture is the newly renovated old Customs House out by the Cardiff Barrage in Penarth Marina. Downstairs is El Puerto (029 2070 5551), while upstairs La Marina is a more formal restaurant with great views. El Puerto houses open kitchens and display cabinets containing huge Bengal Bay king prawns, lobster and sea bass. Dishes are offered simply grilled or fried or in Iberian-style marinades. The Le Monde group also runs the Brasseria El Prado in Laleston near Bridgend (01656 649972), Caesar's Arms at Creigau in Mid Glamorgan (02920 890486) and the Priory Hotel and Restaurant in Caerleon near Newport (01633 421241).

Similar eateries have now sprung up in Swansea. La Brasseria on Wind Street (01792 469683) bears many similarities to Champers; Gilby's, on the outskirts of Cardiff, is a favourite destination for nearby HTV's studio folk – although it lacks the Spanish influence, it has a familiar open kitchen and offers a mouth-watering display of molluscs and fish.

Lunch served noon-2pm, **dinner served** 7-9.30pm daily. **Main courses** £7.95-£12.95. **Set dinner** £26 3 courses. **Credit** MC, V.
This 18th-century harbourside inn has a wonderful quayside location overlooking the Dyfi estuary. As well as the Fisherman's Bar, there is a more formal restaurant – cool and modern with grey surfaces. Food is locally sourced and transformed into tempting brasserie-style dishes by chef Jan Howkins. Crisp whitebait, seared tuna or smoked local trout can be followed by grilled brochette of mixed fish, Welsh Black sirloin or local mountain lamb with aubergines and a mint sauce béarnaise. If apricot frangipane tart with crème fraîche doesn't appeal, then the cheeseboard with ragstone, celtic promise and other Welsh choices almost certainly will. The wine list is a voluminous catalogue, and service retains a welcoming local pub feel.

ABERSOCH

Porth Tocyn

Bwlch Tocyn, Abersoch, Gwynedd LL53 7BU (01758 713303/www.porth-tocyn-hotel.co.uk). **Lunch served** *Mar-Oct* noon-2pm daily. **Dinner served** 7.15-9pm. Closed Nov-Feb. **Main courses** (lunch) £7.50. **Set dinner** £29.50 2 courses, £36 4 courses. **Buffet** (Sun) £20.50. **Credit** MC, V.
Few hotels can claim to enjoy such a dramatic view, with the whole of Snowdonia laid out before you. Situated on a headland above Abersoch, Porth Tocyn combines the jolliness of the bucket and spade experience with old-fashioned standards of food and service. The daily-changing menu might offer starters of smoked goose salad with sauce gribiche or bouillabaisse. Occasionally, there's sashimi (in this location, good quality fish can be expected). Local scallops are sweet and delicious served en brochette. Meat eaters are also well served here with main courses of pork fillet roasted with smoked bacon served with apple compote and a cider reduction. Service is often from the proprietor himself, who treats returning guests so well you may want to become one yourself.

DOLGELLAU

Dylanwad Da

2 Ffos-y-Felin, Dolgellau, Gwynedd LL40 1BS (01341 422870/www.dylanwad.co.uk). **Coffee & cake served** 10am-4pm Thur-Sat. **Dinner served** 7-9pm Thur-Sat (Tue-Sat in holiday periods – phone to check). Closed Feb. **Main courses** £9.80-£14.60. **No credit cards.**
All agree that Dylanwad Da has been a good influence on Dolgellau's slate grey streets since opening in 1988. There's a small bar area and a dining room decorated in bright modern colours and furnished with light-wood furniture. The relaxed atmosphere does not extend to the cooking, which is disciplined and precise. Try chicken, basil and tomato terrine or avocado, beetroot and orange salad. Then there's Welsh sirloin plainly garnished with onions, mushrooms and tomato, allowing the quality of the local ingredients to shine through. Puddings are first rate: Welsh honey and almond ice-cream meringues served with a compote of fresh berries and white chocolate cheesecake. Good quality, relaxed dining in comfortable surroundings.

Penmaenuchaf Hall

Penmaenpool, Gwynedd LL40 1YB (01341 422129/ www.penhall.co.uk). **Lunch served** noon-2pm Mon-Sat; noon-2.30pm Sun. **Dinner served** 7-9.30pm Mon-Sat; 7-9pm Sun. **Main courses** £19.95-£24.50. **Set lunch** £14.95 2 courses, £15.95 3 courses. **Set dinner** £32.50 4 courses. **Credit** MC, V.
High above the Mawddach estuary, this distinguished Victorian residence clings to a terrace on a wooded hillside. It's a salubrious joint: the wood-panelled dining room has upholstered chairs, heavy damask linen and expensive glassware. Justin Pilkington produces dishes with strong, clear flavours. Start with gazpacho, tuna carpaccio or foie gras and chicken liver parfait with toasted brioche. Main courses like creamy wild mushroom risotto with asparagus and truffle are well timed and satisfying. Sea bass from the Cumbrian coast with aubergine caviar, red pepper and tomato sauce shows a Mediterranean influence. All dishes are presented in an attractive but unfussy manner. Puddings might include a milk chocolate mousse with poached raspberries or a fine apple tart with cinnamon ice-cream. Joint proprietor Mark Watson combines his interest with his wine merchant business so it's no surprise that the list here is extensive and enjoyable.

PWLLHELI

Plas Bodegroes ★

Nefyn Road, Pwllheli, Gwynedd LL53 5TH (01758 612363/www.bodegroes.co.uk). **Lunch served** 12.30-2.30pm Sun. **Dinner served** 7-9pm Tue-Sat. Closed Dec-Feb. **Set lunch** £17.50 3 courses. **Set dinner** £38 4 courses. **Credit** MC, V.
Plas Bodegroes sits in its own idyllic gardens on the Llyn Peninsula. This Georgian rectory offers not just Michelin-starred dining but excellent bedrooms. Consistency is the order of the day and chef/owner Chris Chown works to produce imaginative food from the best of local produce. Staff strike a balance between informality and efficiency; the dining room is simple but stylish. Starters include delicate soups such as watercress with nutmeg glaze or ballotine of guinea fowl, apricot and pistachio and red pepper chutney. The monkfish and Carmarthen ham has become a national standard. Main courses include roast cutlets of local mountain lamb with Welsh onion cake and a mustard and rosemary sauce. Welsh beef is also well represented. Puddings are characterful, whether you choose cappuccino crème brûlée or prune and Armagnac parfait with pistachio praline. Consistency, quality and dining with a sense of occasion. Booking is essential.

TALSARNAU

Maes-y-Neuadd ★

Talsarnau, Gwynedd LL47 6YA (01766 780200/ www.neuadd.com). **Lunch served** noon-1.45pm, **dinner served** 7-8.45pm daily. **Set lunch** (Sun) £15.25 3 courses incl coffee. **Set dinner** £31 3 courses, £35 4 courses. **Credit** AmEx, DC, MC, V.
This old mansion in the meadow sits high above Harlech with views of Snowdonia and Cardigan Bay. Appetisers of parsnip crisps, goat's cheese wrapped in ham or smoked duck mousse set the mood. Chef Peter Jackson manages the Welsh National Culinary Team so expect impressive but never intimidating professionalism. Starters of chicken liver parfait with toasted brioche, or fish terrine with lemon and herb yoghurt and mixed leaves lead to a fish course, which could be spicy fish cakes with wilted courgettes and sorrel, or grilled grey mullet with fennel. Main courses are more robust: locally sourced venison with saffron polenta, roasted garlic and pickled walnut sauce. The Francophile wine list is an evening's reading, although Welsh vineyards do get a look in. Service is friendly.

Isle of Anglesey

BEAUMARIS

Ye Olde Bulls Head Inn

Castle Street, Beaumaris, Isle of Anglesey LL58 8AP (01248 810329/www.bullsheadinn.co.uk). Brasserie **Lunch served** noon-2pm, **dinner served** 6-9pm daily. *Restaurant* **Dinner served** 7-9.30pm Mon-Sat. **Main courses** £20. **Set dinner** £25 2 courses, £30 3 courses. **Credit** AmEx, MC, V.
Good beer, smartly dressed bar staff and a buzzing ambience make Ye Olde Bull's Head one of the most attractive watering holes in North Wales. There are also a couple of dining options. A conservatory-based brasserie offers sandwiches and grills as well as mains like black bream fresh from the quay, fried or seared. If you want something grander, then mount the ancient stairway to the dramatic restaurant (soft colours, lots of fabric surfaces and the light off the Menai Strait). The menu focuses on fish, with alluring mains such as cod fillet with spinach, plum tomato confit and caper beurre blanc, though Welsh lamb also features. A good selection of Welsh cheeses is a tempting closer.

Monmouthshire

ABERGAVENNY

Angel Hotel

15 Cross Street, Abergavenny, Monmouthshire NP7 5EN (01873 857121/www.angelhotelabergavenny.com). **Lunch served** noon-2.30pm, **dinner served** 7-10pm daily. **Main courses** £10.50-£16.40. **Set lunch** (Mon-Sat) £8.80 2 courses; (Sun) £14.80 3 courses. **Credit** AmEx, MC, V.
This old coaching inn was once a run-down ruin, but it was bought by Caradog Hotels in 2002 and the bar and dining room now provide an excellent and – by local standards – opulent setting. Chef Mark Turton provides well-planned menus at staggeringly low prices. Starters of cream of mushroom soup and fan of melon with pink grapefruit sorbet are dramatically presented. Main courses include a generous plateful of the local staple, roast leg of Welsh lamb complete with mint sauce and al dente veg. Puddings of chocolate fondant with rum ice-cream and caramelised lemon tart with vanilla mascarpone are hugely tempting. The wine list is short, well chosen and priced to sell.

Allt yr Ynys Country House Hotel

Walterstone, nr Abergavenny, Monmouthshire HR2 0DU (01873 890307/www.allthotel.co.uk). **Lunch served** noon-2pm Mon-Fri, Sun. **Dinner served** 7-9.30pm Mon-Sat; 7-9pm Sun. **Main courses** £15-£19. **Set lunch** £17.50 3 courses. **Credit** AmEx, MC, V.
A local institution. This Grade II-listed, 16th-century farmhouse has provided excellent dining for 14 years; eight under the current owners. The dining room is a masterpiece of understatement with good quality glassware, cutlery and linen and comfortable chairs. Ian Jackson uses underrated fish to great effect and his daily menus feature seasonal produce. Start with a risotto of creamed wild mushrooms with lightly poached egg and truffle-infused bubbles, or caramelised Cornish scallops on creamed celeriac and bacon with a chilli and coriander beurre blanc. Main courses include baked pavé of pollock with herb tapenade crust, puréed potatoes, braised celery and tomato and basil vinaigrette. Even old standards like rack of Welsh lamb are given a new twist, served with garlic cream and a thyme and white wine sauce. Abergavenny is the meeting point for Welsh, Herefordshire and West Country cheesemakers, so the choice is tremendous.

Llanwenarth Hotel

Brecon Road, Abergavenny, Monmouthshire NP8 1EP (01873 810550/www.llanwenarthhotel.com). **Lunch served** noon-2pm Mon-Sat; noon-3pm Sun. **Dinner served** 5.30-9.30pm Mon-Sat; 6-9pm Sun. **Main courses** £9.45-£13.95. **Set lunch** £12.25 3 courses. **Set dinner** (5.30-7pm) £14.25 3 courses. **Credit** MC, V.
Once known as the Pantriwlgoch, this roadside hotel is under new ownership and has reverted to its original name. The interior now boasts cheerful colours and comfortable furniture. The menus has also improved. Starters of black pudding and boudin blanc on mash with red wine reduction, baked filo pastry parcels of goat's cheese with rocket salad or moules marinière are well prepared. Thoughtful vegetarian options include oyster mushroom fettucine with truffle oil and parmesan or baked pepper, tomato and onion tartlet with smoked cheese and spinach. There's also local beef and lamb and lemon sole. A short but user-friendly wine list offers a good house wine and some attractive half bottles.

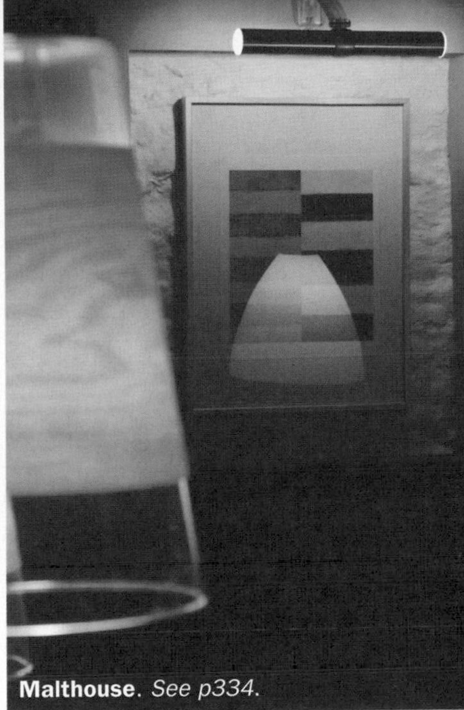

Malthouse. *See p334.*

CHEPSTOW

The Wye Knot

18A The Back Riverbank, Chepstow, Monmouthshire NP16 5HH (01291 622929). **Lunch served** 12.30-2.30pm, **dinner served** 7-10pm Wed-Sun. **Main courses** £12.95-£17.95. **Set dinner** £17.50 2 courses, £21.50 3 courses. **Credit** MC, V.

The Wye Knot has a dramatic situation overlooking the gorge at Chepstow. The interior comprises a series of small, rather awkward spaces, but chef/proprietor Kevin Brookes and his team are constantly trying to make the best of things. Voted Welsh Chef of the Year in 2003, Brookes's dishes use local seasonal produce in a dazzling display of techniques and combinations. Fresh bread and olives set the scene for French onion soup with crispy cheese croutons or warm potato, goat's cheese and provençal vegetable terrine with tapenade dressing. Then there's new season local lamb with a casserole of mixed beans, confit garlic and light lamb jus. For afters, summer fruit terrine is set in vodka jelly with each layer of fruit lined with fresh basil. Service can be slow, but it is always friendly.

CLYTHA

Clytha Arms

Clytha, Monmouthshire NP7 9BW (01873 840206/ www.clytha-arms.com). **Open** noon-3.30pm, 6-11pm Tue-Fri; noon-11pm Sat; noon-10.30pm Sun. **Lunch served** 12.30-2.15pm Tue-Sat; 12.30-2.30pm Sun. **Dinner served** 7.30-9pm Tue-Sat. **Main courses** £12-£17.50. **Set meal** £15.95 2 courses, £17.95 3 courses. **Credit** AmEx, DC, MC, V.

Aficionados of cider will know this great pub as the venue for the Welsh Cider Festival, but this renovated dower house serves great beer and food all year. Chef/owner Andrew Canning offers an excellent bar menu as well as a more sophisticated one for the restaurant. The bar is furnished with wooden benches, tables and bar skittles. By comparison, the dining room is a bit soulless. Dishes vary enormously, so starters could be leek and laverbread rissoles with beetroot chutney, black pasta with cockles, or wild boar rillettes with red onion chutney. Main courses range from the simple yet effective (black bream with leeks and mussels) to the more exotic (Caribbean fruit curry with crayfish). Servings are generous so there's rarely room for treacle pudding and custard. Staff are young, but know their stuff.

LLANTHEWY SKIRRID

Walnut Tree Inn

Llandewi Skirrid, Monmouthshire NP7 8AW (01873 852797/www.thewalnuttreeinn.com). **Lunch served** noon-2.30pm Tue-Sun; **dinner served** 7-10pm Tue-Sat. **Main courses** £12.75-£21.50. **Set lunch** £16.50 2 courses, £19.50 3 courses. **Credit** MC, V.

The opening-up of the old dining room has given this restaurant a more airy feel. The fixed-price lunch menu is still good value but prices on the à la carte have increased noticeably. Food remains Welsh/Italian – a strange hybrid virtually invented by ex-owner Franco Taruschio. For starters, expect fresh asparagus with poached egg. Pasta includes taglioni with sweet, fresh scallops in tomato and basil sauce. Apart from the fresh sewin, pollack, swordfish and turbot, there's a maginificent brodetto of fish served with bruschetta. There's also a well-prepared poached ham hock with baby vegetables in savoury broth. To follow: warm figs with Welsh honey, balsamic and mascarpone. Good wines and delightful service round-off a great experience.

LLANDOGO

Sloop Inn

Llandogo, Monmouthshire NP25 4TW (01594 530291). **Lunch served** noon-2.30pm Tue-Sat; noon-3pm Sun. **Dinner served** 6-9.30pm Tue-Sat. **Main courses** £9.50-£16. **Set meal** (lunch, 6-7.30pm) £11.50 2 courses, £13.50 3 courses. **Credit** MC, V.

Llandogo is the poor relation of glamorous Tintern in Monmouthshire's beautiful Wye Valley with few reasons to visit and even fewer to eat. Caroline Kendrick has changed that with Sloop Inn. Bar and restaurant (which has great views) have been decorated in an uncluttered, modern style. In the bar, chef Steve Jenkins has designed a menu offering stylish, keenly priced sandwiches and pastas. In the restaurant, appetisers of grilled scallops on a tomato pickle reduction precede starters of grilled Cornish sardines with a well-dressed salad or crayfish risotto. Main courses range from shepherd's pie or Welsh steaks to Breconshire venison in a chocolate sauce. Full marks for displaying suppliers on the menu. There's a short, utilitarian wine list with the majority of items priced between £15 and £20.

LLANVIHANGEL GOBION

Llansantffraed Court

Llanvihangel Gobion, Monmouthshire NP7 9BA (01873 840678/www.llch.co.uk). **Lunch served** noon-2pm; **dinner served** 7.30-8.45pm daily. **Main courses** £16.50-£21.75. **Set lunch** £20 3 courses **Set dinner** £29.50 3 courses. **Credit** AmEx, MC, V.

This country house restaurant recently underwent a change of chef, and when we called Simon King was still finding his feet with a menu that was well cooked but unadventurous. Chintz curtains, hunting prints and good quality settings set the tone. An *amuse-bouche* of deep-fried cheese with onion marmalade precedes starters that can include chicken's liver parfait with onion marmalade and brioche or salad of crayfish tails. For main courses choose between Welsh black beef fillet with red wine jus, honey-glazed pork belly with roast parsnips and apples, or Gressingham duck breast with green pepper sauce. Puddings include champagne and summer berry jelly, chilled melon soup with raspberry sorbet. The wine list has a good selection of champagnes, and lists the rest by style.

MONMOUTH

Malthouse

12 St Mary's Street, Monmouth, Monmouthshire NP25 3DB (01600 772052/www.themalthouse.net). **Lunch served** noon-2.30pm Mon-Sat. **Dinner served** 7-9.30pm Mon-Thur; 7-10pm Fri, Sat. **Set dinner** £18 3 courses. **Credit** AmEx, DC, MC, V.

By day the former flour mill is a café serving good coffee and Spanish pâtisseries; in the evening the Malthouse becomes a tapas bar providing a wonderful array of freshly made tidbits to go with a short wine list. The interior is divided into three sections; a dining room; a café area with flagstone floors, kitchen and internet access; a lounge full of plush suede-upholstered sofas, modern art and newspaper racks. The tapas is good: stuffed piquillo peppers, patatas bravas, marinated anchovies, olives and pickled peppers. Prawns sautéed in garlic, and fish casserole are mouth-watering.

NANT-Y-DERRY

The Foxhunter ★

Nant-y-derry, Monmouthshire NP7 9DN (01873 881101/www.thefoxhunter.com). **Lunch served** noon-2.30pm, **dinner served** 7-9.30pm Tue-Sat. **Main courses** £12.95-£17.95. **Set lunch** £18 2 courses, £22 3 courses. **Credit** MC, V.

Matt Tebbutt worked with Alistair Little, Marco Pierre White and Sally Clarke before moving to Wales with his wife Lisa. His menu is modern British but with forays into Tuscany, Catalonia and Andalucia, employing local produce where possible. Starters can include English squid, deep-fried with tartare sauce and lemon or exceptional Scottish langoustine accompanied by preserved lemon mayonnaise. From closer to home comes crisp duck leg and french beans on goat's cheese croûton. Mains include local suckling pig with sautéed peas, broad beans and a slice of potato. Longhorn sirloin from Frank Sutton's award-winning herd was perfectly cooked and served with delicious watercress, pickled mushrooms and tangy herb butter. There's a brace of house whites and house reds at £13.50 and a short but effective list of half bottles. Staff are friendly and knowledgeable. Booking is essential.

NEWPORT

The Chandlery ★

77-78 Lower Dock Street, Newport, Monmouthshire NP20 1EH (01633 256622/www.chandlery restaurant.co.uk). **Lunch served** noon-2pm Tue-Fri. **Dinner served** 7-10pm Tue-Sat. **Main courses** £9.95-£16.95. **Set lunch** £8.95 2 courses, £12.95 3 courses. **Credit** AmEx, MC, V.

It's only taken Simon Newcombe and team a couple of years to establish the Chandlery as the city's restaurant of choice. You have to book to get a table midweek, the commitment to Welsh produce remains evident and the cooking is accomplished. Starters include a rich salmon and lobster fish cake served with buttered spinach and a chive velouté. Trio of duck includes Lady Llanover's salted variety, a confit of foie gras and a lovely spring roll. The Asian interest continues in the main coureses, with five-spice braised belly pork with rice noodles, spring vegetables and king prawns. Welsh meat figures prominently: try beef fillet, blue cheese ravioli, savoy cabbage, smoke bacon and red wine jus.

Junction 28

Station Approach, Bassaleg, Newport, Monmouthshire NP10 8LD (01633 891891/www.junction28.com). **Lunch served** noon-2pm Mon-Sat; noon-4pm Sun. **Dinner served** 5.30-9.30pm Mon-Fri; 5.30-9.45pm Sat. **Main courses** £7.95-£15.95. **Set lunch** £7.95 1 course, £9.95 2 courses, £11.45 3 courses. **Set dinner** (5.30-6.45pm Mon-Sat) £12.95 3 courses. **Credit** AmEx, MC, V.

Find the church in Bassaleg on the Newport outskirts, and behind it is Junction 28. The interior has grown organically to include several rooms and what appears to be the interior of a Pullman dining car. This restaurant reflects the needs of its clientele; what it lacks in finesse, it makes up for with honest food and wine at attractive prices. Starters include soused herring or prawn and cod fish cake with curried hollandaise. Main courses could be monkfish medallions with olive and thyme butter and provençal vegetables, or duck confit on bubble and squeak. All portions err on the side of generosity and are delivered by friendly staff. Puddings such as sticky toffee pudding and milk chocolate and orange mousse are balanced by a lighter crème caramel served with chantilly crème and biscotti. The wine list is notable for its wide choice. Feeding 300 covers an evening causes the occasional hiccup, but this is enjoyable and affordable dining.

Owens at the Celtic Manor

Celtic Manor Hotel, Coldra Woods, Newport NP18 1HQ (01633 413000/www.celtic-manor.com). **Dinner served** 7-10.30pm Mon-Sat. **Set dinner** £45 4 courses, £52 5 courses, £60 6 courses. **Credit** AmEx, DC, MC, V.

Hidden from the bustle of this huge golf resort and hotel complex, Owens is an oasis of comfortable chairs and expensive linen. The bright lighting emphasises that this a place to see as well as be seen. Executive chef Michael Bates and his team produce menus with the focus on Welsh produce such as smoked Caerphilly cheese sausage, Pembrokeshire crab, or tender Monmouthshire beef. Lobster boudin in its own cappuccino foam is followed by a starter of roasted breast of Anjou pigeon cooked to pink perfection. The main courses are complex assemblies like baked supreme of cod with gruyère and herb crust, tomato fondue, choucroute of apple and turnip, rösti and – in case you were feeling short-changed – a fricassee of clams. After a palette reviver of plum compote, biscuit cream and ginger jelly, expect desserts such as rich dark chocolate tart with beetroot ice-cream. After all this exotica, the wine list is a little pedestrian; a matter that is being addressed.

ROCKFIELD

Stone Mill

Steppes Farm Cottages, Rockfield, Monmouthshire NP25 5SW (01600 775424/www.steppesfarm cottages.co.uk). **Lunch served** noon-2.30pm, **dinner served** 6-9.30pm Tue-Sun. **Main courses** £10.50-£18. **Set lunch** (Tue-Sat) £7.95 2 courses, £10.50 3 courses. **Set dinner** (Tue-Thur) £11.95 2 courses, £13.95 3 courses. **Credit** MC, V.

This old farm cider mill has been converted into a rustic beamed dining space. Owner Michelle de Cloedt and her staff provide a welcoming front of house while Dan Vaughn busies himself in the kitchen. Asparagus is accompanied by a rich, smooth hollandaise and perfectly poached duck egg (from the attached farm). Parma ham, figs and parmesan is a simple but winning combination as is crab and chilli linguini with coriander. Main courses range from the house speciality of suckling pig served with braised apple, through to double-cooked poussin with warm grapes and a vermouth sabayon. Puddings have an Italianate flair: fresh raspberries and strawberries served beneath a caramelised layer of mascarpone with crunchy biscotti fragments.

SKENFIRTH

Bell at Skenfrith

Skenfrith, Monmouthshire NP7 8UH (01600 750235/ www.skenfrith.co.uk). **Lunch served** noon-2.30pm daily. **Dinner served** 7-9.30pm Mon-Sat; 7-9pm Sun. **Main courses** £11-£18. **Set lunch** (Sun only) £14.50 2 courses, £ 18.50 3 courses. **Credit** AmEx MC, V.

Even this award-winning restaurant is not immune from staff changes, but the regime here seems more than capable of keeping this establishment on course. New chef Kurt Fleming maintains an emphasis on local produce with suppliers listed in the menu. Starters include ham hock terrine, onion and thyme chutney and mustard dressing, and delicious warm asparagus (from the village) with the caramelised fig relish, blinis and sauce hollandaise. A main of sweet Cornish lobster salad with new potatoes is exemplary. White chocolate crème brûlée with raspberry ice-cream rounded things off perfectly.

TINTERN

Parva Farmhouse

Tintern, nr Chepstow, Monmouthshire NP16 6SQ (01291 689411/www.hoteltintern.co.uk). **Dinner served** 7-8.30pm daily. **Set dinner** £22 4 courses. **Credit** AmEx, MC, V.

Blink and you'll miss this 17th-century farmhouse down a turning opposite Tintern Parva vineyard. The short wine list provides a good choice of fairly priced wines, including some local bottles. Starters included melon with prawns and carrot and orange soup. Mains featured veal escalope cordon bleu, seared tuna with dill sauce or a vegetarian wellington with fresh tomato sauce. A pudding trolley offers banoffi pie, cheesecake and fresh fruit salad. A pleasant interlude in a village that always has lots to see, and lots going on.

TREDUNNOCK

The Newbridge

Tredunnock, Monmouthshire NP15 1LY (01633 451000/www.thenewbridge.co.uk). **Lunch served** noon-2.30pm Mon-Sat; noon-3pm Sun. **Dinner served** 6.30-9.30pm Mon-Sat; 7-8.30pm Sun. **Main courses** £12-£19.50. **Credit** AmEx, MC, V.

The riverside setting may be idyllic in summer but it's dramatic in winter when meltwater turns the Usk into a torrent. Menus retain a bucolic simplicity with starters like locally smoked duck and orange salad and main courses of loin of Gloucestershire Old Spot with grain mustard mash or Carmarthenshire beef with roast parsnips and cocotte potatoes. Cornish seafood and specials are on a blackboard. The single supplier wine list could be more exciting.

WENTLOOGE

Inn at The Elm Tree

St Brides, Wentlooge, Monmouthshire NP10 8SQ (01633 680225/www.the-elm-tree.co.uk). **Lunch served** noon-2pm, **dinner served** 7-9.30pm daily. **Main courses** £12-£17.50 **Set lunch** £7.50 2 courses, £10 3 courses. **Set dinner** £12.50 3 courses. **Credit** AmEx, MC, V.

This 19th-century inn has been comprehensively renovated and now offers fine dining as well as rooms. The restaurant is clean and modern but the wrought-iron fittings and tiled floors make the atmosphere a little clinical. Starters double as light lunches and include Thai-style salmon and crab cakes or seared scallops are on a pea purée base with tomato and lemon dressing. Wild rabbit, pork and Parma terrine with Bloody Mary sorbet and tomato pickle is a treat. Main courses include rack of marinated salt marsh lamb with honey roasted parsnip purée, ratatouille and caper and rosemary butter. South Welsh crab, lobster and salmon appear in a soufflé. An imaginative dessert menu includes white chocolate mousse, raspberry milkshake and Jack Daniels ice-cream. Staff are cheerful.

WHITEBROOK

Crown at Whitebrook

Whitebrook, Monmouthshire NP25 4TX (01600 860254/www.crownatwhitebrook.co.uk). **Lunch served** noon-1.45pm Tue-Sun. **Dinner served** 7-8.45pm Tue-Sat. **Set lunch** (Sun) £18 3 courses. **Set dinner** £30 3 courses. **Credit** MC, V.

The Chandlery. *See p334.*

It's all change at this quiet restaurant with rooms in the heart of the Wye Valley. New owners and head chef have turned a good restaurant into an ambitious one. Appetisers of salmon roulade, butternut squash velouté, spicy lamb kofte, quail's egg with truffle oil, and fried cheese accompany aperitifs. Arrival at the table is celebrated with delicate ginger and pork wun tun with chilli jam. Only after this are you allowed to proceed to starters of hot smoked and baked local eel with sharply pickled radishes and moutard de Meaux dressing. A main of beef fillet is wrapped in layers of braised veal tongue and leek and poached to perfection with a foie gras boudin and gewürztraminer reduction. For dessert, rhubarb trio features sorbet, panna cotta and, served in a shot glass, a vivid rhubarb and vanilla soup.

Pembrokeshire

NEWPORT

Cnapan

East Street, Newport, Pembrokeshire SA42 0SY (01239 820575/www.online-holidays.net/cnapan). **Lunch served** *Apr-Oct* noon-2pm Mon, Wed-Sat. **Dinner served** *Apr-Oct* 6.45-8.45pm Mon, Wed-Sun. **Main courses** £14-£16. **Credit** MC, V.

Opened in the mid-1980s, this is a cross between a tearoom and restaurant. Behind the pink frontage is a light and airy dining room with comfortable, practical furniture, and knick-knacks. Lunches tend to be light with lots of salads, or local crab and lobster. In the evening, the food is more ambitious. Try roast peppers and tomatoes, capers, basil and olive oil topped with good local goat's cheese, or crab and smoked salmon tart, or local seafood chowder. Next, there's Welsh beef and lamb served in a variety of ways. Guinea fowl also makes an appearance either glazed with honey and ginger or with a lemon and elderflower sauce. Presentation is simple and cooking has a light touch. Puddings are rich; service is informal, efficient and friendly. All in all, it seems set for another 20 years.

Llysmeddyg

East Street, Newport, Pembrokeshire SA42 0SY (01239 820008/www.llysmeddyg.co.uk). **Lunch served** noon-2.30pm Tue-Sun **Dinner served** 7-9pm Tue-Sat. **Main courses** £12.50-£22. **Credit** MC, V.

Opened in summer 2004, Llysmeddyg combines a quality restaurant with rooms, with a gallery celebrating the work of artist Peter Daniels. Llysmeddyg is an old house substantially rebuilt with wonderful light, high-ceilinged rooms that have been converted into a bar and double dining room. Chef Ian O'Rawe delivers an exotic lunchtime menu of Californian-style Caesar salad and a wonderful meze of chicken shawarma or lamb kofta, moutabel, tabouleh, olives and fresh veg. Dinner is more complex, with starters such as fresh lobster bisque, prawn ceviche or pan-fried crab cakes served with teriyaki and chilli dips. Main courses include marinated grilled sea bass on a bed of Mediterranean vegetables or pan-fried duck breast with fruits of the forest. Meat – from the town butcher – includes T-bone of veal, lamb cutlets and prime fillet of beef. Dessert includes a dramatic soufflé glacé Grand Marnier. Service is informal and friendly; the wine list is generous. A welcome newcomer.

PORTHGAIN

The Shed

Porthgain, Pembrokeshire SA62 5BN (01348 831518/www.theshedporthgain.co.uk). **Meals served** 9am-5pm, **dinner served** 7-9pm daily. **Main courses** (lunch) £3-£4. **Set dinner** £24.95 2 courses, £27.95 3 courses. **Credit** MC, V.

Attached to the end of the old slate company offices within feet of the quay, settings don't get much saltier than this. Decor is old and the upstairs loft dining room looks like Captain Ahab has just nipped out for a bit of harpoon practice. Sandwiches and light lunches during the day give way to an evening menu based around seafood. Lobster and crab are among the best in the UK. Sea bass often makes an appearance as does monkfish, mackerel and black bream. Main courses are accompanied by seasonal veg. The wine list is truncated but utilitarian.

ST DAVID'S

Morgan's Brasserie

20 Nun Street, St David's, Pembrokeshire SA62 6NT (01437 720508/www.morgans-in-stdavids.co.uk). **Dinner served** *June-Sept* 6.30-9pm Mon-Sat. *Oct-Dec, Mar-May* 6.30-9pm Mon-Fri. **Main courses** £12.50-£18.50. **Credit** MC, V.

This intimate, family-run brasserie is located in a Victorian house just off the main square. The dining area has been created by knocking two rooms into one. The short menu is long on local produce and short on fussiness. Fresh local seafood such as bream, sea bass, salmon, turbot and Dover sole appear regularly. There's usually a soup like pea and mint or Porthgain or Abercastle crab as well as a well-made terrine of duck confit and duck flavoured with Armagnac. Next, try Welsh beef, slow-cooked shoulder of local lamb, or roast turbot with bouillabaisse sauce. Vegetarians can feast on the millefeuille of wild mushrooms in a cream and Pommery mustard sauce. A selection of flavoursome local vegetables accompanies most main courses. The wine list is wide ranging.

Powys

BRECON

Barn at Brynich

Brynich, nr Brecon, Powys LD3 7SH (01874 623480). **Lunch served** noon-2.30pm daily. **Dinner served** 6-9.30pm Mon-Sat; 6-9pm Sun. **Main courses** £7-£15. **Credit** MC, V.

This old farm has been renovated to a high standard. It has a dramatic feel, with the restaurant taking up the whole of the central barn: beams, a stone fireplace and whitewash mixed with local red mud provides a rich roseate glow. Outside, a children's play area makes it a godsend to families. Meals are rudimentary, using organic and local produce wherever possible. A starter of jardinière salad was glorious, with fresh organic rocket, salad burnet, sun-dried tomatoes, preserved artichoke hearts and asparagus finished with Cilowen cheese. Excellent organic vegetable kebabs on tagliatelle come with a rich tomato sauce. 'Barn Favourites' include steak and ale pie or a trio of local sausages with mash and onion gravy. Timings and flavour combinations need to be watched on some dishes – a wonderful trout was ruined by the unnecessary addition of a mushroom and red wine sauce. The wine list is short and predominantly New World.

Felin Fach Griffin

Felin Fach, nr Brecon, Powys LD3 0UB (01874 620111/www.eatdrinksleep.ltd.uk). **Lunch served** 12.30-2.30pm Tue-Sun. **Dinner served** 7-9.30pm daily. **Main courses** £13.50-£17. **Credit** DC, MC, V.
This is one of the country's leading gastropubs and the food is a joy. A sprawling interior with subdued lighting and well-chosen background music puts customers at their ease. Appetisers like butternut squash soup with hazelnut oil are wonderful. Starters include roast scallops with baby gems, peas and lemon butter or salad of seared tuna, baby artichoke, tapenade and gazpacho. Lobster, wood pigeon and spring vegetable salad is not just original but satisfying – the bitter taste of the pigeon offset by the sweetness of the lobster. Main course oak-smoked salmon was brimming with flavour, served on a bed of crushed new potatoes and spinach surrounded by a moat of chive butter. Original desserts like yoghurt mousse with figs marinated in sangria are light and appealing. Felin Fach Griffin is a prince among gastropubs.

Tipple 'n' Tiffin ★

Theatr Brycheiniog, Canal Wharf, Brecon, Powys LD3 7EW (01874 611866/www.brycheiniog.co.uk). **Lunch served** noon-2.30pm, **dinner served** 7-9pm Mon-Sat. **Main courses** £6-£8. **Credit** AmEx, DC, MC, V.
Richard and Louise Gudsell's restaurant is located on the ground-floor corner of the Theatr Brycheiniog that overlooks Brecon's tiny canal basin. The setting is unconventional. So is the menu. All dishes are somewhere between starter and main course in size and designed to be shared. What started as a good idea for theatre-goers has become great venue for everybody. Penclawdd cockles served with crispy bacon, salad and salsa vie for attention with Menai mussels flavoured with white wine, cream and roast garlic. Appealing dishes are pepper and goat's cheese terrine or a substantial chorizo, feta, sun-blush tomato and olive salad. Or try Tamworth pork marinated in hoisin or rabbit cooked with leeks and served with a root vegetable mash. Most dishes have a homely, fresh-from-the-oven feel that adds to the enjoyment. The short wine list is predominantly New World, half available by the glass.

CRICKHOWELL

The Beaufort

Beaufort Street, Crickhowell, Powys NP8 1AD (01873 810402). **Lunch served** noon-2.30pm Tue-Sun. **Dinner served** 7-9.30pm Tue-Sat. **Main courses** £8.50-£14.95. **Credit** MC, V.
Since late 2003, the Beaufort has offered well-planned, seasonal menus and a short but attractive wine list. Chef Heather Matthews cut her teeth at the Daneswood House Hotel in Shipham and seems to enjoy using the abundant local produce. Crickhowell is a town full of rock stars, so if you're lucky you might spot somebody from Oasis downing a sherry or two in this flash, newly modernised lounge bar. Starters include own-cured gravadlax, watercress salad and crème fraîche, or warm duck confit salad. Main courses are tried and trusted combinations that rarely disappoint, say thyme-roasted poussin with parmesan mash and roast vegetables, medallions of local beef with truffled creamed potatoes, wild mushrooms and madeira jus, or fried skate wing with pommes anna, spinach purée and beurre noisette. To finish, try white and dark chocolate terrine or the hazelnut parfait. Most items on the wine list are under £20 and there's a good choice of half-bottles.

Gliffaes

Gliffaes Country House Hotel, Crickhowell, Powys NP8 1RH (01874 730371/www.gliffaes.com). **Dinner served** 7.30-9.15pm daily. **Main courses** £12-£17. **Set dinner** £24.50 2 courses, £29.50 3 courses. **Credit** AmEx, DC, MC, V.
Built in 1885, this romantic Italianate pile enjoys an elevated position in the gorgeous Usk Valley. Thirty-two acres of mature gardens, fishing, walking and an understated approach to country house interiors makes this one of the most relaxing hotels in the country. Menus retain classical and conservative dishes, with an attractive modern twist. French onion soup is lighter than the continental counterpart, while a rich ham hock and foie gras terrine is balanced with nicely sharp pear chutney. Fried calf's liver is balanced on a bed of mash and topped with crispy bacon and shallots. There's also seared tuna with a warm salad of tomato, green bean and olives garnished with hard boiled egg. A supporter of the admirable Slow Food Movement, Gliffaes has a policy of sourcing three quarters of its fresh produce from within 25 miles of the hotel. The wine list includes house wines at £12.50.

Nantyffin Cider Mill Inn

Breacon Road, Crickhowell, Powys NP8 1SG (01873 810775/www.cidermill.co.uk). **Lunch served** noon-2.30pm Tue-Sun. **Dinner served** 7-9.30pm Tue-Sat. **Main courses** £10.95-£14.95. **Set lunch** (Tue-Fri) £10 2 courses, £13 3 courses. **Credit** AmEx, MC, V.

Chef Sean Gerrard has built up something of a local dining empire with his business partners Glyn and Jessica Bridgeman. The flagship enterprise is probably Nantyffin Cider Mill, unmissable in its bold roadside position and with a vivid pink-wash frontage. With comfortable, warm dining rooms in winter, cool interiors and tables outside for summer, the menus have an attractive Mediterranean character. Starters of seared scallops on a richly dressed Caesar salad can be followed by slow-cooked shoulder of lamb or fresh fish from the blackboard. The group also owns the neighbouring Manor Hotel (Brecon Road, Crickhowell, Powys NP8 1SE; 01873 810212) and the wonderfully located Peterstone Hotel (Peterstone Court, Llanhamlach, Brecon, Powys LD3 7YB; 01874 665387), a relaxed bistro in Brecon Beacons National Park. All three restaurants serve organic duck, chicken and lamb from their own farm in Llangynidr.

EGLWYSFACH

Ynyshir Hall

Eglwysfach, Powys SY20 8TA (01654 781209/ www.ynyshir-hall.co.uk). **Lunch served** 12.30-1.30pm, **dinner served** 7-8.45pm daily. **Set lunch** £20-£22 2 courses, £29.50 3 courses incl tea or coffee. **Set dinner** £49 3 courses, £64 7-course tasting menu. **Credit** AmEx, DC, MC, V.

This beautifully maintained country house is one of the handful of Welsh Michelin-starred restaurants. New chef Adam Simmonds has worked at Oxfordshire's Le Manoir aux Quat' Saisons so is equipped to meet the challenge of maintaining the required quality. Starters of confit belly pork with scallops, black pudding and a light curry oil or a millefeuille of roast quail and sweet potato, green beans and truffle jus seem to be a move in the right direction. Main courses of slow-cooked Welsh salt

The Cors. *See p328.*

Gliffaes. See p338.

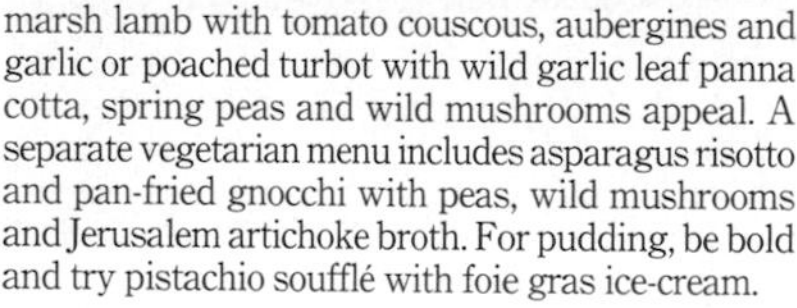

marsh lamb with tomato couscous, aubergines and garlic or poached turbot with wild garlic leaf panna cotta, spring peas and wild mushrooms appeal. A separate vegetarian menu includes asparagus risotto and pan-fried gnocchi with peas, wild mushrooms and Jerusalem artichoke broth. For pudding, be bold and try pistachio soufflé with foie gras ice-cream.

LLANFRYNACH

White Swan

Llanfrynach, Powys LD3 7BZ (01874 665276). **Lunch served** noon-2pm Wed-Sat; noon-2.30pm Sun. **Dinner served** 7-9.30pm Wed-Sat; 7-9pm Sun. **Main courses** £10.95-£14.95. **Credit** MC, V.

Relaunched as a gastropub five years ago, the White Swan's provides a great setting for eating or drinking. The dining room facing the village church looks great – all ancient wood and stone surfaces – but is only open during the evening. Lunch is served in the bar overlooking a cute terrace. Meat and vegetables are local and there's an excellent selection of fish delivered every other day from Swansea. Starters included a massive bruschetta of buffalo mozzarella, rather pale tomatoes and basil leaves with balsamic and pesto. Salads of black pudding and dry cured local bacon with tomato jam are reserved for evening only. Mains included an overdone cod fillet with creamed leeks and parsley sauce, honey-glazed lamb shank or organic chicken wrapped in Parma ham with a lemon and herb risotto. The wine list features some good value New World bottles among Old World stars.

LLANGAMARCH WELLS

Lake Country House

Llangammarch Wells, Powys LD4 4BS (01591 620202/www.lakecountryhouse.co.uk). **Lunch served** 12.30-2.30pm, **dinner served** 7.15-9.15pm daily. **Set lunch** £23.50 4 courses. **Set dinner** £37.50 5 courses. **Credit** AmEx, DC , MC, V.

Courteous, old-fashioned service combined with top quality food and rooms is what you can expect here. The hotel itself is a lovingly restored mid-Victorian hunting lodge, which – judging by the original register in the reception – attracted crowned heads and the well-to-do in their dozens. Four courses start with leek and potato soup enriched with cream and flavoured with roasted almonds and a basil pesto. This is followed by a beautifully made foie gras and duck confit terrine with mango chutney and a dainty clutch of toasted brioche slices, or a warm oyster flan with creamed leeks, champagne butter sauce and caviar. Wonderfully flavoured guinea fowl is served on an intense crab risotto with fresh peas, baby morels and a ginger velouté. Simpler dishes include classic combos like calf's liver with lyonnaise potatoes, pineapple chutney and sherry vinegar jus. Puddings are generous in dimension and fantastic in conception. The wine list has some gems.

LLANWRTYD WELLS

Carlton House ★

Dolecoed Road, Llanwrtyd Wells, Powys LD5 4RA (01591 610248/www.carltonrestaurant.co.uk). **Lunch served** Tue-Fri by arrangement. **Dinner**

served 7-8.30pm Mon-Sat. **Main courses** £22-£26. **Set meal** (lunch; dinner Mon-Thur) £19.95 2 courses, £24.50 3 courses. **Credit** MC, V.
A quiet Victorian spa town provides the location for one of the principality's most dynamic kitchens. The confident pink façade of this wonderful Michelin-starred restaurant with rooms stands out from its more sober neighbours. The split-level dining room is well lit and stylishly decorated with Italian furniture, French porcelain and modish wall lights. Mary Ann Gilchrist's cooking is extraordinary on a number of levels. First, she is self-taught. Second, she runs the kitchen single-handed while husband Alan deals with wine and front of house. Third, the standard of food is consistently high. Modern British in style, there are French influences aplenty. A full-flavoured cream of celeriac soup appetiser enriched with truffle oil is followed by seared scallops with buttered courgettes and a shellfish velouté. Roast lamb is served with crushed new potatoes, courgettes and a pearl onion sauce. Grilled wild sea bass is given a twist with the addition of preserved lemon couscous, baby spinach, roast plum tomatoes and a lime and caper vinaigrette.

LLYSWEN

Llangoed Hall

Llyswen, Powys LD3 0YP (01874 754525/ www.llangoedhall.com). **Lunch served** noon-2pm, **dinner served** 7-9pm daily. **Set lunch** £28.50 3 courses. **Set dinner** £43 3 courses. **Credit** AmEx, DC, MC, V.
Sir Bernard Ashley bought Llangoed Hall in 1987 and launched this luxurious country house hotel on unsuspecting Powys. Its position overlooking the River Wye is among the best. Renovated to act as a showcase for Laura Ashley, and latterly Sir Bernard's own prints and fabrics, the well-lit, yellow-walled dining room glows with promise. It's a lively place with busy, personable, international staff. A lounge menu includes sandwiches, salads and grills, while the dinner menu features cenarth blue cheese soufflé on a rocket and walnut salad and potted shrimps with crab mayonnaise and quails' eggs. Mains might include Breconshire venison loin on a leek and puy lentil stew or crisply presented red mullet on a warm niçoise salad. The wine list is voluminous, with plenty of vintage champagnes.

MACHYNLLETH

Wynnstay Arms

Maengwyn Street, Machynlleth, Powys SY20 8AE (01654 702941/www.wynnstay-hotel.com). **Lunch served** noon-2pm, **dinner served** 6-9pm daily. **Main courses** £7.95-£14.95. **Set lunch** (Sun) £10.95 2 courses, £12.95 3 courses. **Credit** AmEx, MC, V.
The Wynnstay Arms is an ancient coaching inn that has been moving up the culinary ladder. Lunches include juicy sewin and brown trout from the River Dyfi (Dovey); Barmouth lobster and monkfish from the Cambrian coast and lamb and beef direct from local farms. Try Aberdyfi plaice with chips and salad or stuffed lamb shoulder with wild garlic mash and creamed leeks. Gareth Johns, formerly with Alistair Little, produces menus that never fail to engage. Pink pigeon breast comes with a ginger purée. Duck breast is served with strawberries and balsamic. Puddings are substantial. There's a good selection of Welsh cheeses (although they could be served at a higher temperature), and the wine list has keenly priced bottles from around the world.

PONTDOLGOCH

Talkhouse

Pontdolgoch, Powys SY17 5JE (01686 688919/ www.talkhouse.co.uk). **Lunch served** noon-2pm Tue-Sun. **Dinner served** 6.30-9pm Tue-Sat. **Main courses** £11-£15.95. **Credit** MC, V.
When Stephen Garrett got fed up with being a wine merchant in Bermuda (unbelievably, this can happen), he relaunched the Mytton Arms as the Talkhouse. Food critics were wowed by the early display of culinary techniques, but locals less so, menus now reflect a preference for more substantial dishes, which allow the flavours of good ingredients to shine. For starters, try grilled field mushrooms dressed with parmesan or a delicate salad of gem lettuce with bacon and eggs. Main courses include precisely cooked duck breast with bubble and squeak or tender organic chicken breast stuffed with Snowdonia cheddar, served on wilted spinach with mash and a rich red wine reduction. Local pork is served pan-fried with black pudding. The wine list has been shortened but remains skilfully assembled and priced competitively.

Rhondda Cynon Taff

TALBOT GREEN

Brookes

79-81 Talbot Road, Talbot Green, Rhondda Cynon Taff CF72 8AE (01443 239600). **Lunch served** noon-2.30pm Tue-Fri, Sun. **Dinner served** 7-10pm Tue-Sat. **Main courses** £13.95-£18.95. **Set lunch** 2 courses £12.99, 3 courses £14.95. **Credit** AmEx, DC, MC, V.
The only building in Talbot Green with a bright lilac front. Don't be deterred. Inside you'll find a well-lit modern restaurant with glass block walls, whitewashed surfaces, bold modern paintings, light wood furniture and simple table settings. Staff are smartly dressed and knowledgeable. Menus offer modern British dishes with a dollop of Pacific influence. Starters include smooth chicken's liver parfait with red onion marmalade and toasted brioche or a satisfying tempura of king prawns with Caesar salad and aromatic croûtons. Main courses comprise slow braised shank of Welsh lamb or a seared fillet of sea bass on a sauté of tiger prawns, asparagus, spinach and new potatoes.

Swansea

LLANRHIDIAN

Welcome to Town

Llanrhidian, Swansea SA3 1EH (01792 390015). **Lunch served** noon-2pm Tue-Sun. **Dinner served** 7-9.30pm Tue-Sat. **Main courses** £10.50-£18. **Set lunch** £11.95 2 courses, £14.95 3 courses. **Credit** MC, V.

A country pub has occupied this site on the beautiful Gower Peninsula for three centuries. Fresh local and seasonal produce is the basis of the cooking and Gower offers fresh asparagus, excellent lobster, laverbread from the estuary, salt marsh lamb and artisinal cheeses. Chef and co-owner Ian Bennett worked with the Roux brothers and uses his skills to good effect on this array of produce. There's laverbread in an omelette overcoat, pressed terrine of lobster and leek with saffron vinaigrette or simple escabeche of mackerel. After that, try wonderful breast of chicken with rösti, wild mushrooms and truffle ravioli, or a tender fillet of Welsh beef with fondant potatoes and buttered spinach. The wine list is good value; service is competent.

REYNOLDSTON

Fairy Hill

Fairy Hill Hotel, Fairy Hill, Reynoldston, Swansea, SA3 1BS (01792 390139/www.fairyhill.net). **Lunch served** 12.30-2pm daily. **Dinner served** 7.30-9pm Mon-Sat; 7.30-8.15pm Sun. **Set lunch** (Mon-Sat) £14.95 2 courses, £18.95 3 courses; (Sun) £24.50 3 courses. **Set dinner** £29.50 2 courses, £37.50 3 courses. **Credit** MC, V.

Fairyhill occupies a wonderful location in the middle of the Gower Peninsula. Owners Paul Davies and Andrew Hetherington have relentlessly improved this 18th-century house over the years to produce an award-winning hotel. The grounds include idyllic woodland, ponds, a tame swan called Ken, lawns, orchards and a trout stream. Excellent cockles are available from Penclawdd throughout the year and these often appear deep-fried and sometimes accompanied with a quail's egg as appetisers. Then it's laverbread and cockle cakes with crispy fried Camarthen bacon, or twice-baked goat's cheese soufflé. After that, try Welsh beef fillet cooked in a full-on Mediterranean style with sun-dried tomato polenta and a black olive and shallot sauce. Zabaglione with poached plums and cinnamon biscuits rounds things off. The bold wine list features selections from India alongside more usual choices.

SWANSEA

Chelsea Café

17 St Mary's Street, Swansea, SA1 3LH (01792 464068). **Lunch served** noon-2.30pm Mon-Sat. **Dinner served** 7-9.30pm Tue-Sat. **Main courses** £9.95-£16.95. **Set lunch** £10 2 courses. **Credit** MC, V.

Tucked away off Wind Street, this small, stylish bistro is a welcome addition. Plain wood cladding, modern paintings and practical furniture give the interior a business-like feel that's easy on the eye. Matt Hole offers dazzling menus that make the best use of the excellent local seafood and other Welsh supplies. The two-course lunch for under a tenner offers incredible quality. Presentation is cutting edge and dramatic. Starters of spicy, Thai-style beef cakes lacked juiciness but had vivid ginger and coriander flavours. Welsh rump steak with bacon, shallot and red wine jus or breast of chicken with wild mushroom, dolcelatte and port sauce are no less successful. A Mediterranean brodetto contains sea bass, mussels, salmon, prawns and cockles in lobster stock finished with cream.

Didier & Stephanie's

56 St Helens Road, Swansea, SA1 4BE (01792 655603). **Lunch served** noon-1.30pm, **dinner served** 7-8.30pm Tue-Sat. **Main courses** £11.90-£14.50. **Set lunch** £7.70 1 course, £9.70 2 courses, £12.70 3 courses. **Credit** MC, V.

Didier is from Lille and Stephanie is from Burgundy. Four years ago they opened this restaurant on the ground floor of a Victorian terrace, offering lunches and dinners comprising dishes they had grown up with. Snails with garlic, perfectly cooked omelette with prawns and herbs, savoury goat's cheese tart with red onion all vie for attention as starters. Main courses are in a similar vein: confit duck leg with puy lentils or shallots and cassis, a superb rabbit cooked with Dijon mustard or guinea fowl with port sauce and a memorable braised lamb shank with thyme and olives. Puddings include pistachio crème brûlée or poached plums with fresh fruit coulis. The French wine list is particularly good value. Service can start off a bit formal but soon warms up.

Hansons

Pilot House Wharf, Trawler Road, Swansea Marina, Swansea, SA1 1UN (01792 466200). **Lunch served** noon-2pm daily. **Dinner served** 6.30-9.30pm Mon-Sat. **Main courses** £9.95-£17. **Set lunch** £10.95 2 courses, £13.95 3 courses. **Credit** MC, V.

Hansons is located on an upper floor of the boat-shaped Pilot House in Swansea's marina. Given that Trawler Road is full of fish wholesalers and you can see the fishing boats from the dining room, it's no surprise that it is known for its fish. Andrew Hanson ensures there's a good seasonal selection on offer including lobster, sea bass, brill, turbot, scallops, sewin and salmon. Starters include a soup of the day as well as delicately battered monkfish tempura, or haddock fish cakes with tartare sauce. To follow, try hake in batter atop hand-cut chips accompanied by sweet tomato sauce enlivened with balsamic and tartare sauce. Servings are Swansea-style – that is, vast. Even the most robust appetite can falter when confronted by treacle sponge or bread and butter pudding with armagnac and prune. The wine list compliments the unfussy approach to good quality. Efficient, and friendly service completes the picture.

Ireland

Ireland

NORTHERN IRELAND
Rathlin Is.
Giant's Causeway
Carndonagh
Dunfanaghy
Greencastle
Portrush
Ballycastle
Coleraine
Aran Is.
Limavady
ANTRIM
Letterkenny
Londonderry
DONEGAL
LONDONDERRY
Larne
Glencolumbcille
Ballymena
Donegal
Killybegs
Bangor
Omagh
Donegal Bay
BELFAST
Ballyshannon
Portadown
Kircubbin
Enniskillen
LEITRIM
Glaslough
Armagh
Gilford
Sligo
FERMANAGH
ARMAGH
DOWN
Blacklion
Ballina
Monaghan
Newry
Dundrum
Achill Is.
SLIGO
MONAGHAN
MAYO
Cloverhill
Killeary
Warrenpoint
Ballinafad
Carrickmacross
Castlebar
Cavan
Dundalk
Carrick-on Shannon
Clare Is.
Clew Bay
Knock
CAVAN
Dundalk Bay
ROSCOMMON
Westport
LOUTH
Longford
Drogheda
Kells (Ceanannas Mor)
Clifden
Roscommon
LONGFORD
MEATH
Connemara
Tuam
Oughterard
Mullingar
WESTMEATH
GALWAY
Athlone
Ballinasloe
Galway
DUBLIN
Clarinbridge
REPUBLIC OF IRELAND
KILDARE
Dún Laoghaire
Galway Bay
OFFALY
Loughrea
Bray
Aran Islands
Ballyvaughan
Kildare
Kilmacanoge
Doolin
Birr
The Burren
Cliffs of Moher
Port Laoise
Dunlavin
Wicklow Mtns
Ballinderry
Lahinch
Athy
WICKLOW
Wicklow
CLARE
Grangecon
LAOIS
Roscrea
Ennis
Carlow
Aughrim
Arklow
Ballina
CARLOW
Thurles
Kilkenny
Limerick
Adare
TIPPERARY
KILKENNY
Irish Sea
Listowel
LIMERICK
Tipperary
Cashel
Thomastown
KERRY
Abbeyfeale
WEXFORD
Tralee
Wexford
Cahir
Clonmel
Dingle
Killorglin
Rosslare
Waterford
WATERFORD
Mallow
Lismore
Cappoquin
Tramore
Dingle Bay
Killarney
Valentia Is.
CORK
Dungarvan
Cahirciveen
Kenmare
Macroom
Cork
Midleton
Youghal
Sneem
Shanagarry
Bandon
Cloyne
Ballycotton
Glengarriff
Bear Is.
Bantry
Kinsale
Dursey Is.
Clonakilty
Durrus
Kilbrittain
Bantry Bay
Skibbereen
Butlerstown
Ross Carbery
Baltimore
Clear Is.
St George's Channel
0
50
100 Km
0
60 miles

Northern Ireland

BALLYCASTLE

Cellar

11B The Diamond, Ballycastle, Co Antrim, BT54 6AW (028 2076 3037). **Meals served** 4.30-9.30pm Mon-Fri; 12.30-10pm Sat; 3.30-9.30pm Sun. **Main courses** £8.95-£13.95. **Credit** MC, V.

Ideally situated for the monumental scenery of the north coast, the Cellar also offers a rare opportunity to eat well in rural County Antrim. A spruce-clean, country-cosy welcome from cheery staff awaits even the muddiest hillwalkers. The subterranean room is kitted out with a terracotta floor, church pews and convincing make-believe vine. The menu may undermine appetites with hackneyed dishes and exotic aspirations – Italian pancetta Caesar salad, pork and pineapple kebab, vegetable chow mein. However, a sampling of stunning starters such as cracking citrus-buttered crab claws, and pulpy stock-rich broccoli soup restored confidence. A dodgy-sounding Portuguese surf 'n' turf turned out to be brilliant – brothy Irish paella, with slow-cooked steak instead of chicken, piled with fleshy mussels and firm shell-on langoustines. A generous rack of lamb comes with rosemary-crushed, skin-on spuds and a meaty red wine reduction. Desserts such as the finger-licking pavlova roulade are own-made too.

BANGOR

Shanks ★

The Blackwood, Crawfordsburn Road, Bangor, Co Down BT19 1GB (028 9185 3313/www.shanksrestaurant.com). **Lunch served** 12.30-2.30pm Tue-Fri. **Dinner served** 7-10pm Tue-Sat. **Set lunch** £19 2 courses, £23 3 courses. **Set dinner** £42 3 courses. **Credit** AmEx, MC, V.

For many the Michelin-starred Shanks is the ultimate night out. Set in a golf club in beautiful woodland on the Clandeboye estate, its smart, Conran-designed dining room enjoys lovely daytime views. In the evening, with the gentle notes of a twinkly piano in the upstairs bar and the animated chatter of enthused diners, it's even more romantic. An A-list team of chefs led by the charismatic Robbie Millar produce pretty painterly displays of acutely delicious and sumptuously rich food. Gratin of local scallops comes with an intense, sweet shallot purée, spinach, gruyère and chives. Turbot is paired with morels, pommes fondants, braised lettuce and tarragon velouté. The three-course menu ends with inspired desserts such as amaretti stuffed pear with mascarpone, crème anglaise and chestnut honey. While an extensive, steeply priced wine list makes it an extravagant experience, you can also enjoy simpler set lunch and early supper menus midweek. Service is cool but otherwise flawless.

BELFAST

Aldens ★

229 Upper Newtownards Road, Belfast, Co Antrim BT4 3JF (028 9065 0079/www.aldensrestaurant.com). **Lunch served** noon-2.30pm Mon-Fri. **Dinner served** 6-10pm Mon-Thur; 6-11pm Fri, Sat. **Main courses** £8.95-£16.95. **Set meals** (Mon-Thur) £16.95 2 courses, £20.95 3 courses. **Credit** AmEx, DC, MC, V.

It's always a treat to go to Aldens. There are few places in Belfast where you can rely on such consistency. The smart brasserie menu thoughtfully combines classic and modern ideas to provide mouthwatering comfort with dishes that use local and seasonal ingredients. Game and offal abound, such as roast haunch of rabbit with cotechino and mustard sauce or pan-fried lamb's liver and kidneys with green peppercorn jus and sage and onion mash. Aldens also excels at seafood. Innovative pairings, such as mussels with orange fennel and star anise, refresh and revitalise familiar ingredients. And then there's the wine list with a compelling selection of personally chosen wines. Friendly staff swish around, running the room like clockwork.

Bennett's of Belmont

4 Belmont Road, Belfast, Co Down BT4 2AN (028 9065 6590). **Brunch served** 9.30am-3pm Sat. **Lunch served** noon-3pm Tue-Fri. **Dinner served** 5-9.30pm Tue-Thur; 5-10pm Fri, Sat. **Meals served** 9.30am-9.30pm Sun. **Main courses** £4.75-£11.95. **Credit** MC, V.

Pacific Rim chef Colleen Bennett loves zany colours and informal fun. Her newest venture, a retro diner, brings a splash of minty cool turquoise, primrose yellow and chocolate to the neighbourhood. Bennett's serves an all-day menu of high-speed, low-tech super-snacks – pork loin sub with gherkins and mustard mayo; own-made burger with fresh tomato sauce and celeriac remoulade. There's also a nice selection of tasty brasserie dishes – steamed mussels with curried mayo and fries; blue cheese, potato and caramelised onion frittata. Half a roast chicken has a crisp skin, with creamy champ and lemon and thyme gravy. Fontana, Bennett's other restaurant in Holywood (61A High Street, DT18 9AE, 028 9080 9908), offers greater comfort and more cosmopolitan food, but similarly irksome service.

Café Renoir Pizza ★

95 Botanic Avenue, Belfast, Co Antrim BT7 1JN (028 9031 1300). **Lunch served** 11am-4.30pm Mon-Sat. **Dinner served** 5-9.30pm Mon-Thur; 5-10.30pm Fri, Sat; 5-8pm Sun. **Meals served** 9.30am-4.30pm Sun. **Main courses** £7.95-£12.95. **Credit** MC, V.

Acres of beautiful wood, smart earthy colours and splashes of 1970s geometric patterns make this an eye-catching spot. However, it is the alluring warmth of a wood-burning oven that will draw you inside. With over 20 pizzas named after all manner of exotic holiday destinations, the menu is daunting for purists. Such qualms are justified with top-heavy meaty options. However, the idea works a treat with Mediterranean and Mexican toppings, where there is less of a leap between cultures. The Istanbul is heaped with fresh spinach, goat's cheese and caramelised aubergine, and drizzled with zesty cool yoghurt, parsley and spices. With slickly organised service and next-door's popular bistro menu also available, CRP is a hub for students, staff and residents in the University Quarter.

Cayenne ★

7 Ascot House, Shaftesbury Square, Belfast, Co Antrim BT2 7BD (028 9033 1532/www.cayenne restaurant.com). **Lunch served** noon-2.15pm Mon-Fri. **Dinner served** 6-10.15pm Mon-Thur; 6-11.15pm Fri, Sat; 5-8.45pm Sun. **Main courses** £8-£20. **Set lunch** £12 2 courses, £15.50 3 courses. **Set dinner** (6-6.45pm Mon-Thur) £12 2 courses, £15.50 3 courses. **Credit** AmEx, DC, MC, V.

Things don't stand still for a second at Cayenne, the flagship of Paul Rankin's expanding empire. While his cafés and Rain City are hit and miss, Cayenne delivers an uplifting flight from the ordinary. In 2003 the restaurant doubled in size. With a new, smoochy-cool bar area, plus a stunning private dining room designed with Rankin's signature style, Cayenne remains the hottest venue in Belfast. For a typical Cayenne thrill try saffron risotto (with clams, chorizo and borlotti beans), char-grilled veal sweetbreads (with balsamic lentils, rocket and crispy pancetta), and orange crème brûlée (with kumquat compote and hazelnut biscotti). Great wines and pretty perfect service are further pluses.

James Street South

21 James Street South, Belfast, Co Antrim BT2 7GA (028 9043 4310/www.jamesstreetsouth.co.uk). **Lunch served** noon-2.45pm Mon-Sat. **Dinner served** 5.45-10.30pm Mon-Sat; 5.30-9pm Sun. **Main courses** £9.50-£16. **Set dinner** (5.45-6.45pm Mon-Thur) £15.50 2 courses, £17.50 3 courses. **Credit** AmEx, MC, V.

Very nicely packaged in elegantly converted warehouse premises, this attracts a fashionable, well-heeled crowd. Its beautifully lit whiteness is the perfect backdrop for contemporary art and fresh, modern menus. A predominance of appealing Pacific Rim dishes – beef carpaccio or oysters on ice with chilli vodka dressing followed by salmon with creamed fennel and artichokes – shout blue skies and sunshine, making it a particularly good summertime destination. In the winter it could do with more of the warmth and comfort brought by pretty creamed cauliflower soup or butternut squash and mushroom tortellini followed by pork fillet with sweet potato purée, crackling and apple jus. Mind you, expect challenge rather than reassurance with dishes such as cassoulet of crisped belly pork, duck confit, black beans and sweet-spiced liquor. Professional, friendly career waiters provide great service and encourage extravagance.

Nick's Warehouse

35-39 Hill Street, Belfast, Co Antrim BT1 2LB (028 9043 9690/www.nickswarehouse.co.uk). **Lunch served** noon-3pm Mon-Fri. **Dinner served** 6-9.30pm Tue-Thur; 6-10pm Fri, Sat. **Main courses** £7.95-£16. **Credit** AmEx, DC, MC, V.

A consummate host with a passion for wine, Nick Price provides a convivial welcome at his warehouse wine bar. A pioneer of the restaurant trade and the Cathedral Quarter's burgeoning nightlife, Nick's profile guarantees a tremendous turnout and buzzing ambience every night of the week. Menus are informal, edgy and keen on fusion, which means that food can be hit-and-miss, especially when the young brigade of bandana-clad chefs is left to its own devices. Dishes range from falafels and minted mango salsa or spinach and ricotta cannelloni bakes, to seriously meaty choices. Beef and sausage casserole is served with buttery mash. Pan-fried calf's liver comes with pamfrey and ham, shallot and red wine jus. The wine list is full of gems.

Porcelain

Ten Square, 10 Donegall Square, Belfast, Co Antrim BT1 5JD (028 9024 1001/www.ten-sq.com). **Dinner served** 6-10pm Mon-Thur; 6-11pm Fri, Sat. **Main courses** £9-£18.50. **Credit** AmEx, MC, V.

With a regular upheaval of kitchen staff, dinner at Porcelain may not fulfil the expectations raised by executive chef Alistair Fullerton's menus. However, the tantalising choices will reel in those suffering withdrawal symptoms since his departure to Porcelain's sister hotel. Starters are the most captivating. Jerusalem artichoke soup is served with ham hock ravioli and truffle oil; a chilled gazpacho and Bloody Mary sorbet accompanies grilled langoustines. Inventive pairings also give mains an edge. Asian greens and lemongrass beurre blanc are the foil for spiced hake; loin and kidney of lamb are served in a delicious cassoulet with parsley jus. Desserts are also given a spicy or aromatic dimension. The dining room is due to be refitted and it'll be interesting to see how they improve on this beautiful, light-filled space. A new grill room and bar opened in spring 2004 (noon-10pm daily).

Restaurant Michael Deane

36-40 Howard Street, Belfast, Co Antrim BT1 6PF (028 9033 1134/www.michaeldeane.co.uk). **Dinner served** 7-10pm Wed-Sat. **Set dinner** £33 2 courses, £58 8 courses. **Credit** AmEx, DC, MC, V.

Fiercely proud and ambitious Michael Deane became a local celebrity in 1998 when his flagship Restaurant Michael Deane was awarded its first Michelin star. With three restaurants now under his belt (Deane's Brasserie, 028 9056 0000, and the Asian-themed Chok Dee, 028 9024 8800), the strain,

Bar crawl: Belfast

If you haven't got much time in Belfast, then the best place to start a pub crawl is the Cathedral Quarter, a regenerated area just north of the centre. Here you'll find both traditional bars and the hippest kids on the block, all located within walking distance of prime sightseeing spots.

If there's one place you must visit, it's **Whites 1630** (2-4 Winecellar Entry, 028 9024 3080), Belfast's oldest tavern just off Castle Place. Recently restored with simple whitewashed walls and pared-down furnishings, it has the heavenly smell of a smoky turf fire and an afternoon menu of Irish stew, shepherd's pie and fries. It's one of the few places where you can drink unchilled Guinness straight from the keg. Spontaneous, traditional music sessions strike up with regularity. Upstairs (nights only) they've created a confidently cool lounge with flock wallpaper, salvaged furniture and regular jazz.

By way of the **Northern Whig** (2 Bridge Street, 028 9050 9888) – a bold, brash café bar with incongruous but attention grabbing statues of Czech revolutionaries – you'll find the **John Hewitt** (51 Donegall Street, 028 9023 3768). With decent grub, friendly, loyal staff and regular cultural entertainment, it has cultivated the intimate atmosphere of a unique neighbourhood watering hole. It also has a comfortable reproduction interior.

You can enjoy a similar atmosphere at the **Duke of York** (7-11 Commercial Court, 028 9024 1062) before trying out a couple of the more modern bars. **Opium** (3 Skipper Street, off Waring Street, 028 9023 2448) – a dark, intimate Asian-themed den – is a good place to kick-start the evening with cocktails. Across the square, you'll see chairs spilling out under the heat lamps and awnings of the **Quarter** (42 Waring Street, 028 9031 1414), a friendly place in spite of its rather soulless design. Here enthusiastic chefs and resident DJs entertain an eclectic crowd.

Nicholl (12-14 Church Lane, 028 9027 9595) and **Bar Mono** (100 Ann Street, 028 9027 8886) – small, independent bars offering food, cocktails and cosmopolitan style – are further evidence of the revival of the centre's nightlife. Alternatively walk to **Union Street Bar** (8-14 Union Street, 028 9031 6060), a capacious, lively, modern venue and the new heart of Belfast's burgeoning gay scene.

If you have time to explore the city limits, you could get a cab – or train – to the **King's Head** (829 Lisburn Road, 028 9050 9950), originally built in 1868 for the senior managers of the Great Northern Railway. Now it is a rather lavish, food-orientated conglomeration of lounge bars and restaurants. With a Ronnie Scott's inspired nightclub, you may find yourself staying all night.

However, for those who'd prefer a sobering stroll, there's the architecturally splendid **Ta Tu** (701 Lisburn Road, 028 9038 0818), a glamorous bar with outdoor decking. Further down you'll find the **Chelsea Wine Bar** (346 Lisburn Road, 028 9068 7177) – a popular sports bar – and **Ryan's** (116-118 Lisburn Road, 028 9050 9850), which has replaced its TVs and slot machines with funky art and casual food, while maintaining a snug ambience for locals. On the Ormeau Road, another arterial route into Belfast, is **Errigle** (320 Ormeau Road, 028 9064 1410), a maze of lounge bars dating back to 1735. It serves outstanding pub food, as well as a varied diet of musical styles. The wood-panelled oak lounge, although very smoky, offers comfort and charm with table service and genuine retro furnishings.

The high-tech, glass-fronted **Mercury** (451 Ormeau Road, 028 9064 9017) is popular for jazz on a Sunday afternoon. Further down the road, the **Pavillion** (296 Ormeau Road, 028 9028 3283) and the **Limelight** (17 Ormeau Avenue, 028 9032 5968) attract some seriously good gigs.

If you want to hang with a younger crowd, then head to the University Quarter by way of the grungy **Menagerie** (130 University Street, 028 9023 5678). Near Queen's you'll find the **Globe** (36 University Road, 028 9050 9840) and the **Parlour Bar** (2 Elmwood Avenue, 028 9068 6970), which offer drink promotions as well as budget food. The **Bot** (23-27 Malone Road, 028 9050 9740) also promises beer-fuelled fun.

On your way back to town, at **Madison's** (59-63 Botanic Avenue, 028 9050 9800), you'll find a sophisticated interior and outdoor seating. Across the street in the **Empire Music Hall** (42 Botanic Avenue, 028 9024 9276) – a converted church with stage – you get comedy and good old rock 'n' roll. Ken Haddock's Sunday night supper club is not to be missed.

Mill Street Restaurant & Bar. See p349.

exacerbated by stiff competition, is beginning to show. Still, it's worth overlooking the tired furnishings of what was once a lavish, paint-effected room. Although the menus change little from year to year, you cannot fail to enjoy the admirably unadorned, exactly prepared luxuries on offer. French squab comes with an exquisite roast and creamed cauliflower. The sweet, concentrated colours of roast beetroot and parsnip complement tender, pink duck breast. Roulade of chocolate and cherries are delicious modern classics. A loyal team charms with wit and polished service.

Taps Wine Bar

479 Lisburn Road, Belfast, Co Antrim BT9 7EZ (028 9066 3211). **Meals served** noon-11pm Tue-Sun. **Tapas** £1.50-£4. **Credit** MC, V.

Even if the menu isn't strictly authentic, this buzzy café-bar is the first to offer some bona fide tapas in Belfast. Judging by the queues it's just what the city has been missing. Few can resist the lure to order the equivalent of a three-course meal, but the food is surprisingly rich. The tapas vary considerably in size from the dainty canapés of quails' eggs on paper-thin, air-cured serrano ham to the abundant patatas bravas or baby meatballs in almond-enriched tomato sauce. The careful sourcing of ingredients is noticeable in dishes such as the reassuringly irregular rings of squid, and vegetarians will be pleased with the imaginative bolsitas (crisp-fried pastry parcels of fresh, nutmeggy spinach and plump raisins). Diminutive portions make desserts such as the citrus chunk of vanilla custard very excusable indeed.

Tedford's

5 Donegall Quay, Belfast, Co Antrim BT1 3EF (028 9043 4000). **Lunch served** noon-2.30 Mon-Fri. **Dinner served** 5pm-late Tue-Sat. **Set dinner** (5-6.30pm Mon-Fri) £15.95 2 courses, £17.95 3 courses. **Main courses** £10.95-£16.95. **Credit** AmEx, MC, V.

Housed in a landmark building on the shores of the River Lagan, Tedford's is a serious, family-run establishment set up by two friends. Sensibly, in a city of restaurants tending to compete with catch-all cuisine, they have given their food a fishy focus and the menu is characterised by the chef's classical French training and experience of South-east Asia. Mussels with a stunningly authentic Thai red curry clear the nostrils with chilli, coconut and coriander. Mains of sumptuously simple turbot with potato purée, asparagus and mustard sauce or impeccable but over-elaborate barbary duck with black pudding mash, foie gras, roast beetroot and port jus leap from the plate. Desserts are made with the skill and perfection of a dedicated French pâtissier. The partners have yet to take control of the elegant but impersonal dining room. Nervous staff drown the atmosphere with weak smiles and bland music.

Tong Dynasty ★ ★

82 Botanic Avenue, Belfast, Co Antrim BT7 1JR (028 9043 9590). **Meals served** noon-midnight daily. **Main courses** £6.80-£13. **Set lunch** (noon-3pm Wed-Sat) £5.95 3 courses. **Set meal** £16-£24 4 courses. **Credit** MC, V.

Even with a new lick of paint and a modest makeover, Tong Dynasty may not be as ritzy or as popular as other Asian restaurants. But its Cantonese food is the most authentic. It makes concessions to locals with a westernised menu section, but no longer reserves the good or difficult stuff for those in the know. Stir-fried beef comes with bitter melon. Terracotta hot-pots of lamb, eel, or aubergine, minced pork and salted fish arrive bubbling in deliciously spiced liquors. Fresh tofu comes prawn-stuffed with black bean sauce. With speciality chefs for traditional roasts and dim sum, it's also worth popping in by day.

DERRY

Browns

1 Bonds Hill, Derry, Co Derry BT47 6DW (028 7134 5180/www.brownsrestaurant.com). **Lunch served** noon-2.15pm Tue-Fri. **Dinner served** 5.30-10pm Tue-Thur; 5.30-10.30pm Fri, Sat. **Main courses** £8.50-£15.95. **Credit** AmEx, MC, V.

On the outskirts of the city, in a pretty terrace of pastel-painted houses, you'll find Browns, a well-established brasserie that caters for the business trade by day and local residents by night. Stylishly designed – by the owner – with good lighting, comfortable seating, architectural foliage and the odd zebra-print panel, the intimate space has a bustling but relaxed ambience. The menu offers adventurous, casual grub. On rare occasions dishes are compromised with one idea too many or the odd gourmet short cut, but nine times out of ten you can be sure of food with great home-made character. Fresh tagliatelli are coated with a vintage Irish cheddar and scallion cream. Oregano-crusted loin of lamb is paired with a Greek salad. Rhubarb upside-down cake is warm and served with vanilla ice-cream. At lunch, service is speedy, but in the evening proceedings slow to accommodate richer food and the loquacious charm of your host.

DUNDRUM

Buck's Head

77-79 Main Street, Dundrum, Co Down BT33 OLU (028 4375 1868). **Lunch served** noon-2.30pm daily. **High tea served** 5-7pm daily. **Dinner served** 7-9.30pm daily. **Set lunch** (Sun) £14.50 3 courses. **Set dinner** (Sun) £24.50 3 courses. **Credit** AmEx, MC, V.

Originally a small pub with cosy horseshoe seating and fireplaces that glow in winter, the Buck's Head now fills its stunning dining room extension seven days a week. The evening set menu isn't always as daring as the funky new design. However, seafood from nearby Dundrum Bay makes for spankingly fresh tempura oysters with chilli, soy and sesame oil dip. Mains, such as pan-fried lemon chicken with tagliatelli, fennel purée and basil oil, are carefully cooked. Giant, berry-strewn meringues or slabs of warmed brownie with a trail of thickened cream appeal to the sweet-toothed, but even better is the Buck's Head satin-smooth chocolate fudge with whole roasted hazelnuts that comes with coffee. A handpicked selection of wines from local merchants makes this a special place for dinner but it's also great for pub lunches and high teas.

ENNISKILLEN

Restaurant No.6 & Café Merlot

At Blakes the Hollow, 6 Church Street, Enniskillen, Co Fermanagh BT74 7EJ (028 6632 0918). **Lunch served** noon-2.30pm Sun. **Dinner served** 7-9.30pm Tue-Sat. **Set dinner** (5.30-7.30pm Wed-Sun) £9.95 2 courses, £11.95 3 courses. **Main courses** £4.95-£15.25. **Credit** MC, V.

Situated above Enniskillen's oldest pub, the solid, smart Restaurant No.6 is now in the capable hands of an ambitious chef and a passionate wine-enthusiast. This duo's zeal for New World adventure seems to be infectious. Warm smoked duck comes with a salad of bean sprouts, coriander, chilli and mint. A chorizo risotto, and a king prawn in a crisp dry vermicelli shell of kataffi pastry add wow factor to the golden roast fillet of turbot. The lighter menu at No.6's sister Café Merlot offers Asian barbecued pork chop with spring greens, egg noodles, lemon and soy or the inspired penne with cashel blue-cream, balsamic-caramelised red onion and lime-sharp avocado salsa, are more typical. Chatty staff, intricate desserts and reasonable prices also make it worth overlooking the flashy wine cellar theme.

GILFORD

Mill Street Restaurant & Bar

14 Mill Street, Gilford, Co Down BT63 6HQ (028 3883 1166). **Meals served** 12.30-11pm Tue-Sun. **Main courses** £12.95-£15.95. **Credit** MC, V.

Mill Street is great for a frivolous night out. The fabulously flamboyant interior – with twinkling glitterball in the tea-lit cocktail lounge, and purple-tented, chandeliered dining room – is the funkiest in Northern Ireland. Its glamour spills over into the menu. There are a few unintentional clichés from the prawn cocktail years – chef's pâté with redcurrant and port compote; 'black and white' steak with peppercorn and béarnaise sauce. Most dishes veer enthusiastically towards the New World with sunny fruit salsas accompanying local meat, such as Finnebrogue venison, and fish. Deep-fried, Pacific oysters are shell-lickingly good with a lime-laced, fresh tomato jus; a rack of rosy, fat-crisp lamb comes with balsamic-marinated onion and sweet butternut squash. Only the bought-in desserts disappoint.

Oriel

2 Bridge Street, Gilford, Co Down BT63 6HF (028 3883 1543). **Lunch served** 12.30-2.30pm Sun. **Dinner served** 6.30-9.30pm Tue-Fri; 7-9.30pm Sat. **Set lunch** £21 3 courses. **Main courses** £18-£22. **Credit** AmEx, MC, V.

Isolated in the quiet village of Gilford, and housed in a rather makeshift building, the Oriel has never been a very stylish restaurant. However, a Michelin star was top of Barry Smyth's agenda, and with limited resources and hard graft he achieved his ambition in four years. Some question whether a restaurant of such modest means deserves this accolade but Smyth's highly wrought food and assiduously selected wine list puts the Oriel on an equal footing with his local Michelin brothers. Prices have climbed, but remain competitive. Expect decadence such as pressed terrine of braised oxtail and foie gras with Madeira essence and warm brioche, followed by pan-seared fillet of wild salmon with sauté artichokes, braised baby leeks, fennel purée and fresh vanilla, finished with cinnamon and vanilla crème caramel with hot and cold apple.

KILLEAVY

Annahaia ★

Slieve Gullion Courtyard, 89 Drumintee Road, Killeavy, Co Armagh BT35 8SW (028 3084 8084/ www.slievegullioncourtyard.com). **Lunch served** 1-3pm Sun. **Dinner served** 7-10.30pm Wed-Sun. **Set lunch** (Sun) £12.95 3 courses. **Set dinner** £28 7 courses. **Credit** MC, V.

Sheep-strewn South Armagh is not the first place you'd associate with good food, but any hill walkers climbing Slieve Gullion will no doubt return to exercise their taste buds next time they visit the area. The Annahaia exclusively serves a seven-course tasting menu. This seems daunting until you've experienced the skilfully balanced, astutely paced flow of dishes. Innovative, playful and delicious, Michael Rath's food is never overworked. Richer courses of meat (a stunning piccata of veal, encased in a nut brown, billowy parsley batter) and fish (tempura of red mullet and spring onion with caponata, couscous, and sweet shrimp cream) are interspersed with refreshing respites such as the marinated, chilli-edged salad of freshly popped peas, asparagus and artichoke, and perfect passion fruit sorbet. Elegant modern design and the cosmopolitan charms of a charismatic host make this one of Northern Ireland's top five destinations.

KIRCUBBIN

Paul Arthurs ★

66 Main Street, Kircubbin, Co Down BT22 2SP (028 4273 8192/www.paul-arthurs.co.uk). **Lunch served** noon-2.30pm Sun. **Dinner served** 5-9pm Tue-Sat. **Main courses** £10-£15. **Credit** AmEx, DC, MC, V.

In his determination to brighten streets, and enlighten palates in his home town, Paul Arthurs has single-handedly created one of County Down's showcase restaurants. While he earns his bread and butter through a first-rate chippy on the ground floor, the upstairs restaurant in this terracotta terrace offers more sophisticated but simple BYO bistro dining. With a butcher's background and great connections to local fisherman, Arthurs sources fabulous raw materials. Sautéed crab claws with garlic, chilli and coriander butter top a concise menu of dishes such as gnocchi with saffron cream and tomato salsa, summer vegetable risotto with creamy gorgonzola or char-grilled ribeye with chips and Café de Paris butter. Luxuries such as foie gras and lobster make frequent appearances, and the food is laced with cream and butter, but try to save room for gorgeously simple desserts. An effervescent atmosphere offsets any kinks in service.

LIMAVADY

Lime Tree

60 Catherine Street, Limavady, Co Derry BT49 9DB (028 7776 4300/www.limetreerest.com). **Dinner served** 6-9pm Tue-Sat. **Set dinner** £19.95 3 courses. (6-7pm Tue-Fri) £9.95 2 courses. **Main courses** £12.95-£17.50. **Credit** AmEx, MC, V.

Situated in the thriving market town of Limavady, the Lime Tree is a modest, family-owned restaurant. While Maria Matthews does a sterling job running the charming dining room, Stanley, her husband and the Lime Tree's chef, makes frequent appearances to lend a hand or enthuse about food and wine. They have a flexible approach to their à la carte and bargain-priced set menus – you can choose between the two – and dishes can be cooked plainly, the menu advises, for those who don't share Stanley's passion for food that strays from the norm. Fish comes fresh from Donegal for chowders, thermidors, or dressed with simple herb oils and nut butters. Properly matured meat is purchased from the reputable town butcher for delicious mains such as chump of Sperrin lamb with Moroccan spiced sauce or roast stuffed saddle of rabbit with a warm black pudding and bacon salad. Imaginative vegetarian food and classic desserts mean everyone leaves satiated.

PORTRUSH

Ramore Wine Bar ★

The Harbour, Portrush, Co Antrim BT56 8BN (028 7082 4313). **Lunch served** 12.15-2.15pm Mon-Sat; 12.30-3pm Sun. **Dinner served** 5-10pm Mon-Sat; 5-9pm Sun. **Main courses** £4.95-£13.95. **Credit** DC, MC, V.

A sharply designed, well-run group of bars serving feisty food, the Ramore is a haven in the unattractive town of Portrush. The view is out to sea, but with long queues it pays to focus on ordering at the self-service counter. All three venues serve variations on classy fast food with cheap and cheerful wines. Prices are rock bottom but finger-licking sides (such as avocado, coriander and lime salad), competitive fervour and enthusiastic service may encourage you to part with more cash than is necessary. Enjoy huge, crisp pizzas topped with rocket, blue cheese and roast red pepper at Coast, tempura prawns with lobster mayo at the Harbour or opt for the more elaborate, prescribed specialities at the Ramore Wine Bar, where Mediterranean chicken en croute with lemon hollandaise is typical of the food on offer.

WARRENPOINT

Duke's

7 Duke Street, Warrenpoint, Co Down BT34 3JY (028 4175 2084/www.thedukerestaurant.com). **Lunch served** noon-2pm Tue-Sat; 1-3pm Sun. **Dinner served** 6-10pm Tue-Sun. **Main courses** £10-£14. **Set dinner** (Tue-Thur) £12.95 3 courses. **Credit** AmEx, MC, V.

A clamorous restaurant above a rowdy pub, Duke's treads a fine line between the needs of a traditional market and the desires of its ambitious chef. His passion is for fish – fresh from Kilkeel – but many of his customers are still caught in a time warp. So, you'll find two menus. One offers chicken kiev, steaks and deep-fried fish or any combination of these ingredients in the 'chuck wagon' and 'surf and turf' options. The other offers fabulously fresh seafood in rather more refined dishes – prawns with garlic, chilli, coriander and basil cream; monkfish, hake and prawns with caper, courgette and dill butter. The casualties of this choice are desserts – such as the sickly Malteser cheesecake – and service, but on a good night Duke's rocks.

Republic of Ireland

County Cavan

BLACKLION

MacNean Bistro

Main Street, Blacklion, Co Cavan (071 985 3022). **Lunch served** 12.30-1pm, 3.30pm Sun. **Dinner served** 6.30-9pm Wed-Fri; 6-6.30pm, 9.15-9.30pm Sat; 6.30-7.30pm Sun. **Main courses** €21-€25. **Set lunch** €27 4 courses. **Set dinner** €55 6 courses. **Credit** MC, V.

Neven Maguire has quietly, and modestly, become the superstar of Irish cooking, a bloke able to pull big crowds any time he demonstrates his capacious culinary skills. Food lovers always choose the tasting menu because the lightness and balance at the core of the food means a series of courses never overwhelms the tastebuds, instead coaxing and teasing them from one dish to the next: mallard with creamed lentils and roast garlic; quail with a truffle and pea risotto; venison with chocolate sauce; scallops with Fermanagh black bacon; and make sure to have at least two desserts.

CLOVERHILL

Olde Post Inn

Cloverhill, Butler's Bridge, Co Cavan (047 55555/ www.theoldepostinn.com). **Lunch served** 12.30-3pm Sun. **Dinner served** 6.30-9.30pm Tue-Sat; 6.30-8.30pm Sun. **Set lunch** €25 4 courses. **Set dinner** €45 5 courses. **Credit** AmEx, MC, V.

Gearoid Lynch and Tara McCann's sweet little restaurant with rooms is idyllic and romantic. They could pack the place simply by serving gruel, but Lynch is a serious cook and the food in the Olde Post is the charming cherry on a sweet cake of an address. Cheffy concoctions such as bacon and cabbage terrine, roulade of guinea fowl with truffle oil or a smart julienne of Dover sole are just one element of Lynch's style. He can just as easily relax into a soulful dish of fillet of beef with champ or veal with mushroom and Madeira. Execution is sharp, the room is comfortable and prices are very keen indeed.

County Clare

BALLINA

Cherry Tree ★

Lakeside, Ballina, Co Clare (061 375688/www.cherry treerestaurant.ie). **Dinner served** 6-10pm Tue-Sat. **Main courses** €18-€38. **Set dinner** €45 6 courses, €70 10-course tasting menu. **Credit** AmEx, MC, V.

The Cherry Tree offers some of the most exciting and enjoyable modern Irish cooking you can find. Harry McKeogh and his devoted team have created the outstanding destination restaurant of County Clare in just a few years. The cooking offers a real road map of the region: Carrigaholt crabmeat in a crispy spring roll; dry-aged Clare beef with thyme-scented vegetables; Bluebell Falls goat's cheese with wild mushroom crostini; West Clare wild salmon with tortelloni of lobster; Comeragh spring lamb with a ragoût of artichokes, mushrooms and asparagus. The kitchen crew, under chef Mark Anderson, are a dynamic bunch, and this food fizzles with creative energy. Set menus are very good value.

BALLYVAUGHAN

Holywell ★

Newtown, Ballyvaughan, Co Clare (065 707 7322/ www.hollywell.net). **Meals served** 11am-11pm daily. **Main courses** €7-€12. **Credit** MC, V.

Holywell looks as if it has been dropped from out of the sky into the hills above Ballyvaughan when it was really intended for some place in the Italian Alps. No matter: the County Clare locals love it to bits and the only hard bit is actually getting a table so you can enjoy the funky, Tyrolean cooking. They offer four starters, a selection of pastas and pizzas and some splendid ice-creams. The portions are as big as the flavours: pasta e fagioli; herb gnocchi; pizza primavera; and then those sublime ices. You don't need to bring a lot of money, but you do need a big appetite for food and for having a great time. Surreal and quite brilliant.

LAHINCH

Barrtra

Lahinch, Co Clare (065 708 1280/www.barrtra.com). **Dinner served** *July-Aug* 5-10pm Mon-Sat, 1-9pm Sun; *Mar-June, Sep-Dec* 5-10pm Tue-Sat, 1-9pm Sun. Closed Jan, Feb. **Main courses** €21. **Set dinner** (5-6.30pm) €25 3 courses; (6.30-10pm) €37 6 courses. **Credit** AmEx, MC, V.

Paul and Theresa O'Brien's tiny water's edge restaurant is little more than a couple of rooms in their house, but they have been sending happy punters home from here for more than 15 years. Most everyone orders the fish of the day, or the shellfish of the day, knowing that it will be sourced and cooked with care, and that they will have just the right bottle of wine to match the fish. Liscannor Bay chowder to begin, then grilled wild salmon with Dijon mustard sauce, or maybe the tourist's favourite of hot buttered lobster. Everything is simple, logical and lovely. There are some carnivorous things to be enjoyed – sirloin with onion and pepper sauce; Toulouse sausages with chive mash – but the fresh fish really can't be beat.

County Cork

BALLYCOTTON

Grapefruit Moon

Main Street, Ballycotton, Co Cork (021 464 6646). **Dinner served** 7-9.30pm Tue-Sat. **Main courses** €17-€28. **Credit** AmEx, DC, MC, V.

Ivan Whelan and Jean Manning have become noted players in Cork's competitive culinary scene, their success to date built on a rock solid foundation of good food and charming, hospitable service. The strong cooking is explained by smart sourcing, with local fish and shellfish and artisan-standard local foods used to great effect: smoked eel, mackerel and mussels are from nearby Cobh and produced by the peerless Belvelly Smokehouse; fish and shellfish are from Ballycotton Bay, just up the street; local fowl and game are as good as it gets. Ingredients carefully chosen, things are then left well alone: black sole with lobster beurre blanc; mackerel with fresh fennel; hake with asparagus and hollandaise. The cooking is as harmonious as the surroundings.

BALTIMORE

Customs House ★ ★

Baltimore, Co Cork (028 20200). **Dinner served** *Apr-June, Sept* 7-10pm Thur-Sun; *July-Aug* 7-10pm Wed-Sun. **Set dinner** €26-€36 3 courses. **No credit cards**.

The menu here never changes it seems – the fish tasting plate to begin; then the red mullet with tapenade, or hake with salmoriglio, or the token meat dish or duck with red wine sauce and mash, then tarte tatin or poached pears. Yet the truth is that chef Sue Holland never cooks the same dish twice. Like a musician presented with the same sonata, she improvises, embellishes, accentuates, varies, counterpoints, but never allows the song to remain the same. Her skill with fish makes for some of the most extraordinary meals in Ireland, food of rare spirit and artistry. You could pay a fortune for such fine food: happily, you don't have to.

BANDON

Otto's Creative Catering ★

Dunworley, Butlerstown, Bandon, Co Cork (023 40461/www.ottoscreativecatering.com). **Lunch served** 1.30-3.30pm Sun. **Dinner served** 7.30-10pm Wed-Sat. Closed Feb. **Set lunch** €35 4 courses. **Set dinner** €50 5 courses. **Credit** MC, V.

Otto Kunze has been 20 years a-cooking, yet the pioneering culinary signature of this sagacious chef has never seemed stronger or more resolute. Food here means ingredients reared by the chef himself, or collected from the wild, or sourced from select locals who understand the holistic vision that drives this man. The tastes seem supercharged with flavour – this is a man who can make custard that will blow your mind – and throughout a dinner that features own-cured meats, wild game, local fish and shellfish, organic vegetables and leaves, the sensory assault is mighty and unrelenting. The ultra-remote location, close to the sea, is just right; the pair of rooms upstairs a refuge for the traveller.

CORK

Café Paradiso ★

16 Lancaster Quay, Western Road, Cork, Co Cork (021 427 7939/www.cafeparadiso.ie). **Lunch served** 12.30-3pm, **dinner served** 6.30-10.30pm Tue-Sat. **Main courses** €15-€21. **Credit** AmEx, MC, V.

Having written one masterly cookbook, the *Café Paradiso Cookbook*, chef Denis Cotter has promptly followed it up with a second, *Paradiso Seasons*. Anyone who has eaten in this extraordinary vegetarian restaurant will be aware that Cotter knows his stuff. Creative dishes might be grilled artichoke with sweet pepper aïoli, rocket and goat's cheese; vegetable sushi with tempura of pumpkin and cauliflower; noodles in ginger broth with aduki bean and chilli wontons; leek, feta and olive-stuffed aubergine. Great room, great sounds, great staff.

Les Gourmandises

17 Cook Street, Cork (021 425 1959/ www.lesgourmandises.ie). **Lunch served** noon-2pm Fri. **Dinner served** 6-10pm Tue-Sat. **Main courses** €23.50-€28. **Set lunch** €13.50 1 course, €17.50 2 courses, €22.50 3 courses. **Set dinner** €31.50 3 courses. **Credit** MC, V.

Patrick Kiely is a fine cook, one just wishes he had a better room in which to work than the characterless space that is Les Gourmandises. No matter: food this good means you have eyes only for what is on the plate. Ravioli of salmon with parsley and grain mustard; roast chicken with fondant potato, black olives and tomatoes; sea bream with tapenade and roast garlic; confit of duck with parsnip purée; a fine coffee crème brûlée with poached prunes. There is real assurance and skill in this work, a genuine signature and an original style. Here is a chef to watch.

Ivory Tower

Exchange Buildings, Princes Street, Cork (021 427 4665). **Dinner served** 6.30-11pm Wed-Sat. **Set dinner** €50 5 courses. **Credit** AmEx, MC, V.

Devotees of Seamus O'Connell's Ivory Tower restaurant will tell you that every other place to eat is dull, and has none of the wildness and unpredictability that makes the Ivory Tower so special. Opponents of O'Connell's iconoclastic style with tell you that the Ivory Tower is ramshackle, unpredictable and chaotic. Neither side will ever agree, but both are right. The IT offers thrilling food, so long as you aren't alienated by the opinionated service, surreal music and bohemian decor. One taste of the blue cheese soufflé in a globe artichoke, or the amazing carpaccio of wood pigeon, or the mallard with vanilla, will either convince you that you have found the heir of Ferran Adria, or that you want to get out of here.

Jacobs on the Mall ★

30A South Mall, Cork, Co Cork (021 425 1530/ www.jacobsonthemall.com). **Lunch served** 12.30-2.30pm, **dinner served** 6.30-10pm Mon-Sat. **Main courses** €14.80-€30. **Credit** AmEx, DC, MC, V.

Chef Mercy Fenton has taken a stroll to the other side of the swing doors and now runs front of house while her faithful kitchen crew continue to cook in the boss's style. Which is serene, smart and dedicated to flavour: crab salad with ginger and lime mayonnaise; artichoke and mushroom hash cakes with spinach; sublime monkfish with polenta and buttered celery; classics such as sirloin with potato gratin and onions, or a brilliant honey and bay leaf brûlée with satsuma and prune compote. One of the city's most original and accomplished restaurateurs, and Jacob's has a signature style like few others.

DURRUS

Good Things Café ★

Ahakista Road, Durrus, Co Cork (027 61426). **Food served** 10.30am-5pm daily. **Lunch served** *June-Aug* 12.30-4pm daily; *Sep-Apr* 12.30-4pm Mon, Thur-Sun. **Dinner served** 7-8.30pm Mon, Fri-Sun. **Main courses** €5.50-€30. **Credit** MC, V.

Carmel Somers' little café just outside tiny Durrus quickly became the critics' darling after opening, and her simple, expressive style, with its acknowledgement of historical influences and dependence on artisan ingredients, was a real treat. She has since improved upon the high standards set from the outset, and there is such confidence in dishes such as her tribute to the Sugar Club's marinated beef with pesto, or a glorious salad of grilled squid with lemon and parsley, that Good Things could easily trade up to Great Things. The wine list is particularly fine, and the views on a nice day are captivating.

KILBRITTAIN

Casino House

Coolmain Bay, Kilbrittain, Co Cork (023 49944). **Lunch served** 1-3pm Sun. **Dinner served** 7-9pm Mon, Tue, Thur-Sun. **Main courses** €16.90-€24.50. **Credit** MC, V.

Like the dedicated, professional couple they are, Michael and Kerrin Relja simply get on with the business of running a superb restaurant – which also has a charming cottage for rental – without worrying about publicity or fame or media attention. Year after year, they improve and augment their work at Casino House, all the while dedicated to polite, efficient service and great cooking. Relja's lobster risotto is a local cult, but any of his signature dishes – Ballydehob duck with honey and port sauce; saddle of lamb with a rosemary jus; and splendid vegetarian choices such as spinach ravioli with roquefort sauce – are just as adept and delicious. Pretty and romantic.

KINSALE

Fishy Fishy Café ★

Guardwell, Kinsale, Co Cork (021 477 4453). **Lunch served** *Apr-Oct* noon-3.45pm daily; *Nov-Mar* noon-3.45pm Mon-Sat. **Main courses** €12-€18. **No credit cards.**

You can argue the toss about who cooks the best fish in Ireland, but one thing is certain: Martin Shanahan's name will be in the reckoning. Fishy Fishy couldn't be simpler: one room, a tiny kitchen, a menu of fresh fish and shellfish – prawns with garlic and lemon; clams with ginger and rocket; cod with chickpeas and anchovies. Indeed, you could ask yourself: why all the fuss? Why the endless queues? The answer is simple; this is fish sourced and cooked as we see it in our dreams. Grab a table under the awning in the pretty fishing port and enjoy motherly service, stunning flavours and good prices.

Toddies

Eastern Road, Kinsale, Co Cork (021 477 7769). **Dinner served** 7-10pm Tue-Sun. **Main courses** €21-€28. **Credit** AmEx, MC, V.

Pearse and Mary O'Sullivan's restaurant is the emerging star in Kinsale, a town that continues to call itself the gourmet capital of Ireland, without having the restaurants to back up that boast. But Toddies is a star in the making, a place for some serious culinary skills. The menu reads classical – terrine of foie gras; sole meunière; lamb with Mediterranean vegetables; tarte tatin – but a powerful signature style gives these old warhorses a vivid new life. Do take a look at the art collection, which is splendid and personal.

MALLOW

Longueville House ★

Mallow, Co Cork (022 47156/www.longuevillehouse.ie). Bar **Meals served** 12.30-5pm daily. **Main courses** €6.50-€14. *Restaurant* **Dinner served** 6.15-9pm daily. **Main courses** €29.50. **Set dinner** (6.15-7pm Mon-Thur, Sun) €35 2 courses; (6.15-9pm daily) €50 5 courses. **Credit** AmEx, MC, V.

William O'Callaghan is the renaissance man of the Irish kitchen. Using the produce of the large Longueville estate, O'Callaghan weaves a magic that is bewitching. With the estate lamb, for instance, he makes loin of lamb in a herb crust, with a pastry of confit lamb, and a brochette of leg of lamb and lamb liver. A canon of house-smoked salmon has a crab and a sorrel sauce; tripe and oxtail is wrapped in crepinette; a glorious ravioli of shiitake has an intriguing gooseberry pesto. Thrilling food, and the renovated conservatory is wonderfully romantic.

MIDLETON

O'Donovan's

58 Main Street, Midleton, Co Cork (021 463 1255). **Lunch served** 12.15-2.30pm, **dinner served** 6-9.30pm Mon-Sat. **Main courses** €18.95-€27. **Credit** MC, V.

Pat O'Donovan's elegant restaurant in the centre of busy Midleton has a calm, no-nonsense logic to it. When chef Ian Cronin puts together a Caesar salad, he does it by the book, with no post-modern additions that the dish doesn't need. When he gives himself a little leeway, with dishes such as barbary duck with beetroot and horseradish tapenade, or pan-fried turbot with prawn mash and a Bretonne sauce, the result is always sound and considered. An excellent, grown-up restaurant.

ROSS CARBERY

O'Callaghan-Walshe ★

Ross Carbery, Co Cork (023 48125). **Dinner served** *summer* 6.30-9.30pm Tue-Sun; *winter* 6.30-9.30pm Fri, Sat. **Main courses** €26.50-€45. **Credit** MC, V.

O'C-W (as the locals call it) doesn't look or feel like any other restaurant. It's an out-of-the-box place, one of those great, weird, West Cork destinations that you simply don't find elsewhere. Martina cooks fish and shellfish from the locality – wild hake; wild brill; lobster; wild sea bass – and Sean serves it, and as a double-act they would be hard to beat. She cooks like a dream; he is the most sanguine and amusing of hosts. The fish cakes are ace, the lobster cocktail is terrific and the mashed potato is perfect.

SHANAGARRY

Ballymaloe House ★

Shanagarry, Co Cork (021 465 2531/www.ballymaloe.com). **Lunch served** 1-1.30pm, **dinner served** 7-9.30pm daily. **Set lunch** (Mon-Sat) €30 4 courses; (Sun) €35 4 courses. **Set dinner** €55.50 5 courses. **Credit** AmEx, DC, MC, V.

Myrtle Allen, the conscience of Irish cooking, has just turned four score years and, as if in tribute to her youthfulness, Ballymaloe House, despite 40 years in business, seems younger than ever. Try hot oysters with cucumbers and beurre blanc, east Cork beef with red wine sauce and aïoli, or glazed bacon with cranberries and pepperonata – dishes that seem newly minted, with respect for the land and its produce. The calm and dignity of the house is enduring and endearing, and Ballymaloe remains one of the greatest Irish addresses.

SKIBBEREEN

Island Cottage

Heir Island, Skibbereen, Co Cork (028 38102/www.islandcottage.com). **Dinner served** *15 May-15 Sept* 8pm-midnight Wed-Sun. **Set dinner** €40 4 courses. **No credit cards.**

Establish your restaurant on a remote island that can only be reached via a tiny boat. Then make everyone walk for a mile or so. Offer no choice over dinner. Have just half a dozen wines on the list. Make all 20 or so diners in the single room eat at the same time. That is exactly what happens here, and for almost 15 years, this extraordinary adventure in exploration and eating has been one of the success stories of Irish cooking. Surreal, brilliant, and with gorgeous food – the best roast duck; great turbot with mash; sublime lemon soufflé.

County Donegal

CARNDONAGH

The Corncrake

Millbrae, Carndonagh, Co Donegal (074 937 4534) **Dinner served** 6-9pm Tue-Sat. **Main courses** €17-€23. **No credit cards.**

The problem with the Corncrake is simple: once is not enough. When you have made one visit, and enjoyed the crab soufflé to start, then the Donegal lamb with rosemary, then a pitch-perfect lemon and almond tart, you will want to come back, and eat exactly the same things all over again. But, your friends will say, what about the roquefort and celeriac tart, the classic coq-au-vin and the coffee and cardamom brûlée; or the butternut squash soup, the grilled wild salmon and the apple and cinnamon nut crumble? Looks like you'll have plenty more visits to come. The Corncrake is a rare bird, indeed.

DUNFANAGHY

The Mill

Figart, Dunfanaghy, Co Donegal (074 913 6985/www.themillrestaurant.com). **Lunch served** 12.30-2pm 1st Sun of mth. **Dinner served** 7-9pm Tue-Sun. **Set dinner** €35 3 courses. **Credit** AmEx, MC, V.

Derek and Susan Alcorn have a little jewel in the Mill, a beautiful, aesthetically precise little place where the six elegant rooms are complemented by a very fine restaurant. Alcorn has always been an excellent cook, but recently he has moved up a gear. The menus for adults are a treat – superlative oyster carbonara with fresh linguini and pancetta; great chicken livers with black pudding on a rosemary porridge fritter; main courses of Horn Head mackerel with basil mash and a seafood saffron broth, and confit shoulder of lamb with roast rump and some boulangère potatoes – smart, light, deeply pleasing cooking. There are great kids' menus too.

DONEGAL

Coxtown Manor

Laghey, Co Donegal (074 973 4574/www.coxtownmanor.com). **Lunch served** 1-3pm Sun. **Dinner served** *Jun-Aug* 7-9pm daily; *Sep-May* 7-9pm Tue-Sun. **Main courses** €18-€29. **Set lunch** (Sun) €26.50 4 courses. **Credit** MC, V.

Ed Dewael's manor house and restaurant has become one of Donegal's best destinations, boasting a great crew who really enjoy their work and who convey this enthusiasm with unselfconscious ease, determined to ensure that you have a great time. The menu has many echoes of the owner's Belgian background – loads of great beers, lashings of Belgian chocolate desserts and smart main courses such as John Dory cooked in beer – but don't imagine this is some sort of displaced monument to Belgium: Coxtown is a pulsing, animated restaurant, with a great Donegal charm to it. The choice of fish and shellfish from local ports is always excellent – the shellfish cookery is very fine – while meat and game are carefully sourced from the best local producers.

GREENCASTLE

Kealy's Seafood Bar

Greencastle, Co Donegal (074 938 1010). **Lunch served** *winter* 12.30-3pm Fri-Sun; *summer* 12.30-3pm Wed-Sun. **Dinner served** *winter* 7-9.30pm Thur-Sat; 7-8.30pm Sun; *summer* 7-9.30pm Wed-Sat; 7-8.30pm Sun. **Main courses** €15-€50. **Set dinner** €35 4 courses. **Credit** AmEx, MC, V.

James and Tricia Kealy's perennially popular fish bar lies directly opposite the pier at Greencastle. Crisp and classic is the order of the day: stuffed mussels; Greencastle chowder; grilled cod with anchovy butter; beautiful scampi; monkfish Mediterranean-style. All a perfect accompaniment to the relaxed, unfussy bar with its simple adjoining restaurant. Lunch menus are short; dinner offers greater choice, including some meat courses such as chicken and chorizo casserole or steak au poivre. The vegetarian choices are particularly good.

County Dublin

DUBLIN

AYA

49-52 Clarendon Street, Dublin 2 (01 677 1544/ www.aya.ie). **Lunch served** 12.30-3pm Mon-Fri; noon-4pm Sat; 1-4pm Sun. **Dinner served** 5-10pm Mon-Fri, Sun; 5-11pm Sat. **Set meal** (12.30-3pm, 6-7pm Mon-Fri; noon-4pm, 5.30-7pm Sat; 1-4pm, 5-7pm Sun) €19 2 courses, €22 2 courses incl a drink. **Set dinner** €25 3 courses incl coffee. **Credit** AmEx, MC, V.

AYA is some of the best food fun to be had in Dublin. Hip, slick, and on top of its game, Yoichi Hoashi's newly renovated Japanese restaurant in the city centre has conveyor-belt sushi as its main draw, alongside more traditional three-course menus and a pile of gimmicks – a 55-minute sushi offer; AYA T-shirts; manga movies – all backed up by fine cooking. The teriyaki plates are sticky and moreish, the cold noodle salads excellent; salmon comes as tempura or topping nigiri, and kids wolf the pork gyoza and the real prawn crackers. Just so it's not too strange for Dubliners, they have chocolate mousse for dessert. The crew are mainly young Aussies, who are into the idea of making sure you have some fun in this gorgeously designed room. 'Lovelifelovesushi' runs one of the many slogans, and nobody's about to argue with that.

Bang Café ★

11 Merrion Row, Dublin 2 (01 676 0898/www.bang restaurant.com). **Lunch served** 12.30-3pm Mon-Sat. **Dinner served** 6-10.30pm Mon-Wed; 6-11pm Thur-Sat. **Main courses** €10.55-€23.95. **Credit** AmEx, MC, V.

Chapter One. *See p356.*

Local media attention tends to emphasise the cute-boys-about-town status of the Stokes brothers, the owners of Bang. But, for food lovers, the star of this swish city centre restaurant is the less photogenic chef Lorcan Gribbin. He manages to make sense of the food others can't quite get a grip on. His bistro dishes such as chicken chasseur are a statement of the art. His fusion dishes such as Thai beef fillet are perfect rather than pastiche. The level of care shown to even the simplest culinary details is delightful. Book well in advance for weekends, and note that the best seats are upstairs, and not in the basement.

The Cellar

Merrion Hotel, Upper Merrion Street, Dublin 2 (01 603 0600/www.merrionhotel.com). **Breakfast served** 7-10.30am Mon-Fri; 9am-11pm Sat-Sun. **Lunch served** 12.30-2.30pm Mon-Sat. **Brunch served** 12.30-2pm Sun. **Dinner served** 6-10pm daily. **Main courses** €12-€26. **Set Irish breakfast** €26. **Set lunch** €21.95 2 courses, €24.95 3 courses. **Credit** AmEx, DC, MC, V.

The Cellar used to be one of the worst spots in the city, so enveloping and dimly lit that the only sure thing here was claustrophobia. Enter the architect Arthur Gibney, a new design, and one of the city's best front-of-house operators, Damian Corr, and hey presto! A superb makeover. Food is solid, conservative and precise, especially with dishes such as chump of lamb with tarragon, a fine tart of smoked haddock, or a very fine old warhorse such as baked alaska. The service is superlative, and value for money among the best in the capital city.

Chapter One ★ ★

18-19 Parnell Square, Dublin 1 (01 873 2266/ www.chapteronerestaurant.com). **Lunch served** 12.30-2.30pm Tue-Fri. **Dinner served** 6-10.30pm Tue-Sat. **Set lunch** €24.50 2 courses, €28.50 3 courses. **Set dinner** (6-7pm) €29.50 3 courses. **Main courses** €20-€45. **Credit** AmEx, DC, MC, V.

Chef and owner Ross Lewis and his manager Martin Corbett run one of the city's best restaurants. Polished, professional and with a very idiosyncratic, personal modern style that speaks of deep culinary understanding, Chapter One is as good as Dublin gets. Start with a selection of artisan cured meats and salamis from the charcuterie trolley, then enjoy some intriguing combinations – lime-marinated scallops with avocado and crème fraîche; crab-stuffed Dover sole; veal with pancetta and mushroom cannelloni; crab lasagne with fennel velouté. The cheeseboard, like the charcuterie trolley, is a must. This is theatre land, and their pre-theatre dinner with a clever option allowing you to return for dessert has proved astoundingly popular.

L'Ecrivain ★

109a Lower Baggot Street, Dublin 2 (01 661 1919/ www.lecrivain.com). **Lunch served** 12.30-2pm Mon-Fri. **Dinner served** 7-10.30pm Mon-Sat. **Main courses** €39-42. **Set lunch** €30 2 courses, €40 3 courses. **Set dinner** €65 3 courses. **Credit** AmEx, MC, V.

Derry and Sallyanne Clarke's bustling restaurant is not simply part of the culinary culture of the city but part of the culture of the city, full stop. The food is the veritable definition of modern Irish cooking and enjoys a winning swagger and confident deliciousness – veal liver with smoked bacon and champ and shallot cream; rack of lamb with hotpot of carrot and potato; seared monkfish with caramelised fennel; baked oysters with bacon and cabbage and a Guinness sabayon. The energy in the room from both committed staff and delighted punters is electrifying.

Frank's

The Malting Tower, Grand Canal Quay, Dublin 2 (01 662 5870/www.franksbarandrestaurant.com). **Food served** 11.30am-11pm Mon-Fri; 12.30-11pm Sat, Sun. **Main courses** €11-€27. **Credit** AmEx, DC, MC, V.

Frank's is Dublin's newest darling and it is run by two of Dublin's most experienced restaurateurs. Liz Mee and John Hayes were two of the people who made Temple Bar back in the 1980s, and now they are making Grand Canal Dock into the city's hottest new destination. Tucked under a railway bridge on a cobble-stone street, Frank's does back-to-basics food: potted shrimp; native oysters; burger with horseradish sour cream; grilled chicken with mash and spinach; Moroccan lamb. Its secret is to get huge flavours from these ingredients. The room is fun and playful, and everyone from families to courting couples gets exactly what they want.

Halo ★

The Morrison Hotel, Ormond Quay, Dublin 1 (01 887 2421/www.morrisonhotel.ie). **Lunch served** 12.30-2.30pm, **dinner served** 7-10.30pm daily. **Main courses** €24-€36. **Set dinner** €32 2 courses, €35 3 courses. **Credit** AmEx, DC, MC, V.

Fusion cooking has a pretty poor history in Dublin, but in the beautiful, John Rocha-designed Halo, Jean-Michel Poulot shows both the potential and the glory of the style. Poulot will place a black bean sauce alongside mashed potato and roast chicken, and he will make it work. Basil gnocchi with sichuan-peppered tuna? Made for each other. Seared scallops with Indian spices and confit fennel? Why doesn't everyone do it? This ability to find taste symmetries with such unlikely ingredients is masterly, and it makes for luxuriously sensual eating. Prices are not cheap, but they do represent great value for money.

Jacob's Ladder

4-5 Nassau Street, Dublin 2 (01 670 3865/www.jacobsladder.ie). **Lunch served** 12.30-2.30pm Tue-Sat. **Dinner served** 6-10pm Tue-Fri; 7-10pm Sat. **Main courses** (lunch) €14.20; (dinner) €29-€32. **Set dinner** (6-7pm Tue-Fri) €21 2 courses, €26.75 3 courses; (7-10pm Tue-Sat) €37 3 courses. **Credit** AmEx, DC, MC, V.

'The most experimental chef in Dublin,' is how the critics describe Adrian Roche, but they could also add that he is the least well-known of Dublin's cutting-edge cooks, a fact explained by the intrinsic shyness of this gifted cook. He prefers to let his food (and the critics) do the talking, and the menu is fluent in several languages. French-style foie gras is matched with an Irish black pudding. Monkfish is curried, and served with a pearl barley risotto. Salmon has an orange and rhubarb reduction to set the tastebuds zinging. There is no experimentation for the sake of it, however: instead, there is discipline and a determination to please the diner behind every intricately crafted concoction. Service is excellent and the views are charming.

Mermaid Café ★

69-70 Dame Street, Dublin 2 (01 670 8236/ www.mermaid.ie). **Lunch served** 12.30-2.30pm Mon-Sat. **Brunch served** noon-3pm Sun. **Dinner served** 6-10pm Mon-Thur; 6-11pm Fri-Sat; 6-9pm Sun. **Main courses** €18.95-€29.95. **Set lunch** (Mon-Sat) €19.95 2 courses, €23.95 3 courses. **Credit** MC, V.

The Mermaid is funky, unorthodox and inspired, a restaurant with a style and character so left-of-centre that it is a miracle it can survive in a competitive city-centre environment. But the Mermaid positively prospers thanks to Temple Garner's flavour-filled cooking, and a subtle sangfroid that is extremely alluring, especially at weekend brunch. The food is unlike anything else in Dublin: chicken with smoked red peppers and parmesan polenta; mushroom and sage tagliatelle with toasted walnut pesto; osso bucco with tarragon and Jerusalem artichokes; Connemara salmon with mussel and saffron bouillabaisse; kirsch and griottine frozen yogurt. Punky cooking, delivered with real verve, which the confident, charming staff bring off to a T.

Mint

47 Ranelagh Village, Dublin 6 (01 497 8655). **Lunch served** noon-3pm, **dinner served** 6-10pm Tue-Sun. **Main courses** €18-€26. **Set lunch** €21 2 courses, €25 3 courses. **Credit** AmEx, DC, MC, V.

Oliver Dunne is one of the newest stars to emerge from the Dublin cooking scene and the tiny room in suburban Ranelagh that houses Mint has been an ideal showcase for this talented 26-year-old. Of course, you get all the foams and froths beloved of young chefs these days – pied de moton foam with sea bream; parmesan velouté with wild mushroom risotto; vermouth cappuccino with roast hake – but Dunne is no mere fashion-follower. Dishes such as saddle of venison with turnip and prune gratin, or a boudin of veal sweetbreads and wild mushrooms, show real skill. Some folk don't like the fact that the room is so small, forcing the tables together, but that's a small price to pay for such exciting cooking.

Montys

28 Eustace Street, Temple Bar, Dublin 2 (01 670 4911/www.montys.ie). **Lunch served** noon-2.30pm Mon-Sat. **Dinner served** 6-11.30pm Mon-Sat; 6-11pm Sun. **Main courses** €15-€18. **Set dinner** (6-7pm Mon-Thur, Sun) €20 2 courses. **Credit** AmEx, MC, V.

Shiva Gautam's Nepalese place is one of the most popular ethnic restaurants in the city, and a real Temple Bar hotspot. It's a very simple room, with a gloomy basement that you'd do well to avoid. The cooking is creative and enlivening, especially raw, minced lamb kachela, sublime Momo dumplings (order these when you book: they are a must), or the paneer masala (with handmade cheese). Careful and clever use of the tandoor makes for sizzling flavours, and the breads are second to none. The room has a great, informal, laid-back buzz, helped by the fact that everyone who eats here becomes a regular.

O'Connell's ★

Merrion Road, Ballsbridge, Dublin 4 (01 647 3304/ www.oconnellsballsbridge.com). **Lunch served** 12.30-2.30pm Mon-Sat; 12.30-3pm Sun. **Dinner served** 6-10.30pm Mon-Sat; 6-9.30pm Sun. **Main courses** €16.45-€32.50. **Set dinner** (6-7pm) €19.75 2 courses, €22 3 courses; €25 3 courses. **Credit** AmEx, DC, MC, V.

O'Connell's is that rarest of places: a restaurant that manages to be all things to all men, women and children. You will often see large family groups in Tom O'Connell's big, busy brasserie and all will be having a great time, enjoying good savoury cooking, smartly chosen wines and polite and efficient service. And even when the room is heaving, the place never loses an expert polish and charm. The cooking takes fine traditional foods and treats them with respect: Wexford beef with french-fried onions; Gubbeen bacon with spiced cranberries; East Cork smoked fish with dill mayonnaise; Donegal salmon with herb cream. Very tasty, and the consistency shown by the kitchen over the years is admirable.

101 Talbot

101 Talbot Street, Dublin 1 (01 874 5011). **Dinner served** 5-11pm Tue-Sat. **Main courses** €12.50-€19. **Set dinner** (5-8pm) €21 2 courses incl tea or coffee. **Credit** AmEx, MC, V.

Long before O'Connell Street and its environs got tarted up, Paschal Bradley and Margaret Duffy were cooking fine food up the stairs at 101 Talbot Street, over the camping shop. Nothing has changed since this area used to be shabby rather than chic. The food is straightforward, logical and hugely enjoyable, administered by a crack crew who get a real buzz out of their work at this great big eating space. Old-fashioned ideas, such as good value, good humour, good service and good fun, are all put to daily use, which makes the food taste extra good.

Peploe's

16 St Stephen's Green, Dublin 2 (01 676 3144/ www.peploes.com). **Lunch served** noon-3pm, **bar menu** 3-6pm, **dinner served** 6-11pm daily. **Main courses** €12-€24. **Credit** AmEx, MC, V.

Barry Canny's St Stephen's Green restaurant was a long time in the planning and decorating, but it took only 24 hours for Dubliners to take it to their hearts. It's a great, clubby, city-centre room, with simple, meticulously presented food. Deep-fried Cooleeney camembert with port wine figs; asparagus with citrus hollandaise; sirloin steak with béarnaise; and a fine shepherd's pie. It is comforting cooking, but the level of execution raises the food into the zone of real craftsmanship. You can also enjoy small bites with a glass of wine through the day.

Tea Room ★

The Clarence Hotel, 6-8 Wellington Quay, Dublin 2 (01 407 0800/www.theclarence.ie). **Lunch served** 12.30-3pm Mon-Fri; noon-3pm Sun. **Dinner served** 6.30-10.45pm daily. **Main courses** €19-€36. **Set lunch** €26.50 2 courses, €30.50 3 courses. **Set dinner** €65 5-course tasting menu. **Credit** AmEx, DC, MC, V.

The Tea Room, part of the über-stylish, U2-owned Clarence Hotel, is probably the most gorgeous dining room in the city and, with chef Antony Ely at the stoves, it is also home to some of its greatest cooking. Ely's secret is to take gutsy ingredients and then to concentrate on giving them a lush, sensual texture: turnip and potato soup with black pudding straws; partridge with green beans and lentil vinaigrette; monkfish with savoy cabbage and white beans; lamb neck with potato, carrot and onions. Thrilling eating in what is the city's great restaurant for those out to impress somebody special.

Thornton's ★

128 St Stephen's Green, Dublin 2 (01 478 7008/www.thorntonsrestaurant.com). **Lunch served** 12.30-2.30pm, **dinner served** 7-10.30pm Tue-Sat. **Main courses** €45. **Set lunch** €30 2 courses, €40 3 courses. **Set dinner** €65 3 courses. **Credit** AmEx, DC, MC, V.

People complain that the dining room here has little atmosphere, and that the à la carte prices are scarily high, but nobody will argue about the merits of Kevin Thornton's cooking. As pretty and painterly as a Miro sketch, the menu reveals a beautifully sinuous series of experiments with ingredients: loin of veal with a rosemary and lime beurre blanc; ballotine of rabbit with valrhona and hazelnut sauce; blue fin tuna three-ways, with crème fraîche. This is food that is as exhilarating for the brain as for the body, and worth every penny.

DUN LAOGHAIRE

Cavistons

59 Glasthule Road, Sandycove, Dun Laoghaire, Co Dublin (01 280 9245/www.cavistons.com). **Lunch served** noon-1.30pm, 1.30-3pm, 3-5pm Tue-Sat. **Main courses** €15-€23. **Credit** AmEx, DC, MC, V.

Three sittings a day, five days a week, makes for 15 sets of happy customers who have received the weekly lunchtime fix of Caviston's excellent fish. A tiny room – seven tables, that's all – with adjacent fish shop and deli, Caviston's consistently hits the spot. The day's fish is cooked simply – swordfish with dill and lemon; haddock with chervil sauce; mackerel with apple and ginger; scallops with chilli, ginger and spring onion. Booking is essential.

County Galway

BALLINAFAD

Ballynahinch Castle

Recess, Connemara, Ballinafad, Co Galway (095 31006/www.ballynahinch-castle.com). Bar **Lunch served** 12.30-3pm daily. *Restaurant* **Dinner served** 6.30-9pm daily. **Main courses** €18-€35. **Set dinner** €45 5 courses. **Credit** AmEx, DC, MC, V.

Chef Robert Webster and manager Patrick O'Flaherty have been powering the beautiful Ballynahinch Castle towards greatness for the last few years, working on a mandate of affability, affordability and great cooking. The Castle is grand, but democratic and welcoming, a place where locals hang out alongside high rollers. In the sweet and lovely dining room, you can sample Atlantic oysters with red wine and shallot vinegar; rabbit with baby asparagus and chanterelles; black sole with beurre noisette; wild sea bass with fennel and spinach.

CLARINBRIDGE

Old Schoolhouse

Clarinbridge, Co Galway (091 796898). **Lunch served** 12.30-2.30pm Sun. **Dinner served** 6.30-10pm Tue-Thur, Sun; 6.30-10.30pm Fri, Sat. **Main courses** €13-€28.50. **Set lunch** €21 4 courses incl tea or coffee. **Credit** AmEx, MC, V.

Kenneth Connolly's busy restaurant attracts all comers. What they enjoy is modern, stylish food with a confident edge: clam and smoked salmon chowder; grilled goat's cheese with rocket pesto; spring lamb with mint and bacon mash; excellent sea bass fillets with vegetable risotto and lemon balm and thyme dressing. The food has big flavours, which makes for satisfying eating. Good service and value, with particularly good children's menus.

GALWAY

Goya's

2-3 Kirwan's Lane, Galway, Co Galway (091 567010/ www.goyas.ie). **Food served** 9.30am-6pm, **lunch served** 12.30-3pm Mon-Sat. **Main courses** €3.65-€7.75. **Credit** MC, V.

Emer Murray's svelte, handsome dining room is one of the key Galway addresses. Celebrated as one of the finest bakers in Ireland, Murray prepares daytime food that is just as desirable as her baking. Even standards such as vegetable pie or quiche lorraine are transformed into stellar performers. Salads and breads, soups and savoury dishes, are all equally distinguished, and desserts such as poppy seed and blueberry muffin are knock-out.

Nimmo's

Long Walk, Spanish Arch, Galway, Co Galway (091 561114). **Lunch served** 12.30-3.30pm Fri-Sat. **Dinner served** 6-10pm Tue-Sun. **Main courses** €10-€24.50. **Credit** MC, V.

Bar crawl: Dublin

You won't be short of places to go for a drink in this city. Start in Temple Bar: for a beginner's guide to Dublin pubs try the **Auld Dubliner** (17 Anglesea Street, 677 0527) for traditional music and decent pints. The **Front Lounge** (33-34 Parliament Street, 670 4112) is a relaxing joint, oozing class with velvet couches and black marble tables. The back bar is predominately gay, while the front bar attracts a mixed group. The **Globe** (11 South Great George's Street, 671 1220) is good for people-watching, while the equally trendy **Hogan's** (35 South Great George's Street, 677 5904) has a beautifully carved wooden bar and funky art installations. If that isn't fancy enough, try the painfully hip **Octagon Bar** (Clarence Hotel, 6-8 Wellington Quay, 670 9000). More traditional in its charm is the **Long Hall** (52 South Great George's Street, 475 1590) – one of Dublin's unmissables.

The **Market Bar** (14A Fade Street, off South Great George's Street, 613 9094) is Dublin's hottest new superpub, while the **Porterhouse** (16-18 Parliament Street, 679 8847) is its first microbrewery. Finally there's the perennially busy **Temple Bar** (47-48 Temple Bar, 672 5286).

Now head over to Trinity College, where you could pop into the eccentric **Grogan's Castle Lounge** (15 South William Street, 677 9320), and **Mulligan's** (8 Poolbeg Street, 677 5582), a legendary boozer. Continuing the theme is **Bruxelles** (7-8 Harry Street, 677 5362), a raucous late-night dive. In the opposing corner is beautifully decorated **Café en Seine** (40 Dawson Street, 677 4567). In a similar vein comes **Viva** (52 South William Street, 677 0605), a spacious DJ bar. Or you can star-spot at Eddie Irvine's **Cocoon** (Royal Hibernian Way, 679 6259). Round these parts you'll also find trendy **Bailey** (2 Duke Street, 670 4939).

Around St Stephen's Green there's **Doheny & Nesbitt** (5 Baggot Street Lower, 676 2945), a glorious old pub. **Dowling's** (13 Upper Baggot Street, 667 7156) is one of the best wine bars on the southside. Music lovers should try jazz bar **JJ Smyths** (12 Aungier Street, 475 2565) or the **Village** (26 Wexford Street, 475 8555), one of Dublin's best music venues as well as an attractive bar.

Around O'Connell Street is **Kiely's** (37 Upper Abbey Street, 872 2100) – two bars in one: one trad, one trendy. **Metropolitan** (Clifton Court hotel, 11 Eden Quay, 874 3535) is a smart, airy space where DJs play sophisticated sounds for a savvy crowd. Rambling **Pravda** (35 Liffey Street Lower, 874 0076) pulls off the ersatz Eastern European thing pretty well.

Around the North Quays, there's the cosy **Cobblestone** (77 King Street North, Smithfield, 872 1799). Rock star haunt **Dice Bar** (Queen Street, off Arran Quay, Smithfield, 872 8622) has an illicit Noo Yawk street vibe. Another music-y joint is **Voodoo Lounge** (39 Arran Quay, Smithfield, 873 6013). In contrast, **Morrison Hotel Bar** (Ormond Quay Lower, 887 2400) is a modish cocktail bar.

Finally, in the north suburbs, **Kavanagh's** (1 Prospect Square, Glasnevin, no phone) is a Dublin institution. It hasn't changed a jot in a century and a half.

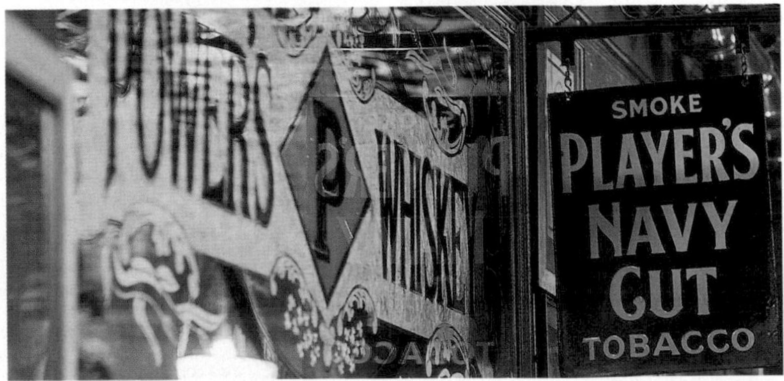

Harriet Leander's stylish, bohemian restaurant is the star turn of the city. Housed in a fine old stone building, there is a splendid wine bar downstairs, with a slightly more formal restaurant upstairs. Funky staff exude Galway bonhomie, while the cooking has style and panache: excellent terrines and pâtés, spot-on renditions of bistro classics such as boeuf bourguignon or coq au vin. Clamorous, raucous fun, you could be nowhere else but Galway.

LOUGHREA

Slatefort House

Slatefort, Bullaun, Loughrea, Co Galway (091 870667). **Lunch served** 1-3pm Sun. **Dinner served** 7-11pm Tue-Sun. **Main courses** €15-€20. **Set lunch** €20 3 courses incl coffee. **Credit** AmEx, DC, MC, V.
Slatefort House looks and feels like a real Italian restaurant, complete with an adorable laissez-faire ambience. The cooking makes no compromises: fresh pasta stuffed with sea bass in a light fish sauce or a perfect breast of duck. Simple vegetable garnishes, fruits poached in wine for dessert, excellent coffee, a modest bill. Maura and Rosario keep things on track with a shy, expert diffidence.

County Kerry

DINGLE

Chart House

The Mall, Dingle, Co Kerry (066 915 2255/www.charthousedingle.com). **Dinner served** 6.30-9.45pm Mon, Wed-Sun; *July-Sept* 6.30-9.45pm daily. Closed 8 Jan-14 Feb. **Main courses** €14.75-€24.95. **Set dinner** €35 3 courses incl tea or coffee. **Credit** MC, V.
Jim and Carmel McCarthy's pretty cottage restaurant has been the destination address in busy Dingle ever since they first opened their half-door, and a crack crew keep this thriving restaurant up to speed with dedicated cooking and service. Classic dishes are delivered with care: spiced chicken sausage with hot pepper marmalade; crab and cod cakes with lime tartare sauce; roast turbot with beetroot and spring onion salad; roast Kerry lamb with a red onion and feta tarte tatin.

Out of the Blue

Strand Street, Waterside, Dingle, Co Kerry (066 915 0811). Mar-Nov **Lunch served** 12.30-3pm, **dinner served** 6-9.30pm Mon,Tue, Thur-Sun. **Main courses** €14-€26. **Credit** MC, V.
A tiny room close to Dingle pier with a few tables arranged outside is the setting where Tim Mason cooks the fish landed that same day. Regulars tend to choose from the dishes scribbled on the blackboard, but the exhilarating freshness of the food guarantees the success of every dish: rock cod with tomato and basil and baby potatoes; John Dory with garlic aubergines; orange roughy with a lemon butter; wild salmon with sautéed potatoes. Simple, straightforward and fresh as seaspray.

KENMARE

Mulcahy's

36 Henry Street, Kenmare, Co Kerry (064 42383/www.mulcahys.com). **Lunch served** 12.30-3pm Sun. **Dinner served** 6-10pm Mon, Wed-Sun. **Main courses** €14.95-€27. **Set lunch** €23 3 courses. **Set dinner** €55 5-course tasting menu. **Credit** DC, MC, V.
Bruce Mulcahy has moved his restaurant across the street to a swish and handsome new room that feels ideal. The food is vivid and exciting, fitting for a chef that is considered the best in town – lime and basil-infused goat's cheese with tomato water; tempura of crab dumplings; spiced duck leg with red wine and prune essence; rhubarb and ginger crème brûlée. For all the international borrowings, the menu remains focused, and the flavours expertly controlled.

Packie's Food & Wine

35 Henry Street, Kenmare, Co Kerry (064 41508). **Dinner served** *Mar-Dec* 6-10pm Mon-Sat. **Main courses** €15-€27. **Credit** AmEx, DC, MC, V.
Martin Hallissey has taken over kitchen duties in this comfortable, simple space, and he has continued the tradition of his mentor, Maura Foley, in creating comfort food that transcends its straightforward ingredients. Fish continues to dominate – excellent seafood sausage with beurre blanc; prawns with a curry sabayon; brill with saffron and orange sauce – but there's also room for trad meat dishes, such as crubeens (pig's trotters) or a fine Kerry lamb stew.

KILLARNEY

Killarney Park Hotel

Kenmare Place, Killarney, Co Kerry (064 35555/www.killarneyparkhotel.ie). **Breakfast served** 7.30-10am Mon-Fri; 8-11am Sat, Sun. *Bar* **Meals served** 12.30-9pm Mon-Fri, Sun; 12.30-7pm Sat. *Restaurant* **Dinner served** 7-9.30pm daily. **Main courses** *Bar* €8-€17.50; *Restaurant* €26-€29. **Set dinner** €57.50 5 courses. **Credit** AmEx, MC, V.
Banish any clichéd thoughts of hotel cooking; creativity, style and real originality are the features here. A pithivier of wild mushroom and quail has a chorizo and raisin jus. Breast of duck has red cabbage braised in cider. Codling comes with creamed salsify and a shrimp beignet. The kitchen prepares a complete vegetarian menu every evening. The room is luxurious, service is right on the money, and this place is a real treat.

LISTOWEL

Allo's

41 Church Street, Listowel, Co Kerry (068 22880). **Meals served** noon-7pm, **dinner served** 7-9pm Tue-Sat. **Main courses** €22.50-€27.50. **Set dinner** (Thur) €22 3 courses. **Credit** AmEx, MC, V.
Fried, battered hake cooked to crispy perfection. Lovely handmade tartare sauce. Excellent fries. A crisp, fresh salad. Great coffee. That's a typical lunch in Allo's, the pioneer of Irish gastropubs. Owner

Helen Mullane and chef Theo Lynch have been doing sophisticated, beautifully executed cooking and serving it in this gorgeous, old-style bar for aeons, and their take on traditional dishes such as bacon and cabbage, or lamb stew, can't be bettered.

TRALEE

Restaurant David Norris

Ivy House, Ivy Terrace, Tralee, Co Kerry (066 7185654). **Dinner served** 5-10pm Tue-Sat. **Main courses** €15-€26. **Set dinner** (5-7pm) €24.95 4 courses. **Credit** AmEx, MC, V.

There is a lightness and elegance about the food served here that gives it a summery trademark. Try crisp spring roll of shellfish with chilli garlic butter or fettucine with onion velouté and tomato confit. There's meatier stuff too – Kerry beef fillet with colcannon, a rich potato and kale mixture, or duck breast with cabbage and smoked bacon. Although the room has a dull location – sandwiched upstairs between shops – there is nothing pedestrian about this cooking, or the excellent service.

County Kilkenny

KILKENNY

Zuni

26 Patrick Street, Kilkenny, Co Kilkenny (056 772 3999/www.zuni.ie). **Lunch served** 12.30-2.30pm Tue-Sat; 1-3pm Sun. **Dinner served** 6.30-9.30pm Mon-Sat; 6-9pm Sun. **Main courses** €17-€30. **Set dinner** (6.30-7.30pm Mon-Thur, Sun) €25 3 courses. **Credit** AmEx, MC, V.

Zuni is the star turn of Kilkenny, a beautiful, energised room where all the elements come together to guarantee a good time. The food is modern in orientation, but it can't resist the lure of creamy comfort cooking, so maple-glazed bacon has a mustard hollandaise, while pappardelle has a rich gorgonzola cream. Dishes from the char-grill, such as fillet steak with peppercorn sauce, or ostrich fillet with port wine jus, are always well judged and based on top-notch ingredients. There's a cute bar out front.

THOMASTOWN

Hudson's

Station Road, Thomastown, Co Kilkenny (056 779 3900). **Dinner served** 6-10pm Wed-Sun. **Main courses** €15-€30. **Set dinner** (6-7pm) €20 3 courses. **Credit** MC, V.

Comfortable rooms, excellent service and some truly fine cooking are Richard and Kyra Hudson's trademarks. The food is described simply – shrimp cocktail; crab spring rolls; breast of duck; tranche of halibut from the char-grill – all the better to create a delightful surprise when artful, colourful and creative dishes arrive. Caesar salad is perfectly executed, with no unnecessary additions; sea bass with a chorizo and pea risotto has a delicate smoky flavour; duck with figs and a balsamic dressing is spot on. This is mature, confident and successful food, and a new star in the offing for Kilkenny.

County Leitrim

CARRICK-ON-SHANNON

Oarsman

Bridge Street, Carrick-on-Shannon, Co Leitrim (071 962 1733/www.theoarsman.com). **Lunch served** noon-3.30pm Mon-Wed; noon-2.30pm Thur-Sat. **Dinner served** 7-9.30pm Thur-Sat. **Main courses** €17-€23. **Set lunch** €18.50 3 courses. **Credit** MC, V.

In this big, arching bar, with a small upstairs restaurant, Conor and Ronan Maher have created one of the destination addresses in the Midlands. Organic pasta dishes, smart sandwiches and wraps, and particularly great puddings (carrot cake with orange syrup) ensure the place is jammed at lunch. Dinner upstairs lets the kitchen crew flex their muscles: supreme of chicken with red pimento mousseline, loin of venison stuffed with morels, and cannon of lamb with ratatouille and sweet potato. Lovely cooking, lovely place.

County Limerick

ADARE

Wild Geese

Main Street, Adare, Co Limerick (061 396451/www.the wild-geese.com). **Dinner served** 6.30-10pm Tue-Sun. **Main courses** €25. **Set dinner** €30 2 courses, €36 3 courses. **Credit** AmEx, DC, MC, V.

David Foley and Julie Randles are one of the great teams in the Irish restaurant business, her front of house skills matched by his distinctive cooking. Put the two of them together in this pretty dining room and you have a sure-fire winner. Dishes are intricate, but subtle: goat's cheese in a curry crust with caramelised pears; deep-fried brie with black olives and a pineapple and cucumber salsa; blackened salmon with roast peppers and rice noodles.

LIMERICK

Copper & Spice

2 Cornmarket Row, Limerick, Co Limerick (061 313620/www.copperandspice.com). **Dinner served** 5-10.30pm daily. **Main courses** €8.50-€16. **Set dinner** (5-7pm) €22.50 3 courses incl glass of wine or soft drink. **Credit** AmEx, MC, V.

Brian and Seema Conroy's Copper & Spice offers fine Indian food, served with style and a winning attitude. The menu reads conventionally – keema matar; chicken karahi; sag aloo – but it is the care and expertise of the cooking that makes these standard dishes shine. Interestingly, the range of Thai dishes is no less expertly delivered, so the green and red curries and the noodle dishes are authentic.

County Louth

DUNDALK

Cube

5 Roden Place, Dundalk, Co Louth (042 932 9898/ www.cuberestaurants.ie). **Lunch served** noon-3pm Mon-Fri. **Dinner served** 5-9pm Mon-Fri; 5-10pm Sat. **Main courses** €26-€55. **Set dinner** €30 2 courses; €75 6-course surprise menu. **Credit** MC, V.

A restaurant that has been designed to within an inch of its life, and so quite a contrast with the rather ramshackle style of Dundalk. The cooking is rock solid: wild boar and apple sausage with mash captures flavours and textures perfectly. The menu has an international span, but recent simplifications have allowed more focus, allowing Cube to deliver with consistent skill.

County Monaghan

CARRICKMACROSS

Restaurant at Nuremore ★

Nuremore Hotel, Carrickmacross, Co Monaghan (042 966 1438/www.nuremore.com). **Lunch served** 12.30-2.30pm Mon-Fri, Sun. **Dinner served** 6.30-9.30pm Mon-Sat; 6.30-8.45pm Sun. **Set lunch** (Mon-Fri) €19.50 2 courses, €25 3 courses; (Sun) €30 4 courses. **Set dinner** €48 5 courses. **Credit** AmEx, DC, MC, V.

Ray McArdle and his crew are forever entering and winning competitions, but while they may like to collect the gongs, it is their work at the Nuremore that really brings home the bacon. The food is outstanding, a luxurious bourgeois blow-out that revels in superb ingredients: caramelised veal sweetbreads with turnip fondant; braised rabbit and wild mushroom pie with sauce foie gras. Fillet of pork with braised stuffed trotter shows a superb ability to combine strong ingredients. The price of such a fine meal offers amazing value for money. One just wishes the room was a little funkier in style.

GLASLOUGH

Castle Leslie

Castle Leslie, Glaslough, Co Monaghan (047 88109/ www.castleleslie.com). **Dinner served** 6.30-9.30pm daily. **Set dinner** €52 5 courses; €57 6-course surprise tasting menu. **Credit** AmEx, MC, V.

Now that owner Sammie Leslie and chef Noel McMeel have made Castle Leslie such a successful destination, it's easy to forget that just a few years ago, this big old pile of a place was a standing joke. No one laughs any more. The restaurant is excellent and food is ace: confit of duck with nutty coleslaw and a sesame and chilli dressing; smoked chicken and walnut terrine with sweet and sour jelly; salmon and brill with creamed leeks and chateau potatoes. Great vegetarian menus too.

County Tipperary

BALLINDERRY

Brocka on the Water ★

Kilgarvan Quay, Ballinderry, Co Tipperary (067 22038). **Dinner served** 6.30-9pm Mon-Sat by appointment only. **Main courses** €20-€25. **Set dinner** €40 3 courses. **No credit cards**.

Anne and Anthony Gernon's little Brocka is the ultimate in bespoke restaurants. It's no more than a couple of rooms in their house, with an adjoining kitchen where Anne's mum, Nancy, does the cooking, but every detail is showered with tender care. Every table is decorated differently, every plate will have some special garnish or decoration according to the individual's taste, every menu is handwritten, every aspect of service is solicitous. And the cooking complements all this with aplomb: baked stuffed sea bass with dill hollandaise, say, or Tipperary sirloin steak Gaelic style.

CASHEL

Café Hans

Moor Lane, Cashel, Co Tipperary (062 63660). **Lunch served** noon-5.30pm Tue-Sat. **Main courses** €7-€13. **No credit cards**.

Just next door to the venerable and ancient Chez Hans, in the stylish Café Hans, Stefan and Hansi Matthiae are knocking out great food, not to mention fabulous chips. The formula is simple: four versions of Caesar salad, four house salads, five open sandwiches (try the coronation chicken), and a variety of soups and other mains. Stefan executes everything with flair, imagination and assurance. Be warned: if you don't get here early, you will have to queue, as the tiny room is usually packed.

Chez Hans ★

Moor Lane, Cashel, Co Tipperary (062 61177). **Dinner served** 6-10pm Tue-Sat. **Main courses** €27-€35. **Set dinner** (6-7.30pm) €23 2 courses, €30 3 courses; (7.30-10pm) €45 3 courses. **Credit** MC, V.

Jason Matthiae is in superb form at the moment in this spectacular, deconsecrated church right under the shadow of the Rock of Cashel. His risotto dishes such as a wild mushroom version with duckling, chorizo and baby spinach leaves are state-of-the-art productions, while cod with potato and artichoke gateau show that being in the centre of the country creates no obstacle to great fish dishes. This place carries the exciting edge of a cook and a restaurant that are currently on top of their game.

CAHIR

Gannon's Above the Bell

Pearse Street, Cahir, Co Tipperary (052 45911). **Dinner served** 5.30-9pm Tue-Thur, Sun; 5.30-10pm Fri, Sat. **Main courses** €16.95-€26.95. **Set dinner** (5.30-7pm) €20 courses, €25 3 courses. **Credit** MC, V.

Tannery

The Bell is a small pub just off the main square. On two floors above the pub Dermot Gannon has plenty of room to show just how star-bound his fine modern cooking is. Working with his brother-in-law, Ricky, Gannon squeezes out a very personal style of fusion cooking: salted black beans with cod and crispy prawns is just right; halibut is made for Thai spiced butter; dipping grill starters are a great way of showcasing grilled meats and vegetables with their signature sauces. This being the somewhat conservative environment of Tipperary, Gannon also shows appropriate respect to prawn cocktail, or sirloin steak with chips and garlic butter for those not quite ready for the fusion experience.

CLONMEL

Cliffords

29 Thomas Street, Clonmel, Co Tipperary (052 70677). **Lunch served** 12.30-2.30pm Thur-Sat; 12.30-4pm Sun. **Dinner served** 6.30-10pm Tue-Sun. **Main courses** €20-€26.50. **Set dinner** (6-8pm) €26.50 4 courses. **Credit** MC, V.

Clifford's has been packed with contented diners just about ever since the doors first opened, and the serene, stylish, classical food explains why well-heeled Clonmel locals are lapping up the food at this great new destination. Dishes such as quenelles of chicken with milleens, and gateau of Clonakilty black pudding are here in all their tastefulness, as well as lovely main courses such as beef with fleurie sauce, Tipperary lamb with pear and thyme, and turbot with fennel and a lemon butter sauce. Enthusiastic young women work the front of house under the guidance of Deirdre Clifford.

County Waterford

CAPPOQUIN

Richmond House

Cappoquin, Co Waterford (058 54278/www.richmondhouse.net). **Dinner served** *summer* 6.30-9pm daily. *Winter* 7-9pm Mon-Sat. **Set dinner** (6.30-7.30pm) €28 4 courses; €47 5 courses. **Credit** AmEx, DC, MC, V.

Paul and Claire Deevy's modest, gracious country house in West Waterford is a lovely place to visit, thanks in no small part to the exciting food on offer. Much country house cooking is conservative fare, but not here. Crab risotto fritters mix with pickled cucumbers. Ostrich fillet has a garlic mousseline. Aubergines team with crispy potatoes in a millefeuille, with a chive dressing. Baked cod is paired with a celeriac purée and an avocado sabayon. The cooking is modern, but it never makes the mistake of being merely fashionable.

DUNGARVAN

Tannery ★

10 Quay Street, Dungarvan, Co Waterford (058 45420/www.tannery.ie). **Lunch served** 12.30-2.30pm Tue-Fri, Sun. **Dinner served** 6.30-9.30pm Tue-Thur; 6.30-10pm Fri, Sat. **Main courses** €16-€28. **Set dinner** (6.30-7.30pm) €25 3 courses and coffee. **Credit** AmEx, DC, MC, V.

Paul Flynn is one of the most significant players in modern Irish cuisine, a brilliant and articulate chef. His writings on food are tempting enough, but they are nothing compared to the fireworks he conjures

Avoca.
See p365.

up in this gorgeous dining room. Flynn takes all the conventions of Irish food, and then turns them sideways: guinea fowl with creamed leeks and a lime syrup; rack of lamb with a saffron, carrot and date risotto; barbary duck with mash, black pudding and a beetroot sauce. Dazzlingly presented, it makes for inspiring, challenging food.

LISMORE

Buggy's Glencairn Inn ★

Glencairn, nr Lismore, Co Waterford (058 56232/www.lismore.com). **Dinner served** 7.30-9pm daily. **Main courses** €21-€25. **Credit** MC, V.

Many people declare that Buggy's (restaurant, bar and rooms) is their favourite. It's ever so slightly magical and mysterious, it's romantic, and the food is superb. It's done very simply – fresh fish fried with fennel seeds, served with amazing string chips, or lovely stews and casseroles that bundle up the umami narcotic of good beef and lamb – but is flavour-packed. The beguilingly surreal decoration of the rooms is charming too.

TRAMORE

Coast

Upper Branch Road, Tramore, Co Waterford (051 393646/www.coast.ie). **Lunch served** 1-3pm Sun. **Dinner served** 6.30-10.30pm Tue-Sat; *July, Aug, bank hols* 6.30-10.30pm Tue-Sun. **Main courses** €18.50-€26. **Set lunch** €24 3 courses. **Set dinner** (6.30-7pm) €26.50 3 courses. **Credit** AmEx, MC, V.

Coast is very hip indeed. Great interior design in both the dining room and their four rooms is complemented by fine cooking: chorizo with polenta cake and tomato cream; the fab prawn cocktail, a marvellous take on retro food; tournedos of salmon with mango and cucumber; ravioli stuffed with mushroom duxelle with truffle oil. Coast is a class act, with style, service and great food.

WATERFORD

Bodéga!

54 John Street, Waterford, Co Waterford (051 844177/www.bodegawaterford.com). **Lunch served** 12.30-2.30pm Mon-Fri. **Dinner served** 6.30-10pm Mon-Sat. **Main courses** €14.50-€22. **Credit** AmEx, MC, V.

Bodéga! is as funky as it gets, a happening space for eating and drinking. It's a long narrow room, the walls lined with wacky works of art, and it always feels like the wee small hours of the morning. Owner Cormac Cronin and chef Arnaud Mary stoke up the atmosphere with some seriously fine meals. Take a tip from the locals; ignore the menus, and choose from the specials chalked on the blackboard. The fish is splendid, and punchy dishes such as chorizo and boudin noir with potatoes are savoury heaven. There's a great selection of good value clarets too.

County Westmeath

ATHLONE

Left Bank Bistro

Fry Place, Athlone, Co Westmeath (090 649 4446/ www.leftbankbistro.com). **Lunch served** noon-5pm, **dinner served** 5.30-9.30pm Tue-Sat. **Main courses** €12-€24. **Credit** AmEx, MC, V.

The Left Bank Bistro is timeless, stylish and all-round excellent, and that's what you'll be thinking even before you get to the food. But when dinner does arrive, in starters such as warm smoked salmon with horseradish cream, or mains such as duck confit on cracked pepper mash, or black pudding with smoked bacon and fried potatoes, the logic and harmony of this cracking little bistro is further magnified. You'll leave smiling.

County Wexford

ROSSLARE

La Marine ★

Kelly's Resort Hotel, Rosslare, Co Wexford (053 32114/www.kellys.ie). **Lunch served** 12.30-3pm, **dinner served** 6.30-9.30pm daily. Closed Dec-Feb. **Main courses** €15.95-€25. **Set lunch** (Sun) €21 3 courses. **Credit** AmEx, MC, V.

Eugene Callaghan's dishes look very simple when they arrive at the table in the funky La Marine. Shoulder of lamb with carrots and spuds. Duck confit with some noodles. Sticky toffee crème brûlée. Panna cotta with rhubarb. And then you taste this basic looking food, and the flavours blow you away. That duck confit, for instance, will be the benchmark against which all others will be measured. La Marine sets a standard that every other bistro has to match. Service is superb and the wine list a thrill.

WEXFORD

Forde's

The Crescent Quay, Wexford, Co Wexford (053 23832). **Meals served** noon-6pm Sun. **Dinner served** 6-10pm daily. **Main courses** €15-€25.50. **Set dinner** (6-7pm) €22 2 courses. **Credit** AmEx, DC, MC, V.

Liam Forde's colourful, unpretentious bistro in the centre of Wexford offers lovely, punchy tasty cooking, with a lot of his dishes harking back to great cordon bleu classics of the 1960s. Medallions of veal with sage leaves; chateaubriand for two; roast suckling pig; beignets of crabmeat with ginger and basil, these are just some of the great tried-and-trusted favourites that are cooked as if they were newly minted. The room is lively, noisy and fun, and it's a big local favourite thanks to good value for money and no-nonsense service.

County Wicklow

AUGHRIM

Strawberry Tree

Brook Lodge, Macreddin, Co Wicklow (040 236444/ www.brooklodge.com). **Lunch served** 1.30-4pm Sun. **Dinner served** 7-9.30pm Mon-Sat; 6.30-8pm Sun. **Set lunch** €35 4 courses. **Set dinner** €55 5 courses. **Credit** AmEx, DC, MC, V.

The selling point of this splendid restaurant, in the ever so hip Brook Lodge Inn, is that all the meals are based around the use of wild and organic foods. The chefs here cook with these ingredients because they provide more interesting textures and tastes: wild rabbit terrine with figs; oxtail and cabbage broth; salad of winter offal with croutons; braised guinea fowl with parsnip purée; fennel-steamed plaice with girolles. It's a mighty achievement to make ideology taste so good and that isn't the only thing that is so impressive: the adventurous wine list is one of the most interesting around, and the dining room itself is a dreamily romantic space.

DUNLAVIN

Grangecon Café ★

The Old Schoolhouse, Blessington, Co Wicklow (045 857892). **Meals served** 9am-6pm Mon-Sat. **Main courses** €9.50-€12.50. **No credit cards**.

Jenny and Richard Street's tiny café has moved from the middle of nowhere – Grangecon – to the middle of somewhere – Blessington – and in the process upgraded to a larger room, which means more food lovers can turn up to sample the delights of this idiosyncratic operation. The Grangecon formula is simple: take fresh, seasonal foods, and conjure up nice things to do with them. Summer gazpacho soup; roasted vegetable sandwiches with fresh pesto; trademark organic sausage rolls; spinach and ricotta tartlets; rhubarb tarts; chocolate chip cookies. All at reasonable prices too. One wishes every restaurant had the same disciplined logic at work in the kitchen, as well as such charming modesty.

KILMACANOGE

Avoca

Kilmacanoge, Co Wicklow (012 867466/www.avoca.ie). **Meals served** 9.30am-5pm Mon-Fri; 10am-5pm Sat; 10am-5.30pm Sun. **Main courses** €9.95-€11.25. **Credit** AmEx, DC, MC, V.

Avoca is one of the cultural institutions of Ireland, a series of delightful shops that also have serious day-time cafés attached to them. The Avoca crew prove something simp le yet fundamental: you can cook well for great numbers of people without collapsing into mere catering. As evidence of this, order the Avoca pizza with peppers, or the spinach and mozzarella lasagne, or the Italian chicken with pasta, and you'll find the consistency, creativity and unabashed deliciousness of the food will help explain the long lunchtime queues.

Also in the area

Avoca Suffolk Street, Dublin (01 672 6019); **Avoca** Powerscourt, Enniskerry, Co Wicklow (012 046070); **Avoca** Avoca Village, Co Wicklow (040 235105); **Avoca** Moll's Gap, Co Kerry (064 34720); **Copper & Spice**, New Town Centre, Annacotty, Co Limerick (061 338791); **Wagamama** South King Street, Dublin 2 (01 478 2152).

Advertisers' Index

Please refer to relevant sections for addresses / telephone numbers

A-Z Index

C

h

i

j

k

l

m

Index

p

S

Index

Subject Index

Index

Index

Gardens

Greek food

Historic premises

Hotels

Indian & Pakistani food

Italian food

Index

Index